Vienna, 1814

ALSO BY DAVID KING

Finding Atlantis:
A True Story of Genius, Madness, and an Extraordinary
Quest for a Lost World

Vienna, 1814

How the Conquerors of Napoleon Made Love, War, and Peace at the Congress of Vienna

David King

Harmony Books

New York

Copyright © 2008 by David King

All rights reserved.
Published in the United States by Harmony Books, an imprint of the
Crown Publishing Group, a division of Random House, Inc., New York.
www.crownpublishing.com

HARMONY BOOKS is a registered trademark and the Harmony Books colophon
is a trademark of Random House, Inc.

Library of Congress Cataloging-in-Publication Data

King, David, 1970–
Vienna, 1814 : how the conquerors of Napoleon made love, war, and peace
at the Congress of Vienna / David King.—1st ed.
Includes bibliographical references and index.

1. Congress of Vienna (1814–1815)   2. Napoleonic Wars 1800–1815—Treaties.
3. Europe—Politics and government—1789–1815.   4. Statesmen—Europe—
History—19th century.   I. Title.
DC249.K46 2008
940.2'714—dc22   2007024680

ISBN 978-0-307-33716-0

Printed in the United States of America

Design by Lauren Dong

1 3 5 7 9 10 8 6 4 2

First Edition

To my parents

Contents

You have come at the right moment. If you like fêtes and balls you will have enough of them; the Congress does not move forward, it dances.

—PRINCE DE LIGNE

Vienna, 1814

PREFACE

May 4, 1814

The tall, sleek frigate HMS *Undaunted* slowly made its way toward the tiny fishing harbor. Two dozen exhausted rowers helped steer the graceful vessel to the hastily constructed wooden quay. Assembled crowds cheered themselves hoarse, and bouquets of flowers floated on the water to welcome the strangers. For on board was the new emperor of Elba, absolute sovereign of every bit of the sixteen-mile-long island.

Everyone was curious, straining to catch a glimpse of the short man in the old green coat, white breeches, and bright red top boots. He was instantly known by his walk, head down, body somewhat stooped forward, hands clasped behind his back, frantically pacing like some "wild animal in a cage." Flakes of snuff frequently dangled from his lips, completing the ruffled, disheveled impression.

Only two weeks before, he had attempted suicide, downing a poisonous concoction of opium, belladonna, and white hellebore carried in a heart-shaped vial worn around his neck. The dose was certainly enough to be fatal, but its strength had been sapped during the brutal Russian winter. Now all the bitter memories of that disastrous time seemed worlds away. Certainly, the island at the other end of his spyglass was no Corsica. But the emperor was resigned to his fate, imagining what lay ahead on his sunny yet confined new home.

For Napoleon Bonaparte, that brilliant maniac, had been stopped after conquering most of the continent. Territory after territory had succumbed with astonishing rapidity to the bold "man of destiny." The

French tricolor had been raised everywhere from Madrid to Moscow; proud members of the Bonaparte clan had been placed on thrones all over the sprawling empire. By 1814, however, overextension, exhaustion, and too many military fiascoes had sent the monstrous edifice crashing down. Napoleon had been defeated, his empire shattered, and the entire web of international relations thrown into utter disarray. It was time to rebuild.

Kings, queens, princes, and diplomats would all pour into the city of Vienna in the autumn of 1814 for the highly anticipated peace conference. More than 200 states and princely houses would send delegates to settle the many unresolved issues. How were the victors to reconstruct the war-torn continent? How were they going to make restitution to the millions who had lost family members or suffered the horrors of Napoleonic domination? The Vienna Congress offered a chance to correct the wrongs of the past and, many hoped, create the "best of all possible worlds."

Reasoned opinion predicted that all negotiations would be wrapped up in three or four weeks. Even the most seasoned diplomats expected no more than six. But the delegates, thrilled by the prospects of a lasting peace, indulged in unrestrained celebrations. The Vienna peace conference soon degenerated into a glittering vanity fair: masked balls, medieval-style jousts, and grand formal banquets—a "sparkling chaos" that would light up the banks of the Danube.

Indeed, while the peacemakers enjoyed themselves, hopes for a timely resolution were quickly fading. Secret intrigues, personal animosities, bitter hatreds, and a host of other unexpected obstacles would prevent the dazzling entourage from agreeing on just about anything. Waging peace, the delegates learned, would be as difficult as defeating Napoleon.

Suddenly, six months into the "happy, unfettered confusion," a courier reached Vienna with a letter marked URGENT. It was slightly past 6 a.m., and the Austrian foreign minister, Prince Klemens von Metternich, was too tired to be bothered with yet another matter claiming immediate attention. He put the letter on his nightstand and went back to bed. An hour and a half later, he opened the dispatch, sent from an imperial and royal consulate general in Genoa (actually, it was Livorno). It read in full:

The English commissioner Campbell has just entered the harbor to inquire whether anyone has seen Napoleon at [Livorno], in light of the fact that he has disappeared from the island of Elba. The answer being in the negative, the English frigate put to sea again without delay.

To his horror, the truth dawned on the dazed insomniac. Napoleon Bonaparte had escaped and no one had any idea where he was headed. The Austrian minister scrambled out of bed, dressed "in a flash," and broke the news to the congress. By the time the curtain fell at the Redoutensaal theater that evening, the hunt was on for the "most feared warlord since Genghis Khan."

THE CONGRESS OF Vienna was indeed quite unlike any other peace conference in history. It was to be the first large peacemaking venture in almost 175 years, and it has been controversial ever since. In addition to the many issues and tensions, one of its most fascinating features is the explosive mix of delegates sent to the decadent Habsburg capital.

Representing the Austrian hosts was the elegant, sophisticated, and vain Prince Metternich, a "Don Juan" who excelled in the arts of seduction. With Napoleon's defeat and exile, France sent a diplomat every bit as polished and devious: Prince Charles-Maurice de Talleyrand-Périgord. Almost all the scandalous accusations about him were true, Madame de la Tour du Pin acknowledged, but Talleyrand was still the most enchanting man she had ever known. His powdered wig, velvet coat, and red heels made him look like the last survivor of the ancien régime. "Shit in silk stockings" was Napoleon's verdict.

The most volatile and hot-tempered of the delegations, however, was undoubtedly Prussia, the north German state that was, at this time, too strong to be a minor power, and yet not quite strong enough to be a great one. Their king, Frederick William III, came in person, bringing one of the largest, most educated, and hardworking delegations to town. The Prussians demanded compensation after their country had been unceremoniously carved up at the whims of the French invaders.

As for Great Britain, Foreign Secretary Robert Stewart, Viscount Castlereagh, made the journey himself. He was an aloof and eccentric gentleman, who had previously caused a scandal in London when, as a member of Parliament, he had hoped to end malicious political intrigues

by challenging a rival cabinet minister to a duel. Now Castlereagh had
turned his energies to strategy, all too aware that he represented an economic powerhouse with a royal navy in a league of its own.

Finally, the last of the great powers were the Russians, and they produced the greatest celebrity of the conference, at least at the beginning:
the Tsar Alexander. Tall, blond, and sporting a dark-green uniform with
a wide hat cocked to the side, Alexander was a man of sudden impulse
and excess. His sexual appetites were insatiable, already rivaling those of
his grandmother Catherine the Great. In addition, the tsar was growing
increasingly mystical and unpredictable. "If he were a woman," Napoleon
once said, "I think I would make him my mistress."

Such were the distinguished and worldly leaders who would come
together for the unforgettable nine-month drama of the Vienna Congress—
the greatest and most lavish party in history. They would plot, scheme,
jockey for position, and, in short, infuriate each other as they competed
in affairs of state and the heart. One participant, the young songwriter
Count Auguste de La Garde-Chambonas, described the spectacle:

> A kingdom was cut into bits or enlarged at a ball; an indemnity was
> granted in the course of a dinner; a constitution was planned during
> a hunt . . . Everyone was engrossed with pleasure.

Yet despite the unabashed frivolity, world maps were redrawn, the neutrality of Switzerland guaranteed, the freedom of the seas and international
rivers proclaimed, diplomatic procedures established, and priceless works
of art restored, along with many other achievements. And by the end of
this historic gathering, the delegates accomplished what they had hoped
to do—the peace was signed on June 9, 1815.

Set in ballrooms, bedrooms, and palaces, *Vienna, 1814* tells the story
of how these unlikely revelers created what Henry Kissinger called the
longest period of peace Europe has ever known.

Chapter 1

BREAD AND CIRCUSES

There is literally a royal mob here. Everybody is crying out:
Peace! Justice! Balance of power! Indemnity!
As for me, I am a looker-on. All the indemnity I ask for is a new hat.

— PRINCE DE LIGNE

$\mathcal{O}$rnate rococo carriages rumbled through a landscape scorched
by twentysome years of revolution and warfare. Dangers
lurked everywhere on the poor, unlit roadways. Cutthroat
highwaymen preyed on isolated travelers, and inns were hardly safe
havens, either, often little better than "murderer's dens." Venturing out
into the bleak postwar world was for "the fearless, the foolish, or the suicidal." During the autumn of 1814, it was also for the idealistic and the
idle. Hordes of pleasure-seekers would flock to Vienna for an unprecedented pageant.

The occasion was the Congress of Vienna, the long-awaited peace
conference to decide the future of Europe. Kings, queens, princes,
princesses, dukes, duchesses, diplomats, and about a hundred thousand
other visitors would make their way to the central European city,
swelling the population by as much as a third. No one, though, it must be
said, really had an idea of what to expect. The invitation for the congress
had been sent by way of an announcement in the newspaper.

The Revolutionary and Napoleonic Wars had ripped Europe apart.
For the first time in history, enormous armies based on universal conscription had marched across the continent to wage a "total war." France
had set the standard for this comprehensive mobilization of the people
with the famous decree of August 1793:

The young shall fight; married men shall forge weapons and transport supplies; the women will make tents and clothes and will serve in the hospitals; the children will make old linen into lint; the old men will have themselves carried into the public squares to rouse the courage of fighting men.

By the end of the war in the spring of 1814, the suffering had been immense—a terrible ordeal that ruined states, wrecked economies, and ravaged families. As many as 5 million people were dead, and many more had been permanently or seriously disabled. Entire villages had been wiped off the map. Lands had been devastated, laws trammeled, and atrocities committed on a horrific scale.

The many issues arising out of this wreckage were, to be sure, tangled, thorny, and controversial. During the war, the Allied powers had understandably hoped to postpone the many difficult decisions until after victory. Now that Napoleon had been defeated, the only matter that had been officially decided was the question of France, which had been settled back in May 1814, after two months of wrangling following the capture of the capital.

According to the terms of the Treaty of Paris, France's frontiers were redrawn as they had been on the first of January 1792. This meant that France would have to surrender the vast majority of its conquests, but not, in fact, all of them. Any territory that France had seized by that date twenty-two years before would be retained, including communities in the northeast, Chambéry in Savoy, the former papal enclave of Avignon, and even some colonies in the new world. Thanks to the treaty, France would actually possess more territory and a greater population than it had under Louis XIV, Louis XV, or Louis XVI.

The Allies had hoped that such generous terms would help the new king, Louis XVIII, establish himself on the throne, and at the same time, reintegrate his country peacefully into the international community. That's also why the victors spared France many of the usual penalties inflicted on a defeated power. There was no indemnity to pay, no foreign occupation army to endure, and no limitation, in any way, on the size of the army. This was, in many ways, a remarkably lenient agreement.

Everything else, however, remained unresolved. The Vienna Congress would have to make some hard decisions about the former empire and its many satellite kingdoms. At stake was virtually all of western Europe, vast realms east of the Rhine, and some highly coveted islands from the Caribbean to the East Indies.

The most difficult of these questions, at least at the beginning, was the fate of Poland. Napoleon had called this country the "key to the vault," and the so-called enlightened despots of the eighteenth century had tried to seize as much of its strategic territory as possible, carving it up no fewer than three times. By 1795, Poland had completely disappeared from the map, devoured, as Frederick the Great had said, "like an artichoke, leaf by leaf."

Russia had ended up with the lion's share of Polish territory, including Lithuania, Ukraine, Belarus, and eastern Poland. Austria had taken the ancient capital of Kraków, along with the rich agricultural region of eastern Galicia and the salt mines of Tarnopol. Prussia had seized Warsaw, Gdánsk, and the strip of territory running north to the sea later known as the "Polish Corridor." For many, such a cynical and ruthless display of power politics was simply indefensible.

During the war, Napoleon had played on these sentiments, blasting the Polish partitions as "unforgivable, immoral, and impolitic." He promised the Poles that if they could prove to him that they were "worthy of being a nation," he would restore their country. But despite the many Polish sacrifices, Napoleon never did more than create the tiny Duchy of Warsaw, and exploit it ruthlessly. The Vienna Congress seemed an excellent opportunity finally to restore Poland, though finding a solution was not going to be easy.

Napoleon, moreover, had been a fertile kingmaker, placing family and friends on thrones all over the continent, from Italy to Holland to Spain. Napoleon had also created brand-new kingdoms in Germany, such as the Kingdom of Bavaria, Württemberg, and Saxony. What were the victors going to do with all the newly minted monarchs desperately clutching their crowns? What, for that matter, was going to happen to the older ruling families who had been ousted in the Napoleonic whirlwind and were now lobbying for a return to their kingdoms? The Vienna Congress was gearing up for an unusual battle royal for the thrones of Europe.

In addition, there was also a controversy brewing about the works of

art that had been stolen. In only a few years, Napoleon and his Grande
Armée had earned a reputation as history's most audacious thieves.
Countless masterpieces from Michelangelo, Raphael, Titian, and Rem-
brandt were carted up and carried off by Napoleon's henchmen. The
emperor's goal was simple: to make the city of Paris, as he put it, "the
most beautiful that could ever exist." The Frenchman in charge of the art
confiscations, Dominique-Vivant Denon, acted with a merciless effi-
ciency, and transformed his museum, the Louvre, into an artistic "wonder of the world."

Now all these sculptures, paintings, jewels, tapestries, and other
stolen treasures were once again up for grabs. The French, of course,
insisted on retaining their war trophies, and the Allied powers had tentatively agreed, adding a clause to the Treaty of Paris allowing France to
keep its loot. But in the autumn of 1814 there was a new call to return
the art to its previous owners, and this motion was particularly popular
among the heavily despoiled lands such as Italy and the Netherlands.

Indeed along with the official delegations, there were many informal
and unofficial representatives, often self-appointed, that came to press
their own hopes and projects. As the form of the congress had been vague,
many believed that they had a right to participate in the decision making
and arrived fully expecting to do so. These private delegations would be
selling everything from constitutions to songs. One American entrepre-
neur, Dr. Justus Bollmann, arrived with a whole portfolio of projects,
including a plan to create the first steamship company on the Danube.

There were delegations coming from Frankfurt, Lübeck, and Prague
to protect the rights of Jewish minorities, so recently granted under
Napoleon and now at risk of being repealed. One group wanted the congress to launch a crusade against piracy around the world, from the corsairs infesting the Mediterranean to the buccaneers raiding the Caribbean.
Representatives of publishing firms came to Vienna to address another kind
of piracy, "the gang of robbers known as literary pirates" who unscrupu-
lously preyed "with impunity against authors and publishers." The hope
was to create an international copyright to protect intellectual property.

Everyone, it seemed, had a vision of how the postwar world should
best be reconstructed. The problem, however, was that the peacemakers
were far more divided than it was imagined. And all the underlying
differences, which had been so successfully suppressed in the life-and-

death struggle against Napoleon, would now reemerge in Vienna with a vengeance.

THE HABSBURG CAPITAL was a good choice for the world meeting. Geographically and culturally, Vienna was the heart of Europe. Until as late as August 1806, Vienna had been the center of the Holy Roman Empire, the gigantic, ramshackle realm that had been dismantled by Napoleon. After nearly a thousand-year run, looming over central Europe at times with a menacing and other times tottering presence, the Holy Roman Empire was no more. Imperial majesty and grandeur, however, had far from faded.

"The city proper," one traveler noted on entering Vienna's gates, "seems like a royal palace." Grand baroque mansions lined the narrow, twisting lanes that snaked their way through the old medieval center. Spires, domes, towers, and neoclassical columns carved in bright white stone, each roof and facade looked more sumptuous and elaborately adorned than the next. Rows of large bay windows predominated, overlooking one of the greenest capitals in Europe, a fact that was due at least partly to the foresight of the eighteenth-century emperor Joseph II, who had decreed that a tree must be planted for every one cut down.

Vienna had indeed an aristocratic flair that many other cities like London lacked, or like Paris had lost since the revolution. Austrian, Hungarian, and Bohemian aristocrats lived there, often in mansions with their own ballrooms, riding schools, and sometimes even private opera houses. Many French émigrés fleeing the revolution had also settled there, though most were considerably poorer now, and lived in cheaper third- and fourth-floor apartments.

The merchant class, if that term can be used about such a small group, was not that visible in Vienna, and the town's artisans overwhelmingly geared their production to meeting the demands of court and society, making saddles, harnesses, carriages, clocks, musical instruments, and other luxuries. The biggest source of production was still wine, which always found a ready market in a town where residents, as one historian put it, "lunched until dinner, and then dined until supper."

The vast majority of the events at the peace congress would take place in the old town, still encircled by its city walls, which ran roughly along the lines of today's sweeping boulevard, the Ringstrasse. According to legend, the thick stone walls had been constructed using ransom money for King Richard I, "the Lion-Hearted," who was captured in 1193 on his way to the Second Crusade. In reality, the walls were built and rebuilt almost incessantly over the centuries, as they withstood various sieges, including two particularly frightful ones from the Turks. After the last attack from the French in 1809, the city walls were not being reconstructed, and the remaining bastions would serve at the congress mainly as a fashionable walkway affording some excellent views of the town.

Vienna was built on a large plain where the Danube divides and can be easily forded, as the Romans who founded a camp there in the first century discovered. During the Middle Ages, the small town lay on the exposed eastern rim of Charlemagne's empire, a fact that survives in the German name for Austria, Österreich. Historically, Vienna has long served as a crossroads between east and west. Crusaders, merchants, friars, and many other travelers would pass through the town, traveling east along its river—the mighty, muddy Danube, flowing on its two-thousand-mile journey from the Black Forest to the Black Sea.

With a population reaching some quarter of a million, and ranked third in size behind London and Paris, Vienna enjoyed a reputation for being a joyous and sensuous, if also irritable and somewhat cranky, place. "Vienna is the city of the world where the most uncommon raptures are experienced," as the French émigré Baronne du Montet put it. Another admirer, the songwriter Count Auguste de La Garde-Chambonas, who had traveled extensively in his search for adventure, called Vienna enthusiastically "the homeland of happiness." That autumn, the visitors to the peace conference would see exactly what he meant.

Hosting the congress officially was the emperor of Austria, Francis I, the last person ever to be crowned Holy Roman Emperor. Born in Florence, Italy, Francis was head of the Habsburg family, Europe's oldest and arguably most illustrious dynasty, occupying the throne in virtual unbroken succession since the thirteenth century. The single exception to this six-hundred-year dominance was Charles VII of the Wittelsbach family, who ruled briefly in the early 1740s, before the crown reverted to the Habsburgs (or more correctly, as they were known, from then on, the House of Habsburg-Lorraine).

Emperor Francis stood about medium height with high, sharply chiseled cheekbones, snow-white hair, and the infamous Habsburg jaw that jutted out from his bony face. He was only forty-six years old, though he looked considerably older. He had already weathered twenty-two stormy years on the throne, facing first the French Revolution and then Napoleon. Indeed, Emperor Francis looked tired and worn-out, or as one put it, "If you blew hard, you'd blow him to the ground."

As insiders knew, Francis was popular among the people and the court. He was called "Papa Franz" and "the father of his country," and was celebrated in music, including Joseph Haydn's "God Save Emperor Franz!" (the melody still used for the German national anthem). Some family members called the white-haired emperor Venus, the goddess of love. This was admittedly something of a Habsburg eccentricity, though the emperor was a well-known lover of statues, seals, and antiquities, and he looked out with a gaze as dreamy and blank as any ancient sculpture.

When the emperor was not trying to make order out of the managed chaos of the administration, which far too often seemed to run in circles after yet another rubber stamp, Francis enjoyed the music of this great *Musikstadt*. The emperor played the violin in the family string quartet, sometimes accompanied by his foreign minister, Metternich, on the cello. Francis also liked to make candy, tend to his plants in the palace hothouses, and study the large collection of maps in his library. The emperor possessed a knowledge of continental geography that, among the sovereigns coming to the congress, was unmatched. His large book collection, which at his death reached forty thousand volumes, would form the core of the Austrian National Library.

The headquarters for the social maelstrom of the Vienna Congress would be Emperor Francis's palace, the Hofburg, or as it was known, the Burg. Originally a functional four-tower fortress built into the old city wall as part of the city's defenses in the late thirteenth century, the rambling palace had grown to occupy several blocks in the city center as the Habsburg rulers continually added new wings and courts.

Emperor Francis had decided to open up this palace to his fellow sovereigns. After some consideration about rank and status, in order not to ruffle any royal feathers, the emperor had offered the Russian tsar the fanciful white and gold paneled rococo suites on the third floor of the

Amalienburg, a late-sixteenth-century addition to the palace named after the wife of Emperor Joseph I, and recently renovated. It was a superb suite with extravagant gilded mirrors, crystal chandeliers, and damask-covered chairs atop shining parquet floors.

The king of Prussia was to have a suite on the third floor of the Schweizerhof, the old medieval center of the castle, the courtyard of which had originally been intended for jousts. At its entrance stood the sixteenth-century Renaissance "Gate of Virtue" with a crowned Habsburg eagle flanked by two large resting lions. This wing had served as the favorite dwelling of the Austrian empress, Maria Ludovika, who moved to another part of the palace in order to make room for this royal guest.

Three other kings, two empresses, a queen, and many princes would also be housed in the palace. The king of Denmark, the tall, thin, and talkative Frederick VI, would also be lodged in the Schweizerhof, and the large, stern, melancholy king of Württemberg on the second floor of the Amalienburg. By the end of the month, the king of Bavaria, Maximilian I Joseph, the popular "Good King Max" and the founder of the Oktober-fest celebration, would take over suites in the early eighteenth-century wing known as the Reichskanzlei, or the Imperial Court Chancellery.

Every night at the palace, some forty or fifty banquet tables would be set at a cost that, it was whispered, ran to wildly exorbitant amounts. They were certainly elaborate affairs, sometimes involving as many as eight courses. The first was usually soup and hors d'oeuvres, brought out in large tureens and platters by wigged and liveried servants, and placed on tables adorned with court silver, crystal, and often gigantic gilded bronze centerpieces that incorporated many flowers and candles.

Guests progressed through a number of other dishes, usually including beef, ham, venison, pheasant, partridge, or some other meat. Years later, the choice of wine and entrée became much more standardized: oysters with Chablis, boiled beef with Rhenish wine, roast meat with Bordeaux or perhaps Tokay, the delicate dessert wine from imperial vineyards in Hungary. Fruits, sweets, cakes, and a wide variety of pies, cheeses, or jellies often followed. Ice cream was served only when Emperor Francis was present, and some six hundred rations of coffee, in mammoth kettles, were set aside daily for the sleep-deprived guests.

The kitchens that turned out such feasts for the congress were a sight unto themselves. In the main kitchen, accessed by a staircase underneath the court chapel, there was a giant spit, large enough to roast an ox, and joined with several other spits that could turn a few geese, ducks, hares, or pheasants. Cauldrons and copper pots and charcoal fumes dominated in the scorching heat—the fire on the largest spit so large, one said, it seemed a vision of hell. In other smaller rooms, a team of chefs, under-chefs, cooks, and other kitchen staff chopped, spiced, and diced on "the poor animals like the devil treats the soul of the damned."

To make sure that his elegant guests were entertained in style, the emperor had appointed a Festivals Committee, and made it responsible for planning, promoting, and managing all the official entertainment. The committee would set the busy social calendar that, as the emperor insisted, should be lively and fresh. The Festivals Committee would be continually challenged to find new or more interesting ways to enhance the "pursuit of pleasure" and make sure that the mood of "universal rejoicing" did not falter—all this for an elite crowd used to the very best and sharply critical when their high standards were not met.

The Festivals Committee was, by most accounts, one of the hardest-working committees at the congress. It would organize a series of lavish balls, banquets, masquerades, hunts, and the whole "preposterous extravagance" that later, more sober generations would come to associate with the Congress of Vienna.

Catering to the whims of their houseguests for an uncertain length of time would sometimes be exasperating. Vienna wits soon put these difficulties in perspective, while also poking fun at the early impressions made by the celebrated guests who would so readily accept Emperor Francis's generosity.

The Emperor of Russia:	*He makes love for everyone.*
The King of Prussia:	*He thinks for everyone.*
The King of Denmark:	*He speaks for everyone.*
The King of Bavaria:	*He drinks for everyone.*
The King of Württemberg:	*He eats for everyone.*
The Emperor of Austria:	*He pays for everyone.*

For a short time, indeed, Vienna would be the capital of Europe, the site of a massive victory celebration, and home to the most glamorous gathering since the fall of the Roman Empire. Palaces and parks, opera houses and ballrooms—the entire town would turn into a shimmering baroque playground. There had been large peace conferences before, but never anything like this. The Vienna Congress was to be the most spectacular peace conference in history. It was also, with its extravagance and decadence, going to be one of the most controversial.

Chapter 2

Two Princes

Good heavens, Madame. Who could resist loving a man with so many vices?

—Count François-Casimir Mouret de Montrond,
describing his friend Talleyrand to one of his mistresses

Silverware was hastily polished, white tablecloths were pressed, and napkins starched and folded. The wine cellars were stocked with the region's finest wines, including some bottles of Tokay, one hundred years old, costing about a year's salary for a junior lecturer at the University of Vienna. Many distinguished arrivals would soon pour into town, as one put it, "like peasants to a country fair."

Imperial carriages received a fresh coat of paint, dark green with a yellow coat of arms on the door, and their coachmen were outfitted in matching yellow livery. All three hundred of the carriages, soon to be placed at the disposal of the guests, would sport a uniform appearance, which would hopefully help avoid unpleasant squabbles over precedence. This was a wise decision, though at least one member of the Naples delegation, Signor Castelli, would have preferred more glitz, comparing his carriage to a "slow-rolling maid's chamber."

In the center of the bustle was Austria's foreign minister, Prince Klemens von Metternich. He was forty-one years old with curly blond hair, pale blue eyes, and the slender toned physique of a fencer. He stood above medium height, and had a handsome, delicate face and a gift for sparkling conversation. Metternich was hailed as the "Adonis of the Drawing Room."

It was hard to believe that this elegant and sophisticated man who had spun so many webs of intrigue for the Austrian Foreign Ministry had not been born in the country whose policy he was now crafting. He had not even seen Vienna itself until after his twenty-first birthday. Metternich was a Rhinelander. He was a native of the city of Koblenz, located on the bank of the Rhine in a region renowned for its towering cathedrals, its terraced vineyards, and its creative blend of Franco-Germanic culture that fostered such an easygoing lifestyle.

Metternich's real name was a tongue-twisting mouthful: Klemens Wenzel Nepomuk Lothar von Metternich-Winneburg-Beilstein, each designation harkening back to a distinguished ancestor or an extensive family estate somewhere in central Europe. Metternich's father, Franz Georg Karl, had been an imperial count of the Holy Roman Empire, one of only four hundred families that enjoyed a privileged status. His mother, Maria Beatrix von Kagenegg, had been a lady-in-waiting for Empress Maria Theresa. Yet by the standards of the time, the Metternichs barely ranked among the elite. There was a definite pecking order, and a number of princes, margraves, dukes, and electors all floated on a social plane high above the count. For many years, Vienna's crème de la crème would not let Metternich forget this tenuous status.

He had gained a social boost, however, when he married into one of Vienna's most distinguished families. His wife, Countess Eleanor von Kaunitz—or Laure, as he called her—was a granddaughter of Prince Wenzel Kaunitz, the famous Austrian minister who guided foreign policy for some forty years in the eighteenth century. "I cannot understand at all how any woman can resist him," she had said of Metternich, swept away by his charm. After overcoming her family's considerable resistance to the match, they had married in September 1795. By most standards, this was not a happy marriage.

Metternich, a notorious harlequin, would have many love affairs over the years, including one with Napoleon's younger sister Caroline, and another with the wife of the French marshal Jean-Andoche Junot. Metternich, indeed, never overcame his weakness for romantic liaisons, those "secret dashes in hired cabs, rendezvous in ghostly grottoes, and moonlight scampering in and out of upper-storey windows." Laure had to settle for amiable compatibility.

While this arrangement was certainly not uncommon among aristocratic families, Metternich was considerably more affectionate with their children. The oldest, seventeen-year-old Marie, was his favorite, with her wit, charm, and good looks that already reminded many of her father. Victor, aged fourteen, was the only surviving son in the family, an excellent student already tapped for a career in the Austrian bureaucracy (two other boys had died in infancy). The two youngest were ten-year-old Clementine and three-year-old Leontine. "If I had not been a minister of state," he said, "I would have been a nursery governess."

What had brought Metternich to Vienna for the first time, in November 1794, was the turmoil of the French Revolution. Fanatical armies had swarmed into the Rhineland on a rampage of destruction, intent to wage war on the aristocracy and its sleek, lacy decadence. The Metternichs, epitomizing this target, were forced to flee for their lives. The family estate on the Rhine was ruined, and their property plundered.

No surprise, Metternich would long be horrified of war, "that hateful invention" that released humanity's most savage urges and almost invariably ended with all sorts of barbaric crimes. Later experience only confirmed these early impressions. In 1809, when the time had seemed right to attack Napoleon, Austria was quickly squashed and almost annihilated as a power. Next time, Metternich knew, Austria might not survive.

It was during that same year of defeat that Metternich was given his chance to manage foreign policy. After a grand tour through the embassies of Dresden, Berlin, and then Paris, Metternich had been named Austrian foreign minister. His career in the five years before the congress had certainly been controversial.

Metternich had arranged the marriage of the Austrian emperor's oldest daughter, Archduchess Marie Louise, to Napoleon, a move highly unpopular in many Viennese circles, which still regarded Napoleon as the devil incarnate and the match as a bitter humiliation. For Metternich, this was a necessary evil that would strengthen Austria, ally it to the continent's strongest power, and allow more time to heal her wounds. Equally controversial, when the French empire started to unravel, Metternich seemed slow to abandon Napoleon and the alliance that, he believed, had kept Austria alive.

Critics were indeed quick to point out Metternich's many shortcomings. He seemed a flippant and frivolous lightweight. One year's essential priority in his foreign office might be discarded the next with an astonishing ease, suddenly dismissed as "antediluvian," as the prince referred to outdated concerns. His policy had a tendency to fluctuate and infuriate, with Metternich bouncing back and forth between colleagues, flittering about like a "butterfly minister."

All the while, Metternich displayed an unshakable confidence in his own abilities—a shocking and annoying arrogance that, as a colleague said, confused "haughtiness for dignity." How easily he brushed aside criticisms, and how little, really, he seemed troubled by the magnitude of the problems he often faced. For many, Metternich was a sly, superficial, and shallow fop, hopelessly out of his league.

Metternich's admirers, on the other hand, were unmoved by this criticism. Sure, there was a kernel of truth in each charge. Metternich seemed lazy, vain, and irreverent, but it was also true that he deliberately cultivated his image of gentlemanly nonchalance. He liked to pose as a playful and idle dabbler, while at the same time he waged diplomacy like a game of chess and did whatever it took to win. His rivals, continuing to underrate his abilities, went right on being checkmated.

In his five years as foreign minister, Metternich had carefully and skillfully guided Austrian diplomacy through a maze of challenges, advancing stage by stage from Austria's utter defeat and subservience to Napoleon in 1809 to becoming an ally of significance, and then, finally, at the right moment, in August 1813, defecting to the Allied coalition that would eventually defeat Napoleon. Austria had helped tip the balance. One historian has called this subtle craftsmanship one of the most remarkable feats in the history of diplomacy.

It was certainly dangerous to underestimate this charming foreign minister with his less than scrupulous means—he himself once summed up his approach as "hedging, evasion and flattery." Austria had benefited tremendously from Metternich's diplomacy, and, on the eve of the congress, seemed poised to do so again.

THE IDEA OF holding a peace conference in Vienna dated back one year to the middle of October 1813, when the Allies achieved a monumental victory over Napoleon at the Battle of Leipzig, the largest single battle in the Napoleonic Wars. Historians call the three-day slaughter the "Battle of Nations"; Metternich called it the "Battle of the World." It was there, at Leipzig, that the Russian tsar Alexander first proposed Vienna as the location for the future gathering. The Austrian emperor immediately agreed, before the unpredictable tsar changed his mind.

Originally, the intention was to invite only the sovereigns of the victorious powers. But in the spring of 1814, the British foreign secretary, Lord Castlereagh, had urged that the conference be expanded to include the representatives of all the states who had fought in the war. Article XXXII of the Treaty of Paris specifically adopted this interpretation, calling for a "general conference" of "all the participating nations" to open in Vienna no later than the fifteenth of July. This date, however, had been pushed back over the summer in response to the tsar's wishes to return first to his capital at St. Petersburg, where he had long been absent. The new opening date for the congress was set for the first of October.

Austria, of course, realized it would be expensive to host a peace conference and celebration worthy of the Allied victory, and it would certainly strain the government's already shaky finances. Austria had, only three years before, declared bankruptcy. Its new banknotes, issued in 1811, had already lost four-fifths of their value, and the government was heavily in debt. Austria had fought France more constantly, since 1792, than any other power except Great Britain, and its governmental income had been severely reduced during the war.

Twice, Vienna had been captured and occupied by Napoleon; twice, the aristocracy and the court had been forced to pack up their valuables and flee the capital. From Ulm to Wagram, the sweeping plains of central Europe seemed to be dotted with names of villages commemorating some defeat or another. Vienna wits had adapted the motto emblazoned on Julius Caesar's chariot to fit Emperor Francis's army: *Venit, Videt, Perdit* ("he comes, he sees, he loses").

Each time after a defeat—1797, 1801, 1805, and 1809—Napoleon had inflicted humiliating terms on the Austrians, demanding enormous cash payments and large amounts of territory. Austria had lost Belgium, Lombardy, Tuscany, Venice, Trieste, Tyrol, Vorarlberg, Croatia, Istria, Dalmatia, and Kraków, along with other former Polish lands and many princely dependencies on the left bank of the Rhine. The 1809 treaty alone had removed 3.5 million Habsburg subjects, sliced off forty-two thousand square miles, and imposed a harsh penalty of 85 million francs. The emperor had been forced to melt down much of the court plate and silverware to pay the sums demanded by Napoleon.

Realistically, Austria had little hope of regaining all of this lost territory, and, actually, the Austrians did not want it all back. They were content to abandon Belgium because of its distance and its proximity to
France, and they were also resigned to relinquishing the crown of the
Holy Roman Empire, deemed too cumbersome with its limitations on the
emperor's power. But Austria did want northern Italy, along with Dalmatia and other territory on the Adriatic coast, which had been completely
removed by Napoleon.

So a country whose fortunes had fallen low in the war had been
selected to host the peace conference. Despite their country's much-
reduced state, and the fact that it was still dangerously close to bankruptcy, Emperor Francis and Prince Metternich were happy to accept
responsibility for the congress. The reasoning was clear. As host, Austria
hoped to take advantage of its well-deserved reputation for hospitality,
and gain as much as possible from the goodwill of its guests.

SEVERAL BLOCKS AWAY from the Hofburg Palace, France's chief delegate,
Prince Charles-Maurice de Talleyrand, had slipped into town around
midnight on September 23. After a six-hundred-mile journey from Paris
completed in only seven days, the traveling carriage dropped him off at
the stately and stylish yellow-gray Kaunitz Palace, centrally placed at
1029 Johannesgasse, right off the busy Kärntnerstrasse and down from
St. Stephen's Cathedral. This was to be the headquarters of the French
embassy at the Vienna Congress.

Despite the excellent address, with its spectacular limestone staircase
and its stocked wine cellar, the house had needed a thorough whipping
into shape. Indeed, the French staff, which arrived one week before, was
appalled. White sheets still covered furniture in the drawing rooms, and
dark cloth shielded the portraits from the sun. The red damask hangings
had long faded from their original splendor. Crystal chandeliers, still
encased in their protective dust bags, needed polishing. Every room, it
seemed, needed a good cleaning and airing out, right down to removing
the moths from the mattresses.

The mansion was named after Prince Kaunitz, the most versatile Austrian diplomat of the eighteenth century, and the man who had played a

major role in achieving the "diplomatic revolution" of 1756 that brought the bitter enemies Austria and France together for the first time in centuries. Talleyrand liked the thought of working in the house of a man who had accomplished such a dramatic reconciliation, and he hoped to achieve his own miracles. But, at the same time, he was very much aware of the challenges that his embassy faced.

"I shall probably play a wretched role," Talleyrand sighed, as he imagined his prospects at the peace conference. He was asked to represent a country that had both launched and lost the war that left Europe in a mess, and many were sure to blame France. Yet despite his concerns for his country's diplomatic position, which he labeled "singularly difficult," Talleyrand was well suited for this mission. He had the talent, the connections, the charisma, and the reputation, not to mention the razor-sharp instincts that had been honed working with nearly every leading figure of the Napoleonic age. In diplomacy as well as society, Talleyrand was a living legend.

Approaching his sixty-first birthday, he stood about five feet eight inches and had a mop of wavy light brown hair tucked under his powdered wig. His face was thin, delicate, and unscarred, despite a dangerous bout of smallpox as a child. He had a slight snub nose, a high forehead, thickset eyebrows, and blue eyes that often fell half closed in boredom. His lips seemed locked in a perpetual smirk. His face, otherwise, was almost expressionless. One might kick him twenty times in the backside, it was said, and not a single muscle on his face would flinch.

Talleyrand looked like he had stepped right out of an eighteenth-century salon, complete with silk stockings, tight knee breeches, diamond buckled shoes, and velvet coats, often in purple, scarlet, or apple green. His starched satin cravat was impeccably tied, and the lace at the end of his cuffs exquisite. His movements were slow and deliberate, as he dragged his lame right foot across the floor. He was known for his elegance, his sophistication, and his immense charm. "If Talleyrand's conversation could be purchased," one admirer said, "I would gladly go into bankruptcy."

But in many ways the limping French minister was the ultimate survivor. In the previous thirty years, he had served everyone from the Church to the Revolution, the upstart Bonaparte to the restored Bourbon king, Louis XVIII. He certainly had an uncanny ability to make himself indispensable, and he also had a way of leaving his mark on every regime that he had served.

Indeed, some in Vienna had never forgiven Talleyrand for his past. He had been a witty and worldly priest who had left a trail of admirers, lovers, and, in some cases, even illegitimate children (including probably the romantic painter Eugène Delacroix). He had scandalized further when, after his consecration as bishop of Autun, he had resigned, and even married. His bride, the beautiful Catherine Grand, had also had a notorious past; it was, as some wits quipped, the former bishop who married the former courtesan.

Additionally, Talleyrand was notorious for having turned his position in the foreign ministry into a highly lucrative enterprise. He routinely collected diamond rings and large payments for his services—gifts, bribes, "user's fees," or whatever one wanted to call them. When France sold the Louisiana Territory to the United States in 1803, for example, Talleyrand had personally pocketed as much as one-third of President Thomas Jefferson's $15 million purchase price.

What troubled his Vienna colleagues most, of course, was not his financial affairs, his romantic liaisons, or even his string of broken oaths. It was instead his relationship with Napoleon. It was Talleyrand, after all, who had helped mastermind Napoleon's seizure of power in the coup of 1799. It was Talleyrand, too, who had helped guide the young, inexperienced, and tactless general through the quagmire of French politics. "Talleyrand is an extraordinarily intelligent man," Napoleon once acknowledged. "He gives me excellent advice."

But it was also Talleyrand who, as everyone knew, had helped bring down Napoleon. By 1805, Talleyrand had realized that the general's many military triumphs had clouded his judgment and rendered him incapable of listening to advice. Again and again, Talleyrand had protested against Napoleon's actions—his blind aggression, his harsh authoritarian rule, and his appalling humiliation of conquered peoples. Repeatedly, Talleyrand had pressed in vain for a more just and humane approach that, he argued, would also better serve France's national interests. By August 1807, Talleyrand had had enough. "I do not wish to become the executioner of Europe," he said, and resigned from office.

Talleyrand had come to realize that Napoleon, despite all his raw charisma, was a frightening figure with an inability to stop waging war. Napoleon had come to power illegitimately, and he could only maintain his authority by extraordinary measures, or, in his case, by waging constant warfare. If France or Europe were ever to know peace any time soon, Napoleon would simply have to be stopped. Of course, with a tyrant, legal opposition was out of the question, and the only effective means of resistance, Talleyrand concluded, was to help Napoleon's enemies. Indeed, over the next few years, he would do just that.

Most prominently, Talleyrand had sent a secret message back in the spring of 1814 to Allied supreme headquarters, encouraging its hesitant leaders to march on Paris at once. Napoleon's regime was tottering, he said, and this was the time to act: "You are walking on crutches, when you should be running." The note, written with his invisible ink and smuggled by an accomplice through the war zone, arrived at the Allied camp at just the right time. Tsar Alexander ordered the army to march, and within a few days, they had captured Napoleon's capital. For Bonapartists, Talleyrand's action was treason. For others, it was a heroic act that saved many lives.

Now, in the autumn of 1814, Talleyrand's arrival in Vienna was causing some concern. To be sure, few diplomats at the congress had not applauded Talleyrand for his services to the Allied cause, and most wanted the newly restored king of France, Louis XVIII, to succeed. But at the same time, many remembered the French minister's checkered past and showed a marked reluctance to deal with him too closely. Talleyrand was a "double-edged sword," Metternich warned; "it was extremely dangerous to toy with him." He was a master of manipulation, a helpful friend who might also turn into a dangerous foe. France's delegate must be treated with great caution.

Chapter 3

ℐLLUSTRIOUS ℐTRANGERS

That's right, those poor kings ought to have a holiday.

—Prince de Ligne

ℐn the late morning of September 25, while church bells clanged and cannons thundered, crowds poured onto the streets and peered out of upper-story windows with great excitement for the arrival of Vienna's most anticipated guest: the Russian tsar Alexander. He was celebrated as a modern Alexander the Great. If Napoleon had been the "Conqueror of Europe," then Alexander was enjoying his reputation as the foremost conqueror of the Conqueror of Europe. Napoleon's invasion of Russia and the burning of Moscow had set his soul on fire, the tsar said to awestruck audiences. Arriving in Vienna, Alexander was ready for the time of his life.

Evidently, the Festivals Committee had been eager to welcome the tsar. That morning, at dawn, cannons had woken the town with news that Alexander had just departed from a nearby village and would arrive in Vienna in just over two hours. How ridiculous this salute was, Metternich noted; it just proved "that nobody has any common sense any more, for never did anyone wake up a whole city with cannon shots to inform them that a sovereign is still forty leagues away."

The weather was beautiful that morning, sunny and warm with a light breeze. The timing was also good, as the tsar's arrival fell on a Sunday, when a large part of the town could turn out to watch the spectacle. Obviously, the crowds were anxious to see the famous tsar in person, and this was particularly the case for many younger women, who adored him like "maniacs at full moon."

The tsar, riding on a white Lipizzaner stallion trained in the Austrian emperor's stables, tipped his hat and waved his large hand, looking and acting like someone accustomed to the cheering crowds. Witty, handsome, and urbane, he stood about six feet tall. Wavy light-brown hair curled around the top of his high forehead, and thick whiskers wrapped around his face. He had a straight nose, a small mouth, very white teeth, and the blue eyes of his grandmother, Catherine the Great. Alexander's cheeks were so rosy that they were often confused with a blush.

Riding at his side on another white stallion was the king of Prussia, Frederick William III, a forty-four-year-old man with dark brown hair and eyes as blue as his uniform. The two were entering Vienna together, just as they had entered Paris in triumph at the end of the war. They were joined by a third monarch, the host, Emperor Francis of Austria, who had ridden through town and crossed the Tabor Bridge to greet his guests.

It was certainly a grand entrance into the emperor's capital. The three victorious monarchs were followed by archdukes, generals, former princes of the Holy Roman Empire, and an escort of soldiers that sported a dazzling array of uniforms from the Napoleonic Wars. The procession passed under the chestnut trees of the Prater, through the Red Tower Gate in the northeast, and then along the narrow streets of the town, ending about an hour later in one of the inner courtyards of the imperial palace. The parade was full of "brilliance and pomp," one police agent in the crowds noted. "Perfect order," he added. "No incident or accident to report."

Later that morning, the tsar and the king of Prussia sat down to a large formal breakfast at the palace, joined by the king of Denmark, the king of Württemberg, and the emperor of Austria. Only the king of Bavaria, who would arrive three days later, was absent. It was rare to see so many monarchs together at the same table—a sight that would soon be almost commonplace in Vienna that autumn.

TSAR ALEXANDER WAS, in many ways, one of the most puzzling and complex figures at the congress. On one hand, he was praised by Thomas Jefferson as a beacon of enlightenment: "A more virtuous man, I believe, does not exist, nor one who is more enthusiastically devoted to better the condition of mankind." Others thought this saint was really a terrible sinner with blood on his hands.

Alexander had grown up in difficult and rather unusual circumstances. His grandmother, Catherine the Great, had fawned on him as her obvious favorite. He was raised in the spirit of the enlightenment, with an upbringing that emphasized the importance of reason, liberty, the happiness of the people, and the value of a written constitution. This education was somewhat strange, some thought, for an apprentice tsar who would one day rule over one of the most autocratic realms on earth.

Catherine's indulgence and obvious preference for her grandson displeased Alexander's father, Catherine's own son and successor, Grand Duke Paul. Intensely jealous by nature, Paul reacted to his rival in his own brutally simple way. He took every opportunity to humiliate his son, and the abuse was mental as well as physical. When Paul became tsar in 1796 (despite Catherine's direct orders to pass the throne to her grandson), life had not gotten any easier for Alexander. Paul's unpredictable outbursts of cruelty gave him the name "the mad tsar" and the bullying only ended in March 1801, when he was violently murdered. A gang of conspirators, including a commander of the elite guard, the Semeonovsky Regiment, stormed the castle, forced their way into the tsar's rooms, and strangled him to death.

It was this murder that placed the young, idealistic Alexander on the throne. The twenty-three-year-old's role in the assassination has long been debated. Some contemporaries, as well as historians, have accused him of outright complicity; others have suggested that he knew of the plot, though made no attempt to prevent it. He certainly did not prosecute or punish the murderers, many of whom would later be at his side. At the very least, Alexander was severely shaken, burdened with a sense of guilt that, by all accounts, only grew worse. He would long be tortured in his sleep, hearing his father's awful screams over and over in his head.

His marriage was not a source of comfort, either. Alexander was married unhappily to Elizabeth of Baden, a German princess with ash blonde hair and sparkling eyes, who was described by one as "certainly one of the most beautiful women in the world." The two looked like angels together—Cupid and Psyche, Catherine the Great had said. But they were not well matched, and ended up living almost separate lives. Elizabeth, for her part, was stuck in a foreign country, feeling, as she put it, "alone, alone, absolutely alone."

Both were certainly having affairs on each other: the tsar with his mistress, Maria Narishkiva, and some speculated even his sister, Grand Duchess Catherine; and Elizabeth with a number of people, ranging from soldiers to a certain "ambiguous intimacy" with a lovely countess. Empress Elizabeth also had an affair with one of the tsar's advisers, Prince Adam Czartoryski, the Polish patriot who had come to Russia as a hostage after the destruction of Poland and won Alexander's trust. The tsar, however, never seemed disturbed by his wife's relationship with his adviser, and in fact, by most accounts, encouraged it as only fair, given the liberties he was taking himself.

When Alexander came to Vienna for the peace conference, he had ruled for thirteen taxing years. During this time, Russia had been invaded by Napoleon and well over six hundred thousand troops, at that time the largest army the world had ever seen. Villages had been destroyed, the countryside devastated, several hundred thousand people killed, and the city of Moscow burned to the ground. Surely Russia should be compensated for its sacrifices in the war against Napoleon. At the very least, its concerns should not be ignored. Under no circumstances would the tsar compromise on an issue as important to him as Poland.

Alexander had yet to specify his exact plans for the region, though privately he had promised to re-create the Kingdom of Poland—that is, he would combine the slice of Poland he had inherited from Catherine the Great with the lands of the Napoleonic Duchy of Warsaw, which his army had occupied since the end of the war. The tsar seemed genuine enough, and many Polish patriots took him at his word. But there was a nagging concern that he might not be able to deliver on these grand promises. Even if he had the best intentions, would the tsar, in the end, allow this creation to be free and independent?

Certainly, no one was comfortable having Russia's enormous realm stretching so far to the west with this satellite kingdom of Poland, and the touchy, unpredictable tsar as a neighbor. Castlereagh and Metternich alike feared the implications. Would this not make Russia the new unrivaled power, potentially enjoying a dominance that not even Napoleon had commanded?

Alexander already had the support of his traveling companion and old friend, the king of Prussia. The tsar and the king had developed a close working relationship, which had been sealed with a melodramatic act, even for that melodramatic age. When Alexander had visited Berlin in 1805, the tsar and the king had descended into the crypt of the enlightened despot Frederick the Great, and, beside the tomb of the dead king, they had sworn oaths of eternal friendship.

Of course, during the stress of the war, the emotional scene had been forgotten, and the two powers had betrayed each other. But later, when the tide had turned in their favor, both had acknowledged their mistakes. This time, they swore that they would stick together, and cemented their renewed alliance with a deal: Russia would gain a free hand in Poland, and Prussia, in return for its support (and surrender of its Polish territory), would receive a part of central and eastern Germany known as Saxony. They had written their promises, in the secret Treaty of Kalisch, signed back in February 1813, and pledged to support each other no matter what.

"YOU CANNOT BELIEVE how beautiful my rooms are when the sun shines through them," Metternich had once said, admiring the tall, well-designed oriental windows of his office study at the Foreign Ministry. The challenge, he knew, was finding the time to enjoy them properly.

By late September 1814, the congress had not yet opened and the foreign minister was appalled to see the staggering amount of work already piling up. There were dispatches to read, protocols to draft, and agendas to juggle, never mind the endless logistical matters of launching the peace conference, for which Metternich was already serving, unofficially, as president. "Interminable chores," it all seemed to the foreign minister in one of his weak moments.

Just as he had feared, visitors were beating down a path to the white stone Chancellery building, home of the Foreign Ministry, a large, early eighteenth-century structure adorned with Corinthian columns and facing out onto the northern end of the Hofburg Palace. The Chancellery was also known as the Ballhaus, after its previous use as a Habsburg tennis court. This was only appropriate, Metternich's critics pointed out, given the foreign minister's frivolous gamelike approach to diplomacy.

Metternich's offices with the lovely large windows were on the second floor. Green damask covered the walls in the main negotiating room, from the parquet floor to the new stucco ceiling. There were dark woodwork, oil paintings in gilt frames, and white marble busts resting on pedestals. The room had been redecorated with a new marble fireplace and many new pieces of furniture that Metternich had purchased a few months before in Paris. He had given the matter some thought, Metternich said, because he feared he would probably be spending a lot of time there.

The large anteroom, with its high, eighteen-foot ceilings, was regularly filled up to capacity. Petitioners hoping to have a word with Metternich found themselves facing what seemed like an interminable wait, and passed the time the best they could, exchanging stories or just staring at the walls, which were lined with mahogany bookshelves holding handsome volumes in red morocco.

One morning that month, for example, Metternich found this room packed yet again with people eager to press some case or other. Prussia's chancellor, Karl August von Hardenberg, who had arrived in Vienna a few days before, had come to request an audience. He was already complaining about the difficulty of gaining a meeting with Metternich the Invisible, as he dubbed him. A representative of the king of Bavaria, Field Marshal Prince Karl Wrede, was also there waiting, probably with his trusty maps in hand. Four officials in long black robes with a shining silver Maltese cross also stood out, representing the Knights of Malta, an elite chivalric order that dated back to the twelfth century.

No doubt the knights wanted to have their treasures returned after Napoleon's plundering in 1798. He had sacked their island, running off with gold and silver chalices, goblets, and jewels from a treasure vault that had been accumulated since the thirteenth century. The knights also wanted their island, Malta, returned. The British had promised a prompt restoration after they liberated it from Napoleon, but they had not yet complied and, in the opinion of the Grand Master of the Order, showed no signs of doing so. The Grand Master was correct. The British had grown attached to the beautiful strategic island with the excellent naval base, and they had secured it in the Treaty of Paris.

Countless other people filled the crowded room, including two or three dozen German noblemen, all former knights of the now defunct Holy Roman Empire. Many of these aristocrats had lost ancient privileges, and often also family property, when Napoleon dismantled the empire and parceled out its western edges, awarding territory to his vassal kingdoms of Bavaria, Württemberg, and Westphalia. Some of the knights would press for restoration of their rights and property, and others went further, hoping for nothing less than the revival of the Holy Roman Empire itself.

"I found all of Europe in my anteroom," Metternich said with vanity and frustration, as he eyed the many petitioners with their bulging leather portfolios and the endless amount of work that they represented. Metternich was not looking forward to the hard wrangling ahead. It was sure to be, he predicted, "four or six weeks of hell."

WHEN THE SHEER magnitude of the problems seemed overwhelming, Metternich could shuffle down a private staircase, cross a cobbled lane, and escape into an eighteenth-century mansion at 54 Schenkengasse.

This was the Palm Palace, and for the past year Metternich had been drawing on all his finesse in arranging a love affair with a woman who occupied one of its large suites: Wilhelmine, the Duchess of Sagan. Metternich had had many liaisons in the past, but this one was different. The duchess was one of the most desirable matches of the day, and Metternich was clearly succumbing to her charms.

The Duchess of Sagan was a slim and petite thirty-three-year-old with dark-blonde hair and deep brown eyes—a ravishing and restless beauty who also happened to be heiress to one of the largest fortunes in Europe. She owned castles all over eastern and central Europe, including Sagan, built by the mercenary of the Thirty Years War, Count Wallenstein, and located a hundred miles south of Berlin.

When Metternich met the duchess, through a mutual friend during his carefree days as a diplomat in Dresden, he had been intrigued. She had grown up in Courland in the Baltic (today's Latvia), traveled all over Europe, and spoke half a dozen languages fluently. She was in her second unhappy marriage, and soon to be her second divorce. "I am ruining myself with husbands," she was said to have quipped.

The duchess had kept her own name, and managed her own estates, a somewhat daunting prospect given her extensive property. She had used some of her fortune for charity, even financing a private hospital for wounded soldiers. At one time, when a maid in her household went into premature labor, Wilhelmine had stepped in as an emergency midwife and helped deliver a healthy baby girl.

The relationship between Metternich and the Duchess of Sagan had first started to heat up in the summer of 1813 when he was working on arranging a peace with Napoleon. The peace at that time failed, but the romance thrived. Metternich saw the duchess as much as he could, and in the midst of the crisis, wrote his first long love letter to her:

> I watched you for years. I found you beautiful; my heart remained silent; why has that sweet peace deserted me? Why out of nothing have you become for me everything?

The duchess was surprised and frankly flattered by the attentions of this dashing statesman, but she had not been won over, at least not yet. Metternich, however, had persisted. One month later, he wrote:

> I am writing because I shall not see you this morning, and I must tell you that I love you more than my life—that my happiness is nothing unless you are very much a part of it.

The duchess could fill a room in her palace with all the gifts Metternich would send, everything from books bound in red morocco to lamps made of lava. Metternich, in turn, cherished every gift that he received. On one shelf in his study was a special black box that had a lock of her hair.

Metternich liked her mind, her judgment, her generosity. He liked how beautiful she looked in her formal gown that sparkled in the ballroom, and he liked the baggy flannels that she wore when she was only lounging around her suite, including her personal favorite, an old "wadded gown with holes in the elbows." Metternich liked the little things, such as the way she drank her cognac, balancing a sugar cube onto the small silver spoon, gently dipping it into the amber drink, and then, at the end, slurping down the rest. "What," he once wrote to her, "don't I like about you."

By the end of that summer, the duchess had finally come around, and confessed her love for Metternich as well: "I do not know how I love you, but I love you very much, and with my whole heart." Metternich had been thrilled with the news—making love was one thing, confessing it was another. He wrote back immediately, feeling like he had been suddenly "transported into the loveliest, most blessed spot on earth."

> You have made me drunk with happiness. I love you, I love you a hundred times more than my life. I do not live, I shall not live except for you.

Their relationship was impossible to keep completely secret, and the Palm Palace was certainly going to be a fascinating place that autumn. With the Duchess of Sagan hosting her fashionable salon on its second floor, there was another woman, in a parallel wing, just as intelligent, witty, rich, beautiful, and it must be said, controversial. This was Princess Catherine Bagration, the thirty-one-year-old widow of Pyotr Ivanovich Bagration, a Russian general and war hero who had fallen at Borodino. She was blonde with light blue eyes and pinkish white skin that one admirer compared to alabaster. Her scandalous evening gowns, very low cut, earned her the nickname "the beautiful naked angel."

For many years now, Princess Catherine Bagration and the Duchess of Sagan had been sworn enemies. The reasons for the hostility were many, buried under many layers of gossip, intrigue, and counterintrigue, though no small part of this animosity stemmed from a long rivalry for honor and influence in high society. They certainly had a lot in common.

Nearly the same age, both had come from the Baltic, and both were the oldest daughters of rich, high aristocratic families, who had traveled and lived all over the continent. Both, after marrying young, were now single and surrounded by many admirers. Both had now ended up in Vienna at the time of the congress, and by "a curious and fatal chance," as one salon regular put it, the two young divas had ended up in the same palace, immediately opposite each other. The windows, in fact, overlooked a shared courtyard.

All throughout the autumn, eyes would peer out from behind silk curtains, keeping careful tabs on the carriages coming and going, and who went to which salon. The two women would compete for everything, from the most prized guests to the greatest social esteem for their evening soirees. They were two queen bees, trying to share the same hive, and their rivalry would both enliven and embitter relations at the congress.

Many intrigues would be spun in the corridors, staircases, and drawing rooms of this palace.

Vienna society would effectively have to make a choice, either taking the left staircase up to Princess Bagration, the "Russian siren," or the right staircase to the Duchess of Sagan, "the Cleopatra of Courland." As for the outcome of the competition between the two women of the north, one society watcher reported, "the bets were open."

But there was something else the two ladies shared: Both had been Metternich's lover. And now, both women, it seemed, were attracting the attentions of Russia's flamboyant tsar.

Chapter 4

DOROTHÉE'S CHOICE

It is essential to make the French embassy a pleasant place.

—TALLEYRAND

espite the distance of the journey, the British had been one of the first official delegations to roll into town. The leader was Lord Castlereagh, tall, blond, and looking twenty years younger than his actual age of forty-five. His thin, almost frail frame was usually draped in black; his somber choice in clothes, it was said, often matched his mood. His long, angular face gave the impression of aristocratic detachment, or, as some dryly noted, made him appear to be in a state of perpetual boredom. It was certainly a champion poker face, which would serve him well both at Vienna's diplomacy and gambling tables.

Castlereagh and his team had reached the Austrian capital back on the thirteenth of September, and immediately hunted down their designated headquarters, a house tucked away in the narrow Milchgasse. The rooms had actually been rented some years before to a young musician named Wolfgang Amadeus Mozart. While living there in the early 1780s, Mozart had worked on his first full German opera, *Die Entführung aus dem Serail (The Abduction from the Seraglio)*, and carried on an affair with the landlady's daughter, Constanze, whom he married in 1782. The cozy flat may have proven a happy place for Mozart and his opera, but its cramped size hardly suited the delegation representing Great Britain, proud financier of Allied victory.

Castlereagh would indeed seek out a new place to stay, and within a week move into a twenty-two-room suite on the Minoritenplatz, an elegant cobbled square lined with aristocratic mansions and the fourteenth-century Church of the Friars Minor. The British delegation was now just a few steps away from both Metternich's offices on the Ballhausplatz and the Hofburg Palace itself. Castlereagh and his wife, Lady Emily, were housed on the top floor, the diplomatic staff on the first floor, and the ground floor was reserved for entertainment. The Castlereaghs would enjoy setting the mood for some evening soirees with the hauntingly ethereal sounds of the glass harmonium, a musical instrument invented by Benjamin Franklin.

Unlike the other major delegations at the peace conference, Britain was actually still at war, fighting across the ocean against the young republic of the United States. In American history, this is known as the War of 1812; in British history, it has not received its own name, generally submerged into the wider conflict with Napoleon. Battles still raged across a number of fronts in Canada, on the Great Lakes, and on the Atlantic. Indeed, just a few weeks before Castlereagh arrived in Vienna, British troops had landed at Chesapeake and burned Washington to the ground, destroying the Treasury, the Library of Congress, and even the President's Palace. James and Dolley Madison had fled, and the war showed no signs of abating.

While this meant that their attention would be divided between America and Europe, Britain clearly prioritized the conference at Vienna, and felt confident in its position. Castlereagh's country had earned immense prestige as the only power that had hung on for the entire struggle against Napoleon, sometimes facing the foe all alone. They had the world's largest navy, its richest economy, and colonial possessions already dotting the globe from South Africa to India. During the war, they had scooped up other colonies from the French and their allies. All of this would, they figured, translate into a strong negotiating position.

National hopes were centered on securing freedom of the seas, so important to the Royal Navy, and one of the many issues in the war with the States. Castlereagh also wanted to make sure that the flatlands and coasts of the area known today as Belgium would not, under any circumstances, fall again into the hands of a hostile country. This meant, above all, that it should be kept away from France. The port of Antwerp was a potential launching pad for an invasion—"the loaded pistol held to England's head."

Castlereagh was pushing for handing over this port, and in fact all of Belgium, to the newly created Kingdom of the Netherlands, whose monarch, William I of the House of Orange, was a good ally of Britain. Actually, Castlereagh had already been assured of success on this point. The handover of territory had been decided as part of a secret clause attached to the Treaty of Paris, and the British foreign minister fully expected that the signing would be a mere formality, no matter how spirited Belgian opposition might turn out to be.

Otherwise, as far as Britain's goals were concerned, Castlereagh was content to promote the general balance of power, a policy that he felt would best serve the interests of world peace. This policy would also, he knew, serve Britain's own commercial interests, the island power already well on its way to becoming the "workshop of the world."

As he saw it, following in a line of politicians including his mentor, former prime minister William Pitt, no single power, or group of powers, should be allowed to dominate the continent, and if any seemed on the verge of surpassing the others, Britain would interfere to restore the "just equilibrium." Traditionally, the biggest threat to this balance had come from France, which had off and on challenged it for the last 150 years. Now, though, with the defeat of Napoleon, there was a potential new menace.

This was Russia, which had been Britain's ally in the last years of the war. While several countries had pretensions of being a Great Power, Great Britain and Russia were the only countries in a league of their own. Russia, of course, was a giant, boasting the continent's largest landmass, equal to some seventy times the size of Great Britain. It had the largest army in the world, and it was now occupying much of the former French empire, including Poland, Saxony, and Holstein, bordering on Denmark. Castlereagh, for one, was worried about the quick rise of Russia—a country whose prestige had been enhanced by its smashing victories, and whose ruler was not exactly known for his moderation.

Prior to his career as foreign minister, Castlereagh had studied at St. John's College at Cambridge, though he left before receiving a degree. He had returned instead to his home in Ireland, Standford Lough in the heart of County Down in the northwest, where he had been elected to the Irish Parliament at age twenty-one. He rose quickly. At every stage in his ascent, as minister of trade, minister of war, and then, in 1812, foreign secretary, Castlereagh had shown himself to be confident, and rather brave in facing stiff opposition. He was dogged in a Churchillian way, and about as stubborn as one might find in the political arena.

Lord Castlereagh had played a pivotal role in founding the modern British Foreign Office. When he had assumed responsibilities two years before, Britain had six diplomatic missions, and only one of them was *not* ruled by a government in exile, prison, or some other greatly reduced state. As Napoleon's empire started to crumble, however, Britain could again establish embassies in the liberated countries. Castlereagh had been in the right place at the right time; he had appointed almost the entire Diplomatic Service of Great Britain.

Castlereagh had also been the first British foreign secretary ever to visit the Continent on an official mission—back in January 1814, during the last stages of the war. Now on his second trip, Castlereagh was bringing one of the larger teams to the peace conference. There were fourteen assistants, including the indefatigable Lord Clancarty, who had previously served as minister to the Hague and would advise on many matters, including the Netherlands, and Lord Cathcart, the former soldier and specialist on Russia, brought along for his good relationship with the tsar. There was also the undersecretary of state, Edward Cooke, and Castlereagh's private secretary, Joseph Planta, both of whom were hardworking assistants loyal to their leader.

Clearly, the most notorious resident of the British embassy was Sir Charles Stewart, a thirty-six-year-old ambassador to Vienna and a veteran of the Spanish campaigns. Loud and obnoxious, Lord Stewart had an outlandish sense of humor better suited to the barrack rooms than the salons, and many critics doubted his diplomatic abilities, to say the least. Far too often, it seemed, after a few drinks, Stewart would stalk around "out to kick everybody in the teeth." His bright yellow boots and extravagant mannerisms would earn him a new nickname, Lord Pumpernickel. Stewart was only there, many thought, because he was Castlereagh's half brother.

Upon his arrival at Kaunitz Palace, Talleyrand began paying his courtesy visits to the embassies scattered around town. He had a new title on his calling card, Prince de Talleyrand, an honor awarded by King Louis

XVIII just before his departure from Paris. The French foreign minister no longer had to use the title Prince de Bénévent, which had been granted by Napoleon. Talleyrand needed to distance himself and his country as far away from Bonaparte as possible.

Although France had happily, as he put it, "escaped destruction" in the Treaty of Paris, Talleyrand knew that the Allied powers had been severely criticized for not being a great deal more demanding. For many, France was still the same reckless and dangerous power full of crusading fanatics simply incapable of allowing their neighbors to live in peace. The congress would run more smoothly without its participation.

Such a negative image, of course, threatened to undermine the efforts of French diplomacy, and this was unfortunate because Talleyrand had many objectives that he hoped to obtain. For one, just as Louis XVIII had been restored as king of France, he wanted to see another member of the Bourbon family, Ferdinand IV, returned to the throne in Naples, which had been lost in 1808 and was now occupied by one of Napoleon's flamboyant marshals, Joachim Murat. As Talleyrand would argue, the Bourbon was the legitimate king, and the best hope for any peace on that peninsula.

Another high priority was saving the king of Saxony, Frederick Augustus, who was in danger of losing both his crown and his country. The king was a cousin of Louis XVIII, an ally of France, and, most important, a counterweight to the rising power of Prussia, which, Talleyrand feared, wanted to dominate all of Germany. Prussian ambitions must be curbed, Talleyrand argued, or that kingdom "would in a few years form a militarist monarchy that would be very dangerous for her neighbors."

That first week in town, Talleyrand would lay the basis for his diplomatic campaign, attending fashionable salons, and calling upon Emperor Francis, the imperial family, the Great Powers, and many of the smaller delegations that were often neglected. He had a good eight or ten days of visits ahead, and it was a task that, he mused, "would weary better legs than mine."

To help achieve his goals, Talleyrand had selected a team of diplomats, experts, and support staff to join him in Vienna. One of the most prominent was an old friend, Emmerich, the Duke of Dalberg, a young man who came from one of the oldest aristocratic families in Germany with considerable property in the Rhineland, especially between Speyer and Worms. Dalberg could be unscrupulous and untrustworthy, not to mention an indiscreet boaster. Talleyrand was not unaware of this fact: Dalberg was chosen, he said, "so that he might broadcast those of my secrets that I want everyone to know."

Talleyrand brought along two other prominent plenipotentiaries, as the chief delegates were called (from the Latin word meaning "someone invested with full authority"). The first was his old friend Gouvernet, the Marquis de la Tour du Pin, a former ambassador to Holland and a handsome and harmless pleasure-seeker who would not be saddled with too many responsibilities. "He will do," Talleyrand said, "for stamping the passports." The second, Comte Alexis de Noailles, an extreme royalist, was selected primarily because he was a well-known informer for the royal family, particularly the king's brother. "If one must be spied upon," Talleyrand explained, "it's best to be surveyed by an agent I have chosen myself."

While these three appointments might not sound the most qualified for complex international negotiations, they had strengths as measured by the standards of early nineteenth-century diplomacy. Each was a nobleman, familiar with the intricacies of drawing-room politics, and boasted many social connections within Europe's cosmopolitan aristocracy, all of which would come in handy at the Vienna Congress.

The best choice for dealing with the hard foreign policy questions was Jean-Baptiste de Gouey, Comte de la Besnardière, a forty-nine-year-old plucked from the Ministry of Foreign Affairs. According to Talleyrand, he had earned a reputation as the department's most promising talent. Besnardière would certainly help with the workload, serving as the unsung coauthor of many of the French delegation's papers.

In addition to these selections, Talleyrand also brought along a team of valets, barbers, hairdressers, cooks, and other staff who would keep the embassy running. Among them was the thirty-six-year-old personal assistant and piano player Sigismund Neukomm. An Austrian from Salzburg and a former student of Joseph Haydn, Neukomm's soft, dreamy keys would help Talleyrand focus, relax, or just escape into his own world of plots and counterplots.

Talleyrand's greatest success in the tricky area of staff selection, however, was arguably his choice of hostesses. He picked a twenty-one-year-old niece by marriage, Dorothée de Talleyrand-Périgord, an intelligent, beautiful woman who, it turns out, was also the Duchess of Sagan's younger sister.

DOROTHÉE WAS A young lady with striking black hair and flashing dark eyes—they were so dark blue that they seemed black, burning, as one admirer put it, "with an infernal fire which turned night into day." Her skin was pale, offset by dabs of rouge, and she had a very thin waistline. By the time of the peace congress, Dorothée was painfully unhappy and very much alone.

Some thirteen years younger than her sister Wilhelmine, Dorothée could not have been more different. Wilhelmine, the oldest in the family, was clearly her father's favorite, adored, indulged, and reared with a stellar education. Dorothée, by contrast, was largely neglected. Her childhood was, in her own words, "sad and miserable." Whereas Wilhelmine could, as a young girl, recite Virgil in Latin, guests at castle were shocked to see the seven-year-old Dorothée unable to read or recognize the letters of the alphabet.

There is some uncertainty about the identity of her biological father. Dorothée always called Peter, the Duke of Courland, her father, though biographers have long noted that it was very likely an impoverished Polish nobleman and captain of a mercenary regiment, Count Olek Batowski, who had briefly stayed at the family castle. At any rate, Duke Peter was almost seventy years old at the time of her birth, and very sick.

Dorothée had never had the chance to know either man. The Polish nobleman had left the castle soon after her birth, and the Duke of Courland died when she was seven. Her mother, Anna-Dorothea, the Duchess of Courland, was also distant, often busy with her own active social life. Dorothée did not grow up close to her three sisters, either; the nearest one in age was ten years older. Dorothée had very few playmates her own age, and, for the most part, she had been left on her own.

Years later, Dorothée described herself and how she had felt as a child:

Small, skinny, yellow in complexion, always ill from the moment of my birth. My eyes were so dark and huge that they were out of all proportion to the rest of my face and seemed to dwarf the other features . . . Sad almost to the point of melancholia, I remember perfectly how I longed to die.

It was one of her mother's lovers, Count Gustav Armfelt, a Swedish guest, who first took an interest in Dorothée's upbringing. He had decided to teach Dorothée personally, and, much to his surprise, he discovered that she was a very quick learner. In fact, he soon became convinced that Dorothée was an unusually gifted child.

All of a sudden, with his prompting, nothing was too much for the family's talented youngest daughter. The Duchess of Courland hired two full-time tutors, one of them being Abbé Piattoli, the former secretary to the last king of Poland. He in turn would take her on excursions that suited her newfound interests, such as many trips to the theater, complete with lessons from the queen of the Berlin stage, Madame Unzelmann. For Dorothée's interest in astronomy, the abbé arranged lessons from the royal astronomer at the Berlin Observatory.

With the help of her encouraging and stimulating teachers, Dorothée was soon showing signs of an exceptionally sharp mind, and the ability to grasp sophisticated subjects quickly. All the while, she was enjoying her new love of reading. She would dash into the family library, scale the ladder to the top, and sit there, under the high ceiling, with a book in her lap.

But by the age of fifteen, Dorothée was under considerable pressure to marry. Despite being promised the freedom to choose a husband herself, she was now being pressured to marry the man of her mother's choice—or rather Tsar Alexander's choice, or more exactly, Talleyrand's choice. Her future had been plotted like an international intrigue.

The French minister had heard of the beautiful heiress Dorothée, and wanted her for his nephew, the twenty-old-year-old Edmond de Talleyrand-Périgord. As Dorothée was a subject of the Russian tsar, Talleyrand had asked Alexander to talk with Dorothée's mother, and persuade her to arrange this marriage. The tsar, being grateful to Talleyrand for his support against Napoleon, agreed. In October 1808, at a visit to their castle, the tsar made his wishes abundantly clear: "My dear Duchess, I refuse to accept any excuse. I have given my word. I ask for yours."

When the duchess approached her daughter about Edmond, Dorothée had flatly refused. She preferred to choose her own husband, and that was going to be the Polish patriot Prince Adam Czartoryski, whom she had heard about from her tutor. Sure, he was twenty-three years older, and they had barely exchanged a word, but for a budding romantic like Dorothée, this was irrelevant. She was determined to make the match work, and no one, including the Tsar of All the Russias, was going to stop her.

At this point, when her mother realized the intensity of her conviction, she resorted to an elaborate scheme to trick Dorothée out of her teenage infatuation with an idealized prince of her imagination.

First, her tutor was threatened and forced to declare, falsely, that the Polish prince had just been engaged to another woman. As Dorothée still held out, her mother arranged for Polish friends to arrive at the castle with confirmation of the lie. All Warsaw was talking of the prince's engagement, they claimed, and in the end, a sad Dorothée agreed to marry this Frenchman she hardly knew.

Edmond was an excellent soldier and cavalry officer who had been decorated several times for his bravery, but he was not a good husband. He was a notorious philanderer, squandering a fortune on his extramarital lovers and his losses at the gaming tables. He racked up considerable debts, too, splurging on his lavish uniforms, adorned with "gold braid, spangles and gems." Worse still, Edmond could not stimulate Dorothée's mind, and the married couple had almost nothing to talk about.

"It was impossible to predict his temperament or his thoughts," Dorothée complained, because "no one has ever relied so heavily . . . on silence." Edmond was only home long enough, it seems, for the couple to have three children: Napoleon-Louis, or Louis since the emperor's downfall; Dorothea-Charlotte-Emily; and the infant Alexander-Edmond. Other than her children, whom she loved dearly, it was a sad and dreary marriage.

Then, that summer of 1814, on the eve of the congress, tragedy struck. Dorothée's daughter had fallen ill to the measles, a frightening situation in the early nineteenth century. Sadly, after an apparent recovery, the little girl had a sudden setback and died.

Dorothée was devastated, and, unfortunately, had to bear most of her suffering alone. Edmond was still away at war—he had not been home for more than a few months of the girl's life. The rest of her family was away in Berlin, Courland, or the spas of central Europe. The only person who came to see her was Talleyrand. He found time from his busy schedule at the foreign ministry to console the poor mother in her grief.

Clearly, Dorothée needed a change of environment, and one day that summer, Talleyrand asked if she would like to accompany him to Vienna for the upcoming peace conference. She could be hostess at the embassy.

Dorothée, for her part, accepted the offer. There was nothing left to hold her back in Paris. She would miss her children, of course, but they could stay with her mother. After all, the congress was only supposed to last a few weeks.

So with a new activity to occupy her mind, Dorothée started selecting dresses, gowns, gloves, fans, masks, stockings, jewels, and many different kinds of shoes, all of which were packed into large trunks and then loaded by footmen onto the traveling carriages. On September 16, the preparations were ready. Dorothée and the chief delegate would travel to Vienna together.

Talleyrand had indeed come to admire her abilities. She was beautiful, graceful, charming, and, above all, very intelligent. She had a love of reading, a talent for the art of conversation, and a knack for putting people at ease. Other salon hostesses might be more worldly or sophisticated, but Dorothée, with her youthful and unstudied innocence, would carve out a niche of her own.

Chapter 5

The Big Four

Pretend to be ignorant of what everyone knows, and to know what others don't, seem to understand what no-one understands, not to hear what all are hearing, and, in particular, appear able to do the impossible.

— The Marriage of Figaro (1784)
Pierre Augustin Caron de Beaumarchais

With so many royalty, statesmen, and other celebrities making their way to the congress, Vienna's street performers were busy honing their acts. New marionette shows appeared in puppet theaters around town, and animal shows flourished as well, including one where the entertainer boasted a monkey, an owl, and what he claimed was a shark that he had fished out of the sea at Trieste. A wider selection of exotic animals could be found at the Schönbrunn Palace Zoo, such as rare birds, bears, buffalo, two camels, and a small collection of kangaroos from New Holland, in what is now Australia.

The giant park known as the Prater, the former royal hunting ground north of the city center, was especially lively. There were cafés, restaurants, dance halls, gambling rooms, some buildings shaped exotically as Chinese pavilions, Indian kiosks, Swiss chalets, and "savage huts." There were good places for fireworks, carriage rides, and pleasant walks. The tall trees of its "magnificent forest" and great lawn, as one visitor, Cadet de Gassicourt, said, "cast shadows that cover the earth with a green carpet that the sun never yellows."

One entertainer in the park had opened his own "mechanical optical theater" to show scenes of the awful war, including "The Fire of Moscow" and "The Battle of Leipzig," to name some of his attractions. He also had a new act depicting the Allied march into Paris, complete with "more than one thousand popular moving figures."

Curious sightseers strolled through the narrow winding streets around St. Stephen's Cathedral and filled the intimate market squares of the inner city. Even Castlereagh's wife, Emily, who was used to the delights of London's West End, was pleased at what she saw. *"Mon Dieu,"* she exclaimed to her husband. "What a fine city! What shops! We almost broke our necks looking."

All around the town, merchants were looking forward to a golden age of business. Innkeepers, restaurateurs, café owners, and theater managers were just some of the entrepreneurs positioning themselves to house, feed, and entertain Europe's richest and most powerful figures, many of whom would also bring their own large retinues. Hatmakers, wigmakers, glove makers, tailors, seamstresses, hairdressers, bakers, butchers, florists, and toymakers were likewise hoping for a good season.

Landlords were calculating their likely profits as the congress dignitaries thronged into the city and competed for housing that was scarce in the best of times. Sometimes mansions were leased to the lucky delegations, such as the Spanish, who moved in near the British on the Minoritenplatz. More often, though, the delegates would have to make do with suites, single rooms, or even just attics.

When Prussian ambassador Wilhelm von Humboldt had arrived in August, he complained that already, at this early date, he could not find anything other than a drab "hole in the wall." Rents had soared. Proprietors of the best real estate near the Hofburg speculated, happily, that if the congress lasted slightly longer than the three to six weeks that most diplomats suspected, then rental intake alone might very well pay for the entire property.

Prices were spiraling higher for many other basic goods. The cost of meat shot up to several times its level just a few months before, and many Viennese blamed the butchers for raising prices arbitrarily. Quality firewood was already hitting 50 gulden a cord, not including additional charges for "cartage, sawing, and splitting." Candles were likewise on the rise, given the demand to fill all the chandeliers and candelabra for all the balls, banquets, and other late-night activities. Soap went up, too, because, someone joked, "the Congress is going to have a heap of dirty laundry to wash."

Winegrowers of the fertile valleys surrounding Vienna were bottling their best vintage, and rushing new ones onto the market, too. Bakers, not to be outdone, had created a special Vienna Congress roll, though some critics complained that a powerful pair of glasses was needed to find the slice of meat on the inside.

Already that autumn, as Metternich pranced, the tsar strutted, and Talleyrand limped, the crowds came to gawk. Notice was taken of the smallest detail—who went to which café, inn, or tavern, and who left the "monstrous tip." Even the most insignificant gesture could attract the curious onlooker. As one observer, Friedrich Anton von Schönholz put it, "Wherever a scaffold went up, equipment was carried in and out, a glass carriage washed, a rug beaten, the pushing crowd was sure to gather."

Indeed, the advertisement about the holding of a congress to decide the future of Europe had stimulated imaginations and brought a whole stream of delegates into town, even from the tiniest principality and the smallest Swiss canton. The pope was sending his secretary of state, Cardinal Consalvi, and the sultan of the Ottoman Empire his adviser, Mavrojény. Even Napoleon's marshals sent an agent to bargain on their behalf for their right to maintain the generous property endowments that the former French emperor had given them, before almost all of them had betrayed him.

Napoleon's stepson, Prince Eugène de Beauharnais, the former viceroy of Italy still in his Napoleonic uniform, had come to safeguard his interests—he had been promised a state by the Treaty of Paris, though it had not yet been specified where it would be. Among the countless German princes, there was Karl August, the Duke of Weimar, the generous patron of Goethe, Schiller, Herder, Wieland, and many other poets and writers who made his small duchy a literary Arcadia.

There were also several members of the Reuss family, whose ancestors had ruled the tiny principality of Reuss since the eleventh century. Every male had been named Henry (at first Henry the Tall, Henry the Short, Henry the Brave, and so on, though by the seventeenth century they had started using numerals, planning to continue until one hundred and then start over again). The family had also split into an elder branch, represented at the congress by Prince Henry Reuss XIX, and a younger branch, by Prince Henry Reuss XXII. Other members of the family who came to Vienna for the congress included Henry LII and Henry LXIV.

Far less conspicuous, of course, was a young erudite twenty-nine-year-old representing the small delegation of Hesse-Cassel named Jacob Grimm. He and his brother Wilhelm had just published, two years before, the *Kinder- und Hausmärchen,* better known as *Grimm's Fairy Tales,* and Jacob Grimm would use his free time in Vienna to work on another collection of folktales that would be published after the congress.

Excitement was indeed in the air, and there was a scramble to participate in the lavish peace conference in any way possible. Vienna's most distinguished families angled to secure a place, as Schönholz noted with surprise, even offering "to don servants' garb only to be close to the wondrous events to come." Prince de Ligne had said that he would not have missed the Vienna Congress for 100,000 florins.

MINGLING, TOO, AMONG these throngs were some spectators with a special mission. Vienna's chief of police, the fifty-four-year-old Baron Franz von Hager, was running an extensive, intrusive, if sometimes highly inept espionage service. He had many agents already watching, following, and befriending the visitors streaming into Vienna. Hager answered directly to the Austrian emperor, Francis, who, like many enlightened despots before him, was particularly keen to stay enlightened about what his people were doing, saying, and thinking.

Austria had considerable experience in the art of surveillance, letter snatching, cipher breaking, and snooping in general. Habsburg agents had honed their skills under the watchful eyes of Joseph II. Emperor Francis would take up where his uncle had left off, increasing the cloak-and-dagger budget by a staggering 500 percent and vastly expanding its activities. An energetic class of agents was recruited, showing the emperor's talent for selecting officers who were, in the words of one well-placed archduke, "repulsive to all decent-minded people."

Stationed in the Hofburg Palace, in a suite of offices in the Imperial Court Chancellery wing of the palace, placed, conveniently, next to the emperor, the Vienna spies would need much more than repulsive qualities to meet the expectations placed upon them. There was indeed a great sense of urgency as the police system finalized its preparations for a large peace conference.

Spies had in fact just uncovered a ring of disaffected Italian patriots who had plotted to open the Vienna Congress by assassinating the Austrian emperor. The suspects were not happy that their homeland would once again fall under foreign rule—passing, as one put it, from the purgatory of Napoleon to the hell of Austria. By the middle of August, however, the police had quietly foiled this conspiracy and expelled the suspects.

Regardless of how dangerous the threat of an assassination actually was, the police acted with quick diligence, and seized upon this occasion to bargain for additional resources to prevent tragedy at the peace conference. It was imperative, they argued, to keep a close eye on the activities of everyone and provide real security for their many royal guests. The emperor agreed.

The official instructions, promulgated at the end of August 1814, suggest the growing ambitions of this revamped espionage network:

> Since a certain number of representatives of the different powers attending the Congress have already arrived in Vienna and the rest will be following them in a steady stream, you should not only keep me informed of the arrival and address of each one, but by virtue of a secret watch intelligently maintained you should also make it your business neither to lose track of their whereabouts nor of the company they keep.

Daily reports, it was added, were to be written and delivered to the emperor's office. Francis would read them closely every morning.

Baron Franz von Hager had entered police administration after his promising career as a cavalry officer, leading a regiment of dragoons, had been cut short by a riding injury. He had been president of the Ministry of Police and Censorship since 1812, and he had hounded rebels, radicals, secret societies, and many other threats to the government, real or suspected. But he would now face a series of challenges in providing security and intelligence that would enervate the most intrepid and dedicated spymaster.

How was he, for instance, to infiltrate the many foreign delegations—French, British, Russian, Prussian, and probably about two hundred sizable others—with all their exotic languages and customs? Even before he could deal with this issue, which he would soon do with zeal, there was another concern. All of Baron Hager's tireless efforts would further be complicated by the fact that the emperor sometimes issued orders and made decisions that quite frankly obstructed the tasks already assigned.

The Austrian emperor had opened up his palace to many sovereigns, a hospitable gesture that brought many guests into close proximity, but it also created a number of problems for the spy baron. For one thing, the royal palaces were technically off limits to his team's prying activities. For another, even assuming that they could overcome this situation with some creative infiltration, there were still serious problems posed by the palace itself.

The Hofburg was a meandering, labyrinthine structure with many back doors, side entrances, and secret passageways—a nightmare situation for even the most skilled surveillance team. Worse still for the information-hungry agents, much of the action at the Congress of Vienna would take place in just these locations—that is, sealed off in the bedrooms where the young delegates would soon, as some grumbled, turn Emperor Venus's palace into a gilded brothel.

As VIENNA PREPARED to stage an unprecedented house party for the royal mob, Talleyrand found the lack of discussion frustrating and disturbing. He had good reason to worry.

Talleyrand had arrived a week before the congress was scheduled to open, but he discovered, just as he had feared, that Prince Metternich had already been busy arranging secret meetings around the green-baize-covered table in his office at the Chancellery. Only a few countries had been invited. "The Big Four," as they were called, were Austria and its major allies at the end of the war: Great Britain, Prussia, and Russia.

In these meetings, Metternich represented Austria and Castlereagh Great Britain. Russia sent Count Karl Nesselrode, a German by birth who had risen spectacularly from a sailor in the Russian navy to the tsar's trusted adviser. Representing Prussia was the state chancellor, Prince Karl von Hardenberg, a sixty-four-year-old who had a head of white hair and was nearly completely deaf. He was joined by the Prussian ambassador to Vienna, Wilhelm von Humboldt, an exemplary classical scholar and linguist who had previously redesigned the Prussian educational system and founded Berlin University. His brother Alexander was a famous explorer and naturalist.

Article XXXII of the Treaty of Paris had called for a "general congress" consisting of representatives from "all the powers that have been engaged on either side in the present war." But in a secret article attached to this treaty, the Big Four had given themselves the authority to organize the peace conference and establish the rules for the deliberations. This had proved more difficult than expected, and the group struggled to agree.

Ever since their first secret meeting, a five-hour affair on September 15, Metternich had emphasized the problems of a congress in the usual sense of a parliament-style assembly. First of all, it would be too large and unwieldy. Too many states with too many demands would hopelessly complicate the negotiations and cause the whole affair to degenerate into a sorry spectacle of disorder. They could, as Metternich put it, poison diplomacy by rekindling "all the maneuvers, intrigues, and plots, which had so great a share in causing the misfortunes of late years."

It was much better, Metternich argued, to adopt a more confidential style of diplomacy, with the four powers making all the decisions themselves, as a cabinet meeting behind closed doors. Compromise-friendly exchange would be much better than a wild free-for-all diplomatic bazaar. The Prussians and the Russians agreed completely. Castlereagh, on the other hand, was skeptical.

While the British foreign secretary also wanted to maintain control over the actual decision making, he advocated establishing a congress of states that would ratify or sanction their decisions. This was more in line with the public articles of the Treaty of Paris, and besides, was not all of Vienna being filled with delegates, who had come on this pretense, and expected to see the congress open soon, presumably in one of the large ballrooms of the imperial palace?

Yes, Metternich conceded, but there were messy problems. Who exactly would be allowed to participate in such an assembly? Take Naples, for example. Would the representative of the current king, Joachim Murat, a former Bonaparte marshal who received his crown from Napoleon, be recognized as the official delegate, or would it be the representative of the exiled King Ferdinand IV, who claimed his throne on the grounds of legitimacy? What about all the princes and knights of the former Holy

Roman Empire? There were hundreds of them—or "millions of them," as someone scoffed—and each had a representative. Would every self-proclaimed delegate in Vienna be permitted in the congress?

On September 22, the day before Talleyrand's arrival in Vienna, the four powers had finally agreed on the organization of the conference. Castlereagh had been outvoted. The Vienna Congress was not in fact going to be a congress. It was no parliament of equal sovereign states, and certainly not any kind of a "deliberate assembly of Europe." Rather, the congress was simply the "site of many individual negotiations." It was only a "Europe without distances."

As for the management of the diplomacy, the Great Powers had agreed simply to take it upon themselves to appoint the Central Committee, or Directing Committee, that would facilitate all the negotiations. More exactly, this committee would control everything from selecting the agendas to making the final decisions:

> This committee is the core of the congress; the congress exists only when the committee is in being, and it is terminated when the committee dissolves itself.

This central committee, further, would be staffed only with members of the four Great Powers—the idea of a "Great Power" enjoying its own special privileges was about to be born in this secret protocol.

This arrangement was only fair, they reasoned. The Big Four were the ones who had carried the brunt of the fight against Napoleon, and, as a result, earned the right to decide Europe's future. All the other states could, of course, voice their opinion, but this would only take place *after* a "final decision" had been reached and the Allied powers had arrived at "a perfect agreement among themselves." The consulting powers could only give "comment and approval." They would have no power to initiate or change anything. Decision making was about to be sealed up in the hands of the Big Four alone.

But there was one glaring obstacle to this plan: How would they inform all the people who had arrived to deliberate in the assembly, or watch its proceedings from the gallery? The French minister, for one, was not likely to respond favorably to this idea of "a congress that was not a congress."

Castlereagh had been pressing his colleagues to include France in their discussions, or at least inform the embassy of their plans. It was not long before Metternich realized that Castlereagh had a point. According to gossip, both in salons and in the spy dossiers, Talleyrand had spent his first week in town whipping up discontent and alarm among the many states about to be shut out of this scheme. Reports also suggested that many were listening.

Why not call him aside and win him over to this plan? Surely as the representative of a defeated country, Talleyrand would go out of his way to be accommodating, if only for the hopes of making gains for his country, or himself. This was, of course, possible. It was also possible that the plan would backfire.

Chapter 6

Bartering Destiny

What took twenty years to destroy can't be rebuilt in thirty days.

—Talleyrand

On the morning of September 30, Metternich sent a note over to Kaunitz Palace curtly inviting Talleyrand to a "private conference" later that afternoon. The invitation arrived between nine and ten in the morning, long before Talleyrand was usually out of the bed.

Getting ready for the day ahead, Talleyrand entered his dressing room and took his seat by the porcelain stove. Three valets waited on him, one supervisor and two assistants dressed in gray livery, covered with long aprons. The team began removing his flannel and stockings from the night before, and placed them in a bucket of eau de cologne. One handed him a cup of camomile tea, and the others set about taking away the rest of the night garments, the "drawers, vests, dressing gowns, with all sorts of odds and ends flopping about."

After the nightcap, a cambric bonnet tied with lace ribbon around his neck, was removed, two valets attacked his hair, "combing, curling, pomading, and powdering him." In the meantime, Talleyrand refreshed himself with a glass or two of warm water, which he then emptied into a silver basin, as one eyewitness described the maneuver, "sucked in through the nose and spit out, much the way the elephant uses his trunk."

A warm cloth was applied to his face, and his feet were washed in unpleasant, medicinal eau de barèges, dried, and then perfumed. His valets put on his white silk stockings, his breeches, and his shoes. As he stood up, the valets skillfully removed the last dressing gowns and maneuvered the shirt over his head—everything was done modestly, as he often entertained guests at the same time. By the end of the lengthy ritual, usually just under two hours, Talleyrand was immaculately dressed in velvet, silk, and satin. He was ready for his first showdown.

Early that afternoon, with the beautiful summer weather still holding, Talleyrand's dark-green coach clattered and clanked its way down the narrow Johannesgasse, lined with impressive palaces. It was a twenty-minute carriage ride out to Metternich's summer villa, a sprawling, rather than towering, classical Italianate structure located on the Rennweg, a main road that passed through another area full of aristocratic palaces.

On the way to the meeting, the French minister met a colleague, Don Pedro Gomez Havela de Labrador, the Spanish envoy, who also found himself unhappily excluded from Metternich's secret meetings. Like Talleyrand, Labrador had received an invitation to the meeting at the summer villa as one of the signatories of the Treaty of Paris.

Spain had played a major role in defeating Napoleon, Labrador could say with justice. Napoleon's invasion of Spain, back in 1808, had been catastrophic. The French army had found itself mired in a long bitter struggle that drained resources, eroded morale, and kept them spread out over a great distance, unable to concentrate effectively in a single arena. As a result, Spain rightly expected to participate at the Vienna peace conference. And its role, Labrador said, would not be simply rubber-stamping the decisions of others. "We are not going to play the role of marionettes."

Talleyrand had a long history of working with his neighbor to the west. Even if the two delegates did not always get along well, they shared several traits: They were aristocratic, haughty, and resourceful when it came to finding ways to attain their own goals. Not everyone, however, had been impressed with the Spanish envoy. "Never have I met a more stupid man," the Duke of Wellington had said after meeting him. Labrador was certainly a dogged and extravagant fellow with a volatile temper.

Arriving early at Metternich's mansion, which was in the final stages of its refurbishment for the congress, including the installation of a brand-new ballroom, the French and Spanish delegates climbed the granite steps, passed through the spacious halls, and entered a large room. It was about two o'clock in the afternoon, and they were right on time. When they crossed the threshold, however, they found other ministers already seated comfortably around a long table. Austria, Russia, Prussia, and Britain were the only powers present, just as they had heard.

Talleyrand calmly took his seat, in the empty high-backed chair between Prince Metternich and Lord Castlereagh, and Labrador sat down on the opposite side near the two Prussian ministers. Britain's foreign secretary, sitting at one end of the table, seemed to be in charge, running the meeting, despite his poor French. At the far end of the table sat Metternich's assistant, Friedrich von Gentz, who had just been appointed secretary for the Vienna Congress.

Glancing around the room and sizing up the handful of men around the table, Talleyrand asked suspiciously: Why was he the only member of the French embassy who had been invited to this meeting?

"It was wished to bring together only the heads of the Cabinets at the preliminary conferences," Castlereagh declared.

"But Count de Labrador is not a head of Cabinet, and he has also been invited," Talleyrand rightly objected, pointing to the Spaniard who accompanied him.

"That is because the Secretary of State of Spain is not in Vienna," Metternich explained in his nasal drawl.

"Even so," Talleyrand countered, looking over at two members of the Prussian delegation. "I see that Herr von Humboldt is here in addition to Prince von Hardenberg, and he is not a Secretary of State."

"This is an exception to the rule," someone said, politely referring to Hardenberg, who used a hearing horn. This exception was "made necessary by the infirmity with which, as you know, Prince Hardenberg is afflicted."

"Oh, well then, if it's a question of infirmities, each of us has one of his own, and we can all claim an exception on that basis," Talleyrand retorted, referring to his limp.

Cantankerous in his disarmingly becoming style, Talleyrand was not one to act like he represented a defeated country, even though he did. His confident approach was already working. In the future, it was agreed that a French diplomatic assistant would also be welcome at the meetings. More important than winning this small point, Talleyrand was demanding equality with the other powers.

Calling the meeting to order, Lord Castlereagh began by reading a letter from the representative of Portugal, the Comte de Palmella, who was disturbed at being excluded from the meetings. His country, after all, had also signed the Treaty of Paris. Why had he not been invited to these meetings, he asked, and why was Vienna's Big Four insulting the crown of Portugal in this way?

When Castlereagh finished reading the letter, both Talleyrand and Labrador voiced their support of the Portuguese count. The other ministers listened politely, and then promptly decided to postpone a decision about who should be invited to the organizational meetings until a later date.

"The object of today's conference," Castlereagh droned in a dry monotone voice, "is to acquaint you with what the four Powers have done since we have been here." He glanced over to Prince Metternich, who on cue handed Talleyrand the protocol. (The protocol, an official summary of policy or a decision, just coming into greater use, remains one legacy of the Vienna Congress.)

The French minister started reading the document, already signed at the bottom by the four powers, and found it sprinkled freely with the term *allies*. Talleyrand stopped reading at once. Allies? "Allies against whom?" Talleyrand asked with displeasure:

> Not against Napoleon, he's on Elba. Not against France, peace has been made. Surely not against the King of France. He guarantees the durability of this peace.

"Gentlemen, let's speak frankly," he added. "If there are still Allied Powers, then I don't belong here."

Talleyrand was hitting upon a potential public relations problem— public opinion becoming an increasingly important force in a close-knit, gossip-ridden town like Vienna. The war was over, and the tasks ahead were daunting. It served no purpose to maintain such divisive vocabulary.

No harm was intended, the leaders explained, trying to brush aside the objection. The word was simply convenient, "chosen only for the sake of brevity."

"Brevity," Talleyrand objected, "should not be purchased at the price of accuracy."

The point evidently hit home, and Talleyrand returned to the protocol, making his way through the dense prose.

"I don't understand," Talleyrand muttered.

The articles were read over again. "I do not understand any better," Talleyrand said. The blank look was deliberately overplayed, he later admitted, to highlight the absolute inappropriateness of the secret meetings. Decision after decision had already been made, even before the other diplomats had had a chance to arrive in town.

Talleyrand was being handed a summary of their conclusions and basically being asked to consent. He was not, however, willing to play along as easily as they had hoped. Talleyrand took a direct shot at the legality of decisions coming from secret, unauthorized meetings:

> For me there are two dates and between them there is nothing—the 30 May, when it was agreed to hold a Congress, and the 1st of October, when the Congress is to open. Nothing that has taken place in the interval exists so far as I am concerned.

Talleyrand's words were greeted with an oppressive silence. Remarkably, when Metternich spoke up, the protocol was immediately withdrawn, and Talleyrand had won another point. How pliable the conquerors of Napoleon seemed before the representative of the defeated power.

No sooner had Metternich retrieved the protocol than he pulled out a second one for consideration, placing it on the table as smoothly as if he were playing a card in a game of whist.

This protocol was more complicated, though, Talleyrand noticed, it hardly seemed any less suspect. This plan proposed dividing every possible issue or territorial question at the Vienna Congress into two categories: general (concerning Europe as a whole) and particular (deemed relevant only on a local or regional basis). But both categories would still be dealt with by committees, appointed by the Great Powers. After the two committees had deliberated and reached their conclusions, the Congress would *then* be assembled. This was proposing, Talleyrand later said, "to finish where I had thought it would be necessary to begin."

Besides, this protocol would also effectively make the four Great Powers, as Talleyrand pointed out, "absolute masters of all the operations of the Congress."

Thinking quickly on his feet, as he was known to do, Talleyrand knew that he had to stall for time. "A first reading," he said, "was not sufficient for the formation of an opinion upon a project of this nature." He would need some time for reflection. "We have assembled to consecrate and secure the rights of each of the powers," he said. After the anarchy of the last war, it would be unfortunate indeed if Vienna's diplomats violated the very rights that they should protect. Working out all the details "before convening the Congress," he added, was new to him.

It was a question of practicality, Castlereagh answered calmly. The smaller number of powers could work with haste and fairness.

Talleyrand also shared these goals, but proved his impatience with his next question: "When is the general Congress going to open?" Why can't it open right now?

Listening to Talleyrand defend the rights of all the states who deserved a voice at the conference, Prussia's Hardenberg blurted out that he would not be dictated to by a bevy of petty princes, such as the Prince of Leyen and the Prince of Liechtenstein. At this point, Castlereagh quickly adjourned the meeting. He did not want to give Talleyrand the chance to score another point.

Talleyrand's opposition was threatening to upset the designs of the Great Powers for transforming the congress into an elite club meeting behind closed doors. That night, Friedrich von Gentz confided in his diary the severity of the crisis. Talleyrand had "savagely upset our plans, and torn them to shreds."

After the meeting, a good two-hour event in which the French delegate had "rated them soundly," Gentz and Metternich cooled down with a casual stroll through the villa's gardens. Austria's foreign minister was showing the preparations that were well under way for an upcoming celebration in honor of Allied victory the previous year at Leipzig. What particularly surprised Gentz, however, was Metternich's attitude. He seemed strangely oblivious to "the embarrassment and the dreadful state of our position."

LEAVING THE SUMMER villa, Prussian ambassador Wilhelm von Humboldt made his way back to the Spielmann mansion on the Graben, a central street lined with boutiques, cafés, and restaurants. Routine business for the embassy would be conducted there on the mansion's second floor. This was a much better environment for concentrating on work than his first temporary lodgings, which were in a room adjacent to Princess Bagration's lively suites in the Palm Palace, where Vienna's beau monde was already gathering.

Forty-seven years old with light hair prematurely turning white, Humboldt was regarded as one of the hardest-working delegates in town. Diplomatic dispatches, memoranda, and drafts of protocols jostled haphazardly on his desk, next to many other projects in progress. When he was not working on another memorandum outlining Prussian policy, Humboldt relaxed by polishing his massive study of Basque languages, already a good decade into the work.

Humboldt was also busy translating the ancient Greek playwright Aeschylus's tragedy *Agamemnon*. He would tinker with the text almost every day of the congress, and, at this point, he was almost happy with the prologue. The challenges of ancient Greek would help Humboldt relieve stress from the day's work around the diplomacy table. "Wars and peace come and go," Humboldt once said, "but a good verse lasts forever."

It is no surprise that Humboldt had made many enemies in the course of his career. His negotiation style was aggressive, and he was blunt for a diplomat. Erudite and intellectually sharp, Humboldt also had a high-handed approach that often manifested itself in a stubborn and inflexible disposition. He was also criticized for appearing overambitious, a tad elitist, and far too much concerned about showing he was right. As he put it himself, he lived for ideas. To many of his colleagues, Humboldt was too enamored by his own "subtleties and paradoxes," which, however delightful to himself, soon wearied them ad nauseam.

Indeed, some wondered if Humboldt, with his scholarly air, would have been better suited to a university, like Berlin University, which he had earlier founded, than the manic high-stakes intrigues that he would encounter at the Vienna Congress. Worse than his pedantic tendencies, which stood out at that worldly conference, some noted a shocking, even chilling detachment to his personality. How could he tour the grim battlefields, strewn with the aftermath of slaughter, and still calmly carry on a discussion of Aristotle's *Poetics*? Like a calculating abstractician, one colleague said, Humboldt only "toys with the world and with human beings as though it were a game."

But the Prussian delegation was in no mood for toys or games in the autumn of 1814. By far the weakest of the Big Four, Prussia was usually viewed as a dangerous and probably the most unsettling delegation at the congress, armed with ambitious, hardworking, and brilliant minds like Humboldt. They seemed aggressive, and they had a formidable scholarly apparatus to back up their belligerency.

No major power had lost such a high percentage of its own territory as Prussia, and, with the exception of Austria, no other power had suffered as many humiliations at the hands of the French. But unlike other victors, who had already made gains during the war, or in the Treaty of Paris, the Kingdom of Prussia remained only a shell of its former self, a "parceled-out territory" that was barely half the size it was on the eve of the war.

Besides that, there was an acute sense of vulnerability that had dogged Prussian rulers for centuries. Flatlands of pine forests, sand dunes, and marshy coastlands in the north afforded no obstacle whatsoever to a determined invader. There were no mountains, oceans, or other natural frontiers demarcating its territory, and this lack of natural defenses only increased the militaristic bent of the kingdom in the exposed center of the Continent. Long before the current king, Frederick William III, Prussian rulers had been notorious for putting their trust in the army.

For several years now, and especially after the embarrassing defeats at Auerstedt and Jena in 1806, Prussia had been reforming its institutions. The army copied French tactics, drill, and conscription, and the government centralized its administration—no longer, as Metternich joked, "a conspiracy of mediocrities held together by the fear of taking a single step." Peasants had been emancipated, education revamped, and the whole tax system made more efficient. Prussia was determined to play a greater role in central Europe.

Like its soldiers, who were feared for looting and destroying more than other armies on campaign, Prussia's diplomats were earning a reputation for their intensity in the conference room. They were the "lions of diplomacy." Humboldt and Hardenberg were among a select few diplomats who would earn a coveted Iron Cross, the famous military honor that had been instituted a few years before by Frederick William III. In fact, both were awarded an Iron Cross First Class with a white band, and they were the only ones ever to receive this honor.

What Prussia wanted most of all at the Vienna Congress was to annex a region that many, including Lord Castlereagh, literally had trouble placing on the map. This was the Kingdom of Saxony, located right in the middle of the Continent. Draw two straight lines, one north-south from Copenhagen to Rome and the other east-west from Warsaw to Paris, and they intersect in Saxony. Castlereagh was no master of geography and the issue of Saxony sounded pretty obscure, but it was soon to be hugely important to the peace conference, and also to the future of the continent.

In the early nineteenth century, Saxony had been a thriving region of towns, farms, and mining, including silver and jade. The capital of the kingdom, Dresden, straddled the Elbe River, and boasted many fine palaces, some "the size of towns," which earned it the distinction of being the "Florence of the Elbe," renowned for its beautiful Renaissance and baroque architecture.

Now this Saxony was under great threat at the Vienna Congress—and that is why the king of Saxony appears in a caricature of the "dancing congress" as the figure desperately "clutching his crown." The problem with Saxony, as far as the Prussians were concerned, was that it had fought on the wrong side of the war. While the Russians, the Austrians, and even the Prussians had also supported Napoleon at one time or another, they had all eventually rallied to the Allies and helped the coalition obtain its victory. The Saxon king, however, had rejoined Napoleon in 1813 after a brief attempt at neutrality, and now many members of the victorious alliance wanted his throne.

Prussia was demanding the entire region, claiming it by right of its sacrifices in the war. Chancellor Karl von Hardenberg asked simply: "Has not Prussia, who made the greatest efforts and the greatest sacrifices in the common cause, the right to claim acquisitions proportionate to those of her neighbors?"

But others were not so sure. Although Prussia had certainly sacrificed, many like Talleyrand feared that this annexation of lands in its immediate south would give Prussia too much influence and upset the balance of power in central Europe. Besides, what right did the Prussians have to dethrone a king and annex an entire kingdom, including Dresden and Leipzig? The king of Saxony was outraged, sending ministers to Vienna to plead his case. He was unfortunately not able to come himself because the Prussians had captured him in October 1813 and locked him away in the Schloss Friedrichsfeld, a fortress prison outside Berlin. As the congress set out to debate his future, the king was still a prisoner of war.

Chapter 7

"ℰUROPE, 𝒰NHAPPY ℰUROPE"

Politics is the art of making war without killing anyone.

—PRINCE DE LIGNE

ll throughout September, Prince Metternich was spending as much time as possible with the Duchess of Sagan. He was as deeply in love with her as he had ever been. Emperor Francis was not merely humoring him when he had said, "I consider her one of the most essential ingredients of the Congress." The duchess was becoming an indispensable part of Metternich's life.

The foreign minister looked forward to each meeting with the duchess, every morning at eleven—"our hour," as he called it—when he came into her pink and white salon in the Palm Palace and they discussed affairs over a cup of chocolate. Metternich was not discreet, and they talked about everything. He respected her opinion so much that he wanted to make her his "secret advisor." "You know—and understand—our problems far better than any of [my] Ministers," he had once confessed to her.

When they were not together, and that was unfortunately too often as far as Metternich was concerned, he would yearn to see her. He would retire to his desk, and late at night, by candlelight, he would plead, in arching swirls: "If the love of my heart grants me another night I shall be repaid for the pains of a lifetime." Wilhelmine would write back, saying that she would be waiting for him, and thinking only of him.

Yet the Duchess of Sagan had many other things on her mind. Behind her glamorous facade, she sometimes seemed melancholy, even depressed. Congress gossipers—and historians, too—had long believed that she was very much concerned about losing properties or income in the territories ruled by the tsar. The duchess was anxious about them, of course, but she had another, much deeper concern that almost no one at the Vienna Congress knew, not even the baron's spies.

Her secret was revealed only in 1949 when the Czech scholar Maria Ullrichová was visiting an old Cistercian abbey at Plass, one of Metternich's Bohemian estates. Underneath the abbey's brewery was a wall—a fake wall, it turned out, that blocked the entrance to a hidden cellar. When Ullrichová noticed the decoy and managed to push it aside, she found a number of blue cardboard boxes marked "Acta Clementina," and among them a small black box with gilded edges. On its side were the words, in Metternich's clear handwriting, "Letters of the Duchess of Sagan."

Metternich scholars knew, of course, of his affair with the duchess, but no one realized that the letters had survived, or had any idea of how close the two lovers had been. The letters tied with a small white ribbon had been hidden by Metternich's descendants sometime in the mid to late 1930s, just before the Nazi seizure of Czechoslovakia. Fortunately, they survived intact, all 616 letters, and they reveal a great deal about the private life of Metternich, the duchess, and her salon at the center of the congress.

What few realized was that fourteen years before, the Duchess of Sagan had given birth to a daughter, and then, under pressure from her mother, given her away. Wilhelmine had only been eighteen years old at the time. Her difficult pregnancy and heartbreaking surrender of her child were explained to her younger sisters as a recuperation from a carriage accident.

The father of the child was unfortunate. It had been the Swedish nobleman and former cavalry officer Gustav Armfelt, who had been forced out of his country in the early 1790s (and the same man who had encouraged Dorothée in her studies). Armfelt had drifted down to the duchess's estate, Sagan, and stayed on as a guest of the family. He looked like a cavalry officer, and his conversation was as glittering as the medals on his uniform. The Swedish gentleman was charming, dashing, and, at that time, regrettably also the lover of Wilhelmine's mother.

Wilhelmine's affair had been discovered in a cruel way. One night before going to bed, her mother, the Duchess of Courland, noticed that a candlestick had been taken from its holder, and wondered who would be stirring at that hour. Following the trail, she entered a room in the large castle, and found the forty-two-year-old man and her teenage daughter in a compromising situation. Shocked, she had slapped her daughter across the face, the sharp edges of her sapphire ring scratching into her skin.

Over the following months, Wilhelmine was forced by her mother into a marriage to Prince Louis de Rohan, a high aristocrat who had fled France during the revolution. Ruined by large debts, he cared little about his rich fiancée who happened to be pregnant with another man's child.

Under further pressure from her mother, Wilhelmine had then handed over her baby, born Adelaide-Gustava, or "Vava," to be raised by Armfelt's cousins back in Finland. The duchess would make sure her daughter had every monetary need fulfilled. Vava's true identity was to be concealed until she turned fifteen, which, by the autumn of 1814, was only months away.

But the duchess had come to regret that decision, and she wanted her daughter returned immediately. How she hated that she had handed over the baby to her lover's family, and how she despised herself for yielding to her mother's demands. Her remorse would at times be all-consuming. She tried to escape by losing herself in the world of the salon, or waltzing "like a lost soul." Yet she suffered increasingly from bouts of depression and intense migraine headaches that lasted three to four days.

There was one person in Vienna who knew her secret, and that was Prince Metternich. The duchess had told him, some ten months before, around Christmas 1813, when she had asked for his help. Could the Austrian foreign minister, she had hoped, use his finesse and influence to help her regain her daughter? Could he perhaps talk with the Russian tsar?

Little Vava was in Finland, a country the tsar had conquered in 1809 and now controlled; he had also appointed the girl's father as its governor. Perhaps Metternich could convince Alexander to intervene—after all, the tsar had done it before, when he had visited Wilhelmine's mother and won Dorothée for Talleyrand's nephew.

Thrilled to be able to help, and confident of his own success, Metternich had at once given his word. He would ask the tsar for this favor immediately, and he added, "I shall make the safety of Russia depend on it."

ACROSS THE CORRIDOR in the Palm Palace, Princess Bagration was making a stir, hosting salons attended by the elite of the congress, particularly from the Russian and Prussian delegations. Prince Hardenberg and Count Nesselrode were regulars, and the salon would sometimes seem like a tiny St. Petersburg in the middle of Vienna. Years later, one admirer left a vivid description of the "lovely princess" who attracted attention wherever she went: "The Princess never wore anything but white India muslin, clinging to her form and revealing it in all its perfection."

As one of Baron Hager's agents pointed out, Bagration had not entirely lost her wild "foolishness of youth." She had had many love affairs over the years, including one, thirteen years before, with none other than Metternich. At that time, both of them had been living in Dresden, then regarded as an opulent, if decadent, backwater. Metternich was a young twenty-eight-year-old ambassador on his first diplomatic mission; Bagration, the beautiful nineteen-year-old wife of a much older Russian general, who was almost always somewhere else. By 1802, the princess had given birth to a daughter and boldly named her Clementine, after the man who almost certainly was the father, Klemens Metternich.

This extramarital affair did not last long, but it had left its scars. Although little remains of the end of this relationship beyond gossip and rumor, there is no sign that the two former lovers parted on anything other than difficult terms. Yet by the summer of 1814, Metternich was again visiting Bagration's salon. Both found themselves in the spa town of Baden bei Wien, nestled in the Vienna Woods, some two hours away by carriage. Metternich was preparing for the congress, and coming over regularly to the princess's fashionable salon for cards, drinks, and the latest gossip. He was enjoying himself so much that he even toyed with the idea of hosting the entire peace conference in this pleasant spa town.

Now, at the Vienna Congress, Bagration seemed interested again in her old lover, "her" Metternich, and seemed determined to win him back. Even if Metternich apparently seemed more interested in the woman across the wing of the Palm Palace, Princess Bagration was not one to sit idly and concede defeat, especially not to the Duchess of Sagan. What's more, if she could not have him herself, then Metternich would suffer the consequences.

ON THE DAY after his initial meeting challenging the Big Four at the summer villa, Talleyrand went over to the Hofburg for an audience with the Russian tsar. Alexander had let it be known that he wished to speak with Talleyrand. The French minister then, in the etiquette of the day, politely requested an audience. This was their first meeting in Vienna, and the first time they had seen each other in months.

Talleyrand and the tsar had come to know each other during the Napoleonic Wars. In September 1808, they had plotted together against Napoleon at Erfurt and collaborated on arranging Dorothée's marriage. The tsar had become a great admirer of Talleyrand's ability. In fact, when the Allies captured Paris, Alexander honored Talleyrand by staying at his house, instead of the royal palace (it was rumored that the palace had been mined, and more than a few historians have wondered about Talleyrand's role in spreading this rumor).

But their relationship had deteriorated greatly in the intervening months. For one thing, the tsar blamed Talleyrand for the king of France's failure to live up to his promises of establishing a genuine constitutional monarchy. This was all the more frustrating for the tsar because he also blamed Talleyrand for convincing him to support the king's restoration in the first place. Alexander had personally been unimpressed with Louis and had preferred placing many other alternatives on the throne, including the former Bonaparte marshal Bernadotte and a younger Bourbon like the duc d'Orléans. Alexander had even considered establishing a republic. Talleyrand, however, had persuaded him to accept Louis, and now that French affairs seemed to be struggling, the tsar was not pleased.

The tension was palpable as the French minister arrived at the Hofburg. After a preliminary discussion about the situation back in France, the conversation switched to diplomacy at Vienna, particularly Russia's intentions in Poland, and immediately took a more menacing turn.

"Now let us talk of our affairs," the tsar said impatiently, "we must finish them here."

"That depends on Your Majesty," Talleyrand replied. "They will be promptly and happily terminated if Your Majesty brings to bear on them the same nobility and greatness of soul as in the affairs of France."

"But each must find what suits it here," the tsar countered.

"And what is right."

"I shall keep what I hold," the tsar affirmed bluntly, referring to the Russian armies in occupation of Poland.

"Your Majesty would only wish to keep that which is legitimately yours," the cunning minister responded provocatively, in his deep guttural.

"I am in accord with the Great Powers."

"I do not know whether Your Majesty reckons France among those Powers."

"Yes, certainly; but if you will not allow each to look after his own interests, what do you propose?" Alexander asked.

"I place right first, and self-interest second," Talleyrand said.

"The self-interest of Europe is what's right," the tsar snapped.

"This language, Sire, is not yours; it is foreign to you, and your heart disowns it."

"No, I repeat it; the self-interest of Europe is what's right,"

As Talleyrand described it, he turned to the wall, and exasperated, rested his head on the fine paneling and muttered, "Europe, unhappy Europe!" After this display of frustration, fearing that the "might is right" mentality would only plunge the Continent into more war and suffering, the French minister turned again to the tsar about the future peace. "Shall it be said that you have destroyed it?"

"Rather war than that I should renounce what I hold," Alexander blurted out.

Talleyrand said nothing, his body language showing, he said later, a combination of displeasure, opposition, and resignation to resumed hostilities, if necessary,

"Yes, rather war," the tsar repeated, breaking the uncomfortable silence.

Then, as the clock struck in the corner, the Tsar of All the Russias beamed. "Ah! It is time for the play; I must go. I promised the Emperor; they are waiting for me."

With these words the tsar abruptly left, nonchalantly dismissing the fate of 2.5 million souls in Russian-occupied Poland, never mind the anxieties of his fellow peacemakers.

Chapter 8

Spies Are Everywhere!

My children cannot sneeze but that Prince Metternich is sure to hear about it.

— ONE VISITOR DESCRIBING VIENNA'S ESPIONAGE NETWORK

andles were already burning late into the night at the Secret Cipher Office in the Hofburg Palace. The minister of police, Baron Hager, was well aware that even with the recent budget increases, Vienna's espionage service was woefully inadequate to cope with the task of keeping track of all the arrivals in town.

Baron Hager was frantically recruiting a large network of agents and underlings to infiltrate foreign missions, maintain surveillance, and trail important dignitaries through town, carefully noting the places they visited, the people they met, and anything that happened out of the ordinary. Special attention was paid to dinner parties and evening entertainments, where a great deal of the Vienna Congress would take place. Every morning, with his café au lait, Emperor Francis would devour the thick dossiers of police reports. He would soon be one of the best-informed people in town.

The spy baron already had some high-placed people on his payroll. Confidants would range from the poet Giuseppe Carpani, Mozart's old friend, to the celebrated Viennese courtesan Josephine Wolters. The identity of the agents was always closely protected, and some of the most active spies have in fact never been identified, known only by their code names, like the prolific agent known as ∞, or the sophisticated, enigmatic informer who signed his daily reports **. The latter was certainly an aristocrat who moved at the highest levels of society, even addressed by Baron von Hager as "Your Highness."

Some would attend the fashionable salons—Mondays at Metternich's, Tuesdays at Castlereagh's, and Fridays either at the Duchess of Sagan's or Princess Bagration's. Talleyrand, who usually dined later than the other hosts, was also a high priority, though he was not attracting Vienna's most powerful guests. Society reflected diplomacy: France was isolated.

Spies were instructed to observe all important happenings with "maximum zeal and vigilance" as they sipped champagne, chatted over tea, or played cards at the small round tables. They were to frequent the cafés and the candlelit taverns in the inner city. They were also to mill about the crowds that invariably gathered around the boutiques of the Graben, the parks of the Prater, and the promenades along the old city walls.

With the help of postal lodges across the empire, many official letters were also intercepted and sent over to the Secret Cipher Office in the imperial palace. There, in this "Cabinet Noir," talented agents pried open the top secret dispatches with a bone knife, copied their contents, and then carefully resealed the envelopes over a smokeless candle. Another team decoded the messages, when necessary, and the spies were always adding to their collection of ciphers.

In addition to tapping into the courier system and covering the ballrooms, drawing rooms, and other meeting places of the plenipotentiaries, Baron Hager was working on extending the reach of his information network around town. Coachmen driving the three hundred imperial carriages were instructed to relay anything they overheard from their distinguished passengers. Porters standing outside the embassies and mansions, staffs in hand, kept tabs on the visitors received and their length of stay. Even some landlords would report on their tenants, such as an editor for the newspaper *Wiener Zeitung,* who would communicate on the activities of Count Anstett of the Russian delegation, who had moved in with him at Weihburgasse 983.

Ideally, the Vienna police would succeed in planting agents inside the main embassies, and, of course, some of the best sources were the servants. Liveried footmen standing behind the chairs at dinner, lackeys carrying the three-branched candlesticks through darkened mansions, observers inside an honor guard attached to a sovereign, and sometimes an assistant to a valet, or even a valet, could be successfully placed near a main delegate.

Some of the most valuable agents of all were the chambermaids, who perused the contents of desks, rummaged through wastepaper baskets, and peered into porcelain stoves and fireplaces looking for any scraps of paper that had not been sufficiently destroyed. These scraps—known in spy parlance as *chiffrons*—were then forwarded to the baron's office and, when possible, painstakingly reassembled. No one knew if some little piece of paper, however meaningless it might seem, did in fact hold a clue that unlocked a secret that puzzled analysts at headquarters.

Astute delegations, however, were soon taking measures to resist unwanted intrusions. "We have enough proofs of the dishonorable passion for opening letters," Prussia's Humboldt wrote back to Berlin, notifying that his delegation was seeking safer channels of communication. One member of his embassy, the influential military strategist General Antoine-Henri Jomini, went further in taking precautions. He had started locking up his papers, and made sure that after changing all his locks, he did not leave the office without taking the set of keys with him.

Castlereagh's own secretiveness was likewise paying off—his annoying "excess of prudence," as one spy complained. The British foreign secretary had insisted on hiring his own staff, including doorkeepers, chambermaids, and kitchen hands. The men and women sent over by the police looking for jobs kept being rejected. Castlereagh was also making sure that all stray documents, however bland and unimportant, were collected and methodically destroyed.

Like the British, Talleyrand was also making it difficult for the eavesdroppers. Anyone who knew Talleyrand, one frustrated agent reported, would not fail to understand the difficulties in gaining information from his headquarters. The spies would have to escalate their efforts. Talleyrand was turning Kaunitz Palace into a veritable fortress.

KINGS AND QUEENS at the Vienna Congress were not exactly used to living in such close proximity with other sovereigns, and, according to police agents, frustrations were mounting at the Hofburg Palace. Some apparently resented it when one of them gained more attention than the others, and in the eyes of many, the Russian tsar was receiving the most attention of all.

Stories circulated that emphasized his narcissistic behavior: how he ordered a block of ice delivered to his room every morning, rumored to improve his rosy complexion, though in fact it might well have been used to treat a skin disease that he already showed signs of developing. It was also said that he thought only of his uniform, and as he had gained weight over of the summer, he could no longer squeeze into it comfortably, and had been forced to order a replacement wardrobe from St. Petersburg. His delegation did not escape gossip, either, accused of boasting irresponsibly of Russian power, spitting on parquet floors, and, in general, behaving as if they were not "housebroken."

The tsar had brought a whole team of advisers to Vienna, and of the Great Powers, they were undoubtedly the most diverse and international delegation in town. Of the tsar's nine most prominent advisers, four came from Germany: Count Nesselrode, Baron Heinrich Friedrich Karl vom Stein, Count Gustav von Stackelberg, and Count Jean Anstett. There was also one from Poland, Prince Adam Czartoryski, and one from Switzerland, Alexander's former tutor, Frédéric-César de La Harpe. There was also one from Corfu, Iōannēs Antōniou Kapodistrias, and one from Corsica, Carlo Andrea Pozzo di Borgo. The tsar had only one prominent Russian adviser at the Congress, and he was Ukrainian: the former Ambassador to Vienna, Count Andrei Kirilovich Razumovsky.

This cosmopolitan set of advisers was certainly puzzling, and some feared that the tsar had only brought them to find ways to increase Russian influence in their home countries. Others feared their pet projects. Would the tsar, for instance, listen to his advisers who wanted him to encourage national sentiments in Germany, or pressed him to undertake a more active policy toward the Ottoman Empire and the eastern Mediterranean? Some wondered, too, if the tsar would take up the cause of oppressed national minorities in the Balkans. So if Alexander's behavior was not difficult enough to predict, Vienna diplomats would also have to gauge which adviser currently had the ear of the impressionable tsar.

Like other monarchs visiting the congress, the tsar did not bother with any special security as he walked the streets—at least not yet. He was spotted slipping into a tavern, ordering a beer, gulping it down, and, then, most unusually, paying for it himself. The tsar was seen, on another occasion, talking to a young Viennese girl he met at a recent ball. Spies were immediately placed on the case. The girl was tracked down, identified, and an agent placed outside her house. Sometimes, indeed, the spies were sent on a wild-goose chase. Nothing else was noted from that address in the bulging dossiers.

The baron's agents had begun in earnest following other sovereigns on their daily excursions and intercepting letters from the foreign missions—royal mail was no exception. Correspondence of the king of Denmark, Frederick VI, was pilfered unmercifully. The Danish king was also often recognized by his green cape, gold-tipped cane, and almost scholarly air, and easily followed. The king liked to visit a young Viennese flower girl, who would soon cause a scandal when she started calling herself the "Queen of Denmark."

One of the best places for gathering information was on the busy Graben, a central street that was once the moat for medieval Vienna. Many delegates were staying in rooms or houses there, which was then, as now, an excellent place for rendezvous or impromptu discussions. It was the home of the "open-air club," as one agent called it, where "loafers, idlers, spouters and disputants" watched the congress go by.

For many people-watchers, the highlight was seeing Prince de Ligne, a delightful seventy-nine-year-old former field marshal from Flanders who, in his long career, had served Frederick the Great, Joseph II, and Catherine the Great. His nickname in Paris salons had been "Prince Charming." With a million stories, and a "delicately malicious wit," he was the Oscar Wilde of his day, having known everybody from Voltaire to Rousseau to Casanova. He was one of the first, for instance, to read Casanova's scandalous memoirs literally as they were written, and one of the last to see the adventurer before his death in 1798.

Prince de Ligne's latest quips were eagerly devoured. It was this prince who gave the congress its lasting memorial: "The congress does not move forward, it dances." He should have known, because he did not miss many of the occasions.

Now, however, he was impoverished. He had lost a fortune when the French revolutionaries seized the vast majority of his landed estates, and he had squandered the rest with his lifestyle. At the time of the congress, he lived in a very small apartment near the old city walls. It was one room wide, with the bedroom doubling as his salon; de Ligne called it his "birdcage." But as its many visitors testified, the pauper prince was still very much the dandy.

The walls were as pink as his cheeks . . . [and his cheeks were as pink] as his humor which was as pink as his talk. Pink as his talk was his stationery, pink as this was his livery, everything in pink.

His cramped quarters had long hosted Vienna's elite; everyone wanted to meet the legendary prince, and hear his stories, anecdotes, and repartee, uttered, as he was known to do, with his eyes "nearly shut." He still drove his old clanky carriage that would have been the height of style a half century before under Louis XV, led by a thin white horse also past its prime. The prince was "the man that time had forgotten."

Another favorite sighting, though rare, was Anna Protassoff, who had, many years before, served Catherine the Great and rendered her invaluable assistance as her "tester," that is, the woman who would try out the guardsmen selected for the empress's bedroom. She was now almost seventy years old and considerably heavier. Prince de Ligne took his protégé, the songwriter Auguste de La Garde-Chambonas, to meet her in her small flat. The young man described his first impressions on meeting this legend: "a huge shape on a sofa" that, when speaking or moving, jingled with jewelry.

On her head, around her neck, covering her arms there was a veritable waterfall of glittering diamonds, bracelets, necklaces, ruby-studded medallions, tremendous earrings that reached down to her very shoulders.

As he looked on, Anna Protassoff and Prince de Ligne conversed, as if they had been magically transported some fifty years into the past— appropriately enough for a congress that would itself sometimes seem anachronistic, and be accused of trying to turn back the clock, as if Napoleon, the French Revolution, and the last two decades of history had only been a bad dream.

WHILE TALLEYRAND WAS displeased with the Big Four and their plans for controlling the congress, he was at least satisfied with the early success of the French embassy. The Duke of Dalberg, the Marquis de la Tour du Pin, Comte Alexis de Noailles, and Comte de la Besnardière had been performing as he hoped, keeping him informed, and spreading news that he wished around town. The French chefs were serving up excellent fare, and the musician Neukomm was playing well, too, though he was under close surveillance by the baron's police, who refused to believe that he was brought along only to play the piano. But Talleyrand was especially pleased with Dorothée.

By her family connections alone, Dorothée had close links to the main delegations. She knew the Russians through her mother, and the Austrians through her sister, Wilhelmine. As for the Prussians, Dorothée was influential in her own right, on account of her own extensive properties in their kingdom. Her mansion in Berlin, built originally by Frederick the Great for his sister and located at 7 Unter den Linden right near the Brandenburg Gate, was one of the most impressive in the capital; in the twentieth century, it would be used as the Soviet embassy.

When Talleyrand had not been invited to the highly sought Monday night soirees at the Metternichs', he had asked Dorothée to appeal to her older sister, the Duchess of Sagan. One simple request was all that it took. The Austrian foreign minister replied immediately that Dorothée and Talleyrand would of course be welcome. They should also, Metternich added, consider themselves as having a standing invitation to the intimate suppers.

This was, of course, a major breakthrough. Salons were ideal settings for diplomacy as Talleyrand preferred to practice it, subtly and informally advancing his interests in a place, like Metternich's, that was sure to be crowded with the people who ruled Europe. At such a gathering, it was really a stroke of bad luck, one salon regular put it, "not to encounter an emperor, a king, a reigning prince, or not to knock into a crown prince, a great general, a famous diplomat, a celebrated minister." On some memorable occasions, too, Metternich would serve on the fine Sèvres china that Napoleon had given him for arranging his marriage to Marie Louise. At Metternich's, diplomats could wrangle over the spoils of Napoleon's empire by day, and then dine on his china at night.

Dorothée was indeed proving herself valuable, not least as an excellent hostess at the French embassy. She ran the salon, presided at the table, and generally lit up the room like a magic lantern. She helped everyone feel welcome and stimulated conversation, guiding it skillfully. If someone harped on a subject too controversial, serious, or just unpleasant, she could gracefully redirect it. The songwriter La Garde-Chambonas, who visited the French embassy that autumn, praised her social skills. Even if France was not at this point attracting the most prominent figures to its salon, Dorothée was performing masterfully: She "did the honors of her drawing-room with an enchanting grace."

Behind the scenes, too, Dorothée was beginning to help Talleyrand in many other ways, apparently even in drafting key documents. In a style reminiscent of the eighteenth century, Talleyrand preferred to avoid the strain of composing his letters and dispatches himself. He would rather dictate as he paced up and down the room, while Dorothée, lying on the bed or sitting at the mahogany desk, scratched away with her quill. Together the two then went over the memorandum or dispatch, line by line, waging "the battle of the words."

Working with Talleyrand must have been an extraordinarily valuable experience, especially for someone as intelligent and observant as Dorothée. She had come to admire his "cool-headed courage"; he had "a presence of mind, a bold temperament, [and] an instinctive type of defiance," all of which, she added, "rendered danger so seductive."

While Talleyrand and Dorothée were trying to lure the congress over to Kaunitz Palace, Metternich was consumed by his affair with Dorothée's older sister, the Duchess of Sagan. To his critics, Metternich's work as foreign minister and host of ceremonies sometimes looked neglected, and now this was getting worse because the Big Four had just voted him "President of the Congress." The Prussian ambassador, Humboldt, for one, complained that "Metternich was mad with love, pride and vanity . . . wasting all his mornings getting up only at ten and then running off to sigh at the feet of Sagan . . ."

Metternich looked forward to seeing the duchess at their morning meetings and everywhere else, from her box at the theater to her commanding presence in a hot, crowded drawing room. He was glad to be able to help the duchess obtain her daughter, and he had put some of his best assistants on the case, including even Gentz, the secretary of the Congress. Metternich continued pouring out his heart to her by night:

If ever the world were lost and you remained to me, I would need nothing more; but if I lose you, I would not know what to do with the world—except for the [plot of land] they'd need to bury me.

With Metternich's regular visits to her salon in the Palm Palace, other leading members of the Austrian Foreign Ministry followed suit. So did the British, who were clearly finding common ground with the Austrians in opposing the Russians. In fact, the duchess's salon was called "Austrian headquarters," and Princess Bagration's, across the way, "Russian headquarters," frequented, as it was, by so many Russian and Prussian well-wishers.

The duchess's salon on Friday night, September 30–October 1, was particularly lively, and Metternich thoroughly enjoyed himself. As the carriages waiting outside in the courtyard gradually took the last lingering guests away, there was no sign that Metternich had left. He was not seen again until the afternoon of the following day, when he arrived at the Chancellery. Almost certainly Metternich spent the night with the duchess. It was then, he later confessed, that he had experienced "the greatest happiness of [his] life."

At the opposite end of the Palm Palace, the same night, Tsar Alexander was also distracted by matters of the heart. He was seen with Princess Catherine Bagration, barely dressed, at his side. The princess had been sending callers away all evening, her servants apologizing that she had a terrible headache. Then the servants themselves were sent away. If this was to quiet rumors, it was not successful.

Vienna heard the stories of the tsar's visit: how he arrived at the palace, rang the bell four times, and the princess descended the staircase in only her negligee. Some also heard of one tense moment: When the tsar had entered her bedroom, he found, to his surprise, a man's hat. Nonplussed, the princess smiled and answered, "Oh, that's the hat of the decorator Moreau. He's the one who is decorating my house for the party tomorrow."

Perhaps the princess was telling the truth, as she did in fact have a ball planned for the next day, and Karl von Moreau, being on the Festivals Committee, was one of the most active decorators in town. The tsar, at least, accepted the explanation, and they laughed at his "unfounded assumptions." The spy who related the gossip remarked ironically, "Evil to him who evil thinks."

The tsar's late-night visit to the princess set Vienna ablaze. "No one," one spy reported, "is talking of anything else."

Chapter 9

Dancing with the World in Their Hands

Truly, the ruins of a ball are as interesting to contemplate as the ruins of monuments and empires.

—Count Z at the Roman Emperor Hotel
one night in the autumn of 1814

The congress was scheduled to begin on October 1, 1814. But that day had arrived, and there still had not been any official word about the peace conference. The opening masked ball at the imperial palace the following day, however, was proceeding as planned. Emperor Francis and Empress Maria Ludovika wanted to make sure it was a success, and as one countess recalled years later, it was "a truly magnificent affair."

Large crystal chandeliers and an estimated eight thousand candles produced a "blinding almost dizzy effect" in the white and gilt paneled ballroom. The central staircase, adorned with a wide array of flowers and plants, led to the upper galleries and balconies, which were draped in red and gold velvet, and overlooked rows of chairs arranged symmetrically on the fine parquet floors below. Some ten to twelve thousand guests had filled the spacious ballroom, spilling over into the smaller ballroom, the Kleiner Redoutensaal, and the indoor arena of the Spanish Riding School. Some of the side rooms had been transformed into a lush orange grove scented with loans from the emperor's greenhouses.

The Grand Ball had been vastly oversold, thanks in part to enterprising counterfeiters who had superbly forged the invitations. Even more responsible for swelling the event beyond capacity were a few doorkeepers, who had apparently adopted a simpler method of cashing in on the enthusiasm: They would take the admission tickets from the guests and then resell them to the crowds eager to experience, if only for an evening, the revelry of emperors and kings.

The waiters, a "broad and noisy phalanx," struggled with the "murderous crush" of the masked guests and gate-crashers. It is not known what exactly the Festivals Committee served that night, but a catering record survives for a similar grand ball for the same number of guests at the congress that called for some 300 hams, 200 partridges, 200 pigeons, 150 pheasants, 60 hares, 48 *boeuf à la mode,* 40 rabbits, 20 large white young turkeys, and 12 "medium-sized wild boar." Among many other things, there was also an assortment of roasted, baked, and cold meats, and other delicacies, including 600 pickled and salted tongues.

The confectionary supplied a range of pies and pastries, as well as almond, pistachio, chocolate, Seville orange, and French puff-pastry gateaux. There were between 2,500 and 3,000 liters of olla soup, 2,500 assorted biscuits, 1,000 Mandl-Wandl (oval-shaped pastries with an almond filling), 60 Gugelhupf (sponge cakes), and other cakes and sweets. Almond milk, lemonade, chocolate, tea, and many kinds of wine were also available, including Tokay and Meneser. Filling the empty wineglasses and replenishing the dishes on the buffet tables must have seemed a never-ending task.

Suddenly, resounding trumpet blasts signaled the arrival of congress royalty. The emperor, the tsar, and many kings entered, with empresses, queens, and archduchesses on their arms. All eyes turned to the glittering promenade that circled the room and ended at their seats on an honored platform, adorned with large white silk hangings "fringed with silver." The empress of Austria sat in the front, along with the empress of Russia; behind them were the queen of Bavaria and the Russian grand duchess Catherine, Alexander's sister. The dignitaries were flanked with elegant women "as beautiful as statues."

Most of the leading diplomats and ladies attended, with a few prominent exceptions, such as Prussian ambassador Wilhelm von Humboldt. He had been to a party the night before, and had evidently had enough of trying to squeeze into a hot room packed elbow to elbow, where he could not move and the sweat poured down his face. He had been so miserable that he found himself somewhat jealous of the delegate of Hanover, Count Münster, who had broken a rib in a recent carriage accident and had a good excuse for staying home.

The young songwriter August de La Garde-Chambonas found his way to the ball that night, and he was thrilled with everything he saw. What impressed this happy adventurer most was not, of course, the leaders of the world:

> You should have seen those ravishing women, all sparkling with flowers and diamonds, carried away by the irresistible harmonies, leaning back into the arms of their partners.

Many of these women would have worn elegantly simple gowns with deep décolletage. The outer dress was usually in petinet or crepe, the underdress in satin of the same color, white being the most popular, followed by light blue, yellow, pink, or pastels. Sleeves were usually long, tight, and edged in lace, embroidery, or satin. Some preferred short sleeves, or combined them with long white gloves. Flowers and ribbons were often fixed into the hair, along with diamonds, pearls, and other precious stones that glittered marvelously from the light of thousands of candles. When dancing, the women looked like "brilliant meteors" lighting up the heavens.

Orchestras had started with a polonaise, the long procession, like a rhythmic march, through the giant room. Alternatively, in one of the smaller rooms, the minuet was danced, it seemed, with a stiff "Teutonic gravity" that drew snickers from young, fashionable wags. The favorite for the younger generation was, of course, the waltz, the graceful gliding and twirling across the floor, as if the first chords of the orchestra sent an electric current through the happy dancers.

The waltz in the autumn of 1814 was not yet the waltz of later Vienna fame, such as Johan Strauss the Younger's "The Blue Danube," "Tales from the Vienna Woods," and "The Emperor Waltz." It was slower and closer to its origins as a southern German or Austrian country dance. Still, it was a "revolving dance," or *Walzer,* that was every bit as controversial. The waltz, after all, divided the dancers into couples, not groups, and involved much more touching than any previous dance in modern history.

It was perhaps only appropriate the congress would be captivated by this intimate dance. Lord Byron described the waltz in a famous ode:

> *Round all the confines of the yielded waist*
> *The strangest hand may wander undisplaced;*
> *The lady's, in return, may grasp as much*
> *As princely paunches offer to her touch . . .*

Just like the waltz, the masquerade was also a central feature of the entertainment in Vienna during the congress. The ballroom, teeming with revelers in mask, became the "the living image of a society devoted to pleasure, to flirting, and seductive pastimes of every description." Elaborate, at times oppressive protocol easily collapsed, on those occasions, behind the mask, which added a rare freedom, not to mention the allure and enchantment of the unknown. The person behind the mask could, in Vienna of 1814, be literally almost anyone at all.

The dresses, the diamonds, and the dances—La Garde-Chambonas was dazzled. He rhapsodized further on the ladies he saw, with their "shimmering silks and light gauzes of their gowns floating and swaying in graceful undulations."

> The continuous music, the mystery of the disguises, the intrigues
> with which I was surrounded, the general incognito, the unbridled
> gaiety . . . in a word, the magic of the whole vast tableau turned my
> head.

"Older and stronger heads than mine," the young man continued, "found it equally irresistible." Unfortunately for Austria's Festivals Committee, many guests found other things irresistible as well. Almost three thousand of the imperial silver tea spoons disappeared that night.

THE DAILY ROUTINE was already emerging at the Vienna Congress. While the delegates of the Big Four worked in their offices, attended meetings, or tried to schedule appointments, the sovereigns generally spent the mornings on hunts, reviews of troops on parade grounds, or some other activity with their fellow monarchs or favorite companions. Afternoons were usually devoted to meetings and sessions, though by no means, as some complained, simply undoing what the diplomats had done during the day. By the evening, they were in dress uniform again, "sparkling in the truly magical festivities given by the Emperor of Austria."

Among the many activities scheduled for the first week of the congress, there was a concert conducted by Vienna's *Hofkapellmeister*, Antonio Salieri, the opera composer who taught Beethoven, and later Schubert and Liszt. The rumor that Salieri had poisoned Mozart was already circulating at the congress, despite the lack of evidence (one of the police agents, Giuseppe Carpani, would later write a defense of Salieri). Salieri would be active in the musical life of the Vienna Congress that autumn, even directing one "monster concert" of some hundred pianos—apparently an arrangement more experimental and innovative than pleasing to the ear.

In accordance with courtesies of the day, the monarchs were busy bestowing honors and awards upon each other. Britain inducted the leaders into its Order of the Bath and the Order of the Garter with the "Diamond George" pendant. The king of Denmark awarded his fellow sovereigns his state's highest prize, the Order of the Elephant, and the king of Prussia the Black Eagle. The emperor of Austria conferred perhaps the most coveted of all, the Order of the Golden Fleece. All of these ribbons, stars, crosses, and collars, along with many others, were slipped around necks or pinned on breasts that first week.

The Festivals Committee was not the only one planning events. Every night there was entertainment at an embassy, salon, tavern, or somewhere else around town. On Tuesday evenings, for example, the Castlereaghs hosted their soiree at the Minoritenplatz, complete with supper, violin and guitar music, and dance. Despite being well attended and usually difficult to gain entrance to before 10 p.m., Agent ** complained of their tediousness. Guests were poorly greeted and often ignored. The room was dimly lit and poorly furnished, and many women who could not find a seat had to stand. Indeed, without the presiding hand of a talented hostess, this drawing room sometimes seemed more like a café than a salon.

When the British delegates ventured out into other salons in town, many seemed awkward and clumsy. "Either they try to impress us," one police agent overheard, "or they skulk like beasts in a cave." Others smiled at their odd selection of clothes, deemed eccentric at best. The effects of being an island power, so insulated from the Continent, seemed evident to more than a few observers that autumn.

One member of the British embassy, Ambassador Lord Stewart, had already gotten involved in a traffic dispute with the driver of another carriage—a common enough hazard in a town with many horse-drawn vehicles racing through the narrow streets. The event made the rounds in Vienna's salons. According to one rumor, the British ambassador almost ended up tossing the coachman into the Danube. Police agents also followed the case, though they learned that it was actually the coachman who was close to pummeling the ambassador.

What had happened was that after the near accident, Lord Stewart, who had apparently "emptied some bottles of Bordeaux," shouted obscenities, clenched his fists, boasted at his record as a boxer, and challenged the other man to a fistfight. The cabdriver, who evidently did not understand English, grabbed the whip and cracked him in the face. Bystanders broke up the scuffle, and police arrived on the scene before it turned worse, though the officers refused at first to believe that the loud drunk was really a high-ranking member of the British delegation.

Lord Stewart was already cropping up in police reports, too, for the vast amount of time he was spending in the company of what the spies called "ladies of easy virtue." He was a regular customer at local brothels, many of them housed in the Leopoldstadt district, a mostly seventeenth-century development in what had once been the city's thriving Jewish quarter. Stewart and his buddies had also discovered the merits of Hungarian wine, and, in the first week in Vienna, the British ambassador had several times been carried to his carriage.

Perhaps the liveliest topic buzzing in the salons the week of the scheduled opening was the reputed imminent arrival of Napoleon's wife, Marie Louise. Since the fall of the empire, the twenty-three-year-old woman had been torn in her allegiance, vacillating between joining her husband on Elba or returning to her father, Emperor Francis, and the family in Vienna. She had spent a great deal of time pondering her choices and had, in the end, decided to return to Vienna. She was supposed to arrive at any moment, and speculation raged on how she would react to the sight of Vienna carried away in its celebration of her husband's downfall.

WHILE ALL THE plenipotentiaries were preparing for the diplomatic duel at the next meeting of the Big Four, Talleyrand decided to take matters into his own hands. Fearing that his ostracization in the conference of the Great Powers would deprive him of any real influence, the French minister played to his strength. Talleyrand was rightly convinced that his conception of the congress as a parliament of states with equal power would resonate with the vast majority of the delegates, who were destined to be excluded from the proposed scheme.

On his own initiative, Talleyrand drafted, signed, and circulated an account of the secret meeting—a maverick breach of diplomatic etiquette. The Great Powers, he announced, had "formed a league to make themselves masters of everything." This was very much against the spirit of the congress and the hopes of establishing a genuine peace. The Great Powers had no right to sabotage the congress, and had set themselves up instead as the "supreme arbiters of Europe."

This note was, needless to say, very unpopular among the Big Four. Not only was the structure of the upcoming congress now out in the open, introduced in an unbecoming and an untimely fashion by an outside party, but Talleyrand's version, in their eyes, blew everything out of proportion. Russia grumbled, Austria took offense, and the Prussians were absolutely furious.

In a meeting of the Big Four on October 2, Wilhelm von Humboldt denounced the French document as a "firebrand flung into our midst." The Prussian embassy, it seems, quickly countered with its own campaign of propaganda, spreading rumors that the French were once again up to their old habits. Talleyrand was accused of sowing discontent among the Allies in order for his country to seize coveted regions of Belgium and the left bank of the Rhine.

Castlereagh, on the other hand, opted for a more constructive approach and went over to Kaunitz Palace, early that same morning, to discuss matters with Talleyrand personally. He had come to respect the French minister and his opinions, though the two men certainly did not agree on everything. Many thought Castlereagh was the friendliest to the French embassy, and among the Big Four, he no doubt was.

The British minister explained to Talleyrand in his calm, reassuring manner that the proceedings at the meeting at Metternich's summer villa were intended to be "entirely confidential." Talleyrand's unexpected publication of his note had "rather excited apprehension" among the Austrian and Prussian ministers. Talleyrand listened, but he did not recant, apologize, or otherwise give any sign of remorse. He only reminded him that Castlereagh had asked his opinion, and "[he] was bound to give it."

Talleyrand further explained that he could not participate in this ill-advised attempt to close off the congress. Napoleonic ideas of seizing power and acting unilaterally should be banished from international politics. Respecting principles of law and justice, on the other hand, was the best way forward. Castlereagh, unimpressed, returned to headquarters.

On October 3, Talleyrand wrote a second note, reiterating his main points, and this time he distributed it more widely. Sure enough, it had great impact. Many princes and delegates outside of the elite club of Great Powers shared Talleyrand's concerns, and they applauded his defiance. He was speaking up for the minor states, and the only one, it seemed, doing so. Indeed, by maneuvering into position to be able to champion law and justice, the foreign minister of a country that had only recently devoured small nations was now, remarkably, being praised as their protector.

THE GREAT POWERS knew that they had to work quickly to rein in the Frenchman. The person that Metternich wanted to draft the official response to Talleyrand's inflammatory paper was his assistant, Friedrich von Gentz, the secretary of the Congress, a short man with red hair and thick small-rimmed glasses. By a combination of talent and his own pushy efforts, he had managed to position himself right in the middle of everything.

In many ways, Gentz had a lot to prove. He was not a prince like Metternich, Talleyrand, or Hardenberg, all of whom had been raised to that title either during or immediately after the war. He was not even a count like his friend, the Russian adviser Karl Nesselrode, a man he had discovered and supported for years. Sure, Gentz had an aristocratic-sounding "von" in his name, but no one seemed to know where it had come from, and many suspected it was on his own initiative, as indeed it was.

A German by birth, the fifty-year-old Gentz had studied at the University of Königsberg under the philosopher Immanuel Kant, and this training showed. He was sharp in debate, adept at manipulating ideas and concepts, and so skillful in his questioning that he sometimes seemed like the Socrates of the Vienna Congress. Like the great philosopher, Gentz would also be unpopular with the people subjected to his painful tactics. He was a very hard worker, shunning many of the entertainments for a quiet evening in a salon discussing politics, which was his main passion. The Socratic comparison, of course, breaks down with Gentz's unabashed worldly streak. He had a love of chocolate, perfume, and flashy rings. "If you want to make him deliriously happy," Metternich said, "give him some bonbons."

Gentz had previously worked as a civil servant in Prussia, where he had edited the conservative *Historisches Journal* and translated political thought, including Edmund Burke's *Reflections on the Revolution in France*. In 1797, he went bankrupt; five years later, his marriage collapsed and he moved to Vienna. He joined the Austrian administration and eventually gained Metternich's attention, becoming one of his most influential assistants. It was Metternich who had given him entrée into the congress and its high society.

Asked to answer the charges made by Talleyrand, Gentz went to work immediately with characteristic intensity. The next day, he was finished. Every decision of the committee was legal, Gentz argued in a frontal assault on Talleyrand's accusations. Every decision, moreover, was shown to be completely in accord with the previous agreements, most importantly with the Treaty of Paris, the international document that legally gave rise to the Vienna Congress. As his colleagues had come to expect, Gentz was a wizard at finding just the right word for the occasion.

Gentz's document was readily accepted and signed by the Great Powers. That night, Tuesday, October 4, at a soiree held by the Duchess of Sagan, it was officially presented to the French delegation. Metternich waited for the right moment, then pranced up to the French minister and, in front of a packed room, made a big show of handing him the protocol.

Talleyrand, of course, was not ruffled in the least. Less than twenty-four hours later, he also had a response, another letter that defiantly stood its ground. The Great Powers had no right, Talleyrand reaffirmed, to "take it upon themselves to decide everything in advance" and leave everyone else outside their cabal. Trying to impose their will as law was no better than Napoleon's tactics and would only have the same result—more war and bloodshed.

When Talleyrand presented this paper at the next meeting of the Big Four at Metternich's summer villa on October 5, the result was another "very tumultuous and very memorable conference," as Gentz put it in his diary. Talleyrand's protest was passed around the table. Both Metternich and Nesselrode frivolously "glanced at it with the air of men who require only to look at a paper to lay hold of all its contents." Metternich turned to Talleyrand and asked him directly to withdraw the letter. He refused. Metternich tried again with more persuasion, but Talleyrand held firm. The French minister then added:

> I shall take no more part in your conferences . . . I shall be nothing here but a member of the Congress, and I shall wait until it is opened.

But Talleyrand was making too many waves in salons and drawing rooms around town, and gaining too large a following to be ignored. Clearly, the French minister was not behaving in the way the Great Powers had hoped when they summoned him to their conference.

Exasperated, Metternich blurted out that he would cancel the peace conference immediately—a threat, at this point, so wildly unrealistic that it did not faze anyone. Russia's Count Nesselrode came to Metternich's assistance, stating unequivocally that the decisions in Vienna needed to be wrapped up quickly because the tsar was leaving town by the end of the month. Talleyrand, still unmoved, only replied, "I am sorry to hear it, for he will not be here to see the end of things."

"How can the Congress be assembled," Metternich asked, "when nothing is ready to lay before it?"

"Well, then," Talleyrand replied in a planned burst of cordiality, "since nothing is ready as yet for the opening of the Congress, and since you wish to adjourn, let it be put off for a fortnight or three weeks. I consent to that." Provided, of course, he added significantly, that the leaders seated around the table accept two conditions. First, they set a firm date for the opening of the congress, and second, they specify the criteria for deciding who will be admitted to the proceedings. He scribbled the terms down immediately and handed the paper over to the Big Four.

This meeting had not gone well for the conquerors of Napoleon, and their disappointment was read in the way the conference ended. It was not adjourned in an orderly fashion, but instead seemed to evaporate, with ministers drifting off at will.

Castlereagh, the last to leave, walked down the wide stone steps afterward with Talleyrand. Like many in Vienna, he preferred to take the personal and informal approach whenever possible. He tried to persuade Talleyrand by hinting at his own help: "certain affairs that most interest [France] could be arranged to my satisfaction."

"It isn't at all a question of certain particular objects," Talleyrand replied, "but rather of the law which ought to serve to rule us all . . . How can we answer to Europe if we have not honored those rights, the loss of which caused all our troubles?"

Turning again to Castlereagh, Talleyrand emphasized the opportunity at hand, a chance to reestablish law, order, and peace:

The present epoch is one of those which hardly occur once in the course of several centuries. A fairer opportunity can never be offered to us. Why should we not place ourselves in a position to answer to it?

Chapter 10

THE PEOPLE'S FESTIVAL

*I have made two mistakes with Talleyrand—first,
I did not take his good advice,
and second, I did not have him hanged when
I did not follow his ideas.*

—NAPOLEON

astlereagh had found himself in an awkward and frustrating position. Besides the fact that he sympathized with Talleyrand's viewpoint, he had another reason for tolerating the sheer defiance of this defeated power. Castlereagh was concerned, more than ever, about the threat of Russia, and its ominously close relationship with Prussia.

In a council of only four powers, the grouping of these two was significant. Castlereagh was about to be left with only one potential ally: Austria, a notoriously ambiguous and tentative partner led by a foreign minister, as a common critique ran, "more polished than steeled." The British minister was worried about how his Austrian ally would stand up under pressure, and wondered if he might in the future need Talleyrand's assistance.

Castlereagh's ideal plan was not, of course, to work with France; he much preferred to win over the Prussians, and shift them away from their Russian ally. He believed that he had a good chance. He related well with the Prussian diplomatic team, and he wanted a strong Prussia anyway. As he saw it, a powerful Prussia would create a "stable foundation" for Germany and, at the same time, provide a valuable counterweight against the temptations of the "devouring powers" from the outside, either France in the west or Russia in the east.

Actually, Prussia's Chancellor Hardenberg and Humboldt shared many of Castlereagh's fears of a mammoth Russian power that could potentially dominate Germany and central Europe, if not also the entire continent. They could not voice these concerns openly, however, because Prussia was still closely allied with Russia. Yet both statesmen made it clear, behind closed doors, that they believed that Prussia had a better future working with Britain and Austria. The problem they faced was convincing their king, who was as determined as ever to stick with the Russian tsar.

Meanwhile, inside Kaunitz Palace, Talleyrand was waiting for an invitation, as promised, to discuss his criteria for admitting delegates to the congress. One day passed, and then another. There was still no word of the meeting. The only invitation in circulation, it seemed, was to the royal hunt in a wooded park outside Vienna.

On October 6, while Talleyrand was still waiting, there was another pageant planned for the vast green span of manicured lawns and shady walkways northwest of the inner town. This was the Augarten, a former royal playground and hunting field that had been opened to the public almost forty years before. It had the oldest baroque garden in Vienna, and an eighteenth-century palace that serves today as the home of the Vienna Boys' Choir. The Augarten also housed a center for porcelain making, and had long staged summer concerts, including Mozart and Beethoven. Now it would host the "People's Festival"—a celebration for the people who had done so much to achieve the Allied victory.

Organizers of the event had erected a grand amphitheater for the sovereigns, along with a large structure built with colored glass to resemble a rainbow. With flags and trophies prominently displayed, veterans of the Napoleonic Wars marched past the tents and crowds to drum and fife. There were footraces, horse races, and an "open-air circus." Acrobats tumbled, equestrian teams performed, and crossbowmen from the Tyrolean Alps competed in sharpshooting contests.

At the end of the games, a Vienna hot-air balloonist climbed into his canvas contraption, about the size of a four-story building, and soared "majestically over the heads of the crowd, waving flags of every nation." Then the honored veterans sat down at sixteen long banquet tables weighed down by food and drink, and enjoyed a feast to military music. They were toasted by fellow soldiers and leaders alike, including the Russian tsar, who stood, drink in hand, and announced in his excellent German, "The Emperor of Russia drinks to the health of you, old men!" Then he sealed the toast by hurling his crystal glass against a nearby garden urn.

Elsewhere in the park, spectators were treated to a group of dancers, in folk costumes, performing regional dances from different parts of the Austrian empire. The grand finale was entrusted to Vienna's fireworks master, Stuwer. His whistling rockets painted the flags of the victorious Allies in the sky.

Later that night, revelers walked through the streets of Vienna, admiring the palaces and mansions illuminated with candles in their windows. While many moved on to ballrooms such as the Apollo Saal and waltzed all night amid its indoor gardens with make-believe grottoes and moss-covered rocks, the sovereigns and their retinues continued to the theater. They saw the ballet *Flore et Zéphire,* which featured the star ballerina Emilia Bigottini, whose graceful dances held the audience in thrall.

The joy that surrounded the People's Festival was fueled, as one observer put it, by "the hope of a durable peace, the price of which had been paid by many years of constant sacrifices." The peacemakers indeed owed it to the people who had suffered so much in the war to make the best peace possible.

TWO DAYS LATER, on October 8, Metternich's invitation to the private meeting to set the terms for the opening of the congress finally arrived. Talleyrand was requested to be at the summer villa at eight o'clock that evening. He was asked to come a little early, if he liked, and Metternich would update him about some developments.

When Talleyrand arrived that evening, Metternich thanked him for his proposal on the opening of the congress, and added that he had taken the liberty of drawing up another plan that differed slightly, but he hoped it would be satisfactory. Talleyrand asked to read it.

"I do not have it yet," Metternich answered. "Gentz has carried it off to put on some finishing touches."

"Probably, it is being communicated to your *Allies,*" Talleyrand snapped back sarcastically, referring to the divisive term that had earlier provoked his displeasure.

"Let us not speak any longer of Allies," Metternich reassured him. "There are no more Allies."

"But there are people here who ought to be Allies," Talleyrand added, wasting no time to remind the Austrian foreign minister that both of their countries had a lot in common, not least the desire to stop an aggressive Russia. The tsar wanted Poland, and should he be indulged in this whim, the situation could potentially be disastrous for Austria. Talleyrand hammered home the risks of a Russian Poland with a direct question: "How can you possibly contemplate placing Russia like a girdle all round your principal and most important possessions, Hungary and Bohemia?"

Metternich remarked coolly that the French minister obviously placed no trust in him, and Talleyrand replied, equally coolly, that so far he had not been given any reason to do so.

"Here are pen, ink, and paper," Talleyrand continued theatrically. "Will you write that France asks nothing, and even that she will accept nothing? I am ready to sign."

"But there is the affair of Naples, that is properly yours." Metternich reminded the French minister of his desire to place the Bourbon king Ferdinand IV back on the throne in southern Italy.

"Not mine, more than everybody else's," Talleyrand replied, implying that the restoration of law was in the interests of everyone.

> For me it is only a matter of principle. I ask that he who has a right to be at Naples should be at Naples; that is all. Now, that is just what everyone, as well as myself, ought to wish.

"Let principles be acted upon, and I shall be found easy to deal with in everything."

One of those principles that Talleyrand urged upon the congress was legitimacy. Although vague and undefined, the word was generally used to mean the rule of law, or the accepted "order of things" based on the sanction of time. As Talleyrand argued, this was "a necessary element of the peace and happiness of peoples, the most solid, or rather the only guarantee of their strength and continuance." Legitimacy, in other words, was "the safeguard of nations," and Talleyrand hoped it would serve as a guiding principle in restoring Europe.

Specifically, he wanted Vienna to maintain the king of Saxony as the *legitimate* ruler of a sovereign state, and restore Ferdinand IV as the *legitimate* king of Naples. As for France's aggressive neighbors, the Prussians, Talleyrand said that he would never consent to their outlandish demands for territory. Nor would he, for that matter, ever allow the Russian tsar to create a "phantom Poland" and thereby advance his empire all the way to the Vistula River in the center of Europe.

Sharing this fear of Russia, Metternich grasped Talleyrand's hand and reassured him: "We are much less divided than you think."

At that point, a footman announced that the other delegates had arrived for the conference, which was, in fact, the first meeting of a new committee, the Committee of Eight. This was actually the Big Four, joined by the four other powers who had signed the Treaty of Paris (France, Portugal, Sweden, and Spain). Reluctantly, the Great Powers had accepted Talleyrand's argument that they had no basis for simply making all decisions themselves, and they had retreated onto more solid ground with this committee. Everyone went into the large meeting room to hammer out the conditions for accepting delegates to the congress. After some negotiation, they agreed to open the congress on the first of November.

As for who exactly could participate, there were two plans for consideration, one drafted by Talleyrand and the other by Metternich. The two plans were similar. The main difference was that Talleyrand's plan, by definition, would not permit the delegate of the Bonapartist Murat to participate in the conference, while Metternich's was vague enough that it did not specify one way or the other. Metternich's plan won.

Talleyrand consented to this arrangement with one small change: The congress "shall then be conducted in conformity with the principles of public law," as international law was then called.

At these words, Prussia's Hardenberg stood up, banged his fists on the table, and shouted, "No, sir, public law is a useless phrase. Why say that we shall act according to public law? That is a matter of course."

"If it be a matter of course," Talleyrand responded, "it can do no harm to specify it."

"What has public law to do here?" Prussia's Humboldt asked.

It was public law, Talleyrand responded, "that sends you here."

The tensions were heating up, and Castlereagh, the force of modera-tion, called Talleyrand aside and discreetly asked him if his colleagues conceded on this point, would he "afterwards be more accommodat-ing"? The French minister agreed.

But the trouble in convincing the Big Four to recognize the authority of law at the peace conference seemed a bad omen. Talleyrand, however, was hopeful that the force of law would help restrain the appetites of the more aggressive powers. Metternich was glad to win another postpone-ment of the congress, and he planned to use the time to find a way to oppose the Russians. He went home to read some poetry, and, as he wrote, think about the Duchess of Sagan.

A FEW DAYS before that important meeting, Talleyrand had gone to a dinner party with Dorothée. It was in many ways typical of the dinners held every night in Vienna that autumn: lavish menus, excellent wine, sparkling conversation led by prominent and often fascinating guests. The Duchess of Sagan was hosting the party and putting her talents to use. But what was most surprising about that party was that the person at her side was not Prince Metternich.

In fact, it was an old lover, Prince Alfred von Windischgrätz, a twenty-seven-year-old from an Austrian aristocratic family who was a cavalry officer with a distinguished record in the war as a colonel in a regiment of cuirassiers, the O'Reilly Light Horse Regiment. He was a soldier's sol-dier, tall and strong, with a taste for smoking cigars, a habit he picked up in Brussels. Prince Alfred is often credited with popularizing this "Bel-gian habit," as it was called, among the Austrian aristocracy.

That evening, the two had carried on, evidently, with more than their usual flirtatious ways, and everyone present had left the party without any doubt that the duchess had rekindled this old flame. The duchess's relationship with Prince Alfred was on a different level than the one with Metternich. Whereas the foreign minister was a sophisticated, worldly charmer, very much at home in elegant drawing rooms and plush opera boxes, Windischgrätz preferred more simple pleasures.

Prince Alfred von Windischgrätz and the Duchess of Sagan had begun their affair in a way that was somewhat characteristic of their relationship. One afternoon, back in 1810, they had ridden out to a country inn in a beautiful wine district just outside Vienna. While they sat together, the duchess nursed her glass, and the prince, cigar in hand, noticed a ring on her finger. It was a giant, impressively cut ruby. The count asked about the gem, wondering no doubt if it had been given to her by a lover.

Actually, the duchess had purchased the ring herself. She had come across it on display at a Vienna jeweler's shop and just had to have it. But for a combination of motives—a sense of pride, mischief, and curiosity about what would happen—the duchess did not wish to say that outright. She was vague and noncommittal in her responses, and this promptly sent the decorated cavalry officer out of his mind with jealousy. At one point, the impulsive prince sprung across the table and snatched the ring from her finger.

As he started to look it over, hunting for an engraving or other sign of its sender, the duchess leaped up and quickly circled the table to take it back. A playful wrestling match ensued, like two teenagers in love, when the duchess, determined to win, sank her teeth into his arm. The prince reacted by locking his hold on her, and then with his free hand, for a prank, put the ring between his tobacco-stained teeth. The duchess broke free, and in the process, the prince accidentally swallowed the ruby. The ring was later recovered and returned to the duchess. Anything could happen on an outing with Prince Alfred.

Now, when word of the Duchess of Sagan's dinner companion made it back to Metternich, he was deeply disturbed. Though he was not unaware of their previous liaison, the thought of them together made him lose his usual cool. He could not stand the idea of anyone taking his place by her side, and wrote to the duchess asking for clarification. Surely, there must be some misunderstanding.

By the time of the emperor's ball at the Spanish Riding School on October 9, Metternich could still not shake the thought from his mind. He wrote to the duchess that day, in the middle of a meeting. He thought of their past, and how during their relationship he had cried "tears of joy." He could not wait to see her.

That evening, the duchess looked more beautiful than ever. She arrived with twenty-three other women, who, arranging themselves in four groups, dressed as the Four Elements. Six young ladies wearing blue and green dresses, adorned with pearls, coral, and other seashells, went

as Water. Six others in blazing red silk dresses and carrying torches were
Fire. Another group of young women wearing wings and the clearest
"flimsiest veiling" was the Air. The Duchess of Sagan was with the group
representing Earth, and wore a brown velvet dress and a headdress in the
form of a "golden basket filled with jeweled fruit." To Metternich, she
outshone everyone.

The ballroom was packed, and maneuvering through the throngs of
dancers was challenging. Yet Metternich started to suspect that the
duchess was avoiding him. Clearly, she had no time for him, and he never
was alone with her. Prince Alfred, on the other hand, seemed to pull off
the feat with no problem at all.

Had Metternich been with the duchess, he could have enjoyed the
magnificent, glittering spectacle of kings and princes at play in the white
stucco hall lit up by silver chandeliers and thousands of candles. The tsar
danced, it was said, with fifty women, apparently doing his best to make
sure the peace conference earned its reputation as the dancing congress.

Metternich was miserable. Late the following night, he penned a long
letter to the Duchess of Sagan describing how he felt: "You have surely
been loved, and you will be loved again, but you will never be more
loved, and you have never been more loved, than by me." Metternich
was even more unused to losing in love than in diplomacy.

Chapter 11

A LAWLESS SCRAMBLE?

Treason, Sire, that is a question of dates.

— TALLEYRAND

While Metternich brooded over the duchess and feared that she was slipping out of his life, Vienna's diplomats were again facing long waits in his anteroom. Two days after the masked ball, Geneva's delegates, Jean-Gabriel Eynard and Charles Pictet de Rochemont, appeared at the Chancellery for a meeting scheduled at one in the afternoon. They had been the first to arrive that day—it was a Tuesday, and Metternich's salons on Monday nights typically lasted until the early morning hours. While they waited for Metternich, a tall, elegant man with a red skullcap, long scarlet gloves, and silk habiliments approached and struck up a conversation.

This man, it turned out, was Cardinal Consalvi, the pope's secretary of state and delegate at the Vienna Congress. For the last fourteen years, he had guided both foreign policy and domestic affairs for the Vatican. He was known as a reformer, and had, among other things, led the excavation of the Forum and the restoration of the Colosseum. He had also ordered names placed onto streets, and numbers given to individual buildings. Above all, Consalvi was known for his work with Napoleon, including the landmark negotiation of the Concordat (1801) that brought about the reconciliation between the Catholic Church and France after the turmoil of the revolution.

It was also Consalvi who, in 1804, had persuaded the reluctant Pope Pius VII to travel to Paris for Napoleon's imperial coronation, the first time a pope had participated in such a ceremony in almost three hundred years, the last time being the coronation of Charles V at Bologna in 1530. Consalvi, meanwhile, back at the Vatican, served as the "Papal-Vicar," the only occasion of this office in the history of the papacy.

Consalvi was indeed a talented diplomat in the league of Metternich, Talleyrand, Castlereagh, and the other giants at the Vienna peace conference. According to the writer Stendhal, Consalvi was actually the greatest of them all because he was "the only honest one" in the lot. Besides his frankness, the pope's secretary of state had earned a reputation as a tough negotiator, as was shown on many occasions when relations between Napoleon and the Vatican later soured. Napoleon called Consalvi "a lion in sheep's clothing" and threatened several times to have him shot. (Consalvi, for instance, refused to recognize Napoleon's divorce from his first wife, Joséphine, and led a group of cardinals in a boycott of the wedding ceremony.)

During the Revolutionary and Napoleonic Wars, the papacy had fallen to one of its lowest points in modern history. The French army invaded the Papal States several times and seized vast amounts of property, including its richest territory, the Legations (Ferrara, Bologna, and Ravenna). The swampy Marches to the south of Rome had also been lost, along with many other places, including Avignon, which had been papal property since 1309, and Venaissin, since 1228.

Napoleon had also plundered the Vatican shamelessly, stealing some one hundred works of art, selected by French commissioners. One observer described the awful spectacle of French "doctrinaire cannibals running around, catalogues at hand," selecting the treasures to be brought back to Paris: the Apollo Belvedere, the Dying Gaul, Raphael's *Transfiguration*, Domenichino's *Last Communion of St. Jerome*, and *Laocoön and His Sons*, to name a few. The French had forced the pope to sign away ownership of these works of art in the Treaty of Tolentino (1797), and subsequent raids brought many more treasures. Two years later, when the pope refused to relinquish his rights as a ruler, Napoleon had him seized from the Vatican. Pius VI actually died in captivity as a French prisoner, and his successor, Pius VII, was only released in January 1814.

Like many others at the congress, the Vatican had strong arguments for regaining its territory and property, especially given the wide support of the principle of legitimacy. But the pope had signed the treaty, and there was no guarantee that congress dignitaries would accept Consalvi's argument that it was done under duress, no matter how self-evident it might appear. There were powerful interests at stake. The current holders of the Papal States wanted to keep them: Murat's army now in the Marches, and the Austrians in the Legations.

Eynard, Pictet de Rochemont, and Consalvi continued to wait on the Austrian foreign minister, who eventually arrived an hour and a half late. Consalvi received the first audience in honor of his position as the pope's delegate. The second meeting went to the Prussian ambassador, Humboldt, who had just arrived and immediately jumped to the front of the line. Urgent business, he said, though it must have seemed to many who now filled the room as just another instance of Prussian arrogance. By the late afternoon, after three hours of waiting, one of Metternich's valets de chambre entered and announced that the Austrian foreign minister could no longer see anyone, as he had a dinner appointment and he had not yet dressed for it. Somehow, though, the Swiss delegates managed to gain entrance, probably with the help of a handsome tip.

"It is impossible to have more agreeable manners than Metternich," Eynard wrote in his diary later that day, after the brief meeting. Metternich, of course, appeared to be on their side—he always seemed on the side of the person he was with. Although the foreign minister was affable and engaging with his usual touch of "lightness and unconcern," Eynard thought he looked "overwhelmed with fatigue." He noted the dark circles under Metternich's eyes, and how the foreign minister fought off yawns. He had no idea about Metternich's current preoccupations with the Duchess of Sagan.

No one knows for certain what Princess Bagration was doing at this time, either, though many rumors were circulating about the mischief she was making at Metternich's expense. Evidently, her attempts to win Metternich had not worked, and as several spy reports began to note, the princess was becoming much angrier at her former lover. She was actively pursuing "revenge for Metternich's neglect," one informed. Another agent reported that she was "openly revealing all she knows, or has heard, that might hurt Austria." Guests to her salon were shocked at her outspoken comments, though the details of her tantrums were discreetly omitted from the police reports.

The Russian tsar, too, was suspected of exploiting Princess Bagration's lingering resentment against the Austrian foreign minister. "Metternich never loved you," Alexander was overheard saying, according to Agent Nota. "Believe me," the tsar was said to have added, Metternich "is a cold fish who is quite incapable of love. Can't you see this plaster-of-Paris figure? He loves no one."

JUST AS GOSSIPERS predicted, Marie Louise had arrived in Vienna back on the seventh of October and moved into the west wing of Schönbrunn, the Habsburg summer palace located south of the town. It was a large residence with a facade in a shade of mustard yellow that the Viennese called "Maria Theresa Gold" after the eighteenth-century monarch who had redecorated the palace. Schönbrunn was originally intended to outshine Louis XIV's Versailles, though the Austrians had run out of money long before they achieved that goal.

Marie Louise had returned to Vienna without fanfare, arriving purposely late to avoid the opening ceremonies of the peace conference. She looked only slightly older now than she did when she had been forced, four years earlier, to marry Napoleon. She still had a youthful face, as one put it, "like peaches and cream," and a figure that looked crafted in a "turner's workshop." She also brought their son, the three-and-a-half-year-old Napoleon Francis, the former infant king of Rome and heir to the throne of France. This "little Napoleon," who resembled his mother with his fair complexion, spoke often of his father and showed a great curiosity about any Frenchman he met. Their carriage still bore Napoleonic emblems, and her servants still dressed in Napoleonic livery.

It had been a stressful six months since Napoleon's abdication, and eight months since Marie Louise had last seen her husband. They had parted in late January 1814, when Napoleon rode out for the brilliant though ultimately unsuccessful spring campaign. Marie Louise had remained in Paris presiding over a council of Napoleon's foremost advisers and administering what was left of his empire. By late March, however, the Allies were closing in on the capital, and Marie Louise had to decide whether to stay or leave for safer territory. Uncertain, though inclined to remain in Paris, she had put the question to the council.

After a long discussion, a vote, and a letter produced at the last minute from Napoleon emphasizing that his family was not, in any circumstances, to "fall into the hands of the enemy," Marie Louise had agreed to leave for temporary residence in Orléans. It was there, on April 12, that a bizarre race for the former empress took place: Napoleon had sent a cavalry escort to "liberate" Marie Louise, while some Austrian officers rode to "save" her and bring her back to her father. The Austrians arrived first.

"I am worried to death for you," Marie Louise wrote her husband as she was forced to accompany the Austrian officers to the castle of Rambouillet, nearly thirty miles southwest of Paris. But once she saw her father, Emperor Francis, she promised Napoleon to make it perfectly clear that she was to join him on Elba, and "nobody is going to prevent me from doing that." By most accounts, Marie Louise had meant every word.

Indeed, despite the politics that inspired their marriage, it is clear that Napoleon and Marie Louise had developed a loving relationship. This fact came as a surprise to most historians when a whole collection of Marie Louise's personal letters was discovered in the twentieth century. "There's no one in the world who loves you as much as your faithful Louise," Marie Louise had written to her husband in one of many affectionate letters composed during this time.

Yet Marie Louise's determination to join her husband on Elba had met some considerable opposition from her father. "He forbids me to come to you to see you," she informed Napoleon. "I told him outright that it was my duty to follow you." But her father had refused, and instead ordered her back to Austria, though he had assured her that she would soon have the freedom to choose her future herself.

Unhappily, Marie Louise had obeyed her father's wishes and returned to Vienna for some five or six weeks before spending the rest of the summer at the spas of Aix-en-Savoie, which were supposed to cure her anxieties. Her doctor had prescribed "absolute rest and tranquility in some suitable spot where she can follow a strict course of treatment." Still, as she left for the healing waters, she had assured Napoleon that she "loved him more tenderly than ever" and planned to come to Elba after that.

It was during that time apart that Marie Louise's resolution apparently began to waver. She had been promised the duchies of Parma, Piacenza, and Guastalla, and this had been written in the Treaty of Fontainebleau (confirmed, too, in the Treaty of Paris). To her great dismay, however, Marie Louise now learned that this might not be a guarantee after all. Her father and Metternich had both written to inform her

that there was a movement to return those duchies to the Spanish Bourbon dynasty that had owned them before the war, and several states supported this view, including Bourbon Spain and France. Marie Louise's
presence in Vienna would be vital, they emphasized, or no doubt overem-
phasized. She should make plans to return home to look after the interests of herself and her son, not to mention her duties as an Austrian
archduchess.

So it was back to Vienna for the congress. "What a sad prospect," she
had confessed to her secretary as she had made her slow, leisurely ride to
a town filled with her husband's conquerors.

AMONG THE MANY unofficial delegates still arriving every day, Johann
Georg Cotta and Carl Bertuch were representing some eighty-one publishing houses and book dealers in Germany. Cotta was head of a major
publishing house in Stuttgart, which owned the newspaper *Allgemeine
Zeitung,* and Bertuch was the son of a publisher in Weimar who printed
the works of many literary giants. Together they hoped to persuade the
Vienna Congress to correct many of the ills that plagued the publishing
business. Specifically, they would petition against censorship and stifling
governmental controls of the press, and, at the same time, appeal for
more protection against rogue printers who pirated their work. The first
problem damaged the quality of publication; the second ate substantially
into the profits.

This was not an easy argument to make with monarchist governments comfortable with the control of the press, whether by censorship
or the licensing of official printing houses. In Austria, for example, a government edict of September 1810 justified the need for "a cautious
hand," as it called censorship, to protect the "heart and head of imma-
ture persons from the corrupting products of a depraved imagination,
from the poisonous breath of self-seeking seducers, and from the dangerous phantoms of perverted minds." Besides this self-interested paternal-
ism that very often squashed dissenting opinion, the state had other
incentives to maintain the status quo. After all, the printers who forged
and plagiarized works also paid taxes and fees.

But a great deal was at stake, Cotta and Bertuch argued. Without
basic freedom and protection, few authors would undertake any serious

work, and even fewer firms would be willing to risk publishing them. Only songbooks and prayer books would be published, they argued, with some exaggeration. At any rate, it would be a shame to miss an excellent opportunity for scholarship and commerce in the newly emerging Germany. There was a large population, growing wealth, and a common vernacular that transcended state boundaries—in short, a potentially large market of readers.

Vienna's police department was leery of many foreign delegations, but these publishers seemed particularly suspicious. Agent Goehausen believed that both Cotta and Bertuch belonged to a banned secret society, the Tugendbund, or "League of Virtue," that flourished amid the patriotism that swept Germany in the wars against France, and promoted unsettling patriotic aims like the unification of Germany. "Agent H"— almost certainly Wilhelm Hebenstreit, the theater critic and future editor of the fashion magazine *Wiener Modenzeitung*—was recruited to keep a close eye on their activities.

Agent H knew that the publishers already enjoyed support among major delegations. The Prussians, in particular, were favorable. Hardenberg and Humboldt had championed liberal and reform policies for years, and Bertuch gained a meeting with the latter, thanks to a friendly letter of introduction written by no less a person than Goethe. Baron vom Stein of Nassau, then serving the Russian delegation, was another easy sell. He saw copyright protections as part of a package of basic rights that he wanted enshrined in the new German constitution: equality of all citizens, the right to study at any university, the right to choose occupations, the right of emigration, and protection against crimes ex post facto, among others.

Both Cotta and Bertuch were engaging, well-rounded conversationalists who could make a strong case, all the while peppering their arguments with anecdotes about famous writers they knew, such as Goethe. They also dangled tempting offers of publishing contracts before some people in town, such as the Swiss strategist serving on the Prussian delegation, Henri Jomini. Cotta, in particular, was someone to watch, being, as Agent H put it, a rich man with many important and diverse contacts.

By the middle of October, the publishers had already secured an audience with Prince Metternich, which was no small feat given his preoccupations at that time. During the conference, held in the afternoon of the fourteenth, Metternich promised his support. He seemed sincere, as he often did. The question was, however, what exactly did his support mean? Metternich sometimes promised assistance, and then the matter went on to die a quiet, mysterious death. The publishing delegates would be well advised not to stop their lobbying.

Among other groups actively seeking support at this time were the Jewish delegations, which came from several cities in Germany and central Europe. During the French occupation, many old laws discriminating against Jews had been repealed, and new ones enacted that extended the rights of Jews. After the war, however, several German states and towns were rebelling against the French legislation, and some were on the verge of reenacting the old discriminatory regulations. The Jewish delegations were working to preserve their equality, which, however incomplete, was still preferable to a return to repression.

There were several different Jewish delegations in town, each working largely independently of the others. Jakob Baruch and J. J. Gumprecht represented the Jews of Frankfurt, and the banker Simon Edler von Lämel represented the Jewish community in Prague. Dr. Carl August Buchholz, a Christian lawyer, worked on behalf of Jewish communities in Bremen, Hamburg, and his native Lübeck. Buchholz was also completing a 157-page booklet advocating Jewish rights, which would soon circulate among congress dignitaries. Fortunately, these delegations had valuable support networks in town, which included some of Vienna's most influential bankers: Nathan von Arnstein, Salomon Mayer Rothschild, and Leopold Edler von Herz.

But the Vienna police were suspicious of these delegations, ordering special surveillance in July 1814, even before the conference had begun. One official in the police bureau responsible for Jewish affairs had been asked to submit a list of names of prominent Jews in town, who were to be investigated; when the delegates began arriving in the autumn, they, too, were followed and their activities scrutinized. Police suspicions were not easily dispelled, and in late October, one agent discovered that Frankfurt's Jewish delegates were posing as "merchants" and tried to have them expelled from town.

It was long suspected that Metternich was behind the harassment, but as the distinguished scholar Enno Kraehe has shown, it was probably the Austrian foreign minister who intervened to prevent their expulsion. He was a friend of one of the delegates in question, Jakob Baruch, whom he had met at the coronation of Emperor Francis in 1792.

The police continued to follow the new arrivals closely, and the more prominent figures were announced in the court newspaper, *Wiener Zeitung*. By the beginning of October, the Grand Duke of Baden had arrived, and his dossier was soon filled with reports of nightly outings at the theater and his pursuit of women, including actresses, maids, and eventually a daughter of an orange and lemon seller. Prince Thurn und Taxis was here as well, hoping to secure a family monopoly on running the postal service in the Habsburg empire. The Prince of Piombino brought a portfolio of arguments explaining why he deserved the island of Elba, rather than its current occupant, Napoleon Bonaparte.

Some tiny rulers indeed had grand pretensions, and one of the most notorious was the Prince of Nassau-Weilburg. The Russian officer and "army historiographer" Alexander Ivanovich Mikhailovsky-Danilevsky described one such audience. Entering into the prince's suite, he had to pass many footmen and chamberlains in gold livery standing at the double doors. The prince, in a distant room, stood completely still, receiving his supplicants like the Sun King. "I nearly laughed out loud," he said, surprised by the ridiculous sight.

Many others slipped into town that autumn for profit and adventure: rogues, charlatans, courtesans, actors, and gamblers, including one of the Continent's most talented whist players, Mr. O'Bearn, and Mr. Raily, a notorious cardsharp, who would die impoverished. The salon run by Madame Frazer was said to be a favorite with many seasoned gamblers. Her gaming tables—"candle snuffers of conversation," as one young socialite said disapprovingly—were the draw, not the tea, which was cold. Two small barking dogs often greeted the guests who arrived hoping to make a fortune.

MEANWHILE, ON THURSDAY afternoon, October 13, three days after touring the battlefield at Aspern-Essling outside Vienna where the Austrians defeated Napoleon in the summer of 1809, the Russian tsar made the dramatic move of paying a visit to Castlereagh's headquarters. It was a breach of etiquette for a monarch to call upon the foreign minister of another power. But the matter was serious, and the tsar maneuvered around the formalities by officially visiting Emily Castlereagh. He then stayed on afterward for a chat with her husband—a tense hour-and-a-half talk.

The tsar was flabbergasted at Castlereagh's opposition to his plans for re-creating Poland. Alexander claimed that his interest was not a matter of power politics, but rather "public morality." The outrageous carving up of the country in the eighteenth century could now finally be corrected. He would, moreover, grant an enlightened constitution. Polish patriots were thrilled about the future, the tsar said, and he himself looked forward to the dawning of a new golden age for this ancient kingdom.

How could Great Britain possibly resist such an act of philanthropy, and besides, the tsar wondered, what business was it really of Castlereagh's what he did in Poland, something so far removed from British national interests? Castlereagh was indeed placed in a difficult position. He feared that this Russian plan would threaten the balance of power, and hence the future peace of Europe, yet he had to show his opposition in an accurate manner without further upsetting the tsar, or violating the complicated rules of protocol that governed relations between a sovereign and a foreign minister.

Russia, of course, had rights, Castlereagh acknowledged, though he was quick to point out that these rights must be limited to what does not harm anyone else, particularly "the security of the Emperor's neighbors." Russia's plan was liable to inspire the Poles who lived in neighboring countries, like Austria's East Galicia, to want independence, which in turn could create much unrest in the region.

When the tsar replied that there was only one possible solution for Poland because his army already occupied it, Castlereagh countered that the tsar's rights to territory must not be based on conquest alone.

It was becoming clear that Britain and Russia had serious differences of opinion, and personal diplomacy was not leading to any reconciliation. Later that day, Castlereagh handed the tsar a memorandum, a written summary of their discussion, which, like the protocol, remains another legacy of the Vienna Congress. He wrote that it was his "solemn conviction" that everything now depended on Alexander—that is, "whether the present Congress shall prove a blessing to mankind, or only exhibit a scene of discordant intrigue, and a lawless scramble for power."

Then, while the tsar went over to Princess Bagration's salon, staying until two in the morning, Castlereagh drew up a second memorandum. He reiterated his concerns that Russian policy in Poland "will plant the seeds of another war" and end by destroying "all hope, rest and real confidence and peace." After writing these words, Castlereagh sent his memo to his fellow allies—all of them, that is, except the Russians.

As MANY HAD predicted, Poland was clearly going to be a major stumbling block—the "aching tooth" of the peace conference. Russia and Britain had both refused to budge, and now the dispute was at a standstill. But there was something else that complicated the Polish question at the Vienna Congress. All discussion of Poland was closely tied to another bitter controversy: the future of the Kingdom of Saxony.

Geographically, the two regions were connected. The Polish plains rolled out into the south, merging without any clear or natural demarcation into the Saxon lowlands. Historically, the two territories had been united under the same ruling dynasty in the late seventeenth century. Although the links had been severed in the 1760s, Napoleon had rejoined them when he created both the Kingdom of Saxony and the Duchy of Warsaw—and then gave them both to the king of Saxony.

Diplomatically, too, there was a connection: If Poland were to be re-created as the tsar demanded, then the congress would have to remove territory from both Austria and Prussia. Now, quite simply, if Prussia lost its former Polish territories, it would then have to be compensated elsewhere to reach its population of 1805, as it had been promised, and the most obvious place was in Saxony. So, in other words, if the tsar would have his way in Poland, then the king of Prussia would most likely receive Saxony. That was the deal the two monarchs had struck and were now supporting with great vigor.

But, of course, many in Vienna were uncomfortable with this arrangement. For one, the king of Saxony refused to yield a single acre of his kingdom, though unfortunately for him, he was still locked up in a Prussian prison. The king of Saxony's representative in Vienna, Count Friedrich Albrecht von Schulenburg, was also protesting, though he, too, had been marginalized. The Prussians had refused to recognize his credentials as an official delegate, and they pressured everyone else to do the same.

It was Talleyrand, then, who had taken it upon himself to lead the defense of the Saxon underdogs. Characteristically, he acted with flair. When the Prussians argued that they deserved Saxony because of the king of Saxony's treachery to the Allied cause, Talleyrand replied simply: Was this not "a sin that we all have on our conscience?" Had not Austria, Russia, and Prussia all at one time or another sworn allegiance to Napoleon? Everyone in Vienna had at one point been loyal to the conqueror—everyone, that is, but a few exceptions like Castlereagh and the British. Why should the king of Saxony be singled out and punished?

From discussions in alcoves of salons to dinners at the embassy, Talleyrand was denouncing Prussian ambitions on seizing this region as a "breach of all public morality" and an "unspeakable crime." It was also, he added, a dangerous folly. If Prussia gained Saxony with its many fortresses, palaces, estates, and rich farmland, then Europe would be creating a powerful state in the center of the Continent that might, Talleyrand warned, be a menace to France and the peace of Europe.

Most of the other German states and princes, in fact, agreed with Talleyrand. One defender, the Duke of Saxe-Coburg-Saalfeld, put this argument well, succinctly dismantling the basis for Prussian claims for seizing Saxony. Did they have a right of conquest? Not by international law. Was it on the basis of surrender? "The king has not ceded and never will cede his rights." Was there a sentence or judgment from an international tribune or trial? No trial had been held, and the king should at least be allowed to defend himself.

What did the Saxon people want themselves? They wanted their king, their *legitimate* king, Frederick Augustus. Besides that, would the congress leaders really like to establish the precedent whereby an aggressive power could legally dethrone a fellow sovereign and seize his territory? How was this any different from Napoleon Bonaparte, and had they not learned anything from the violent chaos of the last twenty years?

But these arguments had almost no impact on the Prussians. They had, after all, not fought a terrible war and sacrificed blood and treasure only to be dictated to by the defeated enemy and some small princes under its influence. They also, for that matter, still had the support of the Russian tsar, who now seemed so frustrated at the diplomatic impasse that he had started threatening to take matters into his own hands. The Russian army had Saxony, Alexander reminded, and he might as well just hand it over to his Prussian ally.

Such a prospect was alarming, as the tsar was certainly not bluffing. Ironically, some of the most concerned were actually Prussia's own ministers Hardenberg and Humboldt. Even though they would have liked to have Saxony, to say the least, neither wanted to receive the realm this way—a simple seizure of territory that would put them in the debt of Russia, and eventually, they feared, also at its mercy.

So with this dilemma in mind, Hardenberg had penned an urgent letter to the foreign ministers of Britain and Austria, appealing to them to act immediately. Prussia would readily support them against the tsar on Poland, he promised, provided that they assure him that Prussia would still be given Saxony. He needed something tangible to take to his king.

Castlereagh had no problem at all making such a concession, as he put it, "for the future tranquility of Europe." Talleyrand, however, was appalled by Castlereagh's "weakness" and warned him that he was about to make a terrible mistake. There was a much better way to save both Poland *and* Saxony: Open the congress at once. Force the aggressive powers to state their claims in front of all Europe, and watch their project collapse under the weight of its own unsustainability.

But the British minister's mind was made up, and that left only one person in a position to resist, and that was Metternich, who was unfortunately very distracted at the moment. "Metternich is in love, he paints himself up, he writes notes, his Chancellery muddles along," Talleyrand observed. Gentz, unfortunately, had to agree. He visited Metternich several times during this Saxon crisis, only to find that Austria's foreign minister was consumed by the Duchess of Sagan, and that "unhappy liaison with Windischgraetz."

One thing was certain: Unless something was done immediately, the Russian tsar was simply going to hand over an entire kingdom to his Prussian allies—with or without the permission of the Vienna Congress.

Chapter 12

Six Weeks of Hell

Hiding behind velvet and purple robes, hostile spirits
fight one another with the daggers of intrigue.

—KARL VON NOSTITZ, A SAXON SOLDIER IN
RUSSIAN SERVICE, LOOKING ON
WITH FRUSTRATION AT THE CONGRESS

Summer seemed to linger a little longer for Vienna's guests that autumn. On October 18, yet another brilliant sunny day, Metternich and the Festivals Committee staged the spectacular Peace Festival to mark the first anniversary of the Allied victory at the Battle of Leipzig. Valets and maids were sent all over town in search of the latest fashions. Hat shops, one said, "were mobbed like bakeries in a famine."

Metternich had wanted this to be a celebration of peace with no military overtures—"No more soldiers!" he had insisted. But he had been overruled. At the last minute, Emperor Francis had preferred to showcase Austrian military strength and asked Field Marshal Prince Schwarzenberg to prepare something appropriate. Complaining in private about the "furious turmoil" that he had been placed in at such short notice, the aged field marshal nevertheless complied. The Vienna garrison, some sixteen thousand men strong, was quickly drilled for the parade.

Almost certainly, it was the growing tensions with Russia that inspired the emperor's decision to march his troops. A little sword rattling just might convince the tsar to abandon his autocratic ways.

That afternoon, sovereigns, soldiers, and spectators assembled in the giant public park, the Prater, for the celebration of peace that now had a more martial air. Over the river, a branch of the Danube, the organizers had constructed a temporary bridge, complete with a rather unique handrailing: muskets captured from Napoleon's armies at the Battle of Leipzig and strewn together with branches of a willow tree.

The focus of attention was a large structure in the center known as the Peace Tent. Trophies and battle standards adorned its columns, and red damask carpets lined the steps up to its altar, covered with a blanket of flowers. Velvet chairs were on the platform for Europe's royalty.

With the crowds hushed into a respectful silence, and hats removed, the archbishop of Vienna led the monarchs, the soldiers, and the enormous throng of spectators in a public celebration of High Mass. The songwriter La Garde-Chambonas described the scene:

At the moment of blessing the Bread and the Wine, the guns thundered forth a salute to the God of Hosts. Simultaneously, all those warriors, princes, kings, soldiers, and generals fell on their knees, prostrating themselves before Him in whose hands rests victory or defeat.

After the smoke of cannons and incense cleared, church bells rang and a large choir sang a German "hymn of peace." The sovereigns moved over to position near the Burg Gate. The soldiers marched past under their view, and afterward received medallions struck from melted-down cannons seized from Napoleon's Grande Armée.

There was another dinner served on tables arranged together in the shape of a gigantic star. Sergeants carried each soldier a bowl of soup, a plate of pork, another three-quarters of a pound of roast beef, rolls, and doughnuts filled with apricot jam, all washed down by a quart of wine. Despite the tensions behind the scenes, both the emperor of Austria and the Russian tsar toasted the soldiers in a public show of solidarity.

That night, invited guests were treated to a Peace Ball at Metternich's summer villa on the Rennweg, where the Austrian foreign minister had built an extension to his estate for this occasion. The building itself was shaped like a dome and ringed by classical pillars. It was made of wood, with walnut parquet floors. Everything was adorned with the new "colorful lights of Bengale," and with many red Turkish tents in the lobby, it seemed like a scene out of *The Book of 1001 Nights*.

As requested, women wore dresses in either blue or white, "the colors of peace," many embroidered in gold or silver, and adorned with diamonds. Several women also wore flower headdresses or wreaths of olive, oak, or laurel, symbolizing the peace. Other ladies preferred a tiara, which along with diamond earrings, pearl necklaces, and a vast array of jewels adorning the dresses made them sparkle from head to toe. The men glittered and clinked as well, with many medals and medallions.

When deciding on the seating arrangements for the feast, Metternich made sure the Duchess of Sagan had a good table. In fact, he sent her the plan beforehand and let her choose the seat herself. She was well placed for the show that evening. A hot-air balloon drifted overhead, to the delight of the eighteen hundred guests. Ballets were danced in his enormous garden, in and around faux temples in honor of the classical gods Apollo, Mars, and Athena, and orchestras hidden behind hedges serenaded the guests.

The evening concluded with a fireworks display that attempted to paint in the sky the horrors of war and then the pleasures of peace. To one guest, Metternich's party surpassed every celebration he had experienced in France, including the heyday of Napoleon's empire. In parties, too, it seemed, Metternich had defeated Napoleon.

THE NEXT MORNING, Gentz had come over to Metternich's for breakfast and to trade stories about the Peace Ball. But despite the apparent success, he found Metternich depressed. "What a sad morning after a festival," Gentz confided in his diary. Evidently, there had been a disturbing incident the night before.

The Russian tsar, who had devoured gossip spread by Princess Bagration, had been loudly bad-mouthing Metternich all evening. The atmosphere of the party had been spoiled, the tsar accused, by the presence of "too many diplomats." They make bad decisions and then "we soldiers," he said identifying himself with the troops, "have to get ourselves shot into cripples." Diplomats, he added, were categorically untrustworthy and he could not stand their falseness.

The tsar's behavior had embarrassed and humiliated Metternich, the host. Along with the tsar's insults, Metternich had also been upset because he had wanted to talk to the Duchess of Sagan that night, even if only for a moment. He had not succeeded. That morning after the ball, as Gentz noted, it had been a "very black scene."

Metternich was also disturbed about the lack of success so far in gaining little Vava for the duchess. He had promised not to let up for "all the treasures of the world," and success had seemed imminent, too, when he had learned that the child's father, Gustav Armfelt, had suffered a stroke and died the previous month. But, unfortunately, instead of helping, the tsar was proving highly uncooperative. At their last meeting, on October 15, when Metternich raised the question again, the tsar abruptly declared that he knew for a fact that Vava preferred to remain in Finland with the Armfelt family. And, indeed, after the last outburst at the Peace Ball, the tsar seemed even less likely to help.

Metternich hung on to the child case—"our child," as he called her. Perhaps his adamancy was his last desperate ploy to win the love of the duchess, as one historian wondered. Metternich certainly seemed to be grasping at any opportunity to have contact with his beloved duchess, no matter how businesslike it might be and how unlikely his chances of success now appeared. He swore he would keep his word, and work even harder on the custody case.

With these disturbing failures absorbing his mind, Metternich was not the most receptive when Talleyrand came over to warn him about relying on the Prussians. Metternich had still not answered Hardenberg's offer of support against Russia in exchange for Prussian gains in Saxony. Talleyrand was determined to prevent Metternich from accepting this proposition, and he thought that he had just the argument to suit the Austrian foreign minister.

If Metternich allowed Prussia to seize Saxony, Talleyrand pointed out, Prussia would surrender its Polish territory to the tsar. Metternich would then end up helping Alexander gain exactly what he wanted. Austria, on the other hand, would be stuck with a much stronger Russia *and* Prussia threatening its borders. Austria simply must resist Prussia, Talleyrand concluded. "Justice, propriety even safety require her to do so."

But Metternich brushed aside Talleyrand's arguments, hatching a plot of his own: He was considering accepting Prussian gains in Saxony, but he would attach so many strings to his consent that Prussia would either accept and serve Austrian interests, or decline and not have his approval at all.

One of these conditions would be that not only must Prussia oppose Russia, but it must also *succeed* in preventing the tsar from having his way in Poland. This way, Metternich would leave it to Prussia's own ministers to convince their king that the dangers of gaining Saxony from the hands of the unpredictable tsar were far greater than any possible benefit.

Metternich did not mention this plan at that time to Talleyrand, who, of course, would have strongly opposed it. After all, as far as the French foreign minister was concerned, it failed to solve the real problem of Prussian aggression, and it might well end by upsetting the fragile equilibrium and endangering the peace of Europe.

THE DUCHESS OF Sagan, meanwhile, was discouraged about the slow progress being made on regaining custody of her daughter. As hostess of one of the most informed salons in town, she knew that the peace conference might in fact erupt into war at any time. Something had to be done immediately. If Metternich could not convince the tsar, then perhaps she would have to do so herself.

On October 20, at a ball given by the Russian ambassador, Count Stackelberg, the duchess wore a sleek red dress, designed by the fashionable Paris designer Louis-Hippolite Leroy, and donned a family heirloom, a "pearl-shaped emerald" that had been set in a "delicate golden circlet" that sparkled from her forehead. She walked up to the tsar and politely requested an audience. The tsar's response was as cordial to her as it was cruel to Metternich, who was standing within earshot.

"My dear Wilhelmine, there is no question of an audience," the tsar said, grabbing her hand and raising her up from her curtsy. "Of course I shall come to see you!" he continued. "Only name the day and the hour—shall it be tomorrow at eleven?"

Eleven o'clock! The tsar had deliberately taken what used to be Metternich's hour with the duchess, and worse, she had allowed it without the slightest hesitation. Metternich's feelings of betrayal and rejection were immense. First she had gone back to Prince Alfred, and now this. Metternich, deeply wounded, left the ball immediately. It must have been a lonely carriage drive home that night.

When he arrived back at the Chancellery, he could not sleep. He went to his desk and poured out his thoughts in another desperate note to the duchess. It was four in the morning. "A relationship, a dream, the fairest of my life has vanished . . . I am punished for having entrusted my existence to a charm only too seductive."

Metternich felt that he was indeed losing the duchess. Heartbroken, the statesman continued:

> You have done me greater harm than can ever be compensated by the whole universe—you have broken the springs of my soul. You have endangered my existence at a moment when the fate of my life is bound up with questions that decide the future of whole generations . . . I have placed everything I have, this life, my trust, my future, all my hope, I have placed everything in the balance.

With this letter, which he did not yet send, Metternich was about to officially end their relationship. Deep down, though, he knew that she had ended it by her own preferences, and he was crushed. "I have lost my last illusion," he mourned, contemplating the implications of this rupture. Without her love, he was condemned to "a world without color and a life without charm."

FROM THE VERY beginning, one of the main subjects in the salons was, of course, Napoleon Bonaparte. Many of the delegates in Vienna had known him personally, and others were curious about this ogre who had once terrorized the world.

Napoleon's successes, failures, and many controversial acts were discussed and debated around town. One delegate, the Duke of Rocca Romana, who represented King Joachim I of Naples (Murat), enlivened the conversations with his rousing tales from the Russian invasion of 1812. At the climax, this "Apollo of a man" would take off his glove and show his hand, where he had lost four fingers from the terrible frost. Listening to the many stories of Napoleon's accomplishments and shortcomings, some delegates seemed to miss his presence on the world stage, openly admitting that he had many more statesmanlike qualities than the victorious sovereigns who were making a royal mess out of the Vienna Congress.

"It's scandalous how the congress behaves," France's Duke of Dalberg

told Agent **, launching into an outspoken critique of how the Great
Powers conspired to shut out Talleyrand, the French embassy, and most
of the other delegations in town. "We do not understand anything of
Metternich's politics," he continued.

> If he gives the crown of Poland to Russia, then in less than fifteen years
> Russia will hunt the Turks out of Europe, and Russia will be more
> dangerous to the liberty of Europe than Napoleon had ever been.

Dalberg, growing more animated as he went along, wanted to sound a
general wake-up call. It was essential, he urged, to "oppose the colossus
that is going to crush Austria and the other powers."

The tension between Russia and Austria was certainly one of the main
problems of the congress. The two powers had been uneasy allies since
the end of the Napoleonic Wars. They had often ended up on opposing
sides on questions of strategy and tactics, most notably in early 1814,
when the Austrian army invaded Napoleonic France through Switzerland—in direct conflict with the tsar's wishes and his promises that the
Allies would respect Swiss neutrality. The relationship between Austria
and Russia had never recovered, Gentz later observed.

Indeed, a vibrant personal rivalry between Metternich and Tsar
Alexander had exacerbated the political problems. As Gentz saw it, the
tsar had come to regard Metternich as "a sworn enemy" and harbored
an intense jealousy of Metternich's flair in the drawing room. He was
witty, mannered, and very popular with women. The tsar had come to
Vienna hoping, as Gentz said, "to be admired," and found it difficult to
share the limelight, especially with a man he had come to detest.

Spies had likewise noticed the tsar's growing interests in Metternich's
private life—his "morbid curiosity" as one agent put it. Alexander was
still suspected of prying for information at the Palm Palace, where both
the Duchess of Sagan and Princess Bagration, of course, were authorities
on their former lover. Princess Bagration, in particular, was glad to comply. She still seemed upset at Metternich for neglecting her in favor of the
Duchess of Sagan, and seemed happy to satisfy the tsar's appetites, spies
reported, feeding him the most intimate details of their previous love
affair.

It was at the congress, Gentz believed, that the tsar's resentment of

Metternich "reached the point of an implacable hatred," and this, in turn, fueled the tsar's "daily explosions of rage and frenzy." All of this, of course, may have delighted gossipers, but it was causing considerable strain on the negotiations. As Gentz concluded, it was Alexander's hatred for Metternich that served as "the key to most of the events of the Congress."

Now, Gentz was often biased in Metternich's favor, and this assessment certainly seems slanted. But Gentz actually no longer regarded Metternich as an infallible "Delphic Oracle," as he had earlier dubbed him. Far from it. At times, Gentz was already emerging as an outspoken critic of Metternich—blasting him not only in his diary, but also openly and indiscreetly at salons and dinner parties around town.

Police agents had noticed, too, that by the middle of October, Gentz was making many visits to Kaunitz Palace. Reportedly, he and Talleyrand were getting along well. They were dining together at the embassy, or with mutual acquaintances like the Duchess of Sagan. The French minister had, it seemed, discovered Gentz's well-known weakness for flattery, perfume, chocolate, and money, and he was increasingly gaining influence over Metternich's assistant.

On October 21, when Gentz arrived at ten in the morning, as usual, for breakfast (only a few hours after Metternich had finished his letter to the duchess), another, more interesting breakfast was about to take place a few blocks away at the Palm Palace. The tsar was coming to the so-called Austrian salon for his meeting with the duchess at Metternich's hour. Their conversation lasted about two hours, though what exactly happened is not known. Presumably, the tsar agreed to do everything he could to help the duchess regain custody of her child. He was certainly in no mood to disappoint her.

Immediately afterward, the ecstatic duchess took a carriage over to Kaunitz Palace to see her sister Dorothée, and rumors soon magnified the morning meeting in countless ways. It was reported and widely believed, for example, that the tsar had forced the duchess to break off her relations with Metternich. Baron Hager's spies thought that this had in fact happened. When Metternich had had an opportunity to ask her about the meeting, the duchess had been coy, replying evasively, "The tsar was at my house and behaved very well, at least with words."

On Saturday, October 22, Metternich was ready to lay his cards on the table. First, he delivered the note ending his relationship with the

Duchess of Sagan, and then, later that evening at a ball over at Count Zichy's mansion, he declared his stance on Saxony in a monumental letter to Hardenberg. He had decided to accept Prussia's offer of support in return for annexation of Saxony. But sure enough, Metternich attached some important conditions to his tentative acceptance: Prussia must give up all other claims to Germany, regard this annexation as part of the larger settlement, and, most important, must actually *succeed* in preventing the tsar from gaining Poland. Alexander, Metternich was now more convinced than ever, must be stopped.

It must have been a stressful night for Metternich. Emotionally, he was a wreck; diplomatically, he had just handed over a letter that would cause, in Gentz's words, "more grief in three months than he has had in all his life."

As AUSTRIA TENTATIVELY approved of Prussian gains, Metternich wasted no time in demanding that Hardenberg fulfill his end of the bargain. Prussia must join Austria at once, and, moreover, they had to act immediately. On October 24, just two days away, the Austrian emperor, the Russian tsar, and the king of Prussia would leave for a weeklong trip to Hungary. Metternich wanted to work out a common strategy before that trip—that is, before the Austrian emperor would be out of town and cooped up with these two close allies.

On the afternoon of October 23, the day before the departure, Metternich and Hardenberg had a rushed meeting. Castlereagh, fearful as ever of a strong Russia, joined them. By the end of their private session, held at Castlereagh's headquarters on the Minoritenplatz, the three ministers had decided to confront the tsar with a united stance and demand that he cooperate on Poland: Alexander would either have to agree to a fully independent Poland, or there would be no Poland at all. Russia, Prussia, and Austria would instead split the territory among them. But under no circumstances would the tsar be allowed simply to impose his will.

They would give Alexander five days from his return to Vienna to comply, or, as Castlereagh suggested, they would threaten to put the question of Poland before the entire community of powers. With this plan agreed upon, it was urgent for Metternich and Hardenberg to gain approval at once from their sovereigns.

The Russian tsar, meanwhile, was feeling his own sense of urgency to wrap up Poland before he went on his trip. He had heard how displeased the French delegation had become with the peace conference, and again let it be known that he wished to speak with Talleyrand. The French minister, obeying etiquette again, then requested an interview with the tsar.

Talleyrand was indeed unhappy. Prussia, his biggest fear, was still pressing its revolting principles, aiming to dethrone kings and destroy kingdoms. Metternich, oblivious to the dangers, was merely "the plaything of the intrigues that he believes he is directing." Castlereagh, worst of all, was fumbling about like a "schoolboy in diplomacy." Diplomats everywhere were moving like tortoises, as he put it, and Saxony, meanwhile, was about to be wiped off the map. Something had to be done.

So on the evening of October 23, Talleyrand and the Tsar of All the Russias had their second interview. After a short exchange of greetings, Alexander brought up Poland and asked where Talleyrand stood on this question. As Talleyrand's correspondence makes clear, he was hoping to barter his cooperation on Poland in return for the tsar's help in saving Saxony.

Talleyrand explained that he was "still the same" on Poland; that is, he favored a restored and independent kingdom. France's only concern, he added, was that the redrawn borders would not in any way endanger Russia's neighbors.

"They need not be alarmed," the tsar said. "Besides, I have two hundred thousand men in the duchy of Warsaw; let anyone try to chase me out."

As the conversation turned to Saxony, the tsar was not any more accommodating. Everything had been arranged, he said bluntly. He had given the territory to the king of Prussia, and Austria had consented.

"I do not know whether Austria does consent," Talleyrand responded. "I should find it difficult to believe that she does—it would be so much against her interest."

Then, raising the question to the level of law, Talleyrand asked if the "consent of Austria" could make Prussia "the proprietor of that which belongs to the King of Saxony."

"If the King of Saxony does not abdicate, he shall be taken to Russia. He will die there; another has already died there," the tsar responded, referring to the last king of Poland, Stanislaw II Augustus, who had been taken hostage by Russian troops in the 1790s and whisked away to finish his days outside St. Petersburg.

"Your Majesty will permit me not to believe that; the Congress has not been called together to witness such an outrage."

"How, an outrage?" the tsar replied. "Why should the King of Saxony not go to Russia?"

Talleyrand did not know where to begin in answering this question, and struggled, as he put it, to control his indignation. Before he could say anything, the tsar launched into a monologue about how much France owed him, and how meaningless all this talk of international law really was. "Your public law means nothing to me," the tsar said. "What do you suppose I care for all your parchments and all your treaties?"

Alexander continued to talk about how he had pledged his word to the king of Prussia to give him Saxony, and he intended to keep it. At this, Talleyrand saw an opportunity to remind the tsar that he had promised him a population of some nine or ten million. "Your Majesty could give them without destroying Saxony," Talleyrand said, handing over a piece of paper outlining some alternatives.

"The King of Saxony is a traitor," the tsar answered, referring to the king's loyalty to Napoleon and conveniently forgetting that he, too, had once been loyal to Napoleon. So had the king of Prussia, and, in fact, most of the leaders and delegates at the congress at one time or another.

Talleyrand had hoped to convince the tsar that he could obtain a satisfactory peace without having to destroy his reputation. He had not succeeded. Alexander was still committed to his policy of annihilating the Kingdom of Saxony and handing its territory over to Prussia. The interview ended, as it began, in irritation and frustration.

By the next morning, the day of the departure for Hungary, Metternich and Hardenberg had not yet gained sanction for their united stance against the tsar. Alexander, instead, had preempted their move and summoned Metternich alone over to his apartments. Their discussion in the white and gold paneled wing of the Hofburg was one of the most difficult of Metternich's entire career.

The tsar flat out demanded Metternich's compliance: "I intend to create an independent state of Poland. I want your agreement before I leave for Hungary today."

"Your Majesty," Metternich replied in a manner that sometimes came across as flippant, "if it is a question of creating an independent Poland, Austria too can create one."

At this, the tsar exploded. Metternich was the only man, he declared, who dared use such a tone with him. In Alexander's words, it was "a tone of revolt," as if the Austrian foreign minister were one of his subjects. The tsar then unleashed a barrage of "haughtiness and violence of language" that left Metternich stunned and visibly shaken.

Metternich compared the talk with the tsar to meeting Napoleon at his most irrational, and felt unsure whether he would end up leaving the palace through the door or through the window, as Alexander allegedly threatened. The Austrian minister never wanted to see the tsar in private again, he said, and predicted "the tsar will end up mad like his father."

Diplomatic relations had hit rock bottom. The tsar set off to Hungary with the emperor and the king, but he did not leave anyone in charge in his absence, and all the pressing problems of the peace conference remained unresolved.

Chapter 13

ℛOBINSON ℭRUSOE

I can never see a throne without being tempted to sit on it.

— NAPOLEON

All over Europe, governments were watching Vienna's victors lose themselves in celebrations and squabbles. One of the most curious observers, it turned out, was Napoleon Bonaparte.

He was, at this time, settling down in his new home on Elba, a rocky isle some seven miles off the northwestern coast of Italy. It is one of six main islands in the Tuscan Archipelago, a circle that also includes, in the south, the tiny, windswept Montecristo, immortalized in the Alexandre Dumas novel. To the north lies the barren Gorgona, which had served as the setting for another work of romantic fiction, *Clisson and Eugénie*, this one about a young Corsican rebel who commands an army only to be betrayed by a trusted friend. The author of the novella was none other than Napoleon himself, at age twenty-six.

The choice of Elba as Napoleon's new home had been made in the spring of 1814, when the Allies captured Paris and demanded his immediate, unconditional abdication. Tsar Alexander had promised, personally, that if Napoleon cooperated, the terms would be generous. Maps were scanned for a place of exile that would encourage the French emperor to vacate the throne without delay.

France, Italy, and other sites within the former continental empire were quickly ruled out as being unacceptable to the victors. As the historian Norman Mackenzie explained, Corsica was objectionable because it was Napoleon's birthplace, and also French property. Sardinia belonged to the House of Savoy, and Corfu was coveted by both England and Russia. Other places were considered, from the Canaries to the Caribbean. Some wanted Trinidad, others the Azores, or even Botany Bay in Australia. Talleyrand pressed for St. Helena in the South Atlantic. It was the Russian tsar who, in the end, proposed the island of Elba.

Actually, Alexander did more than propose the island—he simply refused to consider any other option. The reasons for this stance are open to question. For some, the tsar was relishing his new role as the magnanimous conqueror, an enlightened ruler who would be as forgiving in peace as he had been ferocious in war. Others saw the tiny island as a ridiculous choice intended to humiliate the fallen giant. Austria, however, had a very different explanation.

Behind the tsar's "theatrical generosity," Metternich saw only an attempt to antagonize Austria. The island of Elba was far too close to the Continent, and very near Austria's own interests in northern Italy, especially since it could not be ruled out that Napoleon might one day tire of this new home. He was, after all, only forty-five years old with a promising career ahead, and would likely prove a magnet for the Continent's discontented. Besides that, the island was not the tsar's to give: it belonged to the Habsburg family (as part of the restored Habsburg duchy of Tuscany). As Metternich suspected, the tsar's proposal could only be aimed at placing a source of turmoil in Austria's rear. The southern half of the sprawling Habsburg empire was left highly exposed to the threat of Napoleon's return.

Unfortunately for Austria, there had been very little discussion about sending Napoleon to Elba. The Russian tsar had reached Paris first and started working on his solution immediately. By the time the Austrian delegation made it through war-torn northeastern France in early April 1814, Alexander had already made his proposal and gained Napoleon's consent. The signing of the agreement had to be firmed up as quickly as possible, the tsar said, before Napoleon changed his mind.

But had the Austrians really been held up outside Paris, as they claimed, or were they deliberately holding back? Emperor Francis surely did not want to take part in officially dethroning his daughter Marie Louise, his son-in-law Napoleon, and his grandson, the king of Rome. As for Metternich's best ally, Castlereagh, he was not present, either, and he certainly didn't seem to be in a hurry, hoping perhaps to avoid the unpleasant appearance of imposing a regime change onto France. How long did the tsar have to wait on his Allies? Napoleon was already wavering in his abdication, and this restless man was, as everyone knew, prone to make rash, risky moves. The tsar had made his decision and pressed ahead.

According to the terms of the treaty, known at the time as "the Treaty of Abdication" (history remembers it as the Treaty of Fontainebleau, after Napoleon's palace, though it was not signed there), Napoleon was to maintain the official title "Emperor and Sovereign of the Island of Elba." He was granted this authority for the rest of his life, along with an annual pension of 2 million francs a year, to be paid from the French treasury. His wife, Marie Louise, was to be given the duchies of Parma, Piacenza, and Guastalla in northern Italy, and their son, little Napoleon, would be "the Prince of Parma." Article III of the treaty even incorporated the fiction that the abdication had been Napoleon's choice. As for Napoleon's family members, many of whom had lost thrones, they were also to share a yearly stipend of 2.5 million francs. Just as the tsar had promised, he had been generous indeed.

When Metternich and Castlereagh arrived in Paris, in early April, they had been shocked at the terms of this treaty. Castlereagh refused to sign it. Britain would in fact *never* sign this treaty guaranteeing Napoleon's rights to Elba. Austria was also very disappointed. Confronted with what was essentially the tsar's fait accompli, Metternich had angrily denounced this agreement as malicious and stupid. Within one year, he predicted, Napoleon would be back, and Europe would have to fight him all over again. His protests were in vain. No one was in a position to oppose the tsar, and so, without any more discussion, Napoleon was going to Elba.

WHEN NAPOLEON ARRIVED in early May 1814, some twelve thousand people lived on the small, sun-drenched island. The capital, Portoferraio, facing out onto a secluded bay on the southern shore, was home to about three thousand islanders. The roads were appalling, often mere goat and mule tracks, and the streets were hardly any better, usually little more than dusty stone steps rising steeply up the cliffside. There was a church, a tavern, and a café called Buono Gusto, serving up the island's local wine, *alciato*. The capital, at that time, has been summed up as "no more than a small and seedy Mediterranean port."

From the perspective of a vessel sailing into the island's chief harbor, Elba seemed all rugged mountains, red-tiled rooftops, and whitewashed walls. Relics of its storied past also stood out, like the old castle, built some twelve hundred feet atop a prominent cliff and attributed by local legend to awesome giants. Many legends, in fact, surrounded the isle. It was said, for instance, that Jason and the Argonauts had docked there in their quest for the Golden Fleece, and even the Trojan prince Aeneas had come on a mission to recruit stalwart Elbans for the Trojan War.

Colorful traditions aside, the small island packed a great deal of history within its eighty-six square miles. Much of it, unfortunately, was bloody and tragic. Elba had fallen prey to a long list of conquerors, including Etruscans, Romans, Visigoths, Ostrogoths, and Lombards. Later in the Middle Ages, the towns of Pisa and Genoa captured the exposed island. Then came the kingdom of Spain, which soon handed the island over to the Florentine dynasty of the Medici, who went on to dominate the island for some two hundred years. Others had ruled there at some point, too, including Germans, Turks, and, most recently, English and French.

Elba was, generally speaking, a very poor island. Its soil was rocky and its seasons extreme. Droughts and torrential, almost tropical, storms ravaged the fields and made famines all too common. Many years, Elba had to import as much as two-thirds of its grain, most of it from nearby Italy. But despite the agricultural challenges and the widespread poverty, the island had some valuable natural resources.

At Rio Marina, on the eastern side of the island, men with pickaxes and shovels gathered the iron ore that gave the island its largest source of revenue, and also lent the name to its capital, Portoferraio, literally the "port of iron." To the south, there were rich stone quarries, which shipped hard granite and marble to the mainland for use in the construction of buildings, including the cathedral of Pisa. There were also salt marshes, supplying the large warehouse in the Piazza della Granguardia behind the harbor. Oranges, olives, pomegranates, and grapes grew in abundance, and fishing nets yielded rich hauls, too, particularly tunny and anchovy.

For the most part, Elba had quickly accepted its new sovereign—a tribute, in part, to Napoleon's well-known charisma. He had arrived on the island at a most inauspicious time. After some wild swings of fortune the previous twenty years, ownership had flip-flopped from French to British rule, and then the French gained the upper hand, though the islanders were in revolt, and Elba seemed on the verge of chaos. In fact, guards at the coastal fortifications had fired on the approaching British frigate HMS *Undaunted* as it carried the emperor to his new island.

In all the confusion, however, one thing was certain: The little capital of Elba was unprepared, to say the least, for the strange saga that lay ahead. All the trappings of an imperial court would have to be found or created. As there was no imperial residence, Napoleon was to be housed in a makeshift palace—the unused upper floor of the town hall, which had once been a biscuit warehouse. Chairs, tables, desks, and other furniture were quickly borrowed for the improvised throne room. As for a throne itself, there was none to be found. "What is a throne" anyway, Napoleon had once said; "a bit of wood covered with velvet." On Elba, this was literally the case: Napoleon's throne was a borrowed sofa decorated with paper flowers.

WHILE NAPOLEON WAS playing Robinson Crusoe, as Prince de Ligne put it, Vienna was absorbed with its own gossip and speculation. Count Francis Palffy, it was whispered, was having an affair with the celebrated ballerina Bigottini, and now apparently she was pregnant. The count was said to have just offered her a 6,000-franc pension for life. Prince Eugène de Beauharnais was spotted ducking into a jeweler's shop and splurging on his latest mistress. According to an anonymous police report submitted to Baron Hager in late October, the bill was 32,000 ducats, and the prince paid in part by handing over a cavalry saber given to him by his stepfather, Napoleon.

The biggest source of gossip was still the Russian delegation. While the tsar insisted on making all the main diplomatic decisions himself, many members of his staff found that they had time on their hands, and some were finding their way to Vienna's red-light districts. One member of the delegation was even said to be in charge of inspecting the brothels and procuring for the tsar himself, though others dismissed this as empty gossip. Alexander, they said, needed no help in this regard.

Many high-ranking Russian military officers were also often spotted at the theater in the Leopoldstadt with well-known courtesans, and sometimes they brought them into their suites at the Hofburg Palace. The nineteen-year-old courtesan Josephine Wolters was making a name for herself, slipping past the guards at the palace almost every night, usually wearing the disguise of a man's clothes. Despite complaints from other delegations, police agents were not exactly inclined to put a stop to these escapades. The courtesan was also working for the spy chief.

Apparently, according to police reports, the Russians were upset with many things that autumn, and not just the intrigues of Austria. They did not "hide their discontent with England," particularly with Castlereagh, who was meddling, not mediating, on the question of Poland. They blamed France, too, for stirring up fears among the smaller states and trying to divide the Allies. Some members of the Russian delegation were also unhappy about the growing anti-Russian sentiments expressed around town. Two Viennese wigmakers, for instance, one near St. Stephen's Cathedral and the other on the Schwertgasse, were indecently and offensively using busts of Tsar Alexander as mannequins to display their latest wigs.

Spies were picking up many other signs of tension as they continued their surveillance, interception of letters, infiltration of embassies, and secret rummaging around offices in search of any papers or any scraps left behind. Two crown princes of rival kingdoms, Bavaria and Württemberg, had almost ended up in a duel. They had been playing a game of "blindman's buff" at the salon of Princess Thurn und Taxis when one accused the other of cheating. Fortunately, the duel was stopped in time, by an order from the king of Bavaria.

Remarkably little crime had been reported that autumn, considering how many of the world's richest were in town and that they were not exactly modest about displaying their wealth. Someone had stolen a rare gem from Princess Liechtenstein, and someone else had broken into the Spanish embassy, making off with papers from Labrador's office, but, on the whole, Vienna had so far experienced little criminal activity.

One event that did briefly capture the attention of the police department was an intrigue by the delegate of the Prince of Walachia in today's Rumania. The delegate, Prince Bellio, was responsible for forwarding the correspondence between his sovereign and Friedrich von Gentz. But evidently Bellio had been opening the confidential letters, copying their contents, and then resealing them with a counterfeit seal. By the middle of October, Bellio was trying to arrange a meeting with Princess Catherine Bagration to sell or pass on some of his discoveries to the Russian tsar. Before that transpired, however, police raided his rooms on the third floor of a mansion on the bustling Stock-im-Eisen-Platz and seized his papers. The prince was promptly escorted to the border.

Amid all the rumors, gossip, and intrigues being plotted all over town, the most tantalizing scoop during the first month came from a small scrap of paper retrieved from the French embassy by a chambermaid recently placed inside. The note was vague, enigmatic, and of uncertain reliability. It referred to a French consul in Livorno, the Chevalier Mariotti, who was working on a plan to kidnap Napoleon. The motive for this plot was unknown, and it seemed far-fetched, but, just in case, Baron Hager relayed the information immediately to the Austrian emperor.

As LEAVES TURNED crimson and gold, the temperatures dropped and the sky clouded more frequently into a gray dreariness—weather not exactly suited to lifting Metternich's spirits. He had been desperate to know the duchess's response to his letter, and on October 23 he received it. She explained that she had in fact wanted to break off her relationship with Prince Alfred von Windischgrätz, but even though she realized he was not good for her, she had cared too much to stop seeing him. Bluntly, she added that she no longer regarded Metternich as a lover: "Beyond the enthusiasm of friendship, all remained calm within me."

Hearing that assessment had hardly soothed his nerves. Metternich was still overcome and distraught. "You have had the power to kill me," he wrote back that night. "I told you it would be so." Metternich once again poured out his heart to the duchess, comparing the agonizing last twenty-four hours to one hundred years:

> I am no longer the man I was the day before yesterday . . . the old friend is dead and you have thrown his ashes to the wind.

His heart had been violently ripped out of him, he alleged. Rumors of the tsar prying in his private affairs also continued to bother him. Could she please let him know what exactly she "had promised the tsar"?

Alexander was certainly attacking Metternich's credibility, but could he really have put pressure on the duchess to break all contact with him, as gossipers claimed? The tsar had interfered in the private lives of other subjects in his realm in the past, including the time he virtually imposed a marriage on the duchess's younger sister, Dorothée. Baron Hager's informers were convinced that the tsar was doing so again, threatening his control over her estates and making it clear that "only a formal break with Metternich will satisfy him."

Perhaps the tsar had pressured the duchess—he could, of course, have done so with even more powerful leverage than what the spies suggested: her daughter in Russian-controlled Finland. At any rate, whether the rumors were true or not, Metternich believed that the tsar had ruthlessly used the duchess's daughter as a pawn in diplomacy, and then pressured the duchess to abandon him. "I am no longer astonished at anything, especially when it comes to that man," Metternich said. This belief would influence how he behaved toward his rival.

By the end of October, the emperor, the tsar, and the king had returned from their trip to Hungary. The three sovereigns had visited the cities on the Danube, the pearl of Buda, and the newer, more commercial Pest, which would later that century merge to form Budapest. They had toured the capital, picked grapes, and visited the tomb of Alexander's sister, Alexandra, who had married Archduke Joseph, Palatine of Hungary, and died there thirteen years before.

Despite the hope that a change of environment would ease tensions, the problems had simply moved 150 miles down the Danube. The Russian tsar continued his uncooperative behavior, at odds with prevailing diplomatic etiquette. Rude and crude, he exploded unpredictably, and spies reported a rage of door slamming in the Hungarian palace where they were staying. They also reported that he was insulting his fellow sovereigns by spending most of his time with "pretty women."

The tsar, it was also said, took every opportunity to disparage Metternich and the diplomats he so detested. Alexander told the Austrian emperor that he wanted the two of them, along with the king of Prussia, to band together, in a sort of sovereign's league, to reach solutions about Europe themselves. He wanted to begin by having Metternich removed from office.

But that would not happen, at least not yet. What saved Metternich was undoubtedly the support of Emperor Francis. The Austrian emperor liked his foreign minister and trusted his opinion, no matter what the tsar or Metternich's growing legion of critics had said. Besides, the tsar's domineering behavior showed, if the emperor needed a reminder, how difficult it could be to work with him.

In fact, during this trip to Hungary, Francis suggested that everyone would be better served if the monarchs left the complicated negotiations to their foreign ministers. As diplomats at later conferences would also learn, the differences in rank between a head of state and a foreign minister strained the normal give-and-take consensus-building procedures of the conference room.

So despite Alexander's efforts, Metternich would continue to have his emperor's support and would remain Austrian foreign minister. Emperor Francis, for his part, returned to Vienna, even more wary of the tsar, while the king of Prussia emerged from the royal trip more loyal to Alexander than ever, earning a new sobriquet: the tsar's valet de chambre.

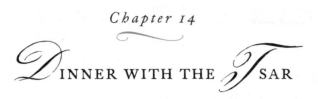

Chapter 14

DINNER WITH THE TSAR

It would be difficult to have more intelligence than Tsar Alexander, but there is a piece missing. I have never managed to discover what it is.

—NAPOLEON

*P*ublic opinion about the Vienna Congress, meanwhile, was falling to a new low. "Our conference is not progressing at all," one member of the Bavarian delegation grumbled. "Nothing is decided, nothing is agreed on." The paralysis was blamed on a simple cause: "Far too few meetings are held; the whole time being consumed with these nauseating, never-ending fetes." Even the king of Prussia was overheard at a ball complaining, "We only seem to be here to amuse ourselves."

It was Metternich's fault, some said: He was devious, deceitful, and, above all, distracted with his love affair. How on earth could he be Austria's foreign minister, let alone president of the congress? Rumors circulated, too, that Metternich would soon resign, be sacked, or even succumb to a nervous breakdown. Others blamed the tsar and his bullying, boasting style of negotiation. Still others, however, traced the ultimate cause for all the discord back to salon intrigues orchestrated by the Duchess of Sagan and Princess Bagration, who, it was said, were playing the leaders of the world like chess pieces.

After the last postponement two weeks before, the congress's new opening date, November 1, was also quickly approaching, and once again there was no sign of an official opening. Many feared that the congress might not take place at all. The peacemakers had never seemed so far apart.

For most of the delegates outside the Big Four, all this wasted time was infuriating and intolerable. How ironic it seemed that the representative of the defeated power, Talleyrand, was emerging as the most prominent spokesman for an immediate opening of the peace congress.

True, Castlereagh, Metternich, and Hardenberg had secretly agreed to threaten the tsar by summoning the assembly of states and throwing the question of Poland before them. But this was Castlereagh's urging, and he really was the only minister inclined to look favorably on the opening of a congress. Talleyrand, of course, realized this fact and saw a potential ally in Castlereagh.

The two foreign ministers related fairly well, both professionally as diplomats and socially as cosmopolitan gentlemen. Both could look over the fact that their countries had been at war the past 20 years, which in turn was part of a larger pattern of hostility that stretched back almost 150 years. Britain and France were used to being enemies, and Talleyrand, at least, hoped to change that.

At Vienna, the biggest difference between the two delegates was a question of priorities. For Castlereagh, the main challenge lay in resisting the growth of Russia, led by a tsar who acted like "another Bonaparte." Talleyrand, on the other hand, was less concerned about an idiosyncratic tsar than angry and belligerent Prussians who might truly launch another war. As he saw it, Castlereagh's views were naive and rather simple-minded, based on the luxury of being a secure island power defended by a strong navy and a stormy English Channel.

Castlereagh, for his part, thought that Talleyrand was overreacting, consumed with unnecessary fears of his German neighbor. "France need never dread a German league," Castlereagh concluded, "it is in its nature inoffensive."

So once again Talleyrand's task, as he saw it, was to set Castlereagh straight and show how dangerous Prussia would become if it gained Saxony. At a private meeting at English headquarters on the Minoritenplatz in late October, Talleyrand limped over to the maps on the table and gave a history lesson to the British minister: "I pointed out to him how that, Saxony and Silesia being in the same [Prussian] hands, Bohemia might be taken in a few weeks."

This was something that Prussia had done three times previously in conflicts with Austria under Frederick the Great, and later that century Prussia would do so again under Otto von Bismarck. And should Bohemia be exposed, then "the heart of the Austrian monarchy would be laid bare and defenseless." As Talleyrand described it, an "astonished" look crept over Castlereagh's long face.

At this point, Talleyrand targeted his appeal more directly to British self-interest: Did they really want to hand over Saxony, with the rich trading city of Leipzig, home to great markets and fairs since the Middle Ages, to a country like Prussia, whose allegiance they could not count on for sure? This was robbing the friendly disposed state of Saxony in order to reward a power whose policy was uncertain at best.

Talleyrand had pounced on a basic problem in British foreign policy: Castlereagh's whole strategy was based on the assumption that Prussia would act as an independent sovereign power and not be subjected to any undue outside influence. But that was simply not the case. Given the king of Prussia's dependence on the tsar, Castlereagh was basically pursuing a policy that would likely end in what he feared most: a much stronger Russia.

Yet it would take more than a few arguments for Talleyrand to change Castlereagh's mind. By the end of the conversation, the French minister began to suspect that there must be another reason for Britain's support of Prussia. Castlereagh was not only preparing for a threat coming from Russia, but he also still harbored a fear of France. Talleyrand tried to assure him that his country posed no threat whatsoever. France would be insane, he argued, to launch another war.

As Castlereagh remained unconvinced, Talleyrand tried yet another line of argument. There was, of course, one way to stop Russian expansion once and for all: Open the Congress. Dare the tsar to make his outrageous demands in front of an assembly of all the delegates. He cherished his image as a war hero, a liberator, and an enlightened thinker too much for that.

There were difficulties in calling a congress, the British statesman said vaguely. When Talleyrand pressed him to specify what exactly those might be, Castlereagh urged him to talk to Metternich. "I conclude from this," Talleyrand wrote, "that something has been agreed to between them," and the two leaders "would not have kept [that agreement] secret from me if they had no reason to believe that I should object to it."

ON OCTOBER 30, as if on cue, Talleyrand received an invitation for a confidential interview with Prince Metternich that evening at eight o'clock. This was immediately before a meeting of the Committee of Eight, which now had to figure out what to do about the congress. Its proposed opening was, as promised, a mere two days away.

Clearly, Metternich was starting to wonder if opening a congress might not be such a bad idea after all. It was the lesser of evils, compared to the risks of a Russian empire creating a satellite Kingdom of Poland and extending its influence all the way to central Europe. His colleagues on the committee likewise felt such a great pressure that they had decided to ask Talleyrand to submit his ideas for the organization of the peace conference.

Ready for this request, Talleyrand brought along his plan to the meeting. His proposal called for a main directing committee that would organize all negotiations and also, interestingly, appoint a series of sub-committees to deal with the more specialized problems the diplomats faced. He proposed three such committees: one dealing with Saxony, another Italy, and the last with Switzerland. As for the tricky problem of who could participate, there would also be a "Commission of Verifications" to examine credentials of the aspiring delegates. The congress of all the states, which would ratify everything, should open immediately.

Castlereagh supported this plan, of course, and now he was joined by Metternich. Russia's Count Nesselrode, however, protested that he could not vote for it because he was not yet well enough informed. The Prussian delegates were even more adamantly opposed; Chancellor Hardenberg, in particular, was said to have a special "horror" at the thought of a congress. By the end of the meeting, with Russia and Prussia sticking together, Talleyrand's proposal was tabled. On the eve of its opening, the congress was postponed once more. A few weeks later, it would be postponed one last time, never in fact to open. The congress, in a sense, would never meet. The Directing Committee and the subcommittees, however, were not scrapped, and the real work of the Congress of Vienna was going to be done there, in small groups meeting behind closed doors.

IT WAS DURING this minor crisis, when it seemed to many that the Great Powers could not agree on anything, that Metternich apparently received a curious, anonymous note. It was probably the same night of the meeting, October 30, at a masquerade in the Hofburg Palace. A masked figure had approached the Austrian foreign minister, handed him a folded paper, and then promptly disappeared into the crowded ballroom.

Opening the note, which was sent from an unnamed source identified only as "a person of the highest distinction" with whom he had recently quarreled, Prince Metternich was promised a handsome sum, if only he would be more cooperative on a certain matter. The rest of the offer must have been much more tempting. The unidentified sender claimed to be in a position to help Metternich solve his problems with "a woman of rank" in whom he was very much interested. All of this was admittedly vague, but the author of the note reassured Metternich: "Your Highness will understand."

Now, of course, Metternich understood perfectly well. The mystery "person of the highest distinction" that he had quarreled with was almost certainly the tsar, and there was only one "woman of rank," at that time, that he was interested in: the Duchess of Sagan. As one of Castlereagh's assistants described the episode, the Austrian foreign minister simply took the note, "tossed it aside [and] pretended not to understand." Later, Metternich regretted that he did not hang on to the paper as proof of the tsar's cheap tricks.

Talleyrand, about the same time, was also receiving some information that might prove useful in future negotiations. This concerned Britain's Castlereagh, who, however helpful with respect to the congress, was proving a tough nut to crack when it came to his Prussian policy. Perhaps that would soon change, Talleyrand hoped, with good reason.

According to Talleyrand's sources, Castlereagh was hiding a secret that, if disclosed, would leave him in a compromising position. Castlereagh apparently had no government sanction for his policy of supporting Prussia. In fact, it seemed that the British foreign secretary was acting in defiance of his own government's orders.

This timely discovery had come from a Saxon officer who had just arrived in Vienna from London bringing news of his recent meeting with the prince regent, who clearly shared Talleyrand's concerns. Other sources had confirmed this discovery, including one of King Louis' ministers in Paris, who had had a revealing conversation with the British ambassador to France, the Duke of Wellington. In other words, Castlereagh, at best, had no authorization for his actions, and quite likely could be exposed for disregarding the wishes of his own government.

While Talleyrand was figuring out how best to use this information, Castlereagh worked frantically with Prussian leaders in their plan to lure the Prussian king away from the Russian tsar.

Indeed, the whole tense and uncertain situation exploded at a dramatic dinner in early November in Tsar Alexander's private suites at the Hofburg Palace. The tsar and the king of Prussia were dining alone, and toward the end of the meal, Alexander turned the discussion to foreign policy, reminding his ally about the importance of reestablishing the Kingdom of Poland. Then, after swearing that he would never yield on this question, the tsar expressed his surprise, disappointment, and anger that the king of Prussia, his "dearest friend," had been scheming against him.

Startled at this accusation, the king uttered a "thousand protestations" and begged his complete innocence. He swore that he had supported the tsar, just as he had promised, and this went for Poland, or any other matter that his ally desired. They had declared their oaths of eternal friendship. Nothing had changed.

"It is not enough that you should be of this mind," Tsar Alexander replied. "Your ministers must agree to support me too!"

"But of course my ministers will support what I choose to support!" the king answered defensively.

At that point, the Prussian chancellor, Hardenberg, was summoned to the dinner table. The aged and sophisticated statesman, who "knew how to make time fly by his charming conversation," found himself in a most uncomfortable and unpleasant situation.

The tsar immediately bombarded him with a series of facts and questions. Russia and Prussia, Alexander said, had reached a "definite and unshakable" agreement about Poland. Will you or will you not listen to the orders of your king, the tsar demanded to know. The Prussian king just sat there, indifferent to his minister's plight.

When Hardenberg tried to explain, at one point, the importance of international consensus on Poland, the tsar said, bluntly, "Those are the arguments of Monsieur Metternich," and then, out of the blue, alleged that Metternich had offered to betray the Prussians. Hardenberg was rightly skeptical. Metternich might have been unpredictable, but this wild assertion was highly unlikely. The Austrian minister was far too upset with the tsar, while Alexander, on the other hand, appeared angry and desperate enough that he might just resort to any means at his disposal to have his way.

What right did the tsar have to treat another king's minister this way? Gentz said afterward that the Prussian chancellor was so shaken by the experience that some friends "feared for his health." When his colleagues on the British and Austrian staffs heard of the dinner, they hoped that he would resign in protest.

The Prussian chancellor was ordered to break off his "intrigues" with Britain and Austria immediately. He would now be bound to carrying out Prussian policy as determined by his king, and that meant, in practice, supporting a policy that he personally felt threatened his country and the stability of the entire continent.

Hardenberg was deeply upset, reportedly afterward denouncing the tsar as "the most perfidious, treacherous, usurping character, and infinitely more dangerous than Bonaparte." Yet he was uncertain about how exactly to proceed. He scribbled his impression in his diary: "Russia, supported by the King [of Prussia] on all points, is wrong. But what to do?"

When Metternich found out about the tsar's accusations, he immediately wrote to Hardenberg to affirm that the allegations were not true: "I deny not only the fact but I am also ready to maintain the opposite in the presence of the Tsar himself."

Another person particularly troubled by this development was Lord Castlereagh. He had been trying to establish a united front with Hardenberg for months—both of them, in fact, working against their own governments for something that they felt would better serve the future peace. Still, their cooperation was a deliberate act of disobedience, and, unfortunately for them, it had backfired. The Russian tsar and the king of Prussia had only been brought closer together.

On November 7, Hardenberg unhappily but officially notified his colleagues that Prussia would now have to support Russia. Castlereagh read this note with a great deal of concern and despondency. "Unless the Emperor of Russia can be brought to a more moderate and sound course of public conduct," Castlereagh sighed, "the peace which we have so dearly purchased will be of short duration."

Chapter 15

PURSUING PHANTOMS

The triumphal chariot of the congress is stuck in the mud.

—BARON FRANZ VON GÄRTNER, IN A LETTER TO COUNT ERBACH,
MAY 16, 1815, INTERCEPTED BY THE POLICE

Seven miles off the coast of northern Italy, Napoleon was still trying to adjust to his life as the emperor of Elba. After staying only one night on the island, he had realized that his current "palace" in the town hall was not working out. Sounds of the city square, with its lively chatter and strumming guitars, wafted up to Napoleon's window late into the night. For such a small capital, the residents of Portoferraio could make a lot of noise.

Rivaling the commotion of the square was the odor that stemmed from the unfortunate habit of simply tossing the trash into the streets. While many cities at that time relied on a similar approach, Elba had far too little rain for most of the year to sweep it away, and the garbage ended up rotting in the gutters. The stench could be overpowering. The first order of business, back in May, had been to find a new place to live.

Obviously, there was nothing on the island that could rival the Tuileries, Fontainebleau, Versailles, Saint-Cloud, or any of the other palaces Napoleon had known back in France. There wasn't anything close. After discounting a couple of possible residences, none of which was particularly enticing, Napoleon had settled for a house on the outskirts.

It was a modest single-story house with eight rooms, four of which had been added in a renovation some fifty years before. Its name, Casa il Mulini, derived from a pair of windmills that had turned there until their destruction in 1808. The house itself, about ninety years old, had originally served as the residence of a Medici gardener. The outside facade was strikingly pink and adorned with emerald green shutters.

What Napoleon particularly liked about the house was the location. On a remote cliff some one hundred feet above the sea, Napoleon could sit comfortably in the villa's breezy garden and scan the blue horizon for incoming ships. With the bay, the fort, and the reefs, no large ship arriving on his island could escape a trained spyglass.

Napoleon's interest in the horizon was not, of course, idle curiosity. He was concerned for his personal safety, and with good reason. During the last twenty years, Napoleon's policies of heavy taxation, forced conscription, mandated legal reforms, and undisguised looting had made many enemies in France and occupied Europe. Royalists, radicals, patriots, and even monks with daggers in their robes—there were many people who nursed grudges and wished to settle vendettas. In addition to aspiring assassins, there was the threat that pirates swarming the Mediterranean might try to kidnap the emperor and ransom him for the rumored treasures stored somewhere on his island. Napoleon was, in other words, potentially in a great deal of danger.

So while guards were posted to keep watch on incoming ships, Napoleon set about immediately to improve the island's dilapidated state of defenses. He was to rebuild the ruined watchtowers, fortify the walls protecting the harbor, and strengthen the firepower atop its ramparts. The best harbor, the only one for sizable ships, must be as secure as possible.

The emperor had been especially glad, too, when his faithful Imperial Guard had arrived safely in the early summer. Four hundred men had been permitted, though their number had already risen to over one thousand. These soldiers were the last remnants of his once invincible Grande Armée. Now they formed the core of his army on Elba, though their functions had to change with the circumstances. The Polish lancers, for instance, who would now have little opportunity for ferocious cavalry charges, were to be retrained for artillery duty.

Napoleon had surrounded himself with loyal followers. Antoine Drouot, a baker's son who had risen to the rank of general, was appointed minister of defense and governor of Elba. Nicknamed the "Wise Man of the Grande Armée," Drouot was looking forward to spending time on his studies. He was learning Italian, reading the Bible daily, and playing chess with Napoleon.

General Pierre-Jacques Cambronne, leader of the Guard, was far less content. "A desperate, uneducated ruffian" who had been wounded so many times that he looked "completely tattooed with scars," Cambronne was a restless soldier bored out of his mind. Another high-ranking loyalist who was frustrated with the lack of action was General Count Henri Bertrand. This engineer turned administrator was now the grand chamberlain at the Elban court, presiding over the etiquette that would be as elaborate as it had been back in imperial France. Bertrand's career advancement seemed to have come to a standstill since moving to Elba, and his wife, Fanny, who had joined him, felt that they had made a mistake.

As for the navy, Napoleon had the small sixteen-gun *Inconstant* (which he used as his flagship), the three-masted *Etoile,* and the twenty-six-ton *Caroline*. In addition, Napoleon was setting up another line of defense with a new police force. A fellow Corsican, Poggi di Talavo, was named chief of police and given the main responsibility for watching all traffic to and from Elba. Permits would be needed for travel, and all newcomers would have to register at the Star Fort, beside the harbor. Police officers piloting small, fast feluccas patrolled the island's isolated beaches. Strangers and suspicious characters were questioned thoroughly. Elba, small and exposed, would be turned into a fortress island.

There were, however, two people that Napoleon deeply wanted to see arrive on his shores: his wife, Marie Louise, and their three-year-old son, the former king of Rome. She had promised to join him on Elba, and Napoleon had been waiting since May, lamenting her absence, his "daily sorrow." At the beginning, he had written her almost every day. He had also started preparing a special wing for them in his palace, repainting and refurbishing it for the expected arrival. Napoleon had everything he needed in his little kingdom, he wrote. "Only you, my dear Louise, are missing, you and my son."

MEANWHILE, BACK IN Vienna, Marie Louise was avoiding the celebrations of the peace conference as much as possible. "Festivities go on every day, so they tell me," Marie Louise wrote to Napoleon, adding that she was "scarcely informed of them" and had no interest in them whatsoever.

All those parties hosted by her husband's conquerors must have seemed distasteful. They must also have highlighted the frustrating new uncertainties over the duchies that she had been promised by treaty. Rumors swirled about how eager some of the treaty's signatories were to break those agreements. "Each day there was a fresh story," her secretary, Baron Claude-François de Méneval, wrote. "To-day Parma was assured to her, on the morrow it had been given to somebody else." The result was that Marie Louise's mood swung rapidly between hope and fear, and all of this, in turn, only increased her anxieties and made her much more willing to submit to the wishes of her father.

While she waited for the congress to decide her future, Marie Louise filled her days by riding in the park, strolling in the gardens, learning Italian, dining with her suite, taking drawing lessons—anything that took her mind away from her worries. One favorite pastime was music, and there was increasingly a new man found at the piano in her salon, a newcomer with a beautiful tenor voice: the handsome and debonair general Count Adam Albert von Neipperg. He had a black silk patch over his right eye as a result of a saber blow received in battle, and a reputation as a ladies' man. Neipperg had been placed in her suite that summer by no less than Emperor Francis. Neipperg was supposed to prevent Marie Louise from going to Elba, and he was instructed to use "any means whatsoever." He had succeeded.

By all accounts, Marie Louise and Neipperg had become lovers on her way back to Vienna from the spas. Their affair had started perhaps by late August 1814, and almost certainly by late September, when they were staying at the inn, Zur Goldenner Sonne, in Küssnacht, just outside of Lucerne, Switzerland. This romantic liaison was, of course, carried on in utmost secrecy. Marie Louise's secretary, the loyal Bonapartist Baron Méneval, already had his suspicions, though. "I can no longer fool myself," he confessed, "that she is the pure and spotless angel whom I held above reproach."

The French members of her suite must also have wondered about Neipperg's growing influence over the former empress, and they, too, cold-shouldered the Austrian officer. The loyal Bonapartists were not inclined to receive him well, anyway. It was Neipperg, after all, who had helped negotiate the agreements that persuaded some of Napoleon's most prominent marshals to desert to the Allies, including no less than Murat, the king of Naples, and Bernadotte, the Crown Prince of Sweden. And now he was trying to steal Napoleon's wife.

Like many in Vienna, Marie Louise's son, the little Napoleon, had no idea how important Neipperg was becoming in his mother's life, of course. The young boy spent his time mainly with his governess, Madame de Montesquiou—"Mamam Q," as he called her. He did, however, pick up some talk from the strongly Bonapartist suite that looked after him at Schönbrunn. The little prince was heard complaining about Louis XVIII, who had taken his father's place back in Paris, and also all his toys. Louis had better return both at once, the little boy had demanded. Actually, the French king would soon send over some toys that had been left behind in the hurried retreat from the Tuileries the previous spring.

In truth, the little prince was lonely and bored. At this stage, few bothered to visit the family locked away in the palace, living symbols of French dominance and occupation. One of the few and, indeed, favorite guests that autumn, however, was Prince de Ligne, who put on his field marshal's uniform spangled with medals from decades of military service. Once on a visit to the palace, the prince was greeted by the king of Rome's obvious joy: The toddler jumped down from his chair, ran excitedly to the old man, and threw his arms around his frail, powdered neck. Separated by almost a century of history, the two played games on the floor with the miniature toy soldiers.

In the words of one observer, this little boy—"Napoleon II"—would tempt any painter with the "angelic cut of his face, the unblemished whiteness of his skin, his sparkling eyes, and the beautiful locks of his curly blond hair cascading down to his shoulders." One of the spies, however, put it slightly differently: "that young Napoleon is an extremely wicked, stubborn child." He must have inherited this quality from his father, many hastened to add.

The Austrian police were vigilant, reporting on all the activities of Marie Louise, Neipperg, little Napoleon Francis, and the French suite that surrounded them. They were also among the first to detect the new relationship between the former empress and Neipperg, whom the Austrian government had named as her lord chamberlain. The baron's spies would have much to report from the west wing of Schönbrunn Palace.

Apparently, Marie Louise was having second thoughts about having returned to Vienna, and all she wanted now was to leave town again, preferably to the Duchy of Parma, though those who did not know of

Neipperg thought she wanted to leave for Elba. But Emperor Francis now was refusing to allow her to go anywhere until the congress had wrapped up its affairs. In the meantime, both Marie Louise and her son, now called Franz to sound more Austrian, were being closely guarded. They were well on their way to becoming virtual prisoners in the palace.

The day of the masked ball at Metternich's summer villa, November 8, was now nearing, and Metternich was going out of his way to make this celebration memorable, as the congress might end abruptly at any time. While the sovereigns wore black, women were asked to appear in regional costumes. Countesses appeared in peasant garb—peasants, that is, with diamonds sewn into their silk dresses. Others dressed as Venetians, Persians, Native Americans, or peasants elsewhere on the Continent. The Duchess of Sagan opted for Carinthian attire. No one was sure about Lady Castlereagh's dress. Was it really supposed to be that of a vestal virgin?

The Prussian diplomat Humboldt had chosen to remain at home, buried in his work. He needed to draft a number of policy papers for the upcoming meetings, and that meant research, marshaling arguments, and putting the final touches on Prussian policy statements. Grand as Metternich's ball was, Humboldt was not sorry to have missed it. "I hate those social affairs unto death."

This time, however, Humboldt missed out. The masked ball had all the color, the excitement, and indeed the magic of many other masquerades—but it also had a special attraction. At midnight, many revelers had switched masks and enjoyed the mischief that followed in the delightful confusion of mistaken identities. At another point that evening, when the dignitaries lined up as usual to march off in the polonaise through the rooms of the villa, the stately promenade degenerated into drunken chaos. The head and tail of the march collided in one of the drawing rooms. The king of Denmark, for one, "laughed so hard he could barely stand up."

Most interesting, despite swearing to the contrary, the Russian tsar had in fact come to Metternich's villa. Alexander and the king of Prussia, together as usual, were seen enjoying themselves, like the fifteen hundred other guests that evening. Even Gentz came out, and did not return home until after four in the morning.

Yet however successful the ball had been, Metternich was almost at his wits' end, suffering what Gentz called a real "state of crisis." It was,

of course, impossible for Metternich and the duchess to end their relationship as neatly as their letters claimed. Meetings were inevitable in the
close-knit society of the congress, and they were often awkward. The
duchess wrote to Metternich:

> Everything is so completely changed in us that it is not at all surpris-
> ing that our thoughts and our feelings no longer meet in anything,
> and that we find ourselves in a situation more than strange to one
> another. I begin to believe that we never did know one another. We
> were both pursuing phantoms.

As she further explained, Metternich had only seen her as an idealized
lady, "a model of perfection." She, in turn, had reciprocated, seeing Metternich before as representing "all there is of beauty and of intellectual
grandeur, something well above honor." Metternich's false idealization
was now swinging to the opposite extreme.

While the duchess denied that she had succumbed to outside pressure
to abandon him, Metternich did not believe it. The tsar must have had a
role in the breakup, and despite everything, Metternich still hoped to
regain his lover. He was consumed as ever. Gentz found the whole situation exasperating. "Long conversation with Metternich," he wrote in his
diary for the eleventh of November, "always more on that cursed woman
than on business."

The exhaustion, physical strain, and sheer mental anguish were taking a toll on Metternich, and this at a time when the Congress of Vienna
needed the full attention of its president. He confessed:

> As to my health, there is no question of it any longer! I am com-
> pletely ill, my body attacked, my soul has not protected it for a long
> time. I am still needed for a few weeks more; those weeks will bring
> to an end the most painful years of my life, and if they finish my life,
> the world will lose only the sad remnants of an existence which I
> myself deserved to lose.

WHILE THE DELEGATES wrangled over Poland and Saxony, teetering on
the verge of war, another major dispute had been uncomfortably placed

on hold: the future of Italy. But it was now becoming increasingly difficult to avoid this delicate subject.

Napoleon had entered the peninsula back in 1796 promising to break the people's "chains of bondage." But by the time the last French troops straggled back across the Alps eighteen years later, the Italian states were left in near chaos. The land had been stripped of valuables, treasure vaults were looted, and countless masterpieces were carted off to Paris.

The extent of Napoleon's looting was shocking. Everything from the Belvedere Apollo to the Medici Venus, the Dying Gaul to *Laocoön and His Sons*—these were just some of the masterpieces in the 288 cartloads of treasures that comprised Napoleon's *first* raid of Italy. They were soon joined by other treasures, including Raphael's *Leo X,* Titian's *Death of Saint Peter Martyr,* Veronese's gigantic *Marriage at Cana,* and the four bronze horses atop St. Mark's Basilica in Venice. Every campaign had added to the collection. As one critic put it, the French would have carried off the Colosseum and the Sistine Chapel, too, if they could have figured out how to do so.

Of all the questions regarding Italy—from old republics destroyed in the war, such as Genoa and Venice, to magnificent art collections ruthlessly plundered, namely, in Florence and the Vatican—the most difficult challenge at this point lay in the southern part of the peninsula. One of Bonaparte's former marshals, Joachim Murat, still ruled as king of Naples, having been placed on the throne in 1808 by Napoleon himself. To allow King Joachim to remain in power was tantamount to "rewarding crime." Conquest, as Talleyrand argued, should not bestow any rights. For the good of Europe, that notion had to be banished forever.

Another problem in allowing Murat to retain his crown was the fact that his presence placed all the states of Italy at risk of another war. Murat was one of the bravest and undoubtedly one of the most talented cavalry officers alive. He was also an unpredictable hothead with the touchiness of someone who had not a shred of legitimacy to his throne. Like Napoleon, Murat would probably have to keep fighting in order to maintain his authority.

Yet to deprive him of the throne would require military intervention, and a large one at that. Murat would certainly not go down without a fight, and after the long war, few wanted to take up arms again over this issue, even if the money were to be readily available, which it was not.

Murat's main supporter at the congress was actually Prince Metternich. This was, by no means, a surprise to insiders at the congress. Salon gossip traced his support back to the fact that Metternich had earlier carried on a passionate affair with Murat's wife, Napoleon's sister Caroline. Many believed that he was still supporting his former mistress. Metternich had certainly had that affair, and he had stayed in contact with her over the years, but he also had many other reasons for hesitating to remove Murat.

Most notably, back in January 1814, during a critical stage in the war, Metternich had signed an agreement regarding Naples: If Murat would desert Napoleon, Metternich would guarantee his right to the throne. Murat had deserted, to the benefit of the Allies. Now Metternich was trying to stick to his end of the bargain, though he did not personally like Murat, and he was taking a lot of heat, from Talleyrand in particular.

In early November, the Committee of Eight had held its first meeting to discuss the fate of Italy. Talleyrand, representing France on this committee, had participated fully. His argument, no surprise, was to remove Murat the usurper, "the last excrement of the revolution," and replace him with the legitimate king, Ferdinand IV.

Metternich reminded him that it would require a bloody campaign. Peasants all over the region were rushing to Murat's support, and who knew what he might do. He could very well call for the unification of Italy, rally the people behind his banner, and end up causing a massive civil war.

"Organize Italy," Talleyrand responded, and Murat would no longer have any supporters. Restore the *legitimate* crown, and Murat would be "no more to Italy than a brigand."

The Austrian foreign minister continued to speak of "complications"—which Talleyrand interpreted as a stratagem employed to "keep up the vagueness which his weak policy requires."

By the end of the meeting, the committee had decided to approach the problems of Italy in a methodical fashion, or at least a geographical one. They would begin their discussions in the north with the fate of the old republic of Genoa, which had been destroyed in the revolution. They would proceed down the peninsula, through Rome and the papacy, until they reached the murky areas of the south, ending with the issue of Naples.

Both Metternich and Talleyrand were happy with this arrangement.

France's minister planned to use the time to gain support for his principles of legitimacy, and Austria's minister hoped to flatter, tack, hedge, and stall the whole uncomfortable subject right out of the congress.

ONE EVENING, A few days after this meeting, Talleyrand returned to Kaunitz Palace and found a troubled Saxon minister waiting impatiently. The guest, Count Schulenburg, held a dispatch straight from the king of Saxony. It was not the usual lament about being uninvited to the congress or imprisoned outside of Berlin. The king had some other disturbing news.

> We have just learnt with great sorrow that our Kingdom of Saxony
> is to be temporarily occupied by the troops of His Prussian Majesty.

According to this report in Talleyrand's hands, the governor-general of Russian-occupied Saxony, Prince Nicolas Grégoriévitch Repnin-Wolkonski, had ordered the army to pull out and hand over the entire kingdom to the king of Prussia. The Prussians were to assume control of Saxony, effective immediately.

Warnings of the tsar's tendency to act unilaterally seemed to have hit their mark with an alarming accuracy. But there was something else unsettling about this announcement. When the Prussian army marched into the region, it made the startling claim that it acted with "the consent of Austria and of England."

Metternich was furious; he had done nothing of the sort. As he put it in his official letter, Austria had promised to accept the seizure of Saxony if—and only if—the Prussians succeeded in preventing Russian gains in Poland. Failure in this question rendered the offer void. Metternich's conditional acceptance was printed as if it had been absolute. It was a complete misrepresentation, he claimed.

Castlereagh also protested against this distortion of the facts, and showed concern about the implications for his diplomatic mission. He had gambled on Prussia and lost. The king of Prussia was now closer to the tsar than ever before; moreover, when the Russian army moved out of Saxony, it marched straight into Poland, fortifying its hold on the disputed territory. Russia was simply acting like the dictator of Europe, imposing its views on the other states. Castlereagh's policy was in shambles.

Chapter 16

The Last Joust

The Congress seemed like a theatrical performance
while the house was burning.

—Countess Elise von Bernstorff

While the congress worked and danced, there was a peculiar forty-seven-year-old in a small flat on the fourth floor of a narrow building on the Mölker Bastei, hunched over a black Auster pianoforte. He was a stocky man of average height, with a mass of dark curly hair, thick eyebrows, and an intense gaze. His nose was "square like a lion," and he had the most "marvelous dimples, formed by two jawbones capable of cracking the hardest nuts." This was Ludwig van Beethoven, and he was composing music for the Congress of Vienna.

During the autumn of 1814, Beethoven was at the height of his popularity. He had moved to Habsburg capital twenty-two years before, from Bonn, where he had been born in 1770. Beethoven had never liked Vienna or its people: "From the Emperor to the bootblack, all the Viennese are worthless," he had generalized. He did, however, enjoy the strolls, particularly out on the slopes of the Kahlenberg at the edge of the Vienna Woods.

Here he walked daily, sometimes "muttering and howling" as thoughts passed through his head. He made sure to bring along paper and pencil for any impromptu jottings—after all, he believed, it is the "woods, trees and rocks [that] produce the echo which man desires to hear." When Beethoven arrived back at his flat, he was known, on a good day, to rush excitedly to his black stool and proceed to lose himself at the keyboard. Walking companions, if there had been any, were quickly forgotten.

His rooms overlooking the old city wall were just as cluttered and untidy as his clothes were shoddy and sloppy. One musician who paid a visit, just after the congress, described them as "dreary almost sordid . . . in the greatest disorder: music, money, clothes lay on the floor, linen in a heap on the unclean bed, the open grand piano was covered in thick dust, and broken coffee cups lay on the table."

Beethoven was one of the first of a new generation of artists, regarded less as a craftsman for hire than as a genius, who, it was believed, could make his own rules and live on his own terms. The concept of genius, influenced by the Romantic movement, was changing, from a particular talent that someone possessed to a description that applied to the whole person, and Beethoven personified this shift. His odd behavior and eccentricities were tolerated as a hallmark of his genius.

Indeed, when he went out to dine at inns or restaurants, Beethoven preferred a table in the far corner, and would often sit there brooding. Gloomy and sullen at times, the musician liked to complain about the endless problems caused by his lazy or scheming servants or friends. He might also, suddenly and unexpectedly, lash out at anyone nearby. He had only recently hurled a plate of food at a waiter.

For the last two years, Beethoven's hearing had been steadily growing worse, and his guests already had to shout. Along with the deterioration, caused, it seems, by a growth in his inner ear by the bone, Beethoven's idiosyncrasies became more marked. He was in pain, and losing contact with the world of sound was only increasing his own sense of isolation. With his rough edges and abruptness, he had already been called an "unlicked bear." He was paying even less attention now to social conventions.

At the moment, the grumpy genius was preparing for the upcoming concert at the Redoutensaal of the Hofburg. His compositions, he knew, should celebrate the Allied victory over Napoleon, and commemorate the Congress of Vienna, convened to reconstruct Europe.

WHEN THE MONARCHS were not acting like "spoiled children" or "playing soldiers," as Baronne du Montet put it, they spent many mornings hunting—often stag, boar, hare, or pheasant. The English physician Richard Bright witnessed one of the hunting parties at the Congress of

Vienna and thought it had all the "barbarity of a bullfight." The carnage, however, was often on a much larger scale.

On November 10, the court traveled to the Lainzer Tiergarten outside Vienna for one such hunt. Some twenty stands had been constructed for the occasion, like an amphitheater. No fewer than six hundred wild boar, and a number of other animals, had been rounded up from nearby forests and were then released, a few at a time, into the small makeshift arena. The monarchs, ready with gun at hand and assistants at their side to help load, shot according to rank. First the emperors fired and then the kings, followed by the princes, dukes, field marshals, and so on. The Swiss banker Jean-Gabriel Eynard was appalled; there was no skill, stamina, or even risk. It was pure slaughter.

Meanwhile, as the Committee of Eight started working its way through the affairs of Italy, proceeding in a geographical fashion, as planned, the first item on the agenda was resolving the fate of Genoa, a port on the northeastern coast that had been a commercial power since the Middle Ages. The ancient republic had been seized by Napoleon, incorporated into his empire in 1805, and transformed, as lamented famously in the first sentence of Tolstoy's *War and Peace,* into the "private estates of the Bonaparte family." Now, with the war over, Genoa was eager to be restored to its independence and regain its former status as a free republic. This was, after all, what the city had been promised.

In the spring of 1814, at the end of the war, Great Britain had assured Genoa that its republic would be revived "as it had been before the Revolution." All the city had to do was officially support the Allied army. The Genoese accepted these terms, and now sent a delegation to Vienna to oversee its promised restoration.

But there was a rude shock awaiting the city's chief delegate, the twenty-eight-year-old scion of a prominent banking family, the Marquis de Brignole-Sale. Britain was now claiming that the man who made the offer of restoring the republic, Lord William Bentinck, the commander of the Mediterranean and minister to Sicily, was not authorized to make such a claim, as indeed he was not. Worse still, rumors circulated that Britain had promised that Genoa itself would be handed over to the king of Sardinia. The rumors were true. Castlereagh had signed his name to that agreement, a secret article attached to the Treaty of Paris.

Castlereagh and the Allies had reasoned that Genoa, a small and relatively weak republic, would be a temptation to future French aggression; moreover, situated as the city was near strategic Alpine mountain passages, the loss of Genoa could threaten all of north Italy as well. The king of Sardinia (Piedmont-Sardinia) could defend the territory much more effectively. Genoa was then just another part of Castlereagh's strategy of building an "iron ring" around France: the greater Netherlands in the north, the stronger Prussia in the east, and now this enlarged Sardinia in the south.

So despite the protests of Genoa's delegate, not to mention the millions he was said to be dispensing to lobby support, the Committee of Eight remained unmoved. Previous promises to the city were now denied and shrugged aside. Arguments for restoring the republic, the legitimate form of government before the war, were made in vain. The delegates simply pointed to the words inked in a secret article of the treaty, "The King of Sardinia will receive an addition to his territory in the state of Genoa," and proceeded to do just that.

As the Great Powers planned to proceed down the peninsula on to the next Italian questions, they were also busy appointing a number of standing committees, not too different from what Talleyrand had proposed. The first of the special committees, the German Committee, had been established in the middle of October to create a federation and write a constitution, though the trouble of Saxony had embittered all its discussions. On the sixteenth of November, the German Committee had actually stopped meeting. It would be some five months before this committee would convene again.

The Great Powers would eventually appoint ten such specialized committees. There would be one, for example, to ensure the free navigation of rivers, and another to sort out the tangled questions that governed diplomatic etiquette. Others would be created as the need arose.

One new committee, appointed on the twelfth of November, was the Swiss Committee, which, like its counterparts, clearly faced some major challenges. Switzerland, at the time of the Vienna Congress, was a federal union of some twenty-two cantons that varied greatly in culture and history. Some spoke French as their official language, others German, and one Italian, not to mention a few places like Engadine and Graubünden, which had a large minority population speaking a fourth language, the Latin-based Romansh. More divisive still, some cantons were predominantly Catholic, others Protestant. Some were bastions of aristocracy, and others fiercely democratic.

The cantons could not agree on their vision for Switzerland. Some wanted closer cooperation between the cantons, and others wanted less; some wanted in the federation, others out. Two different diets—or directing bodies—had been created the past year, one around the aristocratic Bern, the other around the more democratic Zürich. Many feared that their country was headed toward civil war. The Swiss Committee, it was hoped, would find a satisfying solution. It would be difficult to secure peace in Europe as long as war raged in its center.

BY THE MIDDLE of November, as new committees met behind closed doors, two main topics appeared to dominate discussions in Vienna salons. The first was the fate of the king of Saxony, whose kingdom had been seized by the Prussians. The second, more pleasantly, was the upcoming Carousel at the Spanish Riding School, a full-scale attempt to re-create a medieval tournament. Of all the grand spectacles at the Congress of Vienna, many thought that this was the greatest.

Vienna had been eagerly looking forward to the pageant, scheduled for Wednesday evening, November 23. The Festivals Committee had pored over accounts of other elaborate carousels from history, hoping to understand their conventions and then "surpass them in splendor."

The Spanish Riding School, designed by Josef Emanuel Fischer von Erlach and completed in 1735, was a magical setting for the Carousel. Underneath the crystal chandeliers blazing with candles, the arena was shaped in a long rectangle well suited for equestrian maneuvers. At one end was the imperial grandstand, with rows of gilded armchairs waiting for the sovereigns. The balcony at the other end of the hall was reserved for the twenty-four ladies selected to be the tournament's *belles d'amour*, the "Queens of Love," for whom their champions would battle. Galleries ran along the sides connecting the two grandstands. The columns around the hall were hung with the armor, weapons, and mottoes of the knights scheduled to compete.

Crowds started to arrive in the early evening, and by about seven, when La Garde-Chambonas arrived with Prince de Ligne, the arena was nearly full. Counterfeiters had once again produced a number of bogus tickets for the occasion, and the baron's police were put on the case. They wanted to prevent too many uninvited guests from gate-crashing their imagined medieval tournament.

Some thousand to twelve hundred people, it was estimated, packed the good seats in the two main galleries. One section was reserved for the high nobility of the Austrian empire, and another for the ambassadors, diplomats, and ranking plenipotentiaries at the congress. Even Wilhelm von Humboldt had set aside his enormous stacks of paper to attend the Carousel. Talleyrand had run into him that evening, and could not resist teasing him: "Does Your Excellency prefer horse-riding to statistics?"

What a sight it must have been: "an almost unbroken line of glittering gold and diamonds in their Court dresses and uniforms disappearing beneath their orders and embroideries." Dresses had been selected with the greatest care, and jewel boxes ransacked for gems that, in many cases, had been hidden since the turmoil of the French Revolution. One goldsmith in attendance confessed that he could not begin to estimate the worth of all the jewels on display. Princess Esterházy's dress alone was probably valued at 6 million francs. "I do indeed believe," said Dorothée, swept away in the enthusiasm, "we shall wear every pearl and diamond to be found in Hungary, Bohemia, and Austria."

Standing out in the audience, too, with his scarlet hat and silk habiliments, was the pope's delegate, Cardinal Consalvi, along with the sultan's representative, Mavrojény, in his turban and caftan. Castlereagh's wife, Emily, was also conspicuous, once again wearing her husband's Order of the Garter "as a kind of tiara" in her hair.

At eight o'clock, heralds blasted their trumpets to announce the arrival of the Queens of Love. Prince Metternich's seventeen-year-old daughter Marie had been chosen, along with the Duchess of Sagan, her sister Dorothée, Sophie Zichy, and Princess Pauline Esterházy. Each "queen" wore an exquisite velvet dress, La Garde-Chambonas observed, "trimmed with priceless lace, and sparkling with precious stones." Diamonds, emeralds, rubies, and sapphires reflected the glow of the chandeliers with a dazzling brilliance.

"My God," one Prussian had exclaimed with surprise at the ostentation, "three campaigns could be fought with that."

After the ladies promenaded through the arena, their long gossamer veils flowing behind, and reached their seats, the heralds sounded their horns again for the arrival of the Austrian emperor, the empress, and the train of sovereigns. Everyone stood. The Queens of Love removed their veils and the riding school erupted with "a storm of applause."

Scanning the crowds that evening revealed a number of conspicuous absences. Despite persistent rumors that she would attend, Napoleon's wife, Marie Louise, did not show. Notably absent, too, was Metternich. He could not bear watching his beloved Duchess of Sagan, a Queen of Love in her striking green velvet dress with matching jewel-encrusted green velvet cap. Worse still, her champion in the tournament was Prince Alfred von Windischgrätz.

The most obvious no-show, however, was the Russian tsar. Officially, Alexander was sick, though some speculated that this was just a convenient excuse for him to boycott the Austrian-sponsored entertainment. To those gossipers, the tsar's absence suggested deep divisions among the Great Powers, and probably also a sign of the congress's imminent rupture.

But despite this interpretation, plausible enough given the tensions of the moment, it seems that the tsar was in fact sick that night. A few days before the tournament, Alexander had been dancing in one of the ballrooms at the popular Mehlgrube on the Neuer Markt, and then suddenly collapsed on the dance floor. The fall had been so unexpected that many started speculating that the tsar had been poisoned (and one cook in the Hofburg kitchens was fired for his alleged involvement in this plot). Instead, the tsar was probably just exhausted from his long hours, his lack of sleep, and the overall stress from the congress. He had reportedly danced some thirty nights in a row. The night of the Carousel, the tsar was in bed at the Hofburg.

As the orchestra on the top floor of the Spanish Riding School struck up a martial piece, the tournament's twenty-four knights trotted out on powerful black Hungarian chargers, hoofs stomping the matted sand, which had been poured onto the floor to help break the fall of any unseated knight.

To be selected a champion, as La Garde-Chambonas put it, was "tantamount to a diploma in grace and elegance." The champions were generally from the old landed families. There was Prince Vincent Esterházy, Prince Anton Radziwill, and the Duchess of Sagan's lover, Prince Alfred von Windischgrätz. Another knight selected was Prince Leopold of Saxe-Coburg-Saalfeld, the future king of Belgium.

The Carousel at the Vienna Congress was, of course, an imitation of chivalry as it had flourished in a late revival, long after its heyday. The knights looked closer, if anything, to the early sixteenth century than the high Middle Ages. Hence, there were more trunks, hose, and snug velvet doublets with puffed sleeves than hot and heavy plate armor. Instead of cumbersome helmets, too, each knight wore a large diamond-buckled, broad-reamed hat, complete with a "plume of feathers drooping from the side."

The whole procession of champions, joined by squires carrying shields and pages waving large unfurled banners, made its way around the arena, stopping just in front of the sovereigns. The knights did homage, standing in the stirrups, turning to bow to the assembled monarchs, and then "dipping their lances" respectfully to the queens and empresses in the gallery. Then, after paying homage to their Queens of Love at the other end of the hall, they prepared to begin the games.

The first challenge was the so-called *pas de lance,* a "tilting at the rings," which involved champions charging on horseback and lowering the lance to pierce rings hanging from ribbons. Among other events, the knights tossed javelins at fake Saracen heads, or charged forward, scimitar in hand, to slice an apple dangling by a ribbon from the ceiling.

Then it was time for the main event, the mock combat of a joust. This was not like the tournaments of the Middle Ages, when soldiers could and indeed did die on the field, like the unfortunate tournament in 1240 that ended with some eighty knights dead. The Carousel at the Congress, by contrast, was intended to be a highly stylized simulation. The knights were to ride in a gallop and try to unseat their opponent, but the judges had urged that they show the utmost civility. The event did, in fact, go well. The only incident was when Prince Liechtenstein was unhorsed and carried off the field unconscious.

After some further displays of horsemanship, the knights riding to "a kind of dance to the rhythm of the music," the sovereigns, the Queens of Love, and their champions then led the way out of the riding school and into the palace for a banquet. The sovereigns had their own special table, where everything was gilded, from the forks to the fruit baskets. In large rooms, circulating around the banquet tables, acrobats tumbled, jesters juggled, and minstrels, with harp in hand, serenaded the guests. The evening culminated in a grand ball for some three thousand guests.

The Festivals Committee had attempted to create "a never-to-be-forgotten feature of the brilliant" congress, and they had certainly put on a show. The organizers pledged to present another "precise replica" of the tournament for the absent tsar. The details might not have been strictly correct historically, but the sovereigns were happy. The committee had even created a special place for the large king of Württemberg, "five feet in height and six in girth." As few diaries fail to recount, the committee had cut a "large half-moon" shape from the dining table to "accommodate his fabulous paunch."

And so, as kings, queens, champions, and the revelers glided and twirled across the parquet floors, the "dazzling Carousel" drowned out the diplomatic difficulties of the moment.

Chapter 17

"The Glorious Moment"

We make but slow progress in our affairs and yet we are not idle.

—TALLEYRAND

No amount of glitter, however, could obscure the troubles, and the baron's informants detected considerable grumbling outside the palaces, ballrooms, and haunts of the exclusive society at play. The "thinkers and idlers" congregating on the Graben were loudly criticizing the congress for its unrestrained indulgence. Why couldn't the delegates put the same energies into ironing out a just peace as they did in organizing tournaments? Would diplomats ever really have an incentive to wrap up negotiations as long as Emperor Francis continued to open house so freely and set out fifty banquet tables almost every night?

Austrian patriots worried about the great expenses for this lavish entertainment, and wondered how the emperor would ever be able to pay for it all. They also disliked the glaring contrast between the generous Vienna hosts and the countless houseguests, who seemed ungrateful to say the least. Some of the allies from the war, like the Russian tsar, even behaved more like enemies. One spy reported the sentiment that Austria's generosity threatened to cripple its economy if not bankrupt the state: "This is a new way to wage war: eat your enemy."

All the frustration and resentment was only compounded by the exclusiveness of the club of diplomats meeting behind closed doors, and the apparent ridiculousness of some disputes. The leaders were bickering over who entered or left a room first, who sat where at a dinner, who signed a document first. There is a legend that Metternich had several extra doors cut into his office to allow the negotiators to enter and leave at the same time. This is not true, but the issues were real enough.

Protocol was a reflection of power and prestige, especially as diplomats at this time represented monarchs, rather than the state, and everyone could be highly sensitive to any slight. Famously, in September 1661, when a Swedish envoy arrived in London, the Spanish ambassador refused to follow France in the welcoming procession and raced ahead, nearly causing a riot, a scandal, and a declaration of war.

At the congress, business had literally stalled over such issues. The declaration of October 8, which postponed the opening of the congress until November 1, for instance, had been unsigned, in part, because the plenipotentiaries could not agree over the order of signatures. The German Committee experienced countless troubles as its members jostled for precedence—that is, until it stopped meeting entirely.

Perhaps standardizing the rules governing diplomatic transactions would help ease tensions that sometimes bedeviled negotiations. There was no consensus, however, on how to achieve this goal. How much, for instance, should protocol at a negotiation be based on a state's power? What distinctions, if any, should be drawn between representatives of a kingdom and representatives of a republic? What about between the Continent's oldest and most legitimate dynasties, and the newest creations spawned by the sword of Bonaparte? The Congress of Vienna's most recent committee, the Committee on Diplomatic Precedence, which would be meeting by the middle of December under the leadership of Spain's Labrador, was established to sort out those questions.

Still other concerns were heard in Vienna's drawing rooms. Some of the older generation believed that all this hobnobbing with kings would only damage royal prestige. How unbecoming it was, even Talleyrand remarked, "to meet three or four kings, and a still greater number of princes at balls and teas at the houses of private individuals." The situation had almost degenerated into a farce. The Geneva banker Jean-Gabriel Eynard confessed that one night at a party he saw the king of Prussia standing alone against the wall, and confused him with a waiter. He nearly asked the king to fetch him a glass of champagne.

For a number of reasons, many were unhappy with the conference, and the city's discontented sought out places to vent and exchange news. The tavern-inn Empress of Austria was a favorite for a cosmopolitan group of thinkers, who wanted to escape the rigors of court etiquette and speak more freely. Another spot, the Three White Lions Café, was popular especially with many young Germans who met for heated debate over wine and oysters.

Interestingly, some of the most popular centers for information and criticism were churches in the city. Many of the people in town crowded into wherever the energetic priest Zacharias Werner happened to be preaching his provocative and often highly unpredictable sermons. From the pulpit, this tall and thin man with long hair that had been compared to a lion's mane would consistently blast the Vienna Congress as a sorry spectacle of vanity and frivolity. This general theme could be elaborated and varied at will. Most recently, he had preached about how the mob of emperors, kings, and princes in town had clearly fallen under the spell of another ruler, the real ruler of the Vienna Congress: King Foolishness.

Prior to his conversion to Catholicism several years before, Werner had spent much of his career around a theater, and it showed. He had been a playwright who had composed a number of works, including the tragedy *The Twenty-fourth of February,* which had been staged by Goethe. At the age of forty-two, Werner had been overwhelmed by the experience of Mass, and converted. The former vagabond poet renounced his previous debauchery, and traded his activities in the brothel and the stage for the pulpit, and even, for a few years, a monastic cell in southern Italy.

It was during the peace conference that Werner had made his way to Vienna. In a city overflowing with theater, both on the stage and in the streets, Werner had attracted a considerable following. He boasted enthusiasm and passion, though some objected to the language of this fiery preacher, claiming it was as coarse as a coachman and probably better suited to the tavern.

On one Sunday, for example, when the pews were once again packed in the Franciscan church, Father Zacharias veered his sermon onto a discussion of a certain part of the human anatomy—"a tiny piece of flesh . . . on a man's body"—that often led to the most difficult temptations and the most flagrant transgressions. Its effects were evidenced every day at the congress. The audience must have wondered where this unpredictable priest was headed. Then, gripping the edge of the pulpit, Werner leaned his thin face toward the congregation and asked, "Shall I show you that tiny piece of flesh?"

The congregation was "deathly silent," and then, after an "agonizing pause," the priest answered: "Ladies and gentlemen behold the source of our sins." For those who looked up, Father Zacharias was standing there showing the organ in question: He had stuck out his tongue.

To the sound of "nervous giggling" and the relief of the congregation, the priest reminded how the tongue wagged in excess seriously damaged relationships. Gossip, however, was not to be vanquished so easily, and it would continue to rage, dividing the peacemakers until it seemed that it might succeed foolishness as the uncrowned king of the congress.

IN LATE NOVEMBER, the scheduled day for Ludwig van Beethoven's highly anticipated Gala Concert was nearing. The first date picked for the event, November 20, had been moved back a couple of days due to the unexpected illness of the Austrian emperor.

Indeed, as exhaustion seemed pervasive, a vicious flulike virus swept Vienna in late November. Just as the tsar and the emperor had been forced to spend several days at rest, Prince Metternich also succumbed, as did the king of Prussia, Prince Hardenberg, Princess Bagration, Dorothée, and a host of others. In a congress dominated by fashion, it suddenly seemed almost fashionable to be sick. Fortunately, though, this flu—the congress's "uninvited guest"—would leave town as quietly as it had arrived.

Two additional postponements of the concert followed that week, the last one because of English protests against holding a concert on a Sunday. Soon Beethoven's concert seemed uncannily like the Vienna Congress itself, riddled with delays, protests, and postponements.

On Tuesday, November 29, Beethoven was finally able to hold the Gala Concert at the Redoutensaal. The program promised a full afternoon of music, and tickets cost only 3 gulden, or 5 gulden for the better seats upstairs. A stellar audience filled the auditorium, including the Russian tsar, the king of Prussia, and many other princes and princesses.

The concert began with "Wellington's Victory" (also known as "The Battle Symphony"), a triumphant celebration of the Battle of Vitoria, with its creative sampling from "Rule Britannia" and "God Save the King," packed with drumrolls, trumpet fanfares, cymbal crashes, and veritable cannon blasts that re-created the "horrors of battle" and the joyous celebration of the victory over the Napoleonic beast. It was an explosive extravaganza quite unusual for classical music at the time.

Beethoven had originally written the music for an instrument called the panharmonicon, a small handheld box designed to reproduce mechanically the wind, brass, and string sections of a large orchestra. The device had been invented by Beethoven's collaborator, Johann Nepomuk Mälzel, the "Court Mechanician," whose inventions included an ear trumpet and a "Mechanical Trumpeter" that sounded military marches. He also claimed to have invented a mechanical chess player that had supposedly defeated Napoleon in a game of chess during his occupation of Vienna (actually, the real inventor was Wolfgang von Kempelen, and the trick, of course, was a man hidden inside the machine). Another one of his inventions that might have been useful at a congress swarming with spies was a desk with secret compartments guarded by a built-in mechanism that, if disturbed, released a deafening alarm and thick iron locks that automatically gripped the wrists of the transgressor.

It was this rogue inventor and showman who had suggested that Beethoven revamp "Wellington's Victory" for a real orchestra and launch the piece at a public concert packed with Vienna's virtuosos. And in the patriotism sweeping Vienna after the war, Beethoven's work was a hit. The audience in the Redoutensaal received it with rapturous applause.

The second work, the new cantata "The Glorious Moment," was named in honor of the Congress of Vienna. The text was written by a surgeon named Alois Weissenbach, who had come to Vienna for the peace conference, and Beethoven set the patriotic poem to music. This piece has not aged well, often dismissed by critics as "absurdly bombastic." Yet it, too, opened to huge applause. Neither composer, however, could hear this response. Like Beethoven, Weissenbach was deaf.

The concert concluded with the Seventh Symphony, billed as the "new large Symphony." This was, however, not literally new. Beethoven had completed this symphony back in the spring of 1812, and he had actually performed it publicly in December 1813. It was a notoriously difficult piece of music, and the musicians objected at first. Beethoven himself conducted, and was said to "crouch down at the soft passages" and then suddenly leap up for the louder ones. The audience loved it, and Vienna's newspaper, the *Wiener Zeitung*, raved about the performance.

Actually, it seems, Beethoven was not really directing the concert. He was on stage, of course, moving his baton, but the real director was his assistant, Ignaz Umlauf. As historian Ingrid Fuchs rightly shows, Beethoven was no longer capable of directing complicated pieces. Less than a month later, the musician, Ludwig Spohr, heard one of Beethoven's rehearsals and testified to the decline: Beethoven's pianoforte was "badly out of tune," and "the poor deaf musician hammered the keys so hard in forte that the strings rattled." Beethoven made countless mistakes, and the visitor left, as he put it, "gripped by profound sorrow at such a miserable fate."

Beethoven's patron, the Russian ambassador Count Razumovsky, looked on loyally with admiration, claiming that the "world is too small for him." Others were less impressed, prone to judge Beethoven's compositions as too loud, too long, and too heavy, "like Hercules using his club to kill flies." Indeed, just as the congress had split in Russian and Austrian factions, police spies reported that "anti- and pro-Beethoven factions [were] forming." Sure enough, since Beethoven had been supported by a Russian patron and the tsar, the Austrians stayed away from the concert, and the English were not much in evidence there, either. Entertainment, it seemed, was echoing diplomacy.

That night, Beethoven was exhausted, he confessed, by the many "fatiguing affairs, vexations, pleasure and delight, all intermingled and interflicted or bestowed upon me at once." He also complained about the measly tips he received. The king of Prussia, who left halfway through the concert, gave only a "very paltry" 10 ducats, whereas the Russian tsar generously paid some twenty times that.

As BEETHOVEN CONDUCTED "The Glorious Moment," the congress it celebrated was still no closer to resolving its disputes.

The Russian tsar was increasingly viewed as a villain. Besides his rude treatment of foreign ministers, he had arbitrarily handed over one kingdom to his allies, and ordered his army to occupy another. Everything seemed to confirm the worst fears of some diplomats—that he was a dangerous megalomaniac. Gentz summed up the sentiment: "The language of justice and truth is not one Russia understands."

At a ball, for instance, Alexander approached the beautiful Countess Széchenyi-Guilford and asked flirtatiously, "Madame, I note that your husband is not present; may I have the pleasure of occupying his place temporarily?" Her response expressed the frustrations of many: "Does Your Majesty take me for a province?"

Vienna's drawing rooms and makeshift embassy suites also buzzed with heated discussion of Prussia's controversial seizure of the kingdom of Saxony. Outside of the Prussian delegation and its few allies, opinion was overwhelming negative. Many complained of "the detestable Prussians" and denounced their occupation as an outrageous breach of international law.

In fact, many German states had started a petition to resist this aggression. Smaller and midsized states that felt threatened by Prussia signed to protect their "unfortunate brother," the king of Saxony, agreeing that they could not sanction such a dreadful and unjust "act of violence."

This petition against the Prussian annexation made its rounds, and was soon signed by almost every major prince or delegate in Germany. By the middle of December, however, the protest was dead. The reason was simple. The Prussians had made known, in no uncertain terms, that they would regard any state that signed the petition as an outright enemy. One by one, the weaker powers had asked to remove their signatures.

After the Prussian occupation and the intimidation that squashed the protest, tempers were flaring, and feelings of betrayal burned on all sides. Talleyrand took quill in hand and penned one of the more remarkable documents of the Vienna Congress. This paper, a letter addressed to Metternich dated the nineteenth of December, was an elegant combination of philosophy and policy that affirmed the importance of justice and the rights of states in the face of aggression in international affairs.

The French foreign minister first reminded Metternich that his country asked nothing for itself. France was satisfied with its borders and had no desire whatsoever for additional territory. What his embassy hoped instead was to persuade its fellow peacemakers to agree to one guiding principle, namely, "that everywhere and forever the spirit of revolt be quenched, that every legitimate right be made sacred."

France aspired, in other words, to create a situation whereby "every ambition and unjust enterprise [would] find both its condemnation and a perpetual obstacle." This might sound like a grand, unattainable ideal, he said, but Europe really had no choice. Without such principles in place, held firm and rigorously guarded, international affairs would soon degenerate into a reckless pursuit of self-interest and power—just as that reckless scramble had plunged the Continent into that "long and deadly horror" of the last quarter century.

Now that Napoleon was defeated, Europe must take this opportunity to crown justice as the "chief virtue" of international affairs. Leaders of states must pledge that they would never act nor acquiesce in any deed that could not be considered just, "whatever consideration [that] may arise," because only justice, he said, can produce a true state of harmony and stability. Anything short of that would create a misleading and meaningless false order, destined to collapse when the first powerful state decided to take advantage of its superior strength.

"Might does not make right," Talleyrand reminded. Has not Europe, he added, suffered enough from that doctrine, and paid for it "with so much blood and so many tears"? The golden age of peace could be right around the corner, if only every peacemaker would follow this course of action.

Talleyrand had pored over this statement, selecting every word with care, and he made sure it circulated in Vienna. He personally handed a copy of the letter to the tsar's minister, Adam Czartoryski, and sent another one to Castlereagh. Talleyrand's audience, he clearly hoped, was not only Metternich, but also Vienna and, ideally, eventually the Continent at large.

While many praised Talleyrand's masterpiece, as admirers already dubbed it, the Prussians were not so happy. For them, this was, of course, nothing more than another clever yet thinly veiled attempt on the part of France to sow discord among the Allies for her own gain, and the Prussian ministers lost no time trying to undermine and discredit this statement. This was Talleyrand, after all. Was this man, with his string of broken oaths, really to be taken seriously? Some in the Prussian embassy circulated stories that the French were trying to seize the left bank of the Rhine and Belgium, as they had done in the 1790s.

Besides that, Talleyrand's position was being undermined by another rumor, this one undoubtedly true.

News trickled into Vienna that France was becoming highly unstable. King Louis XVIII, after only six months on the throne, was very unpopular, and his whole government was as detested as the French government had been on the eve of the Revolution. Generals were restless. Soldiers missed Napoleon, and so did many veterans who had been reduced to half pay, or even unceremoniously dismissed at the end of the war, and now, in the postwar recession, were forced to beg or steal. A report reached Talleyrand in December from the War Office telling of a regiment of the king's infantry that had "burnt its [Napoleonic] eagles, collected the ashes, and each soldier swallowed a portion of them while drinking a cup of wine to the health of Bonaparte."

All of this made Talleyrand's life more difficult. He seemed to represent a king who was losing his grip on his country, where, unfortunately, "nothing but conspiracies, secret discontent and murmuring" reigned. No matter how confident Talleyrand appeared, and he was as calm as usual, it was easy for the Prussians to cast doubts on his credibility. As they put it, the French minister either did not know the true state of the crisis back home, or he was covering up. Clearly, Talleyrand would have to step up his own campaign, so he called for his chef.

Chapter 18

THE COOK, THE PAINTER, THE BALLERINA, AND THE DIPLOMAT

I was sleeping beside a volcano, without a thought for
the lava that would pour out of it.

— METTERNICH ON THE FRENCH REVOLUTION

lying from the towers on both sides of the island harbor was Elba's brand-new flag, a white banner with a diagonal red stripe adorned with three golden bees. Napoleon himself had designed it, back in May 1814, while still on board the *Undaunted*. A tailor on the ship borrowed some sailcloth and sewed the first two flags for the new empire.

The new palace was not exactly the Tuileries. Napoleon would not be surrounded by his familiar bronze gilt chairs with griffins' heads, or his favorite table, an hourglass-shaped piece of furniture that he had invented to facilitate close collaborative work. Absent, too, was the large oil painting of King Louis XIV, with the head of the Sun King wearing a red, white, and blue republican cockade. The luxurious environment may have changed, but Napoleon was still the same man, only a little older, thinner on top, and rounder in the middle.

The forty-five-year-old emperor would still wear out the floors with his rapid pacing up and down a room, all the while firing off dictation to a secretary who sat there "as silent as another piece of furniture." The faster Napoleon spoke, the quicker he paced, and his secretary hurried to keep up.

Once he had found his house, orders flew out of his mouth in a spirited and disjointed whirlwind. Masons, carpenters, and architects were hired and ordered to complete the renovation plans, which Napoleon had also designed himself. He was adding a second floor, accessed by new pink marble stairs and consisting of two four-room suites, linked by a grand spacious salon. One of the wings was for his wife, and the other his son, who had not arrived and showed no signs of doing so. The eight windows added light to the house's most majestic room. Shutters, however, were necessary. Napoleon's palace had a tendency, in the hot Elban sun, to heat up to a "veritable furnace."

Restless as ever, Napoleon had moved in, back in late May, amid a flurry of remodeling activity in the largely unfinished construction site. Scaffolding had still covered the front facade, and the inside reeked of fresh paint. White and gold armchairs were lugged up to the salon, the workers sidestepping the cement that had not yet dried. The dark wooden chairs with green silk were going to the study, along with his mahogany desk, glass-encased bookshelves, and a gray wooden couch adorned with gold lions and covered with yellow silk.

The ceiling of the bedroom was being painted to resemble a military tent. As for other furniture, he sent a ship to the mainland and raided his sister Élisa's abandoned palaces in Tuscany, now occupied by Austrian troops. Napoleon was still angry at her for deserting him for the Allies. Napoleon's villa was to be decorated with furniture literally stolen from her, including a desk, a clock, and even her famous gilded dark oak bed. It was a superb policy, he joked. He had raided Austria and punished his sister, all at the same time.

To keep up the palace, Napoleon was hiring staff to fill the newly created positions. There was a chief cook and a chief baker to oversee the team of thirteen people preparing meals in the kitchens. There were nineteen other servants in the house, as well as valets, gardeners, coachmen, grooms, harness makers, stablemen, locksmiths, tailors, and many others in their brand-new green coats with gold braids. If the salary was not great, the positions had other benefits. Some of the kitchen boys were so proud of being near the famous man that they strutted about town like "little Napoleons."

The emperor had hired an international group, including French, Italians, Elbans, and Corsicans. A pianist from Florence was recruited as the new director of music, and a woman from a local village selected as the mistress of the wardrobe. A fellow Corsican was named court hairdresser, and his work was cut out for him. Napoleon's hair had become so lumpy and shaggy in the humidity that it was compared to candlesticks.

But there was one other important figure on the island: a soldier from Great Britain who was asked to look after Napoleon and keep in close contact with London. This was Neil Campbell, a thirty-eight-year-old officer, a Highlander by birth, who had fought the French in the West Indies, Spain, and elsewhere. By the end of the war, Campbell was serving as military attaché to the Russian tsar. He had won respect with his bravery, and in fact had been severely wounded in battle, taking a saber blow to the head and a lance point in his back. As he set off for Elba, his head was still wrapped in bandages and his right arm cast in a sling.

That such a relatively unknown man was chosen to accompany the former ruler of the Continent may seem surprising, and many have wondered about the appointment, made by no less than Castlereagh. But the truth of the matter is that few were willing to take on this responsibility. More prominent figures had already declined the post, hardly relishing the prospects of being cooped up with Napoleon on some "little island half forgotten in the sea."

The position would certainly have its difficulties. For one thing, Castlereagh had not explained very clearly what Campbell was supposed to do. It wasn't that he received secret instructions or contradictory orders, but rather that he had had almost no guidance at all. Campbell had not been officially informed of the terms of Napoleon's abdication, or even been shown the treaty itself. What he knew came from reading the newspaper and using his own initiative.

The closest Campbell came to having clear instructions was Castlereagh's general directive to keep Napoleon free from "insult and attack" and not to address him as Your Highness—only "General Bonaparte." It was a vague task that left an enormous amount to his discretion. One historian well summarized Campbell's role as part bodyguard, part spy, and part ambassador. Campbell was effectively turned loose to sink or swim, but, above all, to do so in a way that would not reflect poorly on British leadership. For what was Britain doing there, anyway, a country that had not even signed the treaty?

So there they were, an obscure young officer and the former ruler of Europe. And yet this unlikely pair would get along fairly well. Napoleon seemed to enjoy the company, calling him, in his thick Corsican accent, "Combell." They would talk about everything from Scotland to warfare, and one day, in conversation, Napoleon confessed the greatest mistake of his career: He had not made peace back in 1813, when he had had the chance to save his throne and his empire. All he had to do was to come to Prague and negotiate a settlement in good faith. He refused. "I was wrong," Napoleon said, "but let any one imagine himself in my place." After so many victories, he had faith in his army and chose "to throw the dice once more."

"I lost," Napoleon concluded, "but those who blame me have never drunk of fortune's intoxicating cup."

BACK IN VIENNA, several reports from Elba reached the congress. Talleyrand had heard from many Swiss, Italian, and other travelers who all believed that Napoleon was getting restless. "Bonaparte will not remain in banishment at Elba," one informant bluntly predicted.

With cool, polished finesse honed by years of intrigue, Talleyrand lobbied to have Napoleon moved farther away from Europe. Few, this time, were listening. Napoleon, after all, had been defeated, and banished into exile with an army of only four hundred men. The British Royal Navy was patrolling the waters, as were several French warships. Napoleon might be restless and unhappy, but what exactly could he do? The Vienna Congress hardly seemed distressed by these rumors.

But the king of France knew something that many plenipotentiaries in Vienna did not. Prior to Napoleon's arrival on Elba, the French government had stripped the island's warehouses bare, removing everything from guns and ammunition to government treasuries. Captain Thomas Ussher, the commander of the HMS *Undaunted,* which ferried the emperor into exile, already observed Napoleon's "dismay," as he put it with characteristic understatement. Other insults and injuries had been inflicted on the emperor. None of the 2 million francs promised in the Treaty of Abdication had been paid; worse still, another 10 million francs of Napoleon's personal property had been seized by the king of France.

For many royalists, Napoleon's presence on Elba alone constituted a grave security threat for the restored Bourbon dynasty, whose popularity was plummeting, particularly among soldiers and artisans, many of whom openly mourned the emperor. Leaving Napoleon on Elba was, under the circumstances, risky at best.

While Talleyrand made appeals in Vienna's salons and drawing rooms, someone at the French embassy was apparently planning to take matters into his own hands. The evidence is sketchy, and there are many unanswered questions. But papers uncovered by chambermaids inside the embassy suggest that someone there was in fact working on a plan to kidnap Napoleon. The trail leads to Talleyrand's number two, the Duke of Dalberg, if not also to Talleyrand himself.

The plan was being coordinated with the help of the French consulate in Livorno, which Talleyrand, as foreign minister, had reestablished three months before. Talleyrand had personally selected the consul, Chevalier Mariotti, a Corsican who had once provided security for Napoleon's sister Élisa, and now, for some reason, held a grudge against the Bonaparte family. Mariotti had spent the autumn extending his network of agents and informants, recruiting heavily from nearby seaports. Gradually, he had built up a fairly accurate picture of Napoleon's life on Elba, including the times when he was most vulnerable. The emperor, for instance, often sailed to the neighboring island of Pianosa, traveling with only a fraction of the guard he used at his palace, and then sleeping on board one of his ships. "It will be easy," Mariotti had informed the French embassy in late September, "to kidnap him and take him to Ile Sainte Margueritte."

Apparently, Chevalier Mariotti had hired a young Italian adventurer to pose as an olive oil merchant, travel to Elba, and arrange the abduction. On the last day of November, the "olive oil merchant" arrived at the island capital. According to his passport, he was a thirty-three-year-old Italian patriot from Lucca named Alessandro Forli, though it is by no means certain that this was his real name. He registered with authorities at the Star Fort, and then slipped away amid a crowd of other arrivals, which Britain's Neil Campbell summed up as "mysterious adventurers and disaffected characters." The oil merchant had no difficulty extending his contacts in the capital. Soon he was selling oil at Napoleon's court and waiting to act.

EARLY DECEMBER MARKED the beginning of Advent season, the four weeks of contemplation and reflection that culminate in the celebration of Christmas. During this time, authorities frowned on Catholics who acted frivolously, and some hostesses feared that this might put their salons at a disadvantage, compared with rivals of a different confession. The Duchess of Sagan, a Protestant, and Princess Bagration, who was Russian Orthodox, could continue entertaining as they liked.

Banquets and masked balls would, indeed, take place throughout the season, and there was also a marked increase in intimate dinner parties. One of the favorite sites was Friedrich von Gentz's flat on the Seilergasse. Guests climbed the steep staircase, entered the small apartment on the fourth floor, and squeezed around the table, elbow room only, in the middle of the dining room. On many occasions, with so many at the table, footmen carrying plates had difficulty maneuvering in the narrow space between the chair and the wall. Metternich, Talleyrand, Humboldt, and Princess Bagration were regulars at his highly sought-after dinners.

At one such party, there were many distinguished guests huddled around Gentz's table. During the course of the meal, one of the guests, a German-born American citizen, Dr. Justus Bollmann, started a discourse on the merits of the United States. In particular, he raved about the virtues of a republican form of government—all this to a table of ministers who represented emperors, kings, and princes. Gentz, clearly troubled with the uncomfortable choice of subjects, was said to look "as though murder had been attempted in his presence."

Dr. Bollmann had arrived in Vienna that autumn, hoping to convince some rich patron to invest in his many projects. Among other things, he had drawn up a plan for creating an Austrian national bank and another one for putting a new coin, minted in platinum, into circulation. He also wanted to start a steamship company on the Danube, and increase trade links between Austria and the New World, particularly in quicksilver, linen, watches, and musical instruments. Dinners such as this one were among the best places to make contacts and informally pitch his ideas. So far, though, he was not having any luck.

At another dinner party, hosted by Count Zichy, guests traded ghost stories, very much in vogue in the flourishing Romanticism of the day. Sitting on the floor of a drawing room in the large mansion, to the light of a single candle, Prince Radziwill was telling of a haunted castle back in Poland. Then, all of a sudden, the salon door "creaked slowly open" and then slammed shut again. As one guest in attendance described it, "ladies screamed, gentlemen leapt to their feet," and then Count Zichy, smiling, confessed that he had tied a string to the door. Everyone laughed, particularly the king of Denmark.

It was at the Zichys' where the search for new and exciting ways to pass the time already took on innovative forms. Among other things, there were games of chess in which creatures of the salon, wearing the costumes of kings, queens, bishops, knights, and pawns, moved at command on the large black-and-white squared floor.

Dorothée, too, was relishing the many opportunities for enjoyment, and a new man was often at her side, a young Austro-Bohemian aristocrat and army officer, Count Karl Clam-Martinitz. He was only twenty-two years old and already a reputed favorite of the former Allied commander, Prince Schwarzenberg. It was this same Count Clam who had had the unusual experience of having saved Napoleon's life (eight months before, in April 1814, when he had helped escort the emperor to Elba, and then rescued him from some hostile crowds of southern France).

Dorothée had caught his eye at last month's Carousel, and it was their mutual acquaintance, Gentz, who had introduced them. Count Clam was soon paying visits to the French embassy; the two were seen riding together in the Prater, and dining in restaurants, such as the fashionable Roman Empress. In honor of Dorothée's new beau, Talleyrand's chef had created a new dessert, the divine "Clam-Martinitz Torte."

Talleyrand's chef had actually served several new dishes in honor of the delegates. There was, for instance, "Bombe à la Metternich" and "Nesselrode Pudding." The latter, named after the Russian foreign minister, was a feast of chestnuts, currants, raisins, and whipped cream—and if that weren't sweet enough, it was soaked overnight in Maraschino, and served in a pineapple-sized dome.

No wonder French embassy dinners were becoming increasingly popular and well attended. All the chef's meals—those towering culinary creations, fantastic cream sauces, and rich, sweet desserts—were doing wonders for French diplomacy. "I don't need secretaries, as much as saucepans," Talleyrand was said to have quipped when asked what he required in Vienna.

Someone else helping the French image in town was the ballerina Emilia Bigottini, whose breathtaking performances on stage did not hurt the popularity of the French. This was also true for the French painter

Jean-Baptiste Isabey, who had set up his studio near Café Jungling in the Leopoldstadt, where he was busy painting the portraits of congress dignitaries.

Every Monday, when the painter opened the doors to his studio, guests flocked there to see and be seen amid the half-finished and barely started oils of leading lights that crammed the room. Carriages were parked outside the entrance and lined the street, a testament to the popularity of his studio, "the rendezvous of crowned heads," as Isabey boasted. The painter, with his wit and delightful tales of the foibles of Napoleonic Paris, was a hit.

It was, of course, Talleyrand's idea to invite the cook, the ballerina, and the painter to Vienna—and each one, in his or her own way, was reminding the Vienna Congress that the real France was the civilized champion of sweetness and light, not the Bonapartes and their gang of usurpers.

ALONG WITH THE intimate dinners and the formal feasts, other forms of entertainment were in vogue during Advent, such as the *tableaux vivants,* or "living pictures," which consisted of actors appearing on stage frozen in certain poses that depicted a well-known painting or image. La Garde-Chambonas and Prince de Ligne attended one of these tableaux in December in the grand ballroom of the imperial palace.

Arriving early to an already packed auditorium, the two were taken to their reserved seats next to Princess Marie Esterházy. When everyone was seated, an orchestra of "horns and harps" began playing, and the sovereigns made their entrance. Candles in the white and gold rococo ballroom were extinguished, so as to better focus attention onto the stage.

Scenes of history and mythology were then performed by amateur actors at the congress. There was "Louis XIV kneeling at Madame de la Vallière's feet," and then the ill-starred "Hippolytus refuting Phaedra's accusation before Theseus." The orchestra helped set the atmosphere with the works of Mozart, Haydn, and others, including Napoleon's stepdaughter Hortense, who had briefly, under the empire, been queen of Holland.

The highlight of this particular show was the depiction of the classical gods atop Mount Olympus. Parts were assigned for Jupiter, Juno, Mars, Minerva, Mercury, and the other deities. The person most suited to play

Apollo, famous for his beauty, was the Comte de Wrbna. He was a good match, except for one small thing: his mustache.

The managers tried to convince him to shave in time for the performance—no one had ever seen "the god of light wearing a distinctive hallmark of a hussar." It was a patent absurdity, the stage manager tried to argue; the whiskers had to go. Yet he was having no success, and eventually the empress of Austria intervened, persuading Count Wrbna to remove his "inconvenient ornament." At least diplomacy was making progress somewhere in Vienna, even if it was only on the illusory Mount Olympus of the Hofburg stage.

After the final "loud bravos," the sovereigns and guests went back to the palace for a ball, the actors still in costume. Guests mingled in a crowd that included the tsar, the emperor, and several kings and queens, along with the god of war, the goddess of love, and Louis XIV. The tsar, as usual, opened with a polonaise around the ballrooms, and his train of dancers marched up and down and through nearby rooms of the palace.

They passed Talleyrand, lounging in an armchair, discussing the future of Naples. Spain's Labrador and Cardinal Consalvi, along with a number of other delegates, were standing together deep in conversation. Castlereagh, leaning against a mantelpiece, was talking to an unnamed king. His brother, Lord Stewart, was roaming the rooms aimlessly, like some "golden peacock." Off in a side drawing room, the tsar and his train of dancers marched past some other diplomats locked in silent battles at the whist table.

After another "magnificent supper" at midnight, the ball ended, and the emperor's guests sauntered off "to recruit their strength for the next day by much-needed sleep."

EVENINGS CONTINUED TO be full of opportunities for entertainment, but the excitement did not end, of course, in the early morning hours when the sovereigns went to bed. Often, in fact, it was just beginning.

One night that December, for example, when La Garde-Chambonas was walking home, he took his usual route along the city walls. There on the bastions, much to his surprise, he met his good friend, the aged Prince de Ligne.

"What in Heaven's name are you doing here, Prince, at this hour of the night and in the biting cold?" La Garde-Chambonas asked with concern.

The prince, however, was not his usual self. He muttered something about love affairs, their delightful beginnings, and, afterward, their many painful moments. He was waiting for a rendezvous that apparently was not going to happen. "At your age, though," the prince said, "it was I who kept them waiting; at mine they keep me waiting; and, what's worse, they don't come."

Shaken by his wounded pride, Prince de Ligne showed a new unexpected "tinge of melancholy," noting how all things, at the end, "flee as age approaches." He was, at his advanced age, about to lose his illusions.

At the dawn of life . . . one carries the cup of pleasure to one's lips; one imagines it's going to last for ever, but years come, time flies, and delivers its Parthian darts.

"From that moment," he added, "disenchantment attends everything, the colors fade out of one's existence. Ah me, I must get used to the idea."

The prince went on about how he was no longer "good for anything." It was all a painful contrast to the days he was welcomed by Marie-Antoinette, celebrated by Catherine the Great, and sought after by Casanova. "My time is past, my world is dead."

After bidding good night to the melancholy prince, with assurances that they would meet again soon, La Garde-Chambonas walked home. On the way, he encountered another old friend, a certain "Count Z," who was just returning to his temporary residence at the hotel called the Roman Emperor.

Count Z was a young man about twenty-one years old and rich. His father, who had been a favorite of Catherine the Great, had recently died and left him a fortune. (Was this Count Zavadovsky?) La Garde-Chambonas joined him in his room and, over a few glasses, the two discussed the evening and decided to meet again the next morning, at noon, for a ride in the Prater. But when La Garde-Chambonas returned at the appointed time, he got a surprise.

With curtains drawn, the room was dark and Count Z was still in bed asleep. "Up, up! The horses are waiting for us! Or are you ill?" The count sat up and, holding back tears, said, "I lost two million roubles last night!"

"Are you mad or joking? You are in bed as I left you when I put out the lights."

The count explained that some of his friends had come by shortly afterward, relit the candles, and challenged him to a game. They had played all night.

When La Garde-Chambonas pulled back the curtains, he could see that the floor was still "littered with cards." He was determined to set things right, and went to have a word with the gamblers. No avail. Then he tried the Russian delegation, which might put some pressure on the cardsharps who had despoiled his friend of his inheritance.

He encountered more resistance than he had expected. "Is it worthwhile to make so much ado about the loss of a few boumashkis-boumashkis?" the unnamed diplomat said, referring to the money.

"Europe in Vienna sits round a table covered with a green cloth; she is gambling for states and a cast of the diplomatic dice involves the loss or gain of a hundred thousand, nay, of a million of heads. Why should not I win a few bits of paper when luck favors me?"

Count Z, it seemed, would just be another person that autumn who had lost out in the high-stakes gambling in Vienna.

Chapter 19

$\mathscr{I}$NDISCRETION

It is rumored that the congress will terminate on the 15th December.
Let the thought of the closing of the Congress be
with you every moment, as it is with me.

—Prince de Ligne on how to take advantage of the
last days of the festive peace conference

As the peacemakers struggled over Prussia's seizure of Saxony, Castlereagh was disillusioned with the apparent collapse of his strategy, stumbling around like "a traveler who has lost his way." On December 6, a dispatch from the prime minister's office in London arrived at his headquarters, and it only added to his discomfort.

The British government had learned of their minister's idiosyncratic, indeed disobedient, behavior from many sources, including both Austria and France. The prime minister, Lord Liverpool, ordered him to adhere strictly to British policy in the future. He had now to turn, volte-face, and support the Kingdom of Saxony.

Frustratingly, too, the English dispatch also ordered Castlereagh, in a sweeping and unqualified declaration, to stop antagonizing Britain's allies, meaning particularly, of course, Russia. Britain was still fighting a war across the Atlantic with the United States, Castlereagh was reminded, and the government did not want to risk another war in Europe, especially not over these issues deemed tangential to their interests. The letter clearly stated that this went for "any of the objects which have been hitherto under discussion in Vienna."

With new orders in hand, Castlereagh now faced the unpleasant task of confronting the Prussian chancellor. Uncomfortably yet firmly, Castlereagh stated that Britain's earlier acceptance of Prussian occupation would have to be withdrawn. Britain was no longer at liberty to condone this act.

Hardenberg, stunned at the abrupt change, protested against this "stab in the back." At least, the Prussian chancellor consoled himself, he still had Metternich's assent. But was Hardenberg conveniently forgetting how hedged and tentative this had been, or was he perhaps referring to an oral, off-the-record understanding?

Just a couple of days before, the Prussian chancellor had sent over a message to Metternich, affirming the importance of Prussian-Austrian relations. Hardenberg's means of communication was unusual for diplomacy, though perhaps not so out of place in this dancing congress. It was a poem, celebrating the benefits of their cooperation:

> *Away discord, vanish from our folk.*
> *Give way, thou monster with the snaky hair!*
> *A single perch atop a giant oak*
> *The double eagle and the black one share.*
>
> *From this time forth in all the German Reich*
> *One word, one thought, is uttered by this pair*
> *And where the lutes sound out in German tongue*
> *There blooms one Reich so mighty and so fair.*

On Saturday night, December 10, Hardenberg received Metternich's response: Despite the history of good relations between the two powers, which he recounted in the politest terms, Metternich notified Prussia that his country would join Britain, virtually all of Germany, and other civilized states to resist this seizure of Saxony.

Still claiming to have his friend's best interests at heart, Metternich enclosed a compromise counteroffer. Instead of granting Prussia all of Saxony, he proposed an alternative plan that involved handing over a small part of Saxony, with a population of about 330,000, and also territories farther west in the Rhineland. Together these lands would bring Prussia back up to its 1805 size, as promised, with a population of 10 million. A table of statistics was included in the proposal.

Hardenberg was outraged. One-fifth of Saxony! Prussia must have the entire region, as he still claimed that Metternich had promised. For the past several months, Hardenberg had been trying to rein in extremist Prussian generals who continually pressed their king to make even more vigorous demands. Now Hardenberg was being rewarded with this insult. Many other Prussians in town were equally angry, pouring wrath on Metternich. As Gentz put it, "All the Prussians and all their supporters cried murder."

In the meantime, steaming over the Austrian foreign minister's letter, Hardenberg proceeded to commit an act that Talleyrand would call "a most culpable indiscretion." If Metternich had decided to abandon previous agreements, then Hardenberg knew how to respond: He took all his confidential correspondence with Metternich, marched over to the Hofburg, and showed everything to the tsar.

Metternich's propensity for "tacking, hedging and flattery" was frightfully exposed. Worst of all was the letter Metternich had written in early November, defending himself against the tsar's absurd accusations—which in effect implied that the tsar was a liar. Reading these words, Alexander flew into a rage. He had been personally insulted, and demanded satisfaction. Allegedly, he slammed his sword down on the table and shouted that he would challenge Metternich to a duel.

MEANWHILE, IN HIS small flat on the Mölker Bastei, Prince de Ligne lay sick in bed. Having caught a cold in early December, he lay atop his torn mattress, surrounded by his favorite objects: his books, his etchings, and his paintings, most of which no longer had frames, only "fastened with pins to the walls." His family stayed by his bed, medicine in hand, and guests continued to pay their visits. People looked up to his third-floor window, hoping to see through the light-blue silk curtains for signs of a flickering candle.

"I know it is nature's way," the prince said to the people gathered around him. "We must leave our appointed place in the world to make room for others." After a pause, he continued, "Only leaving all those one loves, oh, this is what makes dying so painful." He muttered some final bits of gossip, and spoke of his plans to travel here and there. He asked about the affairs of the congress, and drifted off imagining himself leading troops into battle. According to one, the prince sighed from his bed, "Oh

I feel it, the soul has worn out its outer garment." Others said that he promised to give the Vienna Congress the spectacle of a field marshal's funeral. By the evening, his doctor was admitting that there was nothing more that he could do. The prince died the following morning, December 13, 1814.

Two days later, and on the day he had feared the congress would end, the prince's funeral took place at the Scottish Church on the Freyung. A large crowd gathered to pay their respects, in the church as well as outside in the square and the streets, while others looked on from balconies and upper-story windows. Marshals, generals, and officers led a long procession through town, past the palace, and out to the Kahlenburg for burial at the edge of the Vienna Woods.

Eight grenadiers pulled the coffin, on top of which were the prince's sword, his baton, his plumed hat, and an array of military orders. A horse followed, riderless and draped in black cloth "spangled with silver stars." At the back of the procession was a knight in black armor, his visor lowered, symbolizing the world of chivalry. The march was slow and silent, except for the sound of a beating drum.

IN DECEMBER, VIENNA was preparing for the Christmas season. The days were shorter, darker, and colder, with snow occasionally falling and whitening the trees. Vienna's residents, both the older and the newer adopted ones of the congress, strolled by markets, shuffled into boutiques in the inner town, and made plans for the celebration of the first Christmas without war in years.

When Agent ** entered the salon of Fanny von Arnstein, wife of a prominent banker in the firm of Arnstein and Eskeles, he had been surprised by what he found in the room: a tall fir tree, decorated with candles and gifts. This was apparently the first Christmas tree that he had ever seen, and he was not alone. Many historians have pointed out that December 1814 saw the first Christmas trees arrive in Vienna—this was called the "Berlin custom."

At the French embassy, Dorothée also convinced Talleyrand to celebrate Christmas "Berlin-style." This meant lots of marzipan, butter cookies, and, in the hallway, a giant fir tree decorated with "colorful garlands and lit candles." Another, even larger tree was placed near the famous stair-case. The French embassy hosted a party on Christmas Eve, and then cel-ebrated afterward, as Dorothée liked, in the German style, exchanging gifts that night, and not, as in Catholic France or Austria, on New Year's Eve.

Talleyrand gave Dorothée a cashmere shawl and some Meissen porce-lain, and she gave him a new Breguet watch, sent over specially from Paris. Inside was a miniature portrait of herself, by the painter Isabey. This watch, she said, would help him make it through the tedious confer-ences that sometimes seemed like they would never end.

Despite the failure of their liaison, Metternich was still thinking very much of Dorothée's older sister, Wilhelmine. That Christmas, he sent over a small jar of fancy English lemon salts that, he hoped, would help ease her migraines. "Little gifts preserve friendships," he added in a letter accompanying the package. "Bon soir, devote a good thought to me, and tell me you are mine!" he added. "I shall see you tomorrow evening."

On the Mölker Bastei, Ludwig van Beethoven continued his work on some new pieces of music, including the Polonaise in C Major (op. 89) which he dedicated to the empress of Russia and for which he received 50 ducats. Beethoven was also working on setting music for a patriotic tragedy written by the king of Prussia's private secretary, Johann Friedrich Leopold Duncker, as well as his previously written Three Violin Sonatas (op. 30), to be dedicated to the Russian tsar. Interestingly, too, Beethoven was polishing another piece that he intended to celebrate the Congress of Vienna. The title was going to be "The Choir for the Allied Princes." The congress, however, would end before he finished; the piece would, in fact, never be completed, and probably never performed—that is, until the 1990s.

On Christmas Day, Vienna's court composer Antonio Salieri conducted the music at High Mass at the palace chapel. Many Protestant delegations headed to Lutheran and Calvinist churches, and houses of worship all over town were packed. Later, Beethoven's concert featuring the Seventh Sym-phony, "The Glorious Moment," and, most popular of all, "Wellington's Victory" was repeated at the Redoutensaal, with proceeds benefiting a local hospital. This time, however, Beethoven neither conducted nor per-formed. Two days before, on the Russian tsar's birthday, he had given a concert, and, as it turned out, this would be the last time that Beethoven ever played the piano in public.

While Princess Bagration planned to host a Christmas dinner for the tsar and the Festivals Committee prepared a ball that evening in the palace, Castlereagh was entertaining at the British embassy on the Minoriten-platz. Guests included Cardinal Consalvi, Prince Eugène de Beauharnais, and the Crown Prince of Bavaria, who apparently spent the evening try-ing to speak in ancient Greek. It was only his fourth language, he boasted, and he needed to keep it fresh. It is unknown how many bottles of wine were consumed that night. When a tally was made of the wine stock in January, the British embassy had finished no fewer than ten thousand.

Baron Franz von Hager, meanwhile, was still at his office, reading the intercepted letters and working on his daily reports. It was business as usual. Some seventy pieces had been forwarded to his Cabinet Noir.

Talleyrand's embassy was no longer an impenetrable fortress. A door-man had been paid to hand over some bits of paper, and chambermaids, securely placed inside, were now roaming the embassy offices. Fortu-nately for the spies, Dalberg left many papers lying around, and not all of them were love letters or lists of his entertainment expenses, which included some 180 florins he had recently spent on the ballerina Bigot-tini. Agents also found it worthwhile to search the carriages used by the French. Comte Alexis de Noailles, in particular, was known to leave a letter or two behind.

Baron Hager had also succeeded in placing both a valet and a door-man with Humboldt, and other agents near the Russian advisers, at least those who were staying outside the Hofburg. As for Alexander, one anonymous agent was gaining valuable information from the tsar's physician, Jacob "James" Wassiliévitch Wylie. The spies even had success with the careful Castlereagh. The key there was finding out the couriers he used in sending his dispatches back to London. From here on in, Britain would be less of a stranger to the Austrian police.

On the day after Christmas, one of the most prominent guests at the congress, the king of Württemberg, left town—or, more accurately, stormed out. Frustrated by the lack of progress, the king had no desire to continue the charade. He had not gotten on well with many of his fellow sovereigns or the Viennese. He refused to tip his hat to crowds and sulked in salons after making only a token appearance. Gossipers called the huge, rude, melancholy king "the Monster," and indulged in tales of his escapades, including an alleged affair with a handsome young guardsman. Yet, as the king of Württemberg's carriage pulled out of the Hofburg early in the morning, palace servants soon had something else to talk about. The so-called Monster had dispensed snuffboxes, rings, and tips freely. His doorman received 300 florins, his hunting personnel 500, and another 1,000 went to the staff at his favorite theater, Theater an der Wien, and he did not forget the clerk in the ticket window.

DURING THE CHRISTMAS season, the humanitarian urge, for a moment, seemed to triumph over the usual squabbles and intrigues. Although it did not as yet lead to any official agreement, many leading sovereigns were coming together for a cause, a pioneering humanitarian fund-raising feast, held in the Augarten, to fight the awful problem of slavery.

The event was arranged by English admiral William Sidney Smith, who had come to the congress to represent the exiled Swedish king Gustav IV Adolf, who had been dethroned in the war, though he remained, Smith argued, the rightful king of Sweden. The English admiral was also hoping to achieve success in another cause dear to his heart: the plight of Europeans kidnapped and sold as slaves in northern Africa. He wanted the congress to abolish, once and for all, the slave trade, a stigma on the civilized world. He had seen the horrible cruelties up close during his time in the Royal Navy, and he would personally lead the crusade against these atrocities as head of a new military order that he proposed, the Knights Liberators of the Slaves in Africa.

Back in 1798, this English admiral had led resistance against Napoleon's siege at the crusader castle of Acre. "That demon Sidney Smith has made Dame Fortune jilt me!" Napoleon had said afterward. Smith had, in fact, a whole range of stories about Napoleon, or the time he escaped from a French prison, or the time, in 1807, when Smith ferried the Portuguese royal family to safety in Brazil. Many enjoyed his colorful stories, though some listeners proved less than patient when the admiral, not known for his succinct qualities, insisted on telling every detail.

Vienna society was inclined to indulge Smith, whose idiosyncrasies, for many, only added to his appeal. Crowds crammed into his apartment for his Wednesday-night salons, spilling over into the hallways and stair-cases. Smith would often appear there, or at a ball, wearing not one honorary order at a time, but proudly displaying his whole collection, sometimes strung together onto his white silk sash. Alternatively, Smith would select one order, wear it for a while, and then change later in the evening, shuffling through his collection of stars, crosses, and insignia, "so as not to insult any guest" or award he had received.

To raise awareness and drum up support for freeing slaves in North Africa, Smith was organizing a series of events, and one of the first was a remarkable banquet scheduled for December 29, 1814. It was a gigantic picnic—a "humanitarian feast"—that would occur in the palace in the Augarten. Guests would pay 3 ducats for the banquet, and an additional 10 guldens for the palace ball afterward, with all proceeds going toward ransoming slaves.

No fewer than 150 kings, princes, generals, diplomats, and other celebrities had accepted his invitation, including the Russian tsar, the Prussian king, and many other leading figures at the congress. They were certainly attracted to the cause. Part of the curiosity, too, it was said, was the experience of paying for a meal themselves, "a novelty of such great charm that not one of the crowned heads . . . would miss it."

Seated around a long table in the form of a horseshoe, the guests enjoyed some of the finest delicacies of the Austrian empire. The food had been catered by Vienna restaurant owner Herr Jann, and some of the best wine from the Rhineland, Italy, and Hungary circulated liberally. The walls of the palace were covered with flags of the assembled states, and two orchestras entertained with national anthems. Royal entrances were further celebrated with a trumpet fanfare, the heralds blowing their horns on horseback and showing the admiral's flair for drama. As La Garde-Chambonas said with admiration, it seemed like something from "the theater of Shakespeare."

The only uncomfortable moment was when Herr Jann's waiter, carry-ing a silver plate with a bill on top, approached the king of Bavaria, Max-imilian I Joseph. The king, well known for his generosity, reached down into his waistcoat pocket to pay the donation. When he came up empty-handed, he shifted his weight and fumbled around in other pockets, soon realizing that he did not, in fact, have any money on him.

With the waiter still standing over his shoulder, "impatiently jingling his money against the dish," the king glanced at one of his courtiers, Count Charles Rechberg, down the table, hoping that he would come to the rescue. Rechberg, however, was deep in discussion with Wilhelm von Humboldt about a new book: his own, two-volume *Les peuples de la Russie*. Another nervous glance down the table, but Rechberg was still oblivious. The king's "torture reached a point where," as Count La Garde-Chambonas jokingly put it, "he would have liked to shout, Three ducats! Three ducats! A kingdom for three ducats!"

The farce ended when the Russian tsar came to the rescue and paid the king's fee. The waiter was "a better bill collector than a courtier," someone observed, and the whole table roared with laughter—the king of Bavaria, afterward, the loudest of all. Admiral Smith also had good reason to be happy. His philanthropic feast had netted several thousand for the cause of fighting slavery.

Chapter 20

KING OF THE SUBURBS

Too frightened to fight each other, too stupid to agree.

—TALLEYRAND ON THE GREAT POWERS AT THE CONGRESS OF VIENNA

With only a few days left in the year, the congress continued to take one step forward, two back, as Cardinal Consalvi noted. The delegates had reached a stalemate over Saxony. While Talleyrand advocated law and justice, Metternich was trying to solve the dispute by striking a bargain.

After the last outburst, when Hardenberg stormed over to the tsar with a portfolio of confidential letters, the Austrian foreign minister had not given up on finding another way whereby Prussia could reach its promised population of 10 million without having to commit the crime of seizing the whole of Saxony. There were, in fact, many possibilities, and Metternich hoped that Prussia would be intrigued enough at least to consider them.

Of these options, the plan that Metternich preferred would offer territory along the Rhine to return Prussia to its promised population size of 10 million "souls"—this was the word for population, the yardstick measure adopted by the congress in carving up the map. Metternich also threw in another five hundred thousand souls to sweeten the deal. This was an interesting proposal, Prussia admitted, but some of the population figures for the territories on the list seemed rather inflated, and given Metternich's track record, Prussia was not inclined to take him at his word.

For weeks, diplomats had pored over numbers, and, typically, they ended up rejecting the statistics claimed by the other side. Accuracy was not easy, even with the best of intentions, given all the loss of life and the vast movements of peoples in the war. For this reason, Metternich proposed another way to resolve the conflict: Why not create an Evaluations Committee to look more closely into the population figures in all the territories, and help obtain the best estimates possible?

Castlereagh also liked the idea of the committee, and he came over to Kaunitz Palace in late December to introduce the issue with Talleyrand. The French minister's support was crucial. Even if he was still outside the inner circle, Talleyrand enjoyed rising popularity for his defense of Saxony and commanded a veritable legion of admiring smaller states that looked to him for leadership. Fortunately, Castlereagh found, Talleyrand did not oppose the idea outright. On the contrary, he liked it, provided, of course, that the committee did not lose sight of the importance of principles in the labyrinth of numbers.

Talleyrand suggested that this new committee should begin, first of all, by recognizing the rights of the king of Saxony. The committee should also consider other factors in evaluating a territory than a simple head count. Peasants "without capital, land or industry," he said, ought not to be counted the same as the prosperous inhabitants of the Rhine, or some other relatively affluent part of Germany. Next, Talleyrand went further and proposed that he, Castlereagh, and Metternich make an agreement to support Saxony.

"An agreement?" Castlereagh asked, taken somewhat aback. "It is, then, an alliance that you are proposing?"

"This agreement can very well be made without an alliance; but it shall be an alliance if you wish," Talleyrand answered. "For my part, I have no objection."

"But an alliance supposes war, or may lead to it, and we ought to do everything to avoid war," Castlereagh said, mindful of his recent orders from London.

"I agree with you," Talleyrand replied. "We ought to do everything, except to sacrifice honor, justice, and the future of Europe."

"War would be regarded with disfavor among us," Castlereagh replied.

"War would be popular with you if it had a great object—one truly European."

Remarkably, when Talleyrand mentioned this idea of a possible British-French-Austrian alliance, Castlereagh, to his pleasure, had not refused outright. He had not even seemed startled. In fact, given his own frustrations with the deadlock, Castlereagh had also been considering the possibilities of working in closer collaboration with France.

The next day, Talleyrand was updated on the proposed Evaluations Committee. There was good news and bad news. The good news was that the idea of establishing it had been accepted; the bad news was that the committee had already been appointed and France had not been invited to participate.

Correctly predicting that this information would provoke an unpleasant scene, Castlereagh had not wanted to convey this message himself. Instead, he sent over his brother, Lord Stewart, who, though not exactly known for his tact or finesse, made a gallant effort to break the news gently.

When Talleyrand learned that the French had been blackballed, he demanded to know who opposed his membership.

"It is not my brother," Stewart replied.

"Who is it, then?"

Hesitating, Stewart started, "Well—it is." He paused before the words escaped his mouth: "the Allies."

At this point, Talleyrand lost his patience. Since the Big Four were still acting as if they were at war against France, he would just let them sort out the congress themselves. He had had enough.

"Europe shall learn what has occurred," Talleyrand threatened. He would make sure that everyone learned how Castlereagh had abandoned Saxony and Poland, and then "rejected the aid by which he might have saved them." All this was highly sensitive, given the recent criticism Castlereagh had received back home.

The conversation ended abruptly, and Stewart rushed back to the British embassy to inform his brother.

Talleyrand's outburst—threatening to call for his horses then and there and leave Vienna immediately, as one English embassy official described it—had made an impression. When the Evaluations Committee met a second time, in late December 1814, Talleyrand's colleague, the Duke of Dalberg, sat comfortably at the table as France's representative.

WHILE THE FOREIGN ministers disputed the number of people in a given province, the Great Powers decided to arrange one last set of meetings to resolve the Saxon crisis peacefully. This problem had, as Gentz put it, "eclipsed" all the others in importance. It was urgent to move quickly before either Prussia consolidated its hold over the seized territory or the congress ended in a fruitless stalemate.

During the meeting on December 30, the Russians proposed, yet again, that all of Saxony would go to Prussia. The tsar, by way of compromise, promised to free the king of Saxony and transfer him to a newly carved-out territory on the left bank of the Rhine. The Saxon king on the Rhine, with a proposed new capital of Bonn, would also receive Luxembourg, and many towns of the former archbishopric of Trier, including Cologne.

Austria was not pleased with these terms. The plan still involved destroying Saxony, handing over the entire territory to Prussia, and leaving its own realm exposed. As for the proposal about the Rhine, was it really a good idea to spirit away a legitimate king and set him up elsewhere in some newfangled kingdom? Why not wait and see what the newly appointed Evaluations Committee could find?

Three full months into the congress, the peacemakers were as divided as ever, and, in fact, they were still lining up in their original constellations. Russia and Prussia stood on one side, and Austria and Britain on the other.

Now, after hearing the Russian proposal, Britain and Austria countered with one of their own. As Saxony was a matter of European concern, why not ask other powers for their opinion? Why not, for that matter, consult the king of Saxony?

At this point, Hardenberg exclaimed that he would rather end the entire Congress of Vienna than allow such a scene to transpire. And should Prussia's temporary occupation be made permanent, then the Prussians would, he added, consider any further opposition as "tantamount to a declaration of war!"

Castlereagh was losing his patience. Such a threat might intimidate "a Power trembling for its existence," he replied, but it would have the opposite effect on a country that valued its dignity, like Great Britain. If that was the way Prussia wanted to conduct business, it might as well "break off the Congress" right now. The tension in the room, Gentz said, felt like "an enormous weight suspended over our heads." The last meeting of 1814 had ended in chaos.

LATER THAT EVENING, the Russian diplomat Count Andrei Razumovsky was throwing his eagerly anticipated end-of-the-year bash. The count was a former Russian ambassador to Vienna, renowned for his wit, good looks, cosmopolitan good manners, and, above all, his enormous fortune. He is remembered in music circles today for his love of the arts, patronizing such Viennese luminaries as Haydn and Mozart. At the time of the congress, he was a generous supporter of Beethoven (hence the "Razumovsky Quartets"), and one of the last noblemen to have his own private orchestra.

The count had, in fact, inherited two large fortunes, one from an uncle who had been the lover of Catherine the Great and a second from another uncle, the lover (and perhaps also secret husband) of Empress Elizabeth. Count Razumovsky had built a large mansion—or, more accurately, a palace—on the outskirts of Vienna. With parties during the congress attended by an array of royalty, the Russian host was earning his own honorary title: "King of the Suburbs."

Some seven hundred guests would make their way out to his palace in the Landstrasse on the thirtieth, where he had turned "a piece of wasteland" into "an Eden of a princely residence." Carriages passed along his own boulevard, manicured park, and bridge to Vienna's "new Winter Palace." Inside, guests marveled at its marble halls, mirrored office, mosaic floor, and library full of rare books and manuscripts, not to mention the hanging staircase. There were galleries of masterpieces, including works by Raphael, Rubens, and Van Dyck, and an entire room devoted to works of the Italian sculptor Antonio Canova. Razumovsky's palace seemed like "a temple erected to art."

The last party at the Razumovskys', three weeks before, had certainly been memorable. The tsar had himself hosted, and no expense was spared. Sturgeon were brought from the Volga, oysters from Ostend, truffles from France, oranges from Sicily, and strawberries from England. On each table was a bowl of cherries, transported that week across Europe from the tsar's greenhouses back in Russia. Guests also admired the pineapples, arranged in the form of a pyramid with exuberance "such as had never before been served on any board." The partygoers danced until dawn, and looked forward to the count's next bash. Little did they know it would end in tragedy.

Early in the morning hours of December 31, Razumovsky's palace caught fire, erupting like a "Vesuvius in full blast." As ringing church bells warned the town of the emergency, Vienna's fire department galloped out to the Landstrasse as quickly as possible. Smoke and flames were soon everywhere, the copper roof glowing a "fiery red."

Volunteers hacked their way through the count's manicured shrubberies to hasten the efforts to fight the fire. Hearing of the emergency, Emperor Francis had come at once, as did other congress members. Talleyrand hurried out as well, because Dorothée had gone to the party with her friend Count Karl Clam-Martinitz, and neither one had yet returned home.

Fortunately, the majority of the partygoers had already left the palace by the time the fire had spread and the "burning beams" began crashing down. But some people were still inside, and the whereabouts of others still unknown. Razumovsky himself could thank a loyal valet and his smelling spices for waking him out of his deep sleep.

Valets and friends alike were frantically tossing the count's belongings out the second-story windows, dropping "dozens of vests, trousers and coats, one after the other," down to the "muddy puddles." Desperate now to save anything, they hurled other goods out the windows. "Expensively bound books, chandeliers, marble tabletops, alabaster vases, silverware, bric-a-brac, paintings, even clocks" crashed down, many shattering on impact, while others were "carted away by the mobs."

Artistic treasures by the hundreds were lost forever, including those in the splendid Canova Hall, consisting solely of the sculptor's marble works. "That's the gallery that held the Dutch genre painting," Dorothée said, safely outside the palace, as she saw a wing crash down. "I sat in it for supper." Tragically, two men died that night, daring chimney sweeps who had entered the burning labyrinth with the hope of rescuing at least some of the embassy papers.

The search for the origins of the fire degenerated into a din of confused and animated speculation. Some believed that the blaze began in the kitchen, the bakery, or maybe with the straw in the stables. Others suggested that it was sabotage. Investigators eventually settled on a flaw in the heating system—or, as one fumed, "the *French* heating system"—installed the previous year. Count Razumovsky had added a wooden extension to his palace for the party, and the fire, it was believed, probably started there.

"One of the ducts concealed in the walls had become overheated by the huge fires maintained around the clock," Friedrich von Schönholz explained, and this "over-heated duct had first charred, then set fire to a wooden beam." The fire then spread ferociously among the combination of wood, wax, and cloth in so many rooms, and, further, the "tapestries and draperies now became the fuses that carried the fire . . . to the remotest corners of the palace."

The tsar had returned to the scene that morning, arriving, it was noted, after the other sovereigns. Walking past the ground, carved with deep ruts made by fire wagons and strewn with plumed hats in the mud, the tsar found Razumovsky, in sable coat and velvet hat, sitting alone under a tree, his head down and sobbing.

All that was left of two decades of the count's collecting and construction were charred, smoking ruins and a few blackened treasures that had been rescued. "This is truly a great misfortune, but we are all in God's hands," the tsar said, trying to comfort the count. But then, in the next breath, he was overheard adding, "This may happen to my knights' hall, also hot-air heated." Maybe it was diplomatic frustrations that solicited the next tactless remark: "That's what we get for aping the French!"

METTERNICH HAD CHOSEN not to attend the Razumovsky ball. He could not bear to participate in an event that was intended to celebrate Russia and its tsar. His relationship with Alexander was as tense as ever.

Happily, Alexander had at least backed down from challenging him to a duel, talked out of it, apparently, by Emperor Francis. The last thing the congress needed, the Austrian emperor had said, was the spectacle of a duel between the Tsar of All the Russias and the foreign minister of His Apostolic Majesty. But the argument that worked most effectively was that a duel would actually hurt Alexander's honor, as it implied a sense of equality between the combatants. The tsar replied that, in any case, he would have no further dealings with a minister "as untrustworthy as Metternich."

Having missed the Razumovsky ball, Metternich was pleading with the Duchess of Sagan for a meeting. He was still desperate to hear from her. He needed her company and her insight, especially given the strains he felt around the diplomacy table. "Write me a word," he said, "I am quite sad, and I certainly need all my strength at this moment!"

In yet another note from the Chancellery, Metternich begged for one last chance to see the duchess before the New Year. It was urgent, he emphasized with the desperation of someone with a superstitious reverence for symbolic dates, but he pleaded in vain. The duchess replied that she was "sick as a dog" and would probably not be well again for a few days.

Interestingly, however, Gentz had stopped by the Palm Palace that night and had a drink with the duchess, as he recorded in his diary. She seemed well enough, surrounded in her drawing room by her sister Dorothée, Count Clam-Martinitz, and many others, including Prince Alfred von Windischgrätz.

It must have been a lonely New Year's Eve for Prince Metternich. He tried a third time to arrange a meeting, adding that "I do not want the first day of the new year 1815 to pass without seeing you."

Indeed, before the champagne toasts were clinked that night, a package would arrive for the duchess from a Vienna jeweler's shop. When the duchess opened the small silk box, she found a handsome gold bracelet, an exquisite piece of craftsmanship, shining with a diamond, a ruby, an emerald, and an amethyst. Each stone symbolically conveyed a message in those romantic times: The diamond and the ruby stood for love and fidelity; the other two were their respective birthstones, amethyst for the duchess and emerald for himself. It had arrived, on Metternich's instructions, "at the stroke of midnight."

Metternich had written an accompanying letter, explaining another symbolism in his gift. Each stone had been engraved with the letter *G*, which stood for the words that, as he put it, "I had hoped to say as I fastened it on your wrist this evening: *Gott gebe Gnade, Glück, Gedeihen*" ("May God grant you Grace, Happiness, and Prosperity.")

What Metternich did that night, after finishing this letter, is not known. The songwriter La Garde-Chambonas claimed to have seen him at Count Zichy's New Year's Eve ball, and that is possible, though the young man was notoriously sketchy when it came to connecting people and places with specific dates. It was probably more likely that when the foreign minister laid down his goose pen at eleven o'clock that night, he rang out the end of the year all alone in the Chancellery office.

Chapter 21

ℛEQUIEM

*I agree with you that Talleyrand cannot be relied upon, and yet
I know not on whom His Majesty can better depend.*

— CASTLEREAGH

After the New Year celebrations, which marked the opening of the Carnival season, Vienna was eagerly anticipating the upcoming social calendar. There was a full schedule of events, including balls, hunts, feasts, plays, concerts, tableaux vivants, and a host of other entertainments to lighten the dark months of winter.

Early morning on New Year's Day, a cold and tired messenger arrived at Castlereagh's embassy on the Minoritenplatz. It had been a hard six-day journey through central Europe, the last leg through rain, snow, and ice. The courier was bringing news that Britain's war with the United States had now ended. On Christmas Eve in Ghent, British and American diplomats had finally agreed on peace.

This was extraordinary news for Castlereagh, who, bogged down with his own negotiations, was thrilled to be released from a difficult war on the other side of the world. Castlereagh sent a messenger over to Metternich and Talleyrand immediately. It was time for a meeting.

"I hastened to offer [Castlereagh] my congratulations," Talleyrand said on hearing the news of the treaty, and then he added, "I also congratulated myself on the event." He knew its importance right away.

With this war over, Great Britain no longer had to divide its attention over such a large amount of territory. Frigates, men-of-war, and ships of the line tied up in the New World would now be freed en masse, and, potentially, so would a large war chest of millions of pounds sterling. Should Prussia insist on pressing its demands, Great Britain could now devote the full might of the British war machine to supporting its diplomacy.

When the British foreign minister was congratulated on the peace agreement at a ball that evening at the Hofburg, Castlereagh enigmatically replied, "The golden age begins." Stories of this response swept through Vienna's salons and drawing rooms, along with speculation on what exactly the foreign secretary meant. Was he implying that the plenipotentiaries would soon reach agreement and avert war? Or was it, as one member of the English delegation sneered, only a reference to the likelihood of more English gold flowing to allies who promised to do his bidding? Castlereagh's words suddenly carried more meaning than before.

Good news had indeed rung in the New Year, but Talleyrand was glad to report, in a dispatch to the king of France, that the end of the war between Britain and the United States was in fact only "the precursor of a still more fortunate event." Enjoying the boost in confidence, Castlereagh had approached Talleyrand with a bold plan: Britain was now willing to offer an alliance with none other than its mortal enemy France.

Castlereagh had been upset at the Prussian and Russian behavior in the last meetings. Prussian arrogance seemed intolerable, and its delegation insisted on adopting a "very warlike" stance unsuitable for negotiation. Castlereagh felt that there was no other way to avoid an all-out war than this pact. The only problem was that it was unauthorized, and again, strictly speaking, against his government's orders.

The whole negotiation was conducted under the strictest secrecy, and the resulting treaty hurriedly written up and signed on January 3, 1815. According to its terms, Britain, Austria, and France pledged to support each other in the case of an attack from any other power, and contribute 150,000 troops, though Britain reserved the right to replace its quota of soldiers with additional financing. There was nothing in the treaty that bound the powers to join an ally in an attack. It was a purely defensive alliance.

That night, at a crowded soiree held at the British embassy, as two Italians strummed a guitar and fiddled on a violin, Talleyrand played cards as usual, Metternich surrounded himself with women, and Castlereagh danced a frantic Scottish reel. The three ministers were not seen together, even for a minute. Few could have imagined that they had just signed a secret agreement that would have a great impact on the negotiations.

Talleyrand, in particular, had reason to rejoice. After only three and a half months in town, representing a shunned, defeated power, he had maneuvered his way right into the council chamber of the Great Powers. The congress had reached such an impasse that Britain and Austria had preferred to work with an enemy they had fought for almost a quarter of a century, rather than with their own allies of the victorious coalition.

RUMORS OF SOME sort of secret pact were soon circulating throughout Vienna, though no one had any confirmation, and they were lost in a sea of other rumors: that war would break out at any moment; the widowed king of Prussia would soon remarry (and his next wife, some wildly predicted, would be Marie Louise!); the tsar had caught a venereal disease; almost every leading figure of the congress would be sacked, and a new team would be appointed to wrap up the negotiations.

Then, all of a sudden, at one of the first meetings of the Big Four in early January, Metternich, rather nonchalantly, proposed that Talleyrand be allowed to join in the deliberations. Castlereagh supported the motion. But while the Prussians fumed and fumbled, there was another surprise that day. The Russian delegation actually gave way and agreed to admit Talleyrand to the committee.

But why would Russia suddenly be so willing to cooperate with Britain and Austria? This is a difficult and important question, because the tsar was now, in many ways, unmistakably proving more accommo- dating. He was, as Metternich put it, experiencing one of his "periodic evolutions of the mind." The tsar was now even willing to discuss Poland, something that he had so far only adamantly refused. Why?

Certainly, the awareness that Britain was no longer restrained by a war across the seas had played a role in causing the tsar to begin to doubt the wisdom of fully supporting Prussia. Alexander had also suspected that some sort of deal had been struck between Britain, Austria, and France. When he met Castlereagh on January 7, for instance, he asked him directly about the rumored alliance, but Castlereagh neither acknowledged nor denied it. He said only that if the tsar "acted on paci- fick [*sic*] principles he would have nothing to fear."

In addition, over the last few weeks, Alexander had seemed more serious and reflective, tired of the frivolous parties and endless bickering. Some historians claim that the tsar was returning to a full-fledged mysticism that had flourished back in 1812 when Napoleon invaded Russia. Alexander was receiving some remarkable letters from an admirer, and apparently he devoured their contents.

The author of these letters was Baroness Julie von Krüdener, a fifty-year-old widow from Latvia, who had preached a fiery apocalyptic mysticism nourished in cold Baltic winters. In letter after letter, Krüdener had instructed the tsar to remember his "divine mission," just as he had in the dark days of Napoleon's invasion. No matter what the tsar suffered at the congress, Krüdener assured him that she knew the "deep and striking beauties in the Emperor's soul."

The flattering letters were increasing in frequency and intensity that winter, reaching the tsar in Vienna with the help of one of Krüdener's well-placed admirers, Roxanne Stourdza, his wife's lady-in-waiting. Alexander had come to look forward to each new letter, and then discussing every shade of meaning with this lady-in-waiting. They would meet in private, away from his foreign policy advisers, and usually in her quarters, a tiny room on the fourth floor of the Hofburg. There they conversed, as the tsar saw it, as "spiritual husband and wife."

Sometimes the letters contained prophecies, or dark troubling visions that awaited the dancing congress: "You do not know what a terrible year 1815 is going to be," Krüdener had predicted that autumn.

> Do you suppose that the Congress will finish its labors? Undeceive yourself. The emperor Napoleon will leave his island. He will be more powerful than ever, but those who support him will be pursued, persecuted and punished. They will not know where to lay their heads.

To the tsar, she was a "divine prophetess," and he hoped, one day, to meet her in person.

Yet even with this rekindled interest in mysticism, there is probably also another factor for the tsar's abrupt change in attitude: Alexander was more cooperative, it seems, because he was tiring of the Prussian alliance. When Hardenberg had shown Metternich's private letters to him a few weeks before, the Austrian foreign minister had retaliated by allowing the tsar to read one of Hardenberg's own letters. In this piece, the Prussian minister had written, in a striking indiscretion, that he was only supporting Russian policy in Poland because it was official Prussian policy, and also because "it would make Russia weaker."

As the tsar looked back over the last few months, he had cooperated with Prussian desire to gain territory, and now he was rewarded, he felt, by treachery from his so-called ally—an ally, the tsar was increasingly convinced, whose aggression would only drag Russia into an unwanted war over Saxony. Alexander, feeling like a man of peace once again, was disillusioned with the Prussians. He now had a reason, or at least a rationalization, for abandoning his ally.

So, indeed, there were many reasons for the tsar's sudden burst of cooperation with Britain and Austria at the congress. Unfortunately for Prussia, she would now suffer the consequences, and find herself an angry but isolated power. As for Talleyrand, he was ready to join the Directing Committee. The former Big Four was now going to be a Big Five, the real center of power and decision making at the Vienna Congress.

MEANWHILE, METTERNICH WAS trying to move on with his life and finally put closure on his ill-starred affair with the Duchess of Sagan. Despite his midnight gift on New Year's Eve, the duchess clearly still preferred Prince Alfred, and Metternich was trying to resign himself to this reality. The same day that he signed the secret treaty with Britain and France, Metternich wrote another letter to the duchess that tried to put the irrational into a meaningful perspective.

I was your lover for two years. I loved you—I ended by adoring you. You ceased even wishing me well the day when I began to love you—natural enough course of human affairs! I was not disheartened; I did not ask you for love at all but only for some certainty—either refusal or hope. You did not cease giving me [hope]; you nourished that feeling in me that you saw as more than imperious; you encouraged it even while you saw it exhaust those faculties of which my honor demanded the full use.

"Called to lead twenty million men," he added, "I should have known how to conduct myself." Metternich was indeed trying to put the past behind him.

Metternich was also busy in January using the secret treaty to great advantage and recruiting other states to join the coalition against Prussia. Bavaria signed on, and so did many smaller German states that wanted a guarantee of their safety. Some were so frightened of Prussia and eager to join that they swore not to deal with any other state without first discussing the matter with Austria. The treaty was thus not only helping break the deadlock of the Vienna Congress, but also, in Metternich's hands, likely to pay rich dividends for Austrian influence in central Europe.

Esteem for Talleyrand had also been growing on the wake of his support for Saxony and his newfound position on the Directing Committee. The French foreign minister likewise knew how to seize this opportunity. The embassy at Kaunitz Palace would entertain even more flamboyantly than before.

One of his great successes that winter was actually a somber event: Talleyrand staged a requiem for the dethroned king of France, Louis XVI, who was guillotined in 1793. January 21, 1815, marked the twenty-second year since that "day of horror and eternal mourning." Talleyrand proposed that Vienna acknowledge the anniversary with a "solemn expiatory service."

When the emperor of Austria heard of Talleyrand's plans for a ceremony, he offered his help—Louis XVI was, after all, his uncle, and Marie-Antoinette his aunt. With the emperor's support, Talleyrand knew that he would now probably have his choice of locations for the service, and it would, moreover, be packed. Sure enough, Talleyrand was offered Vienna's largest and most stately church, the medieval Gothic masterpiece St. Stephen's.

With the emperor's blessing, too, Talleyrand had gained access to the Festivals Committee. Stalwarts of the committee would be turned loose and their "melancholy zeal" would adorn St. Stephen's for a day of public mourning. The cathedral itself was draped in black velvet. A pyramid was placed in the center, with four statues at its base, symbolizing "France sunk in grief, Europe shedding tears, Religion holding the Will of Louis XVI, and Hope raising her eyes to heaven." On every pillar in the church hung the Bourbon crest.

The emperor of Austria appeared, as promised, in mourning. Although the empress could not attend due to her poor health, the other sovereigns had appeared on their platform draped in black velvet and decorated with silver tassels. Members of the noble order Knights of the Golden Fleece and Vienna Congress participants were placed in the choir. Seats in the nave were reserved for other prominent figures, many of the ladies dressed in "flowing veils" and ushered to their pews by the handsome French ambassador, Marquis de la Tour du Pin. Seats open to the public were quickly taken, the crowds everywhere in thick fur and sable coats.

The emperor's confessor, the archbishop of Vienna, celebrated Mass. Antonio Salieri, Vienna's *Hofkapellmeister,* led the chorus of 250 voices, and Talleyrand's piano player, Sigismund Neukomm, composed the music. Another Frenchman in town, the parish priest of St. Anne's, Abbé de Zaignelins, delivered the address, neither a funeral oration nor a lecture nor a sermon. The theme was "The earth shall learn to hold the Lord's name in awe."

The French priest gave a stirring speech that touted the glorious fourteen-hundred-year history of the French monarchy—and the horrors the Revolution committed against the legitimate dynasty. It was a speech that Talleyrand, almost certainly, wrote or edited himself. True to form, Talleyrand had made sure that both the Russian tsar and the king of Prussia were seated prominently in the front of the cathedral. That way, they would not miss the lesson and, equally important, no one could avoid seeing their participation.

Twenty-two years after his execution, Louis XVI finally received his memorial service. Like many of Talleyrand's other projects, the requiem worked on several levels. It honored the past, championed the importance of legitimacy, and, at the same time, subtly though forcefully promoted causes dear to France—from preserving the *legitimate* king of Saxony to restoring the *legitimate* king of Naples. The post-requiem soiree and banquet offered further opportunities for gathering in remembrance of the guillotined king. Although it was an expensive day, indeed, Talleyrand had managed to have all of Vienna celebrate France and its royal dynasty. It was a marvelous success.

Chapter 22

THE GREAT SLEIGH RIDE

One must keep an eye on his allies, no less than on his enemy.

— METTERNICH

On the morning of January 22, Vienna's cold weather had finally created that magical combination of "heavy snowfall" and hard, "biting frost" necessary for the long-awaited sleigh ride. Thirtysome large sleighs were pulled into the Hofburg courtyard, Josefsplatz, each as gilded and grand as any Habsburg carriage. Congress dignitaries were scheduled to arrive in the early afternoon for a ride through the streets of Vienna, the cobblestones covered in snow. They would continue out to Schönbrunn Palace for a gigantic winter party.

The crowds had come to the central square, early in the morning, to take a look at the spectacular sleighs, shining with a bright gold set off by emerald-green velvet upholstery and fine silver bells. Each sleigh was pulled by a team of horses, "caparisoned in tiger skins and rich furs," and each sleigh spared nothing that "taste could imagine and money buy." "Silk, velvet, gold everywhere" was how one observer summed up these veritable winter chariots.

As in many other functions at the congress, the Festivals Committee had struggled with a way to solve the complicated protocol for a sleigh ride that included an emperor, an empress, a tsar, a tsarina, and many kings, princes, and other dignitaries. Who, for instance, would ride first? Who would share sleighs, and how could they allot partners and positions in the procession without offending tender sensibilities? In the end, the Festivals Committee had struck upon a simple solution to the intricate problems: lottery. Let fate decide.

Looking at the results of the draw, however, it seems that the mandate of fate had been tweaked by a committee eager to avoid diplomatic pitfalls. The tsar, who had expressed his displeasure with this sumptuous expedition, had miraculously drawn his current love interest, the salon celebrity Princess Gabrielle Auersperg. The king of Prussia, equally sour at the event, was paired with his favorite, Countess Julie Zichy.

A special cavalry squadron marched in front of the procession, followed by a "leviathan of a sled" containing a small band blasting trumpets and banging on kettledrums. The first of the congress dignitaries were the emperor of Austria and the empress of Russia, dressed in a fur "trimmed in ermine and green silk," a matching plumed green cap, and diamonds once worn by Catherine the Great. Purple, rose, and amaranth-blue fur coats were also all the rage at the sleigh ride; the gentlemen preferred warm Polish long coats also edged with "expensive furs."

Given the biting cold wind that day, some dignitaries had traded their place in the sleigh procession for a seat in a closed carriage. Empress Maria Ludovika, who had fallen ill again recently, opted for the carriage ride to the palace, as did the king and queen of Bavaria. That was fine, and actually probably a good thing, the Festivals Committee knew. A few sleighs should be pulled empty as reserves, in case a sleigh broke down out in the countryside. In the back of the procession was another monstrous sleigh, carrying a second band playing "war-like tunes."

About two o'clock, the emperors, kings, queens, musicians, and other guests climbed into the sleighs. After a grand trumpet fanfare, the Great Sleigh Ride was ready to begin.

Before the sleighs swished out of Josefsplatz, however, there was an unexpected delay. A carriage had slammed into the square and blocked the designated route. When the driver was politely asked to make way for the royal procession, he refused. Another request for the coachman to move his carriage was rebuffed. The court chamberlain then sent one of his trusted officials over to investigate. It turns out that the mysterious haughty coachman was none other than Britain's ambassador, Lord Stewart, and he was apparently drunk.

An order from the emperor did the trick, and off the royal sleighs went, gliding on the packed snow at a stately walking pace, which would allow the curious crowds to watch the parade of sovereigns and sleighs. Once the expedition passed out of the inner town, the drivers turned the horses loose and they galloped, at top speed, to Schönbrunn Palace for the banquet and the ball.

About halfway out of town, the procession stopped at a monument to the Polish king Jon III Sobieski, whose heroic ride with an army of reinforcements in September of 1683 had saved Vienna from the famous siege by the Turks. This was a good opportunity to repair some of the sleighs, whose delicate frames with golden sphinxes on their axles had suffered on the roads, and it was also, undoubtedly, a good opportunity for some subtle diplomacy. The Sobieski monument called to mind the many sacrifices and services that Poland had rendered Europe—a timely advertisement, no doubt, given that Vienna's dignitaries were then weighing the future of Poland.

When they arrived and parked their sleighs, the summer palace seemed a winter wonderland. The lake lay frozen like a "polished mirror." Some skaters entertained with acrobatic jumps, others performed dances on the ice, and one group, dressed as Venetian gondoliers, steered sleighs decked out as gondolas. Others pulled imaginative constructions, such as the "make-believe sleigh" in the form of a swan with silver wings. Enterprising merchants skated out onto the lake, hoping to sell some "fortifying refreshments."

While the guards at the palace tried to prevent the curious crowds from disturbing the festivities, a certain member of the British embassy stole the show with his flashy gliding and twirling, "whirls, loops, and figure-eights." Apparently he was a member of a London skating club, and he really drew admiration when he skated the initials of ladies on the ice. Particularly popular, too, were the women dressed as Dutch milkmaids who gracefully waltzed on the frozen lake.

The party continued at the palace theater with a performance of the opera *Cinderella*, complete with special ballets written for the occasion. Marie Louise and her son were believed to have left the palace earlier that morning, not wanting to witness the elaborate celebration. Another rumor was that she was there the whole time, peering through a specially cut "peephole." After all, some members of the sleigh party swore that they had seen her son, the little prince, on his sled, flying down the palace hillside. The party concluded in the drawing rooms, decorated with orange trees, myrtles, and plants from the emperor's greenhouse.

It was an extraordinary spectacle—surely the most grandiose sleigh ride in history. Count August de La Garde-Chambonas was, as usual, highly impressed, noting that "it was, indeed, a picture which for many centuries will not be repeated." His friend Comte de Witt agreed that it was a "beautiful, marvelous and elegant affair." His only complaint was that the Festivals Committee should have also built an ice palace on top of the lake.

After the "intoxicating pleasures" of Schönbrunn, the revelers returned to central Vienna in a jingling torchlit sleigh ride, racing to make it back for yet another masked ball at the Hofburg. There "they ride with our fifty percent and we must pay more each day," one Vienna resident was overheard complaining, referring to a controversial new tax levied earlier that month, a 50 percent increase needed to pay for this congress, which many thought should have been wrapped up by now.

INDEED, WITH A secret treaty, a more cooperative tsar, and a new majority on the expanded Directing Committee, it seemed that the congress could now finish its pressing business. Few things, however, were easy or simple at the Congress of Vienna.

Britain, Austria, and France had pledged to resist aggression with one voice, but admittedly that left a considerable amount of discretion in interpreting what was considered aggression and how much they should resist. Talleyrand was, of course, urging that they take a firm approach and force Prussia to back down from its demands, even it if meant war. Law, justice, and public opinion were on their side, Talleyrand argued, and a showdown would only rally the rest of Europe to their cause.

Castlereagh disagreed. He did not wish to provoke Prussia, and preferred instead to forge a compromise that he believed would produce a better peace for Britain and Europe. As he saw it, if Prussia wanted a big chunk of Saxony, including the town of Leipzig and the key fortresses of Erfurt and Torgau, why not give it to them? Why risk war over something that he called, at one point, "a mere question of details"? The British government had ordered him to preserve the Kingdom of Saxony, or, more precisely "a kernel of Saxony." He was planning to do just that, though if he had his way, that kernel would be small indeed.

Metternich was stuck in the middle, though now leaning toward Talleyrand. The disputes among the secret allies were growing increasingly acrimonious, and Castlereagh was again finding himself isolated among his partners. On January 24, as the debate about the size of Prussian gains raged, Castlereagh made another desperate gesture and told his allies that they would either have to accept his proposal for a small Saxony or England would leave the peace conference at once.

Actually, Castlereagh was not bluffing, no matter how far-fetched the threat might sound. Under great pressure from London, Castlereagh had just learned that he would soon be leaving Vienna anyway. British policy at the congress was proving highly unpopular, and the opposition party back home, the Whigs, was criticizing them more and more. Castlereagh would have to return to London to defend himself. A government order for his recall, he knew, would arrive at any time.

Desperate to accomplish something before he left, and feeling close to a breakthrough, Castlereagh had backed himself into a corner. If he could just solve the Poland-Saxony crisis, many of the other complicated negotiations would very likely fall into place. He could not imagine returning to London and a hostile House of Commons without anything tangible to show.

So while working frantically in a final diplomatic blitz, and once again finding himself outvoted in the alliance, Castlereagh was ready to make another unexpected move: He swallowed his pride and asked for help from the Russian tsar. Perhaps he could have a word with the king of Prussia and convince him to accept a compromise. So, ironically, the Russian colossus that he feared and worked so energetically to resist would now be his best hope for success.

In *DE L'ALLEMAGNE,* PUBLISHED one year before the congress, Madame de Staël complained about all the time lost in Vienna's fashionable salons:

> Time is wasted on getting dressed for these parties, it's wasted on traveling to them, on the staircases waiting for one's carriage, on spending three hours at table; and in these innumerable gatherings one hears nothing beyond conventional phrases.

The whole experience, which could be repeated three, four, or even more times a week, simply devoured time, not to mention dulling the mind in an endless round of superficiality. The salon, Madame de Staël suspected, was "a clever invention by mediocrity to annul spiritual faculties."

By January 1815, Friedrich von Gentz was another who shared the disillusionment about the tedious follies that sometimes had to be endured in a salon or drawing room. At first, he had been captivated by the environment. He was overjoyed to be in the midst of the beautiful young people who, as he put it, "hold the world in their hands." He later paused and pondered, "Good God, how did I ever get in with this crowd?"

Four months into the Vienna Congress, however, his enthusiasm had begun to fade. Gentz had started to resent the talk about peace, legitimacy, and rule of law, which often seemed to ring hollow. It was all "fine-sounding nonsense," he concluded. The real purpose of the peace conference was only to divide the spoils. Hardened by the revelation, Gentz now laughed at the foibles of this diplomatic farce: "I enjoy the whole spectacle as though it were given for my own private entertainment."

Not all salons were simply glamorous and fashionable centers of intrigue. On Tuesday evenings, Fanny von Arnstein hosted a salon on the second floor of her mansion on the Hoher Markt, overlooking the stands of the fish, crab, herring and geese sellers below. Arnstein was a fifty-six-year-old Jewish woman who had settled in Vienna in the reign of Joseph II. As her friend Karl August Varnhagen, an assistant with the Prussian delegation, described her, she was "a tall, slim figure, radiant with beauty and grace." Her husband, Nathan, was a partner in the prominent firm Arnstein and Eskeles, which managed the accounts for several embassies during the congress; her father had been banker to the previous king of Prussia, Frederick William II.

The Arnstein salon enjoyed a reputation of being the most intellectually stimulating of the major salons. On any given night, guests might encounter the Prussian ambassador, Wilhelm von Humboldt, the pope's delegate, Cardinal Consalvi, or the young poet Friedrich von Schlegel, soon to be famous in Romantic circles and then serving in a minor capacity with the Austrian delegation. Famous physicians also made appearances, such as the opinionated magnetist David Koreff, and an early champion of the smallpox vaccine, Jean Carro, who was then known more for his chest of powders and perfumes as the "doctor of beauty."

Carl Bertuch, who represented German publishing firms and book dealers at the congress, particularly enjoyed the concerts at the Arnstein salon, which were invariably accompanied by generous supplies of "tea, lemonade, almond milk, ice cream, and light pastries." Another hit was Fanny von Arnstein's collection of wax figures. On one occasion that January, Arnstein opened her cabinet of wax figures, which depicted the gods of classical, Norse, and Egyptian mythology, along with Odysseus, Daedalus, the Queen of the Night, and the Four Seasons. The lighting was superb, and the wax figures looked lifelike as usual. But toward the end of the evening, the guests were startled when the wax figures suddenly stirred. Everyone marveled at the ability of the actors who posed as wax dolls.

One person who sometimes attended the Arnstein salon was a young assistant for the Hesse-Cassel delegation, the folklorist and philologist Jacob Grimm. Highly critical of the diplomacy and the drawing room, which he was experiencing up close from his apartment near the domes of the Karlskirche, south of the city center, Grimm described the Vienna Congress to his brother as a maze of rudeness and courtesy, recklessness and reserve, that, so far, had very little to show for its efforts.

In his memoirs, Grimm dismissed his stay at the congress as being "without usefulness." He found his work at the embassy frustrating and mind-numbing, especially the copying of mundane documents. Yet Grimm was also able to spend time hunting for lost manuscripts and pursuing his studies. He was learning Serbian, beginning Czech, and familiarizing himself with the rich traditions of Hungarian and Bohemian folklore. He enjoyed his Wednesday evenings with a group of like-minded writers, intellectuals, and booksellers at the tavern Zum Strobelkopf, where they discussed everything over "a passable roast beef and poor beer and wine."

Interestingly, in addition to preparing *The Spanish Romances* for publication and translating the Norse *Songs of the Elder Edda,* Grimm found an early manuscript of the medieval German epic *Nibelungenlied* ("the *Hohenems* codici") that differed from previous known versions. He was also busy extending his contacts among scholars and working to establish an international folklore society to collect, among other things, folk songs, legends, proverbs, jokes, games, superstitions, idioms, customs, nursery rhymes, ghost stories, and, as he put it, "children's tales about giants, dwarfs, monsters, princes, and princesses, enchanted and redeemed, devils, treasures and wishing-caps." Despite long hours in the office, Grimm was setting the basis for some highly productive years of scholarship that would follow his stay at the Congress of Vienna.

MEANWHILE, ON ELBA, Napoleon had not heard from his wife and son for months, and started to fear that they were being held against their will. He suspected that few of his letters were actually reaching them in Vienna. Although he sent multiple copies, with different messengers, and signed the envelopes with fake names, all his efforts to elude police spies continued to fail.

Napoleon first attributed the cruel obstruction of communications to a faceless Austrian bureaucracy. As time passed, however, Napoleon would blame instead his father-in-law, Emperor Francis, and the Austrian foreign minister, Metternich. Indeed, Marie Louise's secretary, Méneval, soon affirmed that Marie Louise was no longer at liberty to write or receive his letters.

In the meantime, other members of his family had arrived on Elba. His mother, Maria Letizia, had come in early autumn on board the *Grasshopper* and immediately made an impression on the islanders. "I have seen eminent people more intimidated in front of her than in front of the Emperor," one said of the sixty-four-year-old Corsican matron. Napoleon and his mother often played cards and dominoes, with Napoleon, of course, cheating as he tended to do.

Napoleon's favorite sister, thirty-four-year-old Pauline, also arrived on Elba, as she had promised. She brought along her reputation as the wild Bonaparte, having twice modeled nude or seminude for the sculptor Canova. One of the works, now at the Borghese Gallery, depicts her as the goddess Venus, reclining on a couch. By a mechanical device inside the base, the sculpture itself used to rotate to reveal her charms from many angles. Canova also added a thin layer of wax that, when the work was viewed by candlelight, added a more glistening lifelike appearance to the marble. Pauline would certainly enliven court festivities, not to mention the island's social life.

Visitors were coming more frequently to Napoleon's small empire. One day, back in September, rumors circulated that Marie Louise and the little prince had actually arrived on Elba, landing one night in a secluded olive grove at San Giovanni. Eyewitnesses had reportedly seen them travel with the emperor to a remote mountain hermitage, Madonna del Monte, on the western part of the island. A little boy was said to be calling Napoleon "Papa Emperor."

What the curious Elbans had witnessed was not the arrival of Marie Louise and the king of Rome, but in fact Napoleon's Polish mistress, Maria Walewska, and his illegitimate son Alexandre. It is not surprising that the rumors flourished. The two women were of similar age (Maria Walewska was two years older) and looked vaguely similar from a distance; Alexandre was about a year older than the former king of Rome.

Napoleon and Maria Walewska had first met seven years before, when the emperor passed through Warsaw and showed an obvious infatuation with the young Polish woman, then an eighteen-year-old newlywed. Her husband, an elderly patriot, had encouraged her to use Napoleon's interest to the advantage of Polish independence, and she had reluctantly agreed. They had carried on an affair intermittently ever since, and after Napoleon's abdication, Walewska had offered to join him on Elba. He had declined, still hoping, of course, that Marie Louise would arrive. Historians have long suspected that her trip had more than romantic or family purposes, and she was secretly carrying messages between Napoleon and Murat in Naples, though no direct evidence has yet surfaced to confirm that. At any rate, it was just a short weekend visit.

Napoleon was busy on many other projects—building roads, devising schemes for a fire brigade, and even building a kiln to fire bricks for future construction on the island. He was planning a new garbage service to remove the filth that rotted in the streets and to combat some nasty diseases, like typhus, that thrived on the island. In addition, Napoleon was planning a series of aqueducts to bring fresh water to the capital and planting mulberry trees along the sides of the road out to the nearby village of San Martino, hoping, in the long run, that they would furnish enough worms to create a new silk industry. Oaks, pines, and olive trees were also planted, as were chestnuts to stem the erosion on the mountainsides. Napoleon was even landscaping along Portoferraio's main road, striving to create an Elban equivalent of the elegant Champs-Élysées.

Indeed, Napoleon had been running his sixteen-mile-long island with the energy and authority with which he used to rule Europe. Ever since he had arrived, he had marched troops, performed daily maneuvers, and even, on one occasion back in May, brought some forty soldiers and invaded a nearby island. Pianosa, some fifteen miles to the southwest, had been conquered and incorporated into the Elban empire.

This "conquest" was admittedly only a small island, deserted except for its wild goats trampling about some ancient Roman ruins. The island was too dangerous to be settled, and, unlike Elba, it did not have natural defenses and was easily raided. The island was well-named: Pianosa means "flat land."

What it had was fertile soil. Napoleon intended to create a colony to supply grain to Elba. Also on Pianosa, Napoleon planned a hunting reserve, a stud farm to breed horses, and a retirement home for veterans who had served the state. Loyal Elbans had been sent over to start building the island he envisioned.

Pianosa had at least one other advantage that is often forgotten. Unlike Elba's harbor, Portoferraio, which lay in a bay that was easy to close and trap, Pianosa's harbor faced the open sea. If Napoleon were to ever find himself in danger, or wish to leave Elba in secret, he could escape to this island and from there set sail without anyone being too certain of his destination.

Chapter 23

"ODIOUS AND CRIMINAL TRAFFICK IN HUMAN FLESH"

*It is not the business of England to collect trophies
but to restore Europe to peaceful habits.*

—CASTLEREAGH

By early February, Vienna's Carnival season was in full swing. Every night, there was a dinner, ball, concert, play, or some other form of entertainment dreamed up by the Festivals Committee or an embassy around town. Congress dignitaries found themselves shuffling diplomatically from party to party, salon to salon. Big events were pushed later into the evening, to allow everyone to squeeze in as many events as possible, and seldom, it seemed, did any major celebration end before sunrise. It was like "living six weeks in a kettledrum."

The weather—like the spirits—was also improving. "Magnificent weather, spring temperature," Gentz scribbled in his diary that February, "the finest sun in the world; winter such as I've never seen." As the delegates bid farewell to their furs and Polish long coats, the strollers came out again in great numbers. The Graben, the Prater, the Bastions—all the main promenades were once again "positively swarming with people."

At the salon of Princess Bagration, the Russian tsar and Countess Flora Wrbna-Kageneck were in a discussion that somehow veered onto the issue of who could dress the fastest, men or women. The tsar said men were faster, and the countess disagreed. There was one way to find out. And so a few days later, a dressing duel took place at the fashionable salon of Countess Zichy. Both the tsar and the countess showed up in plain attire, giving proof that there were no tricks or cheating. Then, at the given signal, each went into a separate dressing room for the race, or behind a divider placed in the center of the room—eyewitness accounts do not agree.

Several minutes later, the tsar appeared proudly in his full gala uniform shining with "orders and decorations." Snickers were heard, and he looked around the room to see the countess, already there, looking like a vision of the ancien régime. She had not forgotten powder, perfume, rouge, bouquets, beauty spots, or anything else. The countess, it was clear, had won the wager.

"How clever and amusing all this is!" Humboldt snapped sarcastically, marveling how low the congress had fallen. "I am deadly tired of all this partying," he had long complained.

It was during the Carnival season, with its masks, costumes, and sophisticated debauchery, that Vienna received the news that Castlereagh's successor at the congress was to be one of the most popular men alive: the Duke of Wellington, the famous general with a string of victories to his credit in the Spanish campaign, and not a single loss in the war. Vienna society was thrilled.

Wellington was, like Castlereagh, a conservative Tory who had played a vital role in defeating Napoleon. After the war, he had been appointed British ambassador to France, not at first sight the most tactful choice. At any rate, Wellington was well informed. British dispatches between London and Vienna had passed through his office in Paris, the former home of Napoleon's sister Pauline, which Wellington had bought and turned into the British embassy, as it has remained ever since.

Only named a duke nine months before, Wellington was born Arthur Wesley, the third son and fourth surviving child in a large landowning family that belonged to the Anglo-Saxon Protestant Ascendancy of Ireland. His father, Garret Wesley, 1st Earl of Mornington, was professor of music at Trinity College, Dublin. Like Napoleon, born Napoleone Buonaparte, Arthur had changed his name, taking an old-fashioned form of Wellesley that had been his family's name for centuries. The duke always played down his origins. Born in Ireland, he once said, did not make one Irish any more than being born in a barn meant you were a horse.

He was tall and lean with broad shoulders, chestnut-brown hair, and blue eyes. When he appeared in his scarlet field marshal uniform, with its "gold-embroidered velvet collar" and his array of medals, Wellington looked like the "Iron Duke" of his later reputation (the nickname only appeared in the 1820s when he set up a new wrought-iron railing in front of his London house). One thing that did not fit the image, though, was his laugh. Wellington reportedly let out a slightly hysterical cackle like a "horse with whooping cough."

Wellington had been a quiet and introverted young boy who excelled at the violin. He had drifted into a military career after a lackluster record as a student, and after becoming a soldier, he destroyed his violin in 1793, never to play again. He advanced quickly in the military ranks, serving eight years in India, before the Spanish campaign that really won his reputation. Wellington had won big at Salamanca and Vitoria, and, in 1814, he drove Napoleon's army out of Spain.

Confident and distinguished, he could also be smug, brash, icy, and haughty. Few suggested that he was a budding philosopher. When one man asked his views about whether humanity creates the environment, or vice versa, Wellington merely replied, "It would take a volume to answer your question [and] I must go and take off my muddy boots." Others noted that Wellington was not the most engaging conversationalist. He was a stern "master of monosyllables."

Vienna salons were immediately competing for the honor of hosting the new celebrity in town, the excitement coming in part at least because this arrival "supplied something new, for which they were really at a loss." With the famous opera singer and society sweetheart Giuseppina Grassini on his arm, the duke entered Vienna as the "Victor of the World."

Talleyrand won the honor of holding an introductory dinner, Saturday night, February 4, at Kaunitz Palace. Sixty guests feasted on the chef's excellent meal, to the accompaniment of Neukomm's music. Most of the leading figures of the congress were there; in an embassy drawing room, decorated in white carnations and azaleas, the illustrious guests paid their respects to the Duke of Wellington, and, by implication, the host, Talleyrand, and his country, France.

A series of events for the new head of the British delegation followed. Metternich hosted him the next day with a dinner, and then a ball for a few hundred guests. Castlereagh, of course, hosted him at a reception, and then another one that evening, at a salon of the rich banking family the Herzes, "since nowadays," one disgruntled aristocrat observed, "the world's great ones gather at the homes of the moneymen."

With his replacement already in town, Castlereagh's days were numbered. Ironically, only a few months before, Castlereagh could not wait to leave Vienna. Now, with hopes of progress on several diplomatic fronts, Castlereagh wanted to finish the negotiations himself. But sure enough, the order came from London demanding his return. Castlereagh made plans to hand over the portfolios to his celebrated successor, though he stalled as much as he could.

THERE WAS ONE issue that Castlereagh was particularly anxious to address before returning to London: the terrible practice of African slavery. To the horror of an increasing number of reformers, there was an entire industry built on the buying, selling, and trading of human beings.

Conditions were brutal at every stage of the business—human beings seized, bound in chains, strapped together in a yoke, and then subjected to a perilous forced march to the coast. If they managed to survive this ordeal, fighting off extreme heat during the day and cold during the night, the captives were then loaded onto slave vessels, crammed below deck in dark cellar compartments, for a nightmare ocean voyage without sufficient water, air, or space. Sharp irons tore at the skin, and the smell made it difficult to breathe, the stench so bad that it often crept into the porous wood of the ship. Cries, shrieks, and groans further "rendered the whole a scene of horror almost inconceivable."

Once the survivors, often no more than about two-thirds of the cargo, arrived in the New World, whether the United States, Brazil, the Caribbean, or elsewhere, the vast majority would spend the rest of their lives laboring unfreely on large tobacco, rice, coffee, cotton, and especially difficult sugar plantations. They were at all times at the mercy of their masters.

Many reformers had hoped that the Congress of Vienna would abolish this practice entirely, and Castlereagh was one delegate who pushed for action. The problem was that he faced many special-interest groups that benefited from slavery and resisted any limits imposed on their lucrative business. Fortunes and indeed entire industries were built on "the Trade," as it was known, and outlawing it was not going to be easy.

Slave captains, plantation owners, and other defenders had come up with many arguments why they should be allowed to continue business as usual. There would be lost income, the deterioration of tax revenue, and even, some prophesied, the collapse of the British economy. One merchant declared hysterically that banning the trade would "render the City of London one scene of bankruptcy and ruin."

Others pointed out that should the slaves be freed, they would likely rise up, murder their former masters, and then set the entire British West Indies on fire. Recent riots in Jamaica and Haiti provided a chilling reminder, and self-styled pragmatists urged the eager reformers to move slowly on this issue.

Back in December, Talleyrand proposed that the Great Powers establish a committee to look into the question of the slave trade more closely, but this had been blocked by the protests of Spain and Portugal. In the middle of January, Castlereagh renewed the call for a committee, and this time one was appointed by the Committee of Eight. Abolitionists and vested interests alike were represented at the regular meetings, though Castlereagh sometimes felt as if he were the only real spokesman for abolition.

Specifically, one immediate problem that this Slavery Commission encountered was enforcement. If the Vienna Congress banned the slave trade, how would they make sure that this policy was obeyed? What would prevent renegade captains from smuggling contraband slaves, or other nations, for that matter, from trying to meet the enormous demand? Britain's answer—the Royal Navy—did not reassure its colleagues.

In Castlereagh's plan, naval officers would take it upon themselves to board vessels and search for transgressors, a particularly sensitive issue given the resentment this practice had long caused. Britain was the undisputed mistress of the sea, and opponents of the measure tried to position Castlereagh's countrymen as arrogant islanders trying to dominate even more. Wasn't the right to board and search *any* trading vessel all that the British·really wanted, some asked, and wasn't it shameful how they cloaked these ambitions under the idealistic pretext of championing the abolition of slavery?

Another argument that opponents of any restriction on the slave trade used was that Britain, already well stocked with slaves in its colonies, wanted to impose a ban to cement its hold over the lucrative colonial trade. To agree to this abolition was then to submit to losing, permanently, to the British.

While trying to overcome this resistance, the British delegation was also constantly being pressed from the government back home to advance further and faster. Around the country, speeches were made, petitions signed, and many letters written, all demanding that the abomination be ended and pressuring the British government to achieve something in Vienna. In Castlereagh's view, all these efforts, no matter how well-meaning, were actually hampering his ability to make progress.

The word was out that England was desperate, and Castlereagh found himself forced to bargain for each and every concession, no matter how small. States were dangling out hints of possible support—for a price, that is. Talleyrand was not immune to this temptation. Castlereagh offered France the beautiful island of Trinidad in return for his support, but Talleyrand did not at first bother to answer, and when he did, one month later, it was a refusal. The French minister held out for what he really wanted: help in restoring the Bourbon dynasty to Naples. Castlereagh eventually agreed.

It was frustrating and tiresome business wringing out concessions from other powers, and Castlereagh's experiences made him seriously consider employing other tactics. For instance, should the Vienna peacemakers be unwilling to cooperate on banning the slave trade, Castlereagh was looking into the possibility of employing economic sanctions— probably the first ever in peacetime. He did, in fact, threaten, as a last resort, to lay an embargo against the very lucrative colonial products of any country that persisted in this "immoral and pernicious" activity.

With the hope of avoiding such a drastic move and most likely igniting a chain of escalating retaliations, Castlereagh went about his diplomacy with verve, making concession after concession. Countries in southern Europe proved to be most difficult to win over. Portugal finally agreed to end the trade in eight years, in return for 300,000 pounds. Spain, too, showed willingness to agree, though Spain's price seemed odd. In return for banning the slave trade, Spain's diplomats demanded Louisiana.

As Spain's argument went, the U.S. purchase of Louisiana in 1803 was illegal. President Thomas Jefferson had bought the enormous region that comprises some thirteen states today from Napoleon, and, at one stroke, more than doubled the size of the United States. But Napoleon did not have a clean lease to sell, Spain argued. He had only acquired Louisiana three years before from Spain, which had sold it under duress. Besides, Napoleon had promised never to part with the territory until he had first offered Spain the chance to buy it back. He had not done that, either. The Vienna Congress should, the Spanish legal team argued, correct this injustice.

In other words, Spain was arguing that over half of the United States was held inappropriately, if not also illegally. If Britain would support Spain on regaining its rightful territory, then Spain would return the good measure and ban the slave trade.

Such were the challenges that Castlereagh had to face in fighting against this "odious and criminal Traffick in Human flesh." Whatever the merits of Spain's arguments—and its legal advisers, of course, claimed that they had a strong case—this was hardly a realistic proposal at that time. Britain had, only weeks before, ended a war with the United States and had no desire to renew one, especially over the Louisiana Purchase. Castlereagh politely turned down Spain's proposal and offered instead a tidy 400,000 pounds. Spain accepted.

On February 8, 1815, just days before his expected departure, Castlereagh could finally point to some success. France, Portugal, Spain, and others had come on board, and the Great Powers issued a joint declaration condemning the practice as "repugnant to the principles of humanity and universal morality." They further agreed in the importance of putting an end to a scourge that had so long "desolated Africa, degraded Europe and afflicted humanity." The slave trade should be abolished as soon as possible; France promised to do so in five years, Spain and Portugal agreed on eight years. Admittedly, this was slow and tentative, an abolition of neither slavery nor even of the trade itself. Yet it was a start, and human rights, for the first time, had been made a subject of a peace conference.

Chapter 24

BEFORE THE CAKE WAS CUT

Everything is over or nearly over. All the clouds are dispersed.
Europe owes the happy issue of the negotiations to
the departure of Lord Castlereagh.

—CONVERSATION OVERHEARD AT A BALL IN EARLY 1815

The arrival of the Duke of Wellington had not only affected Vienna's diplomatic activity and social calendar; it was also posing a problem to the painter Jean-Baptiste Isabey, who was trying to capture the congress on canvas. He had been working for some time, and he had finally found a way to balance all the strong personalities, many of them patrons, into one single painting, and yet not offend national sensibilities or fragile egos.

The painting, which depicted the delegates gathered in a conference room, turned out to be a compromise in the best spirit of Vienna diplomacy. Metternich, the president of the Congress, draws the eye, as the only standing figure in the foreground. Castlereagh, though, commands the center, sitting with his legs gracefully crossed and elbow resting on the table. The light shining through the window, however, falls onto Talleyrand, sitting across the table with his dress sword at his side. An empty chair on both his right and left make him further stand out, as do the nearby figures who look to him, just as many of the smaller powers had sought his leadership the last few months.

As Isabey was putting the finishing touches to his composition, he had to figure out what to do about the fact that the Duke of Wellington was now also in town. Starting over was out of the question. Omitting a man of his stature was equally impossible. Yet it was not easy to incorporate him into a canvas on which all the best places had already been taken. The painter's solution was simple and elegant: Why not make the painting commemorate the Duke of Wellington's arrival in Vienna?

That way, the duke could simply be inserted on the far left side of the painting, without any insult to his position. As for the duke's reluctance to be painted from a side angle (he was self-conscious about his nose), Isabey had overcome that with a well-targeted compliment: Didn't Wellington look like the handsome and chivalric Henry IV? Pleased with this comparison, Wellington accepted, joking that Isabey was a "good enough diplomat to take part in the Congress."

The painter also had to apply his finesse to convince Humboldt to enter the studio. The Prussian ambassador hated to have his portrait made, and, sure enough, he first declined, claiming that he had "too ugly a face ever to spend a penny" on a portrait. With this statement, Isabey saw his opportunity and emphasized that he would not "ask the slightest recompense for the pleasant trouble I am going to take." Isabey only wanted "the favor of a few sittings."

"Oh, is that all?" Humboldt quickly came around when he realized it would not cost him anything. "You can have as many sittings as you like."

Later, many congratulated Isabey on his portrait, particularly the fine job with Humboldt. The Prussian did not pay anything, as agreed, and Isabey got his revenge, Humboldt joked, by painting "an excellent likeness of me."

Few could complain of the treatment received from Isabey's flattering brush. This famous painting of the Congress of Vienna was pleasing to all, though typical of this peace conference, the scene was purely imaginary. The group of twenty-three delegates had never met in exactly this way before. Isabey had painted the portraits of each figure individually, and then later assembled the whole group together. And so, symbolically, this simulated image would commemorate a congress that never was.

OVER THE COURSE of the next few weeks, the foreign ministers of all the Great Powers worked hard to finish the negotiations, and their efforts, in turn, showed how misleading it was to imply that the congress only danced. They danced, of course, but they also carried substantial workloads. In an attempt to reach an agreement in early February, Castlereagh

was toiling "day and night." Prussia's Hardenberg was working himself
to exhaustion, often collapsing in his chair, falling asleep at his desk, and,
at times, breaking down into tears. Metternich, too, felt glued to his desk,
"like a convict on his chain." The same, of course, went for their assistants.

That February, the Great Powers had finally reached an agreement on
Poland: A kingdom was, in fact, to be established. Its territory was to
come mostly from the former Duchy of Warsaw, though Austria kept
Galicia, while Prussia retained Posen and Gdánsk, and Russia most of its
share of eastern Poland. Kraków was to remain outside as a "free, independent and strictly neutral" city. The new Kingdom of Poland was indeed
much smaller than the tsar had promised (only 3.2 million people, instead
of 10 or 11 million). Its new constitution, moreover, still made Poland
"irrevocably attached to Russia" and its king was to be Tsar Alexander.
While this compromise left many unhappy, the discontent was not spread
equally, and many Polish patriots felt greatly disillusioned.

On February 11, three days after the condemnation of the slave trade,
some real results were finally seen on Saxony as well. Despite all the
Prussian claims the last several months, the Kingdom of Saxony would in
fact be saved. Frederick Augustus would remain its king, and Dresden its
capital. Remarkably, too, Saxony would hang on to the thriving town of
Leipzig and retain about three-fifths of its kingdom, including lands in the
east and south, which were actually its richest and most populous regions.

Prussia would have to settle for the remaining two-fifths of Saxon territory, and one-third of its population, a far cry from its demands for the
entire kingdom, which only months before had looked so certain. Prussia
would not gain any of the largest towns, or the strategic mountain passageways into Bohemia, but instead it would receive a string of fortresses
commanding the waterways of eastern Germany. (These included Erfurt,
Torgau on the upper Elbe, and also the historic fortress town of Witten-
berg, birthplace of the Protestant Reformation.)

To help ease the pain of this deal, the Russian tsar offered some additional territory from his share of Poland, including the fortress town of
Thorn, straddling the Vistula River. The Great Powers had also awarded
Prussia Westphalia, which had recently been ruled by Napoleon's younger
brother Jérôme, and they added Swedish Pomerania, in the north. Former lands of the archbishop of Trier were also transferred to Prussia, as

well as areas from neighboring Hanover and the Netherlands ceded in a last-minute offer made on Castlereagh's initiative. Most important, the Allies handed over a sizable chunk of the Rhineland from the old Holy Roman Empire, including the city of Cologne, with its beautiful soaring medieval cathedral and its prime location on a major central European trade route. Prussia had received its promised 10 million population, and Britain had succeeded in getting a strong Prussia.

Significantly, in one of the most important results of the congress, Prussia had shifted from being a state centered in the east to one pointing to the west—and this, in fact, very much against its own wishes. Significantly, too, Prussia was brought into much closer contact with France. So while the Congress had buried the centuries-old Bourbon-Habsburg rivalry, it had also, by bringing Prussia into the Rhineland, helped create another one that would soon haunt European history.

Few Prussians at the time, however, saw any reason to celebrate. Many were furious. "Where is Germany going to get its security in the future," Humboldt's wife asked him pointedly, if they did not gain Saxony? The army had been promised this region, and they had occupied it, only to be turned out without any significant resistance. No true soldier, Field Marshal Gebhard von Blücher had said, could ever again wear the Prussian uniform with any honor. When the news was announced, Hardenberg's windows back in Berlin were smashed by an angry mob.

Yet while many accused the Prussian delegation of being tricked, corrupted, or simply too weak to resist the "siren charms" of Metternich and the allies, Humboldt realized that there was another side to this story. Despite his formal protests and complaints, he wrote to his wife that Prussia was actually benefiting more by gaining the Rhineland, rather than Saxony. This region was more populous, more productive, and, on the whole, much more valuable. "Prussia is now the greatest German power," he boasted. He was right about the value of the Rhineland, but no one at that time knew the full extent of the wealth, in iron and coal, that would be found in that territory. Fifty years later, the region that they had accepted so reluctantly would be a powerful engine of Prussian industrial might.

For the moment, there would be "two Prussias," as Humboldt saw it, the eastern and the western, separated by sharp cultural and historical differences. Geographically, Prussia would not even be linked together, but sprawled out over and around other independent states, such as Hanover. It was an odd-shaped country. But Humboldt was not too concerned. This unnatural state of affairs would not last long. "With the first war that comes," he added ominously, "Prussia will fill in the gaps."

As DIPLOMATS DISCUSSED affairs in the middle of a ballroom, or the corner of a salon, conversations often ended abruptly, or quickly shifted onto other subjects when someone approached. Spies were still everywhere, and often ended up observing, reporting on, and even following each other.

In this environment, with work and pleasure intermingling in intrigue-rich salons, many agents were working overtime. The police dossiers give an insight into a day in the life of an agent in early February. After a night at the theater, Agent ** paid a visit to the tsar's physician, always a good source for understanding the mood of the Russian embassy, and then he topped it off at a palace ball. Afterward, he went from "one salon to another" in search of entertainment and information, arriving back home at five in the morning.

As Agent ** circulated in high society, or tried to catch a carriage ride with someone well placed, other agents were finding valuable information in the taverns and restaurants. The delicatessen Jean de Paris on Herrengasse was one popular place to swap gossip as the guests "titillated their palate and ruined their stomach." Spies also continued their work posing as servants, or purchasing information from them. Chambermaids, footmen, porters, and coachmen remained the eyes and ears of the Austrian police.

"I am the victim of the lowest kind of espionage," Marie Louise's secretary, Baron Méneval, complained. "A swarm of ignoble spies crawl around me and study my gestures, my steps, and my face." The Prussian adviser General Jomini was still warning of the letter opening and advising his correspondents: "Write only what you would like to see in the newspapers." Knowledge of this advice, of course, comes from one of his intercepted letters.

By early February, Vienna had moved into the season of Lent and the forty days of reflection and contemplation that culminate in the celebration of Easter. Many delegates and guests lined up to see Zacharias Werner deliver his colorful sermons in his flamboyant style, dropping onto his knees, springing up into the air, shouting, and then falling silent.

Lotteries were another form of entertainment that flourished at the congress, never more than during Lent, when the masquerade balls stopped. At one of these occasions, each invitee would bring a gift and then draw a lot for one of the other presents in the salon. "Everyone contributes and everyone wins" was how Talleyrand described it. Guests might walk home with a jewel case, a mosaic box, a fine Persian rug, a set of porcelain vases, or virtually anything at all.

Castlereagh was probably, at least in part, glad to be leaving this vanity fair behind. He had stalled as long as possible—two grueling weeks that witnessed the resolution of the Poland-Saxony crisis and the condemnation of the slave trade. Before he packed his bags and officially handed over all responsibility to the Duke of Wellington, however, the foreign secretary would make one last initiative. He was working on a plan to resolve the Russian-Turkish conflict that sometimes raged and sometimes smoldered over the Black Sea, the Danube, the Balkans, and virtually anywhere the two empires came into contact.

The British foreign secretary wanted the congress to agree to guarantee peace on the basis of the status quo in this turbulent area that would soon be known as the "powder keg of Europe." This would in turn keep Turkey alive, and at the same time help constrain the appetites of an expansionist tsar poised to pick up gains from the crumbling empire. But to Castlereagh's dismay, his plan was being opposed by the sultan of Turkey. Castlereagh spent one of his last meetings in Vienna, literally on his last day in town, pressing unsuccessfully for an agreement. The question was thus left unresolved, and would unfortunately cause a great deal of tension and bloodshed over the next century.

On February 15, after leaving behind parting gifts to his colleagues, among other things a jeweled snuffbox with a handsome miniature portrait of himself on the inside, Castlereagh's carriage clanked its way out of the Minoritenplatz and headed out of Vienna. He was disappointed with the overall results of the conference and feared that the peace that they had worked so hard to settle would not last more than two years. Moreover, he was returning to London, where he would have to answer for his actions before a hostile Parliament.

WITH POLAND AND Saxony solved at last, the congress would surely now finish "cutting up the cake," as some had termed the efforts. Decisions were, in fact, soon reached on other pending issues as well. One of the first was the Netherlands. As the deal was worked out, Holland was to be re-created as a kingdom, and given Belgium, Luxembourg, and other nearby territories. It was a larger kingdom than some had expected or wanted.

Many Belgians resented being shuffled around against their wishes, preferring either their own rule, Austrian rule as in the eighteenth century, or the French as during the happier moments of the Revolution. Indeed, many wanted anything except the Dutch, who had a different religion, language, culture, and historical traditions. But Great Britain had pushed for an enlarged Kingdom of the Netherlands to safeguard the territory from a renewed French attack, and to create a buffer for itself. And Britain had succeeded.

At the same time, Metternich was working to resolve a border dispute with Bavaria over Salzburg, the birthplace of Wolfgang Amadeus Mozart and the home of lucrative salt mines. There was a conflict over the ownership of Berchtesgaden, the mountain resort later notorious as a retreat for Nazi leadership, which had been Austrian before Napoleon took it away and gave it to his ally at the time, Bavaria. The two countries were working on finding some agreement over these territories, a difficult negotiation that showed little sign of progress and would not in fact be completed until after the congress, when Austria gained Salzburg; and Bavaria, Berchtesgaden.

Boosted by the progress on so many fronts, Talleyrand now shifted his attentions to focus on the pressing question of Naples. King Joachim I (Murat) was still in power there, and while no one particularly liked the fact, few were willing to do anything about it. Talleyrand was using all his arguments to rally support, emphasizing the importance of legitimacy for the postwar order, and the vital necessity of removing this unpredictable warrior from the throne. Peace could never be assured, he argued, as long as the last usurper ruled in Europe.

It was important to reach a favorable conclusion on this matter immediately, Talleyrand felt, because the congress seemed to be winding down. Rumors abounded everywhere of imminent departures. Tsar Alexander had already announced his intention to return home by the middle of the month, though the date of departure had been postponed a couple of times. He pledged, at all events, to be back in St. Petersburg in time for the celebration of Easter, which in the Russian Orthodox calendar fell that year on the last day of April.

Following the tsar's lead, other sovereigns had also expressed their desire to return home. Even the host, Emperor Francis, was restless. Officially, he wanted to leave town to make a tour of the banking city of Milan, the ruined marvel of Venice, and other gems of northern Italy that were being restored to Austria. Indeed, after months of putting on a never-ending round of banquets, masked balls, and other forms of entertainment, the emperor was growing weary of his permanent houseguests.

"This desire on the part of every one to go away," Talleyrand predicted, "will expedite the conclusion of affairs." If he had any chance to restore the Bourbon king to Naples, he knew that he had to act quickly.

One morning in mid-February, Talleyrand went over to meet with the tsar, hoping to recruit his assistance on removing Murat. The tsar, however, was more interested in finding out why exactly the king of France had not paid the 2 million francs that he had promised Napoleon.

"As I have been absent from Paris for five months," Talleyrand answered, "I do not know what has been done in this respect."

"The treaty has not been executed; we ought to insist on its execution," the tsar assured him. "Our honor is at stake; we cannot possibly draw back." Alexander added that the emperor of Austria agreed completely.

"Sire, I will report all that you have done me the honor of saying to me," Talleyrand answered politely, and then tried to turn the discussion back onto the subject of Naples. He argued as best he could, but the tsar had a valid point, as would soon be painfully clear.

IT WAS INDEED true that King Louis XVIII had not paid any of the 2 million francs in pension promised to him. Napoleon's own funds, meanwhile, were dwindling. He had to support about a thousand guards, maintain his palace, and pay many other expenses, not to mention the cost of the court life he had wanted as emperor of Elba.

Napoleon had heard rumors about the squabbling heads of state in

Vienna, and, worse, his own informers reported that some delegates were lobbying to have him moved farther away from the Continent. Story after story had also arrived emphasizing the chaos that reigned in France. The army was on half pay, if paid at all. Many had been discharged from service, or relegated to the sidelines to make way for the king's favorites, fit only for the parade ground. The government seemed stuck in a "malevolent muddle," and many openly expressed their regret for the loss of their former emperor.

Napoleon, too, seemed frustrated and bored. On the surface, he had settled down into a modest domestic routine. Evenings ended early, about nine, when Napoleon would stand, walk over to the piano, and, with a single finger, tap the first fourteen chords of Haydn's Symphony no. 94 (Surprise). Then he "bowed and left the room." But those near him knew how much Napoleon resented the way the Allies had treated him, and he feared more treachery. Above all, he regretted that he had abdicated without a fight. Why had he listened to his advisers and not his own inclinations? Just the thought of that made him sick.

In this discontent, a mysterious visitor arrived at Elba that February: Fleury de Chaboulon, a thirty-year-old out-of-work bureaucrat, a former subprefect in Burgundy. Traveling incognito, this man brought reminders of Napoleon's popularity, and, more important, news that a plot was being hatched to overthrow King Louis XVIII and replace him with the king's more popular cousin, the duc d'Orléans. The significance was clear. Napoleon could not sit back on this tiny island while someone else captured the throne of France.

In all likelihood, Napoleon had been planning to leave Elba for some time. But this visit probably convinced him that the time for action had come. In addition, in mid-February, Neil Campbell announced that he was leaving for a trip to the mainland for a cure of his wounds (and a visit with his mistress). Campbell would not be back for two weeks, and Napoleon realized his opportunity.

It was his audacious moves, after all, that had crowned his greatest achievements. A bold strike to seize power had succeeded back in 1799 when many others had plotted and failed. He had crowned himself emperor in 1804, and succeeded, despite the protests of others. A daring decoy maneuver had helped him win big at Austerlitz. Again and again, it was the gutsy moves that had worked best, pushed at breathtaking speed and catching his opponents off guard (of course, they had also failed spectacularly sometimes, like the Russian invasion).

Fed up with the string of broken promises and determined to strike before something worse happened to him, or someone else capitalized on the turmoil back in France, Napoleon had made up his mind. It was time to return to France.

All the energy he had invested in conquering and controlling Europe was now brought to this enterprise. As always, he was careful not to reveal his true intentions. The ship *Inconstant,* which had mysteriously crashed into a roadstead on a routine sail around Elba a few weeks before, was now being refurbished without too much undue attention. He strengthened the masts, revamped the hull, and added a layer of paint that, on inspection, made the brig look remarkably close to an English warship.

On February 26, 1815, the very day of his departure, Napoleon had made sure that everything seemed normal. The soldiers had been planting trees, working in the garden, and carrying out other standard duties, as they had done for months. Napoleon went to Mass in the morning, dined with his mother and sister in the evening, and then rode down to the harbor, passing many curious cheering and waving Elbans. Everything had been loaded onto the sixteen-gun brig *Inconstant.* After nine months and twenty-two days, Napoleon and his crew were ready to set sail.

Napoleon had earned a reputation for daring enterprises, but this one was to be his riskiest venture yet. He was invading one of the most powerful countries on earth, and he had about 1,100 men, seven small boats, and four cannons. The emperor liked the odds. "I shall reach Paris," he announced, "without firing a shot."

Chapter 25

TIME TO SAVE THE WORLD AGAIN

The events are so extraordinary, so unexpected, so magical . . .
it seems that 1,001 Nights is coming true, and everything
happens by the wand of some invisible magician.

—JEAN-GABRIEL EYNARD IN HIS DIARY, MARCH 1815

On Tuesday, March 7, after three in the morning, Metternich climbed the marble steps to his private rooms on the third floor of the Chancellery, where he crawled into bed for a well-deserved sleep. Another lengthy meeting of the Committee of Five had finally ended, and he was exhausted. "I had forbidden my valet to disturb my rest," he said.

Only a few hours later, his valet entered the chamber with a dispatch marked "URGENT." Metternich took the envelope, glanced at the far away sender, and then promptly set it on his nightstand. He then tried to go back to sleep, but as he put it, "sleep once disturbed, would not return." About half past seven, he gave up his tossing and turning, and opened the dispatch. It was a letter that he would never forget.

The commissioner on Elba, Neil Campbell, reported that Napoleon was nowhere to be found and wondered if anyone had seen him. The Austrian foreign minister sprang out of bed, threw on his clothes, and raced over to the Hofburg to inform Emperor Francis. By eight in the morning, they were deep in discussion.

"Napoleon apparently wants to play the adventurer; that is his business," the emperor told Metternich. He continued:

Our business is to secure for the world that peace which he has troubled all these years. Go at once to the Emperor of Russia and the King of Prussia; tell them that I am prepared to order my army once again to march back into France. I have no doubt that the two Sovereigns will join me.

As Metternich described the historic morning, he had a meeting with the tsar over in the Amalia wing of the palace at 8:15 and then hurried across the inner court to meet with the king of Prussia. By nine that morning, he was back at the Chancellery for a meeting with Austrian field marshal Prince Schwarzenberg. "It was in less than an hour," he boasted with some exaggeration, "that war was declared."

Meanwhile, a few blocks away at Kaunitz Palace, Talleyrand was still in bed. Dorothée was seated next to her uncle, drinking chocolate and looking forward to her dress rehearsal later in the day for a theater production that opened that evening. A white-wigged footman in gray livery brought in a note from Prince Metternich.

"It is probably to tell me what time today's meeting of the Congress is to begin," Talleyrand predicted without much concern, as he handed the note to Dorothée. She opened it and read its contents. "Bonaparte has escaped from Elba. Oh, Uncle, what about my rehearsal?"

"Your rehearsal, Madame, will take place all the same," Talleyrand replied with an unruffled composure. Equally calm, he rose from the bed, summoned his assistants, hurried through his ritual levee, and then headed over to the Austrian Chancellery.

By TEN O'CLOCK, the Allies were already gathering in Metternich's study for an emergency meeting.

Talleyrand was the first to arrive at the Chancellery, and Metternich took the opportunity to read the dispatch.

"Do you know where Napoleon is headed?" Talleyrand asked.

"The report does not say anything about it."

"He will land somewhere on the Italian coast and fling himself into Switzerland," Talleyrand predicted.

"No," Metternich answered, "he will go straight to Paris."

This viewpoint was by no means obvious at the time. The road to

Paris would mean progressing through many parts of southern France that had been bastions of royal support and scenes of bitter opposition to Napoleon. Given his unpopularity there, a French destination seemed unlikely, to say the least. If Napoleon "sets foot there," Russia's Corsican adviser, Pozzo di Borgo, would soon predict, "he will be seized the moment he lands, and hanged from the nearest tree."

At this point, Prince Hardenberg and Count Nesselrode entered Metternich's study. The Duke of Wellington also arrived, having quickly changed his plans upon hearing the news. He had hoped to spend the morning hunting in the park.

When the ministers began discussing the dispatch, it was clear that they had no idea of Napoleon's intentions. One thing that they did agree on, however, was the importance of keeping everything quiet, as they did not want to alarm the town. Napoleon's escape would not appear in the next morning's newspapers, *Wiener Zeitung* and the *Österreichischer Beobachter*. On the following day, there was only a small notice in the latter paper, buried in the "Foreign News" section under the headline for Italy.

Even Metternich's assistant, Friedrich von Gentz, who had shouldered so many duties as secretary of the Congress, was not informed. Gentz would come by Metternich's office that same morning, as usual, where the two discussed congress business, though there was no hint of Napoleon being on the loose. Gentz would not find out until later that day, when his old friend Wilhelm von Humboldt told him.

NEWS OF THIS kind could not be hushed up for long in a town buzzing with gossip. Once leaked, it spread rapidly, and, typically for the congress, this happened later that night at the theater.

It was during an amateur production of Kotzebue's *Old Love Affairs* in the Redoutensaal. The tsar, the king of Prussia, and all the leading figures were in the audience, trying to act as if nothing had happened. They did not want to cause panic, nor spoil the performance. After all, Metternich's daughter Marie, Talleyrand's niece Dorothée, and the tsar's "celestial beauty," Gabrielle Auersperg, would all be appearing onstage that night.

Just before the heavy curtain rose, the delegates in their plush red velvet-and-gold-trimmed seats were seen whispering, and then, not long afterward, so were the audience and the actors backstage. It was there at the theater that Countess Bernstorff first learned of the news, and also Countess Lulu Thürheim, the diarist. She described how the dignitaries tried valiantly to keep their opera glasses fixed on the stage. The feigned nonchalance, however, was in vain. Fear could be "read on their faces," as Countess Bernstorff noticed.

As everyone knew, Napoleon was a dangerous threat, and even if he did not yet have an army, that would probably not last long. He was still wildly popular with the soldiers, who remembered with pride how the warlord had triumphed over great odds, humbled kings, and led them to many victories. It was Napoleon who had given France honor and glory, only, in the end, to be unceremoniously betrayed by his marshals. What a miserable sight King Louis and his cronies made in comparison.

There were indeed many angry people in France—the question was how many soldiers and citizens were upset enough to abandon their king and join Napoleon. Also, as the Vienna Congress had alienated many factions the last several months, some feared that Napoleon might attract more international support than originally thought. For example, Joachim Murat, the former Bonaparte marshal, was still ruling as king in Naples, despite all Talleyrand's opposition, and he could potentially rally to Napoleon's side.

There were also many Poles disillusioned with the Russian project for their country. One spy reported that "the Poles overflow with delight" on the news of Napoleon's departure, as many sensed a chance, finally, to realize dreams of a restored kingdom. Napoleon had promised them a kingdom long before, and many believed that unlike the tsar, he might actually fulfill his promise this time.

What if Tsar Alexander, for that matter, had another one of his "periodic evolutions of the mind" and decided to desert his allies at the Vienna Congress? This was a real concern for the Allies; he had already gotten everything that they were going to give him, but Napoleon might soon have a more tempting offer for him.

Indeed, once the shock of Napoleon's voyage wore off, the gravity of the situation settled in, and the Allies began to blame one another. Many accused the English of sloppy work, bungling their vigilance. Where had those famous Royal Navy cruisers been when Napoleon was leaving

Elba? Why did Britain's governor, Neil Campbell, leave the island so mysteriously on the eve of Napoleon's departure? Talleyrand articulated this position when he remarked that "the English, whose duty it was to watch his movements, were guilty of a negligence which they will find it difficult to excuse."

"Are we Napoleon's keepers?" Lord Stewart asked, defensively shrugging off Britain's critics. "What right do we have to keep him under guard?"

Stewart had a point, to an extent. Napoleon was a sovereign ruler of an independent power, and there was, in fact, nothing in the treaty of abdication that prohibited him from leaving Elba. And Britain had never signed the treaty that placed him so close to the Continent. They had, in other words, never recognized Napoleon's right to the island, much less his retention of the title *emperor*. Why exactly was it Britain's responsibility that Napoleon chose to leave Elba?

The French might be quick to point fingers, but matters might have been different if the French government had only fulfilled its obligations. King Louis XVIII had never paid, as promised, the 2 million francs. Many had reminded France of this fact, only to be ignored. To Talleyrand's endless frustration, the king's government had made many blunders. As the Danish foreign minister put it in his journal, the French were acting "as if they had put a dangerous man in prison, refused him bread and then left the door open"—and now complained when he left.

Prussia's Humboldt, for his part, wanted to know where Napoleon had received financing for his departure. Obviously, it was not from the French king, and Napoleon's own funds were supposed to be running low. Rumors of an Austrian general, Franz Freiherr von Koller, making a secretive trip to Elba prior to Napoleon's departure were circulating, and, indeed, it was true. But what exactly was he doing on Elba? The Austrians claimed it was to negotiate a divorce between Napoleon and Marie Louise, though some were skeptical. Would it not be in Austria's interest to have an Austrian archduchess as empress of France, and her son as heir to the French throne? Did Austria have a hand in Napoleon's extraordinary departure?

Then there was the tsar, whose "sentimental politics" had caused Napoleon to be sent to Elba in the first place, over the protests of his allies. Just like the British, Metternich had tried to warn about the close proximity, and during the congress, Talleyrand had attempted several times to have Napoleon moved off Elba. Islands from the Azores to St. Helena in the South Atlantic had all been proposed as a better place for his exile, but nothing had been done.

Of course, with Napoleon's rash actions, everything had changed at the peace conference, and the planned departures that spring would have to be temporarily postponed. Urgent matters were, once again, thrust onto the agenda for the Vienna Congress.

Looking around at his harried colleagues, the British diplomat Lord Clancarty observed how everyone made heroic efforts "to conceal apprehension under the masque of unconcern." Yet, he added, "It was not difficult to perceive that fear was predominant in all the Imperial and Royal personages." Napoleon had to be stopped, it was clear, before he "could set the world on fire again."

Chapter 26

$\mathcal{H}$IS $\mathcal{M}$AJESTY, THE $\mathcal{O}$UTLAW

All that may be only an illusion, but what in our days is real?

—DUCHESS OF SAGAN, SPRING OF 1815

$\mathcal{B}$ack in Paris, the French government pretended not to be overly concerned with the new threat. King Louis XVIII noted that he was sleeping better than ever, and complained more about his gout than the man of Elba. The official newspaper, the *Moniteur,* summed up Napoleon's enterprise as an "act of madness" that would be squashed by "a few rural policemen."

Yet the fact remained that the king's army was deserting in droves, and so were government officials. Given the challenge that Napoleon posed, it was necessary for Vienna's peacemakers to act quickly. But what exactly should they do? One of the French embassy officials, Alexis de Noailles, had no trouble reaching a conclusion about Napoleon: "Now he had escaped, we must hang him!"

"We can't hang him until we've caught him," the king of Prussia responded, "and that won't be so very easy."

In fact, the plenipotentiaries were limited in what they could do until they knew, for certain, where Napoleon was headed. In the meantime, they had to wrap up the remaining disputes of the peace congress. The first order of business was to finish the Saxony affair—that is, convince the king of Saxony to accept last month's solution that he yield two-fifths of his territory and about one-third of his population.

Recently released from prison, the king of Saxony was staying in the old fortress in the nearby town of Pressburg, today's Bratislava, Slovakia. He had no desire to enter Vienna in the presence of his spoliators, and many at the congress returned the sentiment. The congress would send a distinguished delegation to him: Talleyrand, Metternich, and Wellington.

When the leaders arrived at the court of the king on the eighth of March, they were greeted with a cool reception. After a preliminary dinner and general meeting, the king of Saxony received each one individually, and haughtily. The king's men raised objection after objection to the congress's plans for Saxony. "They seemed to nourish a hope," Talleyrand said, "that the terms which have been agreed upon were still open to negotiation."

But the king of Saxony did not change his tune, no more inclined to yield now than he had been earlier, when he had held out as one of the last loyal rulers to Napoleon. No doubt, the king figured that he had more to gain from the emperor than these polished gentlemen, and decided to gamble on better terms in the future. The congress's delegation returned to Vienna without any success.

All over town, people were discussing—and speculating wildly— about Napoleon's actions. In an anonymous police report submitted to Baron Hager, one agent reported that many people now believed that the English had played a role in Napoleon's escape. They had allowed, if not also encouraged and supported, his enterprise. Napoleon had been lured out, it was surmised, so that the congress would have a "pretext to treat him with more severity."

Napoleon's departure from Elba was the topic of every conversation, the Russian soldier Alexander Ivanovich Mikhailovsky-Danilevsky remembered, "if not the only topic of conversation." He had heard it everywhere, on "walks, at gatherings, and meetings in private houses and in cafés." Baronne du Montet recalled, too, how the frightening news caused a great deal of distress. The king of Bavaria, for instance, "walked around for days as if he were deranged." Others were more detached. As spies reported, several people were placing bets on what Napoleon would do next and how far he would go.

On March 10, a messenger arrived with the first real news about Napoleon's destination. He had not, as many suspected, crossed over to Italy, either to seize Genoa or land farther south. He had instead opted for the far more difficult option of France. Moreover, against all odds, he had landed safely at Golfe-Juan, about one mile west of Cannes.

According to La Garde-Chambonas, the shocking news came at a ball

over at the Metternichs', and spread like wildfire among the happy waltzing couples. Metternich's orchestra struggled, in vain, to maintain the
dreamy graceful swirls, but the dancers had merely stopped and stared
at each other in disbelief. Who could really believe that Napoleon was
back in France? "Thousands of candles," La Garde-Chambonas added,
"seemed to have gone out simultaneously."

The songwriter paints a vivid scene. The Russian tsar turned to Talleyrand and snapped, "I told you that it would not last." The French
minister did not say a word in reply, but only bowed politely. The king of
Prussia and the Duke of Wellington hurried out of the ballroom together,
followed by the Austrian emperor and the Russian tsar. "Napoleon, not
wishing to finish by a tragedy, will finish by a farce," Talleyrand predicted to Prince Metternich, who, not responding, "excused himself" and
joined the congress dignitaries who had just left the floor. The French
minister left that evening arm in arm with Dorothée. The crowded ballroom was very soon emptied.

This scene almost certainly never happened. For one thing, Vienna
was still in Lent, and there were no balls then. Yet the scene, despite the
lack of literal truthfulness, is true to the personalities and the tensions of
the time. Talleyrand, for example, faced a whole new set of challenges
now that France was at risk from Napoleon, civil war, and an invasion
from the powers at the congress. The French foreign minister would no
longer be welcome in the deliberations. Having worked his way into the
inner circle, Talleyrand was finding himself at risk of being pushed outside again.

As for the grand balls, where "the quivering violins alternated with
serious negotiations," as Countess Thürheim remembered, they were
occurring much less frequently now. The Carnival season had ended three
weeks before, many sovereigns planned to return home, and the Austrian
emperor had started looking for ways to curtail the expensive entertainment. In a letter dated March 21, Emperor Francis would specifically
instruct his lord chamberlain to decrease expenses and reduce "the number of servants employed." The court was also "to follow the general
guidelines that extraordinary celebrations should no longer be arranged or
given." So despite the make-believe surrounding La Garde-Chambonas's
scene, Vienna's ballrooms were soon to be emptied indeed.

On his way from Elba, Napoleon had enjoyed good fortune in eluding several ships patrolling the waters. The *Inconstant* passed the French frigates *Melpomène* and *Fleur-de-Lys* without incident, and then, rounding Corsica, Napoleon passed yet another enemy warship, the *Zéphir*, without any difficulties. Even the British vessel carrying Campbell back to Elba, the *Partridge,* was sighted on the horizon. No one had stopped him. Conspiracy theories would proliferate for years. Had the winds blown differently, others have speculated, Napoleon might easily have been seized or sunk.

By the first of March, when Napoleon's brig had approached Golfe-Juan, people at first thought it was a small band of pirates about to make a raid. Learning the true identity of the crew, however, did not seem to please them any more. Some scoffed at the ragtag gang that had just been "vomited up from the sea."

But Napoleon had safely disembarked, and managed to pass through the streets without harm. To the thrill of his supporters, at first mainly soldiers and peasants, the initial surprise and cold reception was beginning to thaw. Gradually, there were more cheers and shouts of *"Vive l'Empereur!"*

At this beautiful medieval town, Napoleon faced another major decision. Examining his map sprawled out on a table in the middle of an olive garden, Napoleon calculated his chances either way. He could continue through southern France, a hotbed of royal support, or chance a dangerous mountain path through the French Alps into Grenoble. It was steep and narrow, hardly fit for his cumbersome baggage trains and cannon pieces, and it was covered with ice. Still, that one was deemed the least risky route.

Southern France had suffered tremendously during his empire. Ports like Marseille had been crippled under Napoleon's unsuccessful attempt to boycott English goods, and their shipping business decimated. Taxes had been crushing, and extended to all sorts of items, including alcohol and tobacco. Farmers there, and elsewhere, complained of being forced to furnish the army with supplies, their fields stripped down to the "last kernel of corn and the last forkful of fodder." And, of course, like so many others, they resented the conscriptions into the army and the heavy loss of life in his wars, all of which seemed a high price to pay for Napoleon's so-called glory.

While preparing for the mountain passageway, and abandoning his cannons, which he figured he would not need, anyway, Napoleon finished his own proclamations, one to the French people and another to his soldiers. Both sounded like rallying speeches straight out of those stirring addresses of his early campaigns: "Frenchmen, in my exile, I heard your plaints and prayers; I have crossed the sea amid perils of every kind; I [have] come to you to assert my rights, which are ours."

To the soldiers, he reminded them that they had been not defeated, but rather betrayed by a few marshals who sold out the country, the army, and its glory. He had been summoned back to France by the will of the people, and his symbol, the eagle, would soon "fly steeple to steeple all over the country to Notre Dame."

The emperor's progress was, in fact, astounding. His soldiers marched some fifteen to twenty miles, and often many more, each day under exhausting and very difficult conditions. It was necessary to move quickly, before the Bourbons had a chance to realize what had happened.

King Louis XVIII and the French government were, of course, taking measures to resist Bonaparte. The minister of war, Marshal Nicolas Jean Soult, the former Bonapartist, had some 60,000 troops in the south waiting for deployment, and supposedly another 120,000 on reserve at Melun, south of Paris, that could cover the main roads to the capital. Another marshal working for the king, André Masséna, was marching troops after the invaders. Orders were also made to blow up strategic bridges, such as Ponhaut, and block the way to Grenoble.

On March 7, at Laffrey, some fifteen miles outside Grenoble, Napoleon had the famous confrontation with the Fifth Infantry Regiment. The commander had orders to stop "Bonaparte's brigands," and he was determined to obey. Napoleon's army approached, led by his Polish Lancers and the Old Guard to the rallying anthem of "La Marseillaise." Napoleon himself rode to the front of his troops, dismounted, and advanced straight ahead in the line of fire of the king's soldiers. "There he is, fire," the royalist commander ordered. Napoleon then shouted, "Soldiers of the fifth, I am your Emperor."

"If there is any one among you who would kill his Emperor," Napoleon continued as he opened his greatcoat, "here I am." The tense silence was broken with shouts, *"Vive l'Empereur!"* The soldiers deserted and joined him.

Later that day, only hours after Vienna learned of his escape, Napoleon had already reached Grenoble, some two hundred miles north of his landing. "The inhabitants of Grenoble [were] proud to have the conqueror of Europe within their walls." Five army regiments had come over to his side, and he also gained a large cache of artillery, guns, gunpowder, and other military supplies. No major bridge had been destroyed to slow the advance.

Few orders were, in fact, carried out. Bonapartists in the king's army often refused to obey them, or sabotaged their execution, if they did not desert outright to Napoleon. Other Frenchmen, divided in their loyalties, hedged their bets and waited on the outcome.

Louis XVIII had committed so many mistakes since his restoration that he had effectively obliterated the memories of the worst excesses of the Napoleonic regime. When Napoleon arrived in a town, many rushed to greet him as a liberator. His sympathizers swarmed the popular cafés, looking for supporters and returning encouraged by what they saw. Townsmen stopped their daily activities and talked quietly in their own private enclaves, and street vendors even paused from their tireless railing to observe the astonishing events.

Back in Vienna, the news from France was bad and getting worse. Napoleon was marching with great momentum, and the king's soldiers were rapidly flocking to his side. Fewer symbols of the king, such as lilies and white handkerchiefs, were seen. In fact, when they appeared, the flowers were often trampled, the flags torn to shreds, and the Bourbon coats of arms smashed. Only ten days after his landing, France's second city, Lyon, had fallen. Louis XVIII was having to come to grips with betrayal, desertion, and incompetence on a grand scale.

Vienna's stock exchange had plummeted on this news, and the momentous events surrounding Napoleon's march north were clearly raising the specters of war all over again. The Swiss banker Eynard gave the odds of Napoleon's success, first at 1,000 to 1, and then, a few days later, at 10 to 1. Two additional days, and the bet was even. How on earth could this have happened? Had Napoleon, some asked, made a pact with the devil?

While many of Vienna's diplomats worked with zeal to oppose Napoleon, there were others visibly delighted by Napoleon's success, particularly the many disenchanted, disillusioned, and disenfranchised delegations that deeply resented the way the congress had acted.

The Prussians, for example, seemed happier than they had been for a long time. Extreme opinion not only wanted war, but also hoped to wipe France off the map, carving it up into small states such as Burgundy, Champagne, Auvergne, Brittany, Aquitaine, and others. Territories in the east, like Alsace and Lorraine, would promptly return to a German home. French property would be granted outright to the Allies, or, at the least, used to offset the costs of the new war. Prussian generals looked forward to accomplishing with the sword what the diplomats had failed to secure with the pen.

FOR TALLEYRAND, NAPOLEON'S success caused a lot of concerns. The last thing he had wanted was another Allied invasion of France, and hundreds of thousands of soldiers marching across the country, some undoubtedly preying upon the people again like "ferocious beasts." In this scenario, Talleyrand knew that the suffering would be great, and the chances were slim that France would enjoy such a lenient peace a second time.

Faced with this challenge, Talleyrand had hatched a plan that he hoped would ensure that Vienna's plenipotentiaries made an important distinction between France and Napoleon, and kept the two entities separate. He would draw up a declaration that would specifically name Napoleon, not France, as the enemy. Perhaps, then, all the inevitable anger unleashed in war would be confined to that single person and his supporters and not be projected onto the entire country.

Talleyrand had written a draft, and prepared to present it at a meeting on March 13. The stakes were high. Before his carriage left Kaunitz Palace, he advised his fellow diplomats:

> Watch for my return from the palace windows. If I succeed, you will see me in the carriage window holding up the treaty on which hangs the fate of France and Europe.

As Talleyrand worded it, Napoleon was denounced as a "wild beast" and all of Europe was called upon to rid the world of this "bandit." As he put it, "every measure permissible against brigands should be permissible against him."

Historians have often depicted the outlawing measure as inevitable, but it hardly seemed that way at the time. When Metternich read the draft at the meeting, he was skeptical. Should such words as "wild beast" and "bandit" really be used for Emperor Francis's son-in-law? Wellington also found the terminology inappropriate. Although he had no love for Napoleon, he did not wish to be seen as encouraging outright murder.

Debate raged throughout the night on this declaration that Talleyrand urged on the congress, and it reached a climax—a loud climax—around midnight, when, according to Humboldt, twenty voices were all shouting at once. In the end, Metternich offered a more moderate formulation, and this one was adopted.

In this declaration, drafted by the indefatigable Gentz, Napoleon Bonaparte was in fact declared an outlaw and denounced for his reckless violation of his previous agreement. Napoleon had also, the document continued, "deprived himself of the protection of the law and demonstrated before the world that there can be neither peace nor a truce with him."

However much it was moderated, this solemn document would still cause a scandal. In Vienna, only eight powers were allowed to sign the declaration—the same members of the Committee of Eight. The rest were excluded completely. The king of Denmark and the king of Bavaria, among many others, had not been invited to the meetings, or even consulted on the matter.

Outside Vienna, two passages in the declaration particularly came under fire, one claiming that Napoleon had lost "his sole lawful right to exist," and the other:

> The Powers declare that Napoleon Buonaparte has placed himself outside all human relations and that, as the enemy and disturber of the peace of the world, he has delivered himself up to public justice. (*vindicte publique*)

Some newspapers, when reporting the story of the declaration, translated the phrase *vindicte publique* as "public vengeance," and not, as

Metternich had insisted with his better grasp of French, only as "public justice" or "prosecution." As for the words about Napoleon forfeiting his "sole lawful right to exist," this only referred to legal status, though that was too subtle a distinction for some newspapers' editors. The damage was done. Mistranslations were in print, and critics now had another accusation to hurl at the Vienna Congress: the peacemakers were trying "to deliver Buonaparte over to the dagger of the assassin."

It was Wellington and the British delegation, of course, who would be most criticized for this declaration; after all, they came from a land with a Parliament, an active opposition party, and a relatively free press. One opposition leader, Samuel Whitbread, spoke for many when he criticized this vindictive and "abhorrent" declaration, which branded Napoleon an outlaw and encouraged his murder, when it was the Bourbons who had failed to fulfill their obligations to him. Wellington would be criticized almost daily. Talleyrand, on the other hand, would not have to worry that much. His critics had long accused him of worse.

Indeed, Talleyrand was pleased to put his graceful signature at the bottom of the document. He had obtained his main objective. Declaring Napoleon an outlaw would focus the animosity on him, not the French people, and, moreover, it would serve to "deprive traitors of confidence and to give courage to the loyal." In his letter to King Louis, Talleyrand praised the wording of the document: "It is very strong; there has never been a document of so much power and importance signed by all the sovereigns of Europe."

This was, in fact, the first time in history that states had effectively declared war on a single person. Talleyrand returned to the embassy late that night, waving a copy of the document, signed and stamped with red and black seals. His diplomatic team at Kaunitz Palace was thrilled. "I do not think," Talleyrand concluded in his letter back to Paris, "that we could have done better here."

ONE PERSON INTIMATELY affected by the news of Napoleon's actions was, of course, his estranged wife, Marie Louise. Despite her promises to join him on Elba, she had not done so. She had instead stopped writing, or even answering his letters, and at the same time continued her love affair with General Count Neipperg.

Marie Louise had not immediately been informed of her husband's escape. She only learned the news on Wednesday, March 8, when her son's governess, Madame de Montesquiou, forwarded the information in a letter, before someone else told her. Marie Louise did not take it well. According to agents in the palace, the young former empress "burst into tears," ran to her room, and cried uncontrollably, "sobbing [heard] all the way out in the anteroom."

Only a few days before, after months of uncertainty, Marie Louise had finally been assured the Duchy of Parma as promised. She had been thrilled by the prospects of moving there with her lover, Count Neipperg, and leaving behind the bad memories of the Vienna Congress. Unfortunately, however, Napoleon's flight was threatening to upset her life again. Wouldn't this act of desperation be interpreted by some as breaking the treaty that guaranteed her right to Parma? Her opponents now had another excuse for handing the territory over to the Spanish Bourbons. "My poor Louise, how sorry I feel for you!" her uncle, Johan, Archduke of Austria, said. "For your sake and ours, I hope that he breaks his neck!"

With Bonaparte the outlaw on the loose and advancing closer to the French capital, it was more important than ever to keep the little Napoleon under close surveillance. The four-year-old boy playing on the parquet floors of Schönbrunn Palace was potentially, once again, heir to the French throne, and the link that could solidify Napoleon's dynasty.

The French embassy reported hearing a rumor that someone would soon attempt to kidnap the little prince. Vienna's police chief, Baron Hager, was also worried about this threat. Bonapartist agents were allegedly already in town, and many suspicious people had been seen in the neighborhood of the palace.

By the middle of March, Baron Hager had increased the number of guards patrolling the grounds, and he had planted more policemen in the castle, disguised as servants. In case of emergency, Hager sent a detailed description of the boy to "police stations and customs houses" in the area. Agents were told to be on the lookout for a four-year-old male, tall for his age, with blue eyes, curly blond hair, and a distinctive nose "tip-tilted with wide nostrils." He spoke French and German, and gesticulated greatly.

On March 19, the night before Napoleon's son's fourth birthday, there was allegedly an attempt to kidnap him from his nursery. Rumors of this alleged abduction made their rounds, despite official denials. Soon the culprit was identified as his nurse, Madame de Montesquiou, an ardent Bonapartist. Her son Anatole, who had arrived from Paris just before, was also suspected, and promptly arrested.

It is by no means evident that either one was actually involved, and both would always proclaim their innocence. Madame de Montesquiou was fired the next day, as were many others around her. Spies also stepped up security against another Bonapartist attempt—or even, for that matter, a royalist plot—to seize the heir for their own purposes. Little Napoleon was moved out of Schönbrunn Palace and placed under tight security in the Hofburg.

1. Twenty-three delegates in the negotiation room of the Austrian Chancellery. Standing, from left to right: Wellington, Lobo da Silveira, Saldanha da Gama, Löwenhielm, Noailles, Metternich, La Tour du Pin, Nesselrode, Dalberg, Razumovsky, Stewart, Clancarty, Wacken, Gentz, Humboldt, and Cathcart. Seated, from left to right: Hardenberg, Palmella, Castlereagh, Wessenberg, Labrador, Talleyrand, and Stackelberg.

2. Kings, queens, and princes, as well as rogues, renegades, adventurers, gamblers, and courtesans flocked to Vienna for the congress—"every person a novel," the Prince de Ligne said.

3. Austrian foreign minister and president of the Congress, Prince Metternich—handsome, flirtatious, and seemingly frivolous master of diplomacy.

4. France's foreign minister, the brilliant, unscrupulous "prince of diplomats," Charles-Maurice de Talleyrand.

5. Francis I, the last Holy Roman Emperor and the first Emperor of Austria. He had once wanted a special clock that would slow down in times of pleasure and speed up in times of trial—a device that would have helped him cope with a palace full of houseguests who never seemed to agree, or leave.

6. Russian Tsar Alexander I, the foremost conqueror of Napoleon, whose sexual escapades and mystical experiences fascinated, wearied and alarmed Vienna. Alexander took offense at the Prince de Ligne's famous quip about the "dancing congress," believing that it was aimed primarily at him.

7. King of Prussia, Frederick William III, lived in the shadow of his famous great uncle, Frederick the Great. While he lacked his predecessor's flair for military strategy, he certainly loved uniforms. "How do you manage to button so many buttons?" Napoleon had once teased him.

8. British Foreign Secretary Lord Castlereagh pressed for a balance of power (except, of course, on the seas). He spoke little, smiled less, it was said, though in private, he could be quite charming.

9. The oldest and one of the ablest of the delegates, Prussia's Chancellor Hardenberg, strongly disagreed with many policies that he was forced to carry out.

10. Philologist, scholar, administrator, and ambassador to Vienna, Wilhelm von Humboldt, served Prussia with the same energy that he had used when he had reformed the Prussian educational system and founded Berlin University.

11. The Duke of Wellington was one of the most popular men alive. His arrival in February 1815 raised expectations: peace or war in fourteen days, it was widely believed.

Women had never before and have never since played a more influential role at a peace conference.

12. Hostess of a lively salon and center of intrigue in the Palm Palace, Princess Bagration the "beautiful naked angel" who wore scandalously revealing dresses. She was immortalized in a Balzac novel, as well as *le potage Bagration* and *la salade Bagration*, both coined by Talleyrand's chef.

13. Hostess of a rival salon in the Palm Palace, the glamorous Duchess of Sagan, who, like her archenemy Princess Bagration, seduced Vienna, becoming a major source of tension between Metternich and the tsar.

14. The twenty-one-year-old younger sister of the Duchess of Sagan, Dorothée, served as hostess of the French Embassy. She won many hearts at the congress—not least, it seemed, was that of Talleyrand himself.

15. View of Vienna as seen by many travelers who approached by land. Others arrived on the Danube, which appeared to Jacob Grimm one moonlit night in September 1814 as neither blue nor muddy, but "melting silver."

16. Vienna was one of the most sophisticated cities in Europe. It had welcomed French aristocrats who had fled the French Revolution, and former princes of the Holy Roman Empire who had been dispossessed by Napoleon. The Congress of Vienna added even more luster, leaving a legacy of chic elegance that survives today.

17. On September 25, 1814, the Emperor of Austria (center) met the Russian tsar (right) and the king of Prussia (left), just north of Vienna, prior to their arrival for the congress.

18. During the Congress of Vienna, the Hofburg Palace contained more royalty under one roof at one time than any other place in history. Guards were posted outside entrances to each royal suite, and troop maneuvers were a daily sight. One day in September, a visitor counted no fewer than fifty-three calls to arms.

Month after month, celebrations followed one another in rapid succession, making the Congress of Vienna the most lavish and certainly the most significant party in history. Behind the glittering spectacle, however, tensions were mounting, and war seemed likely to erupt at any moment.

19. Celebration at the Peace Festival on the anniversary of the Allied Victory at the Battle of Leipzig, October 18, 1814.

20. "Quivering violins alternated with serious negotiations, court intrigues alternated with delicate romantic adventures," said Countess Thürheim, describing the charged atmosphere of Vienna's ballrooms. A later rendering of a ball at Prince Metternich's.

21. One of the many masked balls, or *redouten*, held in the spacious ballrooms of the Hofburg during the Congress of Vienna.

22. Grand Carousel held on November 23, 1814, in the Spanish Riding School.

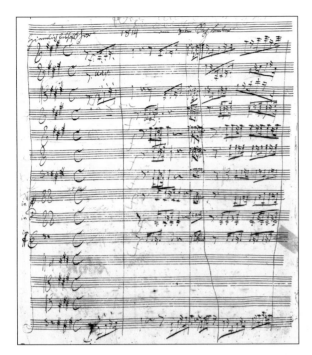

23. This is a page from the score of Beethoven's unfinished celebration of the Vienna Congress, "The Choir of the Allied Princes."

24. On Twelfth Night, the Congress of Vienna cuts up the cake of Europe. Alexander receives Poland, and the King of Prussia Saxony. Austria will take Germany, or at least as much of it as possible. Castlereagh, knife and fork in hand, prepares to serve his colleagues. In the background, marginalized and excluded powers beg in vain for a few scraps. Others watch from the box seats as the orchestra plays, and Justice, overhead, appears wounded, with a bandage over an eye and her scales broken.

25. For the many distinguished guests in town, congress planners had compiled a short list of sightseeing opportunities, ranging from Napoleonic battlefields to a lunatic asylum. The historic abbey on the Danube, Klosterneuberg, was one of the sights, and the print comes from the collection of the king of Denmark, who proved to be the most avid royal sightseer in town.

26. Vienna was one of the greenest cities in Europe, thanks to its many former royal, princely, and aristocratic parks, and the progressive tree-planting policies of Joseph II. The Belvedere Palace, depicted here, also boasted several art exhibits.

27. The Razumovsky Palace, owned by the fabulously rich Count Razumovsky of the Russian delegation, was destroyed by fire on the night of December 30–31, 1814, after one last grand party.

28. The seventy-nine-year-old Prince de Ligne had known everyone from Voltaire to Casanova. His small salon attracted the most distinguished and glamorous guests, and the prince's anecdotes and bons mots circulated in drawing rooms across town.

29. The tsar, the emperor, the kings, queens, and princes—along with an escort of musicians, police, and servants—embarked on a magnificent sleigh ride to Schönbrunn Palace for a banquet and ballet. They returned that evening to the Hofburg for another masked ball.

30. Once ruler of a vast continental empire, Napoleon was now emperor only of the tiny island of Elba. When the original print was held to the light, Napoleon no longer appeared alone, but surrounded by crowds of enthusiastic supporters.

31. After landing at the Golfe Juan in southern France, Napoleon camped in an olive grove outside Antibes (likely near or on the spot of today's railway station). Napoleon had to move quickly, he knew, before news of his arrival spread, along with knowledge of just how small his army actually was.

32. News of Napoleon's flight from Elba struck Vienna, as one put it, "like a flash of lightning and thunder." Painting captures the excitement of Napoleon's march to Paris in March 1815.

33. On March 19, only three days after promising to die in defense of his country, King Louis XVIII left the Tuileries for northern France and then slipped across the border into Belgium.

34. Famous ball, hosted by the Duchess of Richmond, on the eve of the Battle of Waterloo, was less grand than the one celebrated in literature. It took place in a coach house or carriage workshop.

35. "Nothing except a battle lost can be half so melancholy as a battle won," the Duke of Wellington said, surveying the scene of slaughter after the Battle of Waterloo. He hoped that he would never have to fight another battle, and he had his wish.

36. The Congress of Vienna, carving up Europe, trades countries like snuffboxes. The large man to the left was the king of Württemberg, the brash "monster" who stormed out of the conference in December 1814.

LE CONGRÈS.

37. The congress dances. Britain's Castlereagh serves as the dancing master, while Talleyrand, at the far left, observes from the sidelines no doubt awaiting his entry. The jumping figure represents the unhappy Marquis de Brignole, the delegate from Genoa, who protested the fate of his city. On the far right, the king of Saxony, who was in danger of losing his throne, clutches his crown. The "dancing congress" would be a lasting image of the Congress of Vienna.

Chapter 27

With the Spring Violets

The fact is, France is a den of thieves and brigands, and they can only be governed by criminals like themselves.

— Castlereagh

Napoleon's confidence in his success, already high, was growing as he advanced toward the French capital. With expectations of an imminent return to power, he had started appointing his new government: General Armand de Caulaincourt, his former foreign minister, was to be recalled. General Lazare Carnot, "the organizer of victory" in the Revolution, would supervise the Ministry of the Interior, and he wanted his top commander, Marshal Louis-Nicolas Davout, to head the Ministry of War. Fleury de Chaboulon, who had visited him on Elba, was also to find a place as Napoleon's new secretary.

In contrast to Bonaparte's spirited veterans, many in their blue coats, red epaulettes, and tall bearskin hats of the Old Guard, King Louis's men seemed demoralized. Marshal Michel Ney—"the bravest of the brave"— swore to bring Napoleon back in an iron cage. But even he had switched sides. The Paris stock exchange continued its nosedive, the printing of newspapers ground to a halt, and government ministers fled the capital in embarrassingly disorganized retreats.

King Louis XVIII tried to rally his supporters, reaffirming his promise to confront the outlaw Bonaparte. "Can I, at the age of sixty," the king proudly claimed to the French legislature, the Chamber of Deputies, "better end my career than by dying in defense of my country?" Many cheered the brave words, but three days later, just after midnight on

March 19–20, Louis boarded a royal carriage and rumbled away from his capital.

For the sake of safety, six identical carriages left the palace at the same time, separating at the Place de la Concord in different directions. The one with the king headed north. The crown jewels, several millions in the government treasury, and another stash of funds followed in the royal caravan. The king could not be too careful. He did not want to share the fate of his older brother, Louis XVI, whose flight from Paris back in 1791 had ended disastrously with his capture, imprisonment, and eventual execution.

As the king sped away, the palace no longer flew the white flag of Bourbon France, and instead showed an unmistakable "gloomy appearance of its being deserted, with a straggling sentry here and there." Paris itself, as Napoleon approached, looked like "a great city which feels itself to be on the eve of a catastrophe."

Peacemakers in Vienna were clearly facing the prospects of another war. But what was the best way to defeat Napoleon? Where should the armies be placed, and who was to command them?

Appearing to enjoy the challenge again, the tsar volunteered to take personal charge of the Allied troops. Wellington, a far better strategist and tactician, wisely hesitated at the offer. Metternich also balked, having seen the tsar, with all his shortcomings, a little too closely the last six months. With polite firmness, Alexander was persuaded to accept another supreme war council that would include, like last time, himself, the king of Prussia, and the Austrian field marshal Schwarzenberg. Wellington declined to join them, preferring instead "to carry a musket," and the Allies certainly needed his presence on the battlefield.

For the moment, it seemed, the British and the Prussians would take charge in the north, probably somewhere in the Low Countries; the Austrian army would be in the center and south, on the Rhine. The Russian army, still in Poland, was far away from the conflict and would have to hurry to reach the likely battleground, somewhere near France. That, of course, raised an additional concern: Given all the recent tensions with Russia over its claims to occupied Poland, did anyone really want to see the Russian army march across Germany and western Europe?

One of the most important decisions in the series of strategy sessions that followed took place on March 25, when the Great Powers renewed an agreement made at Chaumont at the end of war, and officially created the so-called Seventh Coalition. Each power pledged not to make a separate peace with Napoleon and furnish 150,000 troops for the campaign, with Britain reserving the right to pay additional funds in lieu of its quota. This agreement, moreover, would last for twenty years, or "until Bonaparte should have been rendered absolutely incapable of stirring up further trouble."

BY MARCH, THE Duchess of Sagan had spent months hosting parties in her salon at the Palm Palace, where everything was said to be "debauched, dissolute, unconcerned, extravagant, and racked with debts and blunders." Her personal debts were enormous, and she was having to find ways to raise money to pay off her creditors.

As Metternich had earlier expressed interest in a particular sapphire necklace, the duchess bundled it up in a piece of silk and sent it over to his office. She hoped the jewels would fetch a reasonable price, and asked for his assistance in selling them. Metternich, for his part, was eager to help. "You have not wanted to share the throne with me," Metternich had written before, "but you do not rule less in my realm."

Sure enough, two days later, Metternich had managed to scrounge up a buyer for the duchess's sapphires. The gems were going to Madame de Montesquiou, the former governess of Napoleon's son, who had just been sacked in the alleged kidnapping plot. The price was a solid 3,000 ducats, and the tab was picked up by Emperor Francis. Metternich had convinced the Austrian emperor to buy the sapphires as a farewell gift for Montesquiou's years of services looking after the energetic boy. The necklace traded hands, a small example of Metternich's dexterity, smoothly juggling issues and sometimes managing to have everything fall in the right place.

That Easter weekend, Talleyrand also had to do some juggling of his own. At midnight on Good Friday, the French embassy received an unexpected visitor: the Duchess of Courland, Dorothée's mother and also Talleyrand's mistress.

Like many aristocrats, the fifty-four-year-old duchess had fled Paris in a hurry, and decided to come to Vienna, which had welcomed many French émigrés over the last quarter of a century. The arrival of the duchess, however, must have been awkward, to say the least. A woman of her sophistication could hardly have failed to sense that Talleyrand had come to appreciate her daughter as someone more than a successful embassy hostess.

What a bizarre weekend it must have been, even for Talleyrand, who had seen his share of the unusual. The prospect of the mother and daughter, already suffering a strained relationship, competing for the attentions of the wily Frenchman was simply too much for gossipers. Even Dorothée's older sister, the Duchess of Sagan, could not resist commenting on Talleyrand's rumored affections for her sister: "The great man is at least kept in the family."

ACCORDING TO TRADITION, Napoleon had promised at his abdication to return to France with the spring violets. On Tuesday, March 28, Vienna learned that Napoleon had indeed returned to power. It had taken twenty-three days. Moreover, just as he promised, he had succeeded without firing a shot. The flight from Elba was, in many ways, the most audacious and reckless undertaking in his long career of monumental achievements and colossal blunders. The beautiful flower would be adopted by Bonapartists as a symbol for their hero.

Symbolically, too, Napoleon had returned on March 20, his son's fourth birthday. His supporters went wild with joy. Inside the palace courtyard, cheering enthusiasts swarmed the coach, and, as one put it, "seeing that he could advance no further, the Emperor descended in the midst of the immense crowd, which quickly engulfed him." Eyewitness accounts do not agree on all the details, but give a vivid impression of the euphoria. Some describe the emperor being carried halfway up the palace steps; others claim that he calmly strode them on his own, preceded by a supporter walking backward, repeating in disbelief, "It's you! It's you! It's finally you!"

After Louis XVIII's flight, Napoleon's supporters had prepared the palace for the return of their emperor. Royal emblems were removed from carpets and curtains—in many cases, the fleur-de-lis had only been sewn hastily over the Napoleonic golden bees from the last restoration. "The explosion of feelings was irresistible," one soldier described the enthusiasm, and Napoleon was no less thrilled, calling these days "the happiest period of [his] life."

Street vendors were now hawking small portraits of Napoleon, Marie Louise, and the little prince. A newspaper account in the *Königsberger Zeitung* reported that tailors were gearing up for the task of supplying many new imperial uniforms. Bonapartist cafés and restaurants enjoyed a brisk trade, full of celebrants whose "carousing, feasting, drinking, singing never cease."

As Napoleon's stunning triumph became apparent, Metternich was returning to some old habits, including regular visits to Wilhelmine's salon in the Palm Palace. The duchess was actually delighted, congratulating the foreign minister for having "at last broken the chains that kept you away from my house." Then she added her wish that in the times of uncertainty and the threat of war, they could once again "enjoy peacefully the charms of a friendship and of an agreeable relationship."

But friendship was, of course, not what Metternich wanted. Underneath his cheerful smile, Metternich had not ceased loving her, and it probably seemed at the time that he never would. He had cried a great deal, he confessed, and he had sought help from friends, though without success. Without the duchess, he was only a wanderer adrift in a cruel world—"a man who sees cast up on the shore the wreck of the vessel carrying his whole fortune."

With the news that Napoleon had reached Paris, March 28 was to be the Duke of Wellington's last night in Vienna. "I am going into the Low Countries to take command of the army," he announced. The Duchess of Sagan hosted a farewell party for him that evening, the duke "kissing each lady good-bye and arranging a rendezvous in Paris with one and all."

Britain would once again have new leadership at the embassy. This time, the responsibility would be shared by Lord Clancarty and Lord Cathcart, who had come originally as Castlereagh's advisers. The peace conference was still unfinished, but war was about to begin.

AFTER ANOTHER TENSE late-night session, Friedrich von Gentz, the congress's secretary, woke up and found, at his bedside, a cup of coffee and the morning newspaper *Wiener Zeitung*. As he picked up the paper,

Gentz was struck by an announcement on the front page: "Reward. 10,000 ducats. To whosoever delivers Friedrich von Gentz, the well-known publicist, dead or alive, or simply produces proof of his murder." The manifesto was signed Napoleon.

What a shock it must have been to read his own death warrant. Nervous and high-strung, Gentz already suffered from insomnia for fear that Napoleon would seek revenge on him for drafting the document that branded him an outlaw. Now, presumably with a price on his head, any assassin, mercenary, or bounty hunter eager to make a quick fortune could track him down in his flat on Seilergasse. Everyone knew where he lived. How could he walk home on the narrow dark streets at night, after a salon or late diplomacy session? Would he ever be safe again?

Later that morning, Dorothée and Count Clam-Martinitz came by Gentz's apartment and found him in a terrible state—a wreck amid the half-stuffed suitcases that suggested he was about to leave town in a hurry. "Look at the front page," Gentz explained, flinging the copy of the newspaper to them. "I've got to get out of town." He poured more of his powders into a cup, jerkily stirred them around, and then managed a drink, requiring "both shaking hands to raise it to his lips."

Dorothée could not watch Gentz suffer any longer, and advised him to look at the date of the newspaper. It was the first of April. Prince Metternich had thought it would be amusing to orchestrate an April Fools' prank, and he had overseen its execution, right down to having the paper printed especially for this occasion. That night, at a dinner hosted by Bavaria's Prince Wrede, Gentz had boasted that he had not, in the least, been fooled by the phony paper. People near him, however, knew otherwise. The prince's prank had "almost paralyzed the unfortunate secretary."

Pranks may have helped Metternich cope with the enormous stress, but, unfortunately, what Talleyrand faced was no laughing matter. After seizing power, Napoleon had ordered an immediate halt to the transmission of funds to Vienna. He had also canceled the French embassy's account at the Bank of France, along with its standing credit. In addition, Talleyrand's personal property, worth millions, had been impounded, as had the assets of many other employees at the embassy.

At this time, too, Talleyrand inquired about the state of all his confidential correspondence with the king and the Foreign Ministry since he had arrived in Vienna. "I trust that your Majesty has taken with you all the letters I had the honor of addressing to your Majesty," along with all the other papers sent to the Foreign Ministry, Talleyrand wrote. The reason for his concern was simple: There were many things in his correspondence that Talleyrand feared might upset his new allies, and he did not want it to fall into the wrong hands.

The response came from the acting foreign minister then in the king's temporary headquarters in Brussels, and it was not at all comforting. A few dispatches had been burned, including the secret reports sent from Elba and presumably the documents surrounding the alleged kidnapping and assassination attempts. But, unfortunately, the government had been in a hurry to leave. "I did not take with me, Prince, any important papers," one of the king's officials confessed sadly. None of the other ministers, regrettably, had done so either.

And so the vast majority of Talleyrand's private correspondence during the Vienna Congress, not to mention the secret treaty signed with Britain and Austria, were now lying openly in the ministry offices, just waiting for Napoleon.

Chapter 28

CRIERS OF *VIVE LE ROI!* DOERS OF *NOTHING*

Let us embrace and let all be forgotten.

—TSAR ALEXANDER TO METTERNICH

With the return of Napoleon, the Vienna Congress was now forced to confront the unpleasant fact that the emperor's former marshal, Joachim Murat, was still king of Naples. Murat was still the same restless and swaggering cavalry leader prone to risky moves. He was also eager to play his own role in the unfolding drama. On March 30, while the attentions of the Vienna Congress were focused on events in France, Murat had called for nothing less than the unification of Italy, and launched a surprise attack against the Papal States.

This had been rash, and many of his advisers had argued against it. Murat's wife, Caroline, was one who strongly opposed any action that could be seen as breaking his agreements with Austria. "What need have I of alliances," Murat had said, "since the Italians salute me as their sovereign?"

Even Napoleon had also been against such an invasion. In fact, he had ordered Murat *not* to attack, at least not yet. Timing was everything, and, at the moment, he needed Murat to stay in the south and keep Austria anxious about its Italian holdings. But Murat had been thrilled by Napoleon's successes and wanted to undertake his own. He would succeed, he was confident, just as he had at Marengo, Austerlitz, Jena, Eylau, and many other battles where, with his bold strikes, he had played a key role in Napoleon's victories.

Fortunately for Talleyrand, who had tried to warn diplomats about the dangers of this man for months, Murat's move was now making his job much easier. As Talleyrand put it, this attack "has at last opened the eyes of Austria, and made an end of all her hesitations."

Actually, it was not that Austria suddenly realized the dangers of Murat, but rather that the king of Naples had finally made the fatal error of judgment that Metternich had long expected. Austria declared war. One hundred thousand Austrian troops were ordered to march and restore order in Italy. The whole Naples affair, Talleyrand predicted confidently, "will very soon be definitely settled."

Once this matter was resolved, the remaining issues would most likely fall into place. "All that will then remain for us to do," Talleyrand elaborated, "will be to collect all the articles already agreed upon, and form them into the act which is to terminate the Congress."

As far as France was concerned, the sooner the congress was finished, the better. The embassy was virtually bankrupt. Fortunately, Talleyrand had managed to secure some emergency financial assistance from Great Britain, though this barely covered the embassy's most basic expenses, never mind the stack of unpaid bills. Talleyrand had to send many of his staff home, including his chef and several assistants. While Talleyrand struggled with the new financial realities, Napoleon went one step further and revoked his authority as a French diplomat.

Indeed, messengers were already on their way from Paris with papers officially dissolving the mission of Talleyrand, Dalberg, and the whole "diplomatic phalanx" at Kaunitz Palace. The French embassy had suddenly found itself without anyone to represent—that is, besides a dethroned king who had fled the country.

Opinion in Vienna was becoming increasingly hostile to the Bourbon dynasty, who had abandoned the country without much of a fight. The king's supporters had certainly seemed lackluster; Castlereagh had labeled them "Criers of *Vive le Roi!* Doers of nothing." This was a problem because, as Talleyrand rightly urged, the king needed to show that he maintained the support of his people. The king should, moreover, return to France as soon as possible, and in all events he should not remain anywhere near the coast. This only gave the impression that the king would soon once again flee to Britain.

Frustratingly, days now passed without any news from King Louis

XVIII or anyone in the exiled French Foreign Ministry, which had recently moved from Brussels to Ghent. Talleyrand was used to a fair amount of discretionary power, but at this late stage of the conference, the lack of information was exasperating, and he was forced to wait for every morsel with "extreme impatience."

As SPRING CAME early to Vienna, dinners and salons had been reenergized, though with less of a stellar cast in attendance than before. Many headed out to enjoy the Prater in bloom, or found themselves caught up in the long conferences that had become the rule. A new martial air had also come over the congress. In a series of conferences, with military matters now assuming top priority, Vienna's peacemakers sat down to appoint commanders, assign troops, persuade other powers to join its alliance, and, in short, devise a general strategy to face Napoleon.

"If we are to undertake the job," Castlereagh wrote from London to advise the British delegation, "we must leave nothing to chance. It must be done upon the largest scale." The Allies must amass an enormous force, strike hard, and, as he put it, "inundate France from all directions."

But to do that would be expensive, and, after the last war, few states had the resources for such an undertaking. Indeed, for many plenipotentiaries, the negotiations at the war council were taken as an invitation to barter for financial support from Great Britain. The London government was viewed as an inexhaustible bank freely dispensing its gifts. Such subsidies would help ensure a well-supplied army, and, at the same time, many hoped that they would help prevent the worst cases of pillaging sure to result when the large armies took to the field. The Prussians, in particular, were feared as a modern "Praetorian Guard" drunk with revenge.

Some of the smaller German states also set a price for their participation, promising to cooperate with the Allies in the war in return for a guarantee that the conference would establish a German *Bund,* or union of the German states. This loosely unified Germany should, moreover, be guaranteed a "liberal constitution" with many rights for the people, ranging from a free press to freedom of religion.

In addition, while all these demands were being championed with unexpected intensity, the Great Powers had to wrestle with startling signs of disloyalty among their own troops. Many Saxons, for instance, were manifestly upset about joining the Kingdom of Prussia. The king of Saxony had never agreed to relinquish any part of his country, nor had he freed the troops from their personal oath to him. Many Saxon soldiers plainly preferred to fight their new rulers, the Prussians, rather than Napoleon.

In the unstable environment of Napoleon's return, Bavaria also seemed to be showing just how to profit from the tension. Bavaria was planning to send twice the troops Vienna requested, and this enthusiastic support worried Metternich. As Austria and Bavaria had still not agreed over who should own Salzburg or the surrounding Alpine regions, Metternich feared that Bavaria was cynically exploiting the threat of Napoleon to mobilize a huge force, and then maneuver it, under the pretext of defense, into a strategic offensive position. That way, with the increased leverage, Bavaria could be assured of its gains, either from diplomacy in Vienna or outright seizure on the battlefield.

WITH HIS RETURN to Paris, Napoleon was claiming to be a new man who had learned from his mistakes. He promised to be more moderate in his actions, guaranteeing a liberal constitution with a freedom of the press. He would establish "an empire of liberty," honoring all existing treaties, including the ones that parceled out his previous conquests. All he wanted, in return, was recognition of his authority as the legitimate ruler of France.

Leaders at Vienna had learned from experience to be wary of Napoleon's appeals to peace. This new pledge to respect all existing agreements, many were sure, was as credible as the string of broken treaties he had previously left behind.

Realizing the dangers of Napoleon's usual "divide and conquer" diplomacy, the delegates at the Vienna Congress went to work on another declaration that would reaffirm the aims of their coalition and the basis for the war against Napoleon, "the tiger that had escaped from his cage":

> [Europe] is arming, not against France, but as much for the welfare of France as for her own security. She acknowledges no other enemy than Napoleon Bonaparte, and all who fight in his cause.

The Vienna Congress would not recognize Napoleon's authority, and the many ambassadors he sent to Vienna would be treated merely as "messengers," and then promptly ignored.

But despite the virtual unanimity, ignoring Napoleon's representatives was becoming increasingly difficult. Was not the fact that they had signed a second declaration reaffirming their position a sign that they might not be as unified as they wished to appear?

There was a betting chance, Napoleon gambled, that Austria might be persuaded to accept peace with him as the ruler of France. After all, he had a Habsburg wife and son, and Metternich was known to be the least antagonistic of the Allies. And many at the congress did fear that Metternich was secretly scheming to accept Napoleon as ruler of France.

The Russian tsar was another one who might be lured away from the coalition. Alexander had personally been kind to many Bonaparte family members in Vienna, often visiting Marie Louise at Schönbrunn and spending a great deal of time with Napoleon's stepson, Prince Eugène. In addition, Napoleon now had a copy of the secret treaty that would reveal what the tsar's so-called allies really thought of him.

As for Britain, Napoleon knew that he had virtually no chance at winning over Castlereagh and the Tory Party that controlled Parliament. What he could do, however, was undermine their government. Indeed, on assuming power in France, Napoleon immediately abolished the slave trade, accomplishing at one stroke what the congress had only managed to condemn after endless discussion and countless concessions. Whig opposition leaders, very much impressed, seized the opportunity to denounce the British government for wanting to wage war against such an enlightened ruler.

Napoleon certainly knew how to target his appeals with great skill, and he had a plan for winning over Talleyrand as well. The emperor promised to be forgiving—for he, too, had made mistakes, he admitted. Despite their differences in the past, Napoleon wanted Talleyrand back: "He is still the man, who knows the most about the century, the cabinets, and the peoples." The person he chose to convey this message, Count Auguste-Charles-Joseph Flahaut de la Billarderie, was none other than Talleyrand's son, from an affair back in Paris thirty years before.

When Flahaut had difficulty reaching Vienna, arrested on the way at Stuttgart by officials of the king of Württemberg, Napoleon sent another courier, Count François-Casimir Mouret de Montrond, the charming adventurer known in Paris salons as the "beautiful Montrond" or the "most devilish man in France." He had long been one of Talleyrand's close friends. Montrond's relationship would guarantee an opportunity to present his appeal to the foreign minister. His charm, Napoleon hoped, would do the rest.

Count Montrond made his way to Vienna, arriving successfully by using the false name of Abbé Altieri. On the first evening at the Kaunitz Palace, Montrond asked Talleyrand, point-blank, if he, as French foreign minister, could really support a war against France.

"Read the declaration," Talleyrand responded, pointing to the Vienna papers that outlawed Bonaparte; "it does not contain a single word with which I do not agree." Besides, the French foreign minister continued, "The question, too, is not of a war against France, but of a war against the man of Elba."

This was a firm response, without the equivocation that often shrouded the comments of his gifted colleague Metternich. Or was it, as some of Talleyrand's enemies feared, merely a ploy to raise the price of his cooperation? Almost certainly, Talleyrand had no intention of joining Napoleon, though his former boss continued to raise the stakes.

By the end of the month, another messenger would convey an additional offer intended to appeal to Talleyrand's notorious mercurial streak. All his extensive properties in France, which had been impounded on Napoleon's return, would be restored, along with a salary of some 200,000 livres, if Talleyrand "behaves like a Frenchman and renders me a few services." Refusal to comply, of course, would be interpreted by Napoleon as an insult and a sign of hostility.

WHEN KING LOUIS XVIII fled Paris in March, he risked appearing as a cowardly and unpopular ruler desperate only to protect himself. The king, however, clung to the belief that he maintained the support of the vast majority of Frenchmen. It was only a matter of time before his faithful subjects would rise up against the outlaw. All they needed was a spark to ignite the explosion of support. Perhaps the Vienna Congress could assist in providing that spark.

Yet, as Talleyrand knew, it was going to be a difficult task to convince

Vienna's leaders to restore the Bourbons on the throne for a second time. The king had, among other things, purged the Senate, imposed a strict censorship, and made a mockery of the freedoms that had been promised to the French on the Bourbons' return. Their blunders seemed endless: "They had learned nothing, forgotten nothing," as was commonly said of the Bourbon family.

The Russian tsar, for one, regretted putting them on the throne the last time, and did not wish to repeat that mistake. Metternich, too, was secretly looking into other options. As he confided that spring to the Duchess of Sagan, the Bourbons looked "morally sick" and unable to cope. Opposition to the Bourbons, then, was bringing Metternich and Alexander almost into agreement.

The most prominent spokesmen for the Bourbons, on the other hand, were the British delegates. It was Britain, after all, who had supported Louis' restoration the first time, just as they did before, when he spent many years in exile at Hartwell House in Buckinghamshire. They had, in a sense, invested heavily in him, and presumably did not want to abandon him now. Louis was the best bet, Castlereagh gambled, for a friendly France and a more stable peace.

But imposing the Bourbons over the wishes of Alexander, Metternich, and clearly many Frenchmen would not be easy. Many Englishmen back at home were also opposed to war for this purpose. English debt was already of substantial proportions, amassed in the recent war against the United States and the long, drawn-out struggle against Napoleon. In February, it had passed the £700 million mark, and payments on this debt alone consumed about one-third of the state's annual budget.

In the last war, Britain had paid Russia, Prussia, Austria, Spain, Portugal, Sweden, Sicily, Bavaria, and many German states to fight Napoleon. Was Britain, again, to "subsidize all the world"? Was restoring the Bourbons again really worth risking so much loss in life, not to mention the wartime threats to English commerce and the continued hated income tax, the first in the world?

Members of the opposition Whig Party certainly did not think so. Sir Francis Burdett, for one, did not wish "to plunge this country into a sea of blood to reinstate the Bourbon line in France." This dynasty did not have a good track record. One wit, Richard Sheridan, expressed the discontent rather well, summing up British foreign policy over the previous

150 years: half of it trying to remove the Bourbons, and the other half trying to restore them.

Besides, the Whigs argued, look how easily Napoleon had returned. "No man can doubt that this Napoleon stands as Emperor of France by the will of the French people." Burdett spoke for many when he concluded, "Let then the French settle their own affairs." It was not for Britain or Europe to intervene in their domestic disputes.

While these matters were debated in Parliament, newspapers, and clubs around the country, the Duke of Wellington made a fateful decision: He decided to pledge Britain's full support to the war effort. It was a risky move even in a time of considerable ministerial discretion. Yet he pushed ahead and guaranteed British participation. By the time the Allied troops were marching, none of the opposition—or anyone else in the country, for that matter—had time to realize what had happened. Britain was going to war.

As MATTERS LOOKED grim for the Bourbons in their exiled court at Ghent, Belgium, Talleyrand was praised as their best hope for the future. Arnail François, Comte de Jaucourt, his colleague in the Foreign Ministry, wrote, pleading with him to finish his affairs in Vienna, hurry back to the king, and accept a position of power.

At the same time, many of the other exiled ministers around the king also wanted Talleyrand recalled—but certainly not to offer him any more influence. For many, Talleyrand was to be lured out of Vienna and then sacked. Extreme royalists around the king had never forgiven him for his past; he was an aristocrat who joined the Revolution and then helped bring Bonaparte to power. There was no amount of evidence that would convince them that Talleyrand was not intriguing. The viper would soon again shed his skin.

By late April, King Louis XVIII would, in fact, summon Talleyrand back to his headquarters in Ghent. Talleyrand, however, stalled, and with good reason. He had to be cautious, as he suspected, quite rightly, the motives of many of the king's closest advisers. What's more, he knew that the business in Vienna was about to be wrapped up, and he did not want to leave as the congress approached its climax.

"My anxiety to find myself at Your Majesty's side would make me start tomorrow," Talleyrand answered, "if affairs were sufficiently advanced to render only my signature necessary, or if the termination of the Congress were still in the distance." In another excuse, he argued that as others were preparing to depart, he could leave shortly, so as not to injure the king's interests by being one of the first to leave town.

Two weeks later, Talleyrand was still making excuses for his delay. It was clear that those who wanted his recall, supporters and enemies alike, would have to think of something more powerful than a direct order from the king.

Chapter 29

FAREWELLS

The demon is not far from us, and the Gates of Hell are always open.

—CARDINAL CONSALVI

Determined to strike a deal, Napoleon kept on dispatching messengers to Vienna, and they kept on being stopped. Even his most recent courier, a former chamberlain to Emperor Francis, Monsieur de Stassart, had not succeeded. Arrested in Bavaria, his letters were seized and sent to the congress. Metternich promised to open these confiscated papers in front of his colleagues.

On May 3, Napoleon's secret letters, seals seemingly unbroken, were brought into the conference room and set down on the familiar green table. Did Metternich know their contents already, with the help of the Austrian Cabinet Noir? It was hard to imagine that he did not.

Before he opened the letters, though, Metternich first wanted all nonessential diplomats "politely eased" out of the room. At that particular moment, this included only one person, Prussia's minister of war, General Hermann von Boyen, who had arrived in town the previous month. Ambassador Humboldt was asked to escort his colleague out of the room, which he did, and then rushed back in for the show. The minister of war was left outside, upset and insulted.

With great flair, Metternich broke the seals, unfolded the letters, and began deciphering Napoleon's monstrous scrawl. Sure enough, the emperor was emphasizing his pacific intentions and hoping to persuade Austria to accept peace with him. Metternich promptly affirmed his commitment to the Allies and announced that he would not even dignify Napoleon's request with a response. This scene was exploited for all it was worth as a show of solidarity. He might as well have bowed and blown kisses after his performance.

Later that night, while dining in Chancellor Hardenberg's rooms, Humboldt had the misfortune of running into Boyen again. The Prussian war minister was quite upset with Humboldt—enraged is more accurate. By the end of the tense conversation, on a second-floor balcony, the Prussian minister of war had challenged the ambassador to a duel.

Humboldt, to be sure, was no fighter. Count Carl Axel Löwenhielm, the Swedish delegate, earlier summed up this fact well, when he remarked ironically that if the issues of the Congress of Vienna ended up being decided by physical combat of the participants, then he hoped to draw the Prussian ambassador.

When Humboldt tried to apologize, the proud minister of war refused to listen. The challenge had been issued, and the duel would take place as planned, he insisted. They would meet that Friday, May 5, at three in the afternoon, and drive out to a lonely spot, just outside Vienna.

At the appointed time, after Humboldt had spent the morning in conference and then dined, as he put it, like "Homeric heroes always did before battle," he went to his duel. The location was actually moved to a more secluded place, "a pretty meadow near a wood" in the wine-growing region at Spitz. The minister of war, who had the first shot, aimed his pistol and, at the last second, deliberately shot wide. Humboldt's pistol then also "misfired." As Humboldt wrote home afterward, the two duelists realized the "pure foolishness" of the quarrel, had a good laugh, and walked back to town like old friends. Humboldt said that he had learned a lesson, namely, that it was much braver to reject a duel than it was to fight one.

Meanwhile, with most police resources concentrated on providing information and security in Vienna, the surrounding countryside was left more exposed and preyed upon, as one person complained, by many "plunderers, deserters and discharged soldiers averse to honest labor." Among them was a young veteran, Captain Johann Georg Grasel, who had become so thoroughly disgusted with the prevailing "unequal distribution of wealth" in evidence that he had taken matters into his own hands. Young Grasel had become an outlaw: He would be the Robin Hood of the Vienna Congress.

Legends were quickly developing around this rogue and his gang of robbers, hiding out in a secret lair somewhere in the Vienna Woods. His followers were growing, and sometimes said to number in the fifties, sixties, or even the hundreds. Crimes were traced back to him all throughout the spring, and magnified into mythic proportions. They had a team of horses for quick strikes, always limited, as the story went, to "castles and public offices." As the tradition developed, under the influence of Romanticism, Grasel was celebrated as a people's bandit who would "rob the State and the rich in order to give to those he believed to be unjustly poor and oppressed."

Grasel and his band of forest robbers did not penetrate any of the major delegations, or attack the main figures, but he aroused great interest. Critics of Napoleon saw Grasel as the outlaw emperor in miniature, while others compared the bandits to Prussians seizing territory at will from the Saxons and other Germans. Critics who accused the congress, as a whole, of "robbing the have-nots for the benefit of the haves" found the popular bandit alluring, turning the tables on the rich and powerful. It would not last for long, however. Captain Grasel was arrested later that year, and eventually executed.

NAPOLEON, MEANWHILE, WAS hoping to show the true feelings of the tsar's so-called allies, Britain and Austria, and sent him a copy of the secret treaty that they had signed, with Bourbon France, back in January. Alexander was furious. He threw a fit, stomping around his suites in the palace and glowering so much that, in the words of his adviser Kapodistrias, his face turned bright red and his ears purple. He called for Metternich at once. "Do you know this document?" the tsar demanded.

As Metternich stumbled through his excuses, Alexander interrupted him brusquely—he could be as forgiving as he could be petty. "While we live, there must be no mention of this between us again!" Alexander said, allegedly throwing the paper into the fire. "There are better things for us to do. We must think of nothing but our alliance against Napoleon." The tsar was enjoying the chance to be magnanimous, and in all likelihood, he had suspected this agreement long before.

The Prussian generals also read the secret treaty, which Napoleon had published in newspapers. They were likewise disgusted, though ultimately this had little effect on their already low estimate of Prince Metternich.

Besides, they had already discovered the treaty themselves, when searching a captured French official at Liège. What disturbed them most, however, was the participation of Great Britain. The secret treaty had confirmed their fears about this "Perfidious Albion," as Napoleon had called them.

Back in London, Castlereagh was having difficulty defending his actions in Vienna. He was criticized for abandoning Poland, carving up Saxony, destroying Genoa, and generally making a mockery of diplomacy. His colleague, the Duke of Wellington, was likewise rebuked for his signature on the document that branded Napoleon an outlaw, and his adherence to this so-called doctrine of assassination. Worse still, the Duke of Wellington's pledge that Great Britain would enter the war against Napoleon reached Parliament, and the opposition was outraged.

Britain had been tricked into accepting a war that, essentially, had already been decided upon, opposition party leaders fumed. Castlereagh, Wellington, and the war hawks of the Tory Party were senselessly trying to drown the continent in blood "in order to put down one man," and, moreover, they had guaranteed British funds to pay for it all. "You have deceived us shamefully," declared one member, who spoke for many that spring.

Castlereagh responded by going through a litany of reasons for the war: the impossibility of trusting Napoleon's word—an ironic beginning perhaps, given the critiques against himself. He continued to warn about the dangers of having Bonaparte back in power, and the sheer uncertainty it meant for the future. In this speech, there were many reasons for the war, but, noticeably, no outright denial of any of the charges.

Britain was standing by its commitment to fight and subsidize the Allies in the war. And so the world's first income tax, which had been imposed in Great Britain as "a temporary measure" in the war crisis of the 1790s and was supposed to be repealed in peacetime, would now not be abolished after all.

But even with this tax, the Duke of Wellington was frustrated with the military situation. The British army, gathering in Belgium, was not in the best of shape. Most of the hardened veterans of the Spanish campaign were not available, as many had been released from service at the end of the war and others were now making their way home after service in the American war. In fact, the army Wellington found was only about twelve thousand men, adequate enough perhaps for enforcing the handover of

Belgium to Dutch control. But they were hardly in a position to face Napoleon.

Ever since the duke had arrived in Brussels back on April 4, and moved into the hotel on rue Montagne du Parc, he had worked to whip the troops into shape. Besides the small size of the army, the soldiers were young, poorly trained, and appallingly "ill-equipped," not to mention being encumbered by a "very inexperienced Staff." The commander in chief of the Allied armies in Belgium at this time was the Prince of Orange, a twenty-three-year-old who had been given command as a token of British support for the Dutch royal family. His nickname was "Slender Billy," and the soldiers were not exactly impressed by his leadership abilities.

Indeed, many things had rankled the duke on his arrival. Besides the fact that most of the army spoke German and he did not, Wellington had to worry about the loyalty of some troops. There were Saxons who resented the treatment of their kingdom and refused to be commanded by the Prussians, and Belgians who likewise did not like the prospects of Dutch rule and were reluctant to fight their idol, Napoleon. Wellington had been voicing these complaints and many others, but he was increasingly frustrated by the slow response of the British government. "In my opinion," he wrote to Lord Stewart in Vienna, "they are doing nothing in England."

While the Austrians were mainly on the Rhine, or in Italy facing Murat, and the Russians were farther back as a reserve force, Wellington was to be assisted primarily by the Prussians. Their commander was officially Field Marshal von Blücher, a seventy-two-year-old with silver hair, a pinkish face, and a bushy white mustache. He was rather large—one person who saw him the previous summer thought he was "the stoutest man that ever did live." Blücher may not have been the best general of the Prussian staff, but he certainly was brave. His no-nonsense aggressive approach verged on recklessness, and his usual order, "Attack," earned him the nickname "Old Marshal Vorwarts!"

Blücher's chief of staff, General August von Gneisenau, had considerable authority and actually helped counter this rashness. The king of Prussia had even given Gneisenau authority to assume control, should Blücher again fall sick. The field marshal was prone to some strange delusions, including one belief that he had become pregnant and would soon give birth to an elephant!

Wellington was prepared to shrug aside such beliefs as the harmless idiosyncrasies of an exceptional soldier. The Prussian field marshal, he insisted, was eager for battle—"if anything too eager." At any rate, Wellington preferred Blücher to his assistant, Gneisenau, who had some marked suspicions of the British that would soon be even more pronounced.

Amid the public attempts to display German unity, Vienna learned of trouble in the Prussian army. In early May, the Saxon army had rioted, and in fact almost captured its Prussian commander. Both Blücher and Gneisenau had to "slip out" their back door and flee to safety. Worse still, the rigorous suppression of the mutiny confirmed the worst fears of Prussian brutality.

Allied troops were in the meantime waiting—waiting for orders from their officers, waiting for what Napoleon would do, waiting for what would happen next in the remarkable year of 1815. They passed the time as best they could. The First Regiment of Foot Guards, for instance, played a friendly game of cricket: The soldiers with last names beginning with the letters A through G faced all the rest, and, reportedly, to use a popular phrase of the day, "beat the others hollow."

ALL THROUGHOUT MAY, as dignitaries and guests prepared to leave, awarding jeweled snuffboxes and portraits freely all around, Vienna looked more beautiful than ever. The green expanse of the Prater seemed ideal for a leisurely carriage ride down the boulevard under chestnut trees exploding in brilliant pink. It was "divine weather," and as Gentz noted in his diary, "the most beautiful spring I've ever seen."

With feelings no doubt of excitement, fear, sadness, and exhaustion all at once, the delegates and guests alike made their plans to depart. The tsar of Russia and the king of Prussia, having entered town together, planned to leave together. On May 26, 1815, eight months and a day after their entrance into town, the two sovereigns departed for the new Allied headquarters at Heilbronn. The king of Prussia would stop off first, briefly, in his capital of Berlin.

After some difficult moments, the tsar was nevertheless leaving with Poland, smaller than he liked, though still large enough for him to feel that he had accomplished something. This was, of course, in addition to his previous gains in the war, including Finland and Bessarabia, which were confirmed. Some of his last known appearances were actually in taverns. One person claimed to have seen His Majesty, the Tsar of All the Russias, engaging challengers in a contest to see who "could make the most horrible face." And according to an anonymous informant, Alexander had said, in the end, that if he had not been tsar, he would desire "nothing more than being a general in Austria."

Metternich was also leaving town for his summer villa on the Rennweg. He would spend a couple of weeks there with his wife, his children, and the most recent addition to the family, the pet parrot Polly. This parrot had been given to Metternich by an old English sea captain, though the bird had by now, he joked, "lost his English accent." Metternich would celebrate his forty-second birthday with fellow diplomats at his summer residence on May 15, and return to the Chancellery office periodically in the last month to wrap up the congress.

His assistant, Gentz, was bagging a number of sundry gifts for his many services: honors, payments, snuffboxes, and even a new carriage, which had been dropped off at his apartment by an unnamed benefactor. So many were happy with and grateful to the man who would write the official treaty of the Vienna Congress. One historian called Gentz the most bribed man in history. Although certainly an overstatement, the secretary of the congress did, in fact, pocket a fortune, and as soon as he finished working on the draft, he went house hunting. He found a large, eighteenth-century manor outside town, in the Weinhaus, and felt "as happy as a child" looking forward to moving in there, "as soon as this wretched Congress is over."

Princess Bagration, by contrast, was spending the last days at the congress in deep financial trouble. Already that spring, her chef, Monsieur Bretton, had been forced to stop advancing the princess money for the food and dinners that he prepared himself. He could no longer continue this way until his wages, back wages, and all the other reimbursements were paid. Of all her friends in Vienna the last several months, few were willing or able to help. She wrote her stepfather back in St. Petersburg to send more money.

Ironically, while many had earlier urged the police to remove Princess Bagration from the city, there were a great number in late May trying to make sure that she did not leave, at least before she repaid her enormous debts. According to her close friend Aurora de Marassé, the princess owed a staggering 21,801 ducats, another 18,121 florins, and some 7,860 in promissory notes. There were other outstanding debts to various bankers around town. It was feared that the princess might move straight from the gilded salon to the debtor's prison.

Another matter that bothered the princess was the departure of a new lover she had taken, the Crown Prince of Württemberg. She accompanied the handsome prince out of town, all the way to the first postal stop, Purkersdorf, where they said good-byes so tender that one police agent noted ironically that it might lead to the birth of another "illegitimate child for the virtuous princess."

The Duchess of Sagan was one of the last to leave town. She would, however, vacate the Palm Palace first, leaving Princess Bagration there reigning, though besieged less by admirers than creditors. The duchess's lover, Prince Alfred von Windischgrätz, had left Vienna in April to join his regiment as it prepared to fight Napoleon. The duchess moved into his mansion, the nearby Windischgrätz Palace. The parties were tapering off back in Vienna, she said, and she was "dying of boredom."

In truth, though, the duchess was losing interest in Prince Alfred, and their relationship would soon be over, though Alfred would fight for its continuation, just as Metternich had done before him. While he was away, the duchess had been seeing more and more of the British ambassador, Lord Stewart.

They dined together and rode through the city's many parks, Wilhelmine on a prized horse that she had earlier purchased from Stewart. They took several excursions into the countryside, just as she had done with Alfred. Stewart was like him in many ways, though more wild and unpredictable. "Lord Pumpernickel" had taken advantage of the absence of Castlereagh, Wellington, and Clancarty and, according to one disapproving critic, turned the British embassy into a gambling den and brothel.

Clearly, the Duchess of Sagan and Lord Stewart were struggling to adjust to a city that no longer hosted a spectacular royal carnival. By the end of May, most of the guests had left town, either to face Napoleon, return home, or head off elsewhere in search of the next adventure. "Vienna is becoming a desert," the Duchess of Sagan said with sadness.

Chapter 30

ONQUERING THE PEACE

I have spent the whole day cutting Europe into bits like a piece of cheese.

— PRINCE METTERNICH

On the first of June, Napoleon celebrated his triumphant return with a massive public ceremony, arguably the most grandiose since his coronation as emperor in Notre Dame eleven years before. It was held on the Champs de Mars, a wide parade ground in central Paris that would later hold the Eiffel Tower. A pyramid-like platform and amphitheater had been constructed there for the occasion, outside the officer cadet academy, the École Militaire.

At the center was Napoleon, sitting on a purple throne, wearing a black hat with white ostrich feather and a purple coronation mantle tossed over his shoulders. He was surrounded by his brothers, his marshals, his eagles on columns, and many war trophies. Only his wife and son were missing.

Shouts of *"Vive l'Empereur!"* were heard in the throngs below, estimated at two hundred thousand. After the cannon boomed and Mass was celebrated, a spokesman for the new legislature addressed the crowd, at least those at the very front who could hear:

What do these monarchs desire, Sire, who are advancing against us with such warlike preparations? What have we done to justify their aggressive proceedings? Have we violated any of the treaties of peace?

Posing the question to the crowd, he then promptly answered it. The enemies of France "do not like the ruler we have chosen, and we do not like him, they would impose on us."

After the speech and the applause, the emperor's arch-chancellor introduced the new constitution, the Acte Additional, which the people of France had affirmed in a recent vote. The margin had been large. About 1.3 million approved the constitution, and only 4,206 cast their vote against it—voting under Napoleon always revealed more about his manipulation of the procedures than it evidenced any real freedom of expression. The constitution was then dropped at the foot of the throne for Napoleon's signature.

Napoleon was very good at creating grandiose spectacles to demonstrate, symbolize, and enhance his power. "A government must dazzle and astonish," he had long known, and this was never truer than with a new government. Napoleon needed to fire imaginations, just as he had done in other crucial moments, such as when he first seized power, launched a risky endeavor, or experienced a major setback.

The whole event had originally been planned as a large democratic forum inaugurating the proclaimed new reign of liberty. But only a fraction of the eligible voters had participated, the turnout in Paris estimated at one in ten, indicating that neither Napoleon nor his constitution was as popular as he wished. So he changed his plans and, instead, staged an event with every detail tightly controlled to present a picture of a country rallying around its enlightened emperor.

Tsar Alexander, meanwhile, had arrived at the southern German town of Heilbronn, literally meaning "holy spring," which then temporarily served as Allied headquarters. He was happy about the outcome in Poland, but he agonized over other matters. Why had the French welcomed Napoleon so enthusiastically, and why had the power of the Bourbon king collapsed so easily? Was it really worth shedding more blood just to restore this dynasty?

Even assuming for the moment that this was a worthwhile war aim, the tsar was troubled by the fact that his Russian army, stationed mainly on the other side of the Vistula in the new Kingdom of Poland, was far away from the likely center of action, and would likely be relegated to reserve functions. He had lost his bid to be supreme commander as well. All these concerns nagged at the tsar as he sat alone late one night in early June at his study in the Rauch'sche Palais. It was perfectly clear, at least to him, that he was being punished for all the decadence of the Vienna Congress.

Suddenly, about two that morning, there was a knock on his door, and his aide-de-camp, Prince Volkonski, entered, visibly troubled and apologetic for disturbing the tsar at that hour. He had a message, admittedly strange, to relay to the tsar. There was a woman who insisted on seeing the tsar. It was Julie von Krüdener.

"You can imagine my surprise," Alexander later said. He had just then been thinking about Baroness Krüdener as he contemplated a passage in the book of Revelation: "And there appeared a great wonder in heaven: a woman clothed with the sun." Now the woman who he believed could help him most was standing at the door.

> I thought I was dreaming. I received her immediately, and as if she had read my soul, she spoke strong consoling words which calmed the inner turmoil which had obsessed me for so long.

It was an extraordinary three-hour visit in the middle of the night. The prophetess could illuminate certain passages in the Holy Scriptures that baffled the tsar, and then explain their meaning in the context of the difficulties that he faced. Above all, she assured him that the "white angel" (the tsar) would "conquer the Dragon" (Napoleon). She had a mystic faith in an upcoming apocalypse that, with the tsar's help, would envelop the world with "a great explosion of love."

In the meantime, she explained why inner peace had been so elusive to the Tsar of All the Russias: "You have not renounced your sins and have not humbled yourself before Christ," she said. You must approach God, she further instructed the tsar, "like a criminal begging for mercy."

Few had spoken to the tsar with such blunt criticism of his sins and mistakes before (his favorite sister, Grand Duchess Catherine, was one who did). But Baroness Krüdener knew exactly what she was doing, and Alexander was entranced. She moved into a nearby hut, and during the tense summer, on the eve of hostilities, she came over to visit the tsar virtually every night for study, usually beginning about six and continuing until two in the morning. The tsar's main advisers, on the other hand, were not invited to take part in this spiritual quest.

By June, everyone knew that war might begin at any moment. There was a flurry of activity among those remaining in Vienna to complete the negotiations as soon as possible. The king of Saxony had finally accepted the congress's solution about the fate of his country, and thereby removed one of the last obstacles that the German Committee faced in its deliberations. Its members now went forward in finalizing their decisions, and their series of meetings behind closed doors, seven in all from late May to early June, were among the stormiest of the entire congress.

In discussing the future of the states of Germany, the committee wrangled over everything from writing a constitution to establishing an army. The delegates wrestled with difficult questions about the exact nature of the freedoms that should be granted in the new constitution. Freedom of press, freedom of worship, and freedom of movement, including the right to attend a university, figured prominently on the list for many on the committee. At one point, the Austrian representative noted that he had no fewer than forty-six different drafts of a constitution on his desk.

One of the hotly debated topics in these sessions was the treatment of Jewish minorities in the new German Confederation. The relations varied widely from state to state, but generally, in places the French conquered, occupied, or exerted considerable influence, conditions were better for the Jewish communities. In many places, old laws discriminating against Jews had been repealed, and new laws guaranteeing equality enacted. But now that the French had been defeated, many cities and states wanted the new laws tossed out, along with the unpopular French. Some of the most progressive places, like Westphalia, Frankfurt, and the Hanseatic towns, were now at risk of a vehement backlash.

The Jewish delegations had worked the last eight months behind the scenes in salons like Fanny von Arnstein's to rally support for their cause. Humboldt was a staunch supporter of Jewish rights, joined by the Prussian chancellor Hardenberg. The two had, of course, cooperated well before on this question. Humboldt penned a remarkable treatise calling for full civic equality in 1809, and Hardenberg enacted the law in 1812 that emancipated Prussian Jews. The king of Prussia, less committed personally, had gone along with the reforms.

On January 4, 1815, Chancellor Hardenberg had taken time away from the impending Saxon crisis to appeal for the full equality of Jews. He argued the case well, citing every reason from the humane to the self-seeking; the Jews had made "sacrifices of every kind" in the war, showing "true courage and vaunted disregard of the perils of war." The Jews, he added, had also played a valuable role in the "system of credit and commerce of the various German states." A return to repression would only encourage them to move away, bringing their talents and assets with them.

Another source of support was Prince Metternich and the Austrian team. Friedrich von Gentz was a particularly valuable asset to the Jewish delegates; his diary shows his regular meetings with them that spring. Unlike Metternich and Humboldt, who refused to accept gifts for their support, including fine rings and silver plate, Gentz had no qualms. At meetings with Simon Edler von Lämel of Prague, for instance, Gentz accepted first an unnamed "beautiful present," then another 1,000 ducats, and then another 2,000 ducats, which prompted him to marvel about how all his "financial affairs are working out wonderfully." The Rothschilds had also made appeals on behalf of Jewish rights, both at the Congress of Vienna as well as in London, where the family had played a large role managing the British war effort and financing the huge subsidies that the British government dispensed to enemies of Napoleon.

Opposition, however, came from many circles, including the delegates of Bavaria, Württemberg, Frankfurt, and the former Hanseatic towns of Hamburg, Bremen, and Lübeck. Jacob Grimm's boss, Count Dorotheus Ludwig Keller of Hesse-Cassel, was another opponent. Indeed, when the question of Jewish rights was first officially proposed in the German Committee in late May, the Bavarian delegate, Count Aloys von Rechberg, had started laughing, and, as one eyewitness described it, the laughter ominously became infectious, spreading through the many hostile men in the room.

After many long sessions, however, Humboldt, Hardenberg, Metternich, and their allies had prevailed, and an article guaranteeing Jewish rights would be inserted into the new German constitution. Article XVI specifically instructed the future confederation to find ways to protect its Jewish minorities. In the meantime, all the privileges already granted in the states were to be safeguarded. The Vienna Congress was again launching into a pioneering discussion of human rights at a peace conference. Unfortunately, however, there was a problem that passed unnoticed and soon undermined this victory.

The representative of Bremen, Senator Johann Smidt, had managed to insert a small change in the actual wording of the article. At the last minute, he changed the phrase "[all the rights] granted *in* the several states" to "[all the rights] granted *by* the several states" (italics added). This single preposition would have dire consequences. German states would soon be able to argue that this constitutional guarantee specifically excluded laws passed by outside authorities, like the French. Within one year of the congress, some states were ignoring the rights supposedly guaranteed, and other towns, such as Bremen and Lübeck, even expelled their Jewish populations.

The delegates for the publishing houses and booksellers would also soon be disappointed. After the initial success in October, there had been a long spell without any action. Carl Bertuch's memorandum of April 14 had not restored any momentum. Now, too, as the German Committee deliberated on the constitution, there was a call to postpone a decision about the press and intellectual property rights until the new diet of the German Confederation met later in Frankfurt. This was barely defeated, and discussions continued for several meetings.

On the third of June, another last-minute change was inserted to the draft of Article XVIII, which was to safeguard freedom of the press and literary copyrights. Authors and publishers were still to be protected against forgeries of their works, but the stipulation guaranteeing freedom of the press was quietly dropped, and replaced by a pledge of uniform governmental regulation that would at least level the playing field. The minutes of the meeting do not reveal who initiated this change.

WHILE THE GERMAN Committee labored, leaders of the congress had decided to write one general treaty that would include every decision of the Vienna Congress. This was important, it was believed, to increase the stability of the agreement. Future aggressors were seen as less likely to break a single treaty signed by all the powers than several dozen separate agreements, each contracted by only a couple of interested powers.

Three people were placed in charge of assembling the document: Friedrich von Gentz, the Duke of Dalberg, and Lord Clancarty. The latter two had been added at the last minute after two other delegates declined: Russia's Count Anstett was suffering too much from his gout to focus completely on writing this important treaty, and Talleyrand's assistant, Comte de la Besnardière, was too preoccupied by Napoleon's seizure of his personal property.

The task of this three-man committee was colossal. They were supposed to incorporate the endless committee meetings, negotiations, and resolutions of eight months into one coherent document. And given Napoleon's stunning successes, this was indeed a race against time.

Recently, too, Gentz and his colleagues had encountered another unexpected obstacle. Critics and opponents of a general treaty were coming out en masse. Would not attempting to write such a single document, some asked, give rise to endless dissension among a group of powers that, in wartime, should be united? Even if unity were somehow preserved, would not the war—always full of unexpected consequences—likely end up creating a whole new set of conditions that would make the agreements irrelevant, or worse? The peace treaty could be outdated the very day it was signed.

In the end, the plenipotentiaries decided to take this risk, reasoning that this general treaty would indeed be better for the future security of Europe. Twenty-six secretaries, with scratching quills, labored around the clock on completing the 121-article treaty.

The favorite name for this encompassing document was not at first settled. Some called it simply the Treaty, the "European Treaty," or the "Grand European Treaty," though these were not the most appropriate names for a treaty that not all of Europe had participated in, and many states had only a vague idea of its contents. Others proposed the "New Charter for Europe." Eventually, the name that gained the most acceptance was the "Final Act," which was, as Gentz explained, conceived of as the final act of the victorious coalition against Napoleon.

On June 9, 1815, the delegates to the Vienna Congress gathered in the reception hall of the imperial palace to sign the Final Act—the closest, in fact, that the congress ever came to convening. Even then, it was not exactly a congress, and not everyone was invited to sign. Only the powers on the Committee of Eight would sign, and the rest would be asked to "accede separately." This decision had again insulted and infuriated the many excluded powers, who were once more denied a voice.

Ironically, many of the key figures at the congress were not even present. The host himself, Emperor Francis, had already left for the field of battle. Tsar Alexander and King Frederick William of Prussia were not there, either, having left about two weeks before. As for the British team, Castlereagh was long gone and the Duke of Wellington was somewhere outside Brussels. With the exception of Metternich and Talleyrand, two genuine survivors, none of the main leaders actually signed the treaty that concluded the Vienna Congress. And Talleyrand had only been able to stay for the signature by deliberately and repeatedly disobeying the king's orders.

Cardinal Consalvi had criticized the congress earlier as a Tower of Babel. The diplomats had begun with grand aspirations, but, in the end, they literally could not speak the same language. Consalvi would now issue a formal protest against the Congress of Vienna for its treatment of the pope. Although the Papal States had been restored, the pope had not received his due—either Avignon or Ferrara—Consalvi argued.

Another person who was upset was the Spanish delegate Pedro de Labrador, and he refused to sign the treaty. His government could not sanction the transfer of the Spanish royal territory of Parma to the wife of the detested usurper Bonaparte, nor agree to hand over the town of Olivenza to Portugal, as the congress had demanded. At this point, the delegates refused to make any more changes, either removing articles or adding in qualifications. Labrador would not budge, either. Each of the representatives of the other seven powers, in the meantime, took plume in hand, dipped the tip of the quill in the silver inkwell, and signed one of the most influential documents of the century. Spain would only accept the terms two years later, in May 1817.

The dancing congress ended without a great celebration to mark the occasion of the signing. The remaining participants simply drifted away. Metternich had a last dinner Monday night with Gentz, and then left Vienna at one o'clock the next morning, June 13, for Allied headquarters.

Talleyrand, too, was not to remain in Vienna for long after signing the Final Act. Having bid his farewells and exchanged snuffboxes, Talleyrand made a last tour of Kaunitz Palace, the site of so many parties, dinners, and intrigues the last nine months. As for that "great mass of papers" produced by the embassy, Talleyrand was not about to leave them for the maids, many of whom would surely be employed by the Austrian police. "I have, therefore, burnt the greater portion of these papers, and left the remainder in Vienna in safe hands." He was now ready to return to the king.

Chapter 31

To Conquer or Die

*My dear, with what refinement men go about destroying all the
good things which Providence has showered on them.*

— Prince Metternich

Murat had achieved a number of stunning successes in
rapid succession. He had conquered Rome, Florence,
and Bologna in two weeks, but he could not consolidate his victories. On May 3, the Austrian army caught up with him at
Tolentino in the Apennines and defeated him soundly. Murat's forces disintegrated. The Austrians recaptured the territory and, on the twenty-third, even seized his capital, Naples. Murat fled to France in the disguise
of a sailor, hoping to join Napoleon. After only one month, Murat's rash
adventure had come to an abrupt end.

Napoleon was furious at Murat for his lack of foresight, and he
feared that this defeat would have unpleasant consequences for his own
campaign. The French emperor had lost a potential ally that could have
tied up some one hundred thousand Austrian troops in the Italian peninsula for an undetermined period of time, but now, instead, the Austrians
were firmly in control of the region and free to concentrate on him.
Worse still, Napoleon had started to fear that fortune was abandoning
him, something hard to swallow, with his superstitious reverence for a
force that he believed governed his destiny.

Indeed, troubles were popping up for Napoleon everywhere with a
great deal more frequency. The emperor still suffered serious financial
problems, arising from years of revolution, war, and, most recently, mismanagement. When King Louis XVIII and his royal court left Paris, they

had run off with as much treasure as they could quickly carry away. The state's annual income at the time of Napoleon's return to Paris was barely one-third of the total he had enjoyed back in 1812. He would be forced to take desperate measures to raise money, everything from levying new emergency taxes to selling all state-owned forestlands.

In addition, the army Napoleon inherited was not the one he had left at his abdication one year before. The king's supposed 200,000 soldiers were at best about 120,000, and poorly equipped. Most of Napoleon's talented officers had been removed, and replaced by royalist cronies, many of whom had little or no experience on the battlefield. Veterans had also been dismissed from service or reduced to half pay. Ammunition was in short supply. Muskets, gun carriages, bayonets, and other weapons had been sold as "army surplus," and the money had disappeared.

But during the previous three months, Napoleon had scrambled to turn this unwieldy mass of men into an efficient army. All soldiers officially on leave, some 32,800, had been ordered to report to duty immediately, and the 82,000 known deserters also recalled. Press gangs roamed the capital and the countryside, rounding up even more "recruits." The National Guard was called, gaining an additional 234,000 men between the ages of twenty and sixty. Students at the École Polytechnique and the military academy at Saint-Cyr-l'École were pulled out of classrooms to man fortifications, and sailors lifted from the navy. Napoleon figured he wouldn't need a fleet in the upcoming struggle.

As for equipping the troops, who would have to cover some six hundred miles of exposed frontier in the east alone, Napoleon launched another monumental effort. He placed orders for some 235,000 muskets and some 15,000 pistols for his cavalry. He ordered new cartridges, uniforms, boots, and everything else he needed for his campaign, though it was by no means clear where the money would come from to pay for all these supplies.

Overwhelmed with these demands, ordered at breakneck speed with challenging timetables, many provincial authorities resisted Napoleon's decrees. The new sacrifices and hardships only reminded many Frenchmen of what they had disliked last time about his reign, and the grumbling was getting worse. Even many who had welcomed Napoleon a few months ago were now growing disillusioned.

Supporters of the exiled King Louis XVIII, meanwhile, had been stirring in the west, particularly in the old Bourbon strongholds of Brittany and Vendée, and soon some thirty thousand royalists had rallied under the Marquis de la Rochejacquelin. From the other political extreme, some Jacobins and former revolutionaries were already plotting Napoleon's downfall. Clearly, most radicals had only accepted Napoleon as a temporary ally who could help sweep out the detested Bourbons. Now that this was accomplished, many felt, it was time to remove Napoleon and restore real freedom to France.

As the Allied forces prepared their armies for war, some of Napoleon's advisers suggested that he consolidate his strength and adopt a defensive campaign. His minister of the interior, Carnot, was one who argued for this approach. Britain and Prussia would probably not be in a position to attack for some time, and, moreover, they would likely await the arrival of the other allies. This would mean that the first battle would probably not take place until July at the earliest. Napoleon could use the next few weeks to strengthen his situation at home, both politically and militarily. Let the Allies enter the country as invaders, and discontent with Napoleon would quickly disappear as Frenchmen rallied to his side.

This was certainly an interesting suggestion, but anyone who had studied Napoleon's behavior in critical situations would know that he was inclined to attack. After all, the Allies were only getting stronger. They would soon have as many as seven or eight hundred thousand soldiers marching into France. As for the domestic unrest, Napoleon would address that the best way he knew how: He would fight, and he would win. He knew the stakes. One major defeat could end his reign and his dynasty. A big victory, on the other hand, could cause the fledgling alliance forged at Vienna to collapse from its own internal weakness.

In the early morning of June 12, Napoleon quietly left Paris to launch his invasion of Belgium. Two days later, on the anniversary of his victories at Marengo and Friedland, Napoleon issued a stirring proclamation from Beaumont in northeastern France: Soldiers, he said, "the time has come to conquer or die."

NAPOLEON'S GOAL WAS to make a quick devastating strike and knock out either the Duke of Wellington or Field Marshal Blücher before they could combine their forces. After this first victory, he would then wheel over and defeat the other army. Napoleon had used this general strategy, again and again, in vanquishing larger enemy armies. This time, too, Napoleon actually had a slight advantage in the strength of his troops and fire-power over either Wellington or Blücher, but if they combined their forces, he would be significantly outnumbered.

While the armies were positioning themselves for the upcoming battle, one of the most famous parties in history, the Duchess of Rich-mond's ball, took place on the rue de Blanchisserie in Brussels. Lord Byron celebrated it memorably in *Childe Harold's Pilgrimage,* and William Makepeace Thackeray used it for a scene in *Vanity Fair.* Actually, the his-torical ball was slightly different from the one of literature with its "high halls" of marble: It took place in a carriage house, or rather a coachman's workshop.

Some 224 people appeared on the guest list: Wellington, the Prince of Orange, the Duke of Brunswick, and many other British and Allied offi-cers, including twenty-two colonels. The duke was later criticized for attending such a frivolous event during the time of crisis, though this view fails to appreciate Wellington's intentions that evening. He had come to the ball as a way to dispel fears, and, as he put it, "reassure our friends." He would attend, calm as usual, and show that despite Napoleon's invasion of Belgium, everything was perfectly under control.

During the ball, however, a messenger arrived with the news that Napoleon was again on the march and apparently headed straight for the capital, Brussels. He was also taking an unexpected route (through Charleroi and not, as Wellington had suspected, through Mons). Welling-ton casually stayed on another twenty minutes, as if nothing were amiss, and then departed, pretending to be leaving for a good night's sleep. As he thanked the Duke of Richmond for the evening, he asked if his host happened to have "a good map in the house." The two men retired to a side room. Peering over a map on the table, Wellington confessed that he had misjudged the situation. "Napoleon has humbugged me, by God," Wellington said. "He has gained twenty-four hours' march of me."

The Allies would have to move quickly to protect the capital, the exiled royal court, and, of course, the coastal towns that formed their supply lines back to Great Britain. Wellington would engage the French at Quatre Bras, a strategic crossroads on the main road north, though he well knew that the Allied troops would probably not have enough time

to arrive in strong enough forces to win decisively. At this point, Wellington allegedly ran his finger over the map and said, "I must fight him
here." He pointed to a small village called Waterloo.

A few hours later, on the sixteenth of June, the soldiers were marching, some officers still in silk stockings from the ball. Two battles in fact
would take place almost simultaneously that day. In one of them, at Quatre Bras, the Duke of Wellington and the Anglo-Allied troops drove back
a French detachment under Marshal Ney. The other battle, about seven
miles to the east, at Ligny, was a different matter. Napoleon, in command, won an impressive victory. The Prussians lost some 16,000 troops
and a further 8,000 soldiers deserted. The French, by contrast, suffered
11,500 losses. Field Marshal Blücher had nearly been killed. His horse
had been shot, and its fall had pinned down the seventy-two-year-old,
who was then trampled by two French cavalrymen.

As the Prussians fled the scene in disarray, the French emperor, confident in his success, did not order an energetic pursuit of the defeated. He
was already planning the next stage of his campaign. It was some twelve
hours later—about eleven the next morning—when Napoleon finally sent
away two corps and a force of some thirty-three thousand men under his
most recent marshal, Emmanuel de Grouchy, to catch the Prussian army
and finish them off. By then, the Prussians had managed to escape the
worst danger.

The Prussian military staff, still stunned from the heavy defeat, was
upset, and some blamed Wellington. The chief of staff, General August
von Gneisenau, in particular, felt betrayed. He had had the distinct
impression that Wellington would send several regiments over to aid
them at Ligny. Wellington had, in fact, promised to help the Prussians in
a meeting on the morning of the sixteenth, though he had added an
important qualification that he would only be in a position to send
troops if he were not attacked himself. The ferocity of the French attack
at Quatre Bras prevented him from sending any assistance.

Wellington, meanwhile, learned of the disaster that struck his Prus-
sian allies and realized that he, too, was now in a very exposed position.
He could not remain at Quatre Bras, as a sitting duck, for the armies of
Napoleon and Ney to fall upon him, but would have to march quickly.
Wellington sent a messenger over to his Prussian allies, informing them
that he would retreat north to a place called Mont-Saint-Jean just south

of the village of Waterloo, where he would set up his headquarters. He hoped to engage the French there, and requested that the Prussians send over a corps if they could spare one.

Napoleon's campaign was certainly off to a good start. Having hammered the Prussians, he would now bring the bulk of his troops together, defeat the Duke of Wellington, and watch the alliance unravel.

THIS WOULD ACTUALLY be the first time that the French would fight an army with so many British troops since the Egyptian campaign some sixteen years before, and it was the first and only time that Napoleon and Wellington would face each other on the battlefield. Both were forty-six years old, with outstanding reputations—Napoleon, the bold strategist, inclined to quick surprise strikes, and Wellington, the brilliant tactician who preferred a more cautious and balanced approach. Napoleon was as feared as Alexander the Great and Genghis Khan; Wellington had never lost a battle.

Napoleon, it must be said, had many advantages. Thanks to his zealous efforts rebuilding the army, he had more soldiers, seventy-two thousand to Wellington's sixty-eight thousand, and more artillery, 246 cannons to Wellington's 156. He also had more veterans, compared to Wellington's many raw recruits and troops of uncertain loyalty (some two-thirds of his troops were non-British, mainly Dutch, Belgian, or German; many of them had either served the French in the past or were suspected of having French loyalties, or both). Napoleon, moreover, had a number of marshals who had fought Wellington in Spain and knew his tactics well.

Remarkably, as Wellington marched north on the seventeenth, neither Napoleon nor Ney seized the opportunity to attack. Orders had not been clear or timely, and Ney had hesitated more than usual. Some historians have wondered if Ney suffered from a form of "battle fatigue," or perhaps feared that Wellington's march was another one of his tricks. At any rate, Wellington had advanced his troops unharmed, and when the French realized that a good opportunity of striking the enemy was slipping away, they started marching. They were soon obstructed, however, by a violent storm, with heavy rain and then heavy mud bogging down their movement. By the evening, Napoleon decided to rest his army. "Have all the troops take up positions and we will see what happens tomorrow," he said, moving on to his headquarters a mile away, at a white stone farmhouse called Le Caillou, on the road to Brussels.

Wellington had managed to move into position, and chose the field of battle. It was a classical Wellington selection—a deceptively flat plain with "dips and folds" where he could place his troops on the inverse slope, better to conceal their numbers and protect them from enemy fire. Behind him was the Soignies Forest. Wellington was confident that this would cover his back and, should it be necessary, aid his retreat while also hindering the French cavalry pursuit. Napoleon, on the other hand, thought that Wellington had made a mistake and that the Anglo-Allied troops would end up trapped in the forest. The French emperor wanted to make sure that he did not miss this excellent opportunity to eliminate the British-led army.

In the early hours of June 18, the day of the fateful Battle of Waterloo, the Duke of Wellington was uncharacteristically having trouble sleeping. He got out of bed at three in the morning and wrote a few letters, mainly last-minute orders, though one letter was more personal, to a friend, Lady Frances Wedderburn Webster. Wellington suggested that she prepare to leave Brussels, just in case the battle that day went poorly.

At some point that morning (the time is disputed), a courier arrived at Wellington's headquarters with a message from Field Marshal Blücher. Wellington ripped open the dispatch and read. It was good news: The First and Second Corps of the Prussian army were on their way to join the Allies in battle. This was twice the number of soldiers that Wellington had hoped, but, problematically, the Prussians were not ready to leave for a couple of hours. "The exhaustion of the troops," Blücher explained, "did not allow my commencing my movement earlier."

Would the Prussians really be able to march as Blücher promised? Blücher was notoriously overoptimistic with his predictions, and the slow speed of the courier arriving with the message did not enhance Wellington's confidence. "Blücher picked the fattest man in his army to ride with an express to me," Wellington complained, "and he took thirty hours to go thirty miles." If the Prussian army had any hope of arriving that day, they would have to move faster than that.

About six o'oclock that chilly and damp morning, the duke put on his blue coat, his blue cloak, and his boots, high up on the leg. With his hat in hand, which he typically wore front-back as opposed to Napoleon, who wore it side to side, Wellington walked over to his small charger, the chestnut Copenhagen, stepped into the iron stirrup, and vaulted into the stiff hussar saddle with the high pommel in front. He rode off to be everywhere at once.

Allied soldiers arrived exhausted onto the plateau around Mont-Saint-Jean. Many regiments had marched forty to fifty miles in the previous two days, each soldier carrying some fifty to sixty pounds of equipment. They slept in fields, soaked by the continuous hard rains, and not everyone had a tent. Water had poured down that night like "buckets emptying from the heavens," and "ran in streams from the cuffs of jackets." Many awoke with wet clothes still clinging to their body, and "petrified with cold." The lucky ones had breakfast, even if it was only the "half mouthful of broth and a biscuit" given to the soldiers of the Fifty-second Light Infantry.

Meanwhile, about eight o'clock that morning, at a small whitewashed farmhouse two miles south on the Charleroi-Brussels road, Napoleon was eating breakfast with several senior commanders. After the meal, the imperial silver was removed and maps were spread out on the table.

"We have . . . ninety chances in our favor, and not ten against us," Napoleon said, calculating the odds of success that day.

Marshal Ney, however, was troubled, fearing that Wellington would sneak away in a retreat and the French would miss the opportunity for a decisive victory. Napoleon rejected the possibility outright. Britain could no longer leave the scene, he said. "Wellington has rolled the dice, and they are in our favor."

Marshal Soult, the recently appointed chief of staff, was also concerned, though for a different reason. Soult had fought Wellington in Spain several times, without success—the British infantry was the devil himself, as he had once put it. Perhaps Napoleon should recall Marshall Grouchy and the thirty-three thousand men whom he had dispatched the previous day to pursue the Prussians. Napoleon bluntly dismissed the suggestion: "Because you have been beaten by Wellington, you consider him a great general."

"Wellington is a bad general," Napoleon continued, "the English are bad troops, and this will be like eating breakfast."

"I earnestly hope so," Soult replied.

In truth, Napoleon probably did not believe his harsh indictment of

Wellington's ability as a commander; the emperor often spoke with such dash on the eve of battle, mainly as a tactic to bolster morale, and morale in war, Napoleon said, was everything. Still, the French emperor was probably not too impressed with Wellington so far in the campaign. In the last three days, the British general had been caught by surprise by Napoleon's invasion route, been forced to retreat from Quatre Bas, and now found himself trapped like prey.

All morning, generals, staff officers, and couriers kept coming and going from French headquarters. General Honoré Reille, who would command the Second Corps on the far left or western flank, had just arrived, and on account of his experience fighting in Spain, fielded Napoleon's follow-up question about the British infantry. Reille's answer was not reassuring. The British infantry was fierce, he said, and if they were attacked from the front, "I consider the English infantry to be impregnable." At the same time, Reille noted that the British could be defeated by striking at their flanks. Their infantry was "less agile, less supple, less expert in maneuvering than ours."

Other generals at French headquarters emphasized the importance of attacking on either flank, rather than launching a direct frontal assault on the Allied center. General Maximilien Sébastien Foy, another veteran of the Spanish campaign, pointed out an additional reason why the British were so difficult to defeat: The crafty Duke of Wellington "never shows his troops." Indeed, Wellington had defeated no fewer than eight of Napoleon's marshals in Spain, and many other generals, including several who would take the field later that day.

Prince Jérôme, Napoleon's youngest brother and once widely castigated as the spoiled brat of the Bonaparte family, informed the emperor of a rumor he had heard the previous night at the inn Roi d'Espagne in Genappe. According to a waiter, one of Wellington's aides-de-camp had been boasting, indiscreetly, that the Prussians would return to the field later that day and join the British-led Allies.

"Nonsense," Napoleon snapped, remembering how soundly he had defeated the Prussians two days before. They would require at least two days of hard marching, he added, naturally assuming that the Prussians had retreated north to their supply lines at Wavre. Besides, "the Prussians have Grouchy on their heels."

It was at this morning strategy session that Napoleon's former governor of Elba, Marshal Drouot, advised the emperor to delay the attack a few hours to allow the soggy ground to dry so that they could move and fire artillery more effectively. The emperor agreed. He also knew that his army, which had camped over a large area, needed more time to be in a position for the attack.

By the end of the morning, Napoleon had decided on a general strategy. The French would not concentrate on turning one of the weaker flanks, as several generals plainly hoped, but instead launch a direct frontal assault on the Allied center. The emperor would rely on power, not finesse—a quick strike at the enemy defenses without elaborate feints or maneuvers, which he probably figured would have been useless anyway given the wet ground. Besides that, the small size of the battlefield, barely three miles in width, was not conducive to such grand sweeping maneuvers (Austerlitz, by contrast, was seven miles; Wagram, twelve; and Leipzig, twenty-one). As the emperor's valet Louis Marchand remembered the scene, Napoleon then suddenly rose from the table. "Gentlemen," he concluded confidently, "if my orders are carried out well, tonight we shall sleep in Brussels."

Chapter 32

L A B ELLE A LLIANCE

The ball is at my foot, and I hope I shall have strength to give it a good kick.

—ARTHUR WELLESLEY, THE FUTURE DUKE OF
WELLINGTON, BEFORE THE BATTLE OF TALAVERA

*N*obody knows for certain when the Battle of Waterloo began, but it was probably a little after 11:30 a.m., when Napoleon's youngest brother, Prince Jérôme, leading a division of Comte Reille's Second Corps, launched an attack on the Hougoumont manor on the extreme western flank of the battlefield. Hougoumont commanded the narrow roadway that passed through the rye fields and protected Wellington's right flank against any wide enveloping movements. Napoleon had no intention of concentrating on this outpost, but only wanted to deceive Wellington into thinking that this would be the main thrust of his attack. Then, when Wellington began to shift troops away from the center, Napoleon would slam into his real target with his full strength.

Wellington had selected a Highlander, Lieutenant Colonel James Macdonnell, and five companies of Scots Guards and Coldstream Guards to hold the position at Hougoumont. In addition to the manor with its thick surrounding walls, there was a garden, an orchard, and a forest, as well as nearby hedges and fields. Granaries, storehouses, barns, sheds, stables, cattle pens, two small cottages, and other structures shielded the defenders. The inhabitants of the manor had fled long ago, except for a lone gardener, Willem van Kylsom, who hid in the cellar.

As Prince Jérôme's division of about sixty-five hundred infantrymen attempted to storm the manor, three-quarter-inch iron balls whizzed by from rye fields, woods, and soon also from the manor itself with its windows, loopholes, and makeshift scaffolds. Britain's musket, "Brown Bess," which had only slightly been altered since its introduction in 1745, wreaked a heavy toll on the advancing division. The German light infantry in the forests—*Jäger,* or "hunters"—were deadly accurate, too. Prince Jérôme, however, refused to yield. He had his orders, and he would seize the manor. His reputation was at stake, as was the family name.

Very soon, the fighting became intense hand-to-hand combat in and around the manor, where shots seemed to come from "every crack in the stone," as Victor Hugo put it. The French troops tried to force their way through a gate in the back of the manor, which had been used for supplying the troops. Eventually, a large Frenchman nicknamed L'Enforceur knocked a hole in the defenses and some one hundred Frenchmen streamed into a courtyard. Macdonnell and some fellow Scotsmen managed to close the gate again. The French intruders, trapped on the inside, were slaughtered. The only exception was a young drummer boy.

Undeterred by the lack of success, Prince Jérôme ordered a second attack on the manor, adding another four battalions, despite the protests of General Foy. Prince Jérôme would seize it "at all costs," an order, he later claimed improbably, that came from Napoleon himself. Progress was slow and brief. The French only managed to capture the forest and the orchard for a time. Even the fire that began to rage on the manor roof in the early afternoon, and soon spread throughout the many structures, did not obliterate the defense. A small, exhausted contingent of twenty-six hundred Allied troops was pinning down a force several times their size.

Indeed, rather than diverting troops from Wellington's center, the French assault was proving a drain on Napoleon's main attack. Years later, Wellington attributed the victory at Waterloo to the early action here on the periphery, or, as he put it, "the closing of the gates at Hougoumont."

One of many mysteries about the Battle of Waterloo was why Napoleon did not begin the attack by firing not only cannons but also howitzers, whose high-arced explosive shells would have likely devastated the walls of the manor. Such a bombardment was routine for this type of action, and would have paved the way for Jérôme's brave but ultimately ineffective assaults. Was the strange absence of the howitzers due to the fact that the French simply could not see the terrain and did not know how well the manor would be defended? Perhaps they did not even know the manor was there, as the historian Alessandro Barbero suggested. Orders already seemed confused, and miscommunication was rife; individual commanders were taking major decisions into their own hands, with great repercussions.

Meanwhile, just over fourteen miles away near the village of Walhain, Marshal Emmanuel de Grouchy, commander of the thirty-three thousand men of the Third and Fourth Corps, was eating strawberries in a requisitioned summerhouse when one of his soldiers rushed in with news that the rumble of the guns could be heard from the west. Grouchy's assistant, General Gérard, urged that they immediately turn around the armies and march them in the direction of the cannons.

The firing might well be a "rear-guard affair," Grouchy said. His orders were to advance to Wavre and finish off the Prussians. True, he had written Napoleon earlier that morning, about four o'clock, to ask for further instructions, but no reply had yet arrived. Grouchy reasoned:

The Emperor told me yesterday that it was his intention to attack the English army if Wellington accepted battle . . . If the Emperor had wanted me to take part in it, he would not have detached my army just when he was preparing to attack the English.

Besides, marching on the muddy, soggy roads, he said, would make it difficult to reach the battlefield "in time to be of any use." He insisted on obeying the order precisely.

So over the spirited protests of his assistant and several other officers, Grouchy ordered the army to march away from the guns and away from Napoleon, who would very soon need the thirty-three thousand soldiers of the Third and Fourth Corps, who seemed destined to spend the day vainly roaming the countryside in search of the Prussian troops.

About one o'clock that afternoon, Napoleon was on the hill near the Rossomme farm, sweeping the plain with his telescope. To the northeast, he saw an object that looked like a dark cloud. Was it an approaching army? Some officers near him claimed it was just a cloud, a cluster of trees, or really nothing at all. Napoleon had seen this sight many times before and knew otherwise.

But was it the French corps under Grouchy returning from their mission of finishing off the Prussians? Or was it the Prussians somehow nearing the scene? Napoleon sent scouts out to investigate. A courier was captured and interrogated, removing the last trace of doubt. It was the Prussians, and it was not just a minor detachment. It was the main Prussian army.

Remarkably, after the Prussian loss at Ligny two days before, Blücher's chief of staff, Gneisenau, had made a snap decision to retreat north—one of the fateful orders of the entire campaign. Had he retreated in any other direction, which was more obvious given their supply lines, the location of their headquarters, or the vicinity of strategic fortresses, the Prussians would never have been able to arrive on the scene. That morning, when the Prussians were debating whether to link up with the Allies, Gneisenau had argued against it. Blücher, however, overruled him. Having recuperated from his wounds, he was determined that the Prussians would reach the battlefield in time and fight the French.

When Napoleon first learned of the approaching Prussian army, said to be about six to eight miles away, he was not too concerned. "Even now, we have a sixty percent chance of winning," he said. Napoleon sent messengers to order Grouchy (wherever he was) to return at once. He sent two cavalry divisions, or some two thousand troops, east to distract or lure away the vanguard of the Prussians. In the meantime, he would attack Wellington and win quickly. "A more careful man," Clausewitz judged, "would have broken off the engagement and retreated."

Minutes later, however, some eighty-four French guns thundered onto Mont-Saint-Jean, where Wellington had positioned his troops. After the cannons plowed through the defense, Napoleon planned to order Lieutenant General Jean-Baptiste Drouet, Count d'Erlon, and the First Corps onto the weakened center. Then he would unleash his superior cavalry and complete his victory before the Prussians had time to arrive. Parade uniforms were already in knapsacks waiting for the triumphant march into Brussels.

At 1:30 p.m., Count d'Erlon and the sixteen thousand soldiers of the First Corps began to advance, slowly, through the muddy rye fields to attack the Allies. The columns were enormous, spanning some two hundred men or files across, and twenty-four to twenty-seven deep. This was an intimidating formation that showcased the strength of the attackers, and elevated morale, but it was hardly practical. Packing the soldiers so closely together limited movement, flexibility, and visibility, not to mention restricting firepower to the first two or three ranks. The rest of the soldiers—the vast majority—had virtually no offensive potential. Equally problematic, the deep columns presented a frightfully exposed target to British cannons. Napoleon had not chosen this formation for the assault, but neither had he overruled it. The French infantry would pay terribly for this poor choice.

But as the colossal columns marched forward, twenty-seven steps a minute to keep pace with the roll of the drums, some Allied troops, under the Dutch general Willem Frederik Graf van Bijlandt, fled in terror. British veterans hissed, hooted, and nearly fired at their allies as they raced by, calling them cowards and worse. Actually, many of the Dutch and Belgian soldiers in this brigade were suspected of identifying with Napoleon and hardly relished the thought of fighting their beloved emperor. They were also young troops fighting their first battle. Placed out front, too, they had also been more exposed to Napoleon's cannon salvos than any other troops on the Allied side.

As in all large battles, once it began in earnest, chaos seemed to reign. The thick black smoke of cannons obscured, from many angles, what little coherence might be imposed on the scene, and the low clouds of that overcast morning did not help visibility. In fact, the clouds were so near the ground that they seemed to magnify the roar of the cannons.

That day, some 150,000 men and 30,000 horses would charge, shoot, and hack their way through a muddy plain, not quite three miles long and barely one and a half miles wide. Musket balls struck swords or breastplates like a "violent hailstorm beating upon panes of glass." Sabers, lances, and grapeshot did their worst. Cannons wreaked even more damage. After the first thirty minutes, there were probably more than 10,000 dead and wounded. There were also the awful sights and sounds of the crying horses. It is no surprise that this battle would inspire one of the first modern efforts to protect animals from cruelty.

During the melee, which soon seemed to shift in favor of France, partly out of sheer force, the commander of the Allied cavalry and horse artillery, Lord Henry William Paget Uxbridge, ordered an attack. Outnumbered by perhaps five to one, the Household Brigade and the Union Brigade charged. It was a resounding success, at least initially. The horsemen sabered many Frenchmen, who turned and fled. Advancing quickly, they seized artillery guns, took some three thousand prisoners, and captured two Napoleonic eagles. The French attack had been repulsed.

True to form, the impetuous cavalrymen had difficulty restraining themselves in their triumph. Soon the brigades had overreached, riding deep into enemy ranks. Napoleon, who saw their vulnerability, ordered fresh lancers and dragoons into the fray. The result was devastating, and the "charge of the heavy brigade" came to an abrupt end. No fewer than a thousand of the twenty-five hundred horsemen perished.

As the diversion at Hougoumont turned into a quagmire and Count d'Erlon's attack had been repulsed, Napoleon had to launch his next big offensive against a center that had not been weakened.

Marshal Ney ordered a massive cavalry charge, comprising two brigades of the First Corps, or a total of about five thousand troops. William Gronow, a nineteen-year-old Etonian who fought with the First Foot Guards, described the approach of Ney's horsemen.

> Not a man present who survived could have forgotten in after life the awful grandeur of that charge. You perceived at a distance what appeared to be an overwhelming, long moving line, which, ever advancing, glittered like a stormy wave of the sea when it catches the sunlight . . . [as they approached] the very earth seemed to vibrate beneath their thundering tramp. One might have supposed that nothing could have resisted the shock of this terrible moving mass.

British commanders gave the famous order to form a square: "Prepare to receive cavalry." The soldiers in the front knelt down, readied their bayonets, and formed a human wall, or, as one veteran described it, "a wall bristling with steel, held together by steady hands." Behind this line, two rows of infantry bit off cartridges, loaded, rammed, and prepared to fire their muskets at the attackers.

Britain's infantry squares were actually often closer to rectangles, being larger on the front and the rear than on the sides. The formation was based on the assumption that a horse simply will not ride into a wall of bayonets. Indeed, despite contemporary paintings that depict gory cavalry charges, the horses generally stopped at about twenty yards' distance, no matter how much the riders cursed, or shouted *"Vive l'Empereur."*

The best approach was to fire artillery into the infantry squares first. Cannon fire was, of course, the infantryman's nightmare. Unlike the saber, the lance, or the musket ball, the heavy eight- and twelve-pounders mangled bodies, smashed bones, and lopped off heads. Napoleon had planned to open with them, "his beautiful daughters," as he referred to the twelve-pounders. The problem was that many cannonballs had sunk in the mud rather than richochet through the ranks, and Wellington had protected them well, anyway, on the reverse side of the slopes. The French guns had done much less damage than Napoleon had hoped or expected.

As Wellington issued orders under an elm tree at a crossroads north of the farm of La Haye-Sainte, or riding down the lines encouraging the troops, Napoleon launched attack after attack on the center. The British infantry held firm. Wellington marveled at Napoleon's lack of finesse in varying his tactics: "Damn that fellow! He is a mere pounder after all."

One soldier compared the repeated charges of the French cavalry against the British infantry to "a heavy surf breaking on a coast beset with isolated rocks"; the massive wave crashes "with furious uproar, breaks, divides, and runs, hissing and boiling." Losses were heavy on all sides. One British regiment at the center, the Twenty-seventh Inniskillings, lost 450 of its 750 men, and only an estimated 1 in 18 made it through the grueling day without a wound.

The first cavalry charge, as the historian J. Holland Rose noted, came too soon. It was also plagued by the lack of coordination with artillery and infantry—an unsupported cavalry charge against an unbroken infantry square was recklessly ineffective. In fairness to Ney, it is likely that he misjudged the movements behind the Allied line, thinking that the repositioning of the squares a hundred yards back (to avoid the cannons) and the evacuation of wounded and prisoners was actually Wellington in retreat. Ney had suspected that Wellington would attempt to flee since the beginning of battle, and he was sensitive to any sign that indicated it was taking place. He thought he was cutting off the retreat.

But Wellington was not retreating. The infantry, locked into approximately twenty squares, held firm and the slaughter continued.

DETERMINED TO WIN before the Prussians arrived, Napoleon ordered Ney, about 3:30 p.m., to seize the strategic farm, La Haye-Sainte, on Wellington's left, or eastern, flank that was vital to his center. As at Hougoumont, the result was another intense fight. Against great odds, the King's German Legion on the inside, and the Ninety-fifth Rifles in the nearby gravel pit, held out for hours. But the KGL soon ran out of ammunition, and the standard reinforcements did not fit the Baker rifles used by the specialist sharpshooters. This proved to be another battle within a battle, ending just after six o'clock that evening, when the French captured the farm.

This was certainly a blow to Wellington and the Allies. This eastern flank was one of Wellington's weaknesses—he had deliberately under-defended it because he expected the Prussians to arrive that day and cover his flank. Now that Napoleon had captured La Haye-Sainte, he could place his own artillery and sharpshooters closer in range and apply much more pressure on the Allies.

Soon Wellington was in serious trouble and the center was about to break. Wellington's men were taking a beating, and more Allied regiments had already fled. Basil Jackson, a young staff officer, reported that the forests near the battlefield were full of defectors, entire companies with "fires blazing under cooking kettles, while the men lay about smoking." Most famously, the Cumberland Hussars, a volunteer regiment of Hanoverian gentlemen in splendid uniforms, galloped straight from the battlefield to Brussels with the alarming news that defeat was imminent and the French would soon march through the capital in triumph.

Sensing an imminent Allied defeat, Marshal Ney pleaded with the emperor for more troops to deliver the knockout blow. As military historian David Chandler argued, the situation was critical for Wellington, and with fresh reinforcements, Ney probably would have shattered the Allied center. Napoleon, however, failed to seize the opportunity, answering only in frustration about the impossibility of sending more soldiers: "Where the devil do you expect me to find them! Do you want me to make them?"

Napoleon could have sent in six battalions of the Middle Guard and eight battalions of the Old Guard—the elite troops that he held in reserve. As Chandler further pointed out, had the emperor sent in half of them, Napoleon would probably have won the Battle of Waterloo. Wellington was taking a severe beating, and two brigades had already been destroyed. Others seemed on the verge of breaking.

Napoleon, of course, had no way of knowing just how close Wellington's center was to collapsing—that is the advantage of hindsight. In fairness, too, Ney's record thus far in the campaign could hardly have inclined the emperor to comply with the request. Again and again, Ney had made brave, though ultimately untimely and disorganized, attacks that had proved costly. It would have been easy to see this request in that light. Moreover, Napoleon never liked to use his reserves until the enemy had first committed his, and this was not the case yet.

So, rather than sending in some additional troops for Ney's attack on Wellington's center, Napoleon ordered some eleven battalions of the Guard to take Plancenoit, the largest village in the region, which would hold their position and lines of communication, in preparation for the Prussian arrival. Twenty minutes later, the French had succeeded here as well. Wellington was powerless to help. The British Fifth Division, defending, lost some 3,500 of 4,000 soldiers. "Let us pray to God," Wellington allegedly said on hearing the news, "for the coming of night—or of Blücher."

BY THE LATE afternoon, the army in the distance was unmistakably drawing nearer, and Napoleon was racing against time. A small detachment of Prussians, under General Bülow, was already active on the eastern flank. The French were holding them off, but Blücher, commanding thirty thousand men, was quickly approaching from the east. Wellington, in the meantime, was shuffling troops quickly to shut the hole in his center.

A gambler by nature, Napoleon decided to risk everything, and the French attacks increased in intensity. Marshal Ney, leading charge after charge against the British infantry, had four horses shot from under him. As the vanguard of the Prussian army neared the battlefield, Napoleon told his French soldiers, untruthfully, that the army in the distance was actually Grouchy's.

In the end, Napoleon, desperate, ordered his elite Imperial Guard, "Les Invincibles," to attack. The feared veterans were never used unless the battle was almost over and victory secure, and they had never failed.

So, to drums, "La Marseillaise," and the famous cry *"Vive l'Empereur!"* they started marching. But this time, it was a suicide mission.

Napoleon personally took the lead of some twelve battalions and sixty-five hundred famous veterans of the Grande Armée (fifteen thousand total were in the assault) and marched off in what was to be the warlord's final charge. About six hundred yards out, Napoleon turned aside, handing over responsibility for the attack to Marshal Ney. The Guards marched straight ahead, without any cavalry support, right into the fields where Wellington's troops suddenly rose up from concealed positions and fired with devastating accuracy. Three hundred of Napoleon's veterans died in a minute, according to Captain Siborne's estimate.

Later that evening, when the sun shone brightly for the first time in days and now penetrated the clouds of smoke hovering over the plain, the French were in full retreat. Wellington, standing in his stirrups and waving his hat, urged his men forward to finish the victory. The French flight lost all sense of order. It was "a panic-stricken rabble," as Napoleon called it.

The Prussian leader Blücher, said to have a personal grudge against the French, was determined to catch the French emperor himself. The Imperial Guard, having been repulsed for the first time, had regrouped and now covered the retreat of the French well. Napoleon himself was able to escape, riding away in his bulletproof carriage and then switching to his white charger, Marengo.

The Prussians followed in hot pursuit, continuing the chase long into the night. In the end, the Prussians nearly captured Napoleon himself. They had his carriage, still with his ceremonial sword, a bottle of rum, a bottle of old Malaga, a toothbrush, and a million francs' worth of diamonds, which his sister had given him on Elba. Napoleon's carriage was presented as a gift to the Prince Regent, who put it on show in London and later sold it to Madame Tussaud for her museum, where it remained until it was destroyed in the fire of 1925.

Napoleon himself blamed this defeat—"the horrible piece of bad luck"—on everything from the rain to the mistakes of his subordinates. Marshal Soult had struggled in his new position as chief of staff, sending too few messengers; as a result, many orders never reached their target or arrived too late. Marshal Ney, likewise, had made numerous errors, ranging from unfortunate delays at the opening of the campaign to reckless and untimely attacks that lost many lives. Still "in spite of all," Napoleon added, "I should have won that battle."

For a long time afterward, historians debated the actual causes of this Allied victory. Had Wellington essentially won the battle, or did the arrival of the Prussians prove decisive? Actually, the question is absurd, as the historian Andrew Roberts rightly remarked. Wellington would never have waited on the plain that day for a battle if he had not expected the Prussians to arrive and defend his left flank. At the same time, he would probably not have won without the timely assistance of the Prussians. Both armies deserve the credit.

Wellington's tactics and strategic choice of terrain had been crucial. He had used his information sources effectively and had a sound knowledge of Napoleon's strengths and movements through his spies, including in-depth reports from Napoleon's treacherous minister of police, Joseph Fouché. Moreover, he knew of the Old Guard attack in advance from a defector. The English could also thank the formidable infantry, which withstood Napoleon's increasingly desperate charges. The English, of course, had new weapons such as Congreve rockets, but they were far less important than the human factors.

Napoleon, for his part, had made a number of mistakes that day, some of them bizarre. Besides the large detachment he sent away on the eve of the battle to fight the Prussians, and which might have proven decisive, Napoleon had not used the talents of many of his marshals to the fullest. Davout, an excellent commander, was still in Paris as minister of war. Murat, the greatest cavalry leader of the day, was disdained and not allowed to fight. Another, Louis Gabriel Suchet, was placed in a secondary position defending the eastern approach to France. David Chandler wondered if Napoleon had deliberately "fielded a second team" to preserve the glory for himself.

Napoleon, further, broke many of his own military maxims. Some have claimed that the emperor was suffering from any number of ailments: acromegaly, inflammation of the bladder and urinary tract, or even hemorrhoids. At any rate, Napoleon was not at his best that day. "Everything failed me just when everything had succeeded," he later said.

During that short campaign, there were confusing orders, vague, contradictory, and slow to arrive; personality clashes among his subordinates further hurt their efforts, as did some well-known examples of treachery, such as General Louis August Victor Bourmont's defection to the Prussians. Significantly, too, Napoleon delayed his initial attack almost four hours in the morning to allow the wet ground to dry, a crucial fact that allowed Wellington to dry his weapons and the Prussians to arrive on the scene. And so on. There were countless "ifs" that might have tipped the balance.

The battle was over, and now it was time to name it. Blücher suggested that it should be called "the Battle of La Belle-Alliance," punning on the name of an inn in the Forest of Soignies where the two victors met that evening after the battle. Wellington preferred Waterloo.

SOMETIME AFTER MIDNIGHT, Wellington started drafting the famous Waterloo dispatch. Finishing it the next day at Brussels, he folded it up into the small purple velvet sachet that he had received at the Duchess of Richmond ball and sent it off with a courier to his government back in London. "It is a glorious victory," Wellington announced, though unfortunately "the loss of life had been fearful, and I have lost many friends."

About 40,000 men had been killed that day, and many more wounded. Wellington suffered between 13,000 and 15,000 casualties, and Napoleon's losses are usually estimated between 25,000 and 30,000. Blücher lost about 7,000 men. Total casualties of the four-day campaign were perhaps 115,000 (some 60,000 French and 55,000 Allies).

Nearby Brussels seemed one giant hospital. Carts of mangled, bloodied, and bandaged soldiers rattled through the streets and dropped off the wounded onto beds of straw around the city. Citizens cared for as many in their homes as possible, and carried water to the thirsty. One surgeon described the ordeal of continually operating on the wounded for thirteen hours straight, until, as he put it, his clothes were "stiff with blood, and [his] arms powerless with the exertion of using the knife!" Unfortunately for the soldiers, it was a dreadful experience: The rushed and overworked surgeons labored without the benefit of anesthesia or sophisticated instruments.

Metternich wrote to congratulate the Duke of Wellington for his victory at Waterloo, or, as he put it, "the brilliant opening of the campaign." Wellington, though, was more optimistic about its significance. "I may be wrong," he said shortly afterward, "but my opinion is that we have

Mission Control (during the Apollo 11 landing)

Eugene Kranz: Steely-calm flight director.

Charles Duke: Capcom, the astronaut who communicates with the crew.

Stephen Bales: Responsible for monitoring the spacecraft computer operations.

John Garman: Apollo Guidance Computer expert.

Robert Carlton: Responsible for control of the lunar module.

Edward Fendell: Head of communications.

U.S. Political Leaders

Franklin D. Roosevelt: U.S. president, 1933 to 1945. Led the country through the Great Depression and most of World War II.

Harry S. Truman: U.S. president, 1945 to 1953. Confronted the Soviet Union to start the Cold War.

Dwight D. Eisenhower: World War II general. Later U.S. president, 1953 to 1961.

John F. Kennedy: U.S. president, 1961 to 1963. Embarked on Project Apollo.

Lyndon B. Johnson: U.S. president, 1963 to 1969. Space enthusiast and president during Apollo's coming-of-age.

Russians

Joseph Stalin: Brutal dictator of the Soviet Union, 1922 to 1953.

Nikita Khrushchev: Leader of the Soviet Union, 1953 to 1964. First to grasp the propaganda value of space achievements.

Yuri Gagarin: First human in space.

Jules Verne's astronauts
blast off from a giant
cannon.

Moon map
contemporary with
Verne's novel

MAP OF THE MOON
with the names given by Riccioli in the 18th century

Verne's astronauts approach
the Moon.

GROUP of LUNAR MOUNTAINS. IDEAL LUNAR LANDSCAPE.

Artist's concept of rugged lunar landscape, 1874

BRIEFING:
The Ultimate Destination

In the 1860s, French science-fiction author Jules Verne started work on a new novel. It involved a giant engineering project and an impossibly distant goal. He set the plot in the United States—land of people who think big. His three explorers start out from Florida, travel a quarter of a million miles through space in a large capsule, view the Moon from close-up, and then return to Earth, splashing down in the Pacific Ocean. Along the way, they experience weightlessness and other strange phenomena. Realizing that he had an epic on his hands, Verne split his narrative into two parts. He called the first volume *From the Earth to the Moon*, and the second *A Trip Around the Moon*.

Of course, he made it all up. However, sometimes truth catches up with fiction, which it did . . . a hundred years later.

This book is the true story of Apollo 11, which in the 1960s achieved Verne's amazing vision—down to the country involved, the size of the crew, the launch location, the destination, the splashdown site, and the unearthly experiences. There is another eerie coincidence. In Verne's novel, the technology and expertise that allow his explorers to go to the Moon emerged from the recently ended American Civil War. Apollo, too, was built on the inventions, experiences, and attitudes developed in a catastrophic war.

And therein lies a tale. Do not be misled if the account that follows begins in a place as far from the Moon as one could possibly get, in circumstances that seem to have nothing to with a lunar voyage . . . for they have everything to do with it.

PART 1
WAR

The war made us. It was and is our single greatest moment.
The memory of the war is a key to our characters.

—John F. Kennedy, U.S. senator and later president, 1954

Moonset from space

Astronauts clash on the cover of *Astounding Science Fiction*, 1931.

1

ENSIGN FAGET'S CLOSE CALL

The vessel drifted silently through a limitless realm. Aboard, only row after row of lights and gauges told the crew that, so far, all was well. Out of contact with any other humans on Earth, they felt alone in a way that was primordial. They could have been on their way to another planet. But they knew something was about to happen, and the sweat was already starting to bead on their faces.

Then, *click . . . BANG!* The craft shook.

They all knew what it was.

Then another *click . . . BANG!* An anxious pause. *Click . . . BANG!*

As the junior officer, Ensign Max Faget, age twenty-three, was hyper-alert for any signs of trouble. He was probably too preoccupied to count the explosions. But others kept a tally.

"Three . . . four. They're getting closer."

Click . . . BANG! The hull groaned.

The *click* was the sound of an arriving pressure wave, like the lightning flash that precedes thunder. Then came the main blast of detonating high explosives—depth charges being dropped by Japanese warships trying to kill them, for they were aboard an American submarine and this was World War II.

It was February 20, 1945, the last year of the war, but no one knew that yet. As far as the men in the USS *Guavina* were concerned, it could be their last *minute* of the war.

Click . . . BANG!

"That's six," someone whispered.

●

Like practically every other American at the time, Maxime "Max" Faget (pronounced "fah-ZHAY") was involved in the war effort. The men of his generation were doing the fighting, but millions of others, men and women, were helping out in factories, offices, and hospitals, on farms, railroads, and docks. Those who weren't directly involved participated in other ways—by buying war bonds and, if nothing else, by paying high taxes to support the nation in the largest, most devastating, and most expensive conflict in world history.

It had all started across the sea. In 1937, Japan invaded China. Then in 1939, Nazi Germany, led by Adolf Hitler, invaded and quickly overran Poland. Britain and France came to Poland's defense by declaring war on Germany. Within a year, Germany had defeated France and was poised to invade Britain. Italy joined on Germany's side. In June 1941, the war took a surprising turn when Germany changed course and attacked the Soviet Union—previously its partner in a nonaggression pact.

Even more surprisingly, Japan attacked the American fleet at Pearl Harbor, Hawaii, on December 7, 1941. President Franklin Roosevelt branded it "a date which will live in infamy" and asked Congress to declare war on Japan, which it immediately did. Soon after, Hitler threw his support behind Japan by declaring war on the United States. A war

Max Faget before the war

that had started as a series of regional conflicts in Asia and Europe now encompassed the globe.

What was it all about? Germany wanted control of Europe, and Japan wanted an empire in Asia. American interests in both regions inevitably drew the U.S. into the fighting.

You might think that Germany, Italy, and Japan, known as the Axis powers, would have little chance when most of the rest of the world, known as the Allies, were lined up against them. The Allies included the United States, Great Britain, the Soviet Union, and China, plus the occupied countries and a host of smaller nations. But Germany and Japan had been vigorously preparing for war for years, and their overwhelming success at the outset showed it. By early 1942, they were on the verge of achieving their major war aims. All they had to do was hold on to their winnings.

Faget's small role was to help chip away at those gains.

●

And that's why *Guavina* was at the bottom of the South China Sea, just off the coast of Vietnam. A short time earlier, the submarine had sunk a Japanese tanker carrying badly needed crude oil from Japanese-occupied Indonesia to Japan's home islands. Thanks to American submarines, Japan was increasingly starved of resources. Unfortunately,

Max Faget stands at the depth gauge as *Guavina* dives past 90 feet, 1945.

one of those subs, *Guavina*, was now cornered by enemy ships determined to destroy it.

Click . . . BANG!

The depth charges continued to fall. *Guavina*'s captain, Ralph Lockwood, had ordered "silent running," meaning that all mechanical equipment was turned off—motors, fans, air-conditioning, anything that made noise that could be picked up by the enemy's sonar and betray their location. Most of the crew had nothing to do and waited silently. With the fans and air-conditioning off, the air became stale and hot, making breathing difficult. A thawing turkey in the galley started to smell. No one moved unless they had to. Eighty-five sailors and officers were as still as death.

During the next seven hours, a total of ninety-eight depth charges rocked *Guavina*. It was one of the most relentless anti-submarine actions of the war. "We experienced hell," Captain Lockwood later wrote in his official report.

"Words cannot express the feelings and emotions that surged through my mind while waiting helplessly," recalled one sailor. He saw that most of the men "had the look of fear on their faces. Everyone reacts differently in times of stress," he noted. "One man sat down on the floor and started to giggle, but soon brought it under control." Another, pouring with sweat, began bumping his head against the bulkhead until he was led away.

The closest explosions caused havoc on the boat. Lightbulbs shattered in their sockets. Cork insulation fell to the deck, where the pieces bounced with each new blast. A pipe broke, and seawater gushed into the mess hall; sailors immediately found a safety valve and stemmed the flood. No one could think of anything but the coming catastrophic crash that would break the hull apart and engulf them in a fatal blast of water.

But it didn't come.

Guavina belonged to a new class of submarines built with a strong hull for deep diving. The same high-tensile steel that could resist water pressure at a depth of up to 900 feet also protected the crew from all but the closest hit. During a lull in the action, when the sub chasers returned to a nearby port for more depth charges, *Guavina* surfaced, turned on its diesel engines, and headed back into the open ocean, taking stock of damage and giving sailors a desperately needed dose of fresh air.

For Ensign Faget, a Louisiana native making his first war patrol, there were many lessons. He was a recent graduate of Louisiana State University, where he had studied mechanical engineering, and he had just seen unforgettable proof of how a properly engineered craft can sustain humans under the most perilous conditions. Hull, radar,

USS *Guavina* ready for launching, 1943

sonar, propulsion, control, communications, environmental systems, weaponry—all were perfectly matched to the task of sinking enemy ships and then escaping.

But an engineer with Faget's ceaselessly inquiring mind, who was also an avid reader of science fiction, might imagine using the same technology for another type of vessel, one that could sail a far vaster ocean. "A submarine is a very high-tech ship—very compact, and full of machinery," Faget reminisced much later, adding, "like a spacecraft."

World War II recruiting poster for the Submarine Service

2

PIRATES OF THE WESTERN PACIFIC

Oddly enough, a submarine during World War II was an ideal place for someone who loved the stars.

In the era before nuclear power allowed submarines to submerge almost indefinitely, a sub could stay underwater for no more than a day or two, powered by a bank of storage batteries. When the batteries ran out, the boat had to surface and switch on air-breathing diesel engines. These recharged the batteries and also provided propulsion, just as a gasoline engine keeps an automobile battery charged while simultaneously turning the wheels.

The usual strategy for a sub was to submerge during the day, when enemy planes and ships could easily spot it. At night, the boat would come up and cruise on diesel power beneath a canopy of stars, searching for prey. This was a good time to make celestial sightings with a sextant to confirm the sub's position.

When lookouts spotted a hostile ship, the boat would dive, taking less than a minute to get everyone inside, close the hatches and vents, flood the ballast tanks, and switch to electric power. The captain would

A Japanese destroyer sinks, viewed through the periscope of an American submarine, 1942.

inspect the target through a periscope, maneuver into range, and then fire a salvo of torpedoes. With luck, the underwater missiles would score another success against the Japanese navy or its merchant fleet, bringing the war a little closer to an end.

Lieutenant (junior grade) Thomas O. Paine loved this game. The same age as Faget, he had a more swashbuckling attitude, perhaps because his father was a Navy man and young Paine had grown up with sea yarns. "We were the last of the corsairs," he bragged about the submarine service. "The life of [a] pirate is given to few people. We were part of the tooth-and-claw simplicity of the sea." For Paine, the unpredictability of war gave the experience a strange clarity. You were always focused on the moment. The past and the future meant nothing, for they could be extinguished—along with your life—in an instant.

Paine had been through his share of close calls. On his fourth war patrol, scheduled to last the usual six to eight weeks, a torpedo aimed at a Japanese cargo ship had malfunctioned and circled back toward his sub, USS *Pompon*. Only hasty evasive action saved the situation. It was on this voyage that Paine volunteered for a diving emergency. A certified deep-sea diver, he went over the side at night off enemy shores to repair a broken valve in *Pompon*'s sewage system. He succeeded—to the relief of all—and was rewarded with a stiff drink and ten hours of uninterrupted sleep.

Known as the "silent service" for its tactic of striking without warning, the submarine corps appealed to independent-minded young mariners. What could "a mere ensign do" on the massive ships of the surface navy?—mused an officer on another boat. "But submarines," he marveled, "that was a different story. Submariners were younger men, and they were right there in the front lines delivering telling blows."

During Paine's fifth war patrol in January 1945, *Pompon* was diving just before dawn while stalking a convoy. As the last man to clear the deck pulled the hatch shut, it jammed and wouldn't close. Seawater immediately cascaded into the control room and began filling the vessel. The diving officer shouted, "Surface! Surface!" High-pressure air shot into the ballast tanks, which was the method for increasing the sub's buoyancy to bring it up. But the flooded compartments pulled the boat down, and only the conning tower and bridge poked above the waves.

The situation was dire. There they were, bobbing low in the water 300 miles from Japan, with enemy ships nearby and the sun coming up, exposing them for all to see. The pumps and blowers were knocked out. So were the radar, sonar, and radio. All the

Tom Paine in his college yearbook, 1942

crew could do was organize a bucket brigade to bail out by hand, throwing water over the side, while also trying to fix the most vital equipment. Luckily, they weren't spotted. After seven hours, some of the machinery was working and they resubmerged to finish the repairs in the safety of the deep.

The radio was still out, which meant *Pompon* couldn't communicate with headquarters. And if headquarters didn't know where *Pompon* was, then it was an unidentified vessel, subject to attack by American planes and ships. Threatened by friend and foe alike, *Pompon* gingerly made its way across 3,000 miles of ocean to Midway Island, the only American base that was authorized to receive unscheduled submarines. They arrived on February 11, 1945.

A war-battered American submarine arrives at port.

Seven weeks later, *Pompon* was patched up and ready for another mission. Lieutenant Paine was back aboard, chalking up his sixth war patrol. Surviving that, he embarked in mid-June on his seventh.

Most submariners were transferred to shore duty after four to six patrols. Their nerves were usually shot by then, since submarines had the highest casualty rate of any branch of the U.S. Armed Forces. By the end of the war, nearly one-fifth of America's fighting subs had been destroyed: fifty-two boats. The vast majority were entombed with their crews at the ocean bottom, accounting for the deaths of over 3,500 men.

But the prospect of a watery grave didn't seem to bother Paine. He was having the time of his life. "I saw many strange and wonderful things," he later recalled. "Bali by moonlight, with the smell of the flowers and the spices drifting across the water. Even now I think I could navigate around the island as though it were the back of my hand. Standing watches at night, the heavens became enormously familiar. You could understand the beginnings of myths and legends. Schools of whales accompanied us, sometimes for weeks at a time."

A fan of the writer Joseph Conrad, who penned popular stories about the sea decades before World War II, Paine identified with Conrad's storm-tossed heroes.

"Youth and the sea. Glamour and the sea!" one character exclaims at the end of Conrad's story "Youth." "The good, strong sea, the salt, bitter sea, that could whisper to you and roar at you and knock your breath out of you."

Living at close quarters with men in the prime of life, sharing their dangers, roaming across the wide ocean, diving at a moment's notice, eluding the enemy, and then, at the chosen instant, destroying him in a fiery blast. Above all, playing a part in the greatest war in human history—what more could an adventure-seeking twenty-three-year-old ask?

B-25s return to base after a bombing mission in northern Italy, 1945.

3

LIEUTENANT SLAYTON FLIES
ANOTHER MISSION

If submarines were risky places, then bombers, depending on the mission, could be close to suicidal. World War II saw the birth of strategic bombing, designed to destroy the enemy's morale and its war-fighting industries—as opposed to tactical bombing, which focused on specific battlefield targets such as tanks and supply depots. The improved technology of airplanes made it possible, for the first time in history, to take the battle deep inside enemy territory—not just on a onetime raid but every day, day after day, with the goal of breaking the enemy's will and ability to carry on the conflict.

Since air crews had to be highly trained, the most efficient use of their skills was to keep the crewmembers flying until they were shot down, while having plenty of replacements in training. During World War I—fought between 1914 and 1918—the life span of pilots on combat duty was just a few weeks. And the planes in that war were simple compared to the complex machines being flown in World II, not to mention the sophisticated defenses that had been developed to shoot them down.

Following the fall of France in 1940, the German air force—called the

Luftwaffe—began an eight-month air offensive against Great Britain to soften its defenses for an invasion. Known as the Blitz, this aerial assault on dozens of British cities, carried out mostly at night, failed thanks to Britain's Royal Air Force (RAF), which exacted a heavy toll on Nazi aircraft. The invasion never came. After the Blitz, the British intensified their own bombing campaign against Germany. During July 1941, the RAF averaged over a hundred bombing sorties (attacks by individual aircraft) per day against targets on the European continent. Within two years, the United States had joined the air war, and over 1,000 Allied bombing sorties per day were the norm in Europe, with many more raids by smaller fighter aircraft.

Today it is common to look up in the sky and see an airplane or two. Imagine, though, seeing hundreds at one time. If you lived in eastern England, this was the sight almost every morning during the last two years of the war as Allied bombers headed east toward Germany, flying in tight formation. And every afternoon, you saw a somewhat smaller number returning from their dangerous missions.

●

Second Lieutenant Donald K. Slayton was a nineteen-year-old farm boy from Wisconsin fighting on the Mediterranean front of this war. He was assigned to the 340th Bombardment Group of the Twelfth Air Force, U.S. Army Air Forces. The group was stationed in southern Italy, flying bombing missions against bridges, airfields, railroads, and other targets. Just before Slayton arrived in the fall of 1943, Italy had surrendered to the Allies. But German troops immediately occupied the most important Italian defensive positions, and the war in southern Europe raged on.

Slayton was the copilot of a twin-engine B-25 medium bomber. A typical B-25 crew had a pilot, copilot, bombardier, and three gunners, with one gunner doubling as the radio operator. The lead plane in a formation always had a navigator, and the last plane had a photographer to record the bombing results.

Don Slayton, B-25 copilot

Every evening, Slayton and the other men in his squadron stopped by the operations tent to see if they were scheduled to fly the next day. Working with target orders from headquarters, the staff decided how many planes to send and which crews. The usual mission was a formation of eighteen planes: six from each of three squadrons, with the fourth squadron in the group getting a rest. The operations officer for each squadron determined who would fly from his unit, rotating the men so that everyone on flying status got two or three combat assignments per week, with training flights in between. That was the system.

Crews never stayed intact for long, since one man might be on leave, another might be promoted to a different job, yet another might be transferred out, and someone else would be sick, wounded, or just too rattled to keep flying. Of course, some men would die, get captured, or simply never return from a mission, their fate unknown.

Just as in the submarine service, no one could handle the stress of combat indefinitely, so headquarters set a limit on how many missions an airman had to fly before he was rotated back to the U.S. With a huge pilot-training program, America could afford to do this. Germany and Japan, which were stretched for resources, could not. They flew their crews until they were killed or captured. Eventually, America started feeling the weight of this problem as well, as too many planes were being shot down. The training program couldn't keep up, so the mission limits increased. For medium bombers in the Twelfth Air Force, the limit was originally twenty-five missions. Then it was raised to thirty-five. By the time Slayton arrived, it was fifty missions. Considering the loss rate in the group, fifty missions gave flyers about a 30 percent chance of getting shot down during their combat tour. In other words, one in three airmen either crashed (usually fatally) or bailed out (to be captured, die, or escape back to friendly territory) before reaching the mission limit.

Echoing the feelings of their German and Japanese counterparts, some American airmen chalked a slogan on their T-shirts: *Fly 'til I die.*

On November 16, 1943, the crews assigned for the next morning couldn't believe their bad luck. For the third day in a row they would be attacking Luftwaffe airfields around Athens, Greece. "Same time, same place, same direction!" Slayton later wrote. "We all thought it was kind of stupid going to the same place the same time, three days in a row. But nobody stepped up and said so."

In fact, it couldn't be helped, since a battle for a strategic Greek island was raging 160 miles east of Athens. The mission for Slayton's group and another unit was to keep as many German planes as possible out of that battle. The total air armada would be seventy-two B-25s,

The American P-38 fighter, nicknamed the "fork-tailed devil" by German adversaries, 1944

protected by several dozen P-38 fighters, which were agile single-seat aircraft designed to shoot down enemy planes.

At 10:10 a.m. on the assigned day, they took off. The flight to Athens took a little over two hours. Then "everything happened," according to one pilot.

First there was ack-ack—antiaircraft gunfire, also called flak. German spotters calculated the height of the attackers and then set shells to explode at that altitude. It didn't require a direct hit, since a nearby burst could lacerate an aircraft with jagged chunks of metal, maiming the crew and disabling the plane.

Next were enemy fighters. They "were on us before we hit the target," reported another pilot, "coming at us from the sun"—so they couldn't be seen. "Were we scared? Hell, yes. We continued on our run with the fighters on our tail and ack-ack all around us."

Over the target the bombardiers let go. The bombs hit perfectly, with explosions ripping the airfield from one end to the other. Meanwhile, dogfighting German and American fighters tangled overhead as the bombers zigged and zagged to avoid flak.

Don Slayton (right) leans against his A–26 bomber on a Pacific island, 1945.

On the way back German planes surprised the formation by releasing bombs from above. P-38s came to the rescue, breaking up the attack and downing three enemy aircraft. Miraculously, only one American plane was shot down. It was from Slayton's squadron. Four crewmen out of the six aboard were seen parachuting to enemy-held territory below.

Slayton's plane was safe, but he had experienced the closest of close shaves. When his ship got back to base, it had over 300 flak holes, the tires were blown out, the landing-gear hydraulics were dead, and the crew had to crank down the wheels by hand to land safely. But everyone was alive.

The following day the men learned that the fifty-mission limit was being raised. There were just not enough replacement crews. Slayton went on to fly fifty-six missions. By the time he rotated back to the States, he had been promoted to full lieutenant and first pilot. Since his ambition was to fly fighters like the P-38, he volunteered for more combat. But the Air Force had other ideas and trained him on the latest two-engine bomber. Then they sent him to drop bombs on the Japanese in the Pacific.

German technicians work on a V-2 rocket, the largest in the world, 1942.

CAPTAIN PHILLIPS BOMBS MAJOR VON BRAUN

Don Slayton wanted to be a fighter pilot because that was what the best pilots did. Lieutenant Samuel C. Phillips was a member of this elite group, flying missions over Germany from a base in England. Many years later, he was asked to name his most important experience as a fighter pilot during World War II. "Surviving," he said.

An electrical engineer from Wyoming, Lieutenant Phillips arrived in England in February 1944 with the 364th Fighter Group of the Eighth Air Force. Born the same year as Max Faget and Tom Paine, he was about to turn twenty-three. During the next fifteen months, until Germany surrendered, he saw his original squadron of twenty-eight pilots cut by half. Seven were killed in action, two died in training accidents, and five were shot down and captured. A common event at his and every other combat unit was the arrival of replacements.

Phillips started out in P-38s, the same fighter that Slayton dearly wanted to fly. In July 1944, his group switched to the even more impressive P-51 Mustang. Built by the firm North American Aviation in California, the Mustang had many of the latest advances in aircraft technology.

Sam Phillips in the cockpit of a P-51 Mustang

Other new airplanes did, too, but the Mustang combined qualities that made it the best all-around fighter of the war. Most important was its streamlined shape and powerful engine, which was British-designed. This gave it speed, maneuverability, and the range to accompany bombers from England to Berlin and back—something no other fighter could do.

One of the Mustang's most advanced features was its wing. A little-known U.S. government organization called the National Advisory Committee for Aeronautics (NACA) devoted years to studying the effectiveness of different airfoils. The airfoil is the wing's cross section, as if sliced like a loaf of bread. The shape of this cross section influences lift and also air resistance, or drag. In the late 1930s, NACA researchers discovered an airfoil with remarkably low drag, which translates into greater speed and fuel economy. The Mustang was the first fighter to exploit this discovery.

P-51's innovative airfoil

P-51 on a bomber escort mission, 1944

After the war, the head of Hitler's Luftwaffe, Hermann Göring, re-marked that the arrival of P-51s over Berlin was decisive. "The greatest surprise of the war to us," Göring explained, "was the long-range fighter bomber that could take off from England, attack Berlin, and re-turn to its home base." From then on, Nazi leaders despaired of stop-ping the Allied bombing offensive that was systematically destroying their cities.

But technological surprises work both ways, and the Germans had a big one for the Allies.

On August 25, 1944, having recently been promoted to captain, Phillips took off with his squadron of Mustangs to join an armada of 171 fighters and 376 heavy bombers. Their targets were military installations in and around a secret research facility on a secluded peninsula called Peene-münde, which jutted into the Baltic Sea on Germany's northern coast.

Aerial surveillance showed a new type of weapon being tested at the site. The mission was the third Allied attack on Peenemünde in six weeks and the fourth in a little over a year. The air crews knew the place was important, but they were in the dark about what exactly was going on there.

But Allied leaders knew well and were alarmed. Mounting clues pointed to a new weapon unlike any ever built. Hitler's plan was apparently to obliterate London with unstoppable, long-range, high-explosive projectiles, since evidence showed that his engineers were perfecting the world's most powerful rocket.

The Allied air armada that day hit the test site, a nearby propellant plant, and surrounding airfields. But it was too late. The leaders of the rocket project, including its brilliant technical director, SS Major Wernher von Braun, had moved production of the missiles elsewhere, and hundreds were poised to descend on England.

●

That summer, Wernher von Braun was thirty-two years old. More than a decade earlier, he had been a carefree engineering student in love with the dream of spaceflight.

Von Braun belonged to a club that had built liquid-propellant rockets, which are rockets that produce thrust by burning fuel and oxidizer in liquid rather than solid form. Liquid fuels such as alcohol and kerosene contain much more energy than a comparable quantity of solid chemicals such as gunpowder—the propellant used in fireworks. Although far more complex than solid rockets, liquid-propellant rockets generally go faster and farther; and maybe one day, von Braun and his friends hoped, to the Moon and planets. At the time, rockets were only going a few thousand feet in the air. To reach the edge of space, they would need to go more than a hundred times higher, to an altitude of at least sixty miles. And to reach the Moon, they would have to travel an unimaginably distant 240,000 miles. Obviously, it was crazy even to consider it!

Nonetheless, it was a hobby, and club members were on the lookout for other enthusiasts who might be willing to provide financial support to help move the technology forward. They never expected that the German army would offer to underwrite their experiments. Von Braun's friends were reluctant to submit to army control, but he jumped at the chance, and in 1932 he was made the civilian head of Germany's military rocket research program. The army had no interest in space, but they did see promise in rockets as explosive-carrying projectiles that could travel much farther than artillery shells.

Von Braun threw himself into the assignment. He recruited gifted engineers, including fellow space enthusiasts. On his advice, the army established a secret rocket test center at Peenemünde. Then World War II broke out, and Nazi officials started putting pressure on von Braun to produce results quickly, especially after Allied air attacks began destroying the effectiveness of the Luftwaffe. Feeling that his life was on the line, von Braun worked as he had never worked before.

He had good reason to fear for his safety, because the rocket project had been taken over by the most brutal arm of the Nazi regime—the SS, or special police force, which ran the concentration camps where millions of Jews and other victims of Nazi ideology were being murdered. Ominously, SS chief Heinrich Himmler made von Braun an officer in the terror organization. Von Braun seldom wore his SS uniform, but yearly promotions made it appear he was involved in their crimes, whether he was or not, and by 1944 he was a major.

The SS also kept him supplied with thousands of skilled workers drawn from concentration camps and prisoner-of-war camps. Suspicious of his loyalty, at one point Himmler had him arrested on charges of sabotage, supposedly for advocating spaceflight over military goals.

German generals visit Wernher von Braun (in dark suit) at his secret rocket base, 1941.

It took Hitler's intervention to get von Braun released. "It could have very easily led me to the firing squad," he recalled with a shudder in later years.

On September 8, 1944, two weeks after Captain Phillips flew on the Peenemünde raid, von Braun's rockets began falling on London. Two fell the first day, and an average of two or three more followed every day for the next six months. Other rockets struck elsewhere in England, as well as in Allied-held regions of France and Belgium. Most were launched from German-occupied Holland, about 200 miles from London. During their arcing, five-minute flights, the wonder weapons soared to the brink of space. No human-made object had ever flown so high or so fast. Since they were traveling faster than sound, the rockets arrived without warning, detonating their payloads of high explosives with enough force to demolish a large building.

Von Braun was ordered to target London because of Britain's role in the bombing campaign against Germany, but also because his missiles were not yet advanced enough to reach the U.S. The Germans called the rocket "Vengeance Weapon 2," or V-2. (The V-1 was a less sophisticated, jet-propelled bomb.) During the six months of rocket attack, over 3,000 V-2s took off. More than 1,100 struck England and about 500 hit London. Altogether, they were responsible for some 5,000 deaths—not including the estimated 10,000 forced laborers who died from starvation and maltreatment while building them.

As formidable as the V-2 was, it was a failure as a weapon. It took as much labor to build one as to construct a heavy bomber, yet it was only good for a single mission, and it was barely accurate enough to target an entire city, much less a specific building. It never came close to achieving Hitler's goal of wiping out the British capital, and the V-2 project may actually have hastened Germany's defeat because of the resources it drained from more effective weapons.

Von Braun survived repeated bombing raids on Peenemünde, where most of those killed were Russian prison workers. The bigger risk to him, by far, was the SS. "Once they felt they could do without you, and you were in their way, they'd . . . destroy you," he told an American audience after the war. Defending his work for the Nazis and the SS, von Braun implored listeners to put themselves in his shoes: "The man living under dictatorship adjusts himself to business as usual, whether he likes it or not, because he must, in order to survive."

Soldiers and equipment pour ashore in France a few days after the D–Day invasion, 1944.

5

MAJOR WEBB FACES THE BIG ONE

When Lieutenant Phillips arrived in Britain with his fighter squadron in the winter of 1944, he ran into American troops everywhere. There were a million on the island, plus an even greater number of British, Canadian, French, Polish, and other Allied soldiers, all preparing for the largest seaborne invasion in history. Up to this point in the war, the major land battles in Europe had mostly taken place in eastern Europe, where Soviet troops were fighting toward Germany's eastern border, retaking territory they had lost in the early part of the conflict. The invasion from England would establish a western front, putting further pressure on Nazi forces. Called D-Day, this massive attack took place in the Normandy region of France on June 6, 1944. Some 156,000 troops landed on the first day, and by the end of the month 875,000 Allied soldiers were ashore, fighting stiff German resistance. Pushed back simultaneously from the east and the west, Germany managed to hold out for a little less than a year before finally surrendering unconditionally on May 8, 1945.

But the Pacific war raged on. In the summer of 1945, a year after

D-Day, another mammoth invasion was in the works. Set for November 1 and code-named Operation Olympic, this assault involved an even larger force than D-Day and would target the southernmost of the main Japanese islands, landing Allied troops on Japanese soil for the first time. Then on March 1, 1946, an even bigger invasion, called Operation Coronet, was due to attack the Tokyo area on Japan's central island with the goal of bringing World War II to its apocalyptic end.

Military planners predicted Japan's defeat by 1947, but American soldiers and sailors in the Pacific were not so sure. They had a saying, "Golden Gate in '48," meaning they didn't expect to be returning home beneath San Francisco's Golden Gate Bridge until 1948—if they survived. In fact, Japan's defense of its occupied territories had been so fierce and American casualties so high that it seemed foolhardy to believe *any* prediction about the final end of World War II.

Among the quarter of a million troops assembling for Operation Olympic was Major James E. Webb. Thirty-eight years old and hailing from North Carolina, he had a small but vital role in the coming action. Though he was a veteran aviator in the U.S. Marine Corps Reserve, his flying days were behind him, and he now commanded the First Marine Air Warning Group—2,000 officers and men assigned to wade ashore on invasion day and set up early-warning radar to guard against enemy air attack, particularly at night when radar would provide the only alert. Radar was one of the wonder weapons of the war, and the portable radar units Webb was helping to create seemed almost miraculous.

So important was Webb's assignment that he was temporarily given control over all Marine air transportation in the United States so he could gather radar components from factories around the country for

Jim Webb, put in charge of portable radar units for the planned invasion of Japan

final assembly and testing at his group's headquarters in North Carolina. In early August 1945, he, his men, and their equipment prepared to ship to a staging area in the Far East. Olympic was only three months away.

Like Max Faget and Tom Paine, Webb had a profession outside of the military. Faget and Paine were both engineers, while Webb was a lawyer with a talent for managing complex projects and a taste for trying ambitious new ventures.

When he was in his twenties and struggling to launch a career during the Great Depression, he had taken advantage of a Marine Corps program to train college graduates to be military pilots. The Marines taught him to fly the open-cockpit biplanes of the day. He served on active duty for two years and then went on reserve status. By the time World War II started almost a decade later, the corps had plenty of aggressive young flyers but needed experienced managers, which was what Webb had become. Weighing his own talents, he judged: "My forte was putting things together and getting a team that can play the ball game."

When the war came, Webb was serving as a vice president at the Sperry Gyroscope Company, headquartered in Brooklyn, New York. He had helped build it from 800 employees into a major defense contractor with 33,000 workers. After Pearl Harbor, his first thought was to enlist, especially when his younger brother was captured in Japan's assault on the U.S. base at Wake Island at the end of 1941. But the government preferred him to stay at Sperry, which was flooded with war orders.

"War is a hurly-burly kind of thing," Webb recalled. "We were hiring lots of people every day, training new people, getting rid of people who couldn't make the grade. Worrying about the security problems, finding espionage agents sent over by Germany in our plant. We had to get rid of them. Just a million things to be done . . ."

Many of Sperry's products were based on the gyroscope, a freely spinning disk that holds its position in space no matter how its housing frame is rotated. A gyroscope makes a remarkably reliable reference point for anything that needs to be directed to a precise location, such as an airplane, a submarine, a torpedo, or for that matter von Braun's V-2, which used gyroscopes in its guidance system (its targeting problems were for other reasons).

Educated as a lawyer and not an engineer, Webb still had to know enough about technology to negotiate multimillion-dollar contracts for delivery of devices that had never been built before. He recruited experts to do research and development, while he kept close tabs on their progress to ensure that the products were finished on time. One

The "kamikaze killer" gunsight, developed under Jim Webb's guidance

As Operation Olympic approached, the Japanese put up fierce resistance. Here, two kamikazes have just struck an American aircraft carrier, 1945.

consultant he trusted completely was Charles Stark "Doc" Draper, an eccentric engineering professor at the Massachusetts Institute of Technology (MIT) in Cambridge, Massachusetts. Draper's lab was hired by Sperry for a variety of projects, such as creating a gyroscopic gunsight for the U.S. Navy. This device allowed sailors to target airplanes closing in at 300 miles per hour. Teamed with a powerful antiaircraft gun, the gunsight became known as the "kamikaze killer" for its ability to shoot down Japanese suicide planes targeting ships. More than 85,000 were built, saving countless American lives.

In the third year of the war, Sperry was running so smoothly that Webb was finally allowed to enlist. The Marines gave him a crash course on radar. Then they put him in charge of the First Marine Air Warning Group with orders to produce something that didn't exist yet: portable radar units. To Webb, it was a familiar assignment: do something that had never been done.

"The contractors said it would take us six, maybe eight months," he recalled. "We wanted them yesterday." He didn't get them quite that fast, but as the deadline for Olympic approached, Webb and his men had the radar sets stockpiled and knew how to use them.

They were ready.

This defense worker, known as Rosie the Riveter, displays the attitude that won the war.

6

"WE NEED IT YESTERDAY!"

The news came on the day that Max Faget's submarine, *Guavina*, was cruising out of San Francisco Bay bound for Pearl Harbor and yet another war patrol. That same day, Tom Paine was on Guam where his boat, *Pompon*, was being refitted for more combat. Some 1,400 miles northwest of Guam, Don Slayton was with his new bomb group on Okinawa, the site of a recently concluded ferocious battle with the Japanese that was a grim preview of Olympic. For Slayton, Olympic had already started, since his sorties were targeting defenses around the landing beaches, an hour and a half away by air.

On the other side of the world, Sam Phillips was in Germany with the American occupation forces. Wernher von Braun was also in Germany, under house arrest by the U.S. Army, being questioned almost daily along with other members of his rocket team. And in the United States, Jim Webb was barely a week away from his departure for the Olympic staging area. After almost four years of war, its privations and tragedies, the American people were exhausted, but resigned to more months, even years, of conflict.

But then the news flash came. The date was August 6, 1945. The bulletin said that a Japanese city called Hiroshima had been obliterated by a single, powerful new bomb. "We didn't think that much about it," remembered Slayton. "Nobody was telling us the war was over. Two days later I was on another raid."

But the most destructive war of all time was about to end. In three days' time, another superbomb was dropped, on the city of Nagasaki. The short interval was intended to convince the Japanese that there was an arsenal full of these doomsday weapons, called atomic bombs. In fact, there were very few. Also on August 9, the Soviet Union, which until now had been neutral in the war with Japan, attacked Japanese forces in China with an army of well over a million soldiers. China was where World War II had started eight years earlier.

This devastating series of blows convinced the Japanese emperor to order his government to surrender.

The war was over.

World War I had seen new technology exploited for lethal ends: airplanes, rudimentary submarines, tanks, poison gas, high explosives, and machine guns. But none of these could be called a superweapon. By contrast, World War II produced superweapons of almost unimaginable sophistication: heavy bombers, long-range fighters, deep-diving submarines, guided missiles, mammoth battleships and aircraft carriers, and the superweapon to end them all: the atomic bomb—and then the even more cataclysmic hydrogen bomb that followed a few years later.

The Manhattan Project, which created the atomic bomb, was the prime example of a secret, technically challenging crash program with a no-holds-barred budget. But it was hardly unique; it was only one such effort among many during World War II. The operations that broke the Nazi and Japanese codes on an almost daily basis were no less secret, and the airplane that dropped the atomic bomb, the B-29 Superfortress, came out of a more expensive program of comparable technical difficulty. Radar may have been more crucial to winning the

The atomic bomb—the ultimate superweapon of World War II

war than the bomb. And the lowly Jeep and two-and-a-half-ton truck, built in the hundreds of thousands and the backbone of Allied land armies, were also hurry-up projects that cut corners to get into production and yet delivered outstanding results. Britain made key contributions to some of these projects, but America excelled at them. Through astute management, industrial power, innovation, and healthy budgets, the United States had discovered how to work technological miracles.

One of the secrets of success was a sense of urgency. Workers, managers, and engineers in defense plants everywhere believed that their project, whatever it was, was the most important of all, and they knew only one deadline: "We need it yesterday!" Anyone inclined to business as usual faced getting replaced by someone with a more can-do spirit. A famous story tells how as the war loomed, U.S. Army Chief of Staff General George C. Marshall asked for 150 updated field manuals to train troops in the latest military doctrine. He gave the general in charge a deadline of three months.

"It will take eighteen months," he was told.

"I need them in three," Marshall insisted.

"It can't be done," was the reply.

"I'm sorry, then you are relieved." Marshall sent the general into retirement and found someone who was up to the challenge.

Marshall was known for firing generals who didn't excel at their jobs, and he was a master at spotting new talent. He detected extraordinary ability in a lieutenant colonel named Dwight D. Eisenhower. The relatively young officer was promoted rapidly through the ranks, eventually becoming supreme commander of the Allied forces in Europe—the general in charge of D-Day. Eisenhower was later elected president of the United States.

Another secret of success was that companies figured out how to tackle giant projects of bewildering complexity. The B-29 Superfortress, which dwarfed Slayton's B-25, was the brainchild of General Henry H. "Hap" Arnold, the head of the Army Air Force. In 1939, he had asked Boeing Company executives if they could design a warplane with more than double the range and bomb load of the heaviest bomber then in the U.S. arsenal. But not only that—General Arnold demanded that this plane fly higher and faster, have powerful defensive armament, and be pressurized to allow the crew to fly in comfort at high altitude, without oxygen masks and arctic clothing. The goal was a bomber that could deliver a punishing blow to the enemy across thousands of miles.

It sounded like something in a science-fiction magazine, but the Boeing team got out their slide rules and started calculating. Officially given the job the following year, Boeing broke with aircraft industry tradition by attacking all of the airplane's intricate systems at the same time, assigning thousands of engineers to the effort. Everything about the ship—its airframe, electronics, armament, and other features—had to function in perfect synchrony. This required unprecedented coordination among many separate groups. Boeing also had to work with thousands of suppliers, including the manufacturer of the engines, a crucial component that was as complicated as the rest of the airplane put together.

One manager warned there was no room for error in such a high-performance machine. Success, he said, "depends upon everything working as planned."

For the longest time, it didn't. The worst day was February 18, 1943, when the ninth frustrating test flight of prototype number two started well enough. But after a few minutes in the air, an engine on the left side caught fire. The fire suppression system quickly extinguished it, and the pilot—Eddie Allen, one of the most experienced test pilots of the day—banked the giant B-29 to return to Boeing Field. On the way in, his left wing burst into flames and began disintegrating. Allen lost control and crashed into a meatpacking plant. All eleven crewmen died, along with twenty on the ground.

The most sophisticated aircraft of its day, the B-29 challenged engineers to solve seemingly impossible problems.

The engines were blamed, and there was pressure from Congress to pull the plug on the B-29. Critics argued that the Superfortress was a complex monstrosity destined to fail. But the plane's engineers and managers redoubled their efforts to get things right. A review board ordered changes in the engines. Meanwhile, problems were fixed in the remote-controlled gun turrets, the bomb bay doors, wing de-icers, propellers, and other systems. The government and military tightened their oversight of production, which was behind schedule. They decided to gear up assembly lines before all the kinks were worked out, which was a giant risk. But within fourteen months, the B-29 was flying in combat, and by 1945, it had changed the course of the war. Unlike Germany, Japan had not yet suffered significant attacks on its homeland. Now formations of B-29s, often hundreds at a time, began systematically destroying the cities and factories of the island nation, ultimately dropping two atomic bombs.

For better or worse, the B-29 proved its mettle. With this superweapon, no less than with the atomic bomb, industry and government had found a system for tackling a seemingly impossible task.

But that was war, and now peace had come. Faget, Paine, Slayton, Phillips, von Braun, Webb, and millions of others could thank their lucky stars that they had survived and look to the future. What would that hold?

The Wright brothers' first flight, 1903

Aviation pioneers (including Orville Wright) meet at a 1934 NACA conference.

A captured Japanese Zero in U.S. Army markings, 1943

The rocket-powered X-1, the first aircraft to fly faster than sound, 1947

BRIEFING:
The NACA

Wilbur and Orville Wright made history with the world's first airplane flight in 1903. Success came only after a methodical research program run out of their bicycle shop in Dayton, Ohio, and their flight-test camp in Kitty Hawk, North Carolina. The brothers spent the next few years improving their invention and making it practical. In 1915, the United States government established the NACA—the National Advisory Committee on Aeronautics—to continue the brothers' work. The new agency helped enhance practically every aspect of airplanes: wings, propellers, engines, streamlining, stability, control. Wilbur Wright died in 1912, but Orville served on the NACA advisory board until his death in 1948, only a few months after the first supersonic flight—another NACA project.

The NACA played a key role in making American planes among the top-performing fighters and bombers in World War II. NACA experts focused not just on U.S. aircraft but on the enemy's. During the war, a captured Japanese Zero—the fighter plane that had bombed Pearl Harbor and given American pilots so much trouble in dogfights—was sent to a NACA facility to have its flight characteristics analyzed, so that U.S. planes could counter it more effectively.

In 1958, the NACA became the nucleus for NASA—the National Aeronautics and Space Administration—and many of its aeronautical engineers turned their attention to spaceflight, among them Abe Silverstein, who had directed the Zero study, and Bob Gilruth, an expert on aircraft flying qualities. They and other creative problem solvers approached their new task with the same passion for imaginative thinking and rigorous testing that they had brought to aviation—guaranteeing that the spirit of the Wright brothers lives on in the space age.

PART 2
DREAMS

To place a man in a multi-stage rocket and project him into the controlling gravitational field of the moon, where the passenger can make scientific observations, perhaps land alive, and then return to earth—all that constitutes a wild dream worthy of Jules Verne. I am bold enough to say that such a man-made moon voyage will never occur regardless of all future advances.

—Lee de Forest, electronics pioneer, 1957

The full Moon, seen through a telescope on Earth

20¢

AUGUST
1950

SCIENCE and MECHANICS

The Magazine That Shows You How

Raymond Loewy's
Car of the Futur

The car of the future in 1950 symbolizes the new "rocket age."

7

AMERICA LANDS ON ITS FEET

The fatalistic slogan of Pacific troops was "Golden Gate in '48," and the flippant answer was "Bread Line in '49." The implication was that the booming war economy would grind to a halt after the enemy surrendered. Factories would close and returning veterans wouldn't be able to find work. This was exactly what had happened after World War I ended in 1918. Everyone expected the same after the Axis surrendered in 1945.

Surprisingly, the economy kept booming. Several factors seem to have been responsible. For one thing, there was a huge pent-up demand for consumer goods—everything from bicycles to radios to shoes—that dated to the start of the Great Depression in 1929. The Depression was a decade-long economic crisis, during which up to a quarter of the workforce in the United States couldn't find jobs. The Depression was ended by World War II, when practically everyone who wanted a job could get one, but there was very little to spend money on during the war. With the arrival of peace, factories converted from producing armaments to consumer products, which people now had the savings to purchase.

For another thing, the United States was the only great power to emerge unscathed from the war. Its cities were not bombed, its infrastructure was not destroyed, and the country was not deeply in debt to other nations for food, oil, and weapons (as some of the Allies were to the U.S.). Practically anything the world needed, America could supply. Furthermore, American foreign aid helped rebuild Western Europe under the Marshall Plan, named for its champion, General George C. Marshall, who became the U.S. Secretary of State after the war. The Marshall Plan was a wise investment for many reasons, not least because it created a market for American exports.

Yet another wise investment was the G.I. Bill, which provided education, housing, and business start-up benefits to war veterans, allowing them to land on their feet when they disembarked from troop ships. Instead of a breadline, they could get into a college enrollment line or a line at a bank for a low-interest loan that they could use to buy a house or open a business. With the war over, the energy that had gone into winning battles now went into starting families, getting ahead, and enjoying life.

●

There was also a more fundamental change going on. For many decades, the quality of life in much of the world had been advancing at a remarkable pace, particularly in the United States. In 1945, an American who had been born in 1900 had seen astonishing changes. When that person was an infant, life expectancy was just forty-seven years— which is today considered the prime of one's working life. By 1945, a newborn could expect to live almost two decades longer, thanks to improved public health, better doctor training, and radical new medical treatments. In 1900, only a third of homes had running water, and just half of those were equipped with flush toilets. Electrical lighting, telephones, and central heating were almost unknown. Affordable automobiles, washing machines, and mechanical refrigerators hadn't been invented yet, nor had radios or airplanes. By 1945, all of these dramatic improvements had spread widely.

And they were still spreading after World War II. By itself, this wholesale transformation of society gave an enormous boost to the American economy. It would last until what are now considered the necessities of life—running water, electricity, appliances, telephones, and automobiles—were nearly universal in the United States. For people living in the middle of this revolution, it was easy to think that the dramatic changes would keep coming without limit, as one new invention after another transformed their lives. The technological miracles of World War II reinforced this impression. Atomic energy, radar, electronic computers, and jet planes were straight out of the pages of the pulp magazines that Max Faget read, yet now they existed and had helped win the war. Furthermore, they held the promise that *anything* was possible.

At the end of 1949, a random sample of Americans were asked to look half a century into the future—to the year 2000—and predict progress in three areas. The person-in-the-street's confidence in technology was almost boundless.

"Do you think that fifty years from now trains and airplanes will be run by atomic power?" Yes, said 63 percent. (In fact, no such vehicles have ever been built.)

"Do you think that a cure for cancer will be found within the next fifty years?" A hefty 88 percent responded yes. (Unfortunately, cancer

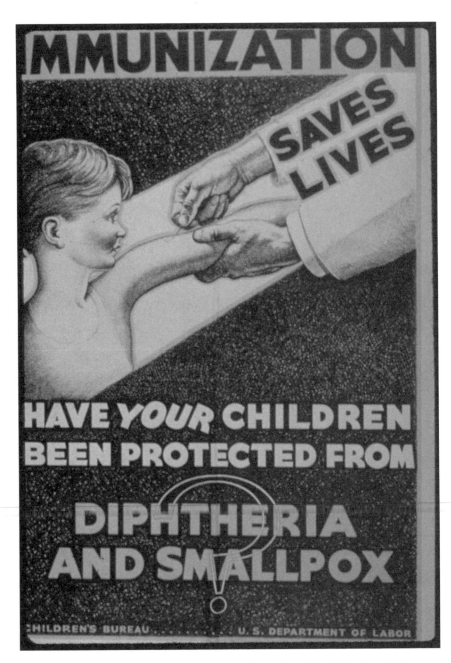

Immunization and other medical advances transformed society in the twentieth century, inspiring almost limitless optimism about the future.

still rivals heart disease as the leading cause of death in the United States.)

But starry-eyed optimism failed with the last question: "Do you think that men in rockets will be able to reach the Moon within the next fifty years?" This was a technological leap too far for 70 percent, who resoundingly answered no. Another 15 percent had no opinion. Only the remaining 15 percent thought that humans would actually fly to the Moon by 2000, fifty years in the future.

Who would have believed that people would make the trip far sooner than that?

Wernher von Braun holds a model of his V-2 rocket in the early 1950s.

VON BRAUN LANDS IN AMERICA

"That guy upstairs wants to go to the Moon." Glancing at the ceiling, Major James P. Hamill was hinting to a reporter that the civilian employee on the next floor was slightly mad. The major added: "That's his passion—space travel. Whether it will be war or peace on Earth comes after that for him."

"That guy upstairs," at the U.S. Army's Redstone Arsenal outside Huntsville, Alabama, in October 1950, was the most sought-after genius from Hitler's Germany: Wernher von Braun. As futile as von Braun's rockets had been during the war, the V-2 still attracted intense interest from the Allies. None of them had a missile nearly as powerful, and all reasoned that if it could be made more powerful still—and accurate—then it might be a decisive weapon in the next war.

Before Germany surrendered, von Braun knew that the Soviets advancing from the east and the Americans and British approaching from the west would be eager to capture him and his rocket team. He guessed that the Soviets would be none too pleased by Germany's treatment of Russian prisoners of war at Peenemünde, and the British might hold a grudge about the V-2 bombardment of London. Therefore, he gambled that the Americans would be the most welcoming.

He had never been to the United States, but his older brother, Sigismund, had studied law in Ohio for a year before the war. Impressed with America's vitality and openness to new ideas, Sigismund told Werner, "America is the place for you to build your Moon rockets."

That settled the matter. As Hitler's empire collapsed around him, von Braun and several hundred of his staff risked execution for treason by the SS and made their way across Germany to the American lines. In early May 1945, a few days before the surrender, the rocket men turned themselves over to U.S. forces. Eventually they found themselves under the charge of Major Hamill.

The Army's first priority was to seize a large number of unused V-2s to ship back to the United States for testing. Army intelligence officers interrogated von Braun and his team, confirming that these men were indeed the talent behind the V-2 and probably had a lot to teach American rocket engineers. If nothing else, they would be essential for assembling and launching V-2s in the U.S.

The Germans were not shy about discussing their interest in space, but none of the Americans took this seriously. In fact, it seemed to exonerate the rocket men from complicity in Nazi war crimes, including the abuse and execution of prison laborers at the V-2 factories. Their sincere, wildly impractical visions of spaceflight made them look like dreamers who had been exploited by the Nazis, not enthusiastic collaborators in an evil regime. Probably, they were a mix of both. No one was as obsessed with spaceflight as von Braun, yet he had still done his best to win the war for Hitler. Even after the war he didn't seem to grasp what victory for Germany would have meant.

"If Germany had won the war," he mused lightheartedly in 1950, "der Führer would probably have lost interest in rockets. His enthusiasm would have shifted to a huge reconstruction project in the Ukraine or some such. I just know it."

The horror that von Braun glossed over was that Hitler's plan was to remake Ukraine as a German colony, exterminating or expelling most of its inhabitants. The Nazis succeeded to the extent of killing virtually all of Ukraine's Jews plus millions of others in the region—this on top of the additional millions who died at their hands in the rest of Europe.

The U.S. Army brought von Braun and more than a hundred of his best engineers and technicians to Fort Bliss, Texas, where they were to live under Army supervision. Their work would be at the nearby missile proving ground at White Sands, New Mexico, where the first atomic bomb had been tested. The rocket team came voluntarily under a one-year contract that paid them a small amount and guaranteed their families back in Germany housing and a degree of security in the postwar chaos of their devastated homeland.

The German rocket team in Texas, 1946. Von Braun is in the front row, right of center, with a white handkerchief in his breast pocket.

At White Sands, the visitors taught their hosts how to fire V-2s, advised them on improvements to the missile, briefed visiting scientists and engineers on the mechanics of the rocket, and assisted with the V-2's new mission of high-altitude research, for it was now launching scientific instruments instead of warheads.

When one year was up, the Army asked the Germans to stay, raising their pay and promising to bring their families over from Germany. The rocket men had proved so efficient that the Army wanted them indefinitely for other missile projects. They were even offered eventual U.S. citizenship. On the one hand, von Braun and most of his team were willing. On the other hand, they were deeply discouraged that they had been given no ambitious new rockets to work on, especially none that could venture higher than the hundred miles or so achieved by the V-2.

Also, the U.S. Congress was less than pleased about their presence. With the war over, legislators had little interest in expensive new weapons, particularly unreliable long-range rockets. The Army tried to make the case that rockets would be as important in future wars as aircraft carriers, submarines, and heavy bombers had been in the last one. But the Army was competing for funds with the other military branches, notably the Air Force, which had become a separate service in 1947. Airpower had strong support in Congress, in part because innovations in warplanes often made their way into civilian aircraft. For rockets, there were no such civilian uses. Certainly, no one in the Army was arguing that rockets could one day carry explorers to the Moon!

Meanwhile, von Braun and some of his colleagues were considering shifting to private industry or returning to Germany. "At Peenemünde, we'd been coddled. Here they were counting pennies," he complained. America was not the paradise for building Moon rockets that he had pictured. Plus, the Germans were beginning to feel unwelcome.

A V-2 rocket topped by a slender second stage takes off, 1950. This series of tests reached a record altitude of nearly 250 miles and a record speed of more than 5,000 miles per hour.

The Army had tried to be discreet about importing German technical advisers, not just in rocketry but in other fields with military applications. Eventually, word got out that hundreds of "former pets of Hitler" were now influential consultants to the U.S. military and might even become U.S. citizens. The Council Against Intolerance in America sent a telegram to President Harry Truman, who had become commander in chief upon the death of Franklin Roosevelt in April 1945. "We hold these individuals to be potentially dangerous carriers of racial and religious hatred," the council objected. The signers included the world's most famous physicist, Albert Einstein, along with Rabbi Stephen S. Wise, a prominent American Jewish leader. Asked their opinion in a national poll, a majority of Americans agreed that harboring Nazi scientists was a bad idea.

The protests might easily have grown until the government felt pressured to send Hitler's engineers back home. But America was starting to forget its old enemies and focus on a new one. In due time, Congress would be sufficiently alarmed to approve funds for a bold new project for the German rocket team.

They would be staying after all.

An American atomic bomb test in the Pacific, 1946

9

THE COLD WAR

In 1947, both Max Faget and Sam Phillips were working at the same U.S. government compound, although they didn't know each other at the time. Faget was a newly hired aeronautical engineer at the Langley Memorial Aeronautical Laboratory—the NACA facility that had developed the airfoil for the P-51 Mustang. Next door at Langley Field, former P-51 pilot Phillips was now Major Phillips with a job in air traffic control. Neither was thinking that another war might be imminent. Little did they suspect they were in the calm before the storm—a very long and chilly storm, for America was about to enter a decades-long conflict with the Soviet Union called the Cold War.

The Soviet Union had been America's ally during World War II, but the relationship was complicated. For one thing, the Soviets had been Hitler's ally at first—until 1941, when the Nazi dictator double-crossed the Russians and invaded their country. If any world leader could be compared to Hitler in bloodthirstiness, it was the Soviet dictator Joseph Stalin, who was responsible for the deaths of millions of his own citizens by execution, starvation, and imprisonment under brutal conditions. On the principle that "the enemy of our enemy is our friend," the United States and Great Britain cooperated with Stalin in the war against Germany, despite what was then known about Stalin's brutality. The U.S. and Britain even shipped millions of tons of military equipment to the Soviet Union, providing a vital lifeline that the Soviet government largely hid from its own people so that they wouldn't feel friendly toward the West. This was one of the many ways that Stalin controlled Soviet public opinion. An additional grievance for the U.S. and Britain was that Stalin did nothing to assist them in their fight against Japan until the last days of the war. And when American B-29s made emergency landings on Russian soil, the planes were impounded and taken apart piece by piece so that the Soviets could see how they were made, and so that they, too, could manufacture this wonder weapon. In short, as an ally Stalin was less than trustworthy.

Then there was ideology. Stalin was only the second ruler of his young nation, which had been established in the Communist Revolution of 1917. Its full name was the Union of Soviet Socialist Republics, or the U.S.S.R. for short. It was often called simply Russia, because that was the largest republic in the union. The United States had been at odds with the Soviets since the beginning, due to the Soviets' promotion of worldwide revolution. Soviet leaders appealed to workers everywhere to organize themselves and seize control of their governments, just as they had done, with all private property to be used for the common good. In practice, this meant total state control of all land, housing, services, factories, and personal freedoms. In 1945, the Soviet Union was the only major country to have taken this drastic step, but the country's leaders were determined to see the system spread around the globe.

They started with their neighbors. No sooner had the war against Germany ended than Stalin began setting up puppet communist regimes in the countries bordering his. Stalin's guarantee that he would allow free elections in these nations—which included Poland, Czechoslovakia, Hungary, and Romania—meant nothing. War-weary, the Americans and British objected but did little to stop the dictator. One outcome was that Germany stayed divided for decades between the eastern part of the country, which Soviet troops had overrun, and the western part of the country, which had been occupied by American, British, and French forces. Divided Germany became a symbol of a world increasingly split between communist and capitalist forms of government, especially after Stalin's successor, Nikita Khrushchev, ordered the construction of the Berlin Wall, a physical barrier preventing communist East Berliners from escaping to the greater prosperity and personal freedom of the American, British, or French zones of the city.

On the one hand, Stalin's policy of installing compliant governments along his borders was easy to understand, since Russia had suffered terribly from attacks by neighbors in wars going back for many centuries. On the other hand, his promotion of universal revolution was a new development in international affairs and threatened the world order that the United States felt obliged to safeguard. World War II had been fought to free the world from tyranny, but now a new tyrant loomed—one that posed a real danger, since the Soviet Union maintained the largest active army in the world. In 1945 President Truman had assured Americans that "we have emerged from this war the most powerful nation in the world—the most powerful nation, perhaps, in all history." The United States was truly a superpower, but the Soviet Union was determined to surpass it.

Joseph Stalin (front row, left) stands next to Harry Truman at their only meeting, July 1945.

Still, the Soviets didn't have the atomic bomb, which was the first weapon to exploit the incomprehensible power of nuclear energy. Invented by the U.S., atomic bombs were at first an American monopoly. Most Americans realized, however, that it was only a matter of time before the Soviet Union broke this monopoly. The man in charge of the Manhattan Project, General Leslie Groves, knew better than anyone what it took to build an atomic bomb, and he assured government officials that twenty years was a good estimate for how long it would take the Russians to catch up. Therefore, it was a profound shock when the Soviets set off their first nuclear explosion in 1949, just four years after the U.S.'s first atomic bomb test.

"The calmer the American people take this, the better," counseled the chairman of the Joint Chiefs of Staff when the news broke. But few took it calmly. One reaction was to believe that the Soviets had stolen the plans. In fact, they *had* stolen the plans, thanks to their spies. But there is far more to building a nuclear weapon than just having the plans. Their achievement hinted at a technical sophistication that was troubling. Moreover, American intelligence officials suspected the Russians were interested in rockets and were being advised by V-2 engineers who had stayed behind at Peenemünde, which was now in the Soviet occupation zone.

Adding to the unease, Chinese communists proclaimed a new Soviet-style government in China just a few days after the Russian atomic bomb surprise. Many Americans felt their backs were to the wall. "Better get out your old uniform," former soldiers told each other.

Emboldened by his ability to challenge American power, Stalin gave the okay to the communist government in North Korea to invade democratic South Korea in 1950. He expected the U.S. to stay out of this conflict, but he was wrong. Determined to block Soviet aggression so it wouldn't spread, President Truman sent in hundreds of thousands of U.S. troops under the auspices of the newly established United Nations, an international organization of countries, including the U.S., with the mission to promote peace. The Korean War raged for three years, ending in a stalemate in 1953, with the border between North and South Korea scarcely changed, despite the deaths of tens of thousands of American soldiers, as well as millions of Koreans on both sides, including civilians. The Soviets were also involved—but only to the extent of providing weapons and medical aid to their North Korean allies. They were careful not to come into direct conflict with American forces—except in one area.

In some aerial dogfights, American pilots suspected they were facing Russian airmen flying North Korea's Soviet-built fighters. This was the first war that saw the widespread use of jets, which flew faster and higher than propeller-powered aircraft like the Mustang. Surprisingly, Russia's jets turned out to be better than America's. Apparently, Russian flight instructors would lead their North Korean pupils into combat in squadrons of these superb flying machines. Communist China also fought on North Korea's side, with ground troops as well as pilots. Therefore, American pilots could be facing either North Korean, Russian, or Chinese adversaries.

The thousands of Americans involved in the air war included a naval aviator named Neil A. Armstrong and an Air Force pilot, Edwin E. "Buzz" Aldrin Jr. The two young men didn't know each other—yet. In the course of scores of sorties, both had their close calls. Flying a flak-riddled jet on one mission, with the wing partially sheared off, Armstrong nursed his ship into friendly territory before ejecting to safety. During the ordeal, he had a remarkably calm discussion with a fellow pilot about the best solution to this life-or-death emergency. For his part, Aldrin's adventures included shooting down two enemy jets, one after a grueling dogfight. Years later, the two coolheaded airmen would join forces for a very different adventure.

The Korean War was the first in a series of wars in which the United States and Soviet Union supported opposite sides—and sometimes sent in substantial numbers of troops—while avoiding, as much as possible, fighting each other. Such a direct conflict could easily have escalated into a nuclear war, with apocalyptic consequences. Throughout the 1950s, '60s, and beyond, armed struggles raged in places such as Korea, Cuba, Vietnam, Chile, and Angola, with the United States backing the democratic, capitalist side, and the Soviet Union sponsoring the totalitarian, communist side. Despite the bloodshed, these were considered engagements in the Cold War. Always, there was the risk that the Cold

Ensign Neil Armstrong (left) and Lieutenant Buzz Aldrin (right) during the Korean War. Aldrin has just returned from shooting down an enemy jet.

War could become "hot"—that it would spiral out of control into a full-scale clash between the two superpowers. Despite the risk, American and Soviet leaders persisted in jockeying for advantage, determined to see their nation's values and interests prevail around the world.

Like World War II, the Cold War drew on the resources of the entire nation. When World War II ended, Americans assumed that the declared state of national emergency would lift and defense expenditures would plummet, which is what happened for a few short years. But by 1950 the military budget had climbed back to about half of what was spent during the peak year of World War II. Many who had expected to enter a peaceful profession found themselves either still in the military or working on military projects.

Although the NACA was a civilian agency, its defense work boomed. Faget belonged to a special group called the Pilotless Aircraft Research Division (PARD), headed by a savvy engineer named Robert R. Gilruth. PARD's work focused on rocketry, particularly experimental rocket planes designed to fly faster than the speed of sound, which is roughly 700 miles per hour at jet altitudes. This research was put to use on missiles and advanced fighters and bombers.

Meanwhile, Major Phillips was sent to the University of Michigan to get an advanced degree in electronics. Then he landed in Ohio,

American F-86 jets patrol the skies over Korea, 1953.

managing weapons programs such as the one that developed the B-52 bomber—a jet-powered behemoth that surpassed the B-29 Super-fortress by as much as the B-29 had dwarfed Slayton's two-engine B-25. The B-52 could fly faster, higher, and farther than the B-29, and carry a much heavier payload. The intended payload was nuclear weapons, and the intended target, should hostilities break out, was the Soviet Union.

For his part, Don Slayton was now a captain with the new nickname Deke, concocted from his initials, DK, to distinguish him from another Don in his unit. He was finally flying fighters as a test pilot for the Air Force's latest supersonic jets at Edwards Air Force Base in California.

Elsewhere, Faget's fellow submariner Tom Paine was leading research in high technology for the General Electric Company, much of it having military applications. Former Marine major Jim Webb was President Truman's budget director before taking the number two job at the State Department during the early stage of the Korean War. Later he joined an energy company as a troubleshooting executive. And almost no one was questioning the presence of Wernher von Braun and his German rocket team in the United States. They were now America's rocket team in the contest with the Soviet Union.

Collier's

OCTOBER 18, 1952 • FIFTEEN CENTS

MAN ON THE MOON

Scientists Tell How We Can Land There In Our Lifetime

Astronauts land on the Moon in a realistic space journey recounted in *Collier's* magazine, October 18, 1952.

10

DISNEY TO THE RESCUE

The Moon orbits Earth at a distance of 240,000 miles, taking a little less than a month to make one complete circuit of our planet. There's no reason the Moon couldn't orbit closer, say at 100,000 miles, where it would complete an orbit in about a week. Or closer still, at 10,000 miles, where it would take less than half a day to go once around. Actually, you wouldn't want the Moon to get *that* close, since Earth's tidal force would cause it to disintegrate into a ring of debris, like Saturn's. However, smaller objects—say, a spy camera, a television relay, or a spaceship with a human aboard—can orbit the Earth as little as 100 miles overhead. Any lower, and the tiny amount of air at the edge of space slows an object, causing it to plunge to Earth's surface in a matter of hours or days.

Objects at this 100-mile distance circle Earth in 88 minutes at a blistering 17,500 miles per hour. Von Braun knew that if he could launch a rocket at least this high and get it going at least this fast, while it traveled horizontal to Earth's surface, then its motor could switch off and it would keep circling. The higher the orbit, the longer it would stay up, possibly for many years. It would be an Earth satellite, just as the Moon is. Moreover, it would be the first step on the long journey to the Moon.

These matters were on his mind one day in the early 1950s, when he excitedly told a colleague, "With the Redstone, we could do it!"

"Do what?"

"Launch a satellite, of course!"

In 1950, von Braun and his rocket team moved into a vacant Army facility called the Redstone Arsenal, near Huntsville, Alabama. It was their first real home in America, and they had a well-funded rocket project to go with it: an advanced version of the V-2 named, appropriately, Redstone. The Army's intended use for Redstone was to loft a nuclear warhead across several hundred miles. The missiles would be stationed in West Germany as a deterrent against a Soviet invasion of non-communist Europe, which was a growing worry.

But von Braun had other plans. If instead of a heavy nuclear bomb, Redstone carried a payload of smaller rockets, stacked on top of one another like scoops of ice cream on a cone, then the rockets could be fired in stages. The first stage—the Redstone missile itself—would exhaust its propellant at a very high altitude and speed, and then drop away. Then the second stage would ignite, boosting the remaining stages even higher and faster. Then the second stage would drop off, the third stage would ignite, and so on. Von Braun figured that four stages would be enough to launch a payload weighing a few pounds into orbit.

Here's another way to think about it. Suppose you want to climb Mount Everest, the tallest mountain in the world. To make it to the top, you require a lot of supplies, such as food, water, cooking fuel, and bottled oxygen (to breathe because of the high altitude). In fact, you need more than you can possibly carry by yourself. So you hire three help-ers. After the first day's climb, the four of you make camp and have din-ner, consuming some of the supplies (you've already been breathing the oxygen). The next day, two of the helpers head back down the mountain, while you and the remaining helper resume the climb, fully replenished with supplies thanks to what the others left behind. The same thing happens at the next camp, leaving you by yourself on the third day. Thanks to the "boost" given by your helpers on stages 1 and 2 of your climb, you can make the final ascent to the top by yourself with all the supplies you need. The principle is much the same with

Two-stage
research rocket,
1951

multi-stage rockets. The bottom stages make it possible for the top stage to reach orbit.

The German rocketeer knew that in a few years' time, after Redstone was designed, built, and working properly, it would be a relatively simple matter to convert one into a satellite launcher. His big problem was to convince his bosses to let him do it.

Collier's magazine was one of the most popular periodicals in America in the first half of the twentieth century, and its March 22, 1952, issue arrived like a trumpet blast from the future. The cover art showed a winged spaceship shedding a lower stage as it rocketed into Earth orbit. The headline proclaimed: "Man Will Conquer Space *Soon*. Top Scientists Tell How in 15 Startling Pages." Turning to the special section

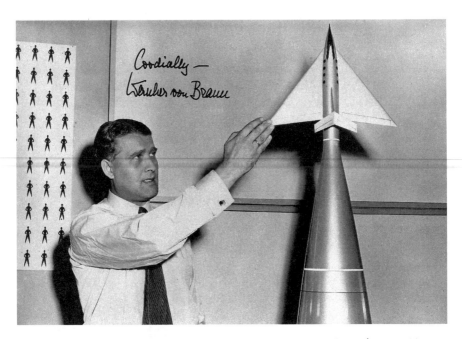

In an autographed photo, von Braun shows a model based on his *Collier's* spaceship.

inside, readers were told, "What you will read here is not science fiction. It is serious fact."

Von Braun was one of the contributors, and his article described in realistic detail the steps for leaving Earth, orbiting the planet, assembling a space station, constructing a deep-space exploration vehicle, and then heading out to the Moon. Just as in science fiction, he pictured humans as a necessary part of the mission. Automated and remote-control devices had advanced greatly since World War II, but most people, including von Braun, assumed that humans would be indispensable on any ambitious space project, since they would be needed to operate the complicated equipment.

A few months earlier, von Braun had met a member of the *Collier's* staff at a small conference on space medicine. Initially skeptical, the editor fell in love with the idea that rocket ships and Moon missions could really happen, and he asked von Braun to write an article about it, sticking to what could actually be done. Von Braun welcomed the opportunity and discovered he had a knack for communicating his enthusiasm to ordinary people. Plus, he had an excellent editor to correct his still-uneven English. The issue was so successful that *Collier's* continued the series with seven more parts, including "Man on the Moon: Scientists Tell How We Can Land There In Our Lifetime." Von Braun was the main contributor, and his enthusiastic readers ventured with him as far as Mars by the close of the series in 1954.

It's hard to recapture the tremendous impact of the *Collier's* articles. It would be almost as if in the early twenty-first century a group of scientists announced that time travel was really possible, and outlined plans for a time machine trip to ancient Egypt. The initial reaction would be that they had lost their minds! Space travel was in a similar boat in the early 1950s. However, the door had opened a crack. Newsreels, which were short news programs preceding the main feature in movie theaters, showed V-2s impressively taking off in New Mexico.

This paved the way in the public's mind for more ambitious achievements in rocketry. In terms of the time-travel analogy, it would be as if scientists already had a machine that could go back an hour or two—in which case, the idea of going back thousands of years might still seem far-fetched, but perhaps not impossible.

Opening the *Collier's* eight-part space series, in the spring of 1952, was an ominous warning from the editors: "The U.S. must immediately embark on a long-range development program to secure for the West 'space superiority.' If we do not, somebody else will. That somebody else would very probably be the Soviet Union."

Collier's made von Braun a national celebrity. He was interviewed on the brand-new medium of television, where he was so captivating, even with his strong German accent, that Walt Disney booked him for three episodes of his *Disneyland* series, broadcast on the ABC television network on Wednesday evenings.

Addressing Disney's audience of children and their parents, von Braun made spaceflight seem as if it were just around the corner. He spelled out the details of rocket stages, propellant weights, cutoff velocities, and other facts with such offhand assurance that he became the classic rocket scientist in the public mind.

"Disney's immediate achievement," wrote a reporter after the first episode aired in March 1955, "is the suggestion that space travel no longer is a wild dream; that it is so near that we can practically feel the Earth tremble under the rocket blast from Dr. von Braun's spaceship." The reporter made a prediction: "Half of the voting population of the U.S.A. has probably reached two impressive conclusions: 'It CAN be done!' and 'Let's get on with it!'"

Among the millions tuning in was U.S. president Dwight Eisenhower.

Walt Disney and
Wernher von
Braun, 1954

He was so intrigued that he called Disney and asked to borrow a copy of episode 1, "Man in Space," to show at the Pentagon. According to Disney's director, the president "made all the generals sit down and look at what was almost a childish primer on how we were going to go into space someday, because the brass had no idea of how this was all done."

A few weeks later, on July 29, 1955, Eisenhower's press secretary announced that the United States would launch an Earth satellite sometime during an upcoming international scientific effort, extending from the second half of 1957 through 1958. Of course, the administration had much more than a children's TV program to go on. Several technical reports recommending a satellite launch had been issued in the preceding years, including one by von Braun involving the Redstone. But whatever the inspiration, America was going into space.

America's Vanguard rocket explodes, December 6, 1957.

11

THE EMPIRE STRIKES BACK

President Eisenhower may have been enthusiastic about launching an Earth satellite, but his predecessor, former president Truman, called it "a lot of hooey!"—using one of his favorite expressions. Truman was no doubt thinking of the foolery about space he had read in *Collier's*.

But Eisenhower was an ex-military man and understood the tremendous promise that satellites had for reconnaissance, communications, and other defense needs. The president was also a strategic thinker, and he recognized the public relations value of a civilian, as opposed to a military, satellite project. The Soviets loved to paint the U.S. as a belligerent capitalist power trying to dominate the world. They would waste no time interpreting a satellite launch as a hostile act, particularly if the U.S. Army's Redstone Arsenal was involved.

Eisenhower agreed with his advisers that the first satellite should be launched on a research rocket, not a military missile, and that it should carry a scientific payload with instruments to measure the properties of outer space. The only problem was, there were no sufficiently powerful rockets available. The launch vehicle his advisers had in mind, called Vanguard, was still on the drawing board. And America's most experienced missile man, Wernher von Braun, had nothing to do with it.

●

The situation was driving von Braun crazy. He knew his Redstone could launch a satellite on short notice and do it at far less cost than Vanguard, which was a low-priority program being run by the scientific research arm of the U.S. Navy. By mid-1955, development work on the Redstone was nearly complete, and it was about to go into production. The following year, von Braun convinced the Army to let him produce an elongated, four-stage version of the Redstone to test missile components for even larger rockets. This souped-up Redstone was tantalizingly close to being able to launch a satellite, but the U.S. government wouldn't let von Braun do it. That was Vanguard's job.

In November 1956, when a scientist connected with Vanguard visited Huntsville, von Braun took him aside and told him that top secret information revealed that the Russians would soon be capable of their own satellite launch. So far, there had been no urgency in getting Vanguard or indeed any American satellite aloft. Von Braun felt like a gold miner in the Old West who was about to see his claim stolen—by the Russians. He implored the man to take a message back to the head of the Vanguard project: "I want you to tell him that if he wants to, he can paint 'Vanguard' right up the side of my rocket. He can do anything he wants to, but he is to use my rocket, not his, because my rocket will work and his won't."

The German rocketeer wasn't finished. He told the scientist he knew exactly what the project director would reply: that it made no difference who launched the first satellite, since what mattered was science. "Will you say to him," von Braun implored, "if that's what he really thinks, will he for Christ's sake get out of the way of the people who think it makes a hell of a lot of difference!"

Less than a year later, on October 4, 1957, von Braun was in his office in Huntsville when he got the bad news: The Soviets had done it. The world's first artificial satellite was now orbiting Earth. Bitterly disappointed but hardly surprised, he reacted with an expression he had picked up in Texas.

"I'll be damned!"

Von Braun was not shocked, but the rest of the U.S. plunged into a nervous breakdown. Russia's success with an atomic bomb in 1949 had been bad enough, but Russia had come in second in that contest. With their satellite, Sputnik (Russian for "traveling companion"), they had achieved a stunning first-place finish. It was all the worse because the entire world could hear and see Sputnik, which periodically passed over practically every inhabited region of the planet. Those below could tune into its radio signal—a steady *beep, beep, beep.* And, if its passage coincided with the time around dusk or dawn, they could see its dim starlike form moving steadily across the sky. More visible still was the giant rocket stage that had boosted Sputnik into orbit. It, too, was circling Earth—a menacing reminder of the Soviet Union's technological prowess.

Politicians wasted no time sounding the alarm. Senator Lyndon B. Johnson from Texas opened a series of hearings by declaring that Sputnik was "a disaster . . . comparable to Pearl Harbor." His fellow Democratic senator Henry M. Jackson of Washington called the Soviet achievement "a devastating blow to the prestige of the United States as the leader of the free world."

Eisenhower, a Republican, tried to play down the significance of the

WEATHER
Fair; not quite so cool.
(Details on Page 2)

The Detroit News

SATURDAY FINAL

SATURDAY, OCTOBER 5, 1957, VOL. 85, NO. 44   THE HOME NEWSPAPER—ESTABLISHED 1873   22 PAGES   SEVEN CENTS

RED 'MOON' PASSES OVER DETROIT TODAY

Arkansas Peace Formula Given to Ike, Faubus

By ROBERT S. BALL
Staff Correspondent The Detroit News

LITTLE ROCK, Ark., Oct. 5.—The White House has been given a new formula for ending the Little Rock school integration crisis, Rep. Harris (D-Ark.) disclosed to The Detroit News today.

Harris said he has submitted his proposal to Gov. Orval E. Faubus and to ranking members of President Eisenhower's staff, and that he has reason to believe Faubus will accept the formula. No word has yet been received from the White House.

Second Riot Is Smashed in Warsaw

WARSAW, Oct. 5. — (P) — Angry students and other Poles battled police and militia in Warsaw's streets last night in the second violent anti-government demonstration in two days.

The street battling rolled on to the doors of Communist Party headquarters before the demonstration was smashed.

Unlike the fighting of Thursday night, which was confined to an area around the Polytechnic School, the violence this time spread in three sections of Warsaw. Other Poles joined the 2,000 students in their defiance of government force.

The demonstration hurled bricks and shouted "Gestapo, Gestapo." They tossed back tear gas bombs thrown by the police.

Government forces beat the demonstrators with rubber truncheons and finally restored order after five hours of fighting.

No figures were available on the number of demonstrators arrested and injured. Many were rushed to hospitals in ambulances.

The rioting began after students had met peacefully for Detroit and southern Michigan through the week-end, but football fans were warned to wear their topcoats this afternoon in Ann Arbor for the Michigan-University of Georgia game.

(Concluded on Page 5)

Cool, Clear for Football

Clear skies are in prospect for Detroit and southern Michigan through the week-end, but football fans were warned to wear their topcoats this afternoon in Ann Arbor for the Michigan-University of Georgia game.

The temperature was expected to be about 61 at game time with gentle north to northeast winds.

The Weather Bureau forecast slightly higher temperatures tomorrow, and a low tonight of 42 to 46.

For the third consecutive day, the temperature dropped below 30 this morning at Grand Manais, in the Upper Peninsula. The reading there was 38 at 1 a.m.

Queen Unworried by Prince's Flu

BALLATER, Scotland, Oct. 5.—(Reuters)—Prince Charles' attack of influenza was taking

U.S. VERSION—Superimposed on a photograph of the southwestern United States from 140 miles up is an artist's version of the earth satellite under construction by U.S. scientists. The Russian "moon" launched yesterday is presumed to be similar. The American satellite will be about 20 inches in diameter.—AP Wirephoto. (Another illustration on Page 2.)

Fear Soviet Has Jump on U.S. in Moon Rocket

WASHINGTON, Oct. 5.—(P)—launching is the fact they are U.S. satellite chief John P. Hagen said under the rocket that blasted the Soviet satellite skyward may have been "closely important" than the United missile (ICBM).

Hagen said the "extremely significance of the Russian satellite-launching program.

Questions, Answers on Earth Satellite

[SPECIAL TO THE DETROIT NEWS]
WASHINGTON, Oct. 5.—Questions and answers on the earth satellite:

Q: What is an artificial earth satellite?

A: It is a small globe that is sent up by rockets to circle the earth. It bears instruments for recording conditions in outer space.

Q: How big is the Russian globe?

A: 23 inches in diameter and 183.82 pounds in weight.

Q: Where is it?

A: It is now about 560 miles above the earth and passes over the United States several times a day.

Q: How fast is it going?

A: About five miles a second. It will go around the earth once every hour and 35 minutes in an elliptical orbit.

Q: Can it be seen with the naked eye?

Saturday Specials

In the Week's Wake .... Editorial, Page 6
Suburban Living .... Page 6
The Three Faces of Eve .... Page 7
Complete Parent-Teacher News .... Page 7
Understanding Our Schools .... Page 7
Teen Guideposts .... Page 7

Mail Call

WELLINGTON, New Zealand, Oct. 5.—(Reuters)—A U.S. Skymaster touched down yesterday at the U.S. Antarctic base at McMurdo Sound with the first delivery of mail since spring.

Speeds 18,000 MPH
560 Miles Over Earth

From AP, UP and Reuters Dispatches

WASHINGTON, Oct. 5.—The earth's first man-made satellite launched by the Russians yesterday, is making at least six trips over the United States today, American scientists said today.

(The "moon" will pass over Detroit between 6 and 7 p.m., according to Detroit experts, but Moscow puts the time much later.)

The satellite, traveling on a north-south axis, passed over the nation three times last night at 95-minute intervals before swinging out over the Pacific Ocean, the scientists reported.

They said the moon passed over Philadelphia at 8:40 a.m., Detroit time, today, then shifting westward, passing over the Middle West states, at 10:15 a.m. and over the Pacific coast region 95 minutes later.

Radio stations around the world today charted the progress made by the satellite and confirmed Soviet reports it is

(Related Stories on Pages 2 and 2.)

circling the globe at a speed approaching 18,000 miles per hour in an altitude of 560 miles.

In London, listeners to early-morning broadcasts over the BBC heard the steady, pulsating sound of "beeps" sent out by a radio inside the "moon."

STEADY COURSE

Reports coming in from Bern, Bonn, The Hague, Copenhagen, Brussels, and Melbourne (Australia) indicated that the satellite was pursuing a steady course around the world.

Dr. Richard W. Porter, chairman of the technical panel on earth satellites for the International Geophysical Year (IGY) program.

Hagen is head of "Project Vanguard," the American satellite-launching program.

Vanguard's job is to get the satellite up and into its orbit. The scientific components of the satellite itself are under civilian scientists.

Hagen said for all U.S. calculations on the size of the Russian rocket were based on the Soviet statement that the satellite weighs 184 pounds and is 560 miles up.

"It certainly was close to an ICBM."

"It would have to have been

(Concluded on Page 2)

SOVIET SATELLITE'S PREDICTED ORBIT / **MAY APPEAR TWICE OCT. 5** / Moscow / EUROPE / AFRICA / SOUTH AMERICA / 560 MILES ABOVE EARTH / EQUATOR / Rotation Of Earth

AROUND THE WORLD IN 95 MINUTES—Global projection illustrates the orbit of the Russians' satellite launched by the Russians. Traveling in a north-south direction, it takes an hour and 35 minutes to encircle the earth.

Look at Satellite Here Is in Doubt

Whether Detroiters will have an early opportunity to spot the Russian satellite was in doubt today because of a lack of definite information and conflicting statements by scientists.

Dr. Everett B. Phelps, professor of physics and astronomy at Wayne State University, said

first picked up the satellite's signal at 8:20 a.m. today. A recording was made and broadcast on morning news program.

Heard on WWJ

Radio master control at WWJ

LISTENS IN GROSSE POINTE PARK BASEMENT

'Ham' Records Satellite's Signals

By ROBERT POPA

While millions of Americans listened to radio and television for news of Russia's newly launched satellite, R. B. Whitehurst sat in his basement listening to the satellite.

Whitehurst, of 501 Pemberton, Grosse Pointe Park, is one of more than 2,000

radio hams in the Detroit area.

He heard of the satellite shortly after 8 p.m. and put his 8:30 bat his receiver banks of radio equipment.

tuned to 20.005 megacycles — the satellite's frequency — where he traced it for nine minutes before it faded.

For the next 35 minutes Whitehurst dipped switches, twisted dials and swung his huge 70-foot-high backyard antenna through a 380-degree arc searching for the signal he had lost.

"Ninety-five per cent of amateur radio operation is sweat, just waiting," he said stiff humbling.

Finally, at 10:04 there was a weak signal from the south — a continuous beep, beep, beep. Seven minutes later it faded. Then it came back with growing strength.

For the next four minutes while the beeps poured monotonously from

INDEX
Amusements 16 Horoscope 13

Sputnik's launch on October 4, 1957, shocked America. (Soviets were known as "Reds" after the color of their flag.)

event, but Senators Johnson and Jackson had raised two issues that deeply worried the American public: that Sputnik gave the Russians a powerful military advantage; and that other countries would be tempted to ally themselves with Russia, which now appeared to be the most technologically advanced nation in the world.

A month after Sputnik was launched, the Soviets succeeded again, with Sputnik 2. Weighing more than half a ton, it was six times heavier than its predecessor and carried a passenger: a dog named Laika. The heavy payload implied that if the satellite launcher was used as a military missile, it could loft nuclear warheads partway around the planet to the United States—a range far in excess of Redstone's. And the living passenger (who sadly died after a few hours) was surely a sign that the Soviets were preparing to send human spacefarers. It was beginning to dawn on Americans that they were in a space race and losing badly.

Soviet leader Nikita Khrushchev, who had seized power after Stalin's death in 1953, enjoyed taunting his capitalist rivals. He would later boast that his intercontinental rockets were coming off the assembly line "like sausages" and that the Soviet system "has triumphed not only fully, but irreversibly."

All was not lost, for America was about to stake its own claim to space with Vanguard. True, Vanguard's satellite weighed just over three pounds, and even with the rocket's maximum payload of roughly twenty pounds, it would need more than fifty launches to put into orbit as much cargo as a single Sputnik rocket. But U.S. officials stressed that Vanguard was aiming for a higher orbit. If all went well, its tiny moon would circle the planet for centuries instead of a few months, as with the Sputniks.

Furthermore, Russia had launched its satellites in secret, but

Vanguard's preparations were taking place in the open—though not yet on television. When the rocket was ready for launch from Cape Canaveral, Florida, on December 6, 1957, a large audience from all walks of life watched from several miles away, searching for clues of the impending takeoff. Peering through binoculars, they saw the rocket servicing platform roll back, a red warning signal appear, and observation planes starting to circle overhead. Meanwhile, in the firing room, the nerve-racking countdown was progressing toward zero.

Reporting to his boss in Washington over a long-distance phone line, the deputy director of the project, J. Paul Walsh, described the climactic moment:

"Zero . . . fire . . . ignition . . ."

With a blast of flame, Vanguard lifted a few feet into the air. It hesitated, as if changing its mind, then fell back toward the pad.

"Explosion!"

According to one reporter, the unfolding cataclysm "bore a remarkable resemblance to atomic-bomb detonations . . . It took the shape of a fiery stem topped by an expanding mushroom-shaped cloud of flame." The newsman continued in a poetic vein: "This configuration lasted for only a few seconds, and was replaced by a pillar of greasy black smoke which gradually dissipated as it was carried inland by offshore breezes." All that was left were smoldering pieces of Vanguard—America's answer to Sputnik—littered across the launch site. Fortunately, no one was hurt.

●

Around this time, movie theaters across the world were screening a Russian short animated film called *After Sputnik—the Moon?* Looking like a mini-episode of Disney's TV series on space, it showed a rocket taking off from Earth, performing orbital maneuvers, and then heading out to the Moon, where it deposited a robotic explorer.

Produced for audiences in the Soviet Union, this charming educational cartoon was picked up for distribution by a British newsreel company, whose announcer asked pointedly at the end: "Propaganda? Wishful thinking? Sober prophecy? We'll have to wait and see!"

Von Braun (right) helps raise a full-scale model of the Explorer 1 satellite at a press conference on February 1, 1958. Scientists William Pickering (left) and James Van Allen (center) were responsible for the satellite, von Braun for the launch vehicle.

12

EXPLORER

A month before the Vanguard disaster, the U.S. Department of Defense gave von Braun the green light to prepare a modified Redstone for a satellite launch. It was an insurance policy against Vanguard's possible failure, a prospect that was starting to worry government officials, including the president. Von Braun insisted that sixty days was all he needed. His boss at the Redstone Arsenal, General John Medaris, asked for ninety days just to be sure. This gave the rocket team until early February 1958.

Von Braun's souped-up, four-stage version of Redstone was called Juno I. It had a longer rocket body than Redstone, which would allow it to hold more propellant. It also required a different type of fuel, since the alcohol and liquid oxygen combination for Redstone didn't produce quite enough thrust to loft a spacecraft into orbit. To avoid costly changes to the rocket, the new fuel had to work in the existing engine and plumbing, which posed a difficult challenge. A chemist named Mary Sherman Morgan formulated an entirely new compound called hydyne, which, when burned with liquid oxygen, gave exactly the right performance. Morgan was one of the many talented women who played a largely unsung role in the early space program. Coincidentally, the launch vehicle propelled by her new fuel was named after a woman, the Roman goddess Juno. It was a rare distinction in a pantheon of American rockets with masculine monikers like Jupiter, Thor, Atlas, and, eventually, the mighty Saturn.

●

In late January, von Braun's team completed preparations for a launch attempt at Cape Canaveral. Their target date was Wednesday, January 29, barely a week before their ninety-day deadline. A series of delays due to high winds in the upper atmosphere pushed the date to Friday, January 31, 1958—probably their last chance. After that, it was Vanguard's turn, since its problems from the December catastrophe had been fixed—although new ones kept cropping up. As commanding officer at the Redstone Arsenal, General Medaris was responsible for the Juno launch decision. Meanwhile, von Braun was in Washington, ready for a high-profile press conference in case of success.

Watching the unruly winds that day was the same Army forecaster who had helped ensure the success of D-Day in 1944. Don Yates, together with his British counterpart, James Stagg, had advised General Eisenhower that a break in bad weather would allow the invasion of Normandy to go ahead. Now Yates was aiding an operation in the Cold War. The battle of winds, his team reported, seemed to be turning in Juno's favor. Measurements showed that airflow in the stratosphere was down to about 100 miles per hour, which Medaris found tolerable. He gave the go-ahead. Juno was to take off at night, so the high-altitude firing of the upper stages could be observed against the black sky.

The countdown went like clockwork. At 10:48 p.m., the firing command was given. Juno slowly came to life. The strange, tublike device atop the missile, which held the upper stages, had already started spinning at 550 revolutions per minute. This would ensure the stability of the second, third, and fourth stages when they eventually fired. Inside the first stage, vents automatically closed, and the propellant tanks began to pressurize. A steam generator started up, which drove a turbine that powered pumps, forcing high-pressure hydyne and liquid oxygen into the combustion chamber. There, an igniter set them ablaze. This all took fourteen seconds.

Then a "tremendous jet burst from the base of the rocket, tearing an incandescent hole in the night," wrote a *New York Times* reporter. For one and three-quarter seconds the rocket stayed Earthbound, as it built up thrust and automatic checks showed that everything was in order.

Only then did the rocket begin to rise—with "incredible slowness," wrote the *Times* man. Few people had ever seen such a giant rocket take off, and reporters outdid each other describing the spectacle. One called it "a flame-footed monster." Another was overcome by the noise of the engine, calling it "terrific" and noting that "observers had to shout at each other, and even then could not make themselves understood." Upward Juno went with ever-increasing speed.

Waiting nervously in Washington, von Braun saw none of this, since there was no live television broadcast. Instead, he listened to a radio reporter in Florida, who was observing the event through binoculars. "Slow rise, faster, faster!" came the excited voice over the speaker. Soon the newsman could only see a bright light against the dark sky—and then he could see nothing. "It is out of sight, but it *must be successful!*" he proclaimed.

●

Juno takes off with Explorer 1 (the pencil-like top stage), January 31, 1958.

And then, seven minutes after launch, the vehicle was in orbit. Or so everyone hoped. General Medaris pestered the technician who was busy calculating the craft's trajectory by hand. Half an hour after launch the mathematician reported "with 95 percent confidence" that there was a 60 percent probability the satellite was in orbit.

"Don't give me that crap," growled the general. "Is it up?"

"It's up."

But definite word had to await reception of the satellite's radio signal in California, as the fourth stage with its radiation and micrometeorite detectors came around Earth near the end of its first orbit. The team waited anxiously. The predicted time for the signal came and went.

Eight long minutes passed before four stations on the West Coast picked up the transmission. "Those moments were the most exciting eight minutes of my life!" von Braun later recalled. The delay meant the payload—now officially a satellite called Explorer 1—had reached a slightly higher orbit than planned, circling Earth every 113 minutes.

Before the launch, von Braun was a TV celebrity with a funny accent. Now he was a national hero. And in his eyes, it was only the beginning. He had often talked about the next step. A few years earlier, at a late-night discussion with friends, he laid it out: "Once the first satellite is in orbit, others will follow. Also, there will be probes to the Moon." Then von Braun envisioned human flights on rockets, first on suborbital flights that would soar briefly into space and back, followed by Earth-orbiting missions. After that, a permanent space station made the most sense.

"We will then begin to make plans for a manned expedition to the Moon," he predicted. "Really, I couldn't think of a serious technical problem that would prevent us from traveling to the Moon."

Von Braun had said similar things countless times—before civic groups, national TV audiences, and congressional committees. The usual response was always, "Amazing! But will it really happen?"

After Explorer 1, people were starting to think it might.

A modern version of the Russian R-7 takes off on a pillar of fire.

With an arsenal of engines, the R-7 packs a powerful punch.

Carrying a Mercury capsule, the Redstone soars aloft on a single jet of exhaust.

The back end of the Redstone—less than a tenth as powerful as the R-7

BRIEFING:
Russia's Rocket

These photos show the back ends of two rockets: Russia's R-7 and America's Redstone. The R-7, which launched Sputnik, produced more than ten times the thrust of Redstone, which was modified into Juno for launching Explorer 1. Why was Russia's rocket so much more powerful than America's?

The reason traces to a meeting Joseph Stalin had with his generals and rocket engineers in April 1947. World War II had been over for a year and a half, and the Cold War was just starting. Russian scientists were hard at work on an atomic bomb, but unlike America, Russia did not have a system of long-range bombers and international air bases for delivering nuclear weapons. As Stalin explained at the meeting, a nuclear-armed intercontinental missile was the perfect device for threatening the United States.

Referring to then president Harry Truman, who years before had run a clothing store, Stalin exhorted, "Do you realize the tremendous strategic importance of machines of this sort? They could be an effective straitjacket for that noisy shopkeeper Harry Truman. We must go ahead with it, comrades. The problem of the creation of transatlantic rockets is of extreme importance to us."

Soviet engineers went ahead and ultimately designed a rocket that could loft Russia's heavy nuclear bombs halfway around the planet. Meanwhile, America had developed lightweight nuclear weapons and relied on its bomber fleet, as well as on medium-range missiles such as Redstone that could be launched from allied countries near the Soviet Union.

When Russia's rocket, the R-7, was finally ready in 1957, it could easily put a satellite into space, which the new leader, Nikita Khrushchev, decided to do for propaganda purposes. America's most powerful rocket at that time, the Redstone, had to be "souped up" to launch a satellite weighing a fraction as much.

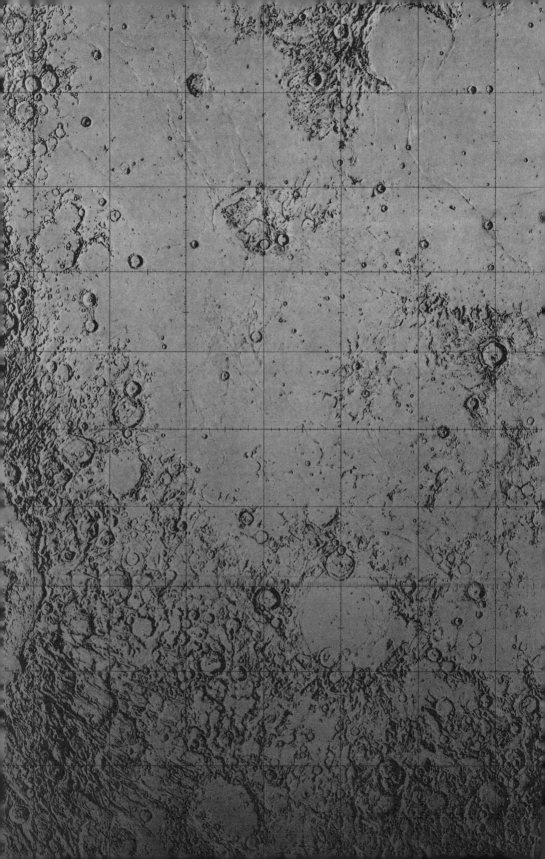

PART 3
SPACEMEN

Your plan will provide the most expensive funeral man has ever seen.

—George Kistiakowsky, presidential science adviser, reacting to the plan to launch a human into space, 1958

Map of the Moon's near side

An unconventional shape for a spacecraft—a blunt cone—is tested in a giant wind tunnel, 1959.

13

MAX MAKES HIS PITCH

Since boyhood, Max Faget had been a fan of science fiction, so he was probably familiar with the skepticism about human spaceflight shown by the editor of one of the most popular sci-fi magazines, *Amazing Stories*. This publication's motto was "Extravagant fiction today . . . cold fact tomorrow," but managing editor T. O'Conor Sloane firmly believed that human trips into space would simply never be "cold fact."

Sloane, a scientist himself, spelled out his objection in a 1929 editorial: "If voyages were to be made from the Earth to any of the planets, or even to the Moon, the distances are so great that starting from rest as the travelers would do, they would have to attain a high velocity in a very short space of time . . . sufficient to kill the person."

In other words, no one could survive the rapid acceleration of launch. Rising slowly wouldn't do, since it would take an unlimited amount of propellant to fight Earth's gravity all the way into space. Any space launch would have to happen relatively quickly. Sloane believed that the force exerted on the human body would be like hitting the ground after falling "from the Washington Monument."

There were other concerns, too. According to experts who had pondered the unknown environment beyond Earth's atmosphere, spaceflight was dangerous in lots of ways. Some had expressed alarm about the potential effects of weightlessness. Once in Earth orbit or on a trajectory beyond Earth, the spacecraft would drift in a state of "free fall"—falling around Earth or on whatever path the ship was following. By contrast with the trip into space, during which travelers would weigh more than their normal weight due to the rocket's acceleration, once the motor was shut off they would appear to weigh nothing at all. If they let go of something, it would float as if suspended in water—and so would everything not bolted or strapped down. The feeling would be like falling without ever hitting the ground. Heinz Haber, a space medicine specialist who appeared on Disney's von Braun program, believed "it will take iron nerves waiting for the impact that never comes." Others speculated that the disorienting feeling of weightlessness would drive people crazy and render them helpless.

Furthermore, there is no air in space, which means a spaceship must have an elaborate life-support system. It's similar to the situation aboard a submarine, except a submarine can get air through a snorkel; in space, there is no such option. Plus, the temperature of an object in space can range from broiling hot in full sun to subarctic cold in shadow, putting extreme stress on the ship and its equipment. Another hazard is that harmful radiation from the Sun and interstellar space rains down on everything—as do meteors, which are mostly dust-grain size but traveling so fast that particles as large as a pebble can puncture the wall of a spacecraft. Earth's atmosphere and magnetic field shield anything close to the ground from most of these hazards, but there is no such protection in space.

Then there is the sheer danger of traveling by rocket, which is both the world's riskiest form of transportation and the only practical way to get into space. All rockets are prone to exploding catastrophically from minor malfunctions, such as a stuck valve or excessive vibration. Returning to Earth is also high-risk, since few materials can withstand the extreme temperature of reentry into the atmosphere, as air friction does the work of slowing a vehicle from 17,500 miles per hour or faster to a safe landing speed.

To an engineer like Faget, these were simply problems to solve. For example, Sloane's worry about high acceleration during takeoff was answered by tests showing that a human can survive acceleration equal to all but the fastest rocket launches—as long as the occupant is positioned like the driver of a car, facing in the direction of travel. In this position, the acceleration pushes the body evenly into a supporting seat. Experts also realized that during reentry, rapid deceleration (slowing down) can exert even more force on the body than the acceleration of launch. Since deceleration pushes the opposite direction from acceleration, a returning space traveler is safest if facing *backward* from the direction of travel, which, again, causes the body to be pushed against the seat.

As for the other problems, Faget subscribed to the optimistic outlook of automobile pioneer Henry Ford, who wrote in 1922: "I refuse to recognize that there are impossibilities. I cannot discover that anyone knows enough about anything on this Earth definitely to say what is and what is not possible."

In mid-October 1957, shortly after the launch of the first Sputnik, Faget attended a secret conference devoted to the future of high-speed flight. The meeting was sponsored by his organization, the NACA, which was involved in rocket plane research that in 1947 had pushed human flight beyond the speed of sound (known as Mach 1); past Mach 2 (twice the speed of sound) in 1953; and even to Mach 3 in 1956. Unfortunately, the Mach 3 flight killed the pilot when his aircraft spun out of control. Now Faget and his colleagues were discussing flights in excess of Mach 17, more than *five* times faster than anyone had ever flown. Eventually, the goal was Mach 25, the speed needed to go into orbit around Earth. No one was seriously considering manned flight in the neighborhood of Mach 35—the speed needed to reach the Moon.

A rocket-powered X-2 drops from its mother ship, 1955. The following year, the X-2 would crash during the first flight to achieve Mach 3.

Most of the engineers at the conference assumed that Mach 25 ships destined for Earth orbit would be upgrades of the rocket planes already built. That is, they would be winged vehicles that pilots could fly like an aircraft during the atmospheric portion of the trip, particularly during reentry. Even von Braun, the world's authority on spaceflight, thought this was the obvious approach—as shown by his proposed spaceship in the *Collier's* and Disney presentations, which had wings on its top stage.

But Faget had his doubts. Alarmed by the surprise launch of Sputnik, he realized that the race was now on to send a human into space. There wasn't time to perfect the sleek, aerodynamic shape of a space plane, heavily clad in an exotic metal alloy that could withstand the searing heat of reentry. Something simpler and cheaper was needed that could be built quickly.

Looking for answers, Faget turned to his NACA colleagues Harvey Allen and Alfred Eggers. They had discovered that the ideal shape for an object capable of surviving the meteor-like plunge through the atmosphere was less like a jet plane and more like a cannonball. The blunt profile would create a shock wave that dissipated heat far more readily than a streamlined shape. And just like a real cannonball, this space "capsule" (for it would be little more than a manned container) would follow a fixed trajectory. Instead of being piloted to a pinpoint landing like a plane, it would come hurtling back and use a parachute in the last few minutes to touch down in a large landing area. This was an unglamorous way for a space pilot to return to Earth, but Faget considered its simplicity a great advantage.

Faget soon discovered that a cone, not a cannonball, was the most effective shape for such a capsule. Sitting atop a rocket, with the cone's pointed end up, it would penetrate the atmosphere with minimal drag during launch. Then the blunt end would be aimed in the direction of travel on the way down, behaving just like a cannonball. The blunt end would be covered with a heat shield to absorb the heat of reentry and protect the occupant inside. On a simple shape like a cone, this vital component could be much smaller and lighter than the extensive shield required for a winged vehicle.

Also ideal, Faget realized, was the pilot's position. Inside the cabin,

Harvey Allen explains his blunt-body concept, 1956. The idea inspired Max Faget to propose a blunt-cone shape for a spacecraft.

the pilot would recline against the blunt end of the ship. During takeoff, the force of acceleration would push him into the seat as the vehicle headed skyward. During reentry, the force of deceleration would also push him into the seat, as the capsule plunged backward toward Earth.

Working with two other colleagues, Faget fleshed out the details and formally presented this brainstorm when the high-speed-flight conference reconvened five months later. The reception was less than enthusiastic.

One member of the audience was Korean War veteran Neil Armstrong, who was now a rocket plane pilot for the NACA. Armstrong looked forward to flying space planes, yet he had just heard a very impassioned and convincing argument that this was not the best approach in the present competition with the Soviets. A trained engineer, Armstrong saw that Faget's analysis made sense, but like practically everyone else in the audience, he had a natural suspicion of unconventional ideas, and this was *very* unconventional. "Max made his pitch," Armstrong later recalled, noting that the zealous engineer appeared "frustrated that everyone could not immediately seem to see the logic of his proposal."

Undaunted, Faget was determined to move ahead. America had lost round one of the space race to Sputnik. He did not want to lose round two.

Neil Armstrong after a flight in the X-15. In 1962 he flew the rocket plane to over Mach 5. For true spaceflight, Mach 25 or faster is needed.

Zazel, the first human cannonball performer, 1887

14

"LET'S GET ON WITH IT"

Hugh Dryden, head of the NACA, was getting testy under questioning by a congressional committee. A month after Faget's presentation at the high-speed conference, Dryden was being pressed to comment on an Army proposal very much like Faget's: loft a human into space inside a capsule atop a Redstone rocket. It was von Braun's idea, and the German rocketeer was pushing it vigorously.

Dryden wanted to keep human spaceflight out of the hands of the military. Like practically all aeronautical engineers, he thought of space travel in terms of winged vehicles, and this was the NACA's turf. He bluntly told the legislators: "Tossing a man up in the air and letting him come back . . . is about the same technical value as the circus stunt of shooting a young lady from a cannon." He had surely heard of Faget's proposal, but he apparently didn't think much of it. He also had a point, since launching a man into space on a rocket just so you could say you'd done it first was beneath the dignity of a serious engineer. To Dryden, it was a trick designed to attract attention.

Meanwhile, thanks to the national panic over Sputnik, the NACA was being transformed right under Dryden's feet. A few months after his testimony, the NACA was reorganized as a new government agency called NASA: the National Aeronautics and Space Administration. NASA kept all of the previous agency's functions in flight research with the added responsibility for space, especially human spaceflight. The new agency also inherited government research centers such as the Jet Propulsion Laboratory, which had created the upper stages of Explorer 1. Within a year, von Braun and his Army rocket team were also transferred to NASA, much to von Braun's dismay, since he had little hope for visionary leadership from the NACA crowd, especially after the harsh words from the man who was now his boss, Dryden. Still, von Braun's new job was to create rockets larger than any ever built, and the new agency's budget would grow sharply, too. The old hands quipped that NA¢A had become NA$A.

Dryden was the logical person to head NASA. However, his "circus stunt" comment had rubbed Congress the wrong way, since a stunt was exactly what Congress and the American people wanted. They wanted to upstage the Russians. They wanted to lead the world in the space race. Dryden was demoted to the number two spot, and T. Keith Glennan, president of Case Institute of Technology, a prestigious engineering school in Cleveland, Ohio, became NASA's first administrator.

●)

Meanwhile, von Braun's Army proposal was practically dead, and Faget's plan was gaining momentum. As stripped down as it was, the plan was more versatile than von Braun's, which was little more than a passenger pod for a test subject, who would be hurled briefly into space before plunging back to Earth—much like a V-2 during the war except with a parachute. Von Braun's defense was that his program was designed to get a human into space at the earliest possible moment—nothing more.

Faget also envisioned such suborbital flights, but only at the start of his program, which was much more ambitious. After the conical capsule proved itself and humans showed they could endure short bouts of weightlessness, he was confident that orbital flights would follow. A rocket like the Redstone would be sufficient for the suborbital tests. But orbital missions would need a more powerful launch vehicle, and the earliest one available would be an intercontinental missile called Atlas being developed for the Air Force. Von Braun had nothing to do with the Atlas, and this may have been the reason he was unenthusiastic about Faget's plan. But the deeper reason was that both men were brilliant and stubborn. They each came up with dazzling proposals that would work and then pushed them relentlessly.

For all its simplicity, Faget's capsule was a true spaceship. It could keep its occupant alive for many hours, point itself in any direction, perform a variety of missions, and exit its hostile environment at a moment's notice. Faget even included a periscope to allow observations outside the ship. In many ways, it was like a submarine.

NASA opened for business on October 1, 1958. The following week, Faget's boss, Bob Gilruth, presented Faget's man-in-space proposal to Glennan, who had little taste for stunts or crash programs. On the other hand, the country wanted dramatic action. After hearing the pitch, the new NASA chief wasted no time: "All right. Let's get on with it."

Surprised by the suddenness of the decision, Gilruth tried to start a discussion about how to proceed. Glennan cut him short: "Just get on with it!"

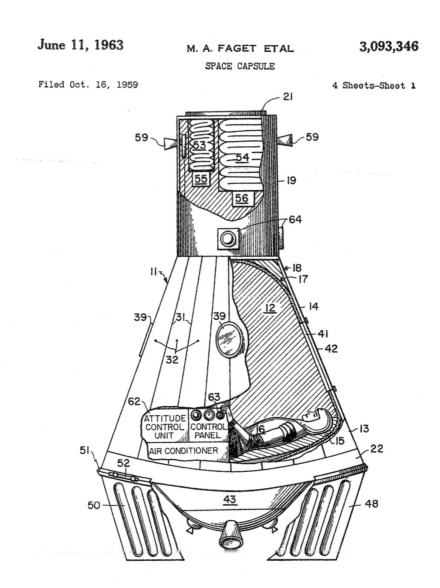

Max Faget's patent for the Mercury spacecraft, approved in 1963

Just like that, America was committed to putting a man in space. The order had all the informality of the command that had set D-Day in motion in 1944. General Eisenhower had listened to the weather report forecasting a break in the storms that were battering the landing areas.

After thinking it over, he said simply, "Okay, we'll go." Now, fourteen years later, President Eisenhower's appointee was being just as terse and decisive. He was setting in motion an invasion that would eventually spread to worlds beyond our own—although no one knew that yet.

●)

Heeding Glennan's order, Gilruth sat down with Faget and two other top engineers, and they started putting together a team. Drawing mostly on talent at the Langley Research Center in Virginia, where Gilruth's PARD rocket division was headquartered, they picked a total of forty-five engineers and other staff, including themselves. The outfit would be called the Space Task Group.

Gilruth also began searching for brave souls to ride the capsule into space. These men would be called *astronauts*, based on the ancient Greek words for "star sailor." The volunteers were to be drawn from jet pilots, balloonists, submarine officers, Arctic explorers, parachute jumpers, combat veterans, and others with a taste for adventure. But when President Eisenhower heard the qualifications, he put his foot down. Only military test pilots would be considered, he ordered. He may have been adamant that manned spaceflight would be a civilian program, but as a practical matter, military test pilots were highly skilled, already on the government payroll, and accustomed to following orders.

"It was one of the best decisions he ever made," Gilruth later admitted. "It ruled out the matadors, mountain climbers, scuba divers, and race drivers, and gave us stable guys who had already been screened for security."

The pieces of America's man-in-space program were falling into place. One loose end was a name for the project. NASA manager Abe Silverstein had a passion for mythology and suggested Project Mercury.

Max Faget wears a pressure suit to test the tight fit inside the Mercury capsule (at left).

It stuck. Mercury was the speedy messenger god with winged sandals. It fit because the astronauts would travel faster than any humans before them. However, if you looked deeper into Roman mythology, you might have noticed that Mercury had another role: he was the god who conveyed the dead to the underworld. That, too, was a distinct possibility with Project Mercury.

The Mercury astronauts in their military flight suits. Left to right: Carpenter,
Cooper, Glenn, Grissom, Schirra, Shepard, and Slayton.

15

THE ORIGINAL SEVEN

Driving around Edwards Air Force Base in the California desert, Deke Slayton passed through entire neighborhoods where the streets were named, one after another, for dead test pilots. Even the base itself was named after Captain Glen Edwards, an acclaimed Air Force test pilot who died on the job. It was easy to imagine a new subdivision where Deke himself would be similarly memorialized should his luck run out.

For this reason, Slayton didn't think he was risking much by applying for the job of astronaut. The newsreels were full of images of missiles blowing up, including the Atlas rocket that he expected to fly into orbit if he was accepted. But how dangerous could it be compared to the Air Force, where a few years earlier sixty-two fighter pilots had died during thirty-six weeks of training? And test pilots lived far riskier lives than fighter pilots! Slayton's chances had probably been better flying bombing missions during the war than flying unproven planes at Edwards.

NASA added a few extra criteria to Eisenhower's test pilot rule. Age, height, weight, and other factors narrowed the pool down to 110 qualified candidates, including Slayton. Gilruth expected only a fraction of that number to be interested. He was surprised and pleased when the vast majority were eager to compete for the half dozen or so slots.

Only men would be considered. At the time, there were no female military test pilots, although some women had thousands of hours of flight time and met the medical requirements for the astronaut corps. Since they were generally shorter and lighter than males, females would have made excellent space travelers in the cramped, weight-restricted Mercury capsule. However, it was not to be. In those days, only men were trained for the extreme dangers that faced astronauts riding rockets. If nothing else, the likelihood of a fatal accident kept women out of the program. NASA administrator Glennan had said that "one tragedy would not stop this project," implying that an astronaut might very well die. That was entirely acceptable if it was a man, but the death of a female astronaut would have been a public relations catastrophe in the family-oriented climate of the 1950s, with stay-at-home mothers and working fathers.

The seven pilots who were finally chosen had remarkable backgrounds. The best known was Marine Lieutenant Colonel John H. Glenn Jr., who two years earlier had made the first supersonic transcontinental flight, jetting from California to New York at bullet-like speed. He had also flown 149 combat missions in World War II and Korea. And of course, like the others, he had risen to the pinnacle of the flying profession as a test pilot.

The others had less publicized records. Navy Lieutenant Commander Alan B. Shepard had served in World War II aboard a destroyer and then entered flight training to become one of the Navy's top air-craft carrier pilots. Air Force Captain Virgil "Gus" Grissom was a veteran of a hundred combat missions in Korea. Navy Lieutenant Commander Walter M. Schirra Jr. was another Korean War veteran, with ninety missions. Air Force Captain L. Gordon Cooper Jr. had served with a peacetime fighter-bomber squadron in Germany, practicing for a possible Soviet invasion. Navy Lieutenant M. Scott Carpenter had flown surveillance missions along the Russian and Chinese coasts during the Korean conflict.

And then there was Air Force Captain Deke Slayton, who was un-characteristically talkative after his selection was announced. "We have gone about as far as we can on this globe," he reflected. "We have to go somewhere, and space is all that is left." Then he made a confession: "I would give my left arm to be the first man in space."

In later years, as the astronaut corps grew, these pioneers would be known as the Original Seven. But when they were notified of their selection in April 1959, they envisioned a short-term project lasting three years at most, after which they would return to their flying careers, while NASA moved on to other things. NASA originally suggested that they resign from the military and become civilians, but this proposal met fierce resistance. "Given the state of NASA and Project Mercury," recollected Slayton, "you'd have had to be an idiot to give up your Air Force or Navy career to join them."

Early in the development of Mercury, Gilruth asked Faget what would happen if the launch vehicle blew up.

"I don't know," Faget replied.

"Well, you'd better figure something out!"

Mercury might never have gotten off the ground had Faget not come up with an escape rocket, attached by a tower to the top of the space-craft, designed to pull the capsule away from an exploding rocket. This had to be done very quickly. A normal Mercury launch would expose an astronaut to a force of six to eight g's (one g equals the pull of gravity at Earth's surface). At eight g's, someone weighing 150 pounds would be pushed back with a force of 1,200 pounds, making it difficult to breathe and impossible to lift an arm. In an emergency, Faget's escape rocket would blast the capsule to safety at up to twenty g's. At that accelera-tion, an astronaut weighing 150 pounds would briefly weigh 3,000 pounds and could suffer internal injuries. The getaway would be brutal but worth it, as a conflagration engulfed the launch vehicle and every-thing around it.

Escape was less of a concern with the Redstone, which would be used for the initial suborbital flights. Von Braun and his team had de-signed the booster to be rugged and reliable. Atlas was a different story. Created for the Air Force to loft nuclear warheads a third of the way around the planet, it was the only available rocket that could get the Mercury capsule into orbit. Pushing the technical state of the art, Atlas was essentially a stainless-steel balloon packed with propellant and at-tached to three rocket engines. The structure was thinner than a dime and had to be pressurized to keep from collapsing under its own weight. Its innovative design was very much like an egg: The eggshell was the rocket body; the yolk and white were the fuel and oxidizer tanks, sepa-rated by a thin bulkhead. The whole structure was amazingly light and strong, if difficult to build.

On May 18, 1959, a little over a month after being introduced to the public, the seven Mercury astronauts were attending an Atlas test flight at Cape Canaveral. Wearing hard hats and standing a quarter of a mile away, the future space travelers watched with great interest as the count reached zero and the engines of the mighty missile ignited, built up thrust, and then the vehicle lifted off the pad and rose into the sky. It was a perfect launch—for about a minute. Then the vehicle tipped to one side and started to veer out of control. The range safety officer hit the destruct switch, producing a gigantic fireball, "like a hydrogen bomb going off right over our heads," recalled astronaut Glenn. Even though the fiery debris cloud was on a path taking it over the Atlantic, the astronauts instinctively ducked.

Al Shepard broke the stunned silence: "I sure hope they fix that."

Being test pilots and trained engineers, the astronauts expected to have a role helping to improve the Mercury hardware and develop the mission procedures. Therefore, they divided Project Mercury into areas where their input could be useful. Deke Slayton got the most unnerving assignment of all: Atlas. He could do nothing about the rocket's habit of exploding, so he focused on the problem of joining a complicated spacecraft to a noisy, shaking, temperamental missile. Looking back on 1960, his first full year as an astronaut, he felt like he had experienced the Fourth of July run amok: "I spent most of my time that year at the Cape, watching Atlases take off and blow up."

Atlas wasn't the only rocket that was blowing up. This is a Juno II going out of control in 1959.

A Russian manned rocket leaves for space.

16

THE VICE PRESIDENT FINDS A SPACE CHIEF

Fall 1960 featured a hotly contested presidential election, pitting Eisenhower's vice president, Richard Nixon, against Massachusetts senator and war hero John F. Kennedy. The Cold War was on everyone's mind, and one of the biggest campaign issues was the supposed "missile gap" between the United States and Soviet Union. Given the Soviets' intense secrecy, it was difficult to say how many nuclear-armed missiles they had. Kennedy cited an informed estimate that gave the Russians a roughly ten-to-one advantage. Eisenhower knew this was incorrect but couldn't say so publicly, since his information was based on intelligence sources that he didn't want to reveal.

Whatever the number of Russia's missiles, it was certain they were far more powerful than America's, as shown by the hefty satellites that these launch vehicles could put into orbit. The Soviets' very obvious superiority in space troubled many Americans, as did the spread of communism to places like Cuba, added to domestic problems such as the sluggish economy and the bitter struggle to end racial segregation and discrimination in the American South. Partly due to these anxieties, combined with the desire for change, Kennedy and his vice-presidential running mate, Lyndon Johnson, won in a very close race.

After he took office, Kennedy was much more focused on military and foreign affairs than on space policy, which he left to Johnson. Possibly because he was a Texan steeped in stories of the taming of the frontier, the vice president was genuinely enthusiastic about conquering space. As a senator responding to Sputnik in early 1958, he had painted a dire picture of America's fate if it did not answer Russia's space challenge. "Control of space means control of the world," he proclaimed. "From space, the masters of infinity would have the power to control the Earth's weather, to cause drought and flood, to change the tides and raise the levels of the sea, to divert the Gulf Stream and change temperate climates to frigid."

Johnson exaggerated, as he often did, but his commitment to the cause made him the obvious person to find a successor to NASA administrator Glennan when the Kennedy administration took power in January 1961. Surprisingly, no one of sufficient stature wanted the job. The problem appeared to be that no one knew where America's space program was going and whether NASA, a brand-new organization, would survive to lead it.

"I don't think I'm the right person for this job," Jim Webb said to Hugh Dryden as they waited for the vice president. "I'm not an engineer and I've never seen a rocket fly."

Dryden was still the deputy administrator of NASA and was there at Johnson's request to help persuade Webb to accept the position that so many others had turned down.

"I agree with that. I don't think you are either," Dryden confided.

"Well, can you tell the vice president?"

"I don't believe that he wants to listen to me on that."

Webb had been summoned, in part, because of his connection to Robert Kerr, the Democratic senator from Oklahoma who had inherited Johnson's chairmanship of the Senate space committee. Since leaving government service in 1953, Webb had run a company for Kerr's oil empire, and the senator thought very highly of him, noting that Webb had "the greatest . . . capacity for sustained mental and physical effort of anyone I know."

Just then, another of Webb's acquaintances entered the room. Frank Pace had been Webb's successor at the Bureau of the Budget and was now working for the company making the Atlas missile.

Webb explained his predicament. Pace agreed that Webb was probably not the right man and promised to try to talk Johnson out of it when the vice president arrived, which he soon did. As Webb and Dryden waited in an adjoining room, Pace had a few words with Johnson and was immediately thrown out of his office. Webb now had to face the music. Johnson tried his usual arm-twisting, but Webb insisted on a meeting with President Kennedy. While this was being arranged, he called a friend who was handling the presidential transition.

"Can you get me out of this?" he implored.

"Ha-ha, I've been recommending you! I am not going to get you out of it."

At the White House that afternoon, the president told Webb the reason that he, and not a rocket scientist or space expert, was the right person to head NASA: "You've had experience in the Bureau of the Budget and the State Department," Kennedy said. "This is a program that involves not science and technology so much as large issues of national and international policy, and that's why I want you to do it."

Webb felt that he couldn't refuse a direct request from the president of the United States. On February 14, 1961, this soft-spoken North Carolinian was sworn in as NASA's second administrator.

President John F. Kennedy (left) greets his new NASA administrator, Jim Webb, 1961.

One of Webb's first problems was what to do about Project Mercury. Kennedy's space advisory committee during the transition had issued a critical report, calling NASA's human spaceflight effort "marginal."

"We mean it's a sick program," a committee member explained to the press. "It was marginal from the beginning, and we should take a hard look at it before we decide to continue it."

With visions of Vanguard exploding on the launchpad and Atlases blowing up in midair, the committee was concerned that "a failure in our first attempt to place a man into orbit, resulting in the death of an astronaut, would create a situation of serious national embarrassment." An even more gruesome spectacle would unfold if an astronaut went crazy in weightlessness, got stuck in orbit and asphyxiated, or was incinerated due to a malfunction on the way down.

Just four days after taking charge of NASA, Webb had to decide whether to go ahead with the launch of an unmanned Mercury capsule atop an Atlas. An identical test the previous July had crashed into the Atlantic. Fretting about the reputation of their Atlas missile and fearing that it might be portrayed as a laughable threat by the Soviets, the Air Force asked Webb to postpone the flight until a sturdier version of the rocket could be substituted. Webb checked with his technical staff, who assured him that the previous problems had been fixed. So he gave the okay. Using a Marine Corps metaphor, he put it this way: "My philosophy has always been . . . if you've got to take that island, you'd better get in there and take it."

On February 21, 1961, the Mercury-Atlas flew flawlessly.

Webb was not only pressing ahead with Mercury, he was also laying plans for the future. Max Faget had already sketched out a more advanced spacecraft—a three-person ship called Apollo (named by NASA manager and mythology enthusiast Abe Silverstein, who had also christened Mercury). Faget decided that three astronauts made the most sense for long missions, since they could rotate on watches in the same way that a naval crew does.

Like Mercury, Apollo was a god with celestial connotations, notably for driving the chariot of the Sun across the sky each day. Of course, no one was thinking of sending astronauts to the Sun, but the Apollo spacecraft would be well suited for a variety of missions, such as ferrying astronauts to a space station in Earth orbit or carrying them on a voyage around the Moon. Hardly anyone was advocating *landing* astronauts on the Moon, but Apollo could be adapted to do that, too. Apollo would require a much larger rocket than Atlas, and von Braun's team was currently working on a powerful family of launch vehicles called Saturn that would serve this purpose.

The president made no commitments, but he gave Webb permission to continue looking at advanced missions. Next, Webb had to convince Kennedy's advisers that it was finally time to launch an astronaut aboard Mercury. After all, the first few manned flights would be up-and-down suborbital trips on von Braun's Redstone, not the far riskier orbital journeys on an Atlas. But the advisers counseled delay. They wanted to be absolutely sure of the astronaut's safety, particularly during weightlessness, and insisted on additional test flights with animals. Events soon made them regret this demand.

On April 12, 1961, long-range radar operated by the United States near the Soviet Union's southern border detected a satellite launch. Twenty minutes later, as the satellite passed over a listening post in Alaska's Aleutian Islands, radio operators heard a human voice, saying in Russian: "I feel splendid, very well, very well, very well. Give me some results on the flight!"

Thirty-five minutes after that, as the vehicle approached the tip of South America, Radio Moscow in the Soviet capital announced: "The world's first satellite-ship, *Vostok*, with a human on board was launched into an orbit about the Earth from the Soviet Union. The pilot-cosmonaut of the spaceship satellite *Vostok* is a citizen of the Union of Soviet Socialist Republics, Major of Aviation Yuri Alekseyevich Gagarin."

Major Gagarin landed in Soviet territory after one orbit. He reported that he was in excellent health and took a congratulatory call from his nation's leader. During their conversation, Premier Khrushchev couldn't resist taunting America: "Let the capitalist countries catch up with our country!"

Round two of the space race had just gone to the Soviets.

A Soviet cosmonaut raises a hammer and sickle, the symbol of the Soviet Union. The text reads: "Long live the Soviet people—the space pioneers!"

President Kennedy, his wife, Jackie, and advisers nervously watch the televised launch of astronaut Alan Shepard. Vice President Lyndon Johnson is at far left.

17

"LIGHT THIS CANDLE"

On April 30, 1961, President Kennedy's first hundred days were up, and they had been a disaster. Americans liked the youth and vigor he brought to the presidency but were dismayed by his handling of the Cold War.

During the campaign, Kennedy had promised to do something about the recently established communist government in Cuba, headed by Fidel Castro. "Those who say they will stand up to Mr. Khrushchev have demonstrated no ability to stand up to Mr. Castro," he said, referring to his opponent in the election, Vice President Nixon.

In a debate with Nixon, Kennedy hammered the point home: "The communists have been moving with vigor—Laos, Africa, Cuba—all around the world today they're on the move. I think we have to revitalize our society. I think we have to demonstrate to the people of the world that we're determined in this free country of ours to be first—not first if, and not first but, and not first when—but first."

Now that he was president, Kennedy's promises were turning to dust. After Major Gagarin orbited the planet, the Soviet Union's claim to be first in technology suddenly looked pretty strong. Then five days after the flight, Kennedy gave the go-ahead for an invasion that was supposed to redeem his Cuba pledge. A U.S.-sponsored force of Cuban rebels landed on the island to retake it from Castro. But the invaders were quickly defeated, giving Kennedy another humiliating setback. Meanwhile in Southeast Asia, communists were gaining ground in Laos, and Kennedy felt forced to negotiate a hasty settlement with the rebels' Soviet backers.

Amid these disasters, who could blame Kennedy if he was nervous about Project Mercury? If his decision to proceed ended up killing an astronaut, his presidency might as well be over.

Ever since the Mercury astronauts were announced, the press had been speculating about who would make the first flight. Would they draw straws? Would it be the most qualified? Would Kennedy make the choice? The press favored John Glenn because of his easy charm, which was very much like the president's. But Bob Gilruth, head of the Space Task Group, chose Al Shepard due to his superb mastery of the Mercury spacecraft. Glenn would be Shepard's backup, and Slayton would be the primary capcom—the capsule communicator who would keep in radio contact with Shepard during the mission. Shepard picked *Freedom 7* for the name of his Mercury capsule in tribute to Kennedy's trademark celebration of freedom. The number seven was used because the capsule was the seventh in the test sequence, but in the public mind it stood for the solidarity of the seven Mercury astronauts.

After a series of delays, Shepard's liftoff was scheduled for early May. Even though this flight was suborbital and would last only fifteen minutes (Gagarin's lasted 108 minutes), the NASA press office was prepared for every contingency. If Shepard died during launch, they had an announcement ready: "Rescue units on the scene report that Astronaut

Shepard has perished today in the service of his country." Similar statements were on file to cover mishaps at every other stage of the mission.

As launch day approached, Kennedy fretted about whether to go ahead. The reality of putting a human atop a rocket was starting to sink in, and it struck him the way it did most Americans: it was crazy. Some of his advisers thought so, too, and tried to get him to postpone the flight at least until the furor over Cuba and Laos died down. But Webb assured the president that every precaution had been taken. Another space official was even more optimistic: "Why postpone a success?" he asked.

Still anxious, Kennedy sought additional assurance and had his press secretary call Cape Canaveral to discuss the details of the Mercury escape system. Clearly, visions of exploding rockets haunted him.

●

On launch day, May 5, 1961, Shepard was almost as cool as the liquid oxygen in the Redstone's oxidizer tank. When the count was stopped with barely two minutes to go, he had been sitting in the capsule for over four hours, waiting through delay after delay as one problem after another cropped up. This was the last straw.

"All right, I'm cooler than you are," he said testily. "Why don't you fix your little problem . . . and *light this candle.*"

Shortly after, the count resumed.

It reached zero.

"Liftoff!" called Slayton over the radio link.

Only Gagarin had ridden a missile into space before, and he had said little publicly about the experience, due to the Soviet government's preference for secrecy. So Shepard didn't know exactly what to expect. To a Navy pilot used to being catapulted off aircraft carriers, liftoff was surprisingly smooth—"a subtle, gentle, gradual rise off the ground," he later recalled. It was not as noisy as he expected either. One oddity was that the cockpit altimeter showed rapidly increasing altitude—40, 50, 60 thousand feet—something every fighter pilot was familiar with. But the craft never leveled off, as an aircraft would have. It just kept climbing and climbing. This was a brand-new experience for the pilot.

About two minutes into the flight, at 70,000 feet, the Redstone broke the sound barrier. Shepard was experiencing 3 g's at this point. Half a minute later, he was passing through 100,000 feet—almost 20 miles up—and feeling 5 g's. He was traveling close to 5,000 miles per hour.

The Redstone exhausted its propellant and the engine cut off. Acceleration dropped to zero and Shepard was weightless. *Freedom 7* separated from the Redstone, turned its blunt end forward, and continued to soar higher against the pull of Earth's gravity, impelled by the tremendous boost given by the rocket. Zero g would last about five minutes, as the spacecraft arced to an altitude of 115 miles—well into space— and then began its plunge back to Earth. Shepard found weightlessness pleasant. As he dropped through 50 miles, the thin atmosphere began slowing the ship and he felt the renewed tug of g-forces. These quickly built to almost twelve times the pull of Earth's gravity, which was the peak g-force during his flight. The heat shield began to glow and flake off, dissipating the energy of reentry. Two minutes later, the main parachute deployed, and *Freedom 7* drifted slowly to the ocean, landing almost 300 miles east of Cape Canaveral, just a quarter of an hour after launch.

Except for one malfunctioning light in the cockpit, the mission had gone off without a hitch. Nervously, President Kennedy watched the television coverage from the White House. Relieved at the happy ending, he called to congratulate Shepard when he was aboard the recovery ship.

In a sense, Shepard's mission had been little more than the stunt described so honestly by Hugh Dryden—not unlike "shooting a young lady from a cannon." But the soaring flight of *Freedom 7* had also been a test in preparation for something far bigger. It had proved the two most crucial operations of any space mission, launch and reentry, which are comparable to takeoff and landing in an airplane. What would come in between—the actual mission—would have to wait.

Alan Shepard lifts off, on his way to becoming the first American in space, May 5, 1961.

Photomosaic of the Moon, assembled from telescopic images, 1966

18

GO TO THE MOON

For all its success, Shepard's flight was frustratingly like Explorer 1. Both missions paled in comparison to the Russian triumphs. Shepard had shot up like a V-2 and then come back down a few hundred miles away, while Gagarin had traveled completely around the globe. As for Explorer 1—it had been a third-place finisher that weighed only a fraction as much as the two Sputniks that preceded it. America had been badly beaten in the first two rounds of the space race.

Still, Al Shepard was a national hero, and his success perhaps foretold a change in the president's fortunes. At least that was the way *Time*, the nation's most influential news magazine, saw it: "The blaze of Alan Shepard's Redstone rocket was a bright light on a dark, Cold War horizon," the magazine wrote. "It was a first step in John Kennedy's fight back from the personal and political Pearl Harbors of Cuba and Laos."

Kennedy was determined to use this piece of good news to reset the country's priorities. A week after Gagarin's flight, he had asked Vice President Johnson to confer with Webb and other space advisers and answer this question: "Is there any . . . space program which promises dramatic results in which we could win?" Now, the jaw-dropping answer came back: it was time to go to the Moon.

The Moon may seem like an easy goal to reach. It's up in the sky where you can see it, and even a small telescope shows details of its rugged landscape, making it appear very close. But the Moon is extraordinarily distant: 240,000 miles away, equal to thirty times Earth's diameter or more than 2,000 times farther than the high point reached during Shepard's flight. The rocket and propellant needed to get astronauts to the Moon and back would have to be at least a hundred times more massive than the Mercury-Redstone. If observers of the Explorer 1 launch, which used a modified Redstone, were awed by the "tremendous jet burst from the base of the rocket" and the terrific "thunder of the rocket engine," then imagine the scene at the launch of a Moon rocket!

Also imagine how difficult it is to go to the Moon, which is a moving target (traveling over 2,000 miles per hour), land safely amid the countless craters, step outside in the complete vacuum to explore an unknown and potentially dangerous world, and finally find your way back to Earth, reentering the atmosphere at more than five times the top speed of *Freedom 7*. Nothing remotely like this had ever been done. However, Webb's advisers assured him and the president that it was possible—expensive, yes, but possible. Webb made doubly sure, since he was a cautious man. "When you decide you're going to do something and put the prestige of the United States government behind it," he said later, "you'd better doggone well be able to do it."

Kennedy was appalled by the price tag, which some experts put at 40 billion dollars. That was four times the combined cost of the B-29 and atomic bomb projects, which were the most expensive weapons systems ever built. He desperately wanted America to take the lead in space, but he also wondered if a less expensive goal than landing a man on the Moon would do. His advisers said no. The Soviets' current advantage in large rockets meant they could accomplish many interim goals in space, but they did not yet have a rocket that could send humans all the way to the Moon and back. America stood a decent chance of beating them to it.

A Moon voyage was a dream as old as humanity. It was also a dream that America could make happen. To anyone who had lived through World War II, daunting tasks were routine. In the weeks following Japan's attack on Pearl Harbor, the Japanese had seized control of the

President Kennedy tells Congress that America will go to the Moon, May 25, 1961. He is the tiny figure at the podium.

western Pacific. At the same time, Nazi forces occupied most of continental Europe. But with the United States in the war, even with its early setbacks, there was never any doubt that the Allies would win, and that America's industries, organizational genius, and fighting spirit would play a decisive role.

America's goal—
240,000 miles
distant

On May 25, 1961, three weeks after the flight of *Freedom 7*, Kennedy stood before a joint session of Congress to reenergize his presidency. His speech was full of new initiatives—in economic, domestic, and foreign policy, and in military affairs—all designed to combat Soviet power. Half an hour into the address, as senators and representatives may have been nodding off, he woke them up with a startling challenge: "I believe that this nation should commit itself to achieving the goal, before this decade is out, of landing a man on the Moon and returning him safely to the Earth."

Kennedy's speechwriter was in the hall and noted the audience's stunned reaction. The president continued: "No single space project in this period will be more impressive to mankind, or more important for the long-range exploration of space; and none will be so difficult or expensive to accomplish."

The president picked up on the air of doubt in the room and departed from his text to encourage the assembled politicians to rise to the challenge and vote in favor of supplying the necessary funds. He closed: "I have not asked for a single program which did not cause one or all Americans some inconvenience, or some hardship, or some sacrifice."

With this, he was echoing the most quoted line from his inaugural address, a patriotic call that had stirred the nation: "Ask not what your country can do for you—ask what you can do for your country." The Moon-landing program would call for the support of every citizen.

●

When they tuned in to the speech, Jim Webb and Bob Gilruth were flying to a meeting aboard a World War II–era transport from the old NACA fleet. The plane was noisy, but they could hear the president's distinctive Boston accent over the radio.

Webb knew what Kennedy was going to say, but Gilruth was shocked when he heard the president's deadline: "before this decade is out." Webb was relieved, since the original deadline had been 1967—the fiftieth anniversary of the Communist Revolution, which was widely assumed to be the Soviets' target date for their own Moon landing, although that was just a guess. Webb had asked the president's advisers for more time. The end of the decade seemed urgent enough but also possible. It was also conveniently vague: it could mean either 1969 or 1970, eight or nine years away, depending on where you started counting. In practice, the deadline came to be considered December 31, 1969.

But one of the managers who had to meet the deadline was sitting right next to Webb, and he was not so confident. Bob Gilruth later said, "I was always a guy that looked at all the things that could go wrong." After tallying that frightening list: "I was sort of aghast."

For the rest of the flight, Webb chatted away about the president's speech, while Gilruth was lost in thought. Below, a small part of planet Earth passed beneath them. A quarter of a million miles away, the Moon beckoned.

67

Space is open to us now; and our
eagerness to share its meaning is not
governed by the efforts of others. We
go into space because whatever mankind
must undertake, _free_ men must fully
share.

I therefore ask the Congress,
above and beyond the increases I have
earlier requested for space activities,
to provide the funds which are needed
to meet the following national goals:

First, I believe that this nation
should commit itself to achieving the
goal, before this decade is out,
of landing a man on the moon and
returning him safely to earth.

Kennedy honors Shepard after his flight.

Kennedy delivers his Moon
speech to Congress.

The Moon speech, continued

68

No single space project in this period
will be more exciting, or more
impressive, or more important for the
long-range exploration of space; and
none will be so difficult or expensive
to accomplish. Including necessary
supporting research, this objective
will require an additional $531 million
this year and still higher sums in the
future. We propose to accelerate
development of the appropriate lunar
space craft. We propose to develop
alternate liquid and solid fuel
boosters of much larger than any now
being developed, until certain which
is superior.

BRIEFING:
The President's Speech

Several years before he ran for president, John F. Kennedy was having dinner with Doc Draper in Boston. As head of the MIT Instrumentation Lab, Draper wanted to get the promising young politician interested in spaceflight. Kennedy made light-hearted fun of the idea, probably thinking of the science-fiction comics he saw in the newspaper. No one would have predicted that one day he would stand before Congress and launch history's most audacious space project.

The key to it, in President Kennedy's mind, was freedom—a concept that had a very special meaning during the Cold War. Eighteen months after the end of World War II, President Truman had invoked freedom again and again in a speech that was a call to arms against Soviet aggression. In his Moon-landing speech, President Kennedy followed suit, mentioning freedom nearly two dozen times, posing this challenge: "If we are to win the battle that is now going on around the world between freedom and tyranny, the dramatic achievements in space which occurred in recent weeks"—meaning the spaceflights of Gagarin and Shepard—"should have made clear to us all . . . the impact of this adventure on the minds of men everywhere." He concluded that something as bold as a Moon landing would make the case for freedom. He was worried that the feats of Soviet scientists and engineers made the Soviet Union look like the most progressive society on Earth.

Kennedy didn't say that the Moon landing would be the realization of an age-old dream, or that humans are born explorers, or that the project would produce unimagined technological innovations or hundreds of thousands of jobs—all of which would have been true. Instead, he appealed to the most powerful idea motivating Americans at the time: freedom.

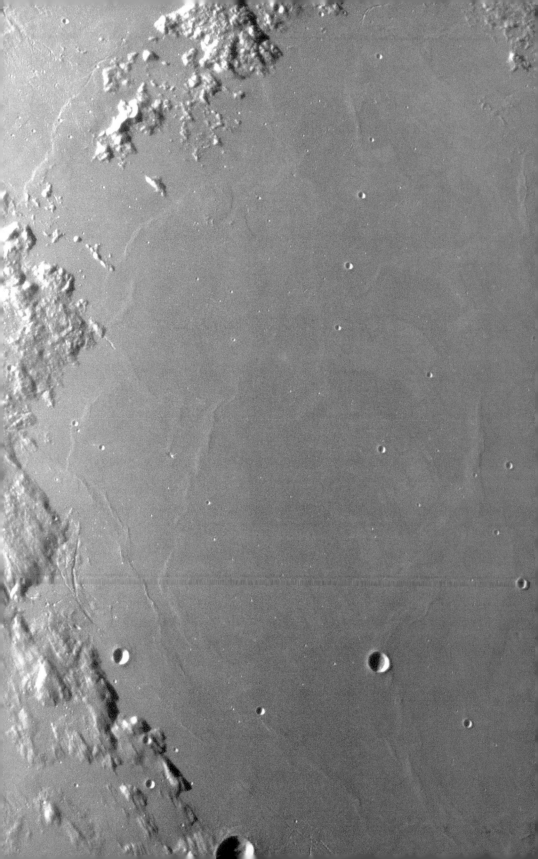

PART 4
THE PLAN

So much happened and it happened so fast. It was almost like being in an accident.

—Rocco Petrone, manager of Saturn V launch operations

The Moon's Sea of Serenity through a telescope

Wernher von Braun stands at the back end of his Moon rocket, with its giant F-1 engines.

19

PIECES OF THE PUZZLE

Thanks to Max Faget, Kennedy's Moon-landing venture already had a name and a design. Faget's three-man Apollo spacecraft could be adapted for landing by adding more rocket motors and other equipment. But what were the other steps? How do you put together the puzzle pieces for a lunar voyage? How do you even know what the pieces *are*? Like generals planning an invasion, Webb's top staff began devising a strategy. NASA's third-in-command, Robert C. Seamans Jr., remembers looking up at the Moon during this period and wondering "if we were all crazy. Intellectually, I believed we could do it. Each step seemed to make sense; yet when I grasped the enormity of the job, I wondered."

Over the next few months, Seamans and his colleagues came up with a plan:

1. Build a Moon rocket

Task number one was building a monstrous rocket that could carry astronauts to the Moon and back. The key component was already under development: a rocket engine called the F-1, designed to produce 1.5 million pounds of thrust—meaning it could lift anything weighing up to 1.5 million pounds. This amount of thrust was equal to nineteen Redstones firing simultaneously. For his Saturn family of rockets, von Braun envisioned boosters that clustered as many as four or five F-1s in the first stage, and he had designs for a behemoth called Nova that would use up to eight F-1s at launch.

These colossal machines could send significant payloads to the Moon. However, one of the big problems was moving them around on Earth. Simply putting one together would be a daunting task, since the completed vehicle would be taller than the Statue of Liberty. Assembly was best done in an enclosed space, out of the weather. Given the need to have several Moon rockets being worked on at the same time, the hangar would have to be the world's largest building by volume. When the rocket was ready, it would need to be moved several miles to the launchpad, since a mishap like the Vanguard explosion would pack the power of a small nuclear bomb.

Von Braun and his team were responsible for the Moon rocket. And a U.S. Army lieutenant colonel named Rocco Petrone was charged with creating the facilities—the assembly building, rocket transporter, launchpad, and other structures—that would send the titanic missiles on their way. These would include the cavernous firing room, where hundreds of engineers would control every aspect of the countdown and launch.

2. Hire a big boss

Webb and Seamans discussed appointing von Braun to head the entire Apollo effort. No one had pushed the dream of a lunar voyage harder than the German rocketeer or done so much to make it happen. But when NASA's long-serving deputy administrator Hugh Dryden heard

Early concept of the Moon rocket

the idea, he said he would rather resign than see the ex-Nazi lead America's greatest technological adventure.

So Webb and Seamans searched elsewhere. They settled on D. Brainerd Holmes, a brilliant engineer who had managed the development of the billion-dollar missile early warning system designed to detect Russian missiles coming over the Arctic region from the Soviet Union. He was an expert organizer of huge, complicated projects, and he looked like the perfect fit for heading not just Apollo, but all U.S. human spaceflight.

3. Expand NASA

In 1961, NASA had 18,000 employees at its centers plus 58,000 contract employees at companies all around the country. This was not nearly enough to mount an expedition to the Moon. The numbers would almost double within a year—the lion's share being contract workers designing and building rockets, spacecraft, and other hardware. The labor force would keep growing until it was at the strength of a major invasion during World War II, topping out at 411,000 workers by 1965.

In addition, a new NASA facility called the Manned Spacecraft Center was being planned to house Gilruth's rapidly expanding Space Task Group. In consultation with Kennedy, Webb selected Houston for the site. Houston met all the requirements, but more importantly, it was in Texas—the home state of Vice President Johnson as well as several top congressional leaders with influence over NASA's budget. (Years later the Manned Spacecraft Center would be renamed the Lyndon B. Johnson Space Center.)

4. Get spaceflight experience

When Kennedy announced that America was going to the Moon, the U.S. had all of fifteen minutes of manned spaceflight experience. Imagine if after the Wright brothers' first flight in 1903, lasting less than a minute, they had announced they were planning a flight around the world! They would have needed a much more sophisticated aircraft and vastly more piloting experience to do it.

NASA was in much the same position. Their Moon ship was in the works, but they needed veteran spacefarers who were familiar with the disorienting effects of takeoff, weightlessness, and reentry; who knew how to navigate by the stars, change orbits, rendezvous and dock with another ship, land on an alien surface, function outside in a pressure suit; and who could cope with other conditions, as yet unknown.

Furthermore, the space travelers had to stand up to these challenges for the full eight days of a round-trip lunar voyage.

Unfortunately, Project Mercury was only able to give astronauts the first three experiences: takeoff, weightlessness, and reentry. Mercury missions were expected to extend into 1963, including orbital flights lasting a day or so, but they would provide no practice in the more sophisticated aspects of spaceflight needed for a lunar voyage. Since Apollo wouldn't be ready for its first Earth orbital missions until 1965 at the earliest, an interim ship was essential. Project Gemini was designed to fill this gap. Named for the constellation that depicts twins from classical mythology, the Gemini spacecraft would carry two astronauts—the "twins"—on orbital missions that would test some of the major challenges of a Moon voyage. One was the maneuver called "rendezvous and docking," in which a spacecraft approaches another and links up with it. It sounds simple, but in space it's tricky and counterintuitive. During Apollo, rendezvous and docking was likely to be an important step for transferring crews, refueling, or other crucial operations.

NASA was also ready to choose the next group of astronauts. Anticipating many Gemini and Apollo flights—at two or three astronauts per mission plus backup crews—officials knew they would need quite a few spacefarers.

5. Reconnoiter the goal

If the Wright brothers really had decided to fly around the world, at least they would have known what they were getting into. Except for the poles, the Earth had been thoroughly explored by the twentieth century. The same was not true for the Moon. The nature of the lunar surface was a major mystery. One prominent scientist argued that billions of years of bombardment by meteorites had ground the Moon's surface into a thick layer of dust. Astronauts attempting to land, he said, would sink out of sight.

To settle this question and answer others, NASA planned three separate programs of robotic exploration to pave the way for Apollo:

- **Ranger**: Designed to plunge kamikaze-like into the Moon, these spacecraft would take pictures until the last instant, relaying them live to Earth while showing closer and closer views of possible landing areas.
- **Surveyor**: This series of automatic landers would come down much like the Apollo spacecraft, firing a braking rocket and settling gently onto the lunar surface, where they would test the soil properties and relay images.
- **Lunar Orbiter**: With the goal of mapping the entire Moon, these spacecraft would go into lunar orbit and use declassified spy-satellite cameras to photograph lunar craters, plains, valleys, and mountain ranges.

6. Develop astronavigation

One of the biggest hurdles facing Apollo astronauts was navigating to the Moon and back. NASA gave this problem such high priority that its first Apollo contract went to the firm best equipped to solve it: the Instrumentation Laboratory at MIT, headed by Doc Draper, who had worked with Jim Webb on defense projects during World War II.

The problem of astronavigation boiled down to designing an on-board guidance system—a gyroscope teamed with a sextant and a computer—that could tell astronauts exactly where they were at any given time, where they needed to be in the next phase of their trip, and what adjustments to make in their trajectory to get there. This information had to be independent of data relayed from Mission Control, since the spacecraft could lose radio contact at any time. In other words, the spacecraft had to be able to navigate on its own like a ship at sea. The difference was that the Apollo ship would be traveling a quarter of a million miles from home.

In 1961, Webb and others at NASA pressed Draper several times about whether his system would really work. He assured them it would. To prove it, the sixty-year-old professor volunteered to make the Moon voyage himself! (His application was politely turned down.)

There was no end to the Apollo to-do list. For example, giant dish antennas needed to be upgraded, as did the techniques for communicating with spaceships at lunar distances. The danger posed by meteors and high-energy solar particles in deep space required study. So did the risk of any hypothetical alien microbes that might be returned to Earth from the Moon. Also, the procedures for the new techniques of mission control had to be perfected; the astronauts would have so much to do, they would require substantial help from the ground. Indeed, the mission controllers would be as much a part of the flight as the crew.

But there was one gigantic piece of the puzzle that hadn't been settled. This was the size of the Apollo spacecraft and the sequence of steps in a mission. Would a single spacecraft proceed directly to the Moon, land, and then return, as in the movies? Or did a piecemeal approach make more sense?

In the early months of the Apollo program, this debate would become surprisingly heated.

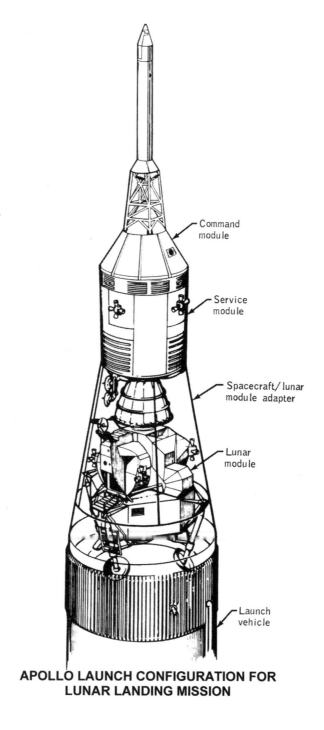

Command
module

Service
module

Spacecraft/lunar
module adapter

Lunar
module

Launch
vehicle

**APOLLO LAUNCH CONFIGURATION FOR
LUNAR LANDING MISSION**

The Lunar Module (LM) nestles behind the Command and Service Module (CSM) at the top of the Saturn V. After launch, the CSM turns around and docks with the LM.

20

HOW TO GET TO THE MOON, AND BACK

"**Y**our figures lie!" shouted Max Faget. He had just seen
a presentation by fellow NASA engineer John C. Houbolt, who was passionate about a cost- and time-saving plan for getting to the Moon.

"He's being misleading," Faget explained to the audience, which included Seamans, von Braun, and other top NASA officials.

Von Braun was also dubious. "No, that's no good," he said about the
scheme.

Such united opposition from the nation's chief spacecraft designer
and premier rocket scientist should have killed Houbolt's idea cold.

But it didn't.

The most crucial step in a round-trip to the Moon is the journey back.
You must be absolutely sure that you have enough propellant to take off
from the Moon and return to Earth. Therefore, mission planners often
started their calculations by examining the return journey. How big a

rocket does it take to get a given spacecraft, consisting of a crew cabin and its support equipment, off the Moon? The bigger the spacecraft sitting on the Moon, the more rocket power is needed to get home.

After you've made this calculation, you can work backward, figuring out how big a braking rocket is needed to land this contraption on the Moon and therefore how big a launch vehicle is required back on Earth to get the whole package traveling at 24,200 miles per hour—the launch speed needed to reach the Moon.

When these calculations were run with Faget's three-person Apollo spacecraft, they showed that the launch vehicle would have to be the largest on von Braun's drawing board: the Nova, packing eight F-1 engines in its first stage, each producing 1.5 million pounds of thrust.

The big assumption here is that you're going to the Moon the way it's done in the movies: leave Earth, land on the Moon, return. This approach is called "direct ascent," and while engineers love it for its simplicity, it's not the only way to go.

Direct ascent made von Braun nervous. He loved building big rockets, but the Nova was too big even for him. So he came up with an alternate strategy, called "Earth-orbit rendezvous." His plan was to use two or more smaller launch vehicles—still enormous but smaller than Nova—to assemble the expedition in Earth orbit. One rocket might send up the complete spacecraft, with its lunar descent and ascent stages attached. Another might launch the fully fueled propulsion unit. The two parts would dock, the propulsion unit would ignite, and off they would go. Other combinations were possible, such as launching a space tanker to "gas up" the Moon ship.

As far as NASA was concerned, Apollo would use one of these two approaches: direct ascent or Earth-orbit rendezvous. Both involved landing the entire Apollo spacecraft on the Moon, with its heat shield, parachutes, and other features intended solely for reentry into Earth's atmosphere. No one saw a practical way around this drawback—except Houbolt.

When Columbus arrived in the New World, he didn't sail his flagship onto the beach only to have to push the massive vessel back into the water on his departure. No, he anchored offshore and climbed into a rowboat that he then used to reach the shore. This was the essence of Houbolt's plan. There was no need to take the entire spacecraft down to the Moon, only to have to lift it off the surface to return to Earth. A small, specialized landing craft—a space rowboat—could do the job, shuttling from the mother ship in lunar orbit, down to the Moon, and back.

Called "lunar-orbit rendezvous," the plan broke down the Apollo spacecraft into modules. Houbolt didn't invent this approach, but he became its tireless champion. As they were later named, the modules became the command module, the service module, and the lunar module.

The command module (CM) is Faget's Apollo capsule, the crew compartment that sits like a nose cone atop the launch vehicle and serves as home to three astronauts. It is the only piece of hardware that returns to Earth, and therefore the only part that needs a heavy heat shield for protection during the scorching reentry into the atmosphere—which, from a lunar voyage, is even faster and hotter than the return from Earth orbit.

Behind the CM is the service module (SM), housing a rocket engine, propellant tanks, a power supply, breathing oxygen, drinking water, and communications equipment. Since the CM and SM remain attached until just before reentry, they can be considered a single unit, called the CSM.

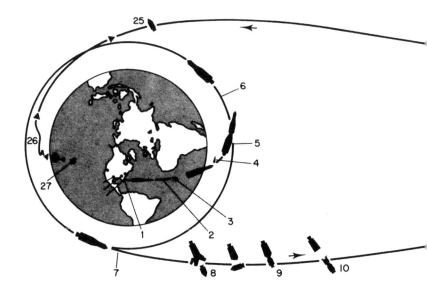

Apollo's Steps to the Moon

The Earth and Moon are not drawn to scale.

1. Saturn V lifts off
2. First-stage burn
3. Second-stage burn
4. Escape tower jettisoned
5. Third-stage burn
6. Earth orbit
7. Relight third stage to leave for Moon
8. CSM separates from LM shroud
9. CSM docks with LM
10. Third stage is cast off
11. Midcourse correction
12. Enter lunar orbit (dashed lines indicate loss of Earth communications)
13. Two astronauts enter LM
14. CSM and LM separate

The lunar module (LM, pronounced "lem") is the rowboat. During launch it is stored behind the CSM, surrounded by a protective shroud. After the firing of the third stage, when the Apollo spacecraft is Moon-bound, the CSM detaches from the top of the shroud, turns around, and docks with the LM, becoming one spacecraft. The third stage and shroud are then cast off. On arrival near the Moon, the CSM fires its engine, putting the combined CSM-LM ship into lunar orbit. Then two

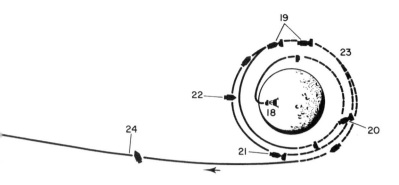

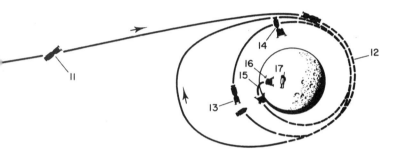

15. LM descent
16. Touchdown!
17. Explore surface, set up experiments
18. LM ascent stage lifts off
19. Rendezvous and docking with CSM
20. LM crew enters CSM
21. CSM detaches from LM

22. Crew prepares for return to Earth
23. CSM fires rocket to leave lunar orbit
24. Midcourse correction
25. CM separates from SM
26. Reentry
27. Splashdown!

astronauts enter the LM through a tunnel, detach from the CSM, and fire the LM's descent rocket, leaving behind the third astronaut in the CSM—the mother ship—to mind the store. They descend to a landing, go outside, and explore the Moon.

Ready to head home, the Moon explorers would climb back aboard the LM and fire its ascent rocket, leaving the descent stage behind on the Moon. Returning to lunar orbit, they dock with the mother ship and rejoin their comrade. The three astronauts then detach from the LM's ascent stage, leaving it behind, and fire the CSM rocket for return to Earth. Just before reentry the CM and SM detach. The CM plummets through the atmosphere (as does the SM, which burns up), roasting the CM's heat shield to a fiery red. In the lower atmosphere, parachutes deploy for a gentle landing in the ocean.

This sounded dangerously complicated to many NASA engineers. They were especially worried about a hair-raising moment of high risk: the rendezvous and docking of the LM ascent stage and CSM in lunar orbit, something that had never been done even in Earth orbit, much less around the Moon. As one NASA official put it, "Houbolt has a scheme that has a 50 percent chance of getting a man to the Moon and a 1 percent chance of getting him back."

Houbolt argued that this wisecrack greatly exaggerated the risk and that no one could dispute the cost-saving. Thanks to the shedding of weight as the flight progressed, a single-launch vehicle with five F-1 engines in its first stage, plus state-of-the-art second and third stages, would suffice for a complete Apollo mission. By contrast, two such boosters were needed for von Braun's preferred Earth-orbit rendezvous plan.

To Houbolt, lunar-orbit rendezvous "offered a chain reaction of simplifications," which significantly streamlined "development, testing, manufacturing, launch, and flight operations." As soon as he encountered the idea, he realized, "Oh my God, this is it! This is fantastic! If there is any idea we must push, it is this one."

After all concerned studied Houbolt's plan, they began to come around. Even Faget and von Braun joined the consensus, recognizing lunar-orbit rendezvous as the most elegant solution to a very difficult problem. It made the most with the least.

It helped that the astronauts far preferred lunar-orbit rendezvous. With the other two approaches, they had to bring a towering spaceship to a landing on the Moon while lying on their backs, watching a televised view of where they were going. The feat would be like backing a Mercury-Atlas onto the pad. By contrast, with Houbolt's plan they got a small, maneuverable lunar module that they could fly like a jet fighter, which naturally appealed to test pilots.

For their part, administrators liked lunar-orbit rendezvous because it avoided the complication of multiple launches and provided the best chance of meeting Kennedy's deadline of a landing by the end of 1969. And so, on July 11, 1962, NASA announced that lunar-orbit rendezvous would be America's path to the Moon. The rocket to start the journey would use five F-1 engines and would be called the Saturn V.

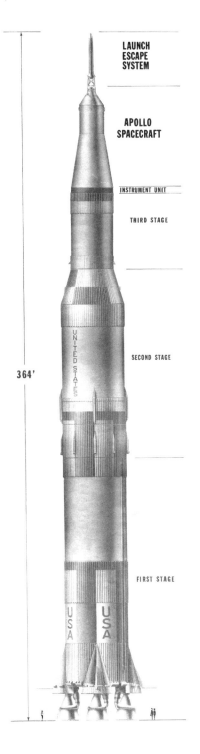

LAUNCH ESCAPE SYSTEM

APOLLO SPACECRAFT

INSTRUMENT UNIT

THIRD STAGE

SECOND STAGE

364'

FIRST STAGE

The Saturn V. (See page 158 for the positions of the CSM and LM.)

Three Russian cosmonauts with Premier Khrushchev (far right), 1963. Left to right: Yuri Gagarin, Pavel Popovich, and Valentina Tereshkova, the first woman in space.

21

THE RACE HEATS UP

Before they were selected as astronauts, the Original Seven were put through the most rigorous medical tests that doctors could devise. All were in superb physical condition. Testing continued during their training as they were subjected to bruising experiments designed to discover how much punishment the human body could take in launches, landings, gyrating space capsules, and other ordeals. Researchers were amazed at their endurance. Then, on the same day that NASA announced the lunar-orbit rendezvous decision, Americans were stunned to learn that Deke Slayton was being grounded due to a heart condition.

The subtle abnormality—irregular heartbeats—showed up briefly about every two weeks. No doctor could say why. Slayton paid no attention to these episodes until he was hooked up to a heart monitor before a training session. A technician noticed the problem and expressed concern. The nation's top heart specialists examined Slayton and found him fit in every way, except this. Just to be safe, they recommended that he be grounded.

Pilots are grounded every day, but this was big news. The Original Seven had been reduced to six. Newspapers treated it almost like a death, reporting in somber detail Slayton's sixty-three bombing missions over Europe and Japan during World War II, his test pilot career, and his memorable quote on joining Project Mercury: "I would give my left arm to be the first man in space." Now it seemed he wouldn't even be the hundredth.

In the summer of 1962, Mercury had come a long way since Shepard's flight a little over a year earlier. Eleven weeks after the launch of *Freedom 7*, Gus Grissom repeated Shepard's suborbital journey in a mission that went perfectly—until the hatch accidentally blew open after splashdown. The capsule sank and Grissom barely escaped with his life. But the perils of rocket flight, as opposed to recovery, appeared to be conquered.

Two weeks after Grissom's quick trip, the Russians countered with their second human spaceflight: seventeen orbits lasting a full day. The headline of one New York paper proclaimed, "Red Spaceman Lands! Covered 434,960 Mi. Can U.S. Still Win Race to Moon?" A British expert on spaceflight didn't think so. He predicted a Russian manned landing on the Moon in 1966 or 1967, and he expected a lunar reconnaissance flight with a dog to pave the way.

Gilruth reacted decisively by canceling the remaining suborbital flights and scheduling the next Mercury mission as Earth-orbiting. John Glenn, who had been backup to both Shepard and Grissom, got the assignment. His capsule, *Friendship 7*, flew on February 20, 1962, giving Glenn the first ride on the trouble-plagued Atlas. The booster behaved beautifully. His main worry during the five-hour, three-orbit trip was a warning light that blinked on at Mission Control, signaling that the

John Glenn heads for orbit aboard an Atlas, February 20, 1962.

capsule's heat shield had come loose. The identical light in Glenn's cabin was off. Mission Control suspected their reading was false, but they couldn't be sure, leading to some anxious moments and a hastily improvised change in the reentry procedure. Had the warning been correct and the heat shield had come off, Glenn would have burned up. Instead it was a faulty sensor, and Glenn had never been in danger. Even so, it was a reminder of the importance of getting every switch, sensor, and other component absolutely right.

America's second orbital mission was supposed to have been Slayton's. But he was grounded and Scott Carpenter took the flight, orbiting the world three times, just like Glenn, in May 1962.

Human spaceflight was soaring. In the following months, Slayton would watch jealously as the other Mercury rookies strapped into their capsules and took off: Wally Schirra for six orbits in October 1962, and Gordo Cooper for a wearying twenty-two orbits lasting thirty-four hours in May 1963.

Cooper's flight was the final Mercury mission and might have set an endurance record, except the Russians had already sent up two manned capsules at the same time, with each cosmonaut staying up more than twice as long as Cooper. More impressively, their orbits brought them within visual range of each other, a difficult feat in spaceflight that was the first step toward rendezvous and docking. A month after Cooper splashed down, the Russians extended their duration record to five days. This was also a dual mission, with the second capsule carrying the first woman in space, Valentina Tereshkova.

Premier Khrushchev crowed. "Bourgeois society always underlines that woman is the weaker sex," he said at a welcome-home rally for the two cosmonauts. "Our Soviet woman showed American astronauts a thing or two. Her flight was longer than that of all the American astronauts put together. There is your weaker sex!" he bellowed as the crowd erupted in cheers.

Khrushchev hit a sore point with American women. In the Soviet Union, females had a more equal status with men and played a major role in technical professions such as engineering. In the United States, a look at the NASA workforce, which was overwhelmingly male, showed that there was a lot of ground to make up. But the men in charge didn't seem to realize it. A prominent female author and politician named Clare Boothe Luce caught America's ambivalent mood in an editorial for *Life* magazine: "News reports after Valentina's blastoff said that women were dancing in the streets of Moscow while men hurled compliments and showered kisses upon them. Not so in America. The flight has become a source of bitter argument between the sexes."

U.S. officials (all male) were either dismissive or defensive. One of New York's senators made a joke about the first woman in space. "It is carrying romance to a new high," he quipped. The commander of military launches at Cape Canaveral called the achievement "merely a publicity stunt," as did a prominent champion of civil rights in the House of Representatives, who labeled it "a sort of stunt." Other critics pointed out that Tereshkova wasn't even a pilot. One NASA official said that the idea of female astronauts "makes me sick at my stomach." Meanwhile, astronaut John Glenn, now a national hero after becoming the first American in orbit, tried to calm the waters by explaining NASA's reasoning: "We felt the qualifications we were looking for . . . were best taken care of by men."

Glenn was right, but only because the deck was stacked. NASA's prime qualification for astronauts was test pilot experience in high-performance jets—a career path open only to men. On the other hand, NASA was loosening the requirement—slightly. As of 1963, non–test pilots could apply to the program, but they would need substantial experience flying military jet fighters—again, something only males were trained to do at the time. The accelerating pace of Apollo, combined with NASA's success with the first group of astronauts, inclined Webb to leave the system as it was. Another factor was that astronauts were on the committee to select new astronauts and tended to prefer their own kind.

Looking ahead, Senator Clinton Anderson of New Mexico remained optimistic. "We will train some women astronauts for sure," he predicted. He was right, but the first American female astronauts wouldn't fly until long after Apollo.

Wernher von Braun (center) explains the Saturn launch system to President Kennedy at Cape Canaveral, 1963. NASA Associate Administrator Robert Seamans is at left.

22

THE GREAT ESCAPE

In the summer of 1963, moviegoers were flocking to see *The Great Escape*. With an all-star cast headed by Steve McQueen, it told the true story of captured Allied airmen who engineer an elaborate bid for freedom during World War II. Confined in a Nazi prisoner-of-war camp designed to be escape-proof, they execute a plot involving multiple tunnels and ingeniously forged documents and uniforms. Their audacious goal is to break out with hundreds of their fellow prisoners. The climactic scene, involving a motorcycle chase through the German countryside, made McQueen famous.

Audiences of the day were obsessed with stories about the war, which had been America's finest hour. The war had been over for almost twenty years, but its memory lingered as a consolation against distressing headlines in the news—about increasing U.S. involvement in Vietnam, violent resistance to racial integration, the pernicious health effects of nuclear testing, military coups abroad, and most upsetting of all, the Cuban Missile Crisis the previous fall, which had been a terrifying close call with possible nuclear war, instigated by Russia's installation of nuclear missiles in Cuba. Fortunately, Kennedy and Khrushchev settled the crisis.

●

In this climate of unease, even America's vaunted space program was starting to draw fire. The most stinging criticism came from former president Eisenhower. This career military man put it bluntly: "Anybody who would spend 40 billion dollars in a race to the Moon for national prestige is nuts."

In fact, Webb's cost estimate for getting astronauts to the Moon and back was half that: 20 billion dollars. As an experienced Washington bureaucrat, he had good reasons for this number. After various rough guesses made the rounds, including some as high as 40 billion dollars, NASA's technical experts came up with a rigorous estimate of 8 to 12 billion. Webb thought this was unrealistic for a project with so many unknowns, so he added an "administrator's discount"—a fudge factor that would provide a cushion for the inevitable setbacks. He told Kennedy he needed 20 billion. No one had ever flown to the Moon before, so Kennedy and Congress accepted the figure, and Webb stuck to it.

Webb was able to get the money from Congress in yearly appropriations thanks to carefully nurtured contacts. He was shrewd in other ways. Bob Gilruth wanted the two-man Gemini program because it was critical for astronaut training. Webb agreed, but he also saw the public relations benefit of keeping human spaceflight in the news during the multiyear gap between Mercury and Apollo. Furthermore, he regarded Gemini as an insurance policy against unpleasant surprises with Apollo. He explained: "If we had an insuperable obstacle and had to stop Apollo, if our equipment wouldn't work or it is too difficult a

The Vehicle Assembly Building under construction, 1965. When completed the following year, it was the largest building in the world by volume. At right are three mobile launchers for the Saturn V.

job, if we really didn't see how to overcome some difficulty in getting to the Moon, we would have still done the next most important thing."

A few years later, two astronauts training for Gemini at the Cape had a premonition of just such a scenario. During time off, David Scott and Neil Armstrong decided to go look at the Apollo buildings under construction. "We walked into the firing room," Scott recalled, which had a sea of 450 consoles designed to control every facet of the Moon rocket.

By contrast, Gemini had about twenty consoles. Scott shook his head: "No way! There's no way this is going to work!" Next, Scott and Armstrong went into the mammoth Vehicle Assembly Building, where the Moon rocket would be put together. They were dumbfounded. "It ain't gonna work!" Scott repeated. "It is too big! It is just too big!"

Apollo, which dared to surmount the obstacles that confine us to our planet, would be humanity's Great Escape—if it worked.

Webb knew that his honeymoon with Congress, the press, and the public could only last so long. In the summer of 1963, Apollo hit its first rough patch. Sir Bernard Lovell, a prominent British scientist, returned from a visit to the Soviet Union reporting that technical advisers to the Soviet space program didn't think a manned lunar journey was feasible. "There are two problems which greatly concern them," Lovell told the press. First was the unpredictable rain of high-energy radiation from the Sun, which could kill Moon voyagers. Second was that once on the Moon, "there may be no solution to getting a man back to Earth safely."

Webb wondered if the Russians were trying to undermine public support for Apollo by painting it as impractical and not a goal they were pursuing. The Central Intelligence Agency (CIA) had advised him there was more than a fifty-fifty chance that the Soviets were, in fact, in the Moon race. Their manned flights, automatic lunar probes, and ambitious launch site construction (photographed by spy satellites) all seemed to support this conclusion.

Webb was also starting to have trouble with his top manager for Apollo. Brainerd Holmes was going behind his back to appeal to Kennedy for more money for the program. This might sound like a good thing, but it undermined Webb's relationship with the president and Congress, and it was an obvious sign that Holmes wanted Webb's job.

Furthermore, to Webb, it signaled that Holmes was running an inefficient operation that couldn't make do with the generous support Apollo was already getting.

When Kennedy asked why he shouldn't listen to Holmes, Webb was frank: "Look, if you want someone else to run the program, I don't know where you'll come out. If you and I stick together we'll both come out all right."

The president was persuaded: "I'm going to stick with you."

With that, Webb fired Holmes and searched for a new manager, ultimately hiring a highly regarded engineer with a knack for running a tight ship. Looking more like a professor than a hard-charging executive, George Mueller (pronounced "Miller") started work on September 1, 1963. Following standard business practice, he asked his staff for "a candid assessment of the real status" of Apollo. President Franklin Roosevelt had done much the same at the outset of World War II, when he asked for a realistic report on what it would take to win the war. The resulting Victory Program for the war was astonishingly farsighted— and successful.

Mueller also got a farsighted report, and it was bad news. Kennedy's goal was a man on the Moon by the end of 1969 at Webb's price tag of 20 billion dollars. There is "no way you're going to be able to do that," Mueller was told. He reviewed the findings with Bob Seamans, who listened quietly. At the end of the meeting, Seamans abruptly told Mueller to destroy the report. "Find out how to do it," he ordered. This was exactly what Mueller wanted to hear, and he spent the rest of that fall putting a new plan into action.

In November, Mueller had the chance to brief President Kennedy. It was a day of show-and-tell for the commander in chief, taking place at Cape Canaveral. Sitting in the firing room flanked by NASA's top brass, Kennedy watched intently as Mueller gave the big picture on the human spaceflight schedule. Particularly impressive were the scale models of

George Mueller gives a briefing to President Kennedy (front row center, with his hand on his chin). Just left of Kennedy is Jim Webb. On his other side are Hugh Dryden and Wernher von Braun.

the assembly building and Saturn V, both several years from completion. At the same scale was a Redstone. Compared to the Saturn V, it looked like a telephone pole next to a skyscraper.

"This is fantastic," Kennedy marveled, probably realizing for the first time the true immensity of Apollo. Mueller talked for about fifteen minutes. Then von Braun led the group out to the launchpad, where a Saturn I was being prepared for a test in a few weeks' time. If all went well, it would orbit a payload far exceeding the Soviet's current weight-lifting record. Kennedy loved that.

●

Before the end of the month, the launch center that the president had just toured would be renamed the John F. Kennedy Space Center, and the location would be called Cape Kennedy. This sudden honor was due to a tragedy that traumatized the nation. On November 22, 1963, less than a week after his visit to Florida, Kennedy was killed by an assassin in Dallas, Texas.

Once considered controversial, wasteful, and even crazy, the Apollo program would continue with more support than ever as a memorial to a fallen leader.

President Kennedy gazes up at a Saturn I, November 16, 1963. Six days later he would be assassinated.

The first Saturn V inside the Vehicle Assembly Building, 1967

23

GENERAL PHILLIPS JOINS THE TEAM

Raised in the tight-lipped American West, Sam Phillips was a man of few words—the type who would sum up his greatest experience in World War II with three syllables: "Surviving." Fourteen months as a fighter pilot escorting bombers through hailstorms of flak had taught him to speak sparingly, focus on the mission at hand, and ignore risks he had no way to control. His motto: "Results are what count."

After the war, Phillips stayed in the Air Force and rose through the ranks as a virtuoso manager of high-technology programs. As the Cold War heated up, new weapons became even more complex than the most monumental defense projects of World War II. New approaches were needed to make these superweapons work and get them finished on time and on budget.

After serving as project officer for the gargantuan B-52, the successor to the B-29, Phillips was assigned the nearly impossible task of producing and deploying a three-stage solid-propellant missile called

Sam Phillips as a major

Sam Phillips gets his general's star at a ceremony with his wife and three daughters, 1960.

Minuteman in just three years. He drew on a discipline called "systems engineering" to coordinate the many complex pieces of the job and meet the deadline. Along the way, he earned a general's star. At 39, he was the youngest general officer in the U.S. Armed Forces.

Before joining NASA as Brainerd Holmes's replacement, George Mueller had worked at one of the contractors for Minuteman. Through colleagues, he heard about the missile's miracle-working program manager, General Phillips. Now that Mueller oversaw human spaceflight, he needed his own miracle to get Apollo back on track, and he knew just who to call. Mueller wanted General Phillips as his deputy. The young general would remain in the Air Force but be on loan to NASA, where his sole responsibility would be Apollo. Although he would report to Mueller, Phillips would effectively be the big boss of the Moon-landing effort.

As Phillips was getting ready for his first day at NASA, a total eclipse of the Moon was in progress. Celestial mechanics brought the Sun, Earth, and Moon into line, so that Earth's shadow swept slowly across the lunar orb, turning it from its dazzling full phase into a gigantic, dark rock suspended in the sky—which is exactly what it is. That forbidding and alien world was General Phillips's new goal.

At end of 1963, lunar-orbit rendezvous had been the official plan for going to the Moon for a year and a half. Its major parts were all in the works: the three stages of the Saturn V rocket plus the Apollo spacecraft, composed of the CSM and LM. Each was among the most complex machines ever conceived. Chosen because it was a money- and time-saver, lunar-orbit rendezvous by itself was not enough to meet Kennedy's deadline. Apollo needed to be streamlined even more, and Mueller and Phillips came up with several measures to speed progress:

1. Reorganize NASA

NASA was like a medieval kingdom made up of warring provinces. The provinces were the old NACA facilities plus the new centers added since NASA formed in 1958. By 1963, the major turf battles over Apollo were between Gilruth's Manned Spacecraft Center in Houston and von Braun's rocket facility in Huntsville, with NASA Headquarters in Washington trying to make things run smoothly but not succeeding. Webb changed the chain of command, giving Mueller authority over Gilruth and von Braun. Mueller then decreed that everything having to do with Apollo would go through Phillips. Nothing would happen without the general's approval.

2. Simplify rocket testing

Multi-stage rockets like the Saturn V were always tested piecemeal. First, a series of launches perfected the first stage. When the first-stage kinks were worked out, a live second stage was added. More tests followed. Then a live third stage completed the process. But that wasn't how Phillips did it. With Minuteman, time had been so short that he followed an audacious strategy. He flew all three live stages on the very first launch. No one had ever done an "all-up" launch on the initial outing. It was considered "crazy" and likely to "blow up on the pad."

But it didn't. Phillips had so carefully managed design, construction, and quality control that everything worked perfectly. This was where systems engineering came in. So many things could go wrong with Minuteman that it would take forever to produce it with the trial-and-error methods used on earlier generations of rockets. Everything about the missile—components, computer programs, tests, timetables, and operations, along with supervising the teams—had to be coordinated like a symphony orchestra. In systems engineering, "if you do your piece right, and you hook it together, it will all work"—just as if you play your part correctly in a symphony, it will meld with all the other perfectly played parts to create beautiful music.

The general's all-up approach was so well known within the rocket community that by the time Phillips arrived at NASA, Mueller had already instituted it for Apollo. Von Braun, who was used to the painstaking, step-by-step German method, was appalled. All-up testing may have worked for Minuteman, he conceded, but for the even more fiendishly complex Saturn, it was likely to end in disaster. Other NASA insiders used words like *impossible, reckless, incredulous, harebrained,* and *nonsense.* But the decision stood.

3. Stop fooling with the design

Engineers love to design things. Perhaps even more, they love to *improve* their designs. Who could possibly object if they came up with a more efficient component for a rocket engine or an enhanced landing radar for the LM? But there is an old saying: "Better is the enemy of good." A change in one place inevitably leads to changes in everything connected to it, and this is rarely a good thing. Therefore, Mueller and Phillips instituted a rigorous system of configuration control, meaning that once a design was approved, any proposed changes faced a large hurdle. A review board had to approve all proposed modifications, taking into account their effects on the cost and schedule.

This policy rubbed Gilruth and other old NACA hands the wrong way, since they had grown up in an era when you built an airplane based on a set of calculations, flew it, tinkered with it, and then flew it again, improving it incrementally. Mueller considered those days over, especially where spaceflight was concerned. "The thing that really kills programs," he said, "is the changing requirements."

4. Meet daily milestones

As the father of two daughters, Mueller almost certainly had strict rules about homework, for he was like a demanding parent in his oversight of NASA employees. "Today's work must be done today," he insisted. The idea was that the path to what seemed like an unattainable goal could be divided into a series of daily tasks. If "we could operate in this fashion for six months we could substantially improve our schedule performance," he said. "And if we could do it for six months, we would find it easy to continue for a year and then two and then five." Mueller's can-do spirit would have done credit to Henry Ford. "We must accept in our minds and hearts that schedules can be met and that it is vital and important to meet them," Mueller urged.

5. Inspire the troops

Mueller practiced what he preached. His boss, Bob Seamans, was amazed. "George was a double whirlwind," he remembered. "The days of the week meant nothing to him. There were meetings on Saturdays and Sundays. George was indefatigable." He preferred to make his frequent trips around the country at night, so he could work all day, sleep on the plane, and then be ready for meetings with contractors or NASA center staff the next morning.

General Phillips was no less driven. A diary entry from his Apollo years records that he made fourteen phone calls, sent out three directives, responded to media, speaking, and congressional requests, and then caught an evening flight to Cape Kennedy, all on a day when he was at home sick.

The enthusiasm was infectious. One of Mueller and Phillips's employees, astronaut Neil Armstrong, noted, "You could stand across the street" from the Manned Spacecraft Center in Houston, "and you could not tell when quitting time was, because people didn't leave at quitting time . . . People just worked, and they worked until . . . their job was done, and if they had to be there until five o'clock or seven o'clock or nine-thirty or whatever it was, they were just there. They did it, and then they went home."

Thinking about how unusual it was to have this level of motivation, Armstrong added: "This was a project in which everybody involved was, one, interested, two, dedicated, and, three, fascinated by the job they were doing. And whenever you have those ingredients, whether it be government or private industry or a retail store, you're going to win."

ALL I ASK ...
DO GOOD WORK

MANNED FLIGHT AWARENESS

Astronaut Grissom's simple request—made into a poster

24

"DO GOOD WORK!"

World War II was won by soldiers, sailors, and pilots, but they couldn't have done it without the industries that supplied the equipment to fight the enemy. Two decades later, many of these same firms were producing the machines to take humans to the Moon, and many of the senior managers at these companies had been there since the early 1940s, moving up through the organization, indelibly shaped by the experience of working night and day to meet the national emergency of the war.

NASA Associate Administrator Bob Seamans had spent the war years at Doc Draper's Instrumentation Lab at MIT, perfecting military guidance and control systems for contractors such as Jim Webb's Sperry Gyroscope Company. His experience had been typical: "Like so many things for my generation," he said, "hard work and a belief in it went back to World War II."

"One year during the war," Seamans marveled, "Doc Draper said he thought it would be a good thing if we took Christmas day off! There were times when I would go to work in the morning, work through the night, then work all the next day in order to get something out on time. My generation built up a do-or-die work ethic. It amazes me when I look back."

○

Six months before America entered World War II, a young engineer named Harrison Storms took a job at North American Aviation in Los Angeles. His early projects included refining the aerodynamics of the P-51 Mustang and adapting the B-25 medium bomber so a squadron of them could take off from the short runway of an aircraft carrier, making possible the famous 1942 surprise attack on Tokyo known as the Doolittle Raid. After the war, Storms helped design the F-86 jet fighter used in Korea, and he was program manager for the X-15 rocket plane, whose elite pilots included Neil Armstrong. When Apollo came along, Storms led the North American teams that won the contracts for two major pieces of the Moon ship: the second stage of the Saturn V and the command and service module.

Alfred Munier came to work at Grumman Aircraft on Long Island in 1943, helping design the company's renowned Navy fighters. These planes had to be especially rugged to survive the stress of landing on an aircraft carrier at sea. Now Grumman was applying this expertise to the lunar module, which would be landing in a place no one had ever gone, under circumstances that were hard to predict. As the head of Grumman's space projects, Munier picked one of his best engineers, Thomas Kelly, to lead development of this unique flying machine.

Meanwhile, at a Boeing Company facility in Louisiana, a dapper, bow-tie-wearing executive named George Stoner was in charge of designing and building the first stage of the Saturn V, with the mighty F-1 engines being supplied by the rocket division at North American. During World

War II, Stoner had been a test supervisor for the dauntingly complex B-29 bomber.

Even a Manhattan Project scientist was involved with Apollo. Nobel Prize–winning chemist Harold Urey had perfected the method for enriching uranium to serve as an atomic explosive. Now he had branched out from chemistry to pursue a hobby: discovering where the planets came from. Convinced that the Moon was the key to this mystery, Urey was eager to get his hands on a piece of the Moon to study in his laboratory. Promising to grant his wish, NASA made him a member of its Working Group on Lunar Exploration.

●

For the NASA engineers who had started it all—Max Faget and Wernher von Braun—it was time to see their concepts turned into working machines. From here on, they would have a supervisory role only, overseeing the efforts of America's hard-driving, hypercompetitive aerospace industries.

Although these companies were in the business of making a profit, they reverted to their World War II outlook and attitude. National survival had been at stake then. It was not that desperate now, but the space program was still something big—something much larger and more important than making a living.

Astronaut Gus Grissom got a glimpse of this spirit when he was touring manufacturing plants during the Mercury program. On a visit to the Convair factory in San Diego that was building the Atlas rocket, Grissom was asked to address hundreds of engineers and staff assembled in the auditorium. He hesitated at this surprise request. Even more sparing with words than General Phillips, he gathered his thoughts and said, "Do good work!" That was it.

The audience reacted as if each and every one of them had been promised a month of paid vacation. They cheered wildly and wouldn't stop. They knew that Gus's message was quite the opposite—that long hours and weekends on the job were ahead as they ironed out the kinks in a vehicle that was all too prone to explode on the pad. But they were primed for the challenge and so inspired by Gus's "speech" that they had posters printed with his image, message, and signature. "Do good work" signs spread to contractors all over the country, putting a real face on the goal of hundreds of thousands of workers. They were doing their best not just for the space program but for Gus, since it was his life that was on the line.

If Grissom's listeners responded like athletes at a coach's pep talk, that was because many of them were barely out of college. Most were in their twenties. One Convair engineer remembered, "We carried responsibilities for very major aspects of the Mercury program . . . on our relatively inexperienced shoulders, and it didn't faze us . . . Atlases blew up, and the next day we went to work and we sat down and tried again." Many were unmarried and practically lived at their offices. Even those with families rarely saw them during daylight, except maybe on Sunday, since it was assumed they would all show up for work on Saturday.

Like a well-oiled machine, the space program was no longer running by fits and starts. It was moving at a fast clip toward Kennedy's goal. There was still much ground to cover and many hair-raising turns ahead, but things were starting to look up for America's race to the Moon. The best-oiled component of all was the astronaut office. As the Mercury program was winding down, it had a new boss, and he was using a system he had picked up during the war to prepare his pilots for a mission like no other.

A common scene during Apollo. Technicians carefully check out a piece of space
hardware—in this case a two-man Gemini—to make sure it is ready for launch, 1966.

Map of Copernicus Crater by Pat Bridges

Margaret Hamilton with the Apollo guidance software

Pat Bridges uses an airbrush on her Copernicus map.

Baerbel Lucchitta sits in a lunar rover trainer.

BRIEFING:
The Women of Apollo

Women may have been excluded from the American astronaut corps, but they filled other vital roles in Apollo.

In the mid-1960s, a mathematician named Margaret Hamilton heard that the MIT Instrumentation Lab was hiring computer programmers to write the software to guide astronauts to the Moon. Programming was a brand-new field, but she already had experience writing code to solve problems in weather forecasting and air defense, so she applied. Hamilton started at the bottom and soon established herself as an expert in the system code that made all the software pieces work together—which they had to do flawlessly. Her code was so error-free that she rose to be manager of command module software and later of all Apollo spacecraft software.

Patricia Bridges had a degree in fine arts and was working as a scientific illustrator for the Air Force mapping center. One day in 1959, her boss asked her to prepare a shaded-relief map of the region around Copernicus Crater on the Moon, based on telescopic images. Her rendering was so lifelike—and accurate—that she was made lead illustrator for a complete set of lunar charts to be used by Apollo planners, scientists, and astronauts.

Born in Germany, Baerbel Lucchitta grew up amid the chaos and devastation of World War II. A U.S. government scholarship brought her to America, where she earned degrees in geology in the early 1960s and went to work for the U.S. Geological Survey. She became an expert on lunar science and taught Moon-bound astronauts what they needed to know about their destination. After they got back, she analyzed the mission data to help redefine our understanding of Earth's far-off companion.

There were more women—in engineering, applied mathematics, rocket propulsion, and other technical fields. But Apollo was a project of its era, and its openness to the female sex was perhaps best symbolized by the near total lack of women's restrooms at Mission Control in Houston. It was still a man's world.

PART 5
CREWS

Any crew can fly any mission.

—Deke Slayton, motto

Chief astronaut Deke Slayton (right) and astronaut Mike Collins have just landed in the T-38 jet behind them.

25

SQUADRON COMMANDER

After Deke Slayton was grounded for an irregular heartbeat in 1962, Al Shepard discussed the situation with the other astronauts and then approached Bob Gilruth. They wanted Slayton to be their chief, Shepard said. Deke might be ineligible to fly in space, but he could run the astronaut office and serve as their supervisor, much like a squadron commander.

Gilruth liked the idea—and so did Slayton, since it would keep him on the scene until the day when his heart problem cleared up and he could finally put on a space suit.

One of his new duties was choosing the crews that would fly in space. It was easy enough with the last Mercury flight, since Gordo Cooper was the only one of the Original Seven besides Slayton himself who hadn't flown. Slayton felt that it was Gordo's turn, plain and simple. But ahead lay the complexities of the Gemini program.

Originally known as Advanced Mercury, Gemini would be a slightly roomier but much more advanced capsule, taking two men on missions in Earth orbit of up to two weeks. Ultimately, ten manned Gemini flights would be launched at roughly two-month intervals, from 1965 through 1966. Each mission required four astronauts: a prime crew who would fly, plus a backup crew who would go through identical training and be available in case illness, accident, or some other mishap put members of the prime crew out of action. The idea was that nothing would delay the schedule. In the end, Gemini involved twenty-one individual astronauts in prime and backup roles—some flying more than once. It was quite a scheduling puzzle for Slayton, and it would only get more complicated with Apollo, which had a crew of three.

The problem was much like assembling crews for bombing sorties during the war. Back then, the squadron operations officer took account of who was on flying status, the slots that needed filling (pilot, copilot, bombardier, etc.), whose turn it was for a combat assignment, and any special requirements for that mission. A well-run squadron rotated airmen at an orderly rate, kept the unit up to strength, and held frequent training exercises. Slayton ran the astronaut office the same way. One of his rules was "any crew can fly any mission"—just as with his bomb group in Italy. If you were accepted by NASA and made it through initial training, then, as far as Slayton was concerned, you were eligible for anything that came up. Not that you would necessarily be picked, but you were eligible.

To keep the astronaut office up to strength, NASA selected new groups of pilot-astronauts in 1962, 1963, and 1966—at which point there were some fifty astronauts, including a handful of scientist-astronauts chosen in 1965. The '62 and '63 groups formed the core of Gemini and Apollo crews and included:

Astronaut Group Two, 1962. Front row, left to right: Conrad, Borman, Armstrong, Young. Back row: See, McDivitt, Lovell, White, Stafford.

1962 Astronaut Group

Neil A. Armstrong, civilian

Frank F. Borman II, U.S. Air Force

Charles "Pete" Conrad Jr., U.S. Navy

James A. Lovell Jr., U.S. Navy

James A. McDivitt, U.S. Air Force

Elliot M. See Jr., civilian

Thomas P. Stafford, U.S. Air Force

Edward H. White II, U.S. Air Force

John W. Young, U.S. Navy

1963 Astronaut Group

Edwin E. "Buzz" Aldrin Jr., U.S. Air Force

William A. Anders, U.S. Air Force

Astronaut Group Three, 1963. Front row, left to right: Aldrin, Anders, Bassett, Bean, Cernan, Chaffee. Back row: Collins, Cunningham, Eisele, Freeman, Gordon, Schweickart, Scott, Williams.

Charles A. Bassett II, U.S. Air Force

Alan L. Dean, U.S. Navy

Eugene A. Cernan, U.S. Navy

Roger B. Chaffee, U.S. Navy

Michael Collins, U.S. Air Force

R. Walter Cunningham, civilian

Donn F. Eisele, U.S. Air Force

Theodore C. Freeman, U.S. Air Force

Richard F. Gordon Jr., U.S. Navy

Russell L. "Rusty" Schweickart, civilian

David R. Scott, U.S. Air Force

Clifton C. "C.C." Williams, U.S. Marine Corps

In addition to this nucleus of twenty-three astronauts, three of the Original Seven were still active in 1964: Gus Grissom, Wally Schirra, and Gordo Cooper. Like Slayton, Al Shepard had been grounded due to a medical problem, and he took a new job as Deke's deputy. John Glenn and Scott Carpenter were pursuing other interests.

Of the new astronauts, all in the '62 group were experienced test pilots in the mold of the Original Seven. The '63 group featured a mix of test pilots, operational fighter pilots, and fighter-pilot-scientists. Interestingly, 80 percent of all NASA astronauts had been Boy Scouts in their younger years, and 16 percent had achieved the top rank of Eagle Scout.

Being an astronaut was a dangerous business. Four astronauts were killed in plane crashes before they had a chance to fly on Gemini or

Apollo. Three others would perish in an accident that almost derailed the Apollo program (recounted in a later chapter). For the '63 group, the loss rate was particularly high. More than a quarter died on the job, a mortality rate that was comparable to that of a combat tour with a bomber squadron during the war.

As new missions approached and Deke announced the crew assignments, astronauts tried to figure out his system. They understood that the key was to get a backup slot, which would clear the way for a seat on a future mission. But how did they land that coveted first assignment? Did buttering up the boss help? Did showing off their flying skills? Most applied the motto of Bill Anders from the '63 group: "Work your tail off, and someone will notice." But that did little to distinguish them from all of their equally ambitious colleagues. If only they had spent

Boy Scout Neil Armstrong (front row, standing next to the schoolmaster), around 1942

time in the operations tent back in southern Italy during the war, they would have understood Deke Slayton's art and science of assembling a crew.

Like a good squadron operations officer, Deke had a method. He always picked the commander first. The commander was the captain of the ship with the authority to make decisions during the flight, subject only to instructions from Mission Control; he also called the shots during training. Slayton gave careful thought to which astronauts would excel in this position. The other slots were filled through private consultation with the commander, aided by Deke's observations of who worked well together. But his principle that any crew could fly any mission meant that in theory anyone could fit in. After all, these were highly motivated professionals who would get the job done even if they didn't like each other.

Slayton also created a rotation system. If you were on a backup crew, you could usually expect to be tapped for a prime crew on the third mission after your backup assignment. For example, the Gemini 3 backup crew became the prime crew for Gemini 6, and the Gemini 4 backups took the prime slots for Gemini 7. A subordinate astronaut who did especially well on his mission could be promoted to commander on a later mission.

Always at the forefront of Slayton's thinking was that he was building a squadron with the skills and working relationships to go to the Moon.

●

Outside of NASA, Slayton's key role went largely unnoticed. Many reporters regarded him as a slightly sad figure. They could see he was staying in shape and keeping up with training in hopes of returning to flight status. But that seemed a forlorn hope, since more and more younger astronauts were coming on board. The press knew he was in charge, but they considered his administrative job a bureaucratic chore.

Furthermore, in interviews Deke made odd comments like, "Going to the Moon is going from point A to point B in a transportation system." There was no poetry or passion to him. Little did they realize, but this ineloquent man was directing the greatest spectacle ever made. He was choosing and coaching the men who would embark on history's most astounding adventure.

One journalist who did get a glimpse behind Slayton's deceptively dull surface was Oriana Fallaci, a feisty Italian writer who jetted around the world interviewing famous people. Like everyone else, she wanted to talk to Shepard and Glenn, but Deke was the chief astronaut, so she had to talk to him first. Naturally, she asked him how it felt to be kicked off his Mercury flight.

"Forgive me for bringing it up," she added.

"Everybody brings it up," he said with resignation. Then he recited the story he had told so many times, about his anger over the decision and his futile attempts to get it reversed.

Searching for another topic, Fallaci got him onto the subject of flying.

Slayton brightened up. "Anything that flies, I'll use it. I'd use an umbrella if an umbrella could fly." Astronauts were famously ignorant of current events, but this remark showed a surprising familiarity with popular culture, since the Disney movie *Mary Poppins* with its umbrella-piloting nanny was about to be released.

He continued: "I've been flying for twenty years. I was nineteen when I was a bomber pilot flying over Italy—"

Fallaci broke in: "Wait, wait, Italy?! And where were you bombing?"

"Here and there, everywhere. Naples. Tuscany. Florence, I remember. In October of '43."

Fallaci had a sick feeling. "Florence? In October of '43?"

"Yes. That cursed railroad."

Fallaci knew it too well. She had been there as a fourteen-year-old girl. Her house had been destroyed, and she had injured her foot getting away.

Slayton was shocked. "I'm sorry. I'm very sorry. It was my job."

"It was the war," she said. It was her turn to be resigned.

And they bonded over this tragedy. Oriana offered Deke a cigarette. He had given up smoking, but he accepted. Like millions of soldiers, he had smoked incessantly during the war. Now, for a moment, he was back, reliving the horror with one of war's innocent victims.

Cosmonaut Alexi Leonov makes history's first space walk, March 18, 1965.

26

THE MOON COMES INTO FOCUS

Sometimes NASA officials felt like the Union Army in the Civil War. During much of that conflict, Union forces in the East were outfoxed again and again by Confederate General Robert E. Lee, whose aggressive style invariably beat them to the punch. At his wit's end, President Lincoln sent for an officer who had been successful in another theater of the war, Ulysses S. Grant, and put him in charge of turning the tide against Lee.

Grant's first job was to convince his demoralized troops that Lee was not invincible. "Oh, I am heartily tired of hearing about what Lee is going to do," he scolded them. "Some of you always seem to think he is suddenly going to turn a double somersault, and land in our rear and on both of our flanks at the same time. Go back to your command, and try to think what we are going to do ourselves, instead of what Lee is going to do."

A century later, the Soviet space program was a lot like General Lee. Invariably, they beat Americans to the punch. They were the first to launch a satellite, the first to send a human into space, and the first to orbit two manned spaceships simultaneously. By 1963, they were in first, second, third, *and* fourth places in the duration of manned missions. (Gordo Cooper's Mercury flight was in fifth place.)

Soviet secrecy kept everyone guessing about their next moves, but one thing was certain: they were reading American newspapers. Alerted by reports of the planned two-seat Gemini spacecraft, they got the jump on the U.S. by launching *three* cosmonauts into orbit some five months before Gemini's inaugural flight (with Gus Grissom and John Young on Gemini 3 in March 1965).

They also knew about NASA's plans for a much-anticipated space spectacular—the moment when an astronaut in orbit would open the hatch and drift out into the void, protected only by a space suit and attached to his craft by a tenuous lifeline. This science-fiction-like feat, popularly known as a space walk but which NASA called "extravehicular activity," or EVA, was scheduled for one of the later Gemini flights. Not only would the EVA provide glorious pictures of an astronaut floating above the blue planet, but it was an indispensable skill for eventually going outside on the Moon.

True to form, the Soviets struck again. They chalked up the world's first EVA in March 1965, eleven weeks before NASA achieved the same feat with Ed White on Gemini 4, advancing its own schedule to try to keep up with the Russians.

"The Russians upstage us every time," an American astronaut lamented.

Premier Nikita Khrushchev was no longer on hand to taunt America. He had been deposed from power the previous year, but his enthusiasm for space lived on with the new leadership. One Soviet space official boldly hinted at the next step: "The target now before us is the Moon, and we hope to reach it in the not-distant future." Oddly enough, political tensions between the United States and Soviet Union were decreasing during this time, helped in part by the departure of Premier

Ed White floats above Earth on America's first space walk, June 3, 1965.

Khrushchev. But the competition in space was becoming fiercer than ever.

●

The Soviets were not just first in manned spaceflight, they were also leading the way in robotic missions. In September 1959, they were the first to hit the Moon with a probe. A month later, they were the first to photograph the far side of the Moon. The photos from the far side mission highlighted the amazing power of space probes, for the images showed the hemisphere of the Moon that is permanently turned away from Earth—something impossible to see without flying hundreds of thousands of miles, taking a series of pictures, and then relaying them by radio signal to Earth, which is exactly what the Soviet probe did.

Although America seemed permanently in second place, its efforts were nonetheless starting to pay off. After six failed attempts, NASA's Ranger program achieved a success in the summer of 1964 when Ranger 7 crashed into the Moon's Sea of Clouds. On the way down it sent back a continuous stream of pictures as it hurtled toward a possible Apollo landing area. Ranger's close-up views were a thousand times better than those from the largest telescopes, and they held good news and bad. The good: lunar dust didn't seem nearly as thick as some scientists had feared. The bad: craters were present at all scales—craters on top of craters on top of craters. The nearer Ranger got, the more craters showed up. Obviously, finding a reasonably flat place to land would be challenging.

NASA adviser Harold Urey suggested the Sea of Tranquility for Ranger's next target. In February 1965, Ranger 8 duly dove into this region, finding it similar to the Sea of Clouds. One area near its southwestern edge offered an expanse of safe-looking terrain that seemed promising for an early Apollo landing site.

A final Ranger expedition took off in March 1965, two days before Grissom and Young's Gemini 3 flight. The highlight of this mission was not the science but the show, aired live on network television. The program put millions of viewers in the driver's seat of Ranger 9, watching the Moon get closer and closer, picture by picture, as the craft plummeted toward self-destruction. Americans viewing at home felt like participants in a thrilling voyage of discovery. Calling it "one of the dramatic moments in television history," an awestruck journalist wrote: "For the first time earthbound people found themselves figuratively transported through space and hurtling toward the Moon at 6,000 miles per hour."

Another newspaper looked ahead to the even more spectacular show to come. "The time is not distant," this reporter prophesied, "when

One of the first views of the Moon's far side—impossible to see from Earth— photographed by a Soviet space probe in October 1959

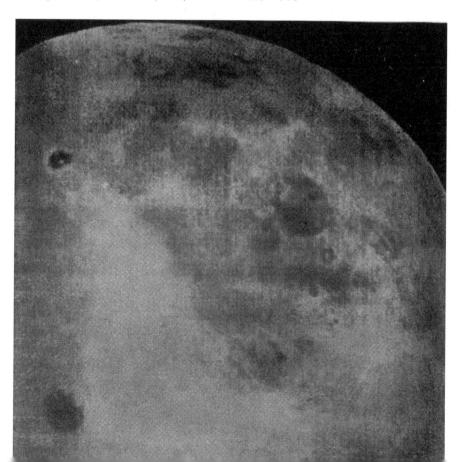

the first men will emerge from a spaceship, carrying cameras with them. Millions all over the world will be able to follow their progress on television as the lunar explorers take man's first step outside the terrestrial sphere. That will be the television show of the century." In his speech announcing the Apollo program, President Kennedy had promised, "In a very real sense, it will not be one man going to the Moon . . . it will be an entire nation."

●

Keeping up the pressure, the next year the Soviets were the first to soft-land a robotic probe on the Moon. Their craft set down in the Ocean of Storms, another of the Moon's bone-dry seas. A soft landing is the most difficult step of all in lunar exploration. Two months later, in April 1966, they scored another coup by putting the first satellite into orbit around the Moon. This would be a crucial maneuver for lunar-orbit rendezvous.

As usual, America was not far behind. In early June, NASA's Surveyor 1 fired its braking rocket and made a gentle touchdown some 400 miles from the Russian landing site. And in mid-August, Lunar Orbiter 1 began circling the Moon, photographing the landscape below in search of more landing possibilities for Apollo. Additional Surveyors and Lunar Orbiters followed.

Also during this time, Gemini missions were going up at an unprecedented rate—an average of one every nine and half weeks—giving American astronauts crucial experience in the complex art of spaceflight. Like General Grant in a much earlier contest, NASA was doing its best to turn the tide.

The American probe Lunar Orbiter 1 records the far side of the Moon, with the crescent Earth in the distance, August 1966.

After a near disaster in space, Neil Armstrong (right) and Dave Scott (left) sit inside their Gemini capsule, assisted by the rescue team, 1966.

27

NEIL ARMSTRONG'S WILD RIDE

During the first few Gemini flights, space rendezvous proved trickier than astronauts had expected. As pilots, their instinct was to accelerate when catching up with a target. But in space, putting on the gas causes the spacecraft to rise to a higher orbit, where it moves *more slowly* than the target. (The higher the orbit, the slower a satellite travels, since gravity grows weaker with distance.) The correct procedure is to *decelerate*, dropping to a lower and therefore faster orbit than the target. When the spacecraft catches up, it must adjust its orbit to be exactly the same as that of the target. Furthermore, the rendezvous must take place under the right lighting conditions, which requires careful timing. The astronauts had trained for all of this, but they still found it frustratingly difficult.

Another difficulty was that Gemini's unmanned target vehicle, a specially adapted Agena rocket stage, was having technical problems. Launched separately from Gemini, Agena was the proxy command module to Gemini's lunar module, designed to re-create the rendezvous and docking circumstances that astronauts would encounter around

A Gemini spacecraft in orbit, photographed from another Gemini during the first space rendezvous, 1965

the Moon. On its much-delayed first launch, Agena blew up. Undaunted, the Gemini astronauts practiced rendezvous—but not docking—with another Gemini spacecraft that had been launched on a separate mission. Not until Gemini 8, the sixth piloted mission, in March 1066, did an Agena finally arrive in orbit, ready for the first rendezvous-and-docking attempt.

Gemini 8 was commanded by Neil Armstrong, teamed with copilot Dave Scott. Aided by radar and a simple onboard computer, Armstrong made rendezvous and docking look easy. After executing a series of precise orbital changes by firing thrusters with a hand controller, he closed in on

Piloted by Neil Armstrong, the Gemini 8 spacecraft approaches an Agena rocket stage (center) prior to the first docking in space, March 1966. Shortly after, the linked vehicles began to gyrate out of control.

Agena during Gemini's fourth revolution around the Earth. Given the final go-ahead, he nudged the spacecraft's nose into Agena's docking collar until capture latches engaged. Announcing, "We are docked!" he added with test pilot nonchalance, "Yes, it's really a smoothie." Back in Houston, mission controllers cheered. This was a space first for America.

Armstrong was relieved that his hardest task of the mission was over. Then, half an hour later, Scott noticed that the two linked vehicles were starting to gyrate slowly. Armstrong righted the situation with his hand controller, but then it started again, growing worse. Assuming the problem was with Agena's control system, which he had been warned about, Armstrong undocked. This only made the oscillations increase, and the Gemini spacecraft soon began tumbling at a rate that approached one revolution per second—about the speed of a figure skater, with arms outstretched, at the start of an Olympic-class spin. Like the skater, Gemini's rotational speed seemed headed for a dizzying finale.

"We have serious problems here," Scott radioed the ground.

Armstrong explained, "We're rolling up and we can't turn anything off. Continuously increasing in a left roll." Both men sounded eerily calm.

Scott later described the event as "like being on a theme-park ride which thrills passengers by spinning at high speed, except theme-park rides don't spin so fast or for so long—if they did, too many passengers would black out."

Close to blacking out themselves, the astronauts diagnosed the problem as a malfunction in their maneuvering system, which consisted of sixteen small thrusters arrayed around the spacecraft. One of the thrusters was stuck and wouldn't stop firing. Fighting vertigo and tunnel vision, and with checklists and other loose items plastered against the walls of the spacecraft from centrifugal force, Armstrong managed to shut down the entire system and activate special thrusters for orienting the spacecraft during reentry. Using these, he gradually got the capsule under control. Mission rules required that they now return to Earth, since they couldn't risk losing more reentry fuel.

And so the flight of Gemini 8 ended prematurely but with two big accomplishments: rendezvous and docking had been demonstrated for the first time, and two coolheaded astronauts had solved the most serious crisis yet in space.

It had been a close call. On the ground, mission controller Bob Carlton, a slow-talking engineer from Alabama who rarely got excited about anything, quickly grasped that the astronauts had been fighting for their lives. "I thought they were gone," he said afterward, calling it one of the most terrifying experiences of his career. Three years later, Carlton would have another hair-raising moment with Armstrong.

Gemini 8 was followed by four more Gemini missions. Surprisingly, the entire Gemini manned program—ten flights stretching from March 1965 to November 1966—took place without a single spaceflight by Soviet cosmonauts. The Russians had preempted the first Gemini mission by a few days with their spectacular space walk, but then they launched no manned missions for the next two years. Given their previous pace of activity, this pause was hard to understand—but nonetheless welcomed, since NASA was now starting to take the lead in the space race.

The agency racked up multiple successes with rendezvous and docking, and also large orbital changes using the Agena engine to propel the docked spacecraft to new heights. Both were crucial techniques for a lunar mission, and the Soviets had done nothing like it. Project Gemini also bested the Russians with the longest-duration spaceflight to date (two weeks, proving that astronauts could survive the minimum eight days of lunar landing roundtrip without ill physical effects); record-breaking space walks (paving the way for lunar field trips); demonstrations of guided reentry (the only way to reduce g-forces to a survivable level when returning from the Moon); and an altitude record of 850 miles (only a third of a percent of the way to the Moon, but a dizzying height for the time).

Even while Gemini was under way, Apollo missions were lining up in the schedule. Deke Slayton had assembled six crews to handle the first three manned Apollo missions, projected for 1967. None would yet go to

Gemini 12—the last of the Gemini series—blasts off in November 1966. Apollo missions were due to start in early 1967.

the Moon, since these early missions would be test flights in Earth orbit of various crucial components. But it was a good guess that Deke's prime crew for the eventual first lunar landing would be picked from among these eighteen astronauts. With the commander listed first, the crews were:

Apollo 1
Prime crew: Gus Grissom, Ed White, Roger Chaffee
Backup: Wally Schirra, Donn Eisele, Walt Cunningham

Apollo 2
Prime crew: Jim McDivitt, Dave Scott, Rusty Schweickart
Backup: Tom Stafford, John Young, Gene Cernan

Apollo 3
Prime crew: Frank Borman, Mike Collins, Bill Anders
Backup: Pete Conrad, Dick Gordon, C.C. Williams

Based on the importance that Slayton placed on the commander, the top-ranked astronauts in his calculations were Gus Grissom, Wally Schirra, Jim McDivitt, Tom Stafford, Frank Borman, and Pete Conrad. Grissom and Schirra were both Mercury and Gemini veterans; Stafford and Conrad had each flown two Gemini missions; and Borman had commanded the record-breaking two-week Gemini flight. The other twelve astronauts were half Gemini veterans, half rookies.

Under Deke's rotation system, a backup crew could expect to skip ahead three missions to the next prime assignment, while the original prime crew became the backup for that mission. In theory, the six crews could keep rotating like this through Apollos 4, 5, 6, and beyond, honing their skills as the hardware was put through its paces in Earth orbit, then near the Moon, and finally on the Moon. Slayton had the option of changing the crews as the Moon landing got closer, sidelining some members and choosing replacements from the remaining pool of astronauts. The important thing was that he now had the system in place to deliver a flight-ready crew for the first lunar landing whenever it was needed—just as during the war his squadron could deliver well-trained crews for any combat mission assigned by headquarters.

Conspicuously missing from his Apollo roster was the heroic commander of Gemini 8: Neil Armstrong.

Apollo 1 crew. Left to right: Gus Grissom, Ed White, and Roger Chaffee.

28

"FIRE IN THE COCKPIT"

Ever since Project Mercury, the media had warned about all the ways that spaceflight could kill astronauts. Launch was the most obvious danger, but reentry was just as risky, and Armstrong and Scott on Gemini 8 had experienced the perils of a minor malfunction in orbit—a simple stuck thruster—that nearly doomed them. At NASA, astronauts, engineers, managers, public affairs officials—everyone—was primed for a tragedy sooner or later, but no one expected the disaster that came.

●

Oxygen is one of the essential requirements for human life. We get it from the air, where it is only one-fifth of any given breath we take; the rest is mostly nitrogen, which we don't need. In a spacecraft, the simplest solution is to skip the nitrogen and fill the cabin with oxygen only—pure oxygen.

A big advantage to this approach is that the cabin pressure can be greatly reduced from ordinary sea-level pressure, since pure oxygen at a lower pressure still gives you all you need. The payoff is that lower cabin pressure means the spacecraft structure can weigh less, since it doesn't have to withstand fifteen pounds per square inch (sea-level pressure) against the vacuum of space. So like the Mercury and Gemini capsules before it, Apollo was designed for a pure-oxygen environment at five pounds per square inch.

The disadvantage of pure oxygen is an increased risk of fire. Most materials need oxygen to burn, and they burn hotter and faster in pure oxygen. However, this problem seemed to be offset by the peculiar behavior of fire in space. Studies suggested that a fire would quickly burn itself out, because the convection currents that feed it don't operate in weightlessness. Just to be safe, NASA ordered that flammable materials be kept to a minimum in the Apollo capsule.

Therefore, fire wasn't on anyone's mind on January 27, 1967, when Apollo 1 astronauts Gus Grissom, Ed White, and Roger Chaffee were sealed into the command module for a simulated countdown at Cape Kennedy in preparation for Apollo's first manned mission—a two-week test of the CSM in Earth orbit, set for the following month. The biggest worry was a frustrating series of equipment problems that had to be worked out before launch day.

The CSM sat atop von Braun's Saturn IB, the largest rocket yet to carry humans, although it was a baby compared to the Saturn V. The rocket was not fueled that day, so the test was not considered hazardous. It should have been, since the cabin was filled with pure oxygen, not at the five pounds per square inch to be used in space, but at the fifteen pounds per square inch at sea level. In fact, the pressure was set a bit higher than sea-level pressure to reveal any leaks in the spacecraft. It was an explosive situation. At seventeen pounds per square inch, practically anything will burn in pure oxygen, even aluminum metal. All it takes is a spark.

Every Mercury and Gemini had been tested on the launchpad with high-pressure oxygen. But they were much smaller spacecraft, much simpler, and with far less wiring.

Somewhere in Apollo's thirty miles of wire a spark jumped between two bare leads where insulation had broken off. In the oxygen-saturated atmosphere, nearby Velcro strips and nylon netting ignited like tissue paper. The netting, which was designed to catch fallen objects, extended throughout the cabin and acted like a trail of spilled gasoline. The fire spread so quickly that the astronauts barely had time to react.

"We've got a fire in the cockpit," one reported tersely. Two of them immediately scrambled to open the hatch, which was impossible against the rising pressure generated by the blaze. Seconds later, all three lost consciousness from the toxic gases and died soon after, thankfully before the raging inferno burned through their space suits.

By the time rescue workers reached the scene, the capsule had burst open and was spouting flames and smoke. The responders did their best to save the crew, but it took five minutes to unbolt the hatch. One glance inside told them it was too late. A reporter who saw the spaceship afterward said it looked like "the cockpit of an aircraft in World War II that took a direct hit."

Aviation veterans were reminded of a catastrophe twenty-four years earlier. In 1943, another mammoth technological project had suffered a similar gruesome setback when a prototype of the B-29 bomber

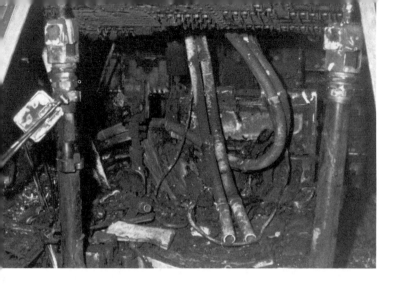

The burned-out Apollo 1 cabin, January 1967. The astronauts' bodies have been removed.

crashed in Seattle, killing thirty-one people. Straining to produce enough power, one of the engines on the super-bomber had burst into flames. With World War II under way, America badly needed advanced weapons, but critics thought the B-29 was impossibly complicated and recklessly being rushed into production.

Now, many felt the same way about Apollo. In the wake of the fire, there were calls to slow down the Moon-landing program or even end it. Walter Lippmann, the most influential newspaper columnist of the day, argued that the success of robotic probes like Ranger and Surveyor proved that humans were not needed in space. "We should abandon the idea of landing a man on the Moon by some arbitrary date," he wrote, "and we should put our minds on the use of machines, already spectacularly promising, to increase our knowledge of the Moon and the space around it." J. William Fulbright, a powerful senator from Arkansas, shared this view. He blamed the fire on "the inflexible, but meaningless, goal of putting an American on the Moon by 1970" and demanded a "full reappraisal of the space program." A handful of others in Congress agreed with him. They were the voices of common sense that had been resisting the lure of human spaceflight since the beginning.

Jim Webb and other top NASA officials were at a diplomatic event in Washington on the day of the accident. President Lyndon Johnson had zealously backed the space program since he assumed the presidency after Kennedy's assassination, and on January 27 he happened to be hosting the signing of an international treaty on the peaceful uses of outer space, marking an easing of Cold War tensions. News of the fire arrived as post-signing celebrations were under way. Everyone was stunned. Some stayed for dinner, but General Phillips and Bob Gilruth immediately left for the Cape to get the full story, while Webb, Seamans, and Mueller went to NASA headquarters to handle the crisis. One badly shaken aerospace official observed, "This is the dreadful price you have to pay in a business like this."

That evening, Webb held a press conference: "We've always known something like this would happen sooner or later," he said, "but it's not going to be permitted to stop the program." Then he brought up the circumstance that made the blow so much worse: "Although everyone realized that someday space pilots would die, who would have thought the first tragedy would be on the ground?"

Astronaut Frank Borman thought the same thing. One of Slayton's Apollo commanders, he later recalled how the accident affected him and his colleagues: "Three superbly trained pilots had died, trapped during a supposedly routine ground test that shouldn't have been any more dangerous than taking a bath. I don't think the grief would have been any less if they had perished in space, but at least it would have been more logical and half-expected."

At Webb's direction, Bob Seamans assembled a review board to investigate the fire. Seamans tapped Borman to represent the astronaut corps and Max Faget to cover spacecraft engineering, together with seven other experts. The night after he inspected the burned-out capsule for the first time, Borman was so overcome that he went out drinking with Faget and Slayton. The three disciplined, dignified men offered toast after toast to Gus, Ed, and Roger. They perhaps overdid it. The agile Faget decided to demonstrate handstands, and they ended the evening by throwing their glasses against the wall.

"It was right out of a World War I movie," Borman wrote. "The only thing we left out was the bravado toast, 'Here's to the next man to die.'"

The review board discovered that work on the command module had been hasty, with large and small problems piling up. It was an impressive ship—in theory. At North American Aviation, the prime contractor, they proudly referred to it as "a labyrinth of systems more complicated than an aircraft carrier packed into a stainless-steel phone booth." But like the B-29 before it, the CM was pushing the state of the art and courting trouble.

At Faget's suggestion, ground operations from then on would be

Max Faget (foreground) and Frank Borman inside a command module mock-up during their investigation of the Apollo 1 fire, 1967

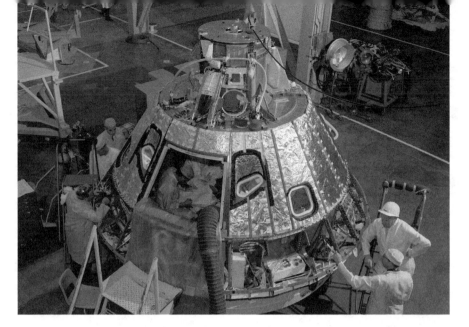

The Apollo 1 command module under construction at North American Aviation, 1966

conducted in nitrogen-rich air, which is far less of a fire hazard. In space, the capsule would operate, as designed, with pure oxygen, but made safer by more stringent rules about flammable materials and wiring. The board also recommended a new hatch that would be much easier for the crew to open.

But the most significant change was something not mandated by the board: a renewed commitment to perfection by all 400,000 people working on Apollo. The new spirit was summed up by Chief Flight Director Gene Kranz. "Spaceflight will never tolerate carelessness, incapacity, and neglect," he told his Mission Control team. "Somewhere, somehow, we screwed up . . . We were rolling the dice, hoping that things would come together by launch day, when in our hearts we knew it would take a miracle . . . From this day forward, Flight Control will be known by two words: *tough* and *competent*. *Tough* means we are forever accountable for what we do or what we fail to do . . . *Competent* means we will never take anything for granted." He closed by ordering that their two watchwords—*tough* and *competent*—be written on every blackboard in every office. "Each day when you enter the room these words will remind you of the price paid by Grissom, White, and Chaffee."

Saturn V emerges from the Vehicle Assembly Building. Note the three workers along the railing at lower right.

29

"GO, BABY, GO!"

"The guys who are going to fly the first lunar missions are the guys in this room." As usual, Deke Slayton was getting right to the point. It was Monday, April 10, 1967—ten weeks since the fire. Deke had called a meeting of his six Apollo crews to get them ready for the tasks ahead.

With the death of Grissom's crew, Slayton had moved their backups into the prime slot for the first manned Apollo mission and readjusted the other assignments. At the end of the line, he added a new crew, picking three astronauts he had been holding in reserve: Neil Armstrong as commander, teamed with Jim Lovell and Buzz Aldrin. The eighteen potential Moon explorers sat around the small conference room, keeping their thoughts to themselves. Gene Cernan was awed but psyched. Walt Cunningham felt at "the climax of a grand competition." Both John Young and Neil Armstrong believed their boss was simply stating the obvious. "Who else would be doing it, flying the first lunar missions, besides us?" wondered Young.

But one thing was certain: in the entire history of exploration, no one had been able to make a promise like this—until now.

●

Issuing his standard warning—"Be flexible, this stuff will change"— Slayton outlined the schedule. A series of unmanned flights up through Apollo 6 would test the Saturn V, the command and service module, and the lunar module before hazarding a manned Apollo flight with the improved CSM, to be designated Apollo 7. Slayton sketched the goals and announced the crew assignments:

Apollo 7
Prime crew: Wally Schirra, Donn Eisele, Walt Cunningham
Backup: Tom Stafford, John Young, Gene Cernan
Mission: Run the CSM through its paces in Earth orbit. Test the Apollo navigation system and guidance computer.

Apollo 8
Prime crew: Jim McDivitt, Dave Scott, Rusty Schweickart
Backup: Pete Conrad, Dick Gordon, C.C. Williams
Mission: Test the CSM and LM in Earth orbit, to be launched separately by two Saturn IBs (later reassigned to a single Saturn V).

Apollo 9
Prime crew: Frank Borman, Mike Collins, Bill Anders
Backup: Neil Armstrong, Jim Lovell, Buzz Aldrin
Mission: Simulate a lunar mission with the CSM and LM in a high Earth orbit, scheduled to be the first manned flight of a Saturn V.

If all went well, then the next mission, Apollo 10, could conceivably be the first lunar-landing attempt, giving the prize to Stafford's crew, assuming that the three-mission rotation system was followed. However, the achievement of Kennedy's goal was more likely to happen on

Apollo 11, 12, 13, or 14. Enough hardware was being ordered for missions through Apollo 20.

The CSM and LM could be perfect in every way, but if the Saturn V didn't work, the Moon landings were off. Webb and Mueller pressed for a test flight as soon as possible to show Congress that Apollo was back on track.

At the time of the Apollo 1 fire in January 1967, all three stages of the first Saturn V were at the Cape to be checked out. Problems kept cropping up. Repairs, new checks, and more modifications extended into the summer. Then much of the fall was taken up with an elaborate rehearsal of the countdown. Only in early November was the Saturn V finally ready for its maiden flight—a risky trial of all three stages at once, carrying an unmanned CSM. This all-up approach was General Phillips's brainchild and George Mueller's decreed policy, designed to save time. Although von Braun went along with it, he was still worried that the tactic courted disaster.

Saturn V (lower right) leaves the assembly building on its 3.5-mile journey to the launchpad.

Phillips and von Braun had had their differences before. During World War II, Phillips piloted an escort fighter on a bombing raid over von Braun's rocket base. Now, the former enemies were colleagues and friends, with utmost respect for each other's dedication and organizational abilities. On the morning of November 9, they stood together in the firing room as the countdown approached 7:00 a.m.—launch time for an event that would make them either heroes or scapegoats. The Saturn V was three and a half miles away. At that distance, you could reach out your arm and blot out the Moon rocket with the width of your little finger. This was the closest that observers were allowed to get to a missile that packed the explosive power of a small atomic bomb.

A few seconds before the count reached zero, the base of the rocket erupted in billowing fire, signaling the start of the ignition sequence. On television, the brilliant light flooded the sensors of the TV camera, making it look like a catastrophic explosion. Then at zero, the mighty rocket started to lift off the pad, propelled by seven and a half million pounds of thrust. It took ten seconds to clear the launch tower—"the longest ten seconds of my life," recalled von Braun, who was shouting, "Go, baby, go!" in his German accent.

At this point, the sound waves from the rocket reached the launch center and press viewing area: "a continuous, pulsating clap of deep thunder," wrote one reporter. With it came bone rattling vibrations like those from an earthquake.

"My God, our building's shaking!" Walter Cronkite of *CBS Evening News* exclaimed over live television. As ceiling tiles rained down and soft-drink bottles clattered to the floor, Cronkite pushed against the plate-glass window to hold it in place.

He couldn't keep his eyes off the spectacle outside. "Look at that rocket go!" he yelled. "Into the clouds at 3,000 feet! The roar is terrific!"

Upward it went, devouring kerosene and liquid oxygen at a rate of fifteen tons per second. Growing lighter as it ascended, while its thrust stayed nearly constant, the thirty-six-story-tall vehicle gained speed. After just over a minute, it was traveling Mach 1 at an altitude of four and a half miles. It would need to go twenty-five times faster and higher before it reached Earth orbit.

At two and a half minutes, the first stage ran out of propellant and dropped away. The second stage ignited, burning liquid hydrogen and liquid oxygen, one of the most potent combinations known. The Saturn V was a hybrid of old and new, with its first stage of five F-1 engines drawing on technology from the 1950s, while its upper stages used more innovative engines designed to handle liquid hydrogen, which is even colder than liquid oxygen. The challenge of developing the second stage had led to long delays before Saturn V's test flight. Developed by North American Aviation, under Harrison Storm's direction, the second stage behaved beautifully, burning for six minutes and taking the ship to an altitude of over a hundred miles.

At this point, the rocket stack was traveling parallel to Earth's surface, 900 miles downrange, at nearly 90 percent of orbital velocity. The third stage ignited for two and half minutes to push the vehicle into orbit. Then it shut off.

On a lunar mission, the CSM and third stage, with the LM nestled between them, would make an orbit and a half. Then the third stage would fire again, propelling the stack to the Moon. On this flight, there was no LM, but a crucial goal was to test the restart capability of the third stage. It reignited and put the CSM into a highly elliptical orbit for the final challenge—a simulation of Apollo's return to Earth. With

an additional boost from the service module engine, the spacecraft plunged back into the atmosphere, reaching a top speed of 25,000 miles per hour, subjecting the heat shield to temperatures double those experienced by reentering Mercury and Gemini capsules.

The test flight ended as the charred but intact command module parachuted to an on-target landing in the Pacific Ocean, almost nine hours after liftoff.

●

Marvin Miles, aerospace editor for the *Los Angeles Times*, had witnessed nuclear explosions and ridden with pilots breaking the sound barrier, but he had never experienced anything like this. He summed up what was at stake: "Had the critical test failed in a giant burst of flame equivalent to one million pounds of TNT, it would have obliterated all U.S. hope of landing astronauts on the Moon by 1970, surrendered the space lead to Russia, and dealt a staggering blow to American technology and national prestige."

Instead, it had dazzled the world, renewed public confidence in NASA, and proved the wisdom of the all-up strategy. And it had taken place the week of the fiftieth anniversary of the Communist Revolution in Russia—the supposed target date for the Soviets' own Moon landing. There was still much to do before America reached that goal, but Russia appeared to be far behind.

"Apollo is on the way to the Moon," proclaimed Sam Phillips. The normally impassive general could hardly stop smiling.

The first Saturn V takes off just after dawn on November 9, 1967.

New NASA manager Tom Paine holds a model of the lunar module, 1968.

30

THE SUBMARINER TAKES CHARGE

After World War II, the fearless submariner Tom Paine was assigned to help disarm enemy subs. During this time, he visited Hiroshima and Nagasaki, the two cities destroyed by atomic bombs. "If you can visualize a molten streetcar," he wrote his parents, "or an area miles square with no object bigger than a fireplace log in it, where it is impossible to tell where the streets and buildings were located, where some 80,000 people were living one second and completely disintegrated along with all their buildings the next, if you can visualize this, you can imagine the process of the atomic bomb." This powerful memory stuck with him for life.

Paine's duties included boarding Japanese submarines, still bristling with weapons as they came into port to surrender. In one case, his small boat approached a sub larger than any in the world. This was the I-400 class, a superweapon able to carry three airplanes. It could maneuver close to a target, surface, and launch a surprise air attack. America had nothing like it. The Japanese planned to use four such vessels to bomb the Panama Canal, the U.S. Navy's vital link between the Atlantic and Pacific oceans. In the end, the Japanese realized that attacking the canal would make no difference in the war, and the supersubs never saw action.

Captured Japanese supersub *I–400*, which Tom Paine navigated from Japan to Hawaii at the end of World War II

A nautical romantic, Paine said that inspecting the supersub was like "carrying out a classic naval 'boarders, away!' operation." "Boarders away!" was the traditional order to scramble aboard an enemy ship. In the old days, the boarding party was armed with cutlasses and pistols. Paine's operation was not quite so dramatic, but it had its elements of suspense. As he and his men toured the giant vessel, they were "wary of the impassive Japanese who stiffly greeted us, curious about the unfamiliar aircraft handling equipment all around us, delighted to be directly involved in this historic finale of the undersea war, and concerned about both the technical and human problems involved in carrying out our orders to disable her torpedo, ordnance, and radio gear before bringing her in." The operation culminated in a 4,500-mile voyage, delivering one of the supersubs to Pearl Harbor. During the journey, Paine was second-in-command, which was his highest military posting—"a fitting finale to my career in the Submarine Service," he wrote.

Twenty-three years later, in 1968, he found himself second-in-command of an even more thrilling enterprise.

In the months after the Apollo 1 fire, NASA deputy administrator Bob Seamans felt he was no longer trusted by his boss, Jim Webb. Traumatized by the deaths of the three astronauts, Webb wanted to make sure it didn't happen again, and he sought out any institutional weaknesses at NASA. If anything, Seamans was a tower of strength, but he knew he had lost his close working relationship with Webb, who blamed part of the negligence that had led to the tragedy on him. Therefore, Seamans resigned to go back to teaching at MIT. The search for his replacement turned up a brilliant executive at the General Electric Company: Tom Paine.

Since his submarine days, Paine had held a series of important jobs at General Electric. Most recently, he headed its innovative think tank, TEMPO, which concentrated on social and technological problems of the future and how they might be solved. When offered the number two spot at NASA, he said yes, in part because he felt the tug of something familiar about the organization. He couldn't put his finger on it, but his wife, Barbara, did.

They had fallen in love during the war, when she was a ground controller for the Royal Australian Air Force in Perth, his submarine's home port. After Barbara and Tom's first tour of NASA installations, she pointed out how the total commitment in the space program was the same spirit they remembered from the war. "These are the RAF types who have just come back from battling the Luftwaffe," she said, "these are the young submariners in Perth," thinking only of the next mission, "taking risks and fighting odds and really doing exciting things."

"It was absolutely true," Paine said later. The experience of working at NASA was "a great recharging of my battery."

●

Paine was nominated to be NASA's deputy administrator almost exactly a year after the fire. In Jim Webb's mind, it was just a matter of time until Paine filled his own shoes. Webb hadn't told anyone, but he was planning to retire from government service. It may seem odd to leave when the organization you have nurtured for seven difficult years is on the verge of its greatest accomplishments, but Webb had mixed feelings about staying. President Johnson had told him he would not be running for reelection in 1968. Whoever was elected that fall would see Webb as Johnson's man and want him replaced. It was vitally important to Webb that someone of Paine's caliber succeed him, and the former submariner had a good chance of being promoted to the top job by the new president, whoever it was.

Plus, the inquiry following the fire had worn Webb down. Congress and the press had searched under every rock for a scandal connected to him. Inevitably, some contracts and political deals were questioned.

They were typical of Webb's no-holds-barred management style, which made him so effective in Washington, where it is notoriously difficult to get things done. Nothing came of these probes. Still, the intense scrutiny meant that Webb had lost his clout with Congress. His turn to resign had come. Privately, he told Johnson he wanted to leave on his sixty-second birthday, October 7, 1968. When the day came, Paine took charge as acting administrator.

A month later, John F. Kennedy's old antagonist, Richard M. Nixon, was elected president in a close contest with the Democratic nominee, Vice President Hubert H. Humphrey. As Nixon's administration was settling in during the following spring, the new secretary of defense, Melvin Laird, called the new secretary of the Air Force, none other than Bob Seamans, and asked him whether Tom Paine should officially be made NASA administrator.

"I can give you a very straightforward, simple answer," Seamans told Laird. "Ask the president if he wants to carry out the lunar landing this year. If he does, make Tom Paine the administrator. But if he wants to run the risk of not going this year, then bring in somebody else."

Tom Paine got the appointment.

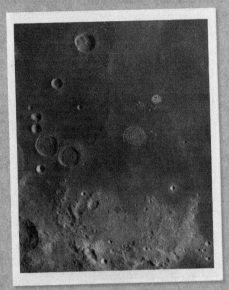

Western Sea of Tranquility from Lunar Orbiter 4, 1967. Apollo Landing Site 2 is in the lower right quadrant. This image is 165 miles across. (Note Moltke Crater at the lower right, also visible in the photos on pages 290 and 291.)

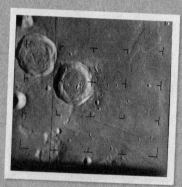

Ranger 8 on its death dive into the Sea of Tranquility, 1965. The two large craters at left are also in the Lunar Orbiter image above.

Ranger 8 two seconds before impact. The image is less than a mile across. The strip of static at right marks the end of transmission on crashing.

Surveyor 5 takes a surface photo from the Sea of Tranquility, 1965.

BRIEFING:
Lunar Reconnaissance

When automatic probes began arriving at the Moon to scout promising landing sites for Apollo, they concentrated on the band along the lunar equator. This region is easier to reach from Earth than are the higher latitudes. Therefore, robotic spacecraft searched there first.

Fortunately, some of the dark areas of the Moon, called lunar "seas," overlap the equator. Telescopic observations showed that these areas are flatter and less heavily cratered than the bright, rugged highlands, and so would make better landing sites, particularly for the crucial early missions. The designation "seas" traces to the pioneering era of telescopes, when the dark spots were thought to be bodies of water. Eventually, it was realized they are dry land, but the original term stuck.

From 1965 to 1967, four Ranger missions successfully crashed into the Moon, five Surveyors soft-landed, and five Lunar Orbiters circled, providing thousands of photographs at all scales. The Apollo site-selection board zeroed in on five potential landing zones that seemed to pose the fewest hazards. Moving from east to west, two were in the Sea of Tranquility, one was in the Central Bay at the Moon's geographic center, and two more were in the Ocean of Storms.

For a variety of reasons, the landing site in the western sector of the Sea of Tranquility was the best option. The selection board called it Apollo Landing Site 2. The automatic probes had found plenty of candidates for more challenging and geologically intriguing missions, once astronauts had a couple of successful landings to their credit. But for the purpose of achieving Kennedy's goal, Landing Site 2 looked like the place to go.

PART 6
THE MOON

"12 02 alarm! 12 02, what's that?"
—Mission controller during Apollo 11 landing, 1969

The surface of the Moon

Apollo 8 mission patch

31

A NEW MISSION TAKES SHAPE

"**A**re you out of your *mind*?" Webb shouted into the receiver.

Two months before he retired as NASA administrator, Jim Webb received a phone call from Apollo program director General Sam Phillips. The normally levelheaded general had floated an idea that made Webb question his sanity.

For his part, General Phillips was grateful that the conversation was taking place by long distance. "If a person's shock could be transmitted over the telephone," he recalled, "I'd probably have been shot in the head."

Also on the line was deputy administrator Tom Paine, who agreed that Webb was "horrified."

What was up?

That summer of 1968, Kennedy's goal of putting a man on the Moon by December 31, 1969, was looking more and more doubtful, since work on the lunar module was falling behind. The LM was unique. No one had ever designed a manned vehicle to land on another world. Not surprisingly, problems kept cropping up, delaying the crucial first manned flight of the LM. This test of the LM's systems, scheduled to take place in Earth orbit on Apollo 8, was now postponed until the winter of 1969, delaying other milestones that had to be reached before humans could walk on the Moon.

These other goals included perfecting techniques for navigation and communications between Earth and the Moon, testing the procedure for entering and leaving lunar orbit, certifying the safety of Apollo landing sites by visual observations from orbit, and demonstrating manned reentry into Earth's atmosphere at 24,200 miles per hour, the speed of a spacecraft returning from the Moon.

However, one NASA official saw the LM's troubles as an opportunity to skip ahead in the schedule and do something truly spectacular. George Low, Apollo spacecraft manager in Houston, proposed forgetting about the LM for Apollo 8 and launching a command and service module by itself on a mission around the Moon and back using a Saturn V. The CSM and Saturn V both appeared to be on track. The CSM still had to prove itself on Apollo 7, set to launch in the fall; and the Saturn V had run into problems on its second test flight earlier in the year, but von Braun was confident his rocket team could fix them. Obviously, the astronauts would be unable to land on the Moon without a LM, but they could test the procedures for traveling there and possibly even for going into lunar orbit, while getting the first close-up look at Earth's nearest neighbor.

Low approached Phillips with the idea. He loved it and checked with Paine, who was equally enthusiastic. When they called Webb, who was with Mueller at a conference in Europe, he hit the roof. Apollo had not yet sent a crew into Earth orbit, and now they were talking about going to the Moon!

Standing from left to right: George Low, Sam Phillips, and Deke Slayton, during an Apollo launch, 1969

But aside from streamlining the schedule, there was another very good reason to attempt this feat. Recent activity by the Russians strongly suggested they were planning to do it themselves.

The path to the Moon, around it, and back is relatively simple. Essentially, it is just an elliptical orbit (really a figure eight) with the Moon at one end. All that's needed is a spacecraft with supplies for several days, a booster that can accelerate the ship to 24,200 miles per hour, and a heat shield that can withstand reentry into Earth's atmosphere at that speed. During the Gemini program, one never-pursued idea called for modifying the Gemini capsule and using a more powerful rocket for exactly this purpose.

The danger of such a circumlunar mission is that once you are outbound, you can't change your mind and come back—a least not without expending more rocket power than you probably have. You are essentially committed to a six-day voyage to the Moon and back. This could be disastrous if you ran into a problem. Nonetheless, the simplicity of the trajectory makes it the poor man's Moon mission. You don't go into orbit around the Moon, you don't land, but you get to see the Moon from roughly a hundred miles away. In a sense, you can say you've been there.

In the summer of 1968, this was what the Soviets were clearly gear-

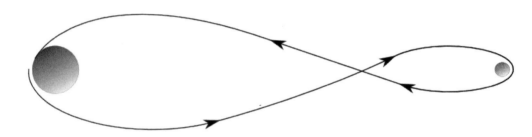

Figure-eight trajectory from Earth (at left) to the Moon and back (not drawn to scale)

ing up to do, and Low was worried that many people would not see the difference between going around the Moon and landing on it. The poor man's Moon mission might easily upstage Apollo. Then it wouldn't matter who landed on the Moon first, because the race would be seen to be over. This would be especially ironic if the Russians had never been in the man-on-the-Moon race in the first place. No one outside the Soviet Union knew whether they had their own Apollo program or not, but their intention to send a cosmonaut crew around the Moon and back had been hinted at by an unusual unmanned flight earlier in the spring.

●

Meanwhile, events were moving quickly in the Apollo program. Starting in October, the space agency was poised to launch manned missions at roughly two-month intervals, just as during Project Gemini. Apollo 7 took off on October 11, commanded by Wally Schirra, with copilots Donn Eisele and Walt Cunningham. Conducting the postponed Apollo 1 mission from nearly two years earlier, except on a redesigned space-craft, Apollo 7 orbited Earth for eleven days and showed that the CSM was a superb spacecraft, ready for more ambitious missions.

Since Webb had retired on October 7, the decision about how ambitious the next flight would be fell to the acting administrator, Tom Paine. He was characteristically bold. "After a careful and thorough ex-amination of all of the systems and risks involved," he told the press, "we have concluded that we are now ready to fly the most advanced mis-sion for our Apollo 8 launch in December, the orbit around the Moon."

In other words, the next mission, Apollo 8, would carry out the most daring version of George Low's plan. It would not just fly out to the Moon and back. When it started to round the Moon on its elongated trajectory, it would fire the service module's rocket engine and enter lunar orbit, exactly as it would do when there was a lunar module at-tached. The CSM would then circle the Moon ten times and finally re-light its engine and accelerate to the speed needed to return to Earth.

Paine added, "Frank Borman and his crew and all of our engineers are unanimously in favor of selecting this mission." As far as the astro-nauts were concerned, this unprecedented journey posed no unreason-able risks. "This will be within the normal hazards of test pilots flying experimental craft," Paine stressed.

Apollo 8 crew. Left to right: Bill Anders, Frank Borman, Jim Lovell.

Many NASA insiders felt that if Webb had still been in charge, he would have been too cautious to authorize such a plan, haunted by memories of the Apollo 1 fire. But Paine was more willing to take a chance. Though he looked like a risk-averse insurance salesman, underneath he was a swashbuckling submariner.

The new mission prompted Deke Slayton to juggle his crews. He wanted Apollo 8's original commander, Jim McDivitt, to stick with his crucial job of flying the first manned test of the LM. That mission would now become Apollo 9. Apollo 9's commander, Frank Borman, was moved to Apollo 8. His original crewmates were Mike Collins and Bill Anders, but Collins had been grounded for a spinal operation and was replaced by his backup, Jim Lovell.

These adjustments had a ripple effect. As Borman's backup, Neil Armstrong was now in line to command the flight three missions after Apollo 8—namely, Apollo 11. Although it was just a number at this point, Apollo 11 would become the most famous manned spaceflight of all time.

Russia's answer to Apollo: the Soyuz spacecraft, seen head-on as it orbits Earth

32

"IN THE BEGINNING"

After a mysterious break during America's Gemini missions, the Soviet manned space program was back in the news in 1967 and 1968. It was a rocky return. One of the reasons for their pause was they were building an advanced capsule called Soyuz. With room for a crew of three, Soyuz was their equivalent of the Apollo command and service module. On its maiden flight in April 1967, Soyuz was piloted by a single cosmonaut—the space veteran Vladimir Komarov. After launch, Komarov faced problems with critical equipment, and the flight director ordered the mission to be cut short. At the end of the eighteenth orbit, Soyuz fired its retrorockets to return to Earth. Unfortunately, the parachute system failed and the ship plummeted to the ground, crashing and killing Komarov instantly. This tragedy took place three months after the Apollo 1 fire.

A year later, in the spring of 1968, a redesigned Soyuz took off on an unmanned flight called Zond 4, which used a new rocket. Although not nearly as powerful as the Saturn V, this booster could send large payloads to the Moon. Zond 4 went nearly as far as the Moon and then returned to Earth, again malfunctioning during reentry.

Then in September 1968, Zond 5 took off, and for a time it seemed there might be a cosmonaut aboard, since a British ground station picked up a voice in Russian calling out instrument readings. It turned out to be a recording for testing communications at lunar distances, clearly in preparation for a manned flight. After passing behind the Moon, Zond 5 returned to Earth. Once again, reentry did not go well, but the craft managed to land intact in the Indian Ocean. It was the first-ever round-trip between Earth and the Moon, and the Russians announced that its cargo included two tortoises and several plants, all of which survived. Also that fall, the Soviets launched another unmanned lunar Zond, as well as an Earth-orbiting Soyuz piloted by a cosmonaut. All objectives were met on both missions, according to Soviet news reports.

The Russians now appeared to be poised for a manned lunar flight. Like a war that flares up after a long lull, the space race had reignited. *Time* magazine caught the mood on the cover of its December 6, 1968, issue, which showed an illustration of two spacemen, one Soviet, one American. They were sprinting toward the Moon over a caption that read, "Race for the Moon."

Queried by a reporter, Wernher von Braun conceded that the Soviets had a good chance of beating Apollo 8 to the Moon. As for who would be the first to land, he predicted it would be "a photo finish."

●

Missions to the Moon have to be launched during specific periods, called launch windows. These fleeting opportunities depend on the location of the launch site, the location of the tracking stations, the lunar phase when the spacecraft is supposed to arrive at the Moon, and the region on Earth where the spacecraft is supposed to land at the end of the mission. If at all possible, launch and landing should take place during daylight.

For the Soviet Union, these stringent requirements meant that the December 1968 launch window opened on the 8th of the month. For the United States, it didn't open until the 20th. Apollo 8 was scheduled to launch the next day, but no one knew what the Soviets' plans were. Therefore, the first part of December was tense with anticipation. On Saturday, December 7, the day before the Russian launch window opened, the newspaper for the town adjoining the Kennedy Space Center ran the headline, "Moon Shot for Soviets Sunday?" When Sunday came, there was nothing to report. Nor on Monday or Tuesday. When the window closed on Thursday, December 12, the Soviets' only space activity had been a routine satellite launch on the 10th. As usual, they said nothing. The following week, on the day before Apollo 8's scheduled takeoff, one of Russia's senior cosmonauts made this remark to journalists: "It is not important to mankind who will reach the Moon first and when he will reach it—in 1969 or 1970."

Had the Russians thrown in the towel?

●

Apollo 8 launched precisely on time, with Earth-shaking power that once again rattled Walter Cronkite's broadcast booth three and a half miles away. So smooth and steady was the Saturn V's rise that Cronkite guessed the astronauts were less jostled than his camera crew on the ground.

Far from it! Frank Borman, Jim Lovell, and Bill Anders were being whipped around like "a rat in the jaws of a big terrier," remembered Anders. The giant F-1 engines at the base of the Saturn V swiveled to keep the rocket upright and avoid knocking into the launch tower, which would have been catastrophic. This feat was like balancing a yardstick vertically in the palm of the hand; tiny movements at the base translate into large fluctuations at the tip—which were what the three astronauts were experiencing.

No one had ever ridden a rocket like this, and the crew could only compare it to a form of transportation they knew from their youth: a freight train. The Apollo astronauts were all children of the Great Depression. Some had hopped freights in their younger days for free rides. Others had held summer jobs on the railroad. Most had ridden troop trains at some point, which had few of the comforts of passenger trains. One astronaut likened the experience on a Saturn V to "a runaway freight train on a crooked track, swaying from side to side."

Then there was the "train wreck," as another astronaut described the instant when the first stage cut off. This happened two and a half minutes after liftoff, as the F-1 engines were burning the last of the first-stage propellant. At this point, the vehicle was 40 miles high and increasing its speed by almost 90 miles per hour every second, as if a racing car could go from 90 to 180 to 270 miles per hour in less time than it takes to read these words. The acceleration pinned the astronauts against their seats with four g's. When the engines quit, the acceleration suddenly dropped to zero and the crew lurched violently forward as if in a head-on collision.

"I suddenly felt like I'd been sitting on a catapult and somebody cut the rope," recalled Anders. In fact, he was experiencing the recoil of the rocket body as it responded to the abrupt loss of thrust, like a spring being released after it is compressed.

Then the second stage kicked in with its hydrogen-oxygen engines, throwing the space travelers back into their seats, this time with a gentler one g, which slowly built to two g's. From here on, the ride was less traumatic except for a periodic back-and-forth oscillation called

The first stage of the Saturn V drops away at an altitude of forty miles.

"pogo," named for the spring-loaded jumping stick. Pogo was one of the problems that von Braun had promised to fix, and his rocket team had been able to reduce it to a safe level but not eliminate it entirely. Therefore, Borman was relieved when the jittery second stage finally shut down and the smoother third stage took over, giving the vehicle a final push to orbital speed—17,500 miles per hour.

They were now in a low, temporary orbit, 119 miles high. Borman, Lovell, and Anders had two to three orbits to check out the spacecraft and confirm it was safe to proceed to the Moon, three days away. After verifying that all was well, they got the okay from Mission Control and relit the third stage for a little over five minutes. For the first time ever, explorers were leaving the Earth behind. No one had ever been on an expedition like this!

The view from Apollo 8, four and a half hours after launch. South America is at the bottom. North America is covered in clouds. No humans had seen the full Earth before.

When Apollo 8 lifted off, more than thirty humans had been into space. But no one had seen our planet from farther away than 850 miles, which was the high point reached during Gemini 11 in 1966. Less than two minutes after the third stage shut down, Apollo 8 beat that record, and half an hour later they were already 7,500 miles from Earth. Frank Borman radioed the ground: "We see the Earth now, almost as a disk."

Jim Lovell filled in the details. "We have a beautiful view of Florida . . . And at the same time, we can see Africa. West Africa is beautiful. I can also see Gibraltar at the same time I'm looking at Florida."

Two and a half days later, the astronauts were so far from their home planet that they couldn't see it at all without carefully orienting the CSM until Earth drifted into view in one of the windows, so small that they could blot it out with a thumb. Anders, who had attended the Naval Academy, said the feeling of isolation was "like being on the inside of a submarine."

Apollo 8 was on a "free-return" trajectory, meaning that if the astronauts did nothing, the CSM would curve around the Moon and return to Earth. As they neared the Moon, they rechecked their systems and confirmed that everything was working properly for the next step: entering lunar orbit. Making sure the CSM was turned so that its big rocket engine was facing backward, they counted down and fired the engine for four minutes, allowing the Moon to capture their craft. Twenty hours later, they would turn the other way and fire the engine again to escape and go home. But for now, they could look down on the Moon from a distance of only seventy miles. Automatic space probes had visited the Moon and taken pictures, but nothing prepared Borman, Lovell, and Anders for what they now saw: a world that was battered beyond belief—"like a war zone," recalled Anders. And it was utterly without color.

"The Moon is essentially gray," Lovell radioed back. "It looks like plaster of Paris or sort of a grayish beach sand." The lack of an atmosphere meant there were no clouds, haze, or suspended dust. Neither was there any sign of water or life.

The far side of the Moon from Apollo 8. The picture is about ninety miles across.

"It's a vast, lonely, forbidding-type existence, or expanse of nothing, that looks rather like clouds and clouds of pumice stone," Borman announced, "and it certainly would not appear to be a very inviting place to live or work."

Like millions of others, Anders had been conditioned by decades of science-fiction movies to expect a landscape of sharp relief, with jagged mountains, ridges, and canyons resembling those in the American West or Swiss Alps. The movie *2001: A Space Odyssey*, one of the most popular films of 1968 and one that every astronaut had seen at least once, was the most realistic depiction of spaceflight ever attempted, and it showed the Moon in exactly this way—which was wrong.

"Let me tell you," Anders said later, "it's sandblasted."

Apollo 8's ten orbits lasted a little less than a day. By the fixed timetable of the December 1968 launch window, that day happened to be the 24th, Christmas Eve. Aboard the CSM was a simple black-and-white television camera, and NASA had instructed the astronauts to do a live broadcast on their next-to-last orbit, which corresponded to prime time in the eastern half of the United States. The content of the program was up to them, but the men were cautioned that they would probably have the largest television audience in history.

When the time came, Borman, Lovell, and Anders focused on the Moon, training the camera out the window and trying to convey the nature of this strange place that had become the object of America's crazy quest.

As the lunar-science specialist on the mission, Anders led the tour, pointing out the changing topography and naming the craters and seas passing below. He interspersed his commentary with long pauses. Lovell and Borman contributed their own commentary, and they used enough scientific jargon to create an aura of esoteric mystery.

Toward the end of the transmission, Anders noted that they were passing over the Sea of Tranquility, "one of our future landing sites," he explained, referring to the prime target zone called Apollo Landing

Site 2. Then, as the camera recorded the lengthening shadows of the approaching lunar night, he began to wrap things up. "For all the people back on Earth," he announced, "the crew of Apollo 8 has a message we would like to send you."

Flying over a world of primordial chaos on Christmas Eve, these men, who were direct witnesses to the wonders of the cosmos, began reading the account of creation from the book of Genesis.

Anders recited, "In the beginning, God created the heaven and the Earth. And the Earth was without form and void; and darkness was

Apollo command and service module over the Moon (made on Apollo 17)

upon the face of the deep. And the spirit of God moved upon the face of the waters. And God said, 'Let there be light,' and there was light."

Taking turns, they read to the end of verse 10, which is just before the creation of life. Then Frank Borman concluded, "And from the crew of Apollo 8, we close with good night, good luck, a merry Christmas, and God bless all of you, all of you on the good Earth."

Earthrise from the Moon, photographed from Apollo 8 on December 24, 1968

33

EARTHRISE

On their fourth orbit of the Moon, Frank Borman was turning the spacecraft to get photographs of features of interest to scientists. Quite by chance, the Earth happened to be rising over the lunar horizon—something the astronauts hadn't seen yet. Bill Anders caught sight of it out his window.

"Oh, my God!" he said. "Look at that picture over there! Here's the Earth coming up. Wow, is that pretty!"

"Hey, don't take that," Borman teased him, "it's not scheduled." In fact, it was true: they had almost no time to depart from the schedule, which booked practically every moment of the trip, but this was an exception. Anders got off several shots that showed the brilliant blue Earth suspended over the ashen lunar landscape.

"It was the most beautiful, heart-catching sight of my life," Borman later wrote. "It was the only thing in space that had any color to it. Everything else was either black or white, but not the Earth. It was mostly a soft, peaceful blue, the continents outlined in a pinkish brown.

And always the white clouds, like long streaks of cotton suspended above that immense globe."

Lovell was also overcome, calling Earth "a grand oasis in the big vastness of space."

After they relit their service module engine and returned home, their hundreds of photographs were developed and distributed to scientists and the press. One of Anders's Earthrise pictures struck a chord. For the first time, ordinary people had the startling experience of seeing their world as an interplanetary visitor would.

It dawned on Anders that the long years of training, focused entirely on the Moon, had led the astronauts, in the end, to discover Earth. "Here we came all this way to the Moon, and yet the most significant thing we're seeing is our own home planet."

The year 1968 had been unusually difficult for the inhabitants of Earth. In the United States, two political assassinations shocked the nation. In April, the great civil rights leader Martin Luther King Jr. was gunned down. And in June, Senator Robert F. Kennedy, the brother of the slain president, was killed. The other great trauma for the U.S. was the ongoing Vietnam War, which was proving to be America's most deadly and costly conflict in the Cold War. Events were no less tumultuous abroad, where France was seized by nationwide unrest, and Czechoslovakia, a Soviet ally, saw its brief experiment in political freedom crushed by Soviet troops in the largest military operation in Europe since World War II. Amid all the chaos, Apollo 8 was a breath of fresh air. In thanks for redeeming 1968, *Time* magazine named Borman, Lovell, and Anders its "Men of the Year," a prestigious journalistic honor.

"For all its upheavals and frustrations," *Time*'s editors wrote, "the year would be remembered to the end of time for the dazzling skills and Promethean daring that sent mortals around the Moon. It would be celebrated as the year in which men saw at first hand their little Earth entire, a remote, blue-brown sphere hovering like a migrant bird in the hostile night of space."

The coming year, 1969, marked the deadline for President Kennedy's quest. Thanks to Apollo 7 and 8, NASA was back on track. If Apollo 9 and 10 were similarly successful, then the first Moon landing attempt would probably fall on Apollo 11, sometime in the summer. According to Deke Slayton's rotation system, that job should go to the Apollo 8 backup crew: Neil Armstrong, Buzz Aldrin, and Fred Haise (Haise joined Armstrong's crew when Jim Lovell moved to the Apollo 8 prime crew to replace the ailing Mike Collins).

Deke's mantra was "any crew can fly any mission." But the first lunar landing was special, and he was ready to break his rotation system for this history-making crew. Had Gus Grissom been alive, Slayton would have preferred him for commander. Gus was just the gutsy flyer who could pull it off; plus, as one of the Original Seven, he had seniority. But Gus was dead, so Slayton had been grooming two other astronauts as potential commanders for the first lunar landing: Frank Borman and Jim McDivitt.

Unfortunately, Borman was out of the running. Before Apollo 8 flew, he told Deke it was his last mission. Managing redesign of the command module following the Apollo 1 fire and then training for Apollo 8 had kept him away from home for almost two years. He felt his family deserved to have him back. When he heard speculation that he could have the first Moon landing, he sensibly pointed out that there wasn't time for him to train on the lunar module, since he was a command module specialist.

Jim McDivitt *was* a lunar module specialist, but he was leading the shakedown cruise of the LM on Apollo 9, due to launch into Earth orbit in the winter of 1969. As commander of Apollo 10, Tom Stafford was next in line. He was scheduled to take a CSM and LM out to the Moon on a mission that could conceivably land. But NASA managers wanted to use it as a dress rehearsal for Apollo 11, testing procedures down to an altitude of 50,000 feet. If delays caused Apollo 10 to slip into the fall, then it could go all the way.

Given all the *if*s—*if* the LM didn't run into problems, *if* pogo didn't return in the Saturn V, *if* the countless other critical systems didn't fail—Slayton decided to stick with his tried-and-true system and assign command of Apollo 11 to the next man in the rotation: Neil Armstrong. If his mission didn't land, then Pete Conrad, the probable commander of Apollo 12, would get a shot. "This is like handling a squadron of fighter pilots," Slayton remarked. "You've got a mission to do and you've got so many flights to fly and you assign guys to fly them." It was that simple.

Mike Collins was healed from his spinal surgery and back in the rotation. Deke had special sympathy for pilots who had been medically grounded, like himself, so he assigned Collins to one of the other seats on Apollo 11. Logically, the third slot belonged to Buzz Aldrin. (Fred Haise was less experienced than either Collins or Aldrin and would stay on backup status for the time being.) Yet Deke had his doubts about Aldrin. Buzz was an expert pilot, a brilliant engineer, and he had flown a flawless mission on Gemini 12. But many of the other astronauts found it hard to get along with him. Personality clashes shouldn't matter; however, Slayton gave Armstrong the option to switch Aldrin for Jim Lovell, who was just coming off duty from Apollo 8. Lovell famously got along with everyone. Armstrong thought it over and decided it wouldn't be fair to Lovell, who deserved a command of his own, much less to Aldrin, who had worked well with Armstrong on the backup crew for Apollo 8.

On January 6, 1969, Deke called the three men into his office. "You're it," he said. Armstrong would command the mission and fly the lunar module. Collins would pilot the command module and stay in lunar orbit, standing by to rescue the LM in an emergency. Aldrin would accompany Armstrong down to the Moon as the lunar module pilot—in reality the copilot, with the all-important job of running the computer and relaying the flight data to Armstrong. In effect, he would talk Neil down to a safe landing—or try to.

Apollo 11 crew, 1969. Left to right: Buzz Aldrin, Neil Armstrong, and Mike Collins.

NASA officials after the launch of Apollo 11. Foreground, from right to left: Sam Phillips, George Mueller, and Wernher von Braun (with binoculars).

34
GO FEVER

The Apollo 1 fire led to a new term, "go fever," which is the tendency to make mistakes while rushing to get a job done, especially when things are going well. Go fever had killed three astronauts aboard Apollo 1. Now, with the near-perfect flights of Apollo 7 and 8, some at NASA worried about go fever in the rush to meet Kennedy's deadline. A truly spectacular disaster was possible—an atomic-bomb-scale explosion on the launchpad, a lunar crash landing, a crew stranded in interplanetary space.

Apollo 8 astronaut Frank Borman knew the risks and worried about the public's reaction to a new catastrophe. "I do not submit that there won't be further tragedy in this program," he cautioned, "but I do say that it's worth the price we have to pay." His remark seemed intended to prepare the public for something frightful.

Since the fire, NASA had tightened contractor management and set up new safety procedures. Still, there were roughly 6 million parts in a typical Apollo mission: 3 million in the Saturn V, 2 million in the CSM, and 1 million in the LM. If those parts were 99.9 percent reliable, that would still mean an average of 6,000 failures per flight. To keep the failure rate even lower than that, every contractor followed Wernher von Braun's advice to encourage "an almost religious vigilance and attention to detail on the part of every member of a development team."

NASA administrator Tom Paine had his own way of dealing with go fever. Starting with Apollo 8, he flew down to the Cape before each mission and had dinner with the crew. He kept it informal, starting out with relaxed conversation. He had two goals. First, he wanted to open a direct channel of communications to the astronauts in case they had concerns they were reluctant to share with their immediate bosses. Second, during dessert or as he was saying goodbye, he had an even more important message. Don't take any unnecessary chances, he told them. "If you don't like the way things look," he said, "come on home and I'll guarantee you three the next flight to try again."

It was a generous offer and one that took some of the pressure off. But it was advice the astronauts were not likely to heed. All the astronauts had been in flight situations where the bad omens kept multiplying, but they had stuck with the mission, intent on solving the problems, which they eventually did. The fact that they were still alive proved they were good at it, and that was why they were chosen as astronauts. To them, a bigger concern than staying alive was not disgracing themselves in the eyes of their peers by playing it safe and aborting a mission needlessly. They prided themselves on having what author Tom Wolfe later labeled "the right stuff," which Wolfe defined as "the ability to go up in a hurtling piece of machinery . . . and have the moxie, the reflexes, the experience, the coolness, to pull it back at the last yawning moment."

That was not what Paine meant when he said not to take unnecessary chances.

●

No one personified the right stuff more than Neil Armstrong. His crewmate Mike Collins compared him to a gourmet who savors perilous situations like fine wines, "rolling them around on his tongue . . . and swallowing at the very last moment." On May 6, 1968, Armstrong had been practicing solo lunar landings in a training vehicle nicknamed the "flying bedstead." It resembled a giant bed frame equipped with a vertically mounted jet engine. Officially called the Lunar Landing Research Vehicle, or LLRV, it was the only way, realistically, to simulate landing on the Moon. And if flying it was extremely hazardous, then that only added to the realism. Armstrong had made several successful landing approaches that day, and he was going up for another practice run. Suddenly, no more than 200 feet in the air, the control system went haywire and the LLRV began tipping over.

"Neil held on as long as he could, not wanting to abandon an expensive piece of hardware," Buzz Aldrin wrote. "At the last possible moment, he realized the thruster system had completely malfunctioned, and he pulled his ejection handles." He was so low that his parachute barely had time to open fully before he hit the ground.

Later that morning, astronaut Al Bean arrived at work and was told, "Do you know that Neil bailed out of the LLRV this morning?"

Bean said, "No way!" He checked Armstrong's office, where he found him sitting calmly at his desk, shuffling some papers.

"Those guys out in the office said you bailed out of the LLRV this morning," Bean reported.

Armstrong gave a distracted reply: "Yeah."

"That was all he said, 'Yeah,'" Bean recalled in amazement. "This

The LLRV, also known as the "flying bedstead," the only realistic practice for landing on the Moon. The pilot is at right.

guy had been a second and a half from being killed. That was it! He didn't say, 'I nearly got killed!'—'Yeah.' That was it!"

Bean himself had a personal connection with crashes, since he had been promoted to an Apollo crew after the death of C.C. Williams, another astronaut. Williams, too, had been in an aircraft that lost control. He, too, had held on and ejected low. But he had been too low.

Armstrong's luck ran out on another mission. Fortunately, it was an Earthbound simulation. The Apollo 11 crew spent hundreds of hours in simulators that mimicked the real spacecraft and real mission in every

Neil Armstrong parachutes to safety after ejecting from a malfunctioning LLRV, 1968.

way possible. Mike Collins recalled that on one of these imaginary flights, "Neil and Buzz had been descending in the LM when some catastrophe had overtaken them, and they had been ordered by Houston to abort. Neil, for some reason, either questioned the advice or was just slow to act on it, but in any event, the computer printout showed that the LM had descended below the altitude of the lunar surface before starting to climb again. In plain English, Neil had crashed the LM and destroyed the machine, himself, and Buzz."

Armstrong later claimed he had been testing the limits to see how Mission Control would respond. This attitude worried Houston. The influential director of flight operations, Christopher C. Kraft Jr., questioned Armstrong's commitment to the rule that Mission Control's orders must be obeyed. And Chief Flight Director Gene Kranz complained that Armstrong obviously "had set his own rules for the landing. I just wanted to know what they were."

Kranz judged that when the moment of truth came, "my gut feeling said he would press on, accepting any risk as long as there was even a remote chance to land."

As for Armstrong, not even Aldrin standing next to him in the LM knew what he was going to do.

Apollo 9 launched into Earth orbit in March and returned with some 150 failures, practically all minor, for a reliability rate of 99.999975 percent. Apollo 10, which went to the Moon in May, was just as trouble-free, with the biggest glitch occurring during preparation for firing the LM's ascent-stage rocket, as a lunar landing crew would have to do to take off from the Moon and rejoin the CSM. On Apollo 10, this test of the maneuver took place in lunar orbit. An incorrectly set switch in the LM caused a tense moment when the LM started tumbling, recalling Armstrong and Scott's harrowing experience with a stuck thruster on Gemini 8. Piloting the LM, Mission Commander Tom Stafford quickly regained control. In less expert hands, the incident might have ended in disaster. It was a lesson in how little room there was for error.

Apollo 11's launch was set for July 16, timed for a landing four days later just after lunar sunrise on the southwestern edge of the Moon's Sea of Tranquility—Apollo Landing Site 2. Inspecting the target area from 50,000 feet on Apollo 10, astronaut Gene Cernan described it as "pretty smooth, like a gummy grayish sand." Stafford warned, "There's still lots of small craters down there, but . . . if you've got hover time, you can probably make it." He added, "If you come down in the wrong area . . . you're going to have to shove off"—meaning Armstrong might have to abort the landing, cutting loose the LM's descent stage and using the ascent engine to rejoin the CSM in lunar orbit.

Deke Slayton awoke the crew on the morning of the 16th, had breakfast with them, and then accompanied them to the transport van after they suited up. On the way out to the pad, he got off at the firing room. There Slayton joined General Phillips, Wernher von Braun, Tom Paine, and other NASA staff. Max Faget usually skipped launches. "To watch a flight is not that big a deal," he often said. "It's just a lot of standing around to watch it go off." There's no record that he attended this one.

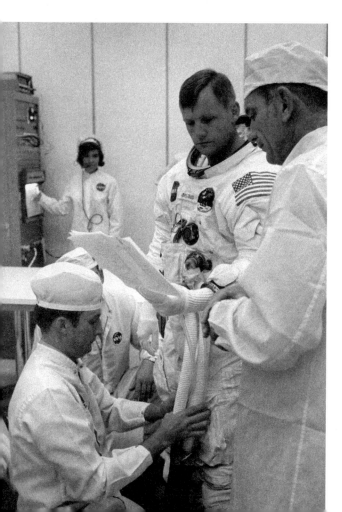

Neil Armstrong suits up on Apollo 11 launch day. Deke Slayton is at right.

Apollo 11 lifts off, July 16, 1969.

Outside on the VIP bleachers, Jim Webb stood with his former boss Lyndon Johnson. Warned about the possibility of delay or worse, the new president, Richard Nixon, wasn't attending and had sent his vice president, Spiro Agnew, instead.

As the count reached zero and the Saturn V rumbled to life, one word was in the thoughts and hearts of the breathless millions who watched.

"Go!"

Former President Johnson (center, in dark suit) watches Apollo 11 rocket skyward. Next to him on the left is Jim Webb. On the right (with the light jacket) is Vice President Agnew.

Mission Control at the moment *Eagle* landed on the Moon. Left to right: Deke Slayton,
Charlie Duke (capcom), and Jim Lovell (Apollo 11 backup commander).

35

TRANQUILITY BASE

Apollo 11 wasn't the only vehicle headed for the Moon on July 16. The Russians had a head start with their surprise launch of an unmanned probe, Luna 15, which was only a day away from entering lunar orbit when Apollo 11 took off. Most experts believed Luna 15 was designed to grab some lunar soil and return to Earth ahead of the Americans, becoming the first mission to obtain samples of the Moon and doing it without an enormously expensive manned flight.

The press went wild with other theories. Some suggested that Luna 15 was a hostile probe designed to jam radio signals from Apollo 11, or that it was on a spy mission to learn how Apollo really worked, or that it was on an errand of mercy to rescue Armstrong and Aldrin if they got stranded.

Von Braun tried to bring reporters down to Earth. "This is undoubt- edly quite a challenging mission, to soft-land a spacecraft on the Moon and scoop up a sample of lunar soil and fly it back to Earth," he ex- plained. He even added a note of admiration: "It would show again that we have very competent competitors in this race . . . I am even quite glad that we are not alone in doing this thing."

But whatever its mission, Luna 15 was a dark horse lurking in the shadows as the most remarkable expedition in history unfolded for all the world to see.

Apollo 11 arrived in lunar orbit on July 19. The following day the CSM and LM undocked, with Collins staying in the command module, named *Columbia*, while Armstrong and Aldrin departed in the lunar module, called *Eagle*. Some 240,000 miles away, in Houston, astronaut Charles Duke was the capcom who would relay information and instructions from flight controllers during the landing attempt. The flight director for this crucial shift was Gene Kranz.

When the time came for Duke to give *Eagle* permission to fire its descent rocket and head down to the surface, he had trouble getting through.

Eagle in lunar orbit. Contact probes extend from the foot pads.

Buzz Aldrin in a composite of photos taken inside *Eagle* prior to landing. Armstrong's station is at the left triangular window; Aldrin's is at the right.

"*Eagle*, Houston," he radioed. "If you read, you're go for powered descent. Over."

The only reply was static. This was not a good sign.

Six seconds later, Collins, whose radio link was working fine, relayed the message to Armstrong and Aldrin: "*Eagle*, this is *Columbia*. They just gave you a go for powered descent."

If the communications stayed this bad, then the landing would have to be canceled for several reasons. One was that Kranz insisted on having as much telemetry as possible to determine what had gone wrong in case the astronauts crashed.

But thirty seconds later, after Aldrin readjusted *Eagle*'s antenna, his ship was back on the air. Five minutes after that, Armstrong lit the descent engine. They were at 50,000 feet and on their way down. Since there was no room for seats in the LM, the two astronauts were standing—as if they were in an elevator on a nine-and-a-half-mile plunge.

Anyone who has ever flown on a commercial jet knows what it's like to be tens of thousands of feet in the air. The ground is a long way down, and you thank your lucky stars that the pilots have plenty of experience landing the plane. Imagine, though, that you are at 50,000 feet—higher than most airliners fly—in a vehicle that *has never landed before.* This violates every rule of flight testing. When the Wright brothers made their first powered flight, they rose a few feet into the air and immediately set down. They repeated this process countless times, going incrementally higher and farther while making steady improvements in their vehicle and their technique. Every airplane ever designed and every pilot who has ever earned a license has gone through a similar process.

Western Sea of Tranquility from lunar orbit. *Eagle's* landing site is just right of center near the edge of darkness.

Not so the LM and its two-man crew. This vehicle had never gone through an actual landing, and neither had the astronauts. They had *simulated* a landing, and Armstrong had practiced the last few hundred feet in the flying bedstead, but no one knew how accurate these exercises were.

Moreover, landing on the Moon presents unique challenges. For one, there are few clues about the size of objects, since there are no cities, buildings, roads, rivers, trees, and certainly no airports to give a sense of how far away things are. There are only craters upon craters upon

The region southwest of *Eagle*'s landing site from 50,000 feet. The large crater is Moltke, four miles wide. On the opposite page, Moltke is barely visible just left of center (also in the top photo on page 246).

craters, of all sizes and all looking much the same. Furthermore, the Moon is considerably smaller than Earth—only one-quarter of Earth's diameter, which means the horizon is closer than it may appear. As you fly over the Moon, features come into view much more quickly than they do on Earth, giving the illusion that you are going faster than you really are. Confusing matters still more, the Moon has no atmosphere, which means that distant objects are not blurred by air. The landscape looks just as sharp from 50,000 feet as it does from 500. Combined with the lack of objects of known scale, this makes it doubly hard to judge distances.

The lack of air has another effect: the LM can't use air resistance to slow down and control its descent, as airplanes do. Apart from crashing like a meteorite, the only way to land on the Moon is to fire a rocket in the direction of travel and gradually slow the spacecraft to a safe landing speed, while using smaller control thrusters to orient the vehicle. This must be done all the way to the ground, and it takes a lot of fuel.

Therefore, you might think the LM would have plenty of gas to give the commander time to survey the landing area, circle it a couple of times, and pick an alternate site if things looked too risky. This was especially important for Apollo, since photos from lunar orbit didn't show features smaller than about six feet, meaning that dangerous boulders and small craters could lurk anywhere. Unfortunately, a properly cautious landing was out of the question. Stringent weight limits meant that the LM had only about a minute of hover time for the pilot to make up his mind.

These formidable hurdles were the reason that practically no one thought Apollo would succeed on its first landing attempt, least of all the flight controllers in Houston. When the inevitable problems accumulated past a certain point, the crew would have to abort, using either the LM's descent stage or the ascent-stage engine to rocket back to the CSM for return to Earth and another try.

Landing on the Moon would have been all but impossible except for two electronic devices: the onboard computer and the landing radar.

Computers in the 1960s were room-size machines that consumed enormous amounts of electricity. In a miracle of engineering devised by Doc Draper's Instrumentation Lab, the CM and LM each carried a suitcase-size computer that used very little power and yet served as the master control for navigation, propulsion, the automatic pilot, instrument readings, and command inputs, allowing the spacecraft to function independently of Mission Control. The computer's performance was similar to that of the earliest personal computers, which became available a decade later—and popularized such games as *Space Invaders* and *Lunar Lander*. Primitive by today's standards, the Apollo computer was so efficiently programmed that it could direct not a crude video game, but a real-life mission to the Moon.

The computer in the lunar module also controlled the landing radar, which told the astronauts their altitude above the surface and their velocity in three dimensions. These readings were crucial pieces of information that Aldrin would be feeding Armstrong.

The landing got off to a bad start. On top of the on-again-off-again communications, Armstrong discovered early in *Eagle*'s descent that he would miss the prime target by several miles, rendering futile all his time spent memorizing landmarks. This meant he was heading for the western end of the landing zone, which Tom Stafford had warned him was much rougher than the aim point.

Things soon got worse—much worse. As *Eagle* passed through 35,000 feet, it was traveling at the fast clip of a supersonic jet coming in for an emergency landing. Aldrin made a routine query to the computer when suddenly the astronauts heard a buzzing tone in their headsets. It was the caution and warning system, informing them there was a computer problem.

"Program alarm," said Armstrong in the crisp voice of a pilot reporting trouble.

He checked the computer display and read out the code: "It's a twelve-oh-two." Neither he nor Buzz had any idea what that meant.

In Houston, capcom Duke had a sinking feeling. A computer problem was a potential showstopper. He didn't know what the code meant either.

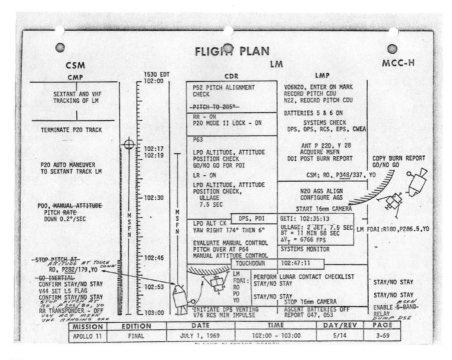

Minute-by-minute flight plan for Apollo 11. This page shows what Collins (CMP), Armstrong (CDR), Aldrin (LMP), and Mission Control (MCC-H) were doing during the landing phase. Everyone involved had this timeline.

Working in a back room, a group of computer experts were linked to Steve Bales, the guidance officer in Mission Control. One of them echoed Armstrong's call: "12 02 alarm!" then muttered, "12 02, what's that?" as he riffled the pages of his checklist.

Seconds passed. Up in the LM, Armstrong calmly radioed Houston.

"Give us a reading on the 12 02 program alarm"—meaning, "What the hell should we do?!"

By now, Jack Garman in the back room knew. "It's executive overflow," he told Bales. "If it does not occur again, we're fine . . . Continue."

Bales passed the word to flight director Kranz. "We're—we're go on that, Flight."

Kranz nodded to Duke, who immediately relayed the message to Armstrong and Aldrin. "We're go on that alarm!"

Twenty seconds later there was another 12 02 alarm.

Quietly observing at Mission Control, astronaut Walt Cunningham worried that the alarms "were creating doubt, one of a pilot's deadliest enemies." And in the press room, British journalist Reginald Turnill couldn't shake a feeling of "impending disaster." He knew enough to realize that problems were piling up. "They're crashing," he kept thinking.

"Okay, all flight controllers, hang tight," urged Kranz.

Executive overflow signaled that the computer had more to do than it could handle, so it stopped and restarted, cutting out less essential tasks. But then something overloaded it again. Fortunately, the computer's design allowed it to stop and restart almost instantaneously, although the vital navigation data disappeared momentarily. There was no time to figure out what the problem was. Garman deduced it was something they could live with as long as the machine's performance didn't degrade further.

Listening in at the MIT Instrumentation Lab in Massachusetts was Don Eyles, the programmer who had written the landing software. He knew the code inside and out, and was thinking, "If it were in my hands, I would call an abort." But he didn't have a direct line to Mission Control.

However, the man at the controls had come to the same conclusion as Garman. "There wasn't anything obviously wrong," Armstrong said afterward. "The vehicle was flying well, it was going down the trajectory we expected, no abnormalities in anything that we saw." He reasoned that "as long as everything was going well and looked right, I would be in favor of continuing, no matter what the computer was complaining about."

As luck would have it, Mission Control had recently run a simulation with another Apollo crew that involved a similar alarm. During that exercise, Bales overreacted and called for an abort. Worried about the mistake, Kranz ordered Bales and Garman to review every possible alarm and come up with the proper action to take for each. It was this list that Garman was consulting for Apollo 11.

Nevertheless, five alarms sounded over a period of four minutes. With their attention-grabbing buzz in the astronauts' headsets, the need to query the computer each time, and the interruption in the crucial navigation numbers, the warnings were hard to ignore.

"I licked my dry lips," Aldrin later wrote. "This was a time for discipline. But the tension had me rigid inside my suit. We *had* to trust Mission Control."

Mission Control responded "go" each time. At MIT, Eyles was practically having a nervous breakdown. "It is as though a terrible screech is coming from the front of your car, but the engine is still running, the steering still works, and you are getting very near your destination."

Duke inadvertently added to the confusion with a constant stream of reassuring chatter. Deke Slayton, who was sitting next to him, punched him in the side and said, "Charlie, shut up and let them land!"

"I think we'd better be quiet, Flight," Duke whispered to Kranz, who announced to the room, "Okay, the only callouts from now on will be fuel."

So far, *Eagle* was being guided by the autopilot, which theoretically could steer the ship all the way to the ground. Armstrong had the option of taking control at any time. After dealing with the computer alarms, he finally had a chance to look out the window. He didn't like what he saw. A mile ahead was a large crater, and the computer was targeting *Eagle* to its debris field, comprised of car-size boulders. When Armstrong activated the manual control to fly over it, the computer suddenly had less to do and the program alarms stopped. Characteristically, Armstrong didn't tell Mission Control—or Aldrin—what he was doing or why. "Pretty rocky area," was all he said—to himself.

At this point, controllers saw something strange on their screens. The data showed that "Neil was flying a trajectory that we'd never flown in the simulator," said Duke. "We kept trying to figure out, 'What's going on? He's just whizzing across the surface at about 400 feet.'"

Aldrin, whose eyes were glued to the instruments, noticed this, too, on the gauge that measured forward speed, which was stopped at its highest setting. Cool as ever, Buzz remarked, "Okay, you're pegged on horizontal velocity"—meaning, "Where the hell are you going?!" Neil didn't reply.

In the back row at Mission Control, Bob Gilruth and Chris Kraft were becoming increasingly edgy. "We could see on our displays that Armstrong was flying manually now and that fuel was getting low," Kraft wrote in his memoirs. "My worry level soared because he should have been descending. He needed an open spot to land, and my worst fear was that he couldn't find one . . . Bob Gilruth squeezed his eyes shut, then opened them with a deep breath. I don't remember if I was breathing or not."

Astronaut Al Bean understood Armstrong's situation as well as anyone, since he was the lunar module pilot for the next mission. He knew that the maneuver Armstrong was performing was wasting gas and must mean there was some kind of emergency. "I wonder if he's going to make it," he thought.

Meanwhile, sitting in Mission Control's viewing gallery, Max Faget had the same reaction: "If they keep doing this, they're going to run out of fuel."

There was one person completely untroubled by the dwindling fuel supply. "If I'd run out of fuel, why, I would have put down right there," Armstrong said later. In the flying bedstead, he often landed with just fifteen seconds of gas left.

"It would have been nice if I'd had another minute of fuel" in the LM, he admitted. "I knew we were getting short; I knew we had to get it on the ground, and I knew we had to get it below fifty feet. But I wasn't panic-stricken."

Aldrin wasn't panic-stricken either, but he was doing his best to convince Neil to land. "Ease her down," he said at an altitude of 270 feet. They were now almost clear of the boulder field.

"Okay, how's the fuel?" Armstrong responded.

"Eight percent."

"Okay. Here's a . . . looks like a good area here," Armstrong said. He had spotted a small crater about 400 feet ahead. Nearby was a reasonably clear patch. It was roughly a minute away.

A minute later, Armstrong was beyond the crater and still searching for a good spot. Aldrin was squirming inside his space suit. "Without wanting to say anything to Neil that might disrupt his focus, I pretty much used my body 'English' as best I could . . . as if to say, 'Neil, get this on the ground!'"

Charlie Duke called up in a tense voice: "Sixty seconds"—meaning a minute of fuel left. The flight surgeon's display showed Armstrong's heart racing at 150 beats per minute.

For millions of Americans watching on television, the networks provided animations, since there was nothing else to see. At this point, CBS showed a replica of the lunar module sitting triumphantly on the surface. According to the landing countdown clock projected on the TV screen, the astronauts should be down by now, and that was what viewers saw. But Buzz's voice continued to recite altitude and velocity figures. In other words, they hadn't landed yet! Neil and Buzz were still out there over the Moon, searching for a safe haven as Houston relayed increasingly alarming numbers on their decreasing fuel.

Flight controller Bob Carlton, who was keeping track of the fuel, had given up hope they would land. He just prayed they'd be able to abort

View out Aldrin's window from an altitude of 220 feet. Armstrong is using *Eagle*'s dwindling fuel supply to fly over the upper left crater, which is about 100 feet wide.

and keep from crashing. Meanwhile, tracking and data manager Bill Easter was spellbound. "It was like watching a man, some snake trainer, put his hand on a cobra; anything can happen any minute and probably will." Another controller, Ed Fendell, felt like he was levitating off his chair.

Garman had a different reaction. When Aldrin reported seeing dust kicked up by the rocket exhaust as they neared the surface, it hit him that this was actually happening, since dust was a detail that had never come up in a simulation. "My God, this is the real thing," he marveled.

The dust was all too real to Armstrong, who was now struggling with the disorienting illusion created by sheets of dust shooting in all directions. He compared it to "landing an airplane when there's a real thin layer of ground fog . . . However, all this fog was moving at a great rate, which was a little bit confusing." As Armstrong looked left, the dust was moving left, which gave the illusion that *Eagle* was moving right. So he instinctively fired the thrusters to push *Eagle* left. But then he glimpsed stationary rocks through the dust, which gave him a reference point. Having overcorrected, he fired the thrusters on the other side to neutralize his sideways drift.

"He's using a lot of RCS," said Bob Nance in the back room, referring to the reaction control system fuel that powered the thrusters.

"Thirty seconds," said Duke.

Armstrong's goal was to come straight down with a hint of forward motion. Too fast and the LM would tip over, but if he was moving in reverse he might back into a crater or boulder he couldn't see.

In his unruffled voice, as if he were helping Neil steer into a tight parking space, Buzz urged him on. "Drifting forward just a little bit; that's good."

Armstrong could see the spidery shadow of the LM growing larger and moving toward him to meet the contact probes dangling from *Eagle*'s footpads. A blizzard of dust engulfed everything.

"Contact light," said Aldrin briskly.

Armstrong intended to shut down the engine at this moment and drop the last few feet to the surface. There was a chance that blowback from the rocket exhaust would cause the engine to explode. Luckily, that didn't happen. Oblivious to the glowing contact light and Aldrin's announcement, Neil piloted *Eagle* to the gentlest possible landing.

"Shutdown," he said.

At Mission Control, they couldn't believe it. Aldrin read through some final instrument settings, then, breathlessly, Duke ventured, "We copy you down, *Eagle* . . ."

Armstrong had a proclamation ready: "Houston, Tranquility Base here. The *Eagle* has landed."

But Duke broke the formality with an expression of overwhelming, jubilant relief: "Roger, Tranquility. We copy you on the ground. You got a bunch of guys about to turn blue. We're breathing again. Thanks a lot."

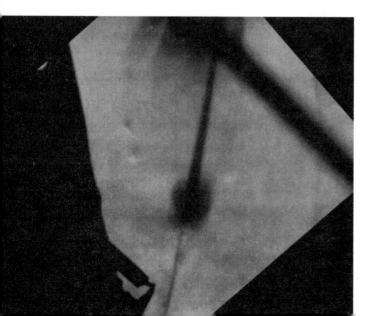

Seconds from touchdown, the shadow of one of *Eagle*'s legs reaches toward the ground.

Astronaut boot print on the Moon, July 20, 1969

36

ONE SMALL STEP

For most of the world, the main act in the Moon-landing drama was yet to come: the first step by a human onto the surface of the Moon. But to Neil Armstrong, that was an almost trivial part of the mission—"not something that I thought was really very important," he said years later. "It has always been surprising to me," he explained, "that there was such an intense public interest about stepping onto the lunar surface, let alone who did it first. In my mind, the important thing was that we got four aluminum legs safely down on the surface of the Moon while we were still inside the craft." On a difficulty scale of one to ten, Armstrong ranked walking on the Moon as a one, whereas "the lunar descent . . . was probably a thirteen."

When he was assigned to command Apollo 11, Armstrong almost certainly assumed that Aldrin would be the first down the ladder. NASA's practice in Project Gemini had been for copilots to make space walks. Science experiments were always the copilot's responsibility due to the heavy workload on the commander. Walking on the Moon was nothing if not a science experiment, and it made sense for the copilot, in this case Aldrin, to go first.

In fact, the original plan had been for the copilot to be the *only* astronaut to go outside. General Phillips felt strongly that a single, brief outing by a single explorer was a reasonable goal for the first landing. However, Bob Gilruth convinced him that both astronauts should go outside and be available to help each other, if necessary.

Neil Armstrong climbs down *Eagle*'s ladder in the television view watched live by 600 million people.

With both astronauts going out, the question then became: Who goes first? To someone like Neil Armstrong, it didn't matter. But to the press it mattered enormously. The first person to plant his foot on the Moon was the *first*—a historically unique individual, even if the second was right behind him.

Unfortunately for Aldrin, personality decided this issue. In a note to President Nixon, Frank Borman described his fellow astronauts this way: Armstrong was "quiet," "perceptive," and "thoroughly decent," while Aldrin was "aggressive," "hard-charging," and "almost humorless." Aldrin's pushy style had won him enemies at NASA. He was respected for his perseverance and intelligence, but top managers thought he was the wrong individual to wear the hero's mantle that the press would inevitably bestow on the first man on the Moon.

Therefore, Neil Armstrong got the assignment. Aldrin was not happy and tried to have the decision reversed, but without success.

On July 20, 1969, six and a half hours after he and Aldrin landed on the Moon, Armstrong backed out of *Eagle*'s hatch and onto the porch. Slowly, he made his way down the ladder. At the bottom, he was not yet on the Moon, since he was standing on one of the LM's broad footpads.

An important duty that went with taking the first step onto the Moon was saying something suitably memorable. People had been pestering Armstrong about this for weeks, asking him what he intended to say. He honestly hadn't decided, because there was a good chance he and Aldrin would have to abort the mission and he wouldn't have to say anything. But now the time had come.

After describing how the LM's footpad was depressed only an inch or two into the soil—an indication that he probably wouldn't sink out of sight as one scientist had insisted would happen—Armstrong said casually, "Okay, I'm going to step off the LM now." More than half a billion people on Earth watched the live television transmission as he leaned to his left—his right hand gripping the ladder just in the case the scientist was right—and took a tentative step into the dirt.

"That's one small step for man; one giant leap for mankind."

Buzz Aldrin climbs down shortly after Armstrong, who takes this picture.

Later, Armstrong said he had intended to say, "*a* man." But people tend to speak in poetic rhythms, and he naturally (and unconsciously) left out the extra syllable. It was actually better that way, since his statement became even more meaningful—contrasting humans as individuals or members of a group, with all of humanity throughout its history.

Fifteen minutes later, it was Aldrin's turn. He slowly slithered through the hatch. Houston had instructed him to close it partially when he was out. He made a sly joke, saying he would be careful not to lock it. Then he started down the ladder, jumped the last three feet from the bottom rung to the pad, leaped back up to test the difficulty of the return climb—an experiment Armstrong had also tried—and paused to take in the panorama.

Armstrong had picked a good landing spot. It wasn't smooth—no place on the Moon is smooth—but it was reasonably flat, amid a sea of small craters, depressions, mounds, and ridges in every direction. Alert to the geology, Aldrin had already looked out the window and described with great enthusiasm the variety of the different rock shapes. Now that he was outside, he felt a different kind of excitement. He blurted out, "Beautiful view!"

Buzz Aldrin stands on the Moon's Sea of Tranquility. Armstrong is the white figure reflected in Aldrin's visor.

Neil agreed. "Isn't it magnificent?"

Buzz summed it up: "Magnificent desolation."

Surveying the landscape, Armstrong said he was reminded of "the high desert of the United States." He was probably thinking of the area around Edwards Air Force Base, California, where he, Deke Slayton, and so many of the astronauts had been test pilots. "It's very pretty out here," he added. This surprised Eric Sevareid of CBS News. "I never expected to hear that word 'pretty,'" he remarked during the network's moonwalk coverage. "The scene he saw on the Moon, what we thought was cold and desolate and forbidding, somehow they found a strange beauty there that I suppose they can never really describe to us."

Armstrong, Aldrin, and later Moon explorers did describe it. One of the most striking things they noted was a sky blacker than any black on Earth, a velvety black you felt you could touch, but when you reached out your hand there was nothing there. No night sky on Earth was that black, even though Apollo landings took place in daylight, with the Sun low in the east, shining so brilliantly that it was impossible to look at it even for an instant. The black sky; the gray landscape sparkling in the dazzling morning Sun; the sharp features visible all the way to the horizon because there is no atmosphere, defeating any attempt to judge distances; and the absence of wind, clouds, sound, or any living thing. It's a breathtaking world of utter barrenness.

Magnificent desolation.

●

Then there was the joy of moving around. Astronauts were used to being weightless, and like everyone on Earth they were used to the one-g pull of terrestrial gravity, not to mention the multiple g's experienced during jet aircraft maneuvers and rocket launches. But the Moon gave them a totally new experience of gravity.

Standing near *Eagle*, Buzz Aldrin sets up an experiment to measure charged particles from the Sun.

The Moon is far smaller and much less massive than Earth. At its surface, gravity is six times weaker than on Earth. No one was quite sure how disorienting the experience would be, so Armstrong and Aldrin were instructed to move with great care to avoid falling. They quickly discovered that one-sixth g is very pleasant, and they were soon bouncing and skipping along. On television, they seemed to be moving in slow motion, and that was how it felt. "When you move" on the Moon, recalled Aldrin, "you just *wait* to be brought down to the surface . . . you've got a lot of time, which means that time slowed down, which gives you this sensation of slow motion . . . you're getting to observe a lot more, and you're aware that you're still not down yet."

Yet there was much to do. Their backpacks carried only four hours of oxygen and cooling water. To be on the safe side, Mission Control had limited their outdoor time to roughly half that. During this period, Armstrong and Aldrin had to set up experiments, collect rocks, take photographs, and explore the general area. Armstrong loped over to the small crater they had flown over in the final minute before landing. Craters are interesting for what they reveal about the geology beneath the surface, and he wanted to get photographs of the inside walls for scientists back home.

"Exploring this place that had never before been seen by human eyes, upon which no foot had stepped, or hand touched—was awe-inspiring," Aldrin later wrote. "But we had no time for philosophical musings." That would come later.

NASA did make time for several commemorative events. Armstrong and Aldrin planted an American flag. They took a short congratulatory call from President Nixon (who had requested that the national anthem be played, but Frank Borman talked him out of it because of the two and a half minutes it would deduct from the astronauts' frantic schedule). And Armstrong and Aldrin unveiled a commemorative plaque mounted between two rungs of the ladder. The plaque reads:

HERE MEN FROM THE PLANET EARTH
FIRST SET FOOT UPON THE MOON
JULY 1969, A.D.
WE CAME IN PEACE FOR ALL MANKIND

It is signed by all three Apollo 11 astronauts and by President Nixon—much as a president's name goes on the dedicatory signs for dams, bridges, post offices, and other federal projects.

Apollo 11's commemorative plaque, mounted on one of *Eagle*'s legs

Surmounting the inscription are the two hemispheres of Earth. Future visitors to the site need only look straight up and lean back a little to see the real thing, always in the same spot of the sky. It's not easy to do in a space suit, said Aldrin, who tried and just managed to catch a glimpse of "our marble-sized planet, no bigger than my thumb."

Earth suspended above *Eagle*. Because the Moon always keeps the same side turned toward Earth, our planet hardly moves in the lunar sky.

No one was celebrating until the astronauts got home, but the landing and moonwalk were feats that brought tears to the eyes of millions. Many people went outside and looked at the Moon while Neil and Buzz were there. It was in its crescent phase, and if you gazed at the center of the crescent, in the sunlit area near the boundary between light and dark—that was where they were. The familiar Moon, origin of myths and bright beacon in the night sky, suddenly looked different.

Like thousands of others who worked on Apollo, Ed Fendell was so busy with his job that he had no time to think about anything else. He had been at Mission Control when Apollo 11 landed. When the new shift came on duty, he stayed to watch the moonwalk. Then he went home to get some sleep. The next morning, he was having breakfast at his usual coffee shop. It was just like any other day. "Two guys walk in and sit down on the two stools next to me," he recalled three decades later. They were from a nearby gas station.

"They're waiting for their breakfast," Fendell went on. "They start talking . . . One of them says to the other one . . . 'You know, I went all through World War II. I landed at Normandy on D-Day . . . It was an incredible day, an incredible life, and I went all the way through Paris and on into Berlin . . . but yesterday was the day that I felt the proudest to be an American.'"

In the year 2000, when Ed Fendell was recounting this story to a NASA historian, it all came flooding back: the excitement, the wonder, the camaraderie, and the pride in being part of a unique adventure. "As you can tell," he said tearfully, "I'm getting a little choked up right now."

NASA managers in the back row at Mission Control celebrate Apollo 11's return to Earth, July 24, 1969. Foreground, left to right: Max Faget, Chris Kraft (with flag), George Low, and Robert Gilruth.

EPILOGUE

"WE MUST STOP"

The real test of John Houbolt's lunar-orbit rendezvous strategy came when Armstrong and Aldrin fired *Eagle*'s ascent-stage engine on July 21. Meticulously timed for a rendezvous with Mike Collins in the orbiting *Columbia*, this do-or-die maneuver was exactly like a Gemini spacecraft ascending to dock with an Agena, except it was happening a quarter of a million miles from Earth. The astronauts used to joke that a launch at the Cape took thousands of people, while the ascent from the Moon needed just two.

It worked. After two orbits, Armstrong and Aldrin rejoined Collins. Later the empty *Eagle* was cut loose and *Columbia* lit its engine for home. Ahead for the three explorers was a short period of quarantine to ensure they had brought home no alien microbes, then parades, speeches, and a lifetime of adulation, which has its frustrations for men who just want to be alone in the cockpit of an airplane. Wherever they went, Armstrong, Aldrin, and Collins said that they weren't the heroes; the American people were the heroes. Still, they had been given a demanding job to do, and they had done it—perfectly.

Shortly before Armstrong and Aldrin took off from Tranquility Base, Luna 15 began its long-delayed descent from lunar orbit. The automatic probe crashed more than 700 miles away. The Soviets put the best possible face on what was supposed to be a headline-stealing sample-return mission, announcing that Luna 15 "achieved the Moon's surface in the preselected area."

The following year, their next attempt, Luna 16, would succeed, returning a canister full of lunar soil to Earth. The Soviets claimed this was the extent of their lunar program and that they had never been in the man-on-the-Moon race to begin with. However, within five years

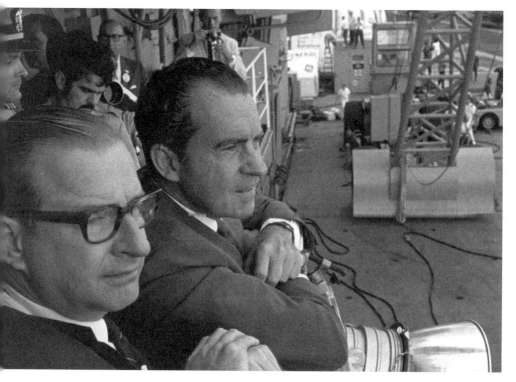

Tom Paine (left) and President Nixon wait to greet the Apollo 11 astronauts on the recovery ship in the Pacific Ocean.

researchers in the West made a convincing case that the Russians had been in the race all along. Later disclosures showed that they had built a monstrous rocket comparable to the Saturn V and secretly tested it four times between 1969 and 1972. Each time it blew up. They had also developed hardware similar to the Apollo CSM and LM, but they never flew it with cosmonauts. Even so, they came close to beating Apollo 8 around the Moon with a less advanced version of their CSM, only to be derailed by technical problems.

What probably doomed their efforts was that the genius behind the Soviet space program, the man responsible for Sputnik, Yuri Gagarin's flight, and the other early triumphs, died during surgery in 1966. Sergei Korolev was the Soviets' Wernher von Braun, Max Faget, Jim Webb, and

New York City welcomes Collins, Aldrin, and Armstrong. Tom Paine is sitting in front of Aldrin.

Bob Gilruth all rolled into one. That may have been the problem. The United States had a deep bench of talent. The Russians had Korolev—until they didn't.

●

After Apollo 11, NASA made six more manned lunar trips: Apollo 12 through 17. One was nearly a disaster. On the way to the Moon in April 1970, a main oxygen tank in Apollo 13's service module exploded due to a faulty switch. It took four days to get back, as vital supplies dwindled. Commanded by Jim Lovell, this mission is one of history's great survival stories. The other Apollo flights are equally notable as some of history's greatest scientific expeditions, which solved the secret of the Moon's origin and energized the field of planetary science.

However, NASA managers were getting nervous. Mindful of the close call on Apollo 13 and the millions of other things that could go wrong, Bob Gilruth lobbied to end the program. "We must stop. There are so many chances for us losing a crew. We just know that we're going to do that if we keep going." His colleague Chris Kraft felt the same way.

And so, in December 1972, three and a half years after Armstrong and Aldrin made history, America closed the book on its incredible lunar adventure with Apollo 17, even though hardware for more flights was available. No one has kicked up the lunar dust and gazed at the Moon's magnificent desolation since then.

●

By the end of the Apollo program, its total cost was just over 25 billion dollars. Taking inflation into account, this was a billion or so less than the 20 billion Jim Webb had said he needed in 1963—and that was just for a single Moon landing! In a way, this was Webb's proudest accomplishment. Landing a man on the Moon is difficult enough, but he had made it happen on time and on budget, which is a miracle in large-scale government projects. Ever since Apollo, advocates for any formidable goal—from curing cancer to solving global warming—preface their pitch with, "If we can land a man on the Moon . . ." What they really mean is, "If we only had Jim Webb . . ."

Wernher von Braun was the dreamer who realized before anyone else that a Moon voyage was possible. After Apollo 11, he tried to make the case for going to Mars. As usual, he had worked out all the details. But with the Vietnam War still raging and America's other problems, it was an impossible idea to sell. He was persuaded to leave his rocket team in Huntsville and take a strategic-planning job at NASA headquarters in Washington, where his promised authority never materialized. It was like tricking a wizard into giving up his magic wand. One of his associates described von Braun's fate this way: "Wernher is like a great conductor who has held the world in awe with his fabulous performances, and who suddenly finds himself without an orchestra, without players and their instruments, without a concert hall, and even without music-loving audiences. He still plays his own violin once in a while, but only few people listen to him."

After the launch of the first Saturn V, when the ground shook and the dawn sky was ablaze with what seemed like a second Sun, when Wernher von Braun yelled, "Go, baby, go!" and the most powerful rocket ever built left Earth for space, Apollo boss General Sam Phillips was asked what he thought. "I was impressed," he said simply. A military man to the core, Phillips reported to the Air Force for his next assignment after Apollo 11. He went on to other high-level posts, including Director of the National Security Agency, the military's intelligence arm, where his tight-lipped style fit right in.

In 1972, Deke Slayton's clean living finally paid off. His heart problem had cleared up and doctors put him back on flight status. As Director of Flight Crew Operations, Deke recommended himself for the next available mission, the docking of American and Soviet craft in Earth orbit, scheduled for 1975. This joint flight would mark a truce in the Cold War and a hoped-for era of cooperation. Using the last flightworthy Apollo CSM, the U.S. crew was commanded by Apollo 10 veteran Tom Stafford and also included Vance Brand, a rookie like Slayton. On their ride into orbit, the two rookies became the seventy-seventh and seventy-eighth persons in space. Deke Slayton had made it after all.

Tom Paine had the top job at NASA and a ringside seat during the exhilarating days of Apollo 7 through 13. He was instrumental in changing the mission of Apollo 8 from Earth orbit to lunar orbit, heading off the Soviet Union's best chance of beating America to the Moon. He presided over the fulfillment of Kennedy's goal, and he promoted an ambitious program of space exploration after Apollo, which was rejected except for the Space Shuttle and Space Station. Paine's account of this pivotal period would have been fascinating. But in retirement he chose to focus on something else: his submarine service during World War II. Paine wrote a memoir about his exploits and amassed a library of some 3,500 volumes on submarines, which was later donated to the United

Deke Slayton suits up for the first joint U.S.–Soviet space mission, 1975.

States Naval Academy. Before Apollo 11's launch, he was given the chance to send a keepsake that would fly to the Moon and back with Armstrong, Aldrin, and Collins. He chose the gold dolphin pin that he had proudly worn as a U.S. Navy submarine officer.

Max Faget, the genius behind the Mercury capsule and the Apollo command module, went on to design the Space Shuttle. In fact, he may have missed the Apollo 11 launch because he was already deep into work on

Submarine officer's pin like the one carried aboard Apollo 11 for Tom Paine

the shuttle in the summer of 1969. Once asked how the U.S. got to the Moon so quickly, he told the story of his submarine, *Guavina*, during World War II. It was built in Manitowoc, Wisconsin, by a firm that specialized in ore haulers and ferries for the Great Lakes. "We weren't going to fight a war on the lake," Faget noted, so the company asked the Navy what kind of ship it needed. Submarines, came the answer. "They had never built a submarine before, didn't know the first thing about it," but they got the plans and worked around the clock to turn them out. "I rode on one, and they were beautifully built," he recalled. "When you've got a real burr up your rear end, boy, you're going to move. So we moved in World War II." Apollo was no different, and in the future, he added, "if we had a real crisis, we could respond a lot faster than you think."

Several years after the end of Apollo, Max Faget and Bob Gilruth were walking on the beach at Galveston, Texas, not far from the space center. The Apollo landings were receding into history, and Americans were starting to forget the anxiety and thrill of the space race, and their tremendous pride in Apollo 11.

This may have been on Gilruth's mind as he looked up at the Moon, shining over the Gulf of Mexico. "You know, Max," he said, "someday people are going to try to go back to the Moon, and they're going to find out how hard it really is."

Gazing up at that distant, glowing orb, Faget nodded. Yes, it had been hard. Most people had no idea how hard. That was the way it always was with a great achievement: in retrospect, it looked easy.

For those involved in Project Apollo—all 400,000 of them—it had been challenging, perplexing, nerve-racking. But for many of them, it was ultimately the most rewarding experience of their lives. Some called it a war without shooting. But it was the crisis of a real war that had made it possible. World War II had taught Faget, Paine, Slayton, Phillips, von Braun, Webb, and thousands of others how to do big things quickly. In submarines, cockpits, research labs, and defense plants, on the front lines and on the home front, they mastered the selfless teamwork that would one day achieve the seemingly impossible—a voyage beyond the atmosphere, through the vacuum of space, to the ultimate destination: the Moon.

Max Faget's submarine, built with speed and skill by a company that was new to submarines. Apollo would spark the same commitment.

Apollo landing sites on the Moon

Apollo 11 (1969)

Apollo 12 (1969)

Apollo 14 (1971)

Apollo 15 (1971)

Apollo 16 (1972)

Apollo 17 (1972)

BRIEFING:
Six Landing Sites

Between 1969 and 1972, the United States landed six Apollo missions on the Moon. Apollo 11 set down on a flat plain, where Armstrong and Aldrin spent barely two hours outside. Each successive mission went to a more challenging site, stayed longer, and explored farther. Unlike Apollo 11, they also made pinpoint landings near their objectives. By Apollo 15, commander Dave Scott was threading his LM between two high mountains to land at their foot next to a canyon as deep as Colorado's Royal Gorge. He and his copilot, Jim Irwin, stayed for three days, exploring the region in an electric moon buggy. "It's absolutely mind-boggling, because you cannot believe it is really that spectacular," Scott said afterward.

The geology during the missions was also spectacular. Practically any rock that astronauts picked up was as old as Earth's most ancient rocks, and many were far older. The specimens told a story of a primordial magma ocean, huge asteroid impacts, and the Moon's origin far back in time, when a rogue planet collided with the infant Earth.

In choosing the astronauts who went to the Moon, Deke Slayton stuck to his rotation system, except he let Al Shepard—America's first spaceman—jump to the head of the line after he was restored to flight status. Below is a rundown of the six landings and crews, with the commander listed first, followed by the command module pilot and lunar module pilot. Along with the crews of Apollo 8, 10, and 13, which flew around the Moon but did not land, these are history's first lunar explorers:

Apollo 11
Crew: Neil Armstrong, Mike Collins, Buzz Aldrin
Landing site: Sea of Tranquility

Apollo 12
Crew: Pete Conrad, Dick Gordon, Al Bean
Landing site: Ocean of Storms

Apollo 14
Crew: Al Shepard, Stu Roosa, Ed Mitchell
Landing site: Fra Mauro highlands

Apollo 15
Crew: Dave Scott, Al Worden, Jim Irwin
Landing site: Hadley Rille

Apollo 16
Crew: John Young, Tom Mattingly, Charlie Duke
Landing site: Descartes highlands

Apollo 17
Crew: Gene Cernan, Ron Evans, Jack Schmitt
Landing site: Taurus-Littrow valley

TIMELINE

1941

Japan attacks Pearl Harbor, Hawaii, bringing the U.S. into World War II.

1957

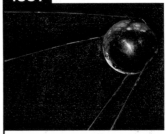

Sputnik 1, the first artificial satellite, is launched by the Soviet Union, using the world's largest rocket at the time. The space age begins.

1945

Germany surrenders. Three months later, the U.S. drops two atomic bombs on Japan, which surrenders, ending World War II.

1958

The U.S. launches its first satellite with a rocket developed from V-2 technology.

1962–1964

The Soviet Union launches five manned Earth-orbiting missions, versus four by America's Mercury program.

German V-2s—the first rockets capable of reaching space—are launched against England with high-explosive warheads.

The Cold War starts, pitting the U.S. and its allies against the Soviet Union and the communist bloc in a largely ideological conflict.

1947

Russian Yuri Gagarin is the first man in space. A month later, Alan Shepard is the first American in space. Shortly after, President Kennedy announces the goal of landing a man on the Moon by the end of the decade, which becomes Project Apollo.

1944

1961

1965

A Russian makes the first space walk. Months later, an American follows suit.

1968

Apollo 8 circles the Moon in a surprise mission, beating an anticipated Soviet manned circumlunar flight.

1966

America's Gemini program ends after ten successful manned spaceflights, including a near disaster for astronaut Neil Armstrong.

1972

Project Apollo ends with its sixth manned Moon landing, Apollo 17.

The Apollo 1 spacecraft is destroyed in a fire on the launchpad, killing the crew. A Russian also dies while testing a new spacecraft.
The first flight of the Saturn V Moon rocket is spectacularly successful.

Apollo 11 astronauts Armstrong and Aldrin become the first humans on the Moon, while their colleague Collins orbits the Moon in the mother ship.

The Soviet Union collapses, bringing an end to the Cold War.

1991

1967

1969

ACKNOWLEDGMENTS

When I was fourteen, I did a science-fair project on rockets that won an award from NASA. It was nothing brilliant, and there were over a hundred winners in the Great Plains states from Texas (where I lived) to North Dakota. We were all honored with a special conference at the then brand-new Manned Spacecraft Center (MSC) in Houston in August 1965.

As luck would have it, the Gemini 5 mission was delayed and ended up coinciding with our visit. Gemini 5 was the longest-duration human spaceflight yet and only the second time that MSC was being used as Mission Control for astronauts in orbit—a function it still serves as the rechristened Lyndon B. Johnson Space Center. Apollo planning was at its peak, and Gemini 5 was intended to show that humans could function in space for the eight days that a lunar-landing mission would take.

Back then, MSC had the look of an Old West boomtown. New construction was everywhere in the middle of what had formerly been ranch land. Our itinerary included tours, a visit to a Gemini press conference (where the big celebrities were the television correspondents we saw on the nightly news), and talks given by insiders such as Apollo spacecraft manager Joseph Shea and astronaut Charles Bassett, who spoke at our banquet on the last night.

Not long after, Bassett was chosen to fly on Gemini 9, scheduled for spring 1966. Tragically, he was to die with his mission commander, Elliot See, when their T-38 jet crashed in bad weather just three months before their launch date. Deke Slayton, head of Flight Crew Operations, said he had had "a lot of plans for Charlie Bassett." After his Gemini assignment, Bassett was slated to be an Apollo command module pilot. Given Slayton's rotation system, he would probably have commanded one of the later Apollo missions and walked on the Moon. T-38s also took the lives of Apollo astronauts Theodore Freeman and Clifton "C.C." Williams—also before they had a chance to fly in space. Astronaut Edward Givens Jr. died in an automobile accident—again before his first mission. In chapter 28, I recount the tragedy of the Apollo 1 fire, which killed three astronauts in a ground test. There were also fatal accidents in the Soviet space program. We should never forget these brave pioneers.

Many years have passed since my teenage visit to Houston, but I have never stopped marveling at the amazing adventure of Apollo. Most recently, conversations with David Michaud and Steven Bressler got me thinking about the importance of World War II to the Apollo program, which drew on the infrastructure, experience, and attitudes developed during the war. David and Steve are talented exhibit designers, and the three of us planned to produce a traveling exhibit on Apollo. It fell through, but the germ of our discussions grew into this book.

My first and closest connections to Apollo veterans have been with the late William R. Muehlberger of the University of Texas at Austin and James W. Head III of Brown University. Both were advisory geologists in the Apollo program, helping pick landing sites, plan exploration, and train the astronauts. Some years ago, I interviewed Jack Schmitt, who actually went to the Moon as a geologist and lunar module pilot on Apollo 17. I was interested in the parallels between the exploration of the American West and the Moon, which as a student of history and a native of New Mexico, Schmitt saw very clearly. Over the years, Apollo historian Andrew Chaikin has been an enthusiastic and indulgent sounding board. Exhibit projects with different museums and galleries allowed me to immerse myself deeply in Apollo images and artifacts. Lorraine Neilan of Mountview Middle School in Holden, Massachusetts, invited me to discuss Apollo with her science students. And Gale Free Library in Holden has been an indispensable resource, for which I thank library director Susan Scott and her superb staff. I am also grateful to space journalist and historian James Oberg for reviewing the manuscript and making a number of excellent suggestions. Any defects that remain are mine alone.

The author's name goes on the title page, but a book is really a joint effort. My collaborators at Roaring Brook include editor Emily Feinberg, designer Monique Sterling, production editor Mandy Veloso, and copyeditor Chandra Wohleber. I am also grateful to former Macmillan executive Simon Boughton, whose enthusiasm for Apollo launched me on this project. This book is dedicated to my delightful daughters-in-law, Jessamyn and Hannah. My wife, Susie, whom I met in the publishing business some four decades ago, has been my guiding star.

NOTES

Abbreviations

    JSC = NASA Johnson Space Center Oral History Project

    LBJ = Lyndon Baines Johnson Library Oral History Collection

    NASM = Smithsonian National Air and Space Museum Oral History Project

Statistics for Saturn and Apollo flights are from Orloff and Harland, *Apollo: The Definitive Sourcebook*. Nautical miles have been converted to statute miles.

PART 1: War

3 *"The war made us"*: Renehan, *The Kennedys at War*, p. 2.

Chapter 1: Ensign Faget's Close Call

6 *It was February 20, 1945*: The depth-charging ordeal is recounted most fully by Faget's fellow crewman Marion L. Shinn in Chap. 18 of his memoir, *Pacific Patrol*. See also "Report of Fifth War Patrol" in "History of U.S.S. *Guavina*"; as well as Hargis, "Boats on Patrol" in *U.S. Submarine Crewman*; and Faget, JSC, June 18, 1997.

9 *"We experienced hell"*: "Report of Fifth War Patrol," p. 12, in "History of U.S.S. *Guavina*."

9 *"Words cannot express"*: From Chap. 18 in Shinn, *Pacific Patrol*.

11 *"A submarine is a very high-tech ship"*: Cooper, "Annals of Space," *New Yorker*, September 2, 1991, p. 57.

Chapter 2: Pirates of the Western Pacific

14 *"We were the last of the corsairs"*: Buckley, "NASA's Tom Paine," *New York Times*, June 8, 1969, magazine section, p. 36.

14–16 U.S.S. *Pompon*: Details of *Pompon*'s patrols are in "History of U.S.S. *Pompon*," a day-by-day log of the submarine's activities. Paine's first war patrol was *Pompon*'s third, his second was *Pompon*'s fourth, etc.

15 *"a mere ensign do"*: Calvert, *Silent Running*, p. 9.

15 *Seawater immediately cascaded into the control room*: The official report on the flooding incident is in "Report of War Patrol No. Seven," pp. 7–8, in "History of U.S.S. *Pompon*." The incident is also recounted by Stanley J. Nicholls in Roberts, *Sub*, pp. 34–35; and by Bailey in "The 7th Patrol of the U.S.S. *Pompon*."

17 *By the end of the war, nearly one-fifth of America's fighting subs*: cited in *United States Submarine Losses, World War II*, p. 1.

17 *"I saw many strange and wonderful things"*: Buckley, "NASA's Tom Paine," *New York Times*, June 8, 1969, magazine section, p. 36.

17 *"Youth and the sea"*: Conrad, "Youth," fourth-to-last paragraph. See Paine's "The Transpacific Voyage," where he says, "In his sea classic 'Youth' Joseph Conrad captures my feelings perfectly."

Chapter 3: Lieutenant Slayton Flies Another Mission

20 *the British intensified their own bombing campaign against Germany*: Background on the bomber offensive in Europe is from Overy, *The Bombing War*. U.S. sortie statistics in this chapter are from *Army Air Forces Statistical Digest: World War II*.

20 *Second Lieutenant Donald K. Slayton*: Slayton's service with the 486th Squadron, 340th Bomb Group, is covered in Chap. 3 of Slayton and Cassutt, *Deke!* Reminiscences by other airmen with the group are in Satterthwaite, *Truth Flies with Fiction*; and Meder, *The True Story of Catch-22*, which covers the experiences of novelist Joseph Heller, who also flew with the 340th.

21 *Working with target orders from headquarters*: The duties of operations staff are described in the chapter "Operations" in Casper, *History and Personnel, 489th, 340th Bomb Group*.

21 *usual mission was a formation of eighteen planes*: Satterthwaite, *Truth Flies with Fiction*, pp. 44–45.

22 *headquarters set a limit on how many missions an airman had to fly*: Changing mission limits are described in Meder, *The True Story of Catch-22*, p. 17.

22 *fifty missions gave flyers about a 30 percent chance of getting shot down*: Data is in Satterthwaite, *Truth Flies with Fiction*, p. 254.

22 *"Fly 'til I die"*: Howard, *Whistle While You Wait*, p. 165.

22 *"Same time, same place, same direction!"*: Slayton and Cassutt, *Deke!*, p. 27. Additional quotes and details on the Athens raid are in "November 17, 1943 Mission to Kalamaki Aerodrome, Greece."

25 *The following day the men learned that the fifty-mission limit was being raised*: Under the entries for November 18 in "History: November 1943."

Chapter 4: Captain Phillips Bombs Major von Braun

27 *"Surviving"*: Phillips, NASM (February 23, 1988).

27 *364th Fighter Group*: For the history of Phillips's unit, see Joiner, *The History of the 364th Fighter Group*.

28 *One of the Mustang's most advanced features was its wing*: For NACA research on laminar-flow airfoils, see Hansen, *Engineer in Charge*, pp. 111–118.

29 *"The greatest surprise of the war to us"*: Irving, *Göring*, p. 469.

29 *On August 25, 1944*: For Phillips's participation, see Stuhlinger and Ordway, *Wernher von Braun: A Biographical Memoir*, p. 201; and *The History of the 364th Fighter Group*, p. 45, where Mission No. 187 is the only raid to the Peenemünde area recorded by the 364th. The raid is broken down in "USAAF Chronology," 25 August 1944, Mission 570, No. 3.

32 *"It could have very easily led me to the firing squad"*: Ward, *Dr. Space*, p. 40.

32 *von Braun's rockets began falling on London*: V-2 launch statistics are from Ordway and Sharpe, *The Rocket Team*, pp. 243 and 251.

33 *responsible for some 5,000 deaths—not including the estimated 10,000*: Neufeld, *The Rocket and the Reich*, p. 264.

33 *It took as much labor to build one*: O'Brien, *How the War Was Won*, pp. 28–29.

33 *"Once they felt they could do without you"*: Ward, *Dr. Space*, p. 39.

Chapter 5: Major Webb Faces the Big One

36 *Major James E. Webb*: Webb's reminiscences of the U.S. Marine Corps and the Sperry Gyroscope Company are in Webb, NASM: February 22, 1985; March 8, 1985; and March 29, 1985. For more details on his life, see Lambright, *Powering Apollo*, and Bizony, *The Man Who Ran the Moon*.

38 *"My forte was putting things together"*: Webb, NASM, February 22, 1985.

38 *"War is a hurly-burly kind of thing"*: Webb, NASM, February 22, 1985.

40 *More than 85,000 were built*: Mindell, *Between Human and Machine*, p. 221.

41 *"The contractors said it would take us six, maybe eight months"*: Webb, NASM, February 22, 1985.

Chapter 6: "We Need It Yesterday!"

44 *"We didn't think that much about it"*: Slayton and Cassutt, *Deke!*, p. 35.

45 *the B-29 Superfortress, came out of a more expensive program*: O'Brien, *How the War Was Won*, pp. 47–48.

46 *A famous story*: Recounted in Ricks, "Whatever Happened to Accountability?"; also in Perret, *There's a War to Be Won*, p. 27.

47 *In 1939, he had asked Boeing Company executives*: Geer, *Boeing's Ed Wells*, pp. 93–94; more B-29 specifications are in Vander Meulen, *Building the B-29*, pp. 12–17.

47 *by attacking all of the airplane's intricate systems at the same time*: Johnson, *The Secret of Apollo*, p. 26.

47 *thousands of engineers*: Vander Meulen, *Building the B-29*, p. 15.

47 *thousands of suppliers*: Bilstein, "Aviation Industry," *The Oxford Encyclopedia of American Business, Labor, and Economic History*, Vol. 1, p. 69.

47 *"depends upon everything working as planned"*: Vander Meulen, *Building the B-29*, p. 86.

47 *The worst day was February 18, 1943*: The accident is recounted in Robbins, "Eddie Allen and the B-29." Also see Herman, *Freedom's Forge*, pp. 301–302 (for the accident) and p. 303 (for the political fallout).

48 *A review board ordered changes in the engines*: For engineering changes and production problems, see Vander Meulen, *Building the B-29*, pp. 32–35 and 90.

48 *within fourteen months the B-29 was flying in combat*: Herman, *Freedom's Forge*, p. 320.

PART 2: Dreams
53 *"To place a man in a multi-stage rocket"*: "Space Travel Impossible, States Dr. Lee De Forest," *Boston Globe*, February 25, 1957, p. 11.

Chapter 7: America Lands on Its Feet
56 *life expectancy was just forty-seven years*: The Berkeley Mortality Database.

57 *In 1900, only a third of homes had running water*: Statistics for modern conveniences are in Gordon, *The Rise and Fall of American Growth*, pp. 114–115.

57 *At the end of 1949, a random sample of Americans*: The Gallup Poll Public Opinion, 1935–1971. Vol. 2: *1949–1958*, p. 875.

Chapter 8: Von Braun Lands in America

61 *"That guy upstairs wants to go to the Moon"*: Lang, *From Hiroshima to the Moon*, p. 180.

62 *"America is the place for you to build your Moon rockets"*: Neufeld, *Von Braun*, p. 190.

63 *"If Germany had won the war"*: Lang, *From Hiroshima to the Moon*, pp. 185–186.

64 *"At Peenemünde, we'd been coddled"*: Lang, *From Hiroshima to the Moon*, p. 189.

65 *"former pets of Hitler"*: Graham, "Nazi Scientists Aid Army on Research," *New York Times*, December 4, 1946, p. 35. For more on this controversy, see Laney, *German Rocketeers in the Heart of Dixie*, Chap. 1.

65 *"We hold these individuals"*: "Opposes Citizenship for Reich Scientists," *The Spokesman-Review*, December 30, 1946, p. 2.

65 *a majority of Americans agreed*: Gallup, *The Gallup Poll Public Opinion, 1935–1971*. Vol. 1: *1935–1948*, p. 618.

Chapter 9: The Cold War

69 *"We have emerged from this war"*: McMahon, *The Cold War*, p. 6.

70 *twenty years was a good estimate*: Rhodes, *The Making of the Atomic Bomb*, p. 633.

71 *"The calmer the American people take this, the better"*: "Red Alert," *Time*, October 3, 1949, p. 10.

71 *"Better get out your old uniform"*: "The Thunderclap," *Time*, October 3, 1949, p. 10.

72 *he had a remarkably calm discussion*: Sears, *Such Men as These*, p. 175.

Chapter 10: Disney to the Rescue
78 *"With the Redstone, we could do it!"*: Stuhlinger and Ordway, *Wernher von Braun: A Biographical Memoir*, p. 122.

80 *arrived like a trumpet blast from the future*: The making of the *Collier's* and Disney series is told in Liebermann, "The *Collier's* and Disney Series"; and in Smith, "They're Following Our Script."

81 *"What you will read here is not science fiction"*: "What Are We Waiting For?" *Collier's*, March 22, 1952, p. 23.

82 *"Disney's immediate achievement"*: Smith, "They're Following Our Script," *Future*, May 1978, p. 59.

83 *"made all the generals sit down"*: Kimball in Ghez, *Walt's People*, Vol. 3, p. 52.

Chapter 11: The Empire Strikes Back
85 *"a lot of hooey!"*: Bracker, "Truman Varies—Airy to Mundane," *New York Times*, February 5, 1956, p. 56.

86 *By mid-1955, development work on the Redstone was nearly complete*: Bulkeley, *The Sputniks Crisis*, p. 158. For von Braun's souped-up Redstone, see Ward, *Dr. Space*, pp. 97–98.

86 *"I want you to tell him"*: Gray, *Angle of Attack*, pp. 15–16.

87 *"I'll be damned!"*: Ward, *Dr. Space*, p. 99.

87 *"a disaster . . . comparable to Pearl Harbor"*: Divine, "Lyndon B. Johnson and the Politics of Space," p. 223.

87 *"a devastating blow to the prestige of the United States"*: Callahan and Greenstein, "The Reluctant Racer," p. 26.

89 "like sausages": McDougall, *The Heavens and the Earth*, p. 240.

90 *a large audience from all walks of life*: "The Death of TV-3," *Time*, December 16, 1957, National Affairs section.

90 *Reporting to his boss in Washington over a long-distance phone line*: Bracker, "Vanguard Rocket Burns on Beach," *New York Times*, December 7, 1957, p. 8.

90 *"bore a remarkable resemblance to atomic-bomb detonations"*: Talbert, "U.S. Moon Rocket Blows Up," *New York Herald Tribune*, December 7, 1957, p. 1.

90 *a Russian short animated film*: "Soviet Movie Shows Reach for the Moon," *Time*, October 28, 1957, p. 26. The film, *After Sputnik—the Moon?*, is posted on YouTube at youtube.com/watch?v=yl5d2EVPMXY (published August 3, 2015).

Chapter 12: Explorer
93 *Redstone was called Juno I*: The rocket was also called Jupiter-C. The Juno designation was to distinguish it from the Redstone and Jupiter programs, which were both military.

93 *Mary Sherman Morgan:* For her life story, see Morgan, *Rocket Girl*.

94 *In late January*: Details of the Juno launch are in Medaris, *Countdown for Decision*, pp. 200–226.

95 *"tremendous jet burst from the base of the rocket"*: Bracker, "Jupiter-C Is Used," *New York Times*, February 1, 1958, p. 7.

95 *"a flame-footed monster"*: "Voyage of the Explorer," *Time*, February 10, 1958, p. 17.

95 *"terrific"*: "U.S. Fires 'Moon'!" *Chicago Daily Tribune*, February 1, 1958, p. 2.

95 *"Slow rise, faster, faster!"*: Neufeld, *Von Braun*, p. 321.

96 *seven minutes after launch*: "U.S. Fires 'Moon'!" *Chicago Daily Tribune*, February 1, 1958, p. 1.

96 *"with 95 percent confidence"*: Bille and Lishock, *The First Space Race*, pp. 131–132.

97 *"Those moments were the most exciting eight minutes of my life!"*: Ward, *Dr. Space*, p. 116.

97 *"Once the first satellite is in orbit"*: Stuhlinger and Ordway, *Wernher von Braun: A Biographical Memoir*, p. 109.

Briefing: Russia's Rocket
99 *"Do you realize the tremendous strategic importance"*: Holloway, *Stalin and the Bomb*, p. 247.

PART 3: Spacemen
101 *"Your plan will provide"*: von Ehrenfried, *The Birth of NASA*, p. 95. See also Gilruth, NASM, February 27, 1987, where Gilruth recounts the July 2, 1958, meeting at which Kistiakowsky made this remark.

Chapter 13: Max Makes His Pitch
103 *"If voyages were to be made from the Earth"*: Sloane, "Acceleration in Interplanetary Travel."

104 *"it will take iron nerves waiting for the impact that never comes"*: "Man in Space," *Disneyland*.

104 *weightlessness would drive people crazy*: Leonard, *Flight into Space*, p. 94.

105 *"I refuse to recognize that there are impossibilities"*: Ford and Crowther, "My Life and Work," p. 14.

105 *secret conference*: Gray, *Angle of Attack*, p. 45.

106 *Most of the engineers at the conference*: For an account of the high-speed-flight conference, known as the Round Three Conference, see Chaikin, "How the Spaceship Got Its Shape."

108 *Working with two other colleagues, Faget fleshed out the details*: See the very readable short paper by Faget, Garland, and Buglia, "Preliminary Studies of Manned Satellites—Wingless Configuration: Nonlifting."

109 *"Max made his pitch"*: Chaikin, "How the Spaceship Got Its Shape."

109 *Faget was determined to move ahead*: Swenson et al., *This New Ocean*, p. 532, n. 54.

Chapter 14: "Let's Get On with It"

111 *under questioning by a congressional committee*: Dryden's tribulations and the birth of NASA are described in Roland, *Model Research*, Chap. 12.

111 *"Tossing a man up in the air"*: Swenson et al., *This New Ocean*, p. 100.

112 *much to von Braun's dismay*: Neufeld, *Von Braun*, p. 330.

112 *NA¢A had become NA$A*: Roland, *Model Research*, p. 300.

113 *stubborn*: See Faget's comments on von Braun in Faget, JSC, June 18, 1997.

113 *who had little taste for stunts or crash programs*: Glennan's attitudes are covered in Glennan, *The Birth of NASA*, pp. 5, 67.

113 *"All right. Let's get on with it."*: Glennan's order to Gilruth is recounted in Hansen, *Spaceflight Revolution*, p. 55; and Detholff, *Suddenly, Tomorrow Came . . .* , p. 20.

115 *"Okay, we'll go"*: Rives, "'OK, We'll Go,'" *Prologue*, Spring 2014.

115 *"It was one of the best decisions he ever made"*: Cortright, *Apollo Expeditions to the Moon*, p. 146.

Chapter 15: The Original Seven
119 *dead test pilots*: Fredrickson, *Warbird Factory*, p. 141.

119 *sixty-two fighter pilots had died during thirty-six weeks of training*: Wolfe, *The Right Stuff*, p. 15.

120 *"one tragedy would not stop this project"*: "Astronaut's Death Will Not Halt Program," *Los Angeles Times*, April 11, 1960.

121 *"We have gone about as far as we can"*: "The Seven Chosen," *Time*, April 20, 1959, National Affairs section.

121 *"Given the state of NASA and Project Mercury"*: Slayton and Cassutt, *Deke!*, p. 70.

121 *"I don't know"*: Faget in Davis-Floyd et al., *Space Stories*, Chap. 2.

122 *up to twenty g's*: Barratt, "Physical and Bioenvironmental Aspects of Human Space Flight," p. 14.

122 *thinner than a dime*: The thickness of Atlas varied from 0.01 to 0.04 inches (Jenkins, "Stage-and-a-Half," p. 76). A U.S. dime is 0.05 inches thick.

122 *very much like an egg*: Logsdon, *Orbital Mechanics*, p. 122.

123 *"like a hydrogen bomb going off"*: Glenn and Taylor, *John Glenn*, p. 207.

123 *"I sure hope they fix that"*: Wendt and Still, *The Unbroken Chain*, p. 14.

123 *"I spent most of my time that year at the Cape"*: Slayton and Cassutt, *Deke!*, p. 87.

Chapter 16: The Vice President Finds a Space Chief

126 *"Control of space means control of the world"*: Divine, "Lyndon B. Johnson and the Politics of Space," p. 224.

126 *"I don't think I'm the right person for this job"*: Quotes and incidents linked to Webb's appointment as NASA administrator are from Webb, NASM, March 15, 1985; and Webb, LBJ, April 29, 1969. Additional details are in Bizony, *The Man Who Ran the Moon*, pp. 16–17; Lambright, *Powering Apollo*, p. 84; and Logsdon, *John F. Kennedy and the Race to the Moon*, pp. 41–42.

127 *"the greatest . . . capacity"*: Holmes, *America on the Moon*, p. 190.

128 *"marginal"*: Logsdon, *Exploring the Unknown*, Vol. 1, pp. 408–409.

128 *"We mean it's a sick program"*: Garwood, "JFK Gets Report," *Austin Statesman*, January 12, 1961, p. A3.

128 *"a failure in our first attempt to place a man into orbit"*: Logsdon, *Exploring the Unknown*, Vol. 1, p. 422.

129 *Fretting about the reputation of their Atlas missile*: Lambright, *Powering Apollo*, pp. 89–90.

129 *"My philosophy has always been"*: Webb, NASM, November 4, 1985; quoted in Lambright, *Powering Apollo*, p. 90.

129 *Max Faget had already sketched out a more advanced spacecraft*: Gray, *Angle of Attack*, p. 166.

130 *"I feel splendid, very well"*: Grahn, "An Analysis of the Flight of *Vostok*."

130 *"The world's first satellite-ship"*: Siddiqi, *Challenge to Apollo*, p. 278.

131 *"Let the capitalist countries catch up with our country"*: Carruthers, "Russian Orbited the Earth Once," *New York Times*, April 13, 1961, p. 14.

Chapter 17: "Light This Candle"

133 *"Those who say they will stand up to Mr. Khrushchev"*: Rasenberger, *The Brilliant Disaster*, p. 90.

133 *"The communists have been moving with vigor"*: *The Fourth Kennedy-Nixon Presidential Debate*, October 21, 1960.

134 *"Rescue units on the scene"*: Thompson, *Light This Candle*, p. 249.

135 *"Why postpone a success?"*: Swenson et al., *This New Ocean*, p. 350.

135 *"All right, I'm cooler than you are"*: Wolfe, *The Right Stuff*, p. 200.

135 *"a subtle, gentle, gradual rise off the ground"*: The Astronauts (Carpenter et al.), *We Seven*, p. 189.

136 *One oddity*: Scott Carpenter, who made the fourth Mercury flight, describes this experience in his memoir, *For Spacious Skies*, p. 256.

136 *About two minutes into the flight*: Technical details of Shepard's flight are from Swenson et al., *This New Ocean*, Chap. 11; also *Post Launch Report for Mercury-Redstone No. 3*; and "Freedom 7 Mercury-Redstone 3."

Chapter 18: Go to the Moon

139 *"The blaze of Alan Shepard's Redstone"*: "It's a Success," *Time*, May 5, 1961, p. 14.

140 *"Is there any . . . space program which promises dramatic results in which we could win?"*: Kennedy's memorandum to Johnson and the reply are in Logsdon, *Exploring the Unknown*, Vol. 1, pp. 423–424, 427–429.

140 *"tremendous jet burst from the base of the rocket"*: Bracker, "Jupiter-C Is Used," *New York Times*, February 1, 1958, p. 7.

140 *"thunder of the rocket engine"*: "U.S. Fires 'Moon'!" *Chicago Daily Tribune*, February 1, 1958, p. 2.

140 *"When you decide you're going to do something"*: Murray and Cox, *Apollo*, p. 81.

140 *40 billion dollars*: Sidey, *John F. Kennedy*, p. 117.

140 *four times the combined cost of the B-29 and atomic bomb projects*: O'Brien, *How the War Was Won*, pp. 47–48. O'Brien gives a combined cost of $5.7 billion for the two programs, or $9.5 billion in 1961 dollars. Inflation calculated with the Bureau of Labor Statistics tool at data.bls.gov/cgi-bin/cpicalc.pl (accessed September 1, 2017).

143 *His speech*: For the entire speech, see Kennedy, "President Kennedy's Special Message to the Congress on Urgent National Needs, May 25, 1961."

143 *a startling challenge*: "Hopes & Misgivings," *Time*, June 2, 1961, p. 13.

144 *the audience's stunned reaction*: The speechwriter was Theodore Sorenson. See Vine, "Walking on the Moon."

144 *When they tuned in to the speech*: Gilruth's reaction is described in Gilruth, NASM February 27, 1987.

144 *the original deadline had been 1967*: Seamans, *Aiming at Targets*, pp. 85, 90–91.

145 *"I was always a guy"*: Gilruth, NASM, February 27, 1987.

PART 4: The Plan

149 *"So much happened and it happened so fast"*: Murray and Cox, *Apollo*, p. 87.

Chapter 19: Pieces of the Puzzle

151 *"if we were all crazy"*: Seamans, *Aiming at Targets*, p. 91.

151 *Seamans and his colleagues came up with a plan*: Apollo plans as of 1962 are covered in Sullivan, *America's Race for the Moon*, based on a series of articles that appeared in the *New York Times* that summer.

154 *In 1961, NASA had 18,000 employees*: Statistics on NASA employment are from *NASA Historical Data Book: 1958–1968*, Vol. 1, p. 106.

155 *ready for its first Earth orbital missions until 1965*: Miles, "Moon Spacecraft Project Speeded," *Los Angeles Times*, April 1, 1962, p. F6.

157 *Webb and others at NASA pressed Draper*: Brooks et al., *Chariots for Apollo*, p. 41.

Chapter 20: How to Get to the Moon, and Back
159 *"Your figures lie!"*: The quotes are from Sheridan, "How an Idea No One Wanted Grew Up to Be the LM," *Life*, March 14, 1969, p. 22. A full account of Houbolt's crusade is in Murray and Cox, *Apollo*, Chaps. 8 and 9.

164 *"Houbolt has a scheme"*: Logsdon, *Exploring the Unknown*, Vol. 7, p. 524.

164 *"offered a chain reaction"*: Sheridan, "How an Idea No One Wanted Grew Up to Be the LM," *Life*, March 14, 1969, p. 22.

Chapter 21: The Race Heats Up
167 *about every two weeks*: Details of Slayton's heart problem are from Slayton and Cassutt, *Deke!*, pp. 85–86, 110–113.

168 *Newspapers treated it almost like a death*: For the typical newspaper reaction to Slayton's grounding, see the wire service story "Heart Forces Slayton Out of Astronaut Role," *Boston Globe*, July 12, 1962, p. 8.

168 *"Red Spaceman Lands!"*: "Red Spaceman Lands!" *New York Journal-American*, August 7, 1961, p. 1.

168 *A British expert on spaceflight didn't think so*: The expert was Kenneth Gatland. See "Russ Cosmonaut Titov Safely Down on Land," *Austin Statesman*, August 7, 1961, p. 1.

168 *canceling the remaining suborbital flights*: Slayton and Cassutt, *Deke!*, p. 104.

170 *"Bourgeois society always underlines that woman is the weaker sex"*: Topping, "Khrushchev Hails Astronauts," *New York Times*, June 23, 1963, p. 11.

170 *an editorial for* Life *magazine*: Luce's comment and the quotes in the paragraph that follows are from Luce, "But Some People Simply Never Get the Message," *Life*, June 28, 1963, p. 31.

171 *"We will train some women astronauts for sure"*: "U.S. Women Still Grounded by NASA," *Chicago Tribune*, June 17, 1963, p. 2.

Chapter 22: The Great Escape

174 *"Anybody who would spend 40 billion dollars"*: Benson and Faherty, *Moonport*, p. 170.

174 *8 to 12 billion*: Lambright, *Powering Apollo*, p. 101. For a condensed version of Webb's budget and political strategy, see Lambright's article "Leading NASA in Space Exploration."

174 *"If we had an insuperable obstacle"*: Trento, *Prescription for Disaster*, p. 52; quoted in Lambright, *Powering Apollo*, p. 110.

175 *"We walked into the firing room"*: Details are from "Apollo 15 Remembered 40 Years Later," starting at 1:07:00. See also Ward, *Rocket Ranch*, p. 129.

176 *"There are two problems which greatly concern them"*: "Reds Not Sold on Trip to Moon," *Washington Post*, July 17, 1963, p. A3.

176 *The Central Intelligence Agency (CIA) had advised him*: David, *Spies and Shuttles*, p. 38.

176 *ambitious launch site construction*: Day, "From the Shadows to the Stars."

176 *Webb was also starting to have trouble*: Lambright, *Powering Apollo*, pp. 114–116.

177 *"Look, if you want someone else to run the program"*: Webb, NASM, October 15, 1985.

177 *"a candid assessment of the real status"*: The assessment and Mueller's meeting with Seamans are recounted in Slotkin, *Doing the Impossible*, pp. 17–18. See also Seamans, *Project Apollo*, pp. 49, 51.

177 *Mueller had the chance to brief President Kennedy*: See the account in Seamans, *Project Apollo*, pp. 51–53.

178 *"This is fantastic"*: Hunter, "President, Touring Canaveral, Sees a Polaris Fired," *New York Times*, November 17, 1963, p. 44. Additional details are in "JFK Sees Polaris Fired," *Boston Globe*, November 17, 1963, p. 16; and "Sub Fires Missile as JFK Watches," *Hartford Courant*, November 17, 1963, p. 1A.

Chapter 23: General Phillips Joins the Team
181 *"Results are what count"*: Neal, *Ace in the Hole*, p. 16.

184 *No one had ever done an "all-up" launch on the initial outing*: Abramson, "Laconic General," *Los Angeles Times*, October 6, 1968, p. F1.

184 *"crazy" and likely to "blow up on the pad"*: Neal, *Ace in the Hole*, p. 12.

184 *"if you do your piece right"*: Guy, JSC (October 30, 2006).

185 *impossible, reckless, incredulous, harebrained, and nonsense*: Seamans, *Project Apollo*, p. 51.

185 *"The thing that really kills programs"*: Slotkin, *Doing the Impossible*, p. 39.

186 *"Today's work must be done today"*: Mueller's words of inspiration in this paragraph are quoted in Slotkin, *Doing the Impossible*, pp. xxiii, 68–69.

186 *"George was a double whirlwind"*: Seamans, JSC, November 20, 1998. See also Seamans, *Aiming at Targets*, p. 110.

186 *A diary entry from his Apollo years*: Bateman, "The Ultimate Program Manager," p. 37.

186 *"You could stand across the street"*: Armstrong, JSC, September 19, 2001.

Chapter 24: "Do Good Work!"
189 *"Like so many things for my generation"*: Seamans, *Aiming at Targets*, pp. 99–100.

190 *a young engineer named Harrison Storms*: Storms's background is covered in Gray, *Angle of Attack*, Chap. 1.

190 *Alfred Munier came to work at Grumman Aircraft on Long Island in 1943*: Saxon, "Alfred Munier, 78," *New York Times*, December 23, 1993, p. B6.

191 *Stoner had been a test supervisor for the dauntingly complex B-29 bomber*: "G. H. Stoner of Boeing Co.," *Washington Post*, March 3, 1971, p. B3.

191 *"Do good work!"*: This anecdote is told in Wolfe, *The Right Stuff*, p. 116. See also Leopold, *Calculated Risk*, pp. 212–213.

192 *"Do good work" signs spread to contractors all over the country*: Tapper, "Throwback Thursday 'Do Good Work,'" May 8, 2014

192 *Most were in their twenties*: "Is NASA's workforce too old?" *Space*, April 11, 2008, *New Scientist Blogs*.

192 *"We carried responsibilities for very major aspects of the Mercury program"*: Fries, *NASA Engineers and the Age of Apollo*, p. 68.

Briefing: The Women of Apollo
195 *Patricia Bridges*: See Kopal and Carder, *Mapping the Moon*, Chap. 7.

PART 5: Crews

197 *"Any crew can fly any mission"*: Cernan and Davis, *The Last Man on the Moon*, p. 239.

Chapter 25: Squadron Commander

199 *discussed the situation with the other astronauts*: Wolfe, *The Right Stuff*, p. 300.

204 *"Work your tail off"*: Chaikin, *A Man on the Moon*, p. 45.

205 *Like a good squadron operations officer*: Slayton's approach to crew selection is covered in Slayton and Cassutt, *Deke!*, Chap. 14, especially pp. 136–138.

206 *"Going to the Moon is going from point A to point B"*: Trafford, "Apollos and Oranges," *Washington Post*, July 19, 1994, p. 6.

206 *Oriana Fallaci*: Fallaci's interview with Slayton is in Fallaci, *If the Sun Dies*, Chap. 8.

Chapter 26: The Moon Comes into Focus

209 *"Oh, I am heartily tired of hearing about what Lee is going to do"*: Porter, *Campaigning with Grant*, p. 70.

210 *"The Russians upstage us every time"* . . . *"The target now before us is the Moon"*: Sullivan, "The Week in Science," *New York Times*, March 21, 1965, p. E3.

212 *a thousand times better than those from the largest telescopes*: Hall, *Lunar Impact*, p. 273.

212 *Urey suggested the Sea of Tranquility for Ranger's next target*: Hall, *Lunar Impact*, p. 282.

213 *"one of the dramatic moments in television history"*: "Live from the Moon," *Hartford Courant*, March 25, 1965, p. 14.

213 *"The time is not distant"*: "Moonstruck," *Washington Post*, March 25, 1965, p. A24.

214 *"In a very real sense"*: Kennedy, "President Kennedy's Special Message to the Congress on Urgent National Needs, May 25, 1961."

Chapter 27: Neil Armstrong's Wild Ride

219 *"We are docked!"*: "Gemini VIII Voice Communications," p. 71.

220 *"We have serious problems here"*: "Gemini VIII Voice Communications," p. 75.

220 *"like being on a theme-park ride"*: Scott, Leonov, and Toom, *Two Sides of the Moon*, p. 168.

220 *"I thought they were gone"*: Houston and Heflin, *Go, Flight!*, pp. 82–83.

221 *Deke Slayton had assembled six crews*: Slayton and Cassutt, *Deke!*, p. 184.

221 *projected for 1967*: For the original Apollo mission schedule, see Shayler, *Apollo*, pp. 112–113. The original Apollo 2 was canceled. Thus Apollo 3 became 2, Apollo 4 became 3, etc. The crews here represent the revised plan.

Chapter 28: "Fire in the Cockpit"

226 *the pressure was set a bit higher than sea-pressure level to reveal any leaks in the spacecraft*: Caldwell Johnson in Davis-Floyd et al., *Space Stories*, Chap. 3. The cabin pressure was set at 16.7 pounds per square inch (*Apollo Accident: Hearing*, p. 156).

227 *Apollo's thirty miles of wire*: Apollo Accident: Hearing, p. 222.

227 *"the cockpit of an aircraft in World War II that took a direct hit"*: "Very Little Left in Cabin of Burned-out Spacecraft," *Baltimore Sun*, January 30, 1967, p. A5.

228 *"We should abandon the idea of landing a man on the Moon"*: Lippmann,

"The Race to the Moon," *Newsweek*, February 13, 1967; quoted in White's dissertation, *The Establishment of Blame*, p. 90.

228 *"the inflexible, but meaningless, goal"*: Benson and Faherty, *Moonport*, p. 394.

229 *at a diplomatic event in Washington*: Accounts of the gathering and its immediate aftermath are in Lambright, *Powering Apollo*, pp. 143–147; Hansen, *First Man*, pp. 304–310; and Slotkin, *Doing the Impossible*, pp. 142–147.

229 *"This is the dreadful price you have to pay"*: Collins, "Celebration Ends Instead as a Eulogy," *Newsday*, January 28, 1967, p. 2.

229 *That evening, Webb held a press conference*: French and Burgess, *In the Shadow of the Moon*, p. 166.

229 *"We've always known something like this would happen sooner or later"*: Collins, "Celebration Ends Instead as a Eulogy," *Newsday*, January 28, 1967, p. 2.

229 *"Three superbly trained pilots had died"*: This quote and the drinking incident that follows are from Borman and Serling, *Countdown*, p. 173.

230 *"a labyrinth of systems more complicated than an aircraft carrier"*: Gray, *Angle of Attack*, p. 255.

230 *At Faget's suggestion*: Collins, *Liftoff*, p. 137.

231 *"Spaceflight will never tolerate carelessness, incapacity, and neglect"*: Kranz, *Failure Is Not an Option*, p. 204.

Chapter 29: "Go, Baby, Go!"
233 *"The guys who are going to fly the first lunar missions"*: Slayton's announcement and Cernan's reaction are in Cernan and Davis, *The Last Man on the Moon*, p. 165. The date of the meeting is deduced from Hansen, *First Man*, p. 310.

233 *"the climax of a grand competition"*: Cunningham and Herskowitz, *The All-American Boys*, p. 202.

233 *Both John Young and Neil Armstrong*: Young's thoughts are in Young and Hansen, *Forever Young*, p. 116. Armstrong's are recorded in Hansen, *First Man*, p. 311.

234 *"Be flexible"*: Stafford and Cassutt, *We Have Capture*, p. 109.

235 *Webb and Mueller pressed for a test flight*: Brooks et al., *Chariots for Apollo*, p. 229.

236 *"the longest ten seconds of my life"*: Von Braun's quotes are from Zinman, "Saturn Success Lifts Moon Hopes," *Newsday*, November 10, 1967, p. 2.

236 *"a continuous, pulsating clap of deep thunder"*: Farrar, "U.S. Scores 2 Space Triumphs," *Chicago Tribune*, November 10, 1967, p. 5.

236 *"My God, our building's shaking!"*: "Launch of Apollo 4" on YouTube, starting at 1:50.

236 *As ceiling tiles rained down*: Cronkite, *A Reporter's Life*, pp. 278–279.

239 *"Had the critical test failed"*: Miles, "U.S. Scores Space Triumph," *Los Angeles Times*, November 10, 1967, p. 1.

239 *"Apollo is on the way to the Moon"*: Zinman, "Saturn Success Lifts Moon Hopes," *Newsday*, November 10, 1967, p. 2.

239 *could hardly stop smiling*: McElheny, "A Double Jump on Road to Moon," *Boston Globe*, November 10, 1967, p. 2.

Chapter 30: The Submariner Takes Charge
241 *"If you can visualize a molten streetcar"*: Mann, "Letters Provide Up-close Descriptions of Nuke Blasts," *Laredo Morning Times*, August 5, 2005, p. 8A.

242 *"carrying out a classic naval 'boarders, away!' operation"*: Paine recounts his exploits in his article "The Transpacific Voyage of HIJMS *I-400*."

243 *he headed its innovative think tank, TEMPO*: Buckley, "NASA's Tom Paine," *New York Times*, June 8, 1969, magazine section, pp. 37–38.

244 *"These are the RAF types"*: Paine in Swanson, *Before This Decade Is Out*, pp. 28–29.

244 *President Johnson had told him*: Levine, *The Future of the U.S. Space Program*, p. 101.

245 *"I can give you a very straightforward, simple answer"*: Seamans, *Aiming at Targets*, pp. 148–149.

Briefing: Lunar Reconnaissance
247 *For a variety of reasons*: For the story of lunar reconnaissance and the rationale for landing in the Sea of Tranquility, see Wilhelms, *To a Rocky Moon*, especially pp. 188–191.

PART 6: The Moon
249 *"12 02 alarm! 12 02, what's that?"*: Flight and guidance communications loops for the Apollo 11 landing, "The Eagle Has Landed," CosmoQuest Forum.

Chapter 31: A New Mission Takes Shape
251 *"Are you out of your mind?"*: Chaikin, *A Man on the Moon*, p. 59.

251 *"If a person's shock could be transmitted"*: Murray and Cox, *Apollo*, p. 322.

255 *"After a careful and thorough examination"*: "News Briefing on Apollo 8 Moon Orbital Flight," p. 2.

255 *"This will be within the normal hazards"*: "News Briefing on Apollo 8 Moon Orbital Flight," p. 44.

256 *he would have been too cautious to authorize such a plan*: Murray and Cox, *Apollo*, p. 323.

Chapter 32: "In the Beginning"

260 *a British ground station picked up a voice*: Siddiqi, *Challenge to Apollo*, p. 655.

260 *"a photo finish"*: Turnill, *The Moonlandings*, p. 134.

261 *opened on the 8th of the month*: Russia's launch window was December 8–12. See "Kamanin Diaries," November 26, 1968.

261 *For the United States, it didn't open until the 20th*: Orloff and Harland, *Apollo: The Definitive Sourcebook*, p. 197.

261 *ran the headline*: "Moon Shot for Soviets Sunday?" *Florida Today*, December 7, 1968, p. 1A.

261 *"It is not important to mankind"*: Siddiqi, *Challenge to Apollo*, p. 667.

261 *"a rat in the jaws of a big terrier"*: "Apollo 8 Reunion," YouTube, starting at 25:01.

262 *"a runaway freight train"*: Woods, *How Apollo Flew to the Moon*, p. 83.

262 *"train wreck"*: Woods, *How Apollo Flew to the Moon*, p. 95.

262 *four g's*: Four g's is a velocity increase of 88 miles per hour for every second.

262 *"I suddenly felt like I'd been sitting on a catapult and somebody cut the rope"*: Chaikin and Kohl, *Voices from the Moon*, p. 23.

265 *"We see the Earth now"*: Apollo 8 voice transcripts are from Woods and O'Brien, "The Apollo 8 Flight Journal."

266 *"like a war zone"*: Chaikin and Kohl, *Voices from the Moon*, p. 45.

267 *"Let me tell you"*: "Apollo 8 Reunion," YouTube, starting at 1:04:18.

Chapter 33: Earthrise

271 *"Oh, my God!"*: Apollo 8 voice transcripts are from Woods and O'Brien, "The Apollo 8 Flight Journal."

271 *"It was the most beautiful, heart-catching sight of my life"*: Borman and Serling, *Countdown*, p. 212.

272 *"Here we came all this way to the Moon"*: Wolfinger, "To the Moon," quoted in Poole, *Earthrise*, p. 2.

272 *"For all its upheavals and frustrations"*: "Men of the Year," *Time*, January 3, 1969, p. 13.

273 *Had Gus Grissom been alive*: Slayton and Cassutt, *Deke!*, p. 191.

273 *Frank Borman and Jim McDivitt*: Slayton and Cassutt, *Deke!*, p. 223. See also Michael Cassutt's post on CollectSpace, March 5, 2005.

273 *he sensibly pointed out*: Borman and Serling, *Countdown*, p. 222.

274 *"This is like handling a squadron of fighter pilots"*: Armstrong et al., *First on the Moon*, p. 105.

274 *Slayton gave Armstrong the option to switch Aldrin for Jim Lovell*: Hansen, *First Man*, p. 338.

275 *"You're it"*: Slayton and Cassutt, *Deke!*, p. 224.

Chapter 34: Go Fever

277 *"I do not submit"*: "Worth the Price," *Time*, January 17, 1969, p. 49.

277 *NASA had tightened contractor management and set up new safety proce-dures*: Levine, *The Future of the U.S. Space Program*, p. 97.

277 *there were roughly 6 million parts in a typical Apollo mission*: Dick, "The Voyages of Apollo."

278 *"an almost religious vigilance"*: Sato, "Reliability in the Apollo Program," p. 23.

278 *"If you don't like the way things look"*: Collins, *Liftoff*, p. 260. See also Paine in Swanson, *Before This Decade Is Out . . .* , pp. 20–22.

278 *"the ability to go up in a hurtling piece of machinery"*: Wolfe, *The Right Stuff*, p. 148.

279 *"rolling them around on his tongue"*: Collins, *Carrying the Fire*, p. 58.

279 *"Neil held on as long as he could"*: Aldrin and McConnell, *Men from Earth*, p. 187.

279 *"Do you know that Neil bailed out of the LLRV"*: Sington, *In the Shadow of the Moon*, 30:16. In the film, Bean mistakenly says "LLTV," which was a later version of the vehicle.

281 *"Neil and Buzz had been descending in the LM"*: Collins, *Carrying the Fire*, pp. 351–352.

281 *Armstrong later claimed that he had been testing the limits*: Hansen, *First Man*, p. 380.

281 *questioned Armstrong's commitment*: Kraft and Schefter, *Flight*, p. 314.

282 *"had set his own rules for the landing"*: Kranz, *Failure Is Not an Option*, p. 262.

282 *returned with some 150 failures*: Nelson, *Rocket Men*, p. 15.

282 *"pretty smooth"*: Woods, Wheeler, and Roberts, "The Apollo 10 Flight Journal."

283 *"To watch a flight is not that big a deal"*: Oberg, "Max Faget," *Omni*, April 1995, p. 62.

285 *Warned about the possibility of delay or worse*: Logsdon, *After Apollo?*, pp. 11–12.

Chapter 35: Tranquility Base

287 *The press went wild with other theories*: Harvey, *Soviet and Russian Lunar Exploration*, p. 211.

287 *"This is undoubtedly quite a challenging mission"*: Turnill, *The Moonlandings*, p. 227.

289 *"Eagle, Houston"*: Air-to-ground and onboard transcripts for the Apollo 11 landing, along with interviews and other background material, can be found at "The First Lunar Landing" in Jones and Glover, "The Apollo 11 Lunar Surface Journal."

292 *the LM had only about a minute of hover time*: Mindell, *Digital Apollo*, p. 203.

293 *which Tom Stafford had warned*: Harland, *The First Men on the Moon*, p. 233.

294 *Duke had a sinking feeling*: Duke, JSC, March 12, 1999.

294 *"12 02 alarm!"*: Selected flight controller audio for the Apollo 11 landing is linked at "Apollo 11 Lunar Landing Audio—Flight and Guidance Loops," NASA Spaceflight.com Forum, July 20, 2014. See also "The Apollo 11 Descent and Landing," Honeysuckle Creek Tracking Station.

295 *"were creating doubt"*: Cunningham and Herskowitz, *The All-American Boys*, p. 217.

295 *"impending disaster"*: Turnill, *The Moonlandings*, pp. 249, 252.

295 *"If it were in my hands, I would call an abort"*: Eyles, *Sunburst and Luminary*, p. 151.

296 *"There wasn't anything obviously wrong"*: Armstrong, JSC, September 19, 2001.

296 *"I licked my dry lips"*: Aldrin, "Lunar Module *Eagle*," *The Bent* of Tau Beta Pi, Fall 1994, p. 15.

296 *"It is as though a terrible screech"*: Eyles, *Sunburst and Luminary*, p. 153.

296 *"Charlie, shut up and let them land!"*: Duke and Duke, *Moonwalker.*

297 *A mile ahead*: Distances during the final approach are based on "Apollo 11 Ground Track Mapped onto LROC Overlay in Google Moon," GoneToPlaid's Apollo website.

297 *"Neil was flying a trajectory"*: Duke, JSC, March 12, 1999.

297 *"We could see on our displays"*: Kraft and Schefter, *Flight*, p. 321.

298 *"I wonder if he's going to make it"*: Sington, *In the Shadow of the Moon*, 59:37.

298 *"If they keep doing this"*: Faget, JSC, June 18, 1997.

298 *"If I'd run out of fuel"*: Armstrong, JSC, September 19, 2001.

298 *with just fifteen seconds of gas left. "It would have been nice"*: Hansen, *First Man*, pp. 471–472.

298 *"Without wanting to say anything to Neil"*: Aldrin and Abraham, *Magnificent Desolation*, pp. 20–21.

299 *150 beats per minute*: *Apollo 11 Mission Report*, p. 158.

299 *had given up hope they would land*: Carlton told an interviewer, "I didn't think there was a chance in the world of us landing." Carlton, JSC, April 10, 2001.

300 *"It was like watching a man, some snake trainer"*: Easter, JSC, May 3, 2000.

300 *felt like he was levitating off his chair*: Fendell, JSC, October 19, 2000.

300 *"My God, this is the real thing"*: Garman, JSC, March 27, 2001.

300 *"landing an airplane when there's a real thin layer of ground fog"*: "The First Lunar Landing" in Jones and Glover, "The Apollo 11 Lunar Surface Journal."

300 *"He's using a lot of RCS"*: Carlton, JSC, April 10, 2001.

Chapter 36: One Small Step

303 *"not something that I thought was really very important"*: Hansen, *First Man*, p. 367.

303 *Armstrong ranked walking on the Moon as a one*: Armstrong, JSC, September 19, 2001.

304 *it made sense for the copilot*: For example, lunar module pilot Rusty Schweickart made the space walk (in Earth orbit) on Apollo 9.

304 *General Phillips felt strongly that a single, brief outing by a single explorer*: Brooks et al., *Chariots for Apollo*, p. 320.

305 *Frank Borman described his fellow astronauts this way*: Logsdon, *After Apollo?*, p. 17.

305 *top managers thought he was the wrong individual to wear the hero's mantle*: The account of this behind-the-scenes drama is in Hansen, *First Man*, pp. 370–372. NASA's official reason for choosing Armstrong to go first was that it was easier for the astronaut at the commander's station to get out the door. Lunar module pilots privately objected that it was a relatively simple matter for the two astronauts to switch places.

305 *"That's one small step"*: The actual first words spoken from the surface of the Moon were when Aldrin said, "Okay, engine stop," just after Armstrong landed.

306 *his statement became even more meaningful*: I owe this insight to poet James Nicola (personal communication).

308 *"I never expected to hear that word 'pretty'"*: "Apollo 11 Moon Walk CBS News Coverage" on YouTube, starting at 4:11:17.

308 *black you felt you could touch*: Chaikin and Kohl, *Voices from the Moon*, p. 68.

310 *Armstrong and Aldrin were instructed to move with great care to avoid falling*: "Apollo 11 Moon Walk CBS News Coverage" on YouTube, starting at 4:10:34.

310 *"When you move"*: Chaikin and Kohl, *Voices from the Moon*, p. 72.

310 *"Exploring this place"*: Aldrin and Abraham, *Magnificent Desolation*, p. 37.

310 *Frank Borman talked him out of it*: Borman and Serling, *Countdown*, p. 238.

311 *"our marble-sized planet"*: Aldrin and Abraham, *Magnificent Desolation*, p. 34.

313 *"Two guys walk in and sit down"*: Fendell, JSC, October 19, 2000.

Epilogue: "We Must Stop"
315 *The astronauts used to joke*: Chaikin and Kohl, *Voices from the Moon*, p. 114.

316 *"achieved the Moon's surface in the preselected area"*: Harland, *The First Men on the Moon*, p. 293.

317 *researchers in the West*: See Oberg, "Russia Meant to Win the Moon Race," *Spaceflight*, May 1975, pp. 163–164.

318 *"We must stop"*: Gilruth, NASM, March 2, 1987.

318 *just over 25 billion dollars*: $25.4 billion according to Logsdon, *John F. Kennedy and the Race to the Moon*, p. 2.

318 *that was just for a single Moon landing*: See Diamond, *The Rise and Fall of the Space Age*, p. 40: "In March 1963, D. Brainerd Holmes . . . testified . . . that the cost of all activities directly related to fulfilling the President's goal would be $20 billion . . . Holmes' figure also made no provision for more than one lunar trip . . ."

319 *"Wernher is like a great conductor"*: Stuhlinger and Ordway, *Wernher von Braun: A Biographical Memoir*, p. 302.

319 *"I was impressed"*: Abramson, "Laconic General," *Los Angeles Times*, October 6, 1968, p. F1.

320 *seventy-seventh and seventy-eighth persons in space*: Counted as those who have flown above the generally accepted boundary of space at 100 kilometers (62 miles).

321 *He chose the gold dolphin pin*: Paine, "The Transpacific Voyage of HIJMS *I-400*."

322 *"We weren't going to fight a war on the lake"*: Faget, JSC, June 19, 1997.

322 *"You know, Max"*: Chaikin, "Management Lessons of the Moon Program," on YouTube, starting at 55:35.

Briefing: Six Landing Sites
325 *"It's absolutely mind-boggling"*: Chaikin and Kohl, *Voices from the Moon*, p. 66.

REFERENCES

Interviews and Oral Histories

Armstrong, Neil A., Jr. NASA Johnson Space Center Oral History Project, interviewed by Stephen E. Ambrose and Douglas Brinkley. www.jsc.nasa.gov /history/oral_histories/ArmstrongNA/armstrongna.htm (updated July 16, 2010).

Carlton, Robert L. NASA Johnson Space Center Oral History Project, interviewed by Kevin M. Rusnak. www.jsc.nasa.gov/history/oral_histories /CarltonRL/carltonrl.htm (updated July 16, 2010).

Duke, Charles. M., Jr. NASA Johnson Space Center Oral History Project, interviewed by Doug Ward. www.jsc.nasa.gov/history/oral_histories/DukeCM /dukecm.htm (updated July 16, 2010).

Easter, William B. NASA Johnson Space Center Oral History Project, interviewed by Kevin M. Rusnak. www.jsc.nasa.gov/history/oral_histories/Easter WB/EasterWB_5-3-00.htm (updated July 16, 2010).

Faget, Maxime A. Robbie Davis-Floyd, Kenneth J. Cox, and Frank White, eds., *Space Stories: Oral Histories from the Pioneers of America's Space Program*, interviewed by Davis-Floyd and Cox. Amazon Digital Services, 2012. Kindle edition.

Faget, Maxime A. NASA Johnson Space Center Oral History Project, interviewed by Carol Butler and Jim Slade. www.jsc.nasa.gov/history/oral_histories /FagetMA/fagetma.htm (updated July 16, 2010).

Fendell, Edward I. NASA Johnson Space Center Oral History Project, interviewed by Kevin M. Rusnak. www.jsc.nasa.gov/history/oral_histories/FendellEI /FendellEI_10-19-00.htm (updated July 16, 2010).

Garman, John R. NASA Johnson Space Center Oral History Project, interviewed by Kevin M. Rusnak. www.jsc.nasa.gov/history/oral_histories/GarmanJR /garmanjr.htm (updated July 16, 2010).

Gilruth, Robert R. Smithsonian National Air and Space Museum Oral History Project, interviewed by David DeVorkin, Martin Collins, John Mauer, Linda Ezell, and Howard Wolko. airandspace.si.edu/research/projects/oral-hist ories/gwspi-p1.html#GILRUTH (revised September 6, 1996).

Guy, Walter W. NASA Johnson Space Center Oral History Project, interviewed by Rebecca Wright. www.jsc.nasa.gov/history/oral_histories/GuyWW /guyww.htm (updated July 16, 2010).

Johnson, Caldwell. Robbie Davis-Floyd, Kenneth J. Cox, and Frank White, eds., *Space Stories: Oral Histories from the Pioneers of America's Space Program*, interviewed by Davis-Floyd and Cox. Amazon Digital Services, 2012. Kindle edition.

Kimball, Ward. Didier Ghez, ed., *Walt's People*. Vol. 3; interviewed by Klaus Strzyz. Theme Park Press, 2015.

Paine, Thomas O. Glen E. Swanson, ed., *Before This Decade Is Out . . . : Personal Reflections on the Apollo Program*, interviewed by Robert Sherrod. Washington, D.C.: NASA, 1999.

Phillips, Samuel C. Smithsonian National Air and Space Museum Oral History Project, interviewed by Martin Collins. airandspace.si.edu/research/projects /oral-histories/gwspi-p2.html#PHILLIPS (revised September 6, 1996).

Seamans, Robert C., Jr. NASA Johnson Space Center Oral History Project, interviewed by Michelle Kelly and Carol Butler. www.jsc.nasa.gov/history/oral _histories/SeamansRC/seamansrc.htm (updated July 16, 2010).

Webb, James E. Lyndon Baines Johnson Library Oral History Collection, interviewed by T. H. Baker. lbjlibrary.net/collections/oral-histories/webb-e. -james.html (accessed September 1, 2017).

Webb, James E. Smithsonian National Air and Space Museum Oral History Project, interviewed by Martin Collins, David DeVorkin, Joseph Tatarewicz, Allen Needell, Linda Ezell, and Michael Dennis. airandspace.si.edu /research/projects/oral-histories/gwspi-p3.html#WEBB (revised September 6, 1996).

Documents and Statistics

"Apollo 11 Ground Track Mapped onto LROC Overlay in Google Moon." GoneToPlaid's Apollo Web Site. Linked at history.nasa.gov/alsj/a11/images11.html (revised February 18, 2018).

Apollo 11 Mission Report. Washington, D.C.: NASA, 1971. www.hq.nasa.gov/alsj /a11/a11MIssionReport_1971015566_Sec12BiomedEvaluation.pdf.

Apollo Accident: Hearing on a Review of Background Information and Systems Decisions Preceding the Apollo Accident of January 27, 1967. Part 1. Senate

Committee on Aeronautical and Space Sciences. Ninetieth Congress, First Session, February 7, 1967. U.S. Government Printing Office: Washington, D.C., 1967. spaceflight.nasa.gov/outreach/SignificantIncidents/assets/apollo -1-hearing.pdf.

Army Air Forces Statistical Digest: World War II, U.S. Army Air Forces, Office of Statistical Control, December 1945. dtic.mil/dtic/tr/fulltext/u2/a542518.pdf.

The Berkeley Mortality Database. u.demog.berkeley.edu/~andrew/1918/figure2 .html (accessed September 1, 2017).

Casper, Jack A. *History and Personnel, 489th, 340th Bomb Group: Combat Campaigns Participated in by the 489th Bomb Squadron*, 1947. warwingsart.com /12thAirForce/squadbook.html.

Ellis, John. *World War II: A Statistical Survey: The Essential Facts and Figures for All the Combatants.* New York: Facts on File, 1993.

Faget, Maxime A., Benjamine J. Garland, and James J. Buglia. "Preliminary Studies of Manned Satellites—Wingless Configuration: Nonlifting," *NACA Research Memorandum*, August 11, 1958. ntrs.nasa.gov/archive/nasa/casi .ntrs.nasa.gov/19930090134.pdf.

The Fourth Kennedy-Nixon Presidential Debate, October 21, 1960. Commission on Presidential Debates. debates.org/index.php?page=october-21-1960 -debate-transcript (accessed September 1, 2017).

Gallup, George H. *The Gallup Poll Public Opinion, 1935–1971.* 2 vols. New York: Random House, 1972.

"Gemini VIII Voice Communications (Air-to-Ground, Ground-to-Air, and On-board Transcription)." NASA Johnson Space Center History Portal. www .jsc.nasa.gov/history/mission_trans/GT08_TEC.PDF (accessed September 1, 2017).

"History: November 1943," 12th Air Force, 57th Bombardment Wing, 321st Bombardment Group. warwingsart.com/12thAirForce/3211143.html (accessed September 1, 2017).

"History of U.S.S. *Guavina* (SS-362)." U.S. Navy Department, Division of Naval History, (October 1953). maritime.org/doc/subreports.htm (accessed September 1, 2017).

"History of U.S.S. *Pompon* (SS-267)." U.S. Navy Department, Division of Naval History, (November 30, 1953). maritime.org/doc/subreports.htm (accessed September 1, 2017).

Joiner, Oliver W. *The History of the 364th Fighter Group*. Marceline, Mo.: Walsworth, 1991.

Jones, Eric M, and Ken Glover. "The Apollo 11 Lunar Surface Journal." NASA History Division. www.hq.nasa.gov/alsj/a11/a11.html (revised December 17, 2015).

Kennedy, John F. "President Kennedy's Special Message to the Congress on Urgent National Needs, May 25, 1961." John F. Kennedy Speeches. John F. Kennedy Presidential Library and Museum. jfklibrary.org/Research/Research-Aids/JFK-Speeches/United-States-Congress-Special-Message_19610525.aspx (accessed September 1, 2017).

Logsdon, John M., ed., with Linda J. Lear, Jannelle Warren-Findley, Ray A. Williamson, and Dwayne A. Day. *Exploring the Unknown: Selected Documents in the History of the U.S. Civil Space Program*. Vol. 1: *Organizing for Exploration*. Washington, D.C.: NASA, 1995.

Logsdon, John M., ed., with Roger D. Launius. *Exploring the Unknown: Selected Documents in the History of the U.S. Civil Space Program*. Vol. 7: *Human Spaceflight: Projects Mercury, Gemini, and Apollo*. Washington, D.C.: NASA, 2008.

NASA Historical Data Book: 1958–1968. Vol. 1: *NASA Resources*. Washington, D.C.: NASA, 1976.

"News Briefing on Apollo 8 Moon Orbital Flight." NASA News, Washington, D.C. (November 12, 1968).

"November 17, 1943 Mission to Kalamaki Aerodrome, Greece," 340th Bombardment Group History, War Diary. 57thbombwing.com/340th_History/487th_History/missions/111743_Kalamaki.htm (accessed September 1, 2017).

Orloff, Richard W., and David M. Harland. *Apollo: The Definitive Sourcebook*. Chichester, U.K.: Springer-Praxis, 2006.

Post Launch Report for Mercury-Redstone No. 3 (MR-3). Langley Field, Va.: NASA Space Task Group, June 16, 1961.

United States Submarine Losses, World War II. Washington, D.C.: Naval History Division, 1963.

"USAAF Chronology: Combat Chronology of the U.S. Army Air Forces, August 1944." paul.rutgers.edu/~mcgrew/wwii/usaf/html/Aug.44.html (accessed September 1, 2017).

Woods, W. David, Ken MacTaggart, and Frank O'Brien. "The Apollo 11 Flight Journal." NASA History Division. history.nasa.gov/afj/ap11fj/index.html (updated March 23, 2018).

Woods, W. David, and Frank O'Brien. "The Apollo 8 Flight Journal." NASA History Division. history.nasa.gov/afj/ap08fj/index.html (updated April 10, 2017).

Woods, W. David, Robin Wheeler, and Ian Roberts. "The Apollo 10 Flight Journal." NASA History Division. history.nasa.gov/afj/ap10fj/index.html (updated January 15, 2018).

Books

Aldrin, Buzz, and Ken Abraham. *Magnificent Desolation: The Long Journey Home from the Moon.* New York: Harmony Books, 2009.

Aldrin, Buzz, and Malcolm McConnell. *Men from Earth.* New York: Bantam Books, 1989.

Armstrong, Neil, Michael Collins, and Edwin E. Aldrin Jr., written with Gene Farmer and Dora Jane Hamblin. *First Men on the Moon.* Boston: Little, Brown and Company, 1970.

The Astronauts (Carpenter, M. Scott, et al.). *We Seven.* New York: Simon & Schuster, 1962.

Benson, Charles D., and William Barnaby Faherty. *Moonport: A History of Apollo Launch Facilities and Operations.* Washington, D.C.: NASA, 1978.

Bille, Matt, and Erika Lishock. *The First Space Race: Launching the World's First Satellites.* College Station: Texas A&M Press, 2004.

Bizony, Piers. *The Man Who Ran the Moon: James E. Webb and the Secret History of Project Apollo.* New York: Thunder's Mouth Press, 2006.

Blair-Smith, Hugh. *Left Brains for the Right Stuff: Computers, Space, and History.* East Bridgewater, Ma.: SDP Publishing, 2015. Kindle edition.

Borman, Frank, and Robert J. Serling. *Countdown: An Autobiography.* New York: William Morrow, 1988.

Brooks, Courtney G., James M. Grimwood, and Lloyd S. Swenson Jr. *Chariots for Apollo: The NASA History of Manned Lunar Spacecraft to 1969.* Mineola, N.Y.: Dover, 2009.

Bulkeley, Rip. *The Sputniks Crisis and Early United States Space Policy.* Bloomington: Indiana University Press, 1991.

Calvert, James F. *Silent Running: My Years on a World War II Attack Submarine.* New York: Wiley, 1995.

Carpenter, M. Scott, and Kris Stoever. *For Spacious Skies: The Uncommon Journey of a Mercury Astronaut.* Orlando, Fla.: Harcourt, 2002.

Cernan, Eugene, and Don Davis. *The Last Man on the Moon: Astronaut Eugene Cernan and America's Race in Space.* New York: St. Martin's, 1999.

Chaikin, Andrew. *A Man on the Moon: The Voyages of the Apollo Astronauts.* New York: Viking, 1994.

Chaikin, Andrew, and Victoria Kohl. *Voices from the Moon: Apollo Astronauts Describe Their Lunar Experiences.* New York: Viking Studio, 2009.

Collins, Michael. *Carrying the Fire: An Astronaut's Journey.* New York: Bantam, 1983.

Collins, Michael. *Liftoff: The Story of America's Adventure in Space.* New York: Grove Press, 1988.

Cortright, Edgar M., ed. *Apollo Expeditions to the Moon: The NASA History.* Washington, D.C.: NASA, 1975.

Cronkite, Walter. *A Reporter's Life.* New York: Knopf, 1996.

Cunningham, Walt, and Mickey Herskowitz. *The All-American Boys.* New York: Macmillan, 1977.

David, James E. *Spies and Shuttles: NASA's Secret Relationships with the DoD and CIA.* Gainesville, Fla.: University Press of Florida, 2015.

Dethloff, Henry C. *Suddenly, Tomorrow Came . . . . : A History of the Johnson Space Center.* Houston: NASA, 1993.

Diamond, Edwin. *The Rise and Fall of the Space Age.* Garden City, N.Y.: Doubleday, 1964.

Duke, Charlie (Charles, M., Jr.); and Dotty Duke, *Moonwalker,* 2nd ed, Rose Petal Press, 2011. Kindle edition.

Eyles, Don. *Sunburst and Luminary: An Apollo Memoir.* Boston: Fort Point Press, 2018.

Fallaci, Oriana. *If the Sun Dies.* New York: Atheneum, 1966.

Fredrickson, John M. *Warbird Factory: North American Aviation in World War II.* Minneapolis, Minn.: Zenith, 2015.

French, Francis, and Colin Burgess. *In the Shadow of the Moon: A Challenging Journey to Tranquility, 1965–1969.* Lincoln, Nebr.: University of Nebraska Press, 2007.

Fries, Sylvia Doughty. *NASA Engineers and the Age of Apollo*. Washington, D.C.: NASA, 1992.

Geer, Mary Wells, *Boeing's Ed Wells*. Seattle: University of Washington Press, 1992.

Glenn, John, and Nick Taylor. *John Glenn: A Memoir*. New York: Bantam, 1999.

Glennan, T. Keith. *The Birth of NASA: The Diary of T. Keith Glennan*, Washington, D.C.: NASA, 1993.

Gordon, Robert J. *The Rise and Fall of American Growth: The U.S. Standard of Living Since the Civil War*. Princeton: Princeton University Press, 2016.

Gray, Mike. *Angle of Attack: Harrison Storms and the Race to the Moon*. New York: Penguin, 1994.

Green, Constance M., and Milton Lomask, *Vanguard: A History*. Washington, D.C.: NASA, 1970.

Hall, R. Cargill. *Lunar Impact: A History of Project Ranger*. Washington, D.C.: NASA, 1977.

Hansen, James R. *Engineer in Charge: A History of the Langley Aeronautical Laboratory, 1917–1958*. Washington, D.C.: NASA, 1987.

Hansen, James R. *First Man: The Life of Neil A. Armstrong*. New York: Simon & Schuster, 2005.

Hansen, James R. *Spaceflight Revolution: NASA Langley Research Center from Sputnik to Apollo*. Washington, D.C.: NASA, 1995.

Hanson, Victor Davis. *The Second World Wars: How the First Global Conflict Was Fought and Won*. New York: Basic Books, 2017.

Hargis, Robert. *U.S. Submarine Crewman 1941–45*. Oxford, U.K.: Osprey, 2003. Kindle edition.

Harland, David. M. *The First Men on the Moon: The Story of Apollo 11*. Chichester, U.K.: Springer-Praxis, 2007.

Harvey, Brian. *Soviet and Russian Lunar Exploration*. Chichester, U.K.: Springer–Praxis, 2007.

Herman, Arthur. *Freedom's Forge*. New York: Random House, 2012.

Holloway, David. *Stalin and the Bomb: The Soviet Union and Atomic Energy, 1939–1956*. New Haven, Conn.: Yale University Press, 1994.

Holmes, Jay. *America on the Moon: The Enterprise of the Sixties*. Philadelphia: Lippincott, 1962.

Houston, Rick, and Milt Heflin. *Go, Flight!: The Unsung Heroes of Mission Control, 1965–1992*. Lincoln: University of Nebraska Press, 2015.

Howard, Fred. *Whistle While You Wait*. New York: Duell, Sloan, & Pearce, 1945.

Irving, David. *Göring: A Biography*. New York: Morrow, 1989.

Johnson, Stephen B. *The Secret of Apollo: Systems Management in American and European Space Programs*. Baltimore: Johns Hopkins University Press, 2002.

Kopal, Zdenek, and Robert W. Carder. *Mapping the Moon: Past and Present*. Boston: D. Reidel, 1974.

Kraft, Christopher C., and James L. Schefter. *Flight: My Life in Mission Control*. New York: Dutton, 2001.

Kranz, Gene. *Failure Is Not an Option: Mission Control from Mercury to Apollo 13 and Beyond*. New York: Simon & Schuster, 2000.

Lambright, W. Henry. *Powering Apollo: James E. Webb of NASA*. Baltimore: Johns Hopkins University Press, 1995.

Laney, Monique. *German Rocketeers in the Heart of Dixie: Making Sense of the Nazi Past during the Civil Rights Era*. New Haven: Yale University Press, 2015.

Lang, Daniel. *From Hiroshima to the Moon: Chronicles of Life in the Atomic Age*. New York: Simon & Schuster, 1959.

Leonard, Jonathan Norton. *Flight into Space: The Facts, Fancies, and Philosophy*. New York: Signet, 1954.

Leopold, George. *Calculated Risk: The Supersonic Life and Times of Gus Grissom*. West Lafayette: Perdue University Press, 2016.

Levine, Arthur L. *The Future of the U.S. Space Program*. New York: Praeger, 1975.

Logsdon, John M. *After Apollo?: Richard Nixon and the American Space Program*. New York: Palgrave Macmillan, 2015.

Logsdon, John M. *John F. Kennedy and the Race to the Moon*. New York: Palgrave Macmillan, 2010.

Logsdon, Tom. *Orbital Mechanics: Theory and Applications*. New York: Wiley, 1998.

McDougall, Walter A. *The Heavens and the Earth: A Political History of the Space Age*. New York: Basic Books, 1985.

McMahon, Robert. *The Cold War: A Very Short Introduction*. New York: Oxford University Press, 2003.

Medaris, John B., with Arthur Gordon. *Countdown for Decision.* New York: Putnam, 1960.

Meder, Patricia Chapman. *The True Story of Catch-22: The Real Men and Missions of Joseph Heller's 340th Bomb Group in World War II.* Havertown, Pa.: Casemate, 2012.

Mindell, David A. *Between Human and Machine: Feedback, Control, and Computing before Cybernetics.* Baltimore: Johns Hopkins University Press, 2002.

Mindell, David A. *Digital Apollo: Human and Machine in Spaceflight.* Cambridge, Mass.: MIT Press, 2008.

Morgan, George D. *Rocket Girl: The Story of Mary Sherman Morgan, America's First Female Rocket Scientist.* Amherst, N.Y.: Prometheus Books, 2013.

Murray, Charles, and Catherine Bly Cox. *Apollo: The Race to the Moon.* New York: Simon & Schuster, 1989.

Neal, Roy. *Ace in the Hole: The Story of the Minuteman Missile.* Garden City, N.Y.: Doubleday, 1962.

Nelson, Craig. *Rocket Men: The Epic Story of the First Men on the Moon.* New York: Penguin Books, 2009.

Neufeld, Michael J. *The Rocket and the Reich: Peenemünde and the Coming of the Ballistic Missile Era.* New York: Free Press, 1995.

Neufeld, Michael J. *Von Braun: Dreamer of Space, Engineer of War.* New York: Knopf, 2007.

O'Brien, Phillips Payson. *How the War Was Won.* Cambridge: Cambridge University Press, 2015.

Ordway, Frederick I., III, and Mitchell R. Sharpe. *The Rocket Team.* New York: Crowell, 1979.

Overy, Richard. *The Bombing War: Europe 1939–1945.* London: Allen Lane, 2013.

Perret, Geoffrey. *There's a War to Be Won.* New York: Ballantine, 1991.

Poole, Robert. *Earthrise: How Man First Saw the Earth.* New Haven: Yale University Press, 2008.

Porter, Horace. *Campaigning with Grant.* New York: Century, 1906.

Rasenberger, Jim. *The Brilliant Disaster.* New York: Scribner, 2011.

Renehan, Edward J., Jr. *The Kennedys at War: 1937–1945.* New York: Doubleday, 2002.

Rhodes, Richard. *The Making of the Atomic Bomb.* New York: Simon & Schuster, 1986.

Roberts, Mark. *Sub: An Oral History of U.S. Navy Submarines*. New York: Berkley, 2007.

Roland, Alex. *Model Research: A History of the National Advisory Committee for Aeronautics, 1915–1958*. Vol. 1. Washington, D.C.: NASA, 1985.

Satterthwaite, Dale J. *Truth Flies with Fiction: Flying B-25 Bombers into Battle during 1944*. Bloomington: Archway, 2014.

Scott, David, Alexei Leonov, and Christine Toom. *Two Sides of the Moon: Our Story of the Cold War Space Race*. New York: Dunne, 2004.

Seamans, Robert C., Jr. *Aiming at Targets: The Autobiography of Robert C. Seamans, Jr.* Washington, D.C.: NASA, 1996.

Seamans, Robert C., Jr. *Project Apollo: The Tough Decisions*. Washington, D.C.: NASA, 2005.

Sears, David. *Such Men as These: The Story of the Navy Pilots Who Flew the Deadly Skies over Korea*. Cambridge, Mass.: Da Capo Press, 2010.

Shayler, David J. *Apollo: The Lost and Forgotten Missions*. Chichester, U.K.: Springer, 2002.

Shinn, Marion L. *Pacific Patrol: A WWII Submarine Saga*. Lewiston, Idaho.: Triad, 1993. Kindle edition.

Siddiqi, Asif A. *Challenge to Apollo: The Soviet Union and the Space Race, 1945–1974*. Washington, D.C.: NASA, 2000.

Sidey, Hugh. *John F. Kennedy, President*. New York: Atheneum, 1964.

Slayton, Donald K., and Michael Cassutt. *Deke! U.S. Manned Space: From Mercury to the Shuttle*. New York: Doherty, 1994.

Slotkin, Arthur L. *Doing the Impossible: George E. Mueller and the Management of NASA's Human Spaceflight Program*. Chichester, U.K.: Springer, 2012.

Stafford, Tom, and Michael Cassutt. *We Have Capture: Tom Stafford and the Space Race*. Washington, D.C.: Smithsonian Institution Press, 2002.

Stuhlinger, Ernst, and Frederick I. Ordway III. *Wernher von Braun: Crusader for Space*. 2 vols.: *A Biographical Memoir* and *A Pictorial Memoir*. Malabar, Fla.: Krieger, 1994.

Sullivan, Walter, ed. *America's Race for the Moon:* The New York Times *Story of Project Apollo*. New York: Random House, 1962.

Swanson, Glen E., ed., *Before This Decade Is Out . . . : Personal Reflections on the Apollo Program*. Washington, D.C.: NASA, 1999.

Swenson, Lloyd S., Jr., James M. Grimwood, and Charles C. Alexander. *This New Ocean: A History of Project Mercury*. Washington, D.C.: NASA, 1966.

Thompson, Neal. *Light This Candle: The Life and Times of Alan Shepard—- America's First Spaceman*. New York: Crown, 2004.

Trento, John J. *Prescription for Disaster: From the Glory of Apollo to the Betrayal of the Shuttle*. New York: Crown, 1987.

Turnill, Reginald. *The Moonlandings: An Eyewitness Account*. Cambridge, U.K.: Cambridge University Press, 2003.

Vander Meulen, Jacob. *Building the B-29*. Washington, D.C.: Smithsonian Institution Press, 1995.

von Ehrenfried, Manfred "Dutch." *The Birth of NASA: The Work of the Space Task Group, America's First True Space Pioneers*. Chichester, U.K.: Springer-Praxis, 2016.

Ward, Bob. *Dr. Space: The Life of Wernher von Braun*. Annapolis: Naval Institute Press, 2005.

Ward, Jonathan H. *Rocket Ranch: The Nuts and Bolts of the Apollo Moon Program at Kennedy Space Center*. Cham, Switzerland: Springer, 2015.

Wendt, Guenter, and Russell Still. *The Unbroken Chain*. Burlington, Ont., Canada: Apogee, 2001.

Wilhelms, Don E. *To a Rocky Moon: A Geologist's History of Lunar Exploration*. Tucson: University of Arizona Press, 1993.

Wolfe, Tom. *The Right Stuff*. New York: Bantam, 1980.

Woods, W. David. *How Apollo Flew to the Moon*. Second ed. Chichester, U.K.: Springer-Praxis, 2011.

Young, John W., and James R. Hansen. *Forever Young: A Life of Adventure in Air and Space*. Gainesville, Fla.: University Press of Florida, 2012.

Articles, Audio, and Video

Abramson, Rudy. "Laconic General—Zero at Small Talk—Is Super Manager of Apollo Project." *Los Angeles Times*, October 6, 1968.

Aldrin, Buzz. "Lunar Module *Eagle*." *The Bent* of Tau Beta Pi, Fall 1994.

"Apollo 8 Reunion." The LBJ Presidential Library (April 23, 2009). youtube.com /watch?v=Wa5x0T-pee0 (published May 15, 2012).

"The Apollo 11 Descent and Landing." Honeysuckle Creek Tracking Station.

honeysucklecreek.net/audio/A11_Network/A11_landing_FD_loop.mp3 (accessed September 1, 2017).

"Apollo 11 Lunar Landing Audio—Flight and Guidance Loops." NASA Spaceflight .com Forum. forum.nasaspaceflight.com/index.php?topic=35230.0 (revised July 21, 2014).

"Apollo 11 Moon Walk CBS News Coverage." YouTube, youtube.com/watch?v =ntyPG1xewJ8 (published January 17, 2017).

"Apollo 15 Remembered 40 Years Later." NASA video. youtube.com/watch?v =zrbS0B3l56A (published July 24, 2011).

"Astronaut's Death Will Not Halt Program," *Los Angeles Times*, via Associated Press, April 11, 1960.

Bailey, Robert G. "The 7th Patrol of the U.S.S. *Pompon* (SS-267)," *Polaris*, August 1994. subvetpaul.com/SAGA_8_94.htm (accessed September 1, 2017).

Barratt, Michael R. "Physical and Bioenvironmental Aspects of Human Space Flight" in *Principles of Clinical Medicine for Space Flight*, edited by Michael R. Barratt and Sam Lee Pool. New York: Springer, 2008.

Bateman, Jeffery S. "The Ultimate Program Manager: General Samuel C. Phillips." *Air Power History*, Winter 2011.

Bilstein, Roger. "Aviation Industry," in Melvyn Dubofsky, ed., *The Oxford Encyclopedia of American Business, Labor, and Economic History*. Vol. 1. New York: Oxford University Press, 2013.

Bracker, Milton. "Army Takes Over Satellite Firing with Jupiter-C." *New York Times*, January 28, 1958.

Bracker, Milton. "Jupiter-C Is Used." *New York Times*, February 1, 1958.

Bracker, Milton. "Truman Varies—Airy to Mundane," *New York Times*, February 5, 1956.

Bracker, Milton. "Vanguard Rocket Burns on Beach," *New York Times*, December 7, 1957.

Buckley, Tom. "NASA's Tom Paine—Is This a Job for a Prudent Man?" *New York Times*, June 8, 1969, magazine section.

Callahan, David, and Fred I. Greenstein. "The Reluctant Racer: Eisenhower and U.S. Space Policy" in *Spaceflight and the Myth of Presidential Leadership*, edited by Roger D. Launius and Howard E. McCurdy. Urbana: University of Illinois Press, 1997.

Carruthers, Osgood. "Russian Orbited the Earth Once, Observing It through Portholes; Spaceflight Lasted 108 Minutes." *New York Times*, April 13, 1961.

Cassutt, Michael. CollectSpace, March 5, 2005. collectspace.com/ubb/Forum38 /HTML/000134.html.

Chaikin, Andrew. "How the Spaceship Got Its Shape," *Air & Space,* November 2009.

Chaikin, Andrew. "Management Lessons of the Moon Program." Knowledge Management Workshop, NASA Goddard Space Flight Center, July 31, 2012. YouTube. youtube.com/watch?v=RaskWhy5pYE (published November 30, 2012).

Collins, Thomas. "Celebration Ends Instead as a Eulogy." *Newsday*, January 28, 1967.

Conrad, Joseph. "Youth, a Narrative," Project Gutenberg, 2012. gutenberg.org /files/525/525-h/525-h.htm (updated September 9, 2016).

Cooper, Henry S. F., Jr. "Annals of Space: We Don't Have to Prove Ourselves," *The New Yorker*, September 2, 1991.

Day, Dwayne A. "From the Shadows to the Stars: James Webb's Use of Intelligence Data in the Race to the Moon." www.thefreelibrary.com/From+the+s hadows+to+the+stars%3a+James+Webb%27s+use+of+intelligence+data . . . -a0126317213 (accessed September 1, 2017).

"The Death of TV-3." *Time*, December 16, 1957.

Dick, Steven J. "The Voyages of Apollo." NASA essays in *Why We Explore*, May 30, 2006. nasa.gov/exploration/whyweexplore/Why_We_20.html.

Divine, Robert A. "Lyndon B. Johnson and the Politics of Space," in Robert A. Divine, ed. *The Johnson Years.* Vol. 2: *Vietnam, the Environment, and Science.* Lawrence, Kans.: University Press of Kansas, 1987.

"The Eagle Has Landed." CosmoQuest Forum. forum.cosmoquest.org/archive /index.php/t-152388.html (accessed September 1, 2017).

Farrar, Fred. "U.S. Scores 2 Space Triumphs." *Chicago Tribune*, November 10, 1967.

Ford, Henry, and Samuel Crowther. "My Life and Work," Part III. *McClure's*, July 1922.

"Freedom 7 Mercury-Redstone 3: The Complete Flight of Alan Shepard, First American in Space." Space Opera France, 2010. youtube.com/watch?v =4LziZpAmMy8 (published March 12, 2011).

"G. H. Stoner of Boeing Co.: Honored by NASA." *Washington Post*, via Associated Press, March 3, 1971.

Garwood, Darrell. "JFK Gets Report: Spaceman Try Delay?" *Austin Statesman*, January 12, 1961.

Graham, Frederick. "Nazi Scientists Aid Army on Research." *New York Times*, December 4, 1946.

Grahn, Sven. "An Analysis of the Flight of Vostok." www.svengrahn.pp.se/his tind/Vostok1/Vostok1X.htm#Tape (accessed September 1, 2017).

"Hopes & Misgivings." *Time*, June 2, 1961.

Hunter, Marjorie. "President, Touring Canaveral, Sees a Polaris Fired." *New York Times*, November 17, 1963.

"Is NASA's workforce too old?" *Space*, April 11, 2008. *New Scientist Blogs*. new scientist.com/blog/space/2008/04/is-nasas-workforce-too-old.html (accessed September 1, 2017).

"It's a Success," *Time*, May 5, 1961.

"JFK Sees Polaris Fired." *Boston Globe*, via United Press International, November 17, 1963.

Jenkins, Dennis R. "Stage-and-a-Half: The Atlas Launch Vehicles," *To Reach the High Frontier: A History of U.S. Launch Vehicles*, edited by Roger D. Launius and Dennis R. Jenkins. Lexington, Ky.: The University Press of Kentucky, 2002.

"Kamanin Diaries." Encyclopedia Astronautica. astronautix.com/k/kamanindi aries.html (accessed September 1, 2017).

Lambright, W. Henry. "Leading NASA in Space Exploration: James E. Webb, Apollo, and Today," *Leadership and Discovery*, edited by G. Goethals and J. Wren. New York: Palgrave Macmillan, 2009.

"Launch of Apollo 4 first Saturn V as seen LIVE on CBS w/ Walter Cronkite." YouTube, youtube.com/watch?v=1uoVfZpx5dY (published November 10, 2010).

Liebermann, Randy. "The *Collier's* and Disney Series," *Blueprint for Space: Science Fiction to Science Fact*, edited by Frederick I. Ordway, III, and Randy Liebermann. Washington, D.C.: Smithsonian Institution Press, 1992.

Lippmann, Walter. "The Race to the Moon." *Newsweek*, February 13, 1967.

"Live from the Moon." *Hartford Courant*, March 25, 1965.

Luce, Clare Boothe. "But Some People Simply Never Get the Message." *Life*, June 28, 1963.

"Man in Space." *Disneyland*. ABC, March 9, 1955. Television.

Mann, William C. "Letters Provide Up-close Descriptions of Nuke Blasts." *Laredo Morning Times*, via Associated Press, August 5, 2005.

McElheny, Victor. "A Double Jump on Road to Moon." *Boston Globe*, November 10, 1967.

"Men of the Year," *Time*, January 3, 1969.

Miles, Marvin. "Moon Spacecraft Project Speeded," *Los Angeles Times*, April 1, 1962.

Miles, Marvin. "U.S. Scores Space Triumph." *Los Angeles Times*, November 10, 1967.

"Moon Shot for Soviets Sunday?" *Florida Today* (Cocoa, Fla.), December 7, 1968.

"Moonstruck." *Washington Post*, March 25, 1965.

Norman, Lloyd. "Army to Try Soon to Send Up Satellite." *Chicago Daily Tribune*, January 28, 1958.

Oberg, James. "Max Faget: Master Builder," *Omni*, April 1995.

Oberg, James. "Russia Meant to Win the Moon Race," *Spaceflight*, May 1975.

"Opposes Citizenship for Reich Scientists." *The Spokesman-Review* (Spokane, Wa.), via Associated Press, December 30, 1946.

O'Toole, Thomas. "Honesty, Distaste for Fanfare Make Apollo Program Chief." *Washington Post*, July 18, 1969.

Paine, Thomas O. "I Was a Yank on a Japanese Sub." U.S. Naval Institute, *Proceedings* 112, September 1986.

Paine, Thomas O. "The Transpacific Voyage of HIJMS *I-400*: Tom Paine's Journal: July 1945–January 1946." Self-published, 1984. Available at freerepublic.com/focus/f-news/1367585/replies?c=6 (revised February 1991).

"Red Alert." *Time*, October 3, 1949.

"Red Spaceman Lands!" *New York Journal-American*, August 7, 1961.

"Reds Not Sold on Trip to Moon, Lovell Says." *Washington Post*, via Associated Press, July 17, 1963.

Ricks, Thomas E. "Whatever Happened to Accountability?" *Harvard Business Review*, October 2012.

Rives, Tim. "'OK, We'll Go': Just What Did Ike Say When He Launched The D-day Invasion 70 Years Ago?" *Prologue*, Spring 2014.

Robbins, Bob. "Eddie Allen and the B-29," November, 29, 2000. avweb.com/news/profiles/182933-1.html.

"Russ Cosmonaut Titov Safely Down on Land: Next Red Target Is Moon?" *Austin Statesman*, via Associated Press, August 7, 1961.

Sato, Yasushi. "Reliability in the Apollo Program: A Balanced Program Behind the Success." *Quest*. Vol. 13, No. 1, 2006.

Saxon, Wolfgang. "Alfred Munier, 78; Worked on Design for Lunar Module." *New York Times*, December 23, 1993.

Setzer, Daniel. "Historical Sources for the Events in Joseph Heller's Novel, *Catch-22*" (2008). dansetzer.us/heller/JHeller.pdf (accessed September 1, 2017).

"The Seven Chosen," *Time*. April 20, 1959.

Sheridan, David. "How an Idea No One Wanted Grew Up to Be the LM," *Life*, March 14, 1969.

Sington, David (director). *In the Shadow of the Moon*. DOX, 2007.

Sloane, T. O'Conor. "Acceleration in Interplanetary Travel." *Amazing Stories*, November 1929.

Smith, David R. "They're Following Our Script: Walt Disney's Trip to Tomorrowland," *Future*, May 1978.

"Soviet Movie Shows Reach for the Moon," *Time*, October 28, 1957.

"Space Travel Impossible, States Dr. Lee De Forest." *Boston Globe*, via Associated Press, February 25, 1957.

Sullivan, Walter. "The Week in Science: A Russian Steps into Space." *New York Times,* March 21, 1965.

Talbert, Ansel E. "U.S. Moon Rocket Blows Up at Start." *New York Herald Tribune*, December 7, 1957.

Tapper, Dan. "Throwback Thursday—'Do Good Work,'" May 8, 2014. Sullivan & LeShane Public Relations. ctpr.com/throwback-thursday-do-good-work/.

"Thomas Otten Paine," *Current Biography Yearbook* 31. New York: Wilson, 1970.

"The Thunderclap." *Time*, October 3, 1949.

Topping, Seymour. "Khrushchev Hails Astronauts, Asks Peace in Space." *New York Times*, June 23, 1963.

Toth, Robert C. "It's Official: Astronaut Grounded for Bad Heart." *New York Herald Tribune*, July 12, 1962.

Trafford, Abigail. "Apollos and Oranges." *Washington Post*, July 19, 1994.

"U.S. Fires 'Moon'!" *Chicago Daily Tribune*, February 1, 1958.

"U.S. Women Still Grounded by NASA." *Chicago Tribune*, June 17, 1963.

"Very Little Left in Cabin of Burned-out Spacecraft." *Baltimore Sun*, via Associated Press, January 30, 1967.

Vine, Katy. "Walking on the Moon." *Texas Monthly*, July 2009. texasmonthly.com /articles/walking-on-the-moon/.

"Voyage of the Explorer." *Time*, February 10, 1958.

"What Are We Waiting For?" *Collier's*, March 22, 1952.

White, Thomas Gordon, Jr. *The Establishment of Blame as a Framework for Sensemaking in the Space Policy Subsystem: A Study of the Apollo 1 and Challenger Accidents* (doctoral dissertation). Blacksburg, Va.: Virginia Polytechnic Institute and State University, 2000. vtechworks.lib.vt.edu/handle/10919 /27037.

Wolfinger, Kirk (director). "To the Moon." PBS *Nova* TV documentary, 1999. Transcript at pbs.org/wgbh/nova/transcripts/2610tothemoon.html (accessed September 1, 2017).

"Worth the Price." *Time*, January 17, 1969.

Zinman, David. "Saturn Success Lifts Moon Hopes." *Newsday*, November 10, 1967.

PHOTO CREDITS

V. Malyshev / CC-BY-SA 3.0/Wikimedia Commons: 166; USAF/NASA: 194A; USAF: 194B; Draper Laboratory/Wikimedia Commons: 194C; USGS: 194D; Neil A. Armstrong Commemorative Archive, University of Cincinnati: 204; FAI: 208; NASA, composited by Jon Hancock: 289; Wisconsin Maritime Museum: 323; White Sands Missile Range: 326(1944); U.S. Department of Energy/Wikimedia Commons: 326(1945A–B)

INDEX